Solving Problems that Matter

AND Getting Paid for It

STEM Careers in Social Innovation and Global Sustainable Development

EDITED BY

Khanjan Mehta

Solving Problems That Matter (And Getting Paid For It)

STEM Careers in Social Innovation and Global Sustainable Development

Copyeditor: Sharon Honeycutt
Cover Design: Peter Lusch
Book Design: Divya Jyoti Darpan

Published in the United States of America

Library of Congress Control Number: 2015948442

ISBN-10: 1514838001
ISBN-13: 978-1514838006

Printed by CreateSpace, An Amazon.com Company

All you aspiring game changers
you dreamers, you workaholics
you brave visionaries who can't sit still
who strive through day and night
armed with science, evidence, and design
tempered by patience, perseverance and grit
who sacrifice blood and sweat and tears
to conquer nature
to reduce human suffering
to launch a million smiles
to build organizations and systems
that advance humanity
that replace arrogance with insight
trade indignity for equity
and fell monolith for mosaic
to build a fairer and friendlier world
to set us free
from poverty, ignorance, and disease
and the shackles of corruption, dogma, and mediocrity
for one and for all
for close and for far
for once and for ever
this book is for you

Go Make Stuff Up
with empathy, rigor, and ethic

Go Get Stuff Done
NOW; life's too short

Go Solve Problems That Matter
whether, or not, you get paid for it
The world is waiting; go make love

Table of Contents

Contents

Contents

Part 7   Personal Considerations   **350**

Index of Innovator Profiles

MULTILATERAL ORGANIZATIONS

GOVERNMENT AGENCIES

❤️ Health   🌾 Food Security   📕 Education   🛡️ Emergency Response

⚡ Energy   🍃 Environment   ⚙️ Multisector   🏠 Infrastructure

NONPROFIT ORGANIZATIONS » INTERNATIONAL MULTI-SECTOR NGOS

NONPROFIT ORGANIZATIONS » GEOGRAPHICAL OR SECTORAL FOCUS

NONPROFIT ORGANIZATIONS » FOUNDATIONS

NONPROFIT ORGANIZATIONS » EDUCATION SYSTEM

NONPROFIT ORGANIZATIONS » PROFESSIONAL ASSOCIATIONS AND SUPPORT ORGANIZATIONS

♥ Health   🌿 Food Security   📖 Education   🛡 Emergency Response
⚡ Energy   🍃 Environment   ⚙ Multisector   🏠 Infrastructure

FOR-PROFIT ORGANIZATIONS » LARGE CORPORATIONS

FOR-PROFIT ORGANIZATIONS » SMALL AND MEDIUM ENTERPRISES; STARTUPS

FOR-PROFIT ORGANIZATIONS » CONSULTING FIRMS

FOURTH SECTOR ORGANIZATIONS

💓 Health   🖊 Food Security   📕 Education   🛡 Emergency Response

⚡ Energy   🍃 Environment   ⚙ Multisector   🏠 Infrastructure

Health   Food Security   Education   Emergency Response

Energy   Environment   Multisector   Infrastructure

Preface

How did this book come about?

There is growing interest worldwide in academic programs and cocurricular activities focused on social innovation and global sustainable development. While such programs and student clubs take on many different names and forms, they share a common goal of actively working with partners to develop and implement practical, innovative, and sustainable solutions to challenges faced by communities in the United States and abroad. Along those lines, my program in Humanitarian Engineering and Social Entrepreneurship (HESE) at Penn State engages students and faculty from diverse disciplines in technology ventures for resource-constrained environments. HESE is one of many programs that provide STEM (Science, Technology, Engineering, Math) students a transformative experience and develop the skills, competencies, and mindsets necessary to launch entrepreneurial ventures and pursue careers in sustainable development. Approximately half the students in HESE are STEM students; the rest come from every other college across campus. Irrespective of their major, these students share a common interest in harnessing the power of science, technology, engineering, mathematics, and design to find practical and sustainable ways to improve the human condition. They value rigorous data-driven and evidence-based approaches to create and deliver new products and services that transform ways of thinking and doing. They value the primacy of trusted relationships and ethical reflection to ensure that the self-determination of all partners is never compromised.

When graduation comes around, the big question facing students, faculty advisors, and parents is: what's next? After pursuing immersive and engaged experiences in academic settings, these passionate, hardworking students are not as excited about taking up well-paying but arguably monotonous jobs in large organizations. They want to directly see the impact of their work rather than designing a widget in a cubicle and becoming another cog in the corporate wheel. While an increasing number of students are starting their own ventures, there are many others who just cannot, or do not want to, start a new entrepreneurial venture and life. Moving to a developing country and jump-starting a social venture poses umpteen professional and personal challenges as compared to undertaking similar endeavors at home. The entrepreneurial pathway is even less attractive when there are student loans to be paid, family and romantic relationships to be respected, and attractive job offers in hand. The question is: what are the other career pathways for these students who want to "change the world"?

While (social) entrepreneurship is the raison d'être of some academic programs, development of an entrepreneurial mindset is emphasized by most of them. The rationale is that students take their entrepreneurial mindset to diverse professions and sectors, finding innovative solutions to compelling problems. While participating in entrepreneurial programs, some students might realize that entrepreneurship is not their cup of tea while others may be drawn to roles and functions in the larger innovation ecosystem. They might realize that, for the problems they care about most, an entrepreneurial venture is not the right approach. Rather, a large corporation, a United Nations agency, or being an elected legislator might afford them a stronger platform to influence change. Few students, and even fewer parents, faculty, and career counselors are familiar with career pathways in global sustainable development and social innovation. With the help of one hundred innovator profiles and fifty-four expert briefs on a wide range of relevant topics, *Solving Problems That Matter (And Getting Paid For It)* illuminates the smorgasbord of career pathways that prioritize social impact. It educates readers about the ins and outs of the various organizations participating in the broader social innovation ecosystem, and the academic, cocurricular, and professional competencies that help prepare individuals for impact-focused careers. Finally, it encourages readers to think through compensation, career advancement, and the personal implications of career choices.

HESE has three goals: impact, impact, and impact. Impact happens through the entrepreneurial ventures related to food security and global health in several countries; through the research publications in refereed journals and conference proceedings; and, most importantly, through the students who spend a semester or four years working on HESE ventures. These students are HESE's most important export, and it is extremely important for me to propel them on their desired career path. With the intention of advising my students better, three years back I set out to understand career pathways in this arena. My initial goal was to speak to twenty-five to thirty professionals in well-known organizations where many of my students aspire to work. I quickly learned that the more prestigious the organization, the harder it is to find people to connect with and to have a longer discussion about what they do and how they got there. Over three years, and with the help of many supporters, I interacted with hundreds of innovators working on a wide range of development challenges across diverse sectors, organization types, and roles within them. I found most innovators to be open, down-to-earth people who were happy to share their work and journey. They graciously agreed to participate in this project and even connected me with their contemporaries. The two key takeaways across these conversations were (1) STEM professionals can be found across all kinds of impact-focused organizations and units (one just needs to look closer), and (2) every single innovator had a unique trajectory to arrive where they are now.

The innovators profiled in this book either have a formal education in the STEM fields or work on challenges that call for STEM competencies. For example, Sebastian Africano has his formal education in business but works on improved cookstoves across Africa and Latin America. Every single innovator's work represents a valid, compelling career path for a STEM professional. This book takes a broader view of STEM and also includes the health sciences, life sciences, medicine, geosciences, and the agricultural sciences. The profiles capture each innovator's educational background, motivations, job functions, a day in their life, major inflection points in their careers, future outlook, and their advice for students. The innovators come from diverse organizations—small and large for-profit corporations to various kinds of nonprofits, academia, consulting companies, governmental agencies, UN agencies, and newer forms of organizations that have recently come about to advance global sustainability. Professionals at various phases in their career are included to demonstrate how certain kinds of advances can come about in a few years while others require decades and centuries.

Alongside the innovator profiles are fifty-four expert briefs, penned by highly experienced (and extremely busy) professionals, that provide candid, poignant insights into a wide range of relevant topics. The briefs in "Part I: STEM for Social Innovation: The Time Is NOW!" capture essential trends and the importance of the STEM fields in advancing the human condition. "Part II: Organizations in the Social Innovation and Sustainable Development Arena" educates readers about the various types of organizations, how they work, and their strengths and limitations. These practical insights deconstruct the glamour, myths, and misconceptions of organizations in order to help readers make informed career decisions. The "Professional Preparation" part discusses various undergraduate and graduate degrees as well as professional development programs, such as the Peace Corps and Fulbright Scholarships. The "Professional Competencies" part delves into the significance of communication skills, fieldwork, and other competencies to impact-focused careers and provides actionable insights into how readers can develop them. The "Finding Your Niche" part has a series of briefs on how to break into, transition into, and transition out of impact-focused careers. Finally, the "Personal Considerations" part takes a deep dive into salaries, benefits, work culture, legal logistics, and special considerations for the LGBTQA community.

Solving Problems That Matter (And Getting Paid For It) seeks to accomplish three things. The first goal, of course, is to educate students, parents, faculty, and career counselors about career pathways and strategies in social innovation and sustainable development. The second objective is to elucidate the "market pull"—the smorgasbord of opportunities available to students and young professionals who have engaged in intensive and immersive engaged scholarship and sustainable development programs. While many faculty members and administrators view programs like HESE as a mechanism to develop soft skills (and assist in program accreditation), that is not why the program exists. HESE strives to address global development challenges while preparing a cadre of social innovators and sustainable development professionals. These career profiles serve as a recruiting tool for academic, cocurricular, and professional development programs struggling to articulate their purpose and position themselves in the university. The objective is to collectively alter the perception of such efforts from a "save-the-world mission with students going to poor countries to save people," to a rigorous, multidisciplinary, integrative discipline that inspires students and faculty to work shoulder to shoulder with communities to deliver impact. The third goal of this book is to help with recruiting and retaining women and underrepresented groups into the STEM fields. The work and stories of the innovators profiled in this book bring to life the relevance and importance of the STEM fields in making the world a better place. This outcome is perfectly aligned with NAE's "Changing the Conversation" mission of changing the perception of engineering (and by extension, STEM) to a caregiving profession vital to advancing the human condition.

While this book chronicles a bewildering array of career paths, it certainly does not capture every possible job profile and trajectory. Neither does it capture how every organization works (or does not work). Such a book would take ten more years of research and have to be carried around in a wagon. It would also be obsolete by the time it was published. This book is not meant to be a "how-to" manual or an encyclopedia either. Rather, it is a diverse mosaic of perspectives, stories, and experiences that provides hundreds of insights into sustainable development careers. It provides a compelling starting point to finding yourself and determining the path forward, into the extremely exciting, somewhat intimidating, and rapidly evolving social innovation and global sustainable development ecosystem.

Why should you read this book?

Like millions of STEM students and professionals around the world, you want to channel your education, expertise, and energy into tangibly improving the human condition. You volunteered at the local food bank all the way through high school, did a mission trip to paint an orphanage in Guatemala, and spent two years in college designing a solar lantern for farmers in Africa. And now you are hooked. This is what you want to do for the rest of your life. But how do you change the world—and get paid for it? Should you pick up your baggage, move to the lovely little town of Arusha in northern Tanzania, and look for opportunities with the aid agencies there? Should you start your own social venture or nonprofit? Should you go back to school, get a PhD in biomedical engineering, and find a position at the Gates Foundation? You do not know whom to ask or where to look for more information on impact-focused careers.

This book will give you a comprehensive, compelling first look into the social innovation and sustainable development space. Here are the kinds of things you will learn, think about, and reflect on as you review the innovator profiles and digest the expert briefs.

#1 The Sheer Diversity of Challenges Facing Our World

Embrace the variety and complexity of sustainable development challenges in different parts of the world. Few, if any, challenges have singular "silver-bullet" solutions. The innovator profiles shed light on the specific problems that game changers are trying to solve in pursuit of the larger challenges. Their profiles illustrate how culture and context inform the way in which each problem is approached and each solution is designed and implemented.

#2 The Different Levels of Abstraction for Development Innovations

You can work on a challenge (say, global health) through the United Nations, the national government, a regional nonprofit, a private sector actor, or one-on-one with rural communities—and every approach is equally valuable. Innovations at higher levels of abstraction can have a much larger impact but are harder to assess, iterate, and implement. You might not even know if the approach is actually working! On the other end of the spectrum, working directly with people can give you immediate feedback and a firsthand view of the human impact, but that impact is constrained to a smaller population.

#3 The Multiplicity of Approaches to Addressing Global Problems

You can address a challenge (say, rural electrification) through policy modifications, advocacy, activism, educational interventions, technological tools, or business operations. Some methods involve direct action while others take an indirect approach by influencing external stakeholders. Some approaches maintain the status quo, provide temporary solutions, or lead to incremental improvements while others are truly disruptive and transformative—solving the problem once and for all.

#4 The Variety of Sectors and Nexuses

The social innovation and sustainable development space is often grouped into sectors such as water, energy, food security, health, education, and human rights. Despite this separation, challenges (and solutions) related to each sector are highly interconnected. Innovators are increasingly focusing on intersections (nexuses), such as the terrorism-trafficking nexus or the water-energy-food nexus.

#5 The Range of Organization Types

The world is full of a bewildering number of organizations interested in social development: government agencies, nonprofits, large corporations, rural startups, and a long list of emergent fourth sector organizations. These organizations offer different kinds of resources and pursue different opportunities and platforms to effect social change. They comply with different legal, operational, and tax regimes across different countries. Some have formal work environments with explicit dress codes while others encourage dogs in the office and offer free backrubs on Wednesdays.

#6 The Different Roles within Organizations

Organizations are composed of employees working together in a structured, collaborative manner—but to many different extents on both fronts. Employees assume a variety of roles, from working directly with people in the field to doing back-office paperwork, to chasing grants and donations to keep the organization alive. There are executives, technical experts, grant writers, managers, coordinators, and as many other jobs as necessary for the organization to accomplish its mission. Some roles afford considerable freedom to explore and define work individually while others are fairly specific with structured responsibilities and processes. The work, and working style, of a coordinator in one organization may be very different from her counterpart at another one. All organizations have a unique culture and style of getting things done.

#7 The Diverse Motivations and Incentives for Engaging

Why do people work in the social innovation space? For some, it is just a job; for others, maybe, it is a more lucrative job. Some love the challenge, some want to give back, while others are looking to "save" or "rescue" people. (Do not do this—empower and cocreate with your partners.) Some may engage to satisfy their ego, to earn bragging rights, or to discover the thrill and adventure of problem solving in an exotic locale. And then, some believe in the Ubuntu philosophy, "I am because we are" (nudge, nudge). There are more reasons than there are people. This book helps you understand and articulate your own reasons; doing so can keep you grounded and help you make better career decisions.

#8 Essential Personal and Professional Competencies, and How to Develop Them

What personal and professional competencies do you need to be successful in this space? How can STEM students prepare for impact-focused careers? Different roles and organizations need different educational levels, expertise, and prior experience. Some organizations do not care about educational qualifications as long as you can get the job done while others have prescribed educational requirements for each role. Some positions may need specific competencies in research methods, engineering design, project management, conflict resolution, or team building—with or without additional STEM skills. There are several graduate and professional degree programs, fieldwork experiences, and fellowship opportunities to cultivate essential competencies and gain relevant experience to help break into the field. One series of expert briefs shares personal experiences and poignant insights on these educational and professional development opportunities.

#9 Compensation and Personal Considerations

Some positions might be career-long, some for six years, and some for just six weeks. Some jobs may involve no travel while others may keep you traveling nonstop throughout the year. Travel might be paid for by the organization and include perks like business-class flights, or you might be expected to cover travel expenses from your own salary. For doing exactly the same kind of work, your annual salary might vary between $25,000 and $250,000! And then, there are benefits, retirement plans, and career advancement opportunities to think about. A dedicated brief deconstructs and demystifies how compensation and benefits work. It also clearly spells out the unknown unknowns, including the kinds of financial, logistical, and legal parameters to think about when negotiating any sort of gig in a developing country.

#10 Inspiration—Hundreds of Times Over

There is not one divine or well-trodden path to a career in social innovation. That would be scary! While journeys share some commonalities, every single innovator profiled in this book carved their own unique path. Each expert brief sheds light on an important facet of working in this enormous, constantly evolving space. Your own personal and professional quest to improve the human condition is not a sprint on the running track; it is a marathon through the jungle. This book seeks to inspire you, share some nuggets of wisdom, and propel you into this exciting arena to solve problems that matter.

On behalf of the innovators profiled, the expert brief contributors, and the editorial team, it is a distinct pleasure and honor to present this book.

Let's get going!

Khanjan Mehta

State College, PA

October 2015

Acknowledgments

I extend my deepest gratitude to Irena Gorski who helped develop and write up the innovator profiles and Siri Maley who helped edit the expert briefs. Rachel Dzombak was there every step of the way. This book would never have come to fruition without their patience and persistence. Shannon Hutchinson, Kelli Herr, Jenny Dobson, Nick Frazette, and Krista Ligouri made up the rest of the editorial team. I am still astounded that we put this volume together. It seems a lifetime ago when I started working on this project. We Are! and we made it happen. Thank you team!

About a couple hundred believers helped identify innovators, connect with them, and proofread the profiles and expert briefs. A few of them deserve special mention: Sarah Ritter, Steve Suffian, Laura Sampath, Jennifer Keller Jackson, Tyler Valiquette, Andy Vidan, Natalie Sisto Means, Sally Mouakkad, and John Lyon. Thanks to all of you for believing in this effort and supporting it. If there is one thing I have learned from this project, it is the importance of continuously building, nurturing, and growing your network. Networking is not a theoretical exercise or a burdensome chore but rather an empathetic mindset and a series of thoughtful actions to help others succeed by facilitating their journey.

The innovators profiled in this book are all game changers, and I am truly grateful to them for giving me the opportunity to take their work to a broader audience. The expert briefs were contributed by incredibly busy people who wanted to give back and help develop the next generation of social innovators. Without their tireless efforts, over years and decades, this book would not exist. It is an honor to be associated with all of these humble world changers.

Sharon Honeycutt copyedited the manuscript meticulously, and I am grateful to her for that. Peter Lusch patiently worked with my team on the cover design and the infographic. All funds for copyediting were generously bequeathed by the family of the late Nagendranath Maley who served the STEM community as an engineer, inventor, and Penn State doctoral alumnus. Divya Jyoti Darpan did the layout for the book and patiently worked with us through umpteen design revisions. The development and dissemination of this book was supported, in part, by a grant from VentureWell and support from the Council on Engaged Scholarship at Penn State. An impact investment from my daughter's college fund allowed for the production and publication of this book.

My parents, Rashmi and Shaila Mehta; brother, Chanakya; and sister-in-law, Priyanka, firmly believe that everything I do is related to changing the world. They express their love for me and their confidence in my work by taking over all household chores and cooking up awesome meals that meet my exacting standards. My wife, Toral, enveloped me with unwavering love, constant encouragement, awesome food, free rides, and great sex. She puts up with my long workdays and nights, incessant new email beeps, and perpetual travels, including a three-month annual trip to the African continent. She is truly my significant other. My two-year-old daughter, Tashvi, inadvertently sacrificed hours and weeks and months and years of playtime with her daddy, just to see a fat book with little elephants in it. I hope that she will read this book someday and forgive me for the time I stole from her.

Khanjan Mehta is the founding director of the Humanitarian Engineering and Social Entrepreneurship (HESE) Program and assistant professor of engineering design at Penn State. HESE is an integrated learning, research, and entrepreneurial engagement program focused on developing and commercializing technology-based solutions in resource-constrained settings. Mehta has led technology-based social ventures in Kenya, Tanzania, India, Mozambique, Zambia, Sierra Leone, and other countries. These ventures range from telemedicine systems and ruggedized biomedical devices to affordable greenhouses and solar food dryers.

Mehta's research interests encompass affordable design; systems thinking; social entrepreneurship pedagogy; agricultural technologies and food value chains (FVCs); global health and telemedicine systems; cellphones, social networks, and trust; indigenous knowledge systems; development ethics and grassroots diplomacy; women in engineering and entrepreneurship; and informal lending systems for microenterprises. The objective of these research endeavors is to democratize knowledge and mainstream HESE as a valid, rigorous area of learning, research, and engagement. He has published over one hundred journal articles and refereed conference proceedings with about forty more in the pipeline. Mehta serves as an associate editor for the *IEEE Technology and Society Magazine* and as a contributing editor for the Engineering 4 Change portal. Mehta publishes a daily cartoon series called *Frame Changers* that captures learning moments in HESE and sustainable development.

Mehta has served on several university-wide and international committees and task forces. He has delivered invited talks and keynote speeches on technology innovation, social entrepreneurship, and global sustainability at several universities and international conferences. The HESE program was the recipient of the 2013 W.K. Kellogg Foundation Engagement Award (Northeast Region) from APLU, 2011 Outstanding Specialty Entrepreneurship Program Award from the US Association for Small Business and Entrepreneurship (USASBE), and was named by *Popular Mechanics* as one of thirty "Awesome College Labs" across America. While these are good accolades, Mehta's primary focus is on the HESE ventures that his students are striving to build up to multimillion smile enterprises.

Mehta lives in State College, Pennsylvania, with his parents; wife, Toral; and daughter, Tashvi.

Irena Gorski is an ecosystem manager for the Council on Engaged Scholarship at Penn State, designing and testing lean, scalable models to expand opportunities for engagement and engaged scholarship for students and faculty. Prior to working for Penn State, she graduated from the university's Schreyer Honors College with a BS in geoscience and worked for an environmental consulting company remediating contamination throughout the tri-state area. Irena was responsible for writing up the innovator profiles in collaboration with the participants and Khanjan Mehta as well as editing the other sections of the book and contributing to the layout design. She considers herself extremely lucky to have been brought into this project because each of those one hundred innovators have inspired her to forge a nontraditional career path of her own at the intersection of public health, nutrition, water resources, and food security.

Siri Maley is a recent graduate of Penn State's Schreyer Honors College with BS degrees in mechanical engineering and political science. She was actively involved with HESE with work spanning from design and in-country construction to venture and curriculum development. Over the last several years, she has authored, presented, and edited numerous articles across HESE's wide range of global health and food security portfolio. She greatly enjoyed working on the book, including aggregating content for many of the expert briefs, editing several innovator profiles, and contributing to the layout design. Siri aspires to use her background in HESE design and development to pursue a career at the intersection of engineering design and change management. She is currently teaching high school science in rural Guyana as a WorldTeach corps member.

Rachel Dzombak is a graduate student in the Laboratory for Manufacturing and Sustainability at the University of California, Berkeley. Prior to attending Berkeley, Rachel graduated from the Penn State Schreyer Honors College with a BS in biomedical engineering. While at Penn State, she actively participated in the HESE program for four years. Rachel's work is focused on integrating the knowledge and ideas of multidisciplinary stakeholders to build entrepreneurial ecosystems. Her research interests include manufacturing productivity in developing countries, social impacts of global supply chains, and mechanisms of eliminating waste from production cycles. Rachel identified and connected many potential participants from diverse circles and assisted in editing the final career profiles and expert briefs. Rachel aspires to teach entrepreneurship and design to undergraduate engineers. She is proud to be part of this book as it includes individuals that set incredible examples for the next STEM generation.

Jennifer Dobson is a junior honors student studying neuroscience at Penn State. As part of HESE, she develops low-cost screening tools for sub-Saharan Africa. Jennifer was responsible for editing career profiles. Jenny feels lucky to have been a part of this project because it has exposed her to a range of role models and career paths. She plans to attend medical school and use her degree to advance her passions of neuroscience, women's rights, and global health.

Nick Frazzette is currently pursuing a combined BS and MS program in biomedical engineering at Penn State through the Schreyer Honors College. As part of HESE, he is involved in low-cost screening tools. Nick edited several innovator profiles. He intends to attend medical school and ultimately combine expertise in biomedical engineering, design, and clinical research to bring new innovations in global health.

Kelli Herr is an undergraduate student majoring in community, environment, and development at Penn State. Kelli is a part of the HESE Program and focuses her studies on indigenous knowledge and international development. Kelli was responsible for transcribing interviews and editing career profiles. She is grateful for the opportunity to work on this project because she feels like it has opened her eyes to some of the realities of the field she wishes to enter.

Shannon Hutchinson is an ecosystem manager for the Council on Engaged Scholarship at Penn State, testing lean, scalable models to expand engaged scholarship opportunities for students. Shannon is grateful for the chance to work on this book and truly believes this will help students get the most out of their college experience and plan their paths ahead. She was responsible for aggregating content for the expert briefs. She aspires to continue working in higher education within the realm of athletics.

Krista Liguori is a recent graduate of Penn State's Schreyer Honors College. Throughout her two years in HESE, Krista worked on a nutritious street food venture, conducted research in Kenya, and aided in teaching a social entrepreneurship course. She edited several profiles featured in this book. Krista begins her master's program in international health at Johns Hopkins this fall. She intends to work on epidemiological control in places with high human rights violations.

Solving Problems that Matter

AND Getting Paid for It

part one

STEM for Social Innovation: The Time is NOW!

SCIENCE AND TECHNOLOGY FOR SOCIETAL IMPACT

Phil Weilerstein

Phil Weilerstein is the executive director of VentureWell, which he has led since its founding in 1995. VentureWell is an innovation and entrepreneurship network focused on higher education and research that cultivates revolutionary ideas and promising inventions. To enable emerging innovators to launch their ideas, VentureWell makes strategic financial investments that have exponential impact. Grants and investments have provided funding to over 500 student teams, more than half of which are still in business today, operating in over fifty countries and reaching millions of people with groundbreaking innovations

We live in a unique time where the passion for scientific discovery and the tools to apply those discoveries are more accessible and interlinked than ever before. We celebrate—almost deify—tech innovators like Steve Jobs and Elon Musk, marveling both at the technologies they create and the ways in which the tools of commerce have made their solutions ubiquitous and affordable. We are also becoming more and more business-friendly as a culture: people today can cross between the worlds of science and business comfortably and without compromising their values, careers, or long-term options. Part of this radical shift toward a tech- and business-oriented world is a greater emphasis on using entrepreneurial approaches to solve issues in international development. The idea of developing products and businesses for the billions of people who live in poverty is generating increasing amounts of interest and attracting resources and talent, from university students and researchers to corporations large and small.

Higher education is playing a significant role in this shift. There is a growing demand for new educational opportunities, particularly in science and engineering. Students want to be taught how to develop products that will empower people to lift themselves out of poverty. Scientists and engineers have always been motivated by the idea that their inventions would be useful to society; what has changed are their propensity and opportunity to participate actively and directly in that process. We are seeing young college innovators develop new approaches to preserving vaccines; expanding access to light, power, and clean water; and developing more sustainable and better forms of building materials, to name just a few.

The combination of a scientific approach, a problem-solving mindset born from creativity and design, and the rigor and embrace of entrepreneurial risk is creating remarkable outcomes. This new culture is collaborative, celebrating successes and respecting failures as opportunities to learn and change. If you are one of these trendsetters fueled by passion, purpose, and drive to make the world better, here are five key concepts to guide your almost boundless potential to create change.

#1 Solve Problems That Matter

The current generation has grown up in a period of great change—and great challenges. Young people have an unprecedented amount of information about the world around them; both global and local problems are streamed into their (and our) lives, confronting us and challenging us to solve them. Students are responding to this by being increasingly interested in solutions, an interest and compassion that transcends culture, nationality, religion, class, and gender and is evident in higher education across disciplines and at every type of institution, from elite universities to community colleges. But to realize this aspiration they need to work on compelling problems—problems that, if they were solved, would have big impact. As Rensselaer Polytechnic Institute Professor Burt Swersey put it: "Don't work on nonsense." Focus on problems that matter and create solutions.

#2 Start with the Science

The world needs more effective, functional, and affordable technology solutions to social and environmental problems. Scientific and technological innovation continues to play a pivotal role in catalyzing the creation of new industries, spawning job growth, and improving the quality of life in the US and throughout the world.

Scientific innovation has led to most of the biggest social impacts in human history in ways that are often taken for granted. Chlorination of drinking water, the development of oral rehydration therapy, solar energy, and many other technological innovations have had huge impacts. The integration of science and technology-based approaches in addressing societal needs is clear and compelling. There is an urgent need to train and engage people from the STEM professions to venture into every kind of organization across every sector, from finance to health care to human rights. As STEM professionals forge their way in the social innovation space, they create paths for future innovators.

#3 Use the Tools of Entrepreneurship

An entrepreneurial approach in which the value of a solution generates the resources needed to implement it is often the best way to approach seemingly intractable problems. For example, Sanergy, which provides safe, sanitary toilets in urban slums in emerging markets, has used the need for clean toilets to develop a business model that creates wealth for local franchisees (toilet owners and operators) as well as Sanergy itself. The scale of implementation is not limited by large, fixed infrastructure and is accessible to alternative forms of capitalization. This approach is now being embraced by aid organizations and is changing the paradigm for providing development assistance.

#4 Take a Systems Thinking Approach

As with any complex challenge, societal development needs a multiplicity of approaches, stakeholders, and organizations. To be effective as an entrepreneur it is critical to understand the system you are seeking to change: who the participants and stakeholders are and how they relate to each other. Entrepreneurs work within ecosystems that (ideally) include proactive governments, supportive investors, trustworthy regulators, and integrated logistics support. In reality it is often difficult to align different stakeholder interests unless you understand them and how they relate to each other. Beginning by mapping your system for effecting change provides insight into the risks and ways to mitigate or avoid them. Designing your strategy and a model for scaling with a clear understanding of the inefficiencies created by such factors as lack of infrastructure, cultural practices, existing alternatives, and regulations is critical.

#5 Take It Personally

First, get to know yourself, and understand what motivates you. Identify your strengths and passions, the issues that resonate with you, and find kindred spirits and build your community. Show up and participate in local events and activities, join professional societies, and frequent maker spaces.

Then get a T-shaped education. That is: become a technical expert in your field; go deep. And then develop your competencies in leadership, entrepreneurship, global awareness and engagement, ethical decision making—the horizontal of the "T." Do not just learn about entrepreneurship—do it! Universities are leading the way in not just educating future change agents, but directly helping them create, develop, and build ventures. This kind of experiential education cultivates empathy, innovation, and entrepreneurship, a mindset and skill set that travels with you everywhere you go.

Find the issue that interests you. Compelling problems are everywhere, from your local food bank to rural clinics in Guatemala to urban slums in Chennai. Whether you are a biochemist, electrical engineer, or statistician, there are millions of problems waiting to be solved. Get out and engage with them!

If you are an aspiring entrepreneur, your time is now. Academic programs that teach you how to do entrepreneurship are proliferating and maturing. Support ecosystems are developing, funding organizations are seeking entrepreneurial solutions, and venture incubators and accelerators want to help you.

The solutions to big problems represent big opportunities for those with the skills and knowledge to understand the context and the will and energy to take action. Peruse a few of the profiles in this book, and you will see how scientific and technical expertise can be transformational and game changing in the right context, for the right problem.

Finally, the journey to social impact is long and winding, but there are many paths to get there. The innovators profiled in this book each carved out their own unique path. We can learn from all of them and all the experts who have shared their insights in this book, but ultimately you must take your own path. Few, if any, innovators and world changers know in advance exactly what they are going to do, or how. They jump in, innovate, collaborate, reflect, and iterate to create impact where there is a need. Take the plunge.

WHAT IS STEM ANYWAYS?

Peter Butler

Peter Butler is the associate dean for education and professor of biomedical engineering in the College of Engineering at Penn State. He has worked on integrating mathematics and biology in a field called mechanobiology and has applied discoveries in this field to drug delivery, global health, and vascular health and disease

STEM stands for science, technology, engineering, and mathematics, and its effects encompass every sphere of human existence, from economic competitiveness to national security to standard of living. STEM research and innovation is the engine that drives technological progress and economic prosperity. Entrepreneurs and corporations need engineering design to make new products and technological infrastructure to streamline their businesses and deliver value. Nonprofits and social enterprises need STEM to help them reach more people and improve more lives. For both financial and social ends, STEM represents many of the tools we use to understand, and change, the world around us. But what is STEM, really? And what role does it play in social innovation and sustainable development? We will start answering that question by deconstructing STEM, its mindsets, and its impact. Then we will turn directly to how STEM can improve our world, and how we prepare future game changers to do so.

#1 Deconstructing STEM

Everything not created in nature is designed by someone, and everything in nature is studied by someone else. The former people are engineers; the latter are scientists. Science seeks to understand everything from fundamental laws of the universe to the specific way this year's flu virus will mutate. And as scientists discover more about our world, engineers apply that knowledge to solve specific problems.

Engineering and science are dynamically interdependent on one another. Whether it is designing a new lens for the Hubble Telescope or developing a new way of reaching patients in rural Chile, engineers must rely on scientists and scientists on engineers. Together, we both rely on mathematics—the language of nature that governs and describes how things work. Math is the common tongue and tool of all STEM professionals, from epidemiologists to theoretical astrophysicists. And the advancements out of these career fields, from the cell phone in your pocket or a new rapid HIV test, are all known as "technology." Technologists are the people that implement, maintain, and adapt advancements within local communities. Together with scientists, engineers, and mathematicians, the STEM community informs, designs, and uses products that (for better or worse) irrevocably impact the world and our lives.

#2 STEM Methods ... and Mindsets

Mentioning STEM in a crowded room might conjure up a story of a scientist in a clean white lab, an engineer on a construction site, or Steve Jobs introducing the MacBook Air. Yes, this is what STEM professionals do. But it is not what *all* STEM professionals do. At its heart, STEM is simply a scientific approach to understanding the world and a problem-solving mindset for making things better. This mindset embraces the rigorous processing of the scientific method and logical flow of mathematical proofs as well as the iterative creativity of the engineering design process and the agile adaptability of software development.

STEM professionals may use these paradigms to conduct basic research into the fundamental workings of our universe or apply research findings to develop new products and services—or both. Beyond even that though, the philosophies of rigorous scientific understanding and systematic engineering design can be applied to all kinds of problems. Being "STEM literate" provides even nontechnical careerists with a different type of critical thinking, new insight into innovation of all types, and a broader appreciation of the world around us and the societies we live in. Fewer than half the undergraduate STEM majors in the US end up in STEM occupations. The rest go on to apply their STEM investigation and problem-solving education to nontechnical challenges, many of them in business and education. Sales managers and political analysts rely on statistical reasoning skills; iterative analysis and improvement is just as important in international relations as it is in engineering design. As our globalized societies confront more and more complex advancements and intricate problems, being STEM illiterate because you are not a scientist will seem just as unlikely as being unable to read because you are not a journalist.

#3 Radical Collaboration for Radical Impact

Solving STEM problems means working with the world. It means operating in the interdisciplinary environments needed to design rural health systems, engineering new agricultural technologies, and implementing efficient distribution networks for vaccines. STEM problems like these are everywhere—in our cars, our bank accounts, the buildings we sit in, and the air we breathe. The world of STEM spans from astronomy and agricultural engineering to vector fields and zoonotics. The effort to create a single rural health-care station relies just as much on basic medical research as on local community health workers. Developing such a station requires clinicians, computer scientists, biomedical engineers, data analysts, medical researchers, electricians, economists, and public health specialists. At the same time, those people may live all around the world in different careers, cultures, languages, and countries. It takes confidence as well as humility to work on such interconnected, interdisciplinary, international challenges. And this is important because these are exactly the kinds of challenges whose solutions will most drastically change our world.

The key to achieving success in the huge, interlocking, multi-sectoral problems of today is radical collaboration. Today's innovation teams do not split up the challenges of global poverty, inadequate infrastructure, or deficient health care into bite-sized chunks labeled "economists," "architectural engineers," or "biologists." Increasingly, they are not even labeled "Sony," "Toshiba," or "IBM." Instead, it is radical collaboration. Radical collaboration means surgeons working beside statisticians and discussing new supply chains with sociologists. It means companies joining research consortiums with their competitors to shorten development times and save resources. Radical collaboration is about people and organizations, from the STEM community and beyond, uniting to make our future brighter.

#4 Primacy of Making Life Better

Early scientists studied domesticated crops while engineers built sewer systems and mathematicians developed statistics. From medicines and germ theory through fertilizers, the telephone, and the microchip, STEM has always been about improving the human condition. We see this today in the mission statements of professional organizations. The Institute of Electrical and Electronics Engineers aims to "advance technology for humanity," Doctors Without Borders wants to "help doctors help patients," and the Royal Society of Chemistry studies "for the sake of knowledge and benefit of mankind." These and other STEM fields underlie many of the advancements and efforts that empower rural farmers in Tanzania, educate grandmothers in India, improve sanitation in Nicaragua, and build better clinics in the Philippines. And yet, today's view of STEM does not consider mechanical engineering or biochemistry to be a caregiving profession.

The days of saving STEM for lab scientists and software "geeks" are over. Throughout the social innovation and international development spheres, we need people who are not just literate but engaged and passionate about using STEM to help others. As members of these fields, we must commit to sharing the stories of game-changing scientists and engineers who achieve radical collaboration with business entrepreneurs and international relations leaders. The world and future world changers need real examples of public health officials and geomappers, agriculturalists and data analysts, who use the principles, methods, and mindsets of STEM for radical improvement and sustainable change. These stories of innovators need to be told again and again to change the conversation about how STEM professionals and skill sets can, and do, solve problems that matter.

#5 Training the STEM Trainers

For STEM education to permeate society it needs to be integrated with service and be infused with values that reflect the needs of all populations. From a higher level, schools and universities must develop frameworks and programs that bring faculty together for interdisciplinary studies that help students prepare for meaningful careers in science and engineering and help them navigate the complexities of the modern workplace. This workplace is global in scope, asks for the deepest ethical introspection, and requires nimbleness of technical skills and depth of thinking in engineering, science, and math fundamentals. So when we talk about providing job skills for students, we are not talking only about showing them how to do mathematical problems. They must also be able to predict outcomes of designs, work in teams, use computational software, and develop useful designs that are responsive to contextual factors of a client who might live thousands of miles away. Of course, K-12 teachers and higher education faculty are also in the business of integrating teaching and research and are the principal providers of a learning environment for students. So it will be equally important for government leaders and society to provide the infrastructure for success and satisfaction of teachers.

There are three main areas where schools, colleges, and universities can improve the delivery of STEM education. First is continuing and distance education. There is a real opportunity to ensure that online education provides unique benefits (even some not typically available through resident instruction) and reaches a much larger audience. Second, schools need to seek out ways to internationalize the curriculum because it has been shown that international contexts motivate students to retain technical information. A third major challenge is to increase the integration of values and ethics into the curriculum.

There are also very practical efforts that could be initiated to ensure that the schools remain innovative and effective at delivering STEM education. These include the development of workshops for new teachers that cover course planning, refinement of teaching philosophies, identification of student learning goals, and avenues to share best STEM practices. Mentoring programs between highly regarded teachers and new faculty (or faculty who want to improve their effectiveness) can be helpful. STEM education needs to be seen as a tool to tackle problems for all genders, ethnicities, and academic backgrounds. With respect to increasing the dissemination of values in the classroom, there might be opportunities to work with the general education curriculum to include courses and topics relevant to engineering training. Skills to develop include creative and logical thinking, leadership, innovation and technology transfer, and fundamentals and applications of ethics. Such skills are often at the core of a liberal arts education. Therefore, attracting students with liberal arts training to STEM could greatly enhance the intellectual diversity of the student body and the impact of STEM education in the world.

#6 Educating World-Class Problem Solvers

As STEM professionals, we hold an immense responsibility for creating and implementing products that will irrevocably impact our world. STEM education needs to take this responsibility as seriously as it takes the duty to teach statistics and biology. Because scientists and engineers *use* technology and mathematics, they *affect* our lives. Technical skill sets, from calculus and computer programming to simulations and structural analysis, are just the tools we use to target constraints, challenge problems, and iterate solutions. They are important, but they are just tools. And the greatest tool for anyone facing the struggles of our societies is not skill or technology—it is thought. At Penn State, world-class engineers are not just taught and tested; they are engaged. They engage through research labs, in internships and co-ops, in real-world projects, in industry-sponsored capstone programs, and in entrepreneurial ventures across the world. And that span of engagement takes a world-class kind of education.

"World class" means many things to many people. At Penn State, the journey to world-class engineering begins freshman year and engenders a lifelong commitment to learning and professional development. World-class engineers are as solidly grounded in fundamentals as they are technically broad across economic, social, and environmental fields. They are emboldened by a concern for our world and tempered by the highest ethical standards of their professions. They are innovative in response to challenges and collaborative in relation to societies. And they are visionary—about their professions, about the world, and about the future.

But making the world "world class" takes far more than just engineers. World-class engineering really is not just about engineering; it is about developing world-class problem solvers. Scientists must be just as understanding, insightful, and cooperative, whether they are unlocking the oceans of the universe or studying the replication of genes. Mathematicians need perception, global concern, and innovation to find answers from epidemiology to cryptography. Public health professionals rely on ethics, understanding, and education to achieve community care and world-class results. As a community, STEM becomes world class only when we unite across our differences and collaborate in the face of the greatest challenges facing humanity.

WHY SCIENCE, TECHNOLOGY, AND INNOVATION?

Sara E. Farley

Sara Farley is the cofounder and chief operating officer of The Global Knowledge Initiative, an organization she built in 2009 to wield the power of networks, science, and collaborative innovation to solve poverty-related challenges. After a decade guiding the World Bank, UN, and others in developing their innovation strategies, today Sara uses her innovation strategy skills to help individuals, institutions, and multi-country teams to solve their challenges collaboratively.

"That is a mouthful," my dad said when I told him I decided to declare my major as an eager university freshman. "It is called STS and it is amazing!" I defended, thinking maybe the acronym would make it an easier sell. STS is science, technology, and society, a tiny melting pot of feisty engineers with a penchant for boundary pushing and a rejection of slandering the "fuzzy" soft sciences. The eight "STS-ers" in my Stanford class found courses exploring the philosophy and technologies of the Industrial Revolution as exhilarating as thermodynamics. We loved the way policy and culture shape the questions that spark scientists, and we endlessly debated how economics influenced the way innovation was diffused or stalled and how that impacts development. Where other classmates saw clear cut "jobs" waiting after graduation, I saw thorny, complex questions everywhere—in law, policy, research, development—that seemed answerable with STS. And so, a lifelong pathway extended from that choice my eighteen-year-old self made through the exhilarating terrain that is the borderland between science, technology, and society. In that space, exquisite questions and world-shaping advances occur. For those asking whether to climb into the intersection, five reasons constitute an invitation for you. These five reasons extol the value of science, technology, and innovation (STI) both for humanity and for the practitioners who devote their lives to understanding and building these tools. It is a pursuit that needs more bright minds. It is a quest that needs you! Here is why:

#1 STI Will Shape the Sustainability of the Planet

Whether you look at population growth, water scarcity, pandemics, or global environmental change, the challenges bearing on our planet are sobering. By the year 2050 our planet will have nine billion mouths to feed, many of whom consume animals that further contend for land, water, and resources. Ours is a planet under pressure. Where resource pressures fester, social tensions escalate. Take water as an example. Just as wars over oil marred twentieth-century history, in *Water: The Epic Struggle for Wealth, Power and Civilization,* writer Steven Solomon argues that water is surpassing oil as the world's scarcest resource, and likely many twenty-first–century conflicts will be fought over it. Predictions about the scarcity of resources harkening conflict are not new. In that same year that I declared STS, I remember being horrified by Malthus's predictions. In 1798, Thomas Malthus wrote: "Famine seems to be the last, the most dreadful resource of nature. The power of population is so superior to the power of the earth to produce subsistence for man that premature death must in some shape or other visit the human race." Malthus predicted the planet's return to subsistence-level conditions once population growth outpaced agricultural production. What overcame Malthus's catastrophic view of the future? Science, technology, and innovation in the form of industrialized agriculture. Spurts of global focus on just that issue ushered in such advances as high-yielding seeds, optimized inputs, and enhanced agronomic practice, which avoided famine in Asia (though Africa's Green Revolution is still to come). In short, STI is what overcame the Malthusian projection.

Solomon's predictions about water wars, like others that project mass migration due to climate-related fiascos, present as bold an invitation as any to join the groundswell of innovators, makers, social entrepreneurs, researchers, scientists, and social impact investors who take part in innovating our way out of these challenges. A life that successfully nudges the trajectory of human development away from peril and toward sustainability is a life well lived. Sustainability is not our divine destiny. It is our choice. And it is work—work that people who wield the tools of science and technology can perform!

#2 STI Turns the Have-Nots into the Haves

Economists like to argue about what makes economies grow. Especially when it comes to phenomena as complicated as innovation, teasing out what investments come first (creating schools and universities that train young researchers) before impact is felt (production of innovations that enable greater productivity and trigger economic growth) gets tricky. However, we do know that where countries invest in science, technology, and innovation you find stronger economic growth. Take the digital revolution and investments in information and communication technologies (ICT) as an example. ICT investment and the use of ICTs result in increased productivity of people and companies as well as job growth. This leads to competitiveness. When this happens, poverty decreases. STI is not just about well-trained scientists getting exciting careers in cutting-edge labs. It is about creating the infrastructure to align tools to humanity's aim for development. At the level of individuals, this spells opportunity. Really, STI matters because it supports social justice. When residents in Oakland, California, use innovative tools such as the website Crimespotting and Everyblock—which automatically use crime report data from police department websites and display it on a map and interface that can be filtered by time, location, and crime type—it enables people to understand the spread of crime across location and time. ICT promotes civil accountability, transparency, and service delivery, not just productivity and wealth increases. Turning the have-nots into the haves is as much a story of economic opportunity as it is about enhanced social justice. These benefits are being felt in the US, Europe, and globally.

#3 STI Is Collaboration

Increasingly humans are building and using new ways to connect. From the networks that organize our collective knowledge—the Internet—to the ways we organize ourselves to work (distributed, teleworking teams), networks shape the organizing principle of mankind. Collaboration is so vital that we have stepped into what I would call "The Collaboration Era." Progress on large, complex challenges demands that problem solvers—be they private sector, government, academia, or civil society—learn effective ways of developing and delivering upon a shared vision. Doing so means mastering "collaborative innovation." The last decade of research offers a compelling rationale for explicitly enabling collaborative innovation through networks. According to the UK's Royal Society, such networks "enhance the quality of scientific research, improve the efficiency and effectiveness of that research, and are increasingly necessary, as the scale of both budgets and research challenges grows." Further, by including implementers, funders, and community members from the beginning of the innovation process, researchers are better poised to ensure that the solutions they envisage may actually work on the ground. Fueled by inspiration across the neuroscience and complexity science communities among others, scientific research can boost our understanding and capability to collaborate intelligently. Technology can amplify the infrastructures needed to connect. Take away the tools of STI or the people who develop them, and collaboration on the challenges that demand our attention simply could not occur. Those who foster collaboration are irreplaceable assets in today's world.

#4 STI Is Where Youth Is Power

In her advice to CEOs and heads of federal science agencies, Megan Smith, the now chief technology officer of the United States, said, "If you want to be relevant in science, technology and innovation, hire a millennial!" Though diminishing in number, many industries—law, medicine, defense—vest power in the seniors. However, if you vacuumed up the millennials (or their younger sisters and brothers) from tech shops like Google, you would barely have a company. Whole areas of technology, like coding, move so quickly that the most capable are those freshly minted, energetic visionaries who are just years (or months), not decades, from a college graduation. The power dynamic in places like Silicon Valley vests substantial influence in the young whose energy, tech-savviness, and willingness to shape technology to meet every possible human need or fancy seem limitless. Looking to the future, by 2050, of the planet's nine billion inhabitants, two billion will be under the age of fifteen. Our planet is getting younger, but the young show a capacity in STI that is undeniable. If influence early in your career sounds attractive, STI offers it.

#5 STI Is a Job (Ask My Dad!)

While no career is impervious to recessions, some are more shock-proof than others. The demand for people with STI skills is so high that in many places (e.g., Rwanda, Uganda, etc.) governments earmark as much as 75% of government scholarships for these areas exclusively. Having passion and a thirst to change the world is one thing. Having a job, a place to apply your skills and capabilities to make things happen, is another. Those with STI in their résumés get jobs. Just ask my dad. He may still forget what STS stands for, but he knows that I never fell out of gainful employment since graduation. More than having a job, however, STS let me answer my calling. Others who love science, find technology fascinating, or yearn to innovate and wish to marry that passion with a desire to make the world a better place have choices. Corporate or nongovernmental, university or military, government or enterprise, the destinations are exciting. The pathway to impact at a global level is yours to follow. And as Ralph Waldo Emerson once said, if there is no path, that is even better. "Go where there is no path, and leave a trail!"

Enjoy the journey and make the most of it, for your benefit and those who share the trail.

CHANGING THE CONVERSATION ABOUT ENGINEERING IN K-12

B.L. Ramakrishna

Dr. B.L. Ramakrishna is the Diane and Gary Tooker Professor and Humanitarian Engineering faculty in the Fulton Schools of Engineering at Arizona State University. He is dedicated to preparing engineers that not only have the necessary engineering skills but also the cross-disciplinary knowledge, entrepreneurial spirit, global perspective, and a sense of mission needed to lead our country and the world to meet the great challenges facing humankind in the twenty-first century. He was recently awarded the Jefferson Science fellowship to serve as a senior science and technology advisor at the Department of State/USAID.

A central issue affecting the enrollment and retention of engineering students, especially from diverse backgrounds that are typically underrepresented in STEM-related professions, is the way engineering is perceived at the K-12 level by prospective students, teachers, guidance counselors, and parents. This is especially hard to tackle as only rarely is engineering explicitly in the K-12 curriculum. It is critical that the K-12 system strive hard to promote the "Engineering Habits of Mind"—systems thinking, creativity, optimism, collaboration, communication, and attention to ethical considerations, particularly because most believe that these are essential skills for all responsible citizens in the twenty-first century.

The engineering profession unfortunately suffers from the perception that it is societally less relevant than many other career options. The teachers, counselors, and parents may unintentionally propagate this stereotype to students and therefore adversely influence the career choices that the students make. Engineers indeed perform an incredibly wide variety of functions applying science and mathematics to solve societal problems. Therefore, it is of paramount importance to highlight the societal context of engineering and the valuable contributions engineering makes to increase the quality of life for everyone.

The fact that the twenty-first–century engineers will have the opportunity and indeed the imperative to address many grand challenges related to health, energy, environment, transportation, etc. needs to be communicated in a meaningful, effective way. Solving these grand challenges requires us to develop leaders, technological experts and workers, and an informed workforce and populace, both within and outside engineering. To develop the scientific and technological expertise and a diverse workforce to address these challenges, we must impact not only the university level, but we must also really start preparing students at the K-12 level.

The Grand Challenges for Engineering offer ideal and coherent themes (such as energy, environment, sustainability, water, and global health) for meaningful K-12 instruction in STEM and beyond. It not only provides a platform to develop and implement a rigorous science and math curriculum, but also contextual learning, motivation, societal connection, and relevance.

Once teachers are inspired to translate their knowledge and excitement into curricular materials and activities that are rooted in context and to illustrate the connections of STEM with societal issues through an interdisciplinary appreciation for the grand challenges, they will be empowered to encourage and stimulate their students to pursue STEM careers and to illustrate to their students how to make a difference in the world around them.

The key question is then how does one change the conversation and carve out a pathway to inculcate the meaning and significance of engineering at the K-12 level? Perhaps one could start by implementing the following ten steps.

1. Discuss the twentieth century's greatest engineering achievements and emphasize how engineering shaped a century and changed the world.[1]

2. Offer compelling contexts for students to understand complicated problems of the twenty-first century and allow them to explore a variety of solutions.[2]

---

[1] Twenty of the greatest engineering achievements of the twentieth century, by the National Academy of Engineering: greatachievements.org.
[2] The National Academy of Engineering's Grand Challenges for Engineering: engineeringchallenges.org.

3. Communicate the value of engineering design and how it relates to solving problems that really matter.

4. Focus on designing and implementing student-led solutions as that is where deep learning really takes place.

5. Stress the importance of interdisciplinarity and systems thinking in addressing the challenges of the global, interconnected world.

6. Establish vibrant partnerships between K-12 and higher education to provide a platform for undergraduate and graduate students to mentor K-12 students and college faculty and K-12 teachers to learn from each other.

7. Engage the larger STEM and public-policy communities in the teaching of and learning about the impact of engineering on society.

8. Emphasize the importance of diversity and inclusion for solving societal problems.

9. Strive for a well-rounded education by incorporating activities that develop key soft skills, such as teamwork and communication, that are critical to a successful engineer.

10. Remind students to keep in mind the ultimate goal of universal accessibility when thinking about solutions. Just as Abraham Lincoln noted that a house divided against itself cannot stand, a world divided by wealth and poverty, health and sickness, and food and hunger cannot long remain a stable place for civilization to thrive.

ARE WE THERE YET?

Cathy Leslie

Cathy Leslie is the executive director of Engineers Without Borders USA, an organization that works with communities that lack adequate infrastructure for basic human needs. EWB-USA equips and connects volunteers to solve these global issues while creating an educational environment to develop skills-based volunteers. The issues of global infrastructure and engineering education find their solution in EWB-USA, which connects the two to build a better world.

I started my career in the Peace Corps in Nepal. In the thirty-plus years between then and now, I have to ask myself, "Are we there yet?" Working in developing communities today seems like it was back then. There were:

- Communities in need
- Organizations wanting to assist
- Volunteers ready to deploy
- Aid money being spent

Today, the same four things still exist, but one would argue that there are maybe fewer communities in need, more organizations to serve, more volunteers ready to deploy, and more money to be utilized and spent. But is that true? Or are we counting the wrong things?

Are we focused on counting outputs instead of outcomes? We can count the number of pumps installed in Africa, but we know that a majority of those are not working. One can argue that those pumps provided clean water for a period of time and that was better than nothing. But was it?

Are we more focused on scale or sustainability? Does one equal the other? Or does the focus on scale take away the focus from ensuring that the project was the appropriate project for the community in the first place? Does it take the focus away from capacity building or behavior change? These two things are known as key sustainability enablers, but they seem to be the place where people focus the least—it seems we just like to build and fund "stuff."

Today, mid-2015, the world is measuring how it did toward the attainment of the Millenium Development Goals. We are now talking about the Sustainability Goals for the future. We are certainly shifting from counting outputs to counting outcomes. According to a policy brief issued in April 2015 by the Global Dimension Engineering Education, "Technical and technological innovative solutions are expected to play a key role in addressing the vast majority of the SDGs."

Today, we know that we need to pay attention to things like:

- Taking the time to make sure we are doing the right project for the right purpose, making sure that the communities we are working in actually believe in, and want, the project.
- Creating an appropriate design that looks at the ever-changing environment, considering global issues such as the effects of climate change, the empowerment of women, etc., and at the same time, considering local issues, such as the capacity to govern and maintain, which have never been more important.
- Taking the time to monitor and evaluate what has been done. Has the intervention accomplished the outcome initially desired? If not, what will be done about it? Failure is failure, and while we certainly need to learn from it, we also need to turn that failure into success.
- It is time to institutionalize organizational learning, to identify promising practices and ensure that we are not making the same mistakes we were thirty years ago.
- It is time to ensure that all volunteers, regardless of profession, are skills-based volunteers capable of creating a solution for a community rather than having an international experience. Volunteers should consider this sort of training as a prerequisite for international service.

The innovative solutions of the future will be the successful incorporation of technology into the approach to sustainable development, rather than the focus on technology itself. These solutions will focus on using technology to improve capacity, whether it is in governance, maintenance, or other means. And we know that works. The innovation in cellular phone networks and their applications has allowed other countries to avoid the expensive infrastructure of a centralized landline system yet allowed access to markets, remote medicine, and remote education.

This is where professionals from the science, technology, engineering, and mathematics fields need to get involved in a much greater way than ever before. It is time for academic prequalifications, design rigor, and analytical frameworks to ensure that the work being done is of the same standard of care in the developing world that it is in the developed world. Working in a community environment takes a special type of person—one who is comfortable in a global environment, one who understands that technology is only a small part of the issue, and one who can understand a complex environment.

It is time to ensure that the developing communities in which service learning is being practiced receive more, or at least as much, benefit as our academic students. True learning happens through authentic experiences that provide positive benefits.

This is not impossible to achieve. There are organizations in the world today that do this work, and do it well. There are academic institutions that have exemplary programs, yet those programs are handicapped by lack of academic support and are vulnerable to the presence of a single faculty person. The future will be to mainstream these programs and to create collaborative partnerships to accomplish both the work and the education, to the mutual benefit of the communities and the students.

My career in international development is not over yet, and hopefully, it will not be for a few years. I will continue to drive the organization I work for to make a significant difference in the communities in which we work, in addition to changing the perspective of the students and professionals that I work with. I have seen much change in the last thirty years that gives me hope.

I see the newest generation of smart, creative, ingenious STEM professionals who are doing incredible work. They are not afraid of hard work or difficult conditions. They are capable of understanding complex issues and are not afraid to look for innovative solutions that change the status quo. They are attracted to their profession because of the potential to make a difference, not just because they are good at math and science. It is this generation that shows incredible potential to get us to where we need to be.

Are we there yet? We are well on our way.

THE FUTURE OF TECHNOLOGY IN THE SOCIAL SECTOR

Edward G. Happ

Edward G. Happ is the global CIO of the International Federation of Red Cross and Red Crescent Societies (IFRC) in Geneva and cofounder of NetHope[5]. He invites all students to connect with him via LinkedIn.

Connecting the dots on how technology is changing our world has been a topic that has fascinated me for the better part of four decades. In my lifetime, personal computers, mobile phones, and the Internet have each disrupted and changed the way we communicate and work. The examples of disruption in the corporate sector have been dramatic (e.g., Kodak, Borders Books, Blockbuster). With change come risks, but also opportunities.

Question: How is technology transforming the very nature of social sector organizations, and what are its implications for tech professionals and social innovators? Let's first look at some critical factors in the digital context and then at how these are impacting humanitarian work.

1. The classic *Did You Know?* video shows how radically technology is changing the world through the eyes of high school students, the next generation of workers. It has been updated six times since 2006[3]. A sample quote is: "The top ten in-demand jobs in 2010 did not exist in 2004."

2. The explosion of technology can be described as a "supernova of multiple dimensions." There is an explosion of information, connected users, mobile applications, and a growing digital divide. For example, forty exabytes (that is 4.0×10^{19}) of new info were created in 2012, and that number is doubling every two years. Mobile users have exceeded desktop users globally[4]. Apps for the iPhone and iPad have passed one million, and most of these apps cost less than a dollar.

3. This has created huge opportunities for the connected in the world, but it has also created a widening digital divide. Based on responses from 116 national societies in the Red Cross Movement, we see that this gap increases as organizations and citizens move up the ICT capacity and learning curve.

Here is how technology is changing social sector organizations.

1. We see five shifts for humanitarian technology: to mobile phones, to local emergency response, to more preparedness, to the beneficiary, and to more collaboration.

2. Shifts are often driven by disruptions, many of which come via new technology. For the social sector, four potential disruptions enabled by technology include:

    a. The renegade in-country partner who links directly with suppliers for emergency relief

    b. The beneficiary-driven relief catalog with beneficiaries placing orders via portable kiosks

    c. In-country corporations taking the lead on programs and relief efforts in functional areas where they have strengths beyond ours (e.g., supply chain) and inviting us to join them

    d. Donor-directed projects in the microfinance and other areas. How we deliver programs will change—either by us or despite us.

3. These shifts are driving seven trends in our sector and how our thinking needs to change:

    a. First, we will need to reach people where they are with information they are seeking and with means of communication with which they are familiar. We need to "think," including a proactive mobile ICT strategy in development programs.

---

[3] Version 6.0 of the Did You Know? video: youtube.com/watch?v=XVQ1ULfQawk. The "Shift Happens" wiki: shifthappens.wikispaces.com.
[4] "By the end of 2012, the number of mobile-connected devices will exceed the number of people on earth, and by 2016 there will be 1.4 mobile devices per capita" (over 10 billion mobile connected devices)—Cisco Visual Network Index Forecast from February 2012 (search on cisco.com).

    b. Second, the vulnerable will be information partners rather than recipients. We need to "think," inviting citizens to join our information networks.

    c. Third, survivors and vulnerable citizens will mobilize into connected advocacy groups faster and with more impact to make their needs known. We need to "think," advocating with beneficiaries and joining their information networks.

    d. Fourth, the vulnerable will look to procure from us rather than us for them. We need to "think," inviting survivors into our supply chain as partners.

    e. Fifth, information and communication technologies for development (ICT4D) are playing a growing role in NGOs as a means for delivering programs far beyond internal information about programs. We need to "think," paying attention to and partnering with those who bring early innovations.

    f. Sixth, technology corporations will be asking us to join and support their development efforts. We need to "think," partnering side by side with corporations in the delivery of programs.

    g. Seventh, citizens from the developed world will increasingly connect and partner directly with vulnerable citizens in the emerging world. We need to "think," partnering with nontraditional innovators who deliver assistance in more direct and connected ways.

4. I am the cofounder of NetHope. NetHope enables humanitarian organizations to better serve the developing world through smarter use of technology. Our mission is to act as a catalyst for collaboration, bringing together the knowledge and power of forty-three leading international humanitarian organizations so that the best information communication technology and practices can be used to serve people in the developing world. NetHope's fundamental principles are the anchors in the storm and provide a framework for thinking about the future. These principles are just as relevant to professionals and other organizations in the social sector, and to all kinds of organizations interested in improving the human condition. Let us look at each of these six values.

    a. First, we believe technology matters; it has impact on our missions and work as nonprofit organizations. We need to continually strive to find pragmatic ways to integrate technology into nonprofit work. We are the glue, the translators, the advocates, and the provocateurs.

    b. Second, we believe that benefitting all benefits one. This is fundamental to our collaboration; the whole is indeed greater than the sum of the parts. Our brand of partnering means shifting from a "do then share" to a "share than do" mentality. That means approaching needs and projects with the question of how we can do this together rather than solo. That may seem like an extra step, but we believe it reduces the massive reinventing of the wheel that goes on within our own far-flung organizations, let alone among us. A further thought: Large organizations, such as my own, need to take a leadership position in collaborating as part of our give-back; where we may have the resources to go it alone, we must begin with sharing and working together. Why? To lead is to serve, and only the humble learn.

    c. Third, we believe in learning through collaboration. This is a variation on the ready-fire-aim approach that Peters and Waters identified as a key theme of excellence thirty years ago. Henry Mintzberg noted that this is fine as long as you get to fire again in a fire-aim-fire-aim sequence. The point here is that we gain a huge opportunity by learning from each other's pilots, successes, and failures in parallel instead of a longer sequential process.

    d. Fourth, we believe in building for the field. This means two important things: cultivating a greater sense of humility in our headquarters, and expecting to learn from the far reaches of your organization and those you serve. The greatest opportunity for us may be a flipping of the pyramid where we learn more about technology that works from beneficiaries and consumers than from the traditional IT department.

    e. Fifth, we have a bias for action. We have always been a group of doers with an impatience for the results that we know technology can deliver. Jim Collins reminds us of a fundamental law from biology: when times are uncertain, smart organizations "vary like mad." Varying means running more pilot programs to increase the chances of a winner that can be taken to scale (and we must scale up to have impact). I believe Michael Schrage made a compelling case for prototyping as a core competency. I would add to that and say agility—the ability to change quickly—is as important in a rapidly changing world.

    f. Sixth, we believe in trust above all else. Trust takes time and is based on the experience of working together. We should be proud of the faith and integrity we have developed with each other. We can depend on each other to face and overcome any obstacle the future throws at us.

5. In these times of accelerating change and increasing unknowns, we need to band together and collaborate to increase our chances of survival. Indeed, we need to collaborate or perish.

6. And as the IBM tagline said for decades: "Think!" Not stop and think, but go forward and think together.

As an existing or prospective technology professional, how can you be ready for change? I recommend applying the principle of agility to greater personal agility: cultivating the potential to embrace change and make changes even when that is uncomfortable. Ask yourself, what does it mean to have an agile career? It does not necessarily mean changing jobs every year. But it does mean embracing change as the new normal; change is not an option—it is a must. So the goal is not to get to a place of no change, but to look to reinvent yourself with each new experience.

---

[5] Edward's publication and writing projects can be found via his website: eghapp.com.

NOW IS THE BEST TIME TO WORK IN TECHNOLOGY FOR GLOBAL DEVELOPMENT

Rob Goodier

Rob Goodier is the manager of the news pages at Engineering for Change where he reports on research, prototypes, and issues in technology that meet basic needs in underserved communities. He is also a freelance journalist for Reuters Health, and his articles have appeared in Scientific American Mind, Popular Mechanics, and other publications.

Now is the greatest time to work as an engineer in global development, and here are ten reasons why:

#1 The Problems Are Entrenched, Systemic, Life-Threatening, and—Yes, Solvable

Consider the lowly cookstove. Cookstoves are the poster children of design for global development, and they are among the first things that come to mind when the topic is mentioned. Aid organizations have distributed cookstoves to almost one billion people around the world, and there is no sign of slowing the pace.

The stoves save money, trees, and lives, making them a no-brainer for development organizations. But there is one glaring problem. They are meant to replace open cooking fires, but the number of fires worldwide has not changed. In fact, the number of fires is projected to stay the same for the next fifteen years. That is an interesting puzzle, and as you begin to place the pieces, you will see that it intersects with other puzzles in the field of technology for global development. They are the kind of problems that are exciting to the right kinds of scientists and engineers. And now, more than ever before in history, we have the tools to solve them.

To start, we need to know more.

#2 You Can Have a Truly Global Career

In 2009 and 2010 Nathan Johnson, an assistant professor of engineering and computing systems at Arizona State University, set out to learn about cookstove usage. He made four trips to a tiny village in southern Mali called Nana Kenieba, where about half the residents were using stoves. He reported his findings in 2014 in *Demand*[6], and I will mention a few of them.

But first, let us let Johnson's work inspire us for a moment. His commitment to solve the cookstove conundrum took him across the world four times. He has stories, and he has data. The facts he gathered in Mali have spanned the globe through publication in online journals so that the cookstove troubles in a small village can influence research and design worldwide. Johnson has a truly global career, and now is the best time to have one. Travel is cheaper and faster than ever before in history. So is communication. Today, more than ever before, problems are not constrained by geography—and neither are solutions. You do not even have to travel far. Your technical skill and creativity can serve people right in your own country. Good design can serve homeless people, community associations in impoverished neighborhoods, school kids, and even marginalized groups that might be off your radar. For example, the San Francisco–based design firm Catapult leads projects around the world, and they also work right in their home country on Native American reservations that have water shortages.

There are opportunities to get involved all around you, which is another reason that now is a great time to take advantage of it.

---

[6] ASME Global Development Review: asme.org/network/media/demand.

#3 You Can Apply Engineering Skills in Tandem with Other Disciplines

Engineers are taught to think in systems, and the interesting problems in global development are embedded within complex systems. Cookstoves can represent the best and worst of global development efforts: the best when stoves are designed and distributed with the cooks and their families in mind, the worst when they are stripped of context and dropped in people's laps.

Johnson's work restored context to a flawed cookstove program. To do it, he had to cross disciplinary borders and work as something of a social scientist. He conducted interviews, watched people cook, noted cultural habits, and so on. He learned that cooks preferred open fires more than stoves because the fires burn for a longer time unattended. If the cook stepped away for a few minutes, the stoves went out, and it was a hassle to light them again. To a social scientist, that might sound like an opportunity for a public education campaign to promote cultural change and save money with proper stove use. But to an engineer, stoves going out sounds like a design problem. As you are reading this, you might already be thinking of ways to keep stoves burning longer—and that is why your skills are sought in global development. You bring to the table the unique, powerful ability to build something useful.

#4 We Are Awash in Data

Mali is not the only country with a cookstove mystery. Each culture, economy, and ecosystem adds nuance to the ways that people cook and the reasons that they do not use stoves the way we expect them to. To solve the mysteries, we need to know more. Fortunately, we are awash in data. At no other time in history has there been so much information available, and new data is flowing in at what must be an exponential rate. The last few years have seen the rise of monitoring sensors that report on the usage of stoves and just about any other device. And new sensors in development can do things like wirelessly transmit air-quality data from inside kitchens. They test whether the stoves are doing what they are supposed to do, which is to make kitchens less smoky for the cooks.

The data is not just limited to stoves, of course. The surge in mobile phone use worldwide has enabled tools like mobile digital survey platforms, data hubs that you can update with text messages to alert people when, say, a water pump is broken; social media mining to track disease outbreaks, natural disasters, traffic, and so on. In fact, just managing the data has become a problem in this field, and software engineers should take note. Engineers should be excited about how cheap sensors are and how easy they are to use. We may not have the time or money to send cookstove investigators to stay for weeks in every village, but we can ship stoves with built-in sensors. And we can equip test kitchens with air-quality sensors to find out if the stoves really are working the way they do in the lab. We can, and we do. We know more than we have ever known before about what is working, why it is working, and what we need to improve. And we will only get better at it.

#5 There is a Convergence of Sectors

Nonprofits, industry, and governments are coming together to take on big hairy challenges. There are more employment opportunities, more resources, and new approaches. A maxim in world travel is that wherever you go, there is a Coke. Coca-Cola appears on shelves in some of the hardest-to-reach corner stores in the world. Social entrepreneurs, charities, and even governments look on the company's powerful supply chain with envy. And Coca-Cola is not stingy with its secrets. The company puts its drivers at the service of government medical suppliers in three African countries and offers advice to startups like Cola Life, which distributes antidiarrheal medicine in sub-Saharan Africa sandwiched between the bottles on Coke crates. The world is coming together to solve poverty. Poverty's roots span sectors, and so does its solutions.

#6 Abundant Resources Are Becoming Available

It is easier than ever to raise money for a startup, a product launch, a prototype, research, or even just a good idea. Impact investing is a new thing. So is online crowdfunding. Design contests and grants abound, with money available from governments, universities, investment firms, businesses, and nonprofits. E4C hosts a continuously updated list of design contests[7], humanitarian technology development grants from the US government[8], and a short guide on crowdfunding device development[9].

---

[7] E4C's list of design contests: engineeringforchange.org/news/2011/04/16/sustainable_design_contests_and_awards_roundup.html.

[8] E4C's list of US government grants: engineeringforchange.org/news/2011/10/16/humanitarian_tech_development_grants_roundup.html.

[9] E4C's guide to crowdfunding: engineeringforchange.org/news/2013/07/19/where_to_crowdfund_device_development_and_projects.html.

#7 It Is Easier Than Ever to Learn What to Do

If you do not know what you are doing, you are in luck. Now it is easier than ever before to learn something new. Johnson and his colleagues in academia around the world take a leading role in building new technology for global development. They represent a growing number of universities that offer degrees and individual courses in the field. E4C hosts a list of dozens of relevant academic programs.[10]

But you do not need to take the formal route through academia. Instead, you can learn by doing. Your skills will be useful as a volunteer with a local Engineers Without Borders chapter or a trade organization, a church, a school, or other groups. You can also learn at home. Ivy League and other credible universities put their engineering and science courses online for free or reduced costs. The list above includes online education and publications in this field, and E4C also has a quick guide to a free online education in STEM.[11]

#8 You Can Make Your Own Job

In fact, it is recommended. If you are looking for paid work, those who have jobs in this field often suggest that you make your own. As you become familiar with the space through the educational tools you choose and the organizations that you work or volunteer with, you might think about which idea of yours deserves a shot as a startup.

#9 The Momentum Is with Us

The things we have done seem to be working. People are living longer worldwide, and economies in low-income countries are growing. From 2005 to 2012, the life expectancy in low-income countries increased from fifty-eight to just over sixty-one years. And in that same period, the gross domestic product of low-income countries grew by 5–6.7% while the world's GDP grew at 2.2–3.6% with a dip down to -2.1% during the recession in 2009. Poverty might be a problem that we can solve in our lifetimes, and now is the best time to help out.

#10 A Technological Future Could Be a Beautiful Thing!

The often-quoted fact that more people in India have access to a mobile phone than to a toilet might sound like an indictment of Indian infrastructure shortcomings, but it is also a testament to the head-spinning proliferation of cheap communication tools. Another frequently overheard fun fact about mobile phones is that they are a leapfrog technology. They skipped over the need for laying landlines to give telecommunications to impoverished communities in hard-to-reach corners of the world.

Now other technologies are coming online that inspire hopes for similar leapfrogging. Things like 3-D printers and cargo-carrying aerial drones might someday help a village manufacture its own goods while skipping over the need for roads and rails from city factories. In the future, a cookstove might be designed on a laptop in Nairobi, emailed to a village in southern Mali, printed in a community workshop, and delivered by drone to a family of farmers that had ordered it from a mobile phone. That kind of thing might be a key way to catch everyone up economically. If we ever get there, it will be the engineers who guide us. And that is why now is the greatest time to work in technology for global development.

[10] E4C's list of academic programs: engineeringforchange.org/news/2013/02/04/education_with_conscience_academic_programs_for_engineering_for_global_development.html.
[11] E4C's guide to online STEM education: engineeringforchange.org/news/2012/06/27/ten_best_sites_for_free_online_education.html.

GO NOW!

John Gershenson

John Gershenson is a professor of mechanical engineering at Michigan Technological University (MTU) and the cofounder of Baisikeli Ugunduzi, a company that makes components for people who depend on bicycles to earn their living in sub-Saharan Africa.

Four years ago I cofounded Baisikeli Ugunduzi, a company that makes components for people who depend on bicycles to earn their living in sub-Saharan Africa. By the time the company had its first products on the market, I was forty-six with two sons in high school and a steady career and income as a mechanical engineering professor. I found a way to work on the company on nights and weekends and managed to get to Kenya several times, including a roughly fourteen-month stint to launch our first product (while working full-time at a Kenyan university). The excitement, opportunity for hands-on learning, and personal fulfillment from starting a social venture was like nothing else in my professional life. I was left with three very strong emotions: (1) I should have done this earlier in my career because I feel like I have wasted so much time; (2) with two children about to begin college, a house, and a career, this is a horrible time to want to switch gears into something that cannot possibly pay for the life that I live; and (3) once you have the opportunity to use your skills to potentially have a significant impact on the lives of tens of millions of people, it is tough to work on less than that.

Along the journey to starting this venture with my cofounder Ben Mitchell, I have learned several relevant lessons that apply equally well to starting a venture or to taking the next career step for any a person who views creating impact as a driving force in their work life.

#1 Business Plans Pivot, and So Do Life Plans

The original plan that we set out with in our venture is long in the rearview mirror. However, the mission that we set out with is still the road sign in front of us. I would say that, given the ups and downs of that venture—and the ups and downs of any career—the idea of "pivoting" the plan but staying true to the mission is key. Your career and activities will change, probably greatly, as you move on. Therefore it is not necessary to view decisions as being forever. However, for real impact it is important to see how these decisions and plans fit into your overall mission. At the end of the day, mission rules and happiness wins.

I was a somewhat successful professor with a decent design research program. When along came an opportunity to begin work in product development for the developing world, I knew it was time to pivot. I did not know if such a focus was possible for a faculty member (it is far less desirable by most administrators), let alone for a business. I decided to pivot my interests in that direction as I felt my talents would have more impact on customers in that sector, and I knew that what I learned would give me more impact on the students that I teach and work with.

The results have been amazing. The lessons learned in this venture have had a huge impact on every other part of my life. It has significantly improved my activities at the university, with a unique and significant experience that is applicable to nearly every class I teach. It has made me more focused and settled at home. I am significantly more mission-focused in almost any undertaking and much more fearless in pivoting any undertaking to get it more aligned with the mission. For me, the mission is experiences, passions, and impact. So what is your life mission, and how are you pivoting toward that?

#2 It Is Never That Simple or Easy, and It Is Never That Complex or Hard

The doing, the going, the making, the funding, or whatever is the next hurdle is simpler and easier to jump than you make it out to be. It just takes a running start and the guts to try. Even if you miss, you will learn enough in the trying to get it next time. Sometimes it takes getting over yourself—I am not as important as I think I am, and if this does not work out, it will not ruin my life. That being said, the sum of what you view as all the necessary components for success are likely incomplete. There is something harder and more complex to the problem that will be key to its eventual success. The issue is that you may not find out what that something is until you get closer to it. Just take the time to build up the capabilities, partnerships, and confidence to get over it when it comes. I read a lot outside my area and take many online courses to prepare for those opportunities/hurdles.

#3 Prototype Everything—Products, Services, Ventures, Lifestyles

When in doubt, take your ideas to the street. Do not ask people what they think; prototype it and see what they do with it. Anything can be prototyped, and most anything can be prototyped cheaply and quickly. Even the mission or lifestyle you are committing to can be tried on for size.

Prototyping builds creative confidence, and creative confidence is a very powerful thing. An important element of prototyping is often context, however. Make it, and take it to the customer; take it to the environment and place; take yourself there; and see how it works. In my latest venture, I was not sure if I could handle living in Kenya for a long period of time, working on this venture. So we went to Kenya and did it for three weeks. Of course, we were there prototyping and testing the venture, but we were also prototyping and testing the lifestyle. We realized we needed to be somewhere else, and that we needed our own place. We then did a prototype and test for three months. That one went very well, and we realized we needed some more people around us. We prototyped that a third time for two months. It went so well that my partner stayed in Kenya. For me, that was the prototype of the lifestyle and the big question, "Would I move my family to Kenya?"

#4 It Is About Developing Partnerships, Both Formal and Informal

Your success both in a venture and in your career, and probably your enjoyment as well, will depend more on your ability to create productive and fair partnerships and collaborations than it will depend upon your deep technical expertise. Yes, it IS whom you know. But it is more whom you get to know over time and how and why you work with them.

You can rarely achieve any scale of impact alone. Work hard to cultivate relationships and partnerships with like-minded people and organizations. Like-mindedness with respect to mission rather than method is a good indicator of fit. In starting Baisikeli Ugunduzi, I was surprised to find the best fit was someone more than fifteen years younger than I who, despite our many differences, shared the same core reasons for doing this right. When anything would go wrong, we always had that fit to fall back on, and we knew we could trust each other's motivations. I maintain a list of people that I have come across that I would love to have as part of future ventures. I am frequently editing the list. You should start collecting your people BEFORE the venture or idea comes along. Then, do not to wait to work with them; find a way to practice. Get them to do some small project with you for fun or pro bono.

#5 Find Balance Overall, but Do Not Require It at Every Moment

There should be times to work hard, but there should be times to play hard. That was not original. The balance is over a long period of time. It is okay to work your tail off to achieve an opportunity that will yield significant fun. It is tough if you are always working for that next thing and never take time to have fun. The best way to get the balance is to take the right people along with you on these ventures. People with whom spending time is a reward in itself, people who bring out the best and the fun in you, and people who balance you.

I love to race bikes, travel, coach math teams, and, of course, spend time with my family. To get all of that done requires that I work hard when I am working and play hard when I am playing. If each moment is balanced, you are doing nothing fully (and nothing well). There are times, days, weeks, months, even seasons when you will be all-in on one side of your life or the other. Make sure to make it up by being all-in on the other side of your life in short order. However, when you are all-in on one side, do not shortchange that by feeling guilty about what you are missing. Only feel guilty if you are wasting your time doing something for which you have no passion.

#6 Be Proud and Celebrate the Steps

Whatever it is that you are doing—your job, your venture, your life—it is important to celebrate. Pro sports have so many days of high-fiving each other for rather small successes. Why do other jobs not celebrate the small things like that? In a social venture in particular, the road is hard and possibly long. Each positive step (and even some of the backward slides) should be celebrated. If you set out to alleviate poverty for ten million people but only do it for one million, lose funding, and then fold without ever celebrating your success in changing lives for each of those people, that would be a shame.

It cannot be all about the destination. The destination often never arrives; it moves—you get on a new trip; you do not make it. The journey is the learning that makes the next destination more achievable, that makes you understand where the next journey should take you, and that helps you to build the skills necessary for that next journey. The journey is also where the fun is. My partner and I have made a habit of not only high-fiving each other, but also maintaining a collection of celebration bottles representing important milestones in our work. Let me be the first to congratulate you for taking enough interest in choosing a career path of impact to read this. High five! Now read the next suggestion before you get too proud.

#7 Go Now!

What are you doing tomorrow that is so important? Go prototype the first/next step and stay there a while. What is the barrier to going or getting started that you have created—money, time, lifestyle? Understand that YOU have fabricated these barriers, and none are insurmountable.

I was a forty-five–year-old guy, with two kids in high school, a job that I could not risk leaving because I had to pay for my kids to go to college, a mortgage, no ability to pay for the venture myself, no real experience in Africa, an idea that was not getting traction with significant funders, and a boss at my day job who absolutely did not back what I was doing … and I uprooted everything to make this happen. The only thing I regret is not doing it earlier. That is the key: the day you start doing this you will look back on the days before and feel that it was time wasted.

So GO! GO NOW!

part two

Organizations in the Social Innovation and Sustainable Development Arena

ORGANIZATIONS IN THE SOCIAL INNOVATION AND SUSTAINABLE DEVELOPMENT ARENA: AN OVERVIEW

Editorial Team

Social innovation and sustainable development are championed by a bewildering array of actors across the public, private, social, and emerging fourth sector. The definition of development varies widely across different contexts. For the purpose of this book, we consider "development" to be social, economic, and/or political change that improves the quality of life for people around the world. "Social innovation" refers to creating and integrating new ways of thinking, doing, working, interacting, and living into society so as to improve lives and livelihoods. Social innovations encompass products and services, practices and policies, collective thoughts, and individual actions that move society forward. Societal advances necessitate fluidity between the individual and larger society and balance between empowering individuals (people), building a just and prosperous economy (profit), and creating a sustainable world (planet). Social innovation is about people, prosperity, and the planet. Social innovation applies to every sphere of human existence and progress. It is just as important in the Western world as it is in developing countries. Sustainable development, as defined by the Brundtland Commission and accepted by most multilateral institutions, is development that meets the needs of the present without compromising the ability of future generations to meet their own needs. "International development" refers to social innovations and advances applied in low- and middle-income countries (LMICs) and the least developed countries (LDCs). A fundamental premise of this book is that science, technology, engineering, and mathematics (STEM) can play a larger role in fostering development and social innovation. The STEM fields bring with them the tools, processes, competencies, and mindsets that can enable and catalyze social innovators.

There are three traditional sectors of society: public, private, and social. The government and its allied organizations constitute the public sector. The public sector sets and enforces rules in order to maintain a level playing field and an enabling environment for all societal actors. The private sector is comprised of enterprises that produce and sell products and services that enhance our quality of life. Enterprises spur innovation and reward entrepreneurial efforts. The implicit incentive mechanism and market feedback system embedded in enterprises make them particularly suitable for investing, developing, and scaling practical, inclusive, and sustainable social innovations. Finally, the social sector comprises organizations such as nongovernmental organizations, foundations, and trade unions that strengthen and sweeten civil society. Organizations in the social sector safeguard inclusion and sustainability, build the capacity of at-risk populations, and reduce investment risk for the private sector. A particularly important social subsector includes universities, think tanks, and research organizations that create and disseminate new knowledge for the benefit of all actors.

Do social innovations emerge from the public sector, private sector, or the social sector? In reality, success is interdependent among all actors. Innovations know no boundaries—they come from individuals, informal groups, and established organizations. They come from startups, large corporations, nonprofits, governmental agencies, and increasingly, at the intersection of these entities. In this globally interconnected world, game-changing innovations are as likely to emerge from the backstreets of Bamako or bazaars of Bombay as the barrios of Brasilia or basements of Boston. Over the last two decades, the three traditional sectors have realized that their operations, outcomes, and destinies are intertwined and are gradually converging to create a hybrid "fourth sector" that strives to add social and economic value simultaneously. While these hybrid organizations (e.g., faith-based ventures, for-profit social enterprises, blended value organizations, community-supported agricultural cooperatives) are rapidly emerging and gradually maturing, related support systems (e.g., legal frameworks, investment vehicles, professional recognition and norms, technical assistance resources) are not yet fully developed. While some fourth sector organizations such as the B Corps, L3Cs, and cooperatives have legal frameworks, other emergent organizations legally establish themselves as, but not necessarily function similar to, the traditional private and nonprofit sectors.

STEM PROFESSIONALS DELIVER SOCIAL IMPACT

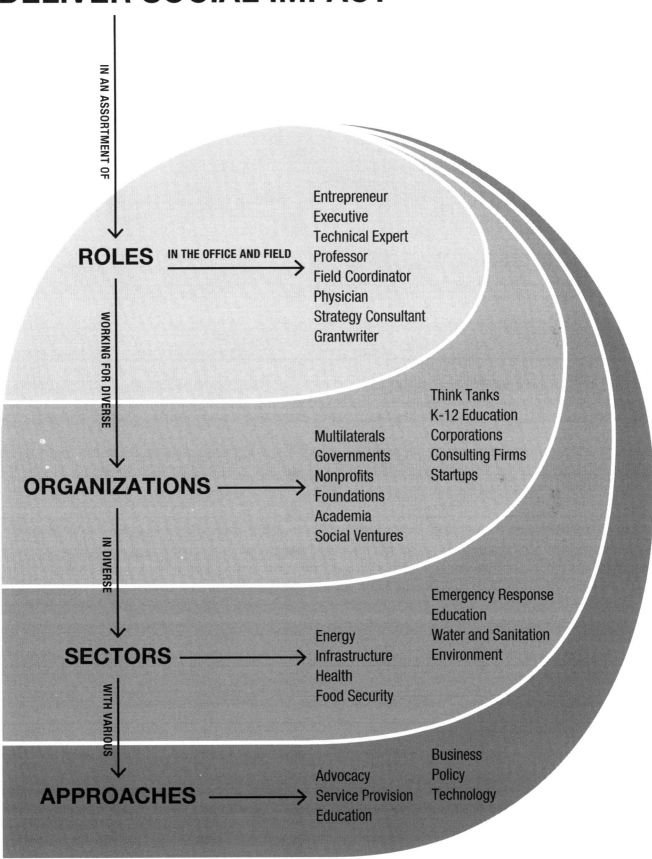

IN AN ASSORTMENT OF

ROLES IN THE OFFICE AND FIELD →

Entrepreneur
Executive
Technical Expert
Professor
Field Coordinator
Physician
Strategy Consultant
Grantwriter

WORKING FOR DIVERSE

ORGANIZATIONS →

Multilaterals
Governments
Nonprofits
Foundations
Academia
Social Ventures

Think Tanks
K-12 Education
Corporations
Consulting Firms
Startups

IN DIVERSE

SECTORS →

Energy
Infrastructure
Health
Food Security

Emergency Response
Education
Water and Sanitation
Environment

WITH VARIOUS

APPROACHES →

Advocacy
Service Provision
Education

Business
Policy
Technology

Design: Peter Lusch

This chapter reviews the various kinds of organizations that play a role in social innovation and international development. Each of these organization types represents hundreds, or even thousands, of organizations—each with its own unique mission, culture, and philosophy of engagement. Some of these organizations provide funding, whereas others provide expertise or work directly with people. Some of them are three-person outfits while others are behemoth organizations that employ ten thousand people. This chapter provides a 30,000-foot view of the different kinds of organizations. The innovator profiles provide deeper insights into how these organizations actually work and how STEM professionals can play a multiplicity of roles within them. Finally, it must be noted that while there are parallels across some kinds of organizations, every organization, and every unit within, has its own unique work culture.

Multilateral Organizations

"Multilateralism" refers to countries working together for a specific cause. Multilateral organizations, such as the United Nations (UN) ecosystem of intergovernmental agencies, bring resources from a multitude of countries to address specific issues on a regional or global scale. Multilateral organizations stand in contrast to bilateral organizations (e.g., USAID and the CDC) that receive funding from their own (in this case, the US) government to help developing countries. For example, the World Health Organization combats global disease and improves public health. UNICEF (the UN Children's Fund) directly works to improve the lives of children and mothers, with particular focus on the developing world. UNICEF derives funding from voluntary donations from all sectors of society: governments, private individuals, corporations, foundations, and nongovernmental organizations.

The UN also includes specialized programs focused on peacekeeping (UN Protection Forces and UN Transitional Authorities), refugee relief (UNHCR), global hunger (World Food Programme), and environmental sustainability (UN Environment Programme, or UNEP). The UN Development Programme underpins their global development network, and UNOCHA (Office for the Coordination of Humanitarian Affairs) coordinates emergency response and disaster relief efforts. While many UN programs and agencies have their own protection forces, HIV/AIDS educators, or civil engineers, the vast majority of the UN's work is completed by other organizations that have been awarded grants and contracts. For example, the World Food Programme partners with both private corporations and governments to ensure students are fed in school. The UN Human Rights Office provides grants to assist anyone, from victims of modern slavery to marginalized indigenous communities. Many agencies also run regional "small grants" programs to support community-level projects. For example, UNEP offers small grants to facilitate knowledge transfer of sustainable living practices among individual rural communities, NGOs, governments, and aid organizations.

Not all multilaterals are within the UN ecosystem. Some multilateral organizations, such as the World Bank and regional versions like the African Development Bank, directly invest in infrastructure development. From 1990 to 2005, for example, these banks loaned some $4 billion USD toward power and electricity sector development, with the majority of funds going to greenfield projects (i.e., new projects that are not related to prior work). Typically, with the exception of a few designated "small grants" programs, these funding opportunities are large and directed at broad systems. The World Bank, for example, loans money interest-free to governments for development projects—including education, health, water and sanitation, infrastructure, and institutional reforms—and it also provides policy and technical advice as needed. Twenty years ago, the World Bank had no competitors for loaning money to countries for large infrastructure projects. However, the World Bank is no longer the only player in town and is instead part of an investment portfolio. Commonly, countries approach the World Bank when they need the rest of the package (i.e., advice) because obtaining these loans, which come with a lot of strings attached, is a slow and bureaucratic process.

US Governmental Agencies

Governments play a variety of roles in international and domestic development, including funding sources, executors, regulators, and arbitrators. In the US, funders such as the National Science Foundation (NSF) and National Institutes of Health (NIH) are key contributors to the creation and dissemination of new scientific knowledge that spurs innovation across all sectors of society. NSF supports research into all fields of fundamental science and engineering, except for medical sciences, by providing funding to researchers at universities and other research institutions throughout the US. NSF employees and prominent scientists from around the country review research proposals to identify the most promising ideas at the frontiers of science and engineering and award them funding. NIH's mission is to seek fundamental knowledge about the nature and behavior of living systems and the application of that knowledge to enhance health, lengthen life, and reduce illness and disability. The vast majority of NIH funds are granted to scientists at universities, medical schools, hospitals, and research institutions throughout the country. Although NIH is primarily a funding organization, it also conducts its own research—for example, by contributing to the Human Genome Project and AIDS research. Researchers working for NSF and NIH are on the frontlines of advancing science through their own research and by supporting the research they identify as most promising.

Environment and health are interconnected global challenges, particularly when it comes to human-generated pollutants in the air and water. The Environmental Protection Agency's (EPA) primary focus is writing and enforcing regulations to protect the US biosphere. However, it also conducts internal research aimed at improving environmental monitoring and repairing damaged resources. For instance, EPA researchers have developed low-cost air-quality monitors to help underserved urban communities. They are creating new technologies to monitor air and water quality by satellites, thereby enabling a better understanding of the pollution challenges in isolated communities. In addition, the EPA offers numerous grant opportunities, including a college-level competition (P3 Grants), that encourage innovative solutions to address water, energy, agricultural, chemical, and human structure sustainability challenges.

The Centers for Disease Control and Prevention (CDC) protects Americans from health threats, including diseases, injuries, disabilities, and other health problems associated with natural disasters and bioterrorism attacks. They do this by conducting research to detect, prevent, and cure diseases; disseminating this knowledge to provide guidance to health-care professionals; and responding to disease outbreaks. The CDC offers a number of grant opportunities for research and other initiatives. A separate entity, the CDC Foundation, provides funding to partner organizations to advance the CDC's work on specific health threats that range from fighting childhood obesity to reducing tobacco use to preventing partner violence. The CDC is the driving force behind the prevention of many infectious diseases, such as the virtual eradication of polio in the US and the identification of malaria-related anemia as a major cause of death in Kenyan and Malawian populations.

The US Agency for International Development (USAID) is a bilateral development agency that promotes resilient, prospering, democratic societies while advancing US foreign policy and security interests. USAID programs range from providing disaster relief after the 2015 Nepalese earthquake to conserving forests in Jamaica. USAID concentrates heavily on global health support and research. For example, in 2014, the President's Emergency Plan for AIDS Relief (PEPFAR) provided antiretroviral treatment to 7.7 million people and supported HIV counseling for over 14.2 million. The agency also sponsors numerous funding opportunities and competitions. For instance, the Securing Water for Food (SWFF) program is cosponsored by USAID, the Swedish International Development Cooperation Agency (SIDA), and the Ministry of Foreign Affairs of the Kingdom of The Netherlands to find and accelerate innovations that increase the availability and efficient use of water in food production, processing, and distribution. Competitors propose diverse technological innovations ranging from low-cost desalination and water efficiency systems to supply chains and financing tools. Programs like SWFF are highly competitive; in 2014, sixteen teams were selected and funded from an initial pool of 520 applicants.

A number of other US federal agencies and departments support domestic and international development and innovation initiatives. These include agencies with mission-centric causes, such as the Federal Emergency Management Agency (FEMA) and military disaster relief efforts, as well as programs like the Department of State's overseas innovation teams and the Department of Energy's Innovation Hubs. The innovation teams bring together technology and civil-society experts to seek technological solutions to grassroots challenges. The Innovation Hubs serve as centers for integrated basic and applied research, focusing on the integration of different sectors of society—both domestic and abroad—to catalyze practical solutions. In addition, departments and their subordinate agencies offer external funding opportunities to support social innovations. For example, the Department of Agriculture offers rural development grants while the Department of Justice runs small-business and community-policing initiatives.

Nonprofit Organizations

Nonprofits represent an enormous force in the development sector, particularly as actors and executors of development. A "nonprofit" refers to any organization that does not function to make a fiscal profit. Rather, nonprofits prioritize social value; they exist for the common good. Nonprofits must return all revenues (through charity or earned income) back to the organization rather than distribute them to the owners/shareholders. Nonprofits follow specific laws pertaining to incorporation, operations, and taxes. While these laws vary significantly from country to country, typically nonprofits pay lower (or no) taxes, and people get a tax deduction on contributions made to nonprofits. The social innovation world includes a wide range of nonprofits: from some consulting firms and media outlets, to most universities and hospitals, to museums, community charities, and volunteer societies.

Nongovernmental Organizations

Nongovernmental organizations (NGOs) are a major subcategory of nonprofits that exist to strengthen civil society without insight from the government. The World Bank defines NGOs as private organizations that pursue activities to relieve suffering, promote the interests of the poor, protect the environment, provide basic social services, or undertake community development. NGOs are typically named as such because they offer government-type support without actually being related to a government or multilateral organization. There are many hospitals and medical research centers around the world that operate as nonprofits. Although they might conduct outreach in neighboring communities and create screening programs for low-income patients, their primary identity is that of a hospital. On the other hand, Doctors Without Borders is a nonprofit that provides medical services in humanitarian crises and is typically referred to as an NGO. In the US, NGOs that provide social services within the country are commonly referred to as nonprofits while organizations that conduct international outreach are referred to as NGOs. In most developing countries, NGOs are called NGOs! Many people, including those in the international development industry, use the terms "nonprofits" and "NGOs" interchangeably, thus adding to the confusion.

Let us consider another example. PATH is an international nonprofit organization on the frontlines of global health innovation. PATH accelerates innovations across five platforms—vaccines, drugs, diagnostics, devices, and system and service innovations. Their work is funded by foundations, the US government, other governments, multilateral agencies, corporations, and individuals. PATH works in over seventy countries with diverse local partners, many of which are nationally, regionally, or locally recognized NGOs. While PATH calls itself, and is referred to as, a nonprofit in the US, it is commonly referred to as an NGO in Kenya or India. PATH was ranked as the sixth-best NGO in the world on the 2012 "top 100" list published by *The Global Journal* and received the 2009 Conrad N. Hilton Humanitarian Prize, a $1.5 million award honoring a charitable or nongovernmental organization that has made extraordinary contributions toward alleviating human suffering. So, is PATH a nonprofit or an NGO? It is both, depending upon whom you ask. All NGOs are nonprofits, but all nonprofits are not NGOs. This book chronicles the work of innovators associated with large international NGOs, small mission-specific NGOs, as well as faith-based NGOs. Depending on their mission and resources, these organizations can have a local, regional, or international scope.

Large international NGOs typically operate on budgets of $50 million or more, and counterintuitively, many receive most of their funding from single sources. Some, such as Habitat for Humanity, are household names whose missions are easy to guess from their titles. Others, such as Youth Villages, are less recognizable but can be just as important to the same social missions. Small organizations are also important players on the NGO stage as they often have the ability to focus more clearly on a mission, scope, or region. For example, Grameen Foundation provides microfinance support in poor regions of Bangladesh; Sustainable Bolivia provides financial and human resources to educational groups in Cochabamba, Bolivia. Many nonprofits are also religious organizations, either founded out of a church, mosque, synagogue, or temple or very closely associated with one. Faith-based organizations (FBOs) are typically not officially designated as such and may or may not have explicitly religious primary purposes. Depending on how explicit the religious mission is, some FBOs cannot receive government grants and therefore work entirely from private donations. However, they still work closely with governments and other public development organizations. USAID, for example, has a subdivision, the Center for Faith-Based and Community Innovations, that serves as a unique avenue for FBOs to access and connect with external support.

Foundations

The Council on Foundations defines a foundation as an entity that supports charitable activities by making grants to unrelated organizations, institutions, or individuals for scientific, educational, cultural, religious, or other charitable purposes. There are three kinds of foundations: private, corporate, and public (also known as public charities). Private foundations usually derive their principal funding from a single source, typically an individual or family. Corporate foundations, on the other hand, are created and funded by companies as separate legal entities. Companies set up foundations through an endowment and/or by providing periodic contributions from their profits. Large corporations also have corporate giving and/or corporate social responsibility (CSR) programs. Such programs are operated from within the company and are legally and operationally disconnected from their foundations. Private and corporate foundations do not directly engage in charity work; rather, they empower others to solve critical development issues. Public foundations, on the other hand, can include charitable hospitals, schools, and temples/churches in addition to grant-giving organizations. Public charities receive funds from multiple sources, including other foundations, private and corporate donations, individuals, government agencies, and fees they charge for charitable services they provide. These funds are used to support their own programs and/or fund other organizations with aligned missions.

Private foundations range in size from small family versions with assets of less than $1 million USD to the Bill & Melinda Gates Foundation, the largest in the world with over $40 billion USD in assets. Small foundations tend to have a sharper focus so as to maintain efficiency and optimize impact. For example, the Segal Family Foundation supports grassroots organizations engaged in finding local, scalable solutions to sub-Saharan Africa's most pressing challenges, with a focus on supporting healthy, productive, and empathetic youth. Similarly, the Lemelson Foundation has a specific focus on supporting the education and praxis of technology innovation in the US and abroad. Larger foundations, because of their significant resources, tend to have broader goals and multiple focal areas. The

Gates Foundation, for example, has two broad missions: global development, with foci such as financial services for the poor, women's empowerment, and water sanitation; and global health, with foci such as combating infectious diseases. Large foundations often have the staying power to address major concerns in tandem with world governments on domestic and international challenges. For example, the Gates Foundation supports a $1.37 billion USD endowment to the United Negro College Fund and $1.5 billion USD endowment for GAVI Alliance, a global childhood vaccination venture.

Though the largest foundations are private, corporate foundations are also major contributors in terms of total giving. For instance, the Gates Foundation gave the most of any foundation in the US in 2013, but second place went to Bristol-Myers Squibb. In fact, excluding the Gates and Ford Foundations, the rest of the top ten were corporate "access-to-care" foundations. Access-to-care or patient-assistance foundations are typically run by pharmaceutical companies and serve to subsidize the cost of their donor company's medications for patients that cannot afford them. Other large corporate foundations include a focus on their donor company's industry; for instance, the GE and ExxonMobil Foundations contribute grant money and volunteer hours toward STEM education, and the Ford Motor Company Fund runs the Driving Skills for Life program.

Many of the largest public charities are either hospitals or private universities, whose nonprofit function is synonymous with their mission. According to the National Center for Charitable Statistics, Harvard University and Kaiser Hospitals top the list followed by Stanford, Yale, Princeton, and the Howard Hughes Medical Institute. University endowments typically yield about 5% per year and are used to pay professors, provide scholarships, support student engagement and new initiatives, and upgrade facilities. In a similar vein, hospital foundations raise money to subsidize health care for uninsured and underinsured patients. In essence, public foundations, just like their private and corporate counterparts, address diverse challenges, including humanitarian relief, civil rights, environmental sustainability, and community development.

Universities

While some colleges and universities are nonprofit public entities and others are for-profit private entities, they all serve in broader capacity building as well as focused engagement roles. They educate the future workforce—the next generation of social innovators and problem solvers. Universities are major centers of knowledge creation through fundamental research as well as application-oriented research and development. For instance, university medical centers may conduct research into immunology and toxicology while also developing specific therapeutic regimens for treating breast cancer. Academic researchers disseminate their findings to the broader ecosystem of social innovators through publications. Research findings inform novel solutions and lead to deeper questions, both of which are essential to advance the state of the art and to inform innovations by other ecosystem actors. Universities also participate in social innovation at a more direct level by fostering collaboration between academic units and community partners—in their backyard and across the world. Some professors work shoulder to shoulder with their students and community partners to design and implement context-appropriate solutions.

While research and engagement in contemporary societal challenges were always part of the university ethos, over the last decade, many universities have developed focused programs on social innovation and entrepreneurship. For instance, the Humanitarian Engineering and Social Entrepreneurship program engages students from all colleges within Penn State University to develop solutions that follow sound engineering design and business principles within resource-constrained settings. In addition to a lecture component, students acquire hands-on and in-country experience that is invaluable regardless of their continued involvement in the social innovation sector after graduation. In addition, some of the actual projects become independent ventures. Academic programs of this type include Humanitarian Engineering at the Colorado School of Mines, Global Resolve at Arizona State University, D-Lab at MIT, Design for Extreme Affordability at Stanford University, Development Engineering at the University of California, Berkeley, and the Mortenson Center in Engineering for Developing Communities at the University of Colorado, Boulder.

Finally, universities' outreach, extension, and public scholarship efforts directly engage local and global communities on societal challenges. Most universities, including all land-grant universities, offer extension programs on agriculture-related topics ranging from animal handling to pesticide use, water quality monitoring to business, and nutrition to youth development. Many universities also offer ecosystem services such as small business consulting services, sustainability outreach centers, and continuing education programs. As our society has become more urbanized, universities have expanded their ecosystem services traditionally aimed mostly at rural farmers to issues facing urban communities. In addition to their responsibilities at the university, faculty members often leverage their expertise in consulting roles and partnerships with outside organizations to directly help with programs across their life cycles.

When professors invent new technologies, they want the fruits of their research to reach the people. They work with the technology transfer office in the university to license the technology to companies. Sometimes, with the concurrence of the technology transfer office, they might even spin off their own companies. For example, a professor with research focused on preventing alcohol abuse among college students developed a phone app that lists nonalcoholic activities around town. The research forms the nucleus and informs a self-sustaining business that aims to reduce alcohol abuse and related problems on college campuses. Finally, the climate for faculty and student entrepreneurship has never been sunnier. Today's college students are growing up in a society with umpteen challenges and high unemployment rates. Many are jumping at the opportunity to solve problems and create jobs by becoming entrepreneurs. While some students are going it alone, universities are increasingly channeling this entrepreneurial zeal through formal education and incubation programs.

K-12 Schooling Systems

University students are educated in the K-12 education system, which is undergoing fundamental changes in terms of STEM teaching, project-based learning, technology integration, and global awareness. Some people have taken on the challenge of creating future STEM professionals head-on by creating nontraditional charter schools focused on the STEM areas. One example is the North Idaho STEM Charter Academy that teaches all subjects but aims to pique student interest in STEM fields through special emphasis and project-based learning. More traditional schools offer extracurricular activities to get students interested in STEM fields, from geography bees to programs run by outside entities. For instance, the Intel Science Talent Search is the nation's most prestigious science research competition for high school seniors, and Lemelson-MIT Inventeams is a program to support high school students that have formed teams with their teachers and partners in the community to pursue invention projects.

The effort to get students passionate about global challenges and innovative solutions relies on prepared, motivated teachers. Hence, many organizations focus on providing hands-on STEM educational opportunities to teachers. Such efforts include Teach For America and its international counterparts, nonprofits such as WorldTeach, and government programs like the Peace Corps.

Professional Organizations

Professional organizations seek to further a particular profession through supporting individuals engaged in that profession and piquing public interest in it. Entities like Engineers Without Borders (EWB) and Engineers for a Sustainable World (ESW) support community-driven development projects around the world to provide engineering solutions to community problems spanning agriculture, water quality, and disaster readiness. At the same time, college students and professionals who volunteer their time and expertise have transformative experiences that enrich their global perspectives. Discipline-centric organizations such as the American Society of Mechanical Engineers (ASME), the American Chemical Society (ACS), and the Institute of Electrical and Electronics Engineers (IEEE) are equally important for providing innovation support through research dissemination in published journals and networking opportunities in their communities. Many professional associations also develop standards for their field in terms of safety and performance and thus act as certifying organizations. In addition, professional organizations consult with governmental agencies and legislators on developing and amending relevant policies. Separately, think tanks are independent professional organizations that focus specifically on conducting research and performing advocacy around specific issues. Think tanks, also known as policy or research institutes, are typically nonprofit but can also be funded by larger businesses, interest groups, or governments. Regardless, think tanks perform many functions similar to universities and professional organizations in terms of converging experts and catalyzing dialogue, in addition to focusing on policy research and advocacy. Prominent think tanks in the US include the Institute for Homeland Security Studies, the Center for American Progress, and the Carnegie Endowment for International Peace.

Catalysts and Support Organizations

Social innovation and international development need money. Creating, developing, testing, and iterating solutions require financial, intellectual, human, and social capital. If a program to educate midwives in a rural area costs $10,000, it might be covered by a grant from a charitable organization. An intervention to educate solar technicians might cost $50,000 and be supported by a private foundation. However, most grant makers and social investors tend to be picky, with specific criteria and idiosyncrasies on what they will, or will not, support. Larger projects, especially those that require capital over a longer time period or that stand to make a profit and lean toward self-sustainability, might not be fundable by private donations. Alongside the mission-centric foundations, a variety of financing institutions contribute to domestic and international development without directly participating in ventures. While traditional nonprofit foundations provide donations and grants, for-profit firms and a growing number of nonprofits provide "impact investments." Impact investors are socially responsible organizations (for-profit and nonprofit) that invest money to yield financial and social returns on their investment.

A manufacturer of low-cost greenhouses might need an investment of $500,000 to reach smallholder farmers in a new country. If this company was working in the US, they would be able to get loans and investment capital from venture capitalists, angel investors, banks, and other sources. Venture capital and angel firms provide capital in return for partial ownership in startup companies. The investors earn significant gains if and when the startup grows. These large funding sources are not available in the developing world, or even in resource-constrained communities in the Unites States, because of the associated low gains and high risks. Impact investors support ventures like these that have the potential to become financially self-sustaining and hence viable in the longer term. This market-centric approach drives the social innovation sector toward self-sufficiency and scale. Examples include Spark Capital in Boston, which invests in startups focused on media, software, and transportation, and Angels' Forum in Palo Alto, which invests in startups focused on life sciences, technology, and consumer products.

There are also smaller financing institutions that do not have the scope of regional banks or NGOs. For instance, Village Capital is a nonprofit that runs programs to support entrepreneurs tackling social problems. At the end of each program, the entrepreneurs peer-select which of them most deserves an investment from their affiliated for-profit investment fund, VilCap Investments, LLC. Kiva, a peer-to-peer micro-lending platform, takes on a different business approach by uniting people around the world with entrepreneurs in underserved communities. Anyone with an Internet connection can offer a microloan to a startup company.

Given the complexity of the social innovation organization landscape, there is a real niche for matchmakers and catalyzers among programs. Matchmakers find promising mission-oriented organizations and connect them to consultants, foundations, and other entities that can provide transformational resources. D Capital Partners, for instance, matches underserved communities and initiatives with capital investors. As an investment advisory firm, D Capital Partners manages finances, transactions, and investment strategies. For example, they matched a private sector investor interested in improving global health with organizations on the ground in sub-Saharan Africa to provide them with up-front funding for malaria medication for them to pay back once their cost savings were achieved. Villgro provides technical insight to young technology-based ventures in addition to financial support. Their funding partners and industry mentors support health care, education, energy, and agricultural businesses across rural India. Villgro is one of many social business accelerators and incubators that support entrepreneurs in financial and nonfinancial ways, often through competitive scholarships for educational programs. These accelerators run programs to help entrepreneurs overcome the challenges of startup and scale-up in their ventures. Echoing Green takes this a step further by providing a two-year stipend for selected entrepreneurs along with health insurance and professional development allowances as well as access to pro bono partnerships, technical support, expert conferences, networking, and one-on-one counseling.

Certifying Organizations

Legal certification, or governmental regulation, is handled by governmental or intergovernmental bodies such as the EPA mentioned previously. These agencies legally regulate what development projects occur, and continue, within their jurisdiction. They also have a number of other responsibilities, often including research and grant making. However, there are also nongovernmental certifying organizations that focus on specific protections of environmental and socioeconomic ecosystems. These organizations are targeted at specific social problems—for instance, Good-Weave International, a coalition of NGOs, businesses, government entities, and multilateral groups, aims to raise demand for certified child-labor-free rugs so that manufacturers will employ only skilled, adult artisans, and children will no longer be exploited in the carpet industry.

In contrast to governmental regulations that are backed by law, some popular certifications are enforced by private consumers. For instance, the authority behind a Fair Trade USA logo comes from consumers that want to buy products certified to protect farmers and their ecosystems. Building developers may pursue certifications like the Leadership in Energy and Environmental Design (LEED) label for "green buildings." These independent LEED certifications set comprehensive standards for assessing the sustainability of construction, interior design, and neighborhood development. These standards also bridge the gap between independent and regulatory certifications since many US federal and state agencies reward LEED certification, and some even require it. This pursuit of a single standard unifies the efforts of many different social innovators and gives the community a common language and set of goals to strive toward.

Industry and Profit-Driven Organizations

Some of the biggest players in socioeconomic development are actually corporations that prioritize financial returns but balance them with environmental and social bottom lines. This balance can be difficult and controversial to strike, but profitable companies are critical for both economic sustainability and job creation. Companies of all types can support social innovators through financial assets and sociopolitical clout. Even social ventures can be run as for-profits because ventures that are not economically self-sustaining are difficult to scale! And to achieve the really big goals of social innovation—poverty eradication, full access to health care, universal education—the world needs lean, practical, economically viable approaches on a massive scale!

For the purposes of this book, we will focus on three kinds of for-profit companies: contractors, large corporations, and small startups. As mentioned earlier, organizations such as USAID and the World Bank do not directly implement their programs and agendas. Rather, companies such as Development Alternatives Inc. (DAI), Dalberg, and Chemonics bid on, and win, contracts to actually implement projects. For instance, DAI manages the East Africa Trade and Investment Hub, the flagship of the US presidential Trade Africa initiative. As the contractor, DAI tries to increase regional trade in staple foods, introduce policies that improve trade and investment, facilitate technology use and information sharing, and promote export trade.

Large corporations serve as the economic backbone of a country. Large corporations create jobs that stabilize communities and infuse money to enable innovation. People with stable salaries donate to nonprofits and support society. Companies manufacture and sell products, from toilet paper to cereal bars to light bulbs, that improve our quality of life and enable entrepreneurs to work smarter and faster. What company would be able to operate efficiently without electricity and cell phone service? What emergency response team could identify optimal locations of health centers without GPS? We owe gratitude to a large number of research labs and corporations for cell phones and electricity. We can thank NASA for the basic research on GPS technology and a bunch of corporations for the GPS units.

Realizing their potential to make a large social impact, large corporations are becoming increasingly interested in emerging markets. One example is GE. GE has an incredibly large portfolio of technologies that have traditionally been marketed within Western countries. However, they also have a Global Research and Development Center that identifies technologies in their portfolio that can address unmet needs in developing countries at scale and then identifies partners who can bring complementary resources to solve the problem. GE still makes some profit from these projects but also values their social return. Another example is Safaricom, the largest telecom provider in Kenya, which provides much more than communication services. The company has partnered with financial institutions, such as the Commercial Bank of Africa, to offer mobile financial services to people living in extreme poverty. M-Pesa, their mobile phone-based money transfer and microfinancing service, has enabled millions of Kenyans to streamline personal and business finances while increasing Safaricom's bottom line. These are just two examples of large corporations that seek a social return alongside their financial return; they help others while helping themselves—a win-win situation.

In essence, large corporations bring with them sustainability models and supply chains that can be harnessed to deliver other products. Large companies bring in huge amounts of financial capital, corporate experience, buying power, and public influence. Corporations and employees leverage this into social change by way of corporate giving, nonprofit advising, advocating for marginalized communities, and altering supply practices. Large corporations depend on a talented, dedicated workforce and are playing an increasingly larger role in important societal issues. For example, many companies stood against homosexual discrimination by states and other actors in the US, eventually resulting in changed government policies and new legislation against discrimination on the basis of sexual orientation. In terms of supply chains, sustainable sourcing has become important in many agriculture-based businesses: large corporations are able to control where they buy raw goods, and thus, can enforce social and environmental sustainability standards. For instance, Starbucks works with the Ethical Tea Partnership to ensure fair, sustainable sourcing. The Partnership ensures and monitors factory health and safety, fair and equitable worker treatment, and proper environmental and agrochemical management. The Hershey Company has sustainable sourcing programs in Ghana for cocoa. Hershey provides farmers with support and education to sustainably increase their cocoa yields, which improves and sustains incomes for farmers and ensures Hershey has a continued source for their cocoa.

Small companies and startups lack the immense resources of large corporations, but they can be much more agile and responsive to localized and rapidly changing needs. At the same time, their profitability also primes them to scale up quickly. In fact, most, if not all, startups in underserved communities can arguably provide scalable social impact. Entrepreneurship is crucial in low-resource settings, and virtually all ventures from energy to food security to health care provide marked improvement to customers' quality of life. More importantly, they create jobs and provide hope and encouragement in tough conditions. In 2011, Husk Power Systems was a small startup in Bihar, one of the poorest states of India. It has now installed eighty-four miniature power plants to provide sustainable electricity to 300 villages and over 33,500 households. Small companies like Husk Power Systems can experiment with technologies, business models, and collaborations quickly to figure out what can work and what can sustain.

Consulting Companies

Consulting firms provide subject-matter expertise to other organizations that need additional insight or skills. Many large and small organizations hire consultants to expand their institutional knowledge, acquire external views, or increase their overall output. Expertise in some areas, such as strategic redirection, process improvement, and renewed design, is not needed on a regular basis. Hence, it is rare for organizations—even large, successful ones—to retain and develop all the expertise they might need in-house. This is where consultants come in: they work with companies to understand the problem(s) and provide expert advice on how to address challenges. Most consulting firms leave the implementation of the advice to the host companies. As one might expect, only some of the recommendations are actually implemented, and the implementation can be limited or disjointed at best.

The largest consulting agencies are huge corporations that provide management, strategy, international business, and/or information technology support to large companies. Accenture, for instance, innovates across four platforms for their clients' ventures: strategy, operations, technology, and digital connections. Over 323,000 employees in 200 cities work across these four areas. Several large consulting companies have allied units dedicated to working with mission-centric organizations. For instance, Accenture Development Partnerships is a nonprofit arm of the company that collaborates with NGOs to help them deliver sustainable, global, market-driven social impact solutions using Accenture's institutional knowledge. Besides the large consulting companies and their impact-focused business units, there are small to large consulting firms that cater exclusively to nonprofits and mission-centric organizations. ICF International is a mission-oriented consulting company that offers political and managerial consulting to governmental organizations, major corporations, and multilateral institutions from more than seventy offices worldwide across the topics of energy and environment, health and social impact, and public safety and defense. Smaller nonprofit consultants can have even more specific clientele; for instance, IBS Global Consulting specializes solely in helping small and medium-sized businesses create sustainable growth through successful expansion into international markets.

Smaller consulting companies, often called boutique consultancies, often specialize in specific skill sets. They may, for example, specialize in emerging markets, life-cycle analysis, environmental impact mapping, product design, or strategic communications. Boutique consulting firms tend to provide chosen clients longer-term support from ecosystem mapping through implementation, rather than providing more hands-off support to a large number of clients. This enables the consultancies to provide creative, context-specific problem solving for their customers. While some consulting agencies are profit-driven enterprises, there are quite a few agencies established as nonprofits themselves. For example, the Foundation Support Group offers support ranging from financial advice for community charities to scale-up assistance for major NGOs. Their expertise and largest area of practice is in results-based monitoring and evaluation of social ventures. There are thousands of small consulting firms that rely on their professional networks to sustain and grow their businesses. A substantial number of these agencies are actually single consultants, hired independently for their insight and experience in a specific subject. No matter what the sector, geographical area, or specific problem, one can find consultants to come in and resolve the issue. Alongside the full-time professional consultants, experts from nonprofits, large corporations, and academia moonlight as pro bono or professional consultants, too.

Fourth Sector Organizations

The fourth sector encapsulates a wide range of hybrid organizations working at the intersection of the public (government), private (business), and social (nonprofit) sectors. Organizations in this emergent sector prioritize social value while being independent of charitable donations. In this hybrid space, businesses take an active interest in delivering social and environmental value while governmental and nonprofit organizations operate in a more businesslike manner. The goal of this new sector is to build sustainable and scalable solutions that optimize social impact. There is recognition that prioritizing social returns may limit growth or profitability in exchange for preserving social outcomes and core values. Organizations in the fourth sector have many names and flavors: social enterprises, sustainable enterprises, blended value organizations, nonprofit enterprises, benefit corporations, social businesses, community wealth organizations, ethical social institutions, new profit companies, faith-based enterprises, civic/municipal enterprises, cross-sectoral partnerships, community interest corporations, social economy enterprises, and community development corporations[12]. One of the most prominent types of fourth sector organizations is a blended value organization. A blended value organization is one that measures its success by its ability to holistically create social and environmental impact on society alongside financial performance.

For instance, Greyston Bakery sells brownies and cookies just like normal bakeries, but their motto says it all: "We don't hire people to bake brownies, we bake brownies to hire people." Their goal is to hire and empower people who would not otherwise be employable because of previous criminal history or lack of relevant skills. Greyston focuses on giving such individuals a chance at a job and helping them onto the path of self-sufficiency. They are for-profit, but they are for people. On the other side, Aravind Eye Hospitals are not like other nonprofit hospitals supported by donations through foundations and external funding. Aravind, which works to eradicate cataract-related blindness in India, now includes five hospitals, a research institution, a lens factory, an eye bank, and a training facility. It subsidizes its services for poor customers, often helping them travel from remote villages and providing low- or no-cost surgery and glasses—and they do it all by earning a profit. By operating with unparalleled efficiency in eye care and developing a sterling reputation in the field, they are also able to attract India's more affluent customers, who subsidize similar services for poor customers.

Another prominent type of fourth sector organization is a social enterprise. Although there is no uniform legal definition, a social enterprise is an organization that applies commercial strategies to maximize improvements in human and environmental well-being. Social enterprises can be structured as for-profit or nonprofit entities. In fact, they are often nonprofit entities that function according to for-profit sustainability principles, but with tax-exempt status. In the US, social enterprises may even form a new legal entity known as a low-profit limited liability company (L3C), which bridges the nonprofit-profit gap by providing a structure that facilitates investments in socially beneficial, for-profit ventures by simplifying tax requirements for program-related investments by private foundations. For example, Kickstart uses a similar hybrid model—legally a nonprofit but functioning as a business—to sell manual irrigation pumps that to date have raised 850,000 Africans out of poverty. Different enterprises can have widely disparate focuses, from organizations like Kickstart and Greyston selling irrigation pumps and brownies to entities like Kiva, which facilitates loans to underserved entrepreneurs from anyone with an Internet connection. Finally, organizations like Essmart focus on developing distribution channels to underserved communities, in Essmart's case throughout southern India. The different types of fourth sector organizations overlap, but the defining characteristic of all of them is that they integrate social and environmental outcomes with business approaches.

Concluding Thoughts

A recent article by Henry Mintzberg in the *Stanford Social Innovation Review* calls for grouping social organizations into "the Plural Sector," one that is neither public nor private, owned neither by the state nor by private investors[13]. It is a sector about shared "communityship" and made up of members with a purpose rather than employees with a job. Our society has three basic needs: protection, provided predominantly by governments; consumption, offered mainly by the private sector; and connection, found especially in our communities. A healthy society balances respected governments in the public sector, responsible businesses in the private sector, and robust communities in the plural sector. In the past, we have seen these three sectors fall out of balance, with the public sector dominating communist societies and the private sector dominating capitalist societies. Governmental and private sector organizations each have their own role in the ecosystem of sustainable development and social innovation. Organizations in the plural sector have a unique emerging role in advancing the ecosystem as a whole, and doing so in a balanced fashion. The expert briefs and innovator profiles in this book soundly validate Mintzberg's call for organizations in the plural sector to unleash an era of radical purpose-driven collaboration that optimizes the collective impact.

---

[12] "The Emerging Fourth Sector": fourthsector.net/learn/fourth-sector.

[13] "Time for the Plural Sector" by Henry Mintzberg (2015): ssireview.org/articles/entry/time_for_the_plural_sector.

TO E, OR NOT TO E

Carl Hammerdorfer

Carl Hammerdorfer is the managing director for Small Enterprise Assistance Funds' first African fund in Dar es Salaam, Tanzania. He is an amateur linguist, inveterate traveler, enthusiastic musician, and a pathological optimist.

So you say you want to be a social entrepreneur, but you are not sure you are cut out for the pressure, the risk, the criticism, those painful slings and arrows of outrageous fortune.

No worries. In case you missed it (possibly you are living under a rock or in a van down by the river?) there is a new, cool dude in town. And she is called the social entrepreneur!

That is right. She is that bold, hip, brave, clever iconoclast who is marching to her own drummer, sticking it to the man, doing her own thing, and building a great new company like nobody has ever seen . . . against all odds. Sure, she is smart enough to know that 90% of new ventures will fail. But she is also just dumb enough to think that there is a 90% chance that she is in the other 10%. You know, those ventures that could be HUGE! When you meet this hip world changer at your local coffee shop and ask her what she does, she will look you straight in the eye and say, "I am an entrepreneur." And you are like, "Whoa! That is cool!"

Most people today do not even remember that there was once a time when entrepreneurs were rumpled and hard-bitten, not all sunshine, energy, and light—more like a James Dean with a Rolodex or a Hell's Angel with a flip phone. Thought a fool by many. An eccentric. Possibly shunned by family and society, a wolf of the steppe.

Well, okay. Maybe not that dramatic, but nothing like today. Entrepreneurs in this third millennium are both totally in vogue *and* common as muck. Any guy-gal with an idea, a little money, and a website can now proudly proclaim, "I am an entrepreneur." And while it is true that for some that is just a more artful way of saying they are "in between jobs," or "consulting" (it sounds a lot better than, "I am unemployed at the moment"), let us not forget the added bonus that people like to buy entrepreneurs beers, listen to their ideas, maybe even give them a couch to lie on. . . . that is, if they ever sleep.

Thankfully, it is not just business students who are jumping on the entrepreneurship bandwagon. Engineers are all over it, scientists are trying to turn their inventions into companies, and even (gasp!) liberal arts graduates are donning the nametag. This E-rush could simply be fallout from corporate downsizing, offshoring, or the recent abysmal economy. Or it could be a fundamental change in how young people view life and work. But there is also the fun factor. I mean, come on? You work when you want, where you want, on what you want? Who can say no to that? Particularly if you can get other people to finance the whole deal.

The uber-cool of the entrepreneurship set are the social entrepreneurs. Not only are they building the next great company, but they are doing it to make a difference, to lift people out of poverty, to save the world, to. . . . you get the picture.

Social ventures are a unique type of business that make life better for their customers and for all of us, theoretically. They sell products that improve health, education, the environment, happiness, equality, etc. So the more they sell, the more good they do, and the more money they make. What is not to like about that?

Frankly, a lot, if you are not cut out for this line of work. All the aforementioned cache notwithstanding, this whole entrepreneurship thing can break your heart, your bank, and your relationships. It is not to be dabbled in if you are at all interested in success. So before you take that leap, ask yourself a few questions:

1. Are you that brilliant engineer or designer who thinks that inventing the solution or machine is 90% of the work? Do you so clearly see the beauty and utility of your product or service that you believe that commercializing said product/service is really just a simple, final step? If so, STOP RIGHT NOW! Nothing could be further from the truth. Just as objects in our mirror may appear smaller than they are, the challenge of building a venture to work financially is much larger than it appears. If you take this leap, be prepared for a long, frustrating process much more apt to fail than succeed (see "failure" below).

2. If you think you can invent cool stuff in a lab or at a whiteboard with a handful of your smartest friends and, in so doing, build a successful venture, STOP! Cool ideas on a whiteboard or a napkin may be the kernel of many a great venture, but the part that came after the great times in the design room is the real stuff of success. And that stuff is called customer contact, customer discovery, customer development, and a bunch of other things that have the word "customer" in them. The people who are going to give you money to build this company will love to hear about your product, but they are not likely to write you a check unless you can show them customers, their need, and the product that meets that need.

3. If you see parallels between how a widget moves through a machine or manufacturing process and the way humans behave, STOP! Products, science, and the physical world are rational and predictable. Smart engineers and scientists can solve all kinds of problems using materials, math, and the laws of physics. But in entrepreneurship it is usually some combination of human factors that doom a venture. Somebody on the team or in the transaction path does something irrational that stops your forward progress, and it just does not make sense to the entrepreneur. "Why are they not buying my solution!? It will save them money and make them healthier! Do they not understand?" No, they do not.

4. If you think you can build a company in Kenya or Guatemala while living in Austin or Boston, STOP immediately. As Woody Allen said, "80% of success is just showing up." And it is very hard to show up when you are 7,500 miles away. "But, we have a guy on the ground," or "I get to Cambodia five times a year" in almost all cases does not swing it. If you want to be a social entrepreneur in country X, then you must be willing to move to country X for (let me make a figure up) a minimum of eighteen months but more likely for three to five years. Cannot do that? Then consider building your social venture right where you live.

5. If you are super tenacious and simply refuse to fail, STOP. An operating rule of entrepreneurship is to fail . . . preferably fast. Another significant accomplishment of entrepreneurs is that they have failed often, at least in their early days. But be careful with this rule. Failing over and over without ever succeeding does not necessarily qualify you to say you are a serial entrepreneur. Several successful entrepreneurs are on record for saying that they did not even refer to themselves as such until their first success.

6. If you are not willing to endure the ridicule of friends and strangers or to submit your idea to my favorite website—WhyYourIdeaSucks.com—then STOP. Yes, you can have an ego in business, but no, you cannot attach that ego to your idea. The idea, product, and/or solution must live outside of you and be subjected to economic Darwinism and all the attendant criticisms that that entails—which kind of means you do too, if you have attached your ego to said idea.

7. If you are uncomfortable asking people for money, with a smile on your face and confidence in your heart, then STOP. It is most unlikely that you will be able to build something great without some cash (if you are a Rockefeller or a Kennedy, please disregard this rule). Someone who owns your business, you or a partner, needs to be happy asking for money.

8. If you place more weight on your inner Mother Teresa than on your inner Ray Kroc, you are lowering your opportunity to go big. The social enterprise world is littered with gaggles of lovely people sounding the charge for social and economic justice, but so many of them cannot make a payroll, often even their own payroll. If you cannot do that, you probably do not have enough customers to accomplish the social end that drove you to this path. Do not be afraid to make money!

None of the above is meant to discourage you. No, really! These are big questions that are meant to save you unnecessary effort, hardship, and possibly even heartbreak. (That is right; entrepreneuring can be hard on relationships too!) Starting a social venture provides all the aforementioned cache, benefits, and excitement, but it is not the only way to work for human or environmental benefit.

For example, the problem of global hunger is being grappled with by many different actors in many different ways. You can do your part as a writer, a researcher, a scientist, an investor, working through NGOs, or even getting into politics. If it is the problem that animates you, decide whether you are cut out to solve that through a business venture or via one of these other, often safer channels. It is very possible that you will learn a great deal about the problem you hope to solve by working one of these other avenues *and* getting a regular paycheck. And, while you tend to have more energy and less to lose in your twenties, you might be well served by the wisdom and savings that you will have by the time you are thirty-five or forty-five. On the other hand, you might also be too fat, dumb, and happy to take that leap at that point in your life.

Whatever you choose, the entrepreneur's crooked, rocky path or another way, there is one piece of advice that applies almost regardless. Remember the customer. Listen to their voices, understand their needs and challenges, and do not build your solution from the comfort of your air-conditioned office with three of your smartest friends. That is a sure path to disaster.

WHY YOU MIGHT WANT TO WORK IN RELIEF AND DEVELOPMENT (AND WHY YOU MIGHT NOT)

Nick Macdonald

Nick Macdonald is a relief and development professional with over fifteen years of experience. He has managed programs in conflict-affected areas of the Balkans, Indonesia, and Central Asia for a variety of international aid agencies and currently consults for international and US–based organizations as well as teaching "Conflict and Development" at the University of Oregon. His blog and book about Getting Your First Job in Relief and Development are at HumanitarianJobs.info.

Choosing a career path calls for self-reflection and an analysis of your interests, passions, and experiences. Congratulations if you have discovered what you want to do with your life! If that discovery has led you to think you might want to work in humanitarian relief and international development, here are some of the pros and cons of working in this field. While these are generally true, you should understand that organizations, roles, and assignments vary greatly.

Why should you work in development?

#1 A Job with Meaning That Aligns with Your Values

It seems to me that a lot of people have made peace with the idea that work is something that is separate from your values, from your passions, and from your interests—something that fills the workday and pays the bills, but what you really want to do happens on the weekends, evenings, and vacations. Mission-driven organizations provide one way to reconcile the two elements of seeking professional fulfillment and paying the bills. There is often no sharp distinction between work and the rest of your life, between your interests and passions and your job description. The upside of this is that you are doing work that you feel passionately about and are not doing so simply because you are getting paid to. Being a humanitarian aid worker is a lifestyle (a calling, if you will), not just a job.

#2 Opportunities to Make a Difference

On a good day, it can be the best job in the world. Really. I cannot imagine anything else being as interesting, challenging, exhilarating, and rewarding as some of the jobs I have had. Plus, every now and again, things go right, and you walk away feeling that, for some people, in some places, the world is a better place because of something you did. That is tremendously powerful and motivating, and it is what keeps many people doing this.

#3 A Community of Motivated Coworkers

The people I have met in this line of work are among the most wonderful friends and colleagues I can imagine. The bonds that are formed working together in intense situations are very powerful, and friendships formed over even a few days can be long lasting (although on occasion this intensity can produce equally high levels of acrimony!). Being part of this community of people who share similar values and aspirations is hard to quantify, but it is definitely a positive aspect of the job.

#4 Challenge and Responsibility

You will likely have more responsibility and authority earlier in your career than you would have in the corporate world. It can be a sink-or-swim situation, but if you swim, people will give you more and more responsibility. I vividly remember arriving in the office of a major NGO in Albania just as millions of refugees were fleeing war in Kosovo and being put in charge of a major part of the logistics of supplying the food for hundreds of thousands of people. I tried to explain that I was new and did not know how to do this; I was told that I would have to figure it out because no one else was there on the ground to do it. I swam, just about, and you likely will too. It is not that there is no support and training; it is just that you need to be ready to step up to challenges and expect to be given tasks that are overwhelming. It is part of the nature of the work: the problems we face are enormous and extremely challenging, and there is often no choice but to attempt to address a problem, even though the skills and resources available are not sufficient.

#5 See the World, Experience Different Cultures

Living and working in cultures other than your own can be fascinating and very rewarding. It is quite different from tourism and lets you get to know a society and understand more about it than many other types of travel. There are very few other careers that give you such an opportunity to experience a range of different countries than relief and development work. You will also see things that no one else will see—not all of them will be good, mind you, but they will be fascinating, challenging, and sometimes exciting!

Why should you reconsider if you want to work in development?

#1 Conditions

I've been stationed in some truly fantastic places, but the reality is that much relief and development work takes place in some of the more challenging locations in the world. In emergencies you may occasionally be called on to live in a tent or share a small room with coworkers; more frequently, in insecure environments you may live in the same house or compound as colleagues. You may not have reliable access to the normal amenities of the Western world, such as electricity, hot and cold running water, reliable heat and cooling, and the freedom of movement to explore at your leisure. While aid agencies very rapidly find solutions for providing many of these things to their staff (through generators, water-purification systems, etc.), the conditions in some postings can be tough.

#2 Workload

The flip side of a values- and passion-driven business that is focused on changing the world is that the employees are often expected to work hard and make personal sacrifices. Long hours and unpaid overtime are often the norm, and many jobs in the field are "meat grinders"—they are emotionally and physically exhausting, and people tend to burn-out in a few years. This is not to say that organizations themselves are always unreasonably demanding of their staff, but that they often have cultures and work ethics that are very demanding.

#3 It Is Not Always a Feel-Good Business

Some people want to work in this line of business because they want to help people and feel good about what they are doing. There is nothing wrong with that, but it is worth bearing in mind that it is not always a feel-good job. In places with high levels of need and suffering where resources are insufficient, neither you nor the beneficiaries of your work will likely feel particularly uplifted by the amount you are able to do. You may spend a lot of your time refusing requests because of inadequate resourcing and dealing with donors who are unsympathetic, officials who are uncooperative, or combatants who are unwilling to help. Do not expect to get a high level of recognition or praise for your efforts, or to feel that you are able to solve all the problems you will encounter.

#4 Relationships and Roots

While it creates intense friendships among colleagues, the business can place enormous strains on marriages and relationships. The pace of work, the upheaval of constant and unpredictable travel, separation from loved ones, and other stressors can make stable relationships difficult. Think seriously about the strains that this kind of work will place on your family relationships and friendships. Not only will you be away for long periods of time, but your experiences will change you and may make it more difficult for you to fit back into old relationships. It is not impossible by any means, but go into it with your (and your partner's) eyes open.

A Consideration That Cuts Both Ways: Pay

Many expats are able to pay less income tax (or even avoid it entirely) in their home country while they are living overseas (you should consult a tax advisor on the specifics of this as tax law changes frequently and is different in each country). Many postings are in relatively affordable locations where the currency you are earning will go a long way. Many international organizations have generous packages of housing, insurance, education for dependent children, etc., reducing expenditures further. Sometimes there are ways to have some student debt deferred or forgiven if you work for a nonprofit.

While there is a huge range of salaries and benefits, ranging from agencies that really "employ" only volunteers to organizations that pay extremely well, the pay even at the top end with the United Nations and some contractors is generally less than the equivalent in the corporate world. Furthermore, for most people working in the nonprofit world, it is decidedly mediocre compared to careers in the private sector. It is very hard to generalize, but most of the larger international NGOs have pay scales that allow their employees to live very comfortably, and if you are working overseas, the equation changes again.

TEN MYTHS OF WORKING IN THE NONPROFIT SECTOR

Triparna Vasavada

Triparna Vasavada is an associate professor of public administration in the School of Public Affairs at the Pennsylvania State University at Harrisburg. She teaches and does research in the field of nonprofit management. Her research interests include complexities and networks, gender issues, and leadership in nonprofits. She is active in professional organizations and enjoys reviewing journal manuscripts and nonprofit grant proposals.

The cross-sector partnership is not a new phenomenon anymore. Especially in the recent decade, business and nonprofit organizations have mingled and sectorial boundaries have blended. Nonprofits are being more entrepreneurial, and businesses are being more socially responsible. This convergence has fueled growth in both sectors that created jobs across the board. The nonprofit sector is growing fast and offers great avenues for career development. Nonetheless, there are several misconceptions about the nature of the nonprofit sector that might cause individuals to resist exploring this career path. Though the diversity of the sector offers an opportunity for individuals to work in a stimulating environment with flourishing innovative ideas, there are fallacies that are damaging the image of the nonprofit sector. It is important to burst the common myths to bring forth the real characteristics of the sector.

#1 Name Says It All . . . Nonprofits Cannot Earn a Profit

What is in the name? The terms "nonprofit," "not-for-profit," "voluntary organizations," etc. are misleading. Like any other organization, nonprofits can make a profit, and they absolutely should. For nonprofits, making a profit is as important as a business organization to ensure sustainability. However, they differ in their organizational goals. Nonprofit organizations are formed to benefit the public, not private interests. Therefore, they receive tax-exempt status and cannot distribute their profits to any private individual. They cannot register as a public limited company. This leads to popular myth #2.

#2 Salaries Are Low and Caring about Money Is Frowned Upon

Like any other organization, employees of nonprofit organization care about their own salaries. The "nonprofit" term indicates that the organization is not making a profit for itself. It is reinvesting the profits in the organization and its mission. Therefore, employees are paid competitive salaries. Though the level of salaries varies in the nonprofit sector, smart nonprofit organizations make all attempts to pay competitive salaries and benefits to hire strong talent. More and more nonprofits are paying salaries that are on par with for-profit salaries.

#3 Nonprofits Are Mainly into Service Work in Communities

The biggest strength and weakness of the field of the nonprofit is its diverse nature. Though the word "nonprofit" immediately brings an image of neighborhood soup kitchens and homeless shelters, there are many different kinds of organizations that are categorized as nonprofit organizations (e.g., advocacy groups, which work for social change; trade associations and professional association, which offer membership activities such as research support and training for a particular industry or profession; and religious institutions, like churches and temples). Nonprofits have the same organizational functions to perform as for-profits, such as website design and maintenance, accounting, database management, lobbying, human resource management, and others. They hire employees from the same pool of skilled people that for-profits are looking for.

#4 Working for a Nonprofit Is Just Like Volunteering—Laid Back, Less Professional, and Less Rigorous

This is illusive. Nonprofits are fast-paced, demanding, and disciplined. The nonprofit work environment is at times more challenging than the for-profits mainly because employees in nonprofits are encouraged to do more using fewer resources.

They are required to consider opinions of beneficiaries, communities, and funding sources when making decisions. Also, keep diversity in mind when you think about nonprofits. Although it is true that nonprofits engaged in direct services do rely on volunteers for certain tasks, volunteers often do not play a large role in organizational, financial, or other strategy makings. Therefore, nonprofit employees play a bigger role and face more challenges than volunteers in the organization.

5 Working in the Nonprofit Sector Is Not Competitive as Nonprofit Organizations Rely Heavily on Collaborations

Fierce competition exists in the nonprofit sector as organizations compete for the same pool of funding resources and for recognition. Though competition seems to be detrimental to organizations with a shared mission, it could be a promoter for innovative solutions. Nonprofits strategically enter into collaborations to work on similar problems to find different solutions. Collaborations are also considered as strategy to overcome the lack of certain expertise or resources. Therefore, collaboration does not dilute the innovative nature of nonprofit work environment; it makes it even more challenging and stimulating.

#6 Passion Is an Important Qualification for a Nonprofit Job

Passion is great for any job! However, it is not a reality that only people with a passion for changing the world work in nonprofits. Like any other organization, nonprofits are looking for a professional fit. An employee's skills and experience are more important. Although some nonprofit workers are passionate about the mission of their organization, they are employed because their skills are a good fit with the demand of the organization. Passion is a plus. A proven track record of achieving strong results matters more, and there are employees who are not quite as passionate but work in the nonprofit due to a strong professional fit.

#7 Nonprofits Get Most of Their Funding from Foundations

Nonprofit organizations have several types of revenue sources, including individual donations, fees for services, government grants and contracts, private foundations, corporate foundations, and other types of grants. Though it is difficult to generalize because of the diverse nature of the nonprofit sector, foundation grants represent only a small part of the total number of dollars. Many organizations earn the major part of their revenue from charging fees to their clients; think about medical research hospitals. Some nonprofits depend solely on government contracts and individual donations. There are diverse financial resources available, and it is impossible to generalize about foundations as the main source of funding for nonprofits.

#8 Nonprofits Are Flat and Nonhierarchical

It is a common belief that nonprofits have flat organizational structure and are nonhierarchical. They pursue more democratic decision making and provide open channels of communication with executives. Nonprofits that are relatively small in size might have a flat structure, and interns can have a similar level of input as its CEO in decision making; however, not all nonprofits are in the same category. Think about research institutes and large nonprofit higher education institutes. There is a line of authority just as there is in the for-profit sector with hierarchical structure and bureaucracy. The blending of the for-profit and the nonprofit sectors is on the rise, and employees bring their management practices from the business environment to drive success in nonprofits. The hierarchical organizational structure is one of those.

#9 The Economy Does Not Depend on Nonprofit Jobs

No, this is no more the reality. In recent decades, nonprofit organizations have been shown to play an important role in the nation's overall economic growth. According to a report by the Urban Institute, approximately 1.58 million nonprofits were registered with the Internal Revenue Service (IRS) in 2011, an increase of 21.5% from 2001. An estimated $836.9 billion was contributed to the US economy by the nonprofit sector in 2011, which made up 5.6% of the country's gross domestic product (GDP). In addition to the growth in the number of nonprofit organizations, employment within the nonprofit sector has shown growth, even beyond employment growth in other sectors. Therefore, the nonprofit sector is now considered an important contributing sector for the nation's economic growth.

#10 Nonprofit Sector Is for "Business Rejects"

Yes, nonprofit and for-profit organizations are distinctly different, yet jobs in the nonprofits require similar skills that are required for-profit jobs. The lines between the two sectors are blurring. Now people often change jobs from one sector to the other; each sector presents its own set of challenges, but there are many talented people in both sectors. The differences in both sectors are understood better, and employees capitalize on skills they learned in one sector to grow their career in the other sector.

FIVE REASONS NOT TO START YOUR OWN NGO (AND THE ONE TIME YOU CAN CONSIDER IT)

Alanna Shaikh

Alanna Shaikh is an international development consultant based in Cairo, Egypt; she focuses on helping small NGOs achieve big impacts. Her experience includes work with USAID and the UN as well as NGOs and private companies involved in international development. She is the author of What's Killing Us: A Practical Guide to Understanding Our Biggest Global Health Problems published by TEDbooks in 2012, and she currently writes about global health and development for UN Dispatch, Global Dashboard, and her own blog, Blood and Milk[14]. Alanna is a senior TED Fellow, and she holds an MPH from Boston University.

"Directing the African Prisons Project is a great privilege. I am excited by the transformation I see in the lives of the prisoners and prisons staff in Kenya and Uganda with which we work. I learn a huge amount from these men and women, who are change makers, and I look to the change they will bring in their communities and nations with great interest. However, this work is hard; relentlessly, constantly hard and I wonder if it must be this way."

– Alexander McLean, founder of the African Prisons Project

Why Should You Not Start Your Own NGO?

#1 Your Idea Is Not That Good, or That New

It is really not. I know it feels exciting and innovative, but development is littered—littered like Miami Beach after spring break—with exciting ideas that did not turn out like anyone expected them to. Check out the Hippo Roller, One Laptop per Child, or the entire concept of microfinance if you do not believe me. It is just about 100% certain that someone has tried your idea before. If they made it work, you should go find them and work with them. Why would you start a competitor to a successful, good idea?

Good development work is all about knowing your context. That means the context of the place where you are working—the village, hospital, or nation you are working with. It also means the context of your intervention. You need to know if anyone else has ever tried offering solar energy, or distributing baby warming wraps, or outsourcing their work to refugee camps[15]. Other people's failures are your best education, and you do not get that by starting an NGO and hoping to sort things out as you go.

#2 You Have No Idea Where to Get Funding

Getting money for your good idea is really hard. If you plan on going the government-donor/foundation route, it is a difficult, ugly path of conforming to what donors want from you. At some point, if you are doing exactly what donors want, you need to wonder what value your cookie-cutter organization brings. You are just a competitor with a bunch of other, similar groups.

And if your plan is to sell a product at low cost to the intended users, it is not going to work. No one is going to buy your social entrepreneurship product, at least not easily. Not even in the BRICs. Sorry. Customers, be they individual or institutional, do not automatically recognize a useful product. The Coca-Cola logo is recognized by 94% of the world's population. They are selling cheap, nearly addictive caffeinated sugar, and they still have to spend $2.9 billion a year on marketing.

---

[14] These writings can be found at: UNDispatch.com (*UN Dispatch*), theglobaldispatch.com (*Global Dispatch*), and bloodandmilk.org (*Blood and Milk Blog*).

[15] For examples of these three, see Solar Sister (solarsister.org), Embrace (embraceglobal.org), and Samasource (samasource.org).

Your product will require marketing. In fact, the more innovative your product is, the more marketing it will require. Are you a marketing expert? Are you ready to hire one? It is going to be years before your sales cover your costs.[16]

#3 You Do Not Know How to Manage People

Management is both a talent and a learned skill, and it is a stunningly rare individual who is a good manager based on talent alone. You learn to manage from being managed. Good managers give you behavior models. Bad managers show you what not to do. It is much easier to lead a team when you have real experience being part of a team.

Starting an NGO means you do your management learning in the highest-stakes situation possible. Your beneficiaries and your team depend on you. Mistakes could be the actual end of your whole organization. And you are doing it all from scratch?

#4 It Is Boring

Running an NGO is a lot of administrative and organizational work that will take you away from your core passion and technical skills. Have a passion for water engineering? Tough luck. The head of a water-engineering NGO spends her time talking to donors, dealing with the media, and managing the people in her organization. Being a small NGO actually makes that effect worse because you do not have a human resources or public relations department to help you. You have to do it all yourself. Kjerstin Erickson, founder of FORGE, a refugee NGO that died a sad, quiet death, talks about inexperience and its impact in an article for GuideStar.[17]

#5 Failure Has Major Consequences

Poor people spend most of their time trying to survive—earning money and otherwise acquitting the means to provide for their basic needs and the needs of their families. (Read *The Poor and Their Money* if you do not believe me.) When you waste the time of poor people, you waste something very precious. That means your NGO can potentially have high impact of the worse possible kind (think meteor). If you try and fail, you have lost a couple years where you could have been earning a better salary, going to grad school, or learning the cello. But your community—the people who gave their time and energy and limited resources—will have lost a lot more. Their opportunity cost is much, much greater. They did not lose the chance to learn French. They lost the chance to feed their children a better diet.

One Exception:

There are times when it actually might make sense to found an NGO. If you are a member of the community affected by the problem you are trying to solve, you have unique knowledge that helps make up for everything I just listed. If you have a unique, guaranteed funding source that no one else can access, then even an inefficient NGO is probably doing more good than harm[18]. And if you have deep background on your chosen issue (I am thinking at least a decade of experience) and you can say with certainty that no one is covering the specific issue you care about, you are probably adding value by creating an NGO.

You will still probably collapse. Most startups fail, be they NGO or for-profit. But if you have one of those advantages going for you, it may be worth a try.

---

[16] The life cycle of a useful, culture-appropriate product that still did not sell: gcstz.com/history.

[17] The story of the end of an international nonprofit: trust.guidestar.org/2013/06/20/nonprofit-emaciation.

[18] I admit, I have trouble envisioning this situation. Perhaps your eccentric billionaire uncle will help the endangered puffins only if you are leading the effort? Even so, your time might be better spent convincing him to support the Audubon Society: projectpuffin.audubon.org/puffin-faqs.

THE EVOLVING ROLE OF LARGE CORPORATIONS IN SOCIAL INNOVATION

Renee Wittemyer

Renee Wittemyer is the director of social innovation in the Corporate Affairs Group at Intel Corporation. In her role she leads Intel's efforts to engage young people in innovation and entrepreneurship programs globally and works across Intel's business to develop social innovation opportunities. She also manages Intel's global relationships with strategic alliances such as USAID, the World Bank, NGOs, and UN Women.

The public may believe that economic and social bottom lines are at odds with one another, that major corporations are focused only on profit, and that social endeavors beyond the needs of public relations are not relevant to profit. This is an oversimplification. In truth, large corporations do something for social innovation and development that even governments, corporate foundations, and major nonprofits cannot: mobilize the power of vast, sustainable private resources. Corporations are increasingly embracing this unique role in social innovation, and in turn they are shaping the development landscape and society as a whole in important ways.

#1 The Importance of Large Corporations

Large corporations have both the stability and the perspective to think in advance. Their amassed resources mean they know what has worked in the past and want to maintain their positions by paving the way into the future. They have the human, financial, and knowledge capital to not just identify gaps and opportunities, but to quickly design products and services to fill them. Compared to donation-based entities or startup entrepreneurs, large corporations can achieve economies of scale very quickly, even in new market niches. This gives them the opportunity to be both efficient and agile in new markets if they adopt the right strategies.

#2 The Evolving Role of Large Corporations in Society

Consumers and employees are increasingly coming to expect responsible social practices from global companies. In fact, more corporations are realizing that employees prefer working for responsible companies, and consumers will pay more for positive societal and environmental impact. This has led to a widely adopted business philosophy that intertwines purpose and profits, "doing well by doing good." This attitude cuts across industries and business models, from Kellogg's and Pepsi, to 3M and Microsoft, to Gap and Nike.

In the world of public-private partnerships, there has been a significant shift from a focus on partnerships driven by philanthropic interests of companies to those driven by principles of "shared value." Such partnerships seek to align the core business capabilities of a company to advance efforts that both deliver societal impact and drive business growth and long-term sustainability.

Companies like Intel have embraced this directly with its corporate mandate to "create and extend technologies to connect and enrich the lives of every person on Earth." For example, on the sourcing side, in 2014, Intel became the first company to manufacture only "conflict-free" microprocessors. Technology companies like Intel are also on the cutting edge of environmental sustainability in general, from pioneering research in energy efficiency to building socially responsible supply chains. In terms of employment, many technology companies are investing in developing the pipeline of women and underrepresented minorities in STEM fields and in the technology industry. Intel Capital announced the Intel Capital Diversity Fund—the largest of its kind—to invest $125 million in businesses led by women and underrepresented minorities. Intel also pledged a $300 million investment to increase the company's workforce diversity. In addition, many large corporations directly support employee volunteerism, whether by matching grant programs or flexible work practices. In essence, large corporations arc increasingly interested in helping employees and customers find their niche. What would be more compelling than Intel even helping retirees transition into local nonprofit organizations?

#3 Large Corporations as Platforms for Social Innovation

In addition to creating shared value, large corporations also play an important role in preparing and supporting future game changers. As resilient and well-resourced companies, they can be a very good place to learn and experiment with opportunities. Professionals in large companies get immediate exposure to successful processes, workflows, and teammates. They learn how, and why, organizations work and how to navigate within them, and with partners. Corporations, particularly those with strong social innovation missions, also provide the resources and encouragement that professionals need to experiment quickly and efficiently without taking on the risks of entrepreneurship. Whether you intend to stay in your company as an intrapreneur or use your knowledge and experience for entrepreneurship, large corporations can be a great place to start your career or provide a platform to achieve certain kinds of impact . . . at scale.

THE SECRET LIFE OF UNIVERSITIES AS ECONOMIC AND SOCIAL DEVELOPMENT HUBS

James K. Woodell

Jim Woodell is assistant vice president for innovation and technology policy at the Association of Public and Land-grant Universities (APLU). He is the staff director for APLU's Commission on Innovation, Competitiveness, and Economic Prosperity (CICEP) and for the association's Council on Engagement and Outreach (CEO), working with members in both organizations to advance the impact of public research universities in their communities and around the world. Jim's research interests lie in how institutions of higher education adapt to evolving engagement missions.

These days, universities are about a lot more than teaching students and conducting research. More and more, they are hubs for innovation and economic development. University leaders are increasingly concerned with what happens to students and scientific discoveries once they leave classrooms and laboratories. They are interested in making sure that knowledge has impact.

#1 Why do universities care so much about impact?

Universities are made up of people—students, faculty, and staff—and four of the key reasons these groups are engaged in economic development are problems, relevance, pressure, and resources. They are all interrelated, but individuals at universities might see one or two of them as more important than the others.

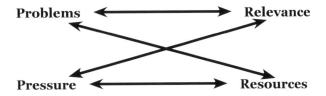

Problems. Every minute of every day, our world gets more complex. The social and economic problems that we face seem to grow ever more complicated. People at universities are good at complicated problems, but they are finding that they have to do things in new ways—collaboratively, across disciplines—in order to tackle today's level of complex problems. Solving problems is rewarding in and of itself, of course, but also because it can result in real improvement in people's lives. Finding these solutions helps individuals see the value and relevance of their work. At the same time, ever more complex problems press the limits of the resources available.

Relevance. University people like to solve problems because they like seeing that their work, which can sometimes feel detached from the real world, plays a role in making society better. A lot of what universities focus on is "curiosity-driven" research—looking for answers to fundamental questions. Universities also undertake "applied" research, which is more focused on practical problems. Whether engaged in fundamental or applied research, students and faculty are inspired when they can see how pursuing their curiosity can lead to meaningful change and improvement in the lives of others.

Pressure. Relevance is also of interest to the general taxpaying public and the politicians who represent them. They expect that most things universities do will have relevance—that we will not waste our time and money on things that do not help us get healthier, stronger, safer, and/or more prosperous. Particularly in tough economic times, they apply pressure on our universities to focus their intellectual and other assets on activities that can have immediate impact.

Resources. Tough economic times for society in general also mean lean budgets for universities. As resources become more and more limited, people at universities look for ways to justify resource expenditures in hopes of getting access to what is needed to continue to work on the complex problems to which they wish to contribute solutions.

#2 How Universities Contribute to the Social and Economic Good

As universities become more problem-focused and interested in relevance, their work increasingly focuses on economic and social development. Universities are traditionally known for pursuing three missions: learning, discovery, and engagement. When you think about these missions in terms of the outcomes they produce, you get the central ways in which universities contribute to social and economic development: talent, innovation, and place. Each of these unfolds in this framework of problems and relevance described above.

Talent. Ask any university president what their institution does to promote economic development and the first thing they are likely to say is "graduation." By preparing students for the working world, institutions of higher education feed the economy with the talent necessary to create value, turning ideas into products and solutions.

Colleges and universities are looking at how to better connect the talent development they do to the needs of the economy. They are developing programs that help students and faculty alike understand what it takes to be an effective entrepreneur. They are rethinking student learning, how professors teach, and what is taught. Institutions are implementing "high-impact practices"—things like undergraduate research, co-ops, internships, learning communities, and capstone projects—that engage students in problem solving and better prepare them for life and work after college.

Innovation. Just as students entering the workforce represent a significant economic contribution made by universities, so do ideas entering the marketplace—that is, innovation. Some researchers spend a lot of time trying to unlock answers to the most fundamental questions of the universe, and others focus their work on more practical issues. While working at either kind of discovery, researchers create knowledge and spark ideas about how to solve problems in the real world. Efforts to capitalize on knowledge and ideas—supporting faculty and student businesses, undertaking technology transfer and commercialization efforts—illustrate the ways in which universities contribute to economic development through innovation.

Innovation is part and parcel to the work of most universities like never before. Institutions are building innovation parks where university researchers and students can interact with industry. They are creating maker spaces and fab labs. They are emphasizing inventions and patents as important outcomes of research, along with publications and advancing knowledge. With this increased emphasis comes a focus on new ways to recognize student and faculty invention and entrepreneurship. Engagement with the economy and with society around innovation is being woven into the fabric of the university.

Place. Universities and other higher education institutions help to create great places to live and work. Contributing to the economy also means addressing social, cultural, and community needs. Universities engage with key partners in their regions and around the world to improve the environment, public education, health care, and civic life.

Creating great places means trying new approaches to helping communities. Universities are building academic and research centers in the middle of urban downtown neighborhoods and placing research and teaching centers alongside residential and shopping districts. They are making themselves a more integrated part of "K-20" education systems, creating better connections to elementary and secondary schools to improve student success. Institutions are talking with regional leaders to find out how institutional assets can be mapped to the needs of the community to create stronger ties. Colleges and universities are often considered "anchor institutions"—place-based organizations that are not going to pull up stakes and leave, therefore playing an important role in the health and prosperity of their regions. More and more, universities are recognizing and committing to this role, while continuing to work toward global impact.

#3 Frontiers of Social and Economic Engagement

To achieve outcomes in talent, innovation, and place development, universities and other higher education institutions need to address some important gaps if they are to have impact.

Knowing. First, there are gaps in what institutions of higher education know about social and economic engagement and how best to do it. Universities must reflect on their work and contributions in these arenas; define their role in their communities, regions, and the world; and have an awareness of what they are good at as well as where they need to improve. They must know their capacity.

Measuring. Part of knowing is measuring. As institutions engage in economic development and other efforts to benefit the public good, it is important that they work to set goals and measure their impact. A frequently used phrase is "what gets measured gets done." Economic and social development are about getting things done, so measuring is critical.

Telling. Knowing and measuring are only as good as telling. Universities have to be able to tell their story with regard to the contributions they make to social and economic development. Public institutions in particular rely on the support of lawmakers and the citizenry. People want to know how universities and other institutions of higher education are relevant to the challenges their communities face. If universities are unable to tell their story, public support can wane, and their capacity to continue this work will wane along with it.

Universities do not accomplish social and economic outcomes on their own. It is only through partnerships with communities, business and industry, government, and nonprofit organizations that institutions of higher education can accomplish these kinds of goals. Knowing, measuring, and telling must be done in partnership with these stakeholders. Universities cannot simply hand over knowledge or discoveries. They must ask what partners need and invite them to co-lead the exploration for solutions.

#4 Your Engagement as a Higher Education Social Innovator

Institutions of higher education are at a crossroads, and they need the skills and mindset you can bring as a social innovator. As universities increasingly seek to have and make clear their impact, your passion for making a difference can lead the way. As they look to translate ideas into action, your focus on value creation is critical. You and other social innovators are the engines that will continue to drive institutions of higher education as hubs for social and economic development.

The time is ripe to make a difference. How can your work in STEM or other areas of social innovation respond to the ways universities work and help them bridge the gaps that are discussed above?

ACADEMIA: BASE FOR INNOVATION AND ENTREPRENEURSHIP

Sven Bilén and Gari Clifford

Sven G. Bilén, PhD, PE, is professor of engineering design, electrical engineering, and aerospace engineering and head of the School of Engineering Design, Technology, and Professional Programs (SEDTAPP) at Penn State. He believes that innovation happens at the interface of disciplines, which has led him to pursue interdisciplinary approaches in his job as an academic.

Gari Clifford, DPhil, MA, MS, SMIEEE, is an associate professor of biomedical engineering and biomedical informatics in the Departments of Biomedical Engineering and Biomedical Informatics at Georgia Institute of Technology and Emory University. Gari believes innovation is a form of gradient descent and enjoys the odd local minimum from time to time, but not for too long.

It has often been said that all academics are entrepreneurs, even if they are not starting companies. To be successful as an academic (particularly in engineering or the sciences), you need to run a successful research group (company) by writing research grants (business plans) to granting agencies (funders, investors), then finding and mentoring students (hiring and managing employees) to engage in new discoveries (products and publications). Of course, research is not the only role expected of academics; we are also expected to provide impactful teaching and service, and innovation in these areas is required in order to be successful. No longer is "chalk and talk" the only style of teaching; rather we are trying "flipped classrooms," hands-on design labs, online delivery, and MOOCs. Stuffy faculty service committees are giving way to enhanced connections with the community and an ability to manage increasingly complex interactions among academia, industry, government, and society.

In this brief, we will examine the role of academics and how academia can be used as a base for innovation and entrepreneurship. Along the way, we will also help dispel some myths about academics, which is important because students may have only a narrow view of the profession because of limited interactions with faculty during their time in college. Given our own backgrounds, our focus here is on faculty positions in the STEM fields at research universities in the Western world.

#1 Types of Academic Positions

First, it is very important to understand that there is a variety of academic appointments. The one most people think about when we say "professor" is that of a tenured/tenure-track faculty member. This appointment type is highly desired, and competition for new positions is extremely fierce (often hundreds of applicants for every open position). It almost always requires a doctorate degree, has a prescribed timeline to the tenure-and-promotion decision (usually six years), and can be quite stressful given the performance expectations in the areas of teaching, research, and service. Tenure is granted for demonstrated impact at the national level and promotion to full professor for impact at the international level.

More and more, universities are employing faculty off the tenure track. There are many reasons for this: having the ability to employ people with nonacademic backgrounds in areas of specific needed expertise; workforce flexibility for both the academic and the university; and, quite frankly, as a cost-saving measure. One of the myths is that all faculty want a tenured appointment. Some non-tenure track (NTT) faculty have worked their careers in a relevant field and wish to give back by teaching the next generation without being put through the tenure ringer so late in their career. The university benefits from their wealth of practical knowledge and connections to the "real world." A few NTT faculty have other "day jobs" and appreciate the opportunity to teach one or two classes, interact with students and other faculty, and bring material from their job into the classroom and from academia into their day job. Others enjoy the flexibility to care for their children or parents, pursue a startup or consulting career, or have the ability to take off a semester if need be. Postdocs are another kind of academic appointment, which is often used by recently minted PhDs to get additional training and to begin to define their own research agendas—indeed, in some fields having completed a postdoc may be a requirement before applying for a tenure-track position. Given their growing numbers, most universities are grappling with how to create an inclusive environment for their NTT faculty, one which fully utilizes their skills and experiences and makes them feel connected to the complete mission of the university and not just the teaching mission.

Appointment type also describes what is expected of you. A tenure-track faculty member is expected to do teaching, research, and service. NTT faculty may have appointments that are focused primarily in one of these areas, with the expectation to contribute at a lower level in the other areas. Regardless of the type of appointment, we like the analogy that an academic position is like holding a ticket to the amusement park: you are inside the gates, so you can try all the rides! That is, avail yourself of the many opportunities, facilities, resources, colleagues, etc. within the university to pursue a career with maximum impact.

#2 Teaching

One of the myths is that faculty who excel at research perform poorly as a classroom instructor. Sure, there are examples of this, but in general, the data show otherwise. And when you think about it, it make sense. Faculty translate complex concepts into readily learnable nuggets and also contextualize what students are learning. For material on the bleeding edge, faculty whose research is also on the bleeding edge are those best equipped to create the right learning environment. In the area of social innovation, this is especially true. Those who have been out in the field, collecting and interpreting data, working to establish ventures, etc., are those best able to teach what it takes, with "real-world" examples and, most importantly, a true understanding of context.

Our responsibility as faculty is to create the best environment for learning, exploration, and application that we know how, and the student's responsibility is to do the learning, exploring, and applying. We wish we could just open up your head and pour in the knowledge, skills, and understanding, but this is not possible—nor would it be as much fun or as meaningful! A quote from the great author Mark Twain is particularly apropos: "I have never let my schooling interfere with my education." It is important for faculty to show students that much learning goes on outside the classroom—indeed, it is those environments where the greatest learning will occur!

Another aspect that falls under teaching is the mentorship of undergrads, graduate students, and postdocs. This tends to be more one-on-one, and the impact we have on our mentees' futures can be quite impactful. We can list numerous cases where our input and contacts led to great job postings; our knowledge of the state of the art enabled a student to achieve more, faster; and our experience helped smooth over a particularly bad setback or failure. The personal relationships are one of the most rewarding aspects of our jobs.

Perhaps the best part of academia is teaching a class and spotting the student(s) who you are sure will surpass you and go on to greater things. It happens to us all at some point, and it is a great thing to know the world passes into more and more skilled hands with every generation. Perhaps the best moment of innovation and creativity comes in the classroom—from both sides. When you teach a subject and *really* prepare for it, you find out just what you do not understand about the subject yourself, and you learn as much, if not more, than the students themselves. This constant learning (through teaching) is what reinvigorates an academic's research, provides them with new ideas, and helps them to reach a deeper understanding of the subject. It is often said that teaching gets in the way of research—and the volume of teaching can sometimes do that—but it is a myth because teaching can be an integral part of the innovation process. When students are aware that they are actively involved in helping shape the curriculum (for future years), then they tend to react more positively to the material, and to learn more deeply.

Teaching is assessed through student feedback, innovation of the courses, and through mentorship. Perhaps another myth is that academics do not care what their students think of them. In fact, we are delicate creatures who hope for ubiquitous popularity while providing challenging, rewarding material. However, this is impossible for several reasons. First, not everybody will like you. That is a good lesson for life. Some people will dislike you whatever you do, so it is best to just move on. Second, everybody learns in a different way, so you cannot satisfy the enormous distribution of skills and learning styles you will encounter. Finally, data collection methods are imperfect, and feedback tends to be biased—only the very effusive and annoyed are inclined to provide feedback.

The feedback process is part of the fun and innovation, though, particularly when it leads to positive "reverse mentoring." Often we are asked to list who we have mentored and where they are now. A long list of successes is expected, with positions in academia and industry, or less frequently, in related areas such as government or nongovernmental organizations (NGOs). The reason for this is that perhaps the most important thing we do in academia is to ensure our mentees leave our research groups and are themselves successful. However, there is another, perhaps unspoken, reason for this: we can leverage our connections to develop unique collaborations both inside and outside academia, resulting in continued innovation through industrial-academic partnerships that would not exist otherwise in either organization. This is perhaps the most exciting of innovation platforms because research can progress into a product rapidly, and an academic can initiate innovative applied research that might take a long time to fund or that might sit outside conventional funding mechanisms.

#3 Research

In general, academics enjoy the freedom to set their own agenda in terms of what they research and how they teach. This is perhaps our primary motivation for being in this type of job, and in fact, a good academic reinvents their research agenda every decade or so in order to adapt to the changing funding climate, which reflects the rapid changes in society that we see nowadays. However, the need to obtain funding is often a strong shaper in terms of an academic's focus, and the most exciting and innovative ideas require innovative funding approaches (such as crowd-funding). In particular, a steady drop in funding levels (per academic) over the past decade has led to searches for funding from sources other than the government, including startups. This has led to some interesting tensions in academia between the need to innovate and the need to satisfy investors who expect a return on investment. If an academic is not careful, they can find themselves in a position where the board of a company and the investors do not understand the product well enough and take a "safe harbor" view to publication of raw data and source code, seeing any public dissemination of this as threatening to the business. This is, in effect, the antithesis of academia (which tries to promote open dissemination of the science behind an innovation). Academics are generally itching to publish their code and data for others to use. One of the fun parts of academia is seeing someone else copy your work, reuse it, thank you, find bugs in your code, and then improve it.

Research is often valued by the number and size of grants, number of high-quality publications (in high-impact journals), patents, and the resultant tangible products (such as databases, code repositories, and sustainable training programs). More recently, researchers are also being evaluated by their personal impact factor, such as the h-index, which reflects the number of times their work is reused or influences others through citations. This is an interesting notion because it encourages a researcher to spend time posting open source code and well-documented open access data. In doing so, it is more likely that their work is cited, and rightfully so, as they are providing the only truly repeatable scientific documentation. This opportunity to add to the creative commons is a key driver for many academics and leads to a disproportionate level of innovation.[19] Although grant authorities have been mandating such activity over the last decade, the mandates often fall short of the prescriptive needs of researchers, and barriers to open innovation remain. The opportunity to lead the field and develop new models of innovation based on open data and open source code is an exciting opportunity that is rarely seen in industry. The myth that it is impossible to protect and commercialize open source code is slowly dying, and companies from Google to General Electric Medical are using patent-free and patent-protected open source code.

There are also a growing number of social media platforms specifically for academia, such as Google Scholar, ResearchGate, and, to a lesser extent, LinkedIn. These platforms allow academics to see the research others in (and outside) their field have published, who their coauthors are, and the impact the research has had based on who has cited it in their own research. Although mechanisms existed in the past, these new platforms have leveraged the power of social media to allow people outside academia and in developing countries to easily access research publications. This is especially important for social innovators.

#4 Service

Contributions to service in academia are often perceived to be rather nebulous, and although traditionally they have included editorial work on journals; sitting on various department, college, university, local, national, and international committees; and organizing conferences, the term "service" is starting to encompass a wider perspective. Academics routinely consult, sit as expert witnesses, or act as advocates. They are also beginning to start their own NGOs, institutes, or centers for innovation that address disadvantaged populations. This sector is increasingly becoming a focus for innovation both from within and from without, with universities taking on an increasing role.[20] This is in part due to the facilitatory effect of the explosion of ubiquitous mobile communication technology and also the enormous passion that a younger generation (both students and faculty) is taking in the subject.

It is important, however, to remember Sayre's law as applied to academia: "The politics of the university are so intense because the stakes are so low." We have been in faculty meetings where passions became heated over a seemingly trivial matter. It is important to keep your head on straight and seek to work for the betterment of the institution and those you engage with.

---

[19] Example of a creative commons community: PhysioNet.org.
[20] Example of innovation using academia: UNICEF's Innovation Labs.

#5 Collaboration

It is a myth that all research in academia exists in silos, i.e., that faculty are focused on only very narrow areas of inquiry and do not collaborate with others. Increasingly, academics are recognizing that, in order to solve the hard problems of the twenty-first century, we need to take a systems-oriented, interdisciplinary approach, which means building teams with a broad representation of expertise and backgrounds. Indeed, universities may perhaps be uniquely positioned in this regard because you have subject-matter experts on almost every topic you can imagine, particularly at large, research-oriented institutions. This creates a rich environment for pushing the boundaries and recognizing that innovation happens at the intersection of concepts, disciplines, cultures, and countries. Another unique aspect of academia is that it is probably the most neutral of all forums to bring together people and organizations of various backgrounds to understand and address complex problems.

One other aspect about academic appointments that addresses the growing need for interdisciplinary collaboration is the increase in the number of joint appointments, i.e., faculty who hold titles in more than one department or college. This is perhaps especially true for institutions who are interested in social innovation, e.g., they seek an engineer with a global heath background or a geographer with a social science background. Although there are challenges to successfully holding these joint positions (double the committee work, staying visible in your "other" department), the benefits—such as access to students, additional funding sources, and research facilities—make them worthwhile.

#6 Consulting

Faculty are afforded the opportunity to consult for organizations external to the institution, and how much is permitted is generally governed by specific university policy (e.g., a maximum of one day per week, provided it does not interfere with university activities). Compensation for consulting efforts may or may not be provided by the organization. Many faculty elect to consult as they are often experts in a field and sought after to provide guidance to the organization, and it provides mechanisms for broader engagement as well as visibility. Regardless of whether or not there is compensation, any such association external to the institution, however, must be disclosed, lest there be an appearance of conflict of interest. As examples, a civil engineering faculty member may be asked by a development NGO to assist in the development and/or deployment of a water cistern in an arid region for people without access to clean water. A biomedical engineer might consult on a SBIR[21] project with a small company to address compatibility with bodily tissues.

#7 Sabbatical

One of the benefits of a (tenure-track) faculty position is the sabbatical. As suggested by its name, this is a time, every seven years or so, during which an academic is released from their teaching and committee responsibilities to "recharge their batteries." This is a time when a new research direction might be pursued, a book written, a visit to another institution arranged to see (and appropriate) their teaching and research innovations, or, increasingly, a startup venture worked on. The benefit to the institution is that the academic returns afresh with new ideas and connections, strengthening the institution.

#8 Spin Out and Technology Transfer

Faculty are getting more and more support to translate their research and knowledge into practical innovations that improve the human condition. Increasingly, academics are being "strongly" encouraged to commercialize their research. This is, in part, due to the recognition that nonacademic pursuits can be equally or sometimes more valid and impactful on society than the traditional research and publication route. The more skeptical might also note that universities may see the commercialization of research as another significant source of long-range income, or that academics, traditionally paid much less than their industrial counterparts, need to supplement their income. However, in general, academics are not "in it for the money," so the latter explanation is rarely a realistic one.

#9 Academic Freedom

Lastly, we discuss the notion of academic freedom that we enjoy as faculty members. Although each institution defines this concept slightly differently in practice, generally it is the belief that faculty members should have freedom of inquiry and freedom to teach ideas (especially those that may be viewed as political or inconvenient to authorities) without fear that they could lose their jobs. This is an important principle in academia, but it is also important to realize it is not "freedom from"; rather it is "freedom to." It is the freedom to pursue your own research agenda, to address

---

[21] Small Business Innovation Research: sbir.gov.

sensitive topics, and to create the learning environment you feel facilitates the most learning. It is not freedom from service requirements, requirements to be civil in discourse, or "undesirable" teaching assignments.

With this great freedom comes great responsibility. Your paycheck is still issued by the university (or, at some places such as state universities, the government), so it is important to figure out how to forward the mission of academia. Your performance will be evaluated annually by your department head and/or dean, during which they will look at your accomplishments and outputs of your efforts and activities. Yes, you might have won that huge grant, but where were the results published and how many students received degrees? Yes, you taught that new course, but how much did students learn?

The fact that these assessment criteria are not applied with firm cutoffs, are annual at most, and in reality are only seriously evaluated every few years, means that there is plenty of room for an academic to explore ideas with long lead times, high risks, and possibly unconventional rewards. Moreover, without a political or financial agenda, academia provides the credibility to be considered an independent voice (with a rich tradition of ignoring their employer's demands to tow the party line). These reasons, perhaps above everything else, spur unique innovation and are perhaps the driving impetus that means an academic would find it hard to consider life in another profession.

It should also be stated that, while you are free to pursue your own research directions, they need to be aligned with market trends and larger societal needs. Faculty need to "sell" their ideas and figure out how they advance the larger agendas. Successful faculty figure out how to do some "blue sky" research while pursuing more specified research agendas. Indeed, universities are pretty much the only places still doing far-reaching research, i.e., that which might not have any short-term applications.

#10 Closing Remarks

Academia is an exciting place to be, particularly right now, for the reasons we have described above. Academia provides you with a platform, a voice, and the credibility to accomplish all kinds of impactful things. Society still looks to academia to provide thought leadership (that is why we are call professors, after all!), and academics have respected positions to question practices and policies and to advocate for change. This might be through traditional research and classroom teaching, or through informal channels such as blogs, opinion pieces in newspapers, and social media. However you seek to make an impact, it is this impact—on society, the next generation, our understanding of nature—that makes the academic career one of the best there is.

part three

Innovator Profiles

Photo by Jasmine Johnston

MULTILATERAL

♥ **Rick Johnston, 47**

World Health Organization
Technical Officer, Joint Monitoring Programme for Water Supply
and Sanitation | ~$140,000

PhD, Environmental Engineering, University of North Carolina
at Chapel Hill (2008)
MSc, Environmental Engineering, Johns Hopkins University (1996)
BA, French Literature and History, Grinnell College (1989)

Job Description

The World Health Organization (WHO), a United Nations' agency, is responsible for improving health conditions around the world. WHO employs 7,000 people from over 150 countries to work on preventing and treating communicable and noncommunicable diseases; promoting mental, physical, and social health throughout the life cycle; and providing emergency preparedness and response. WHO works toward these goals by providing leadership on health issues and engaging their employees directly in projects where necessary; working together with policy makers, academia, and the private sector to support countries to develop national health plans; and coordinating health responses during emergencies. One key part of WHO's work involves improving access to safe drinking water and sanitation in low-income settings. Rick Johnston, water-quality expert, leads WHO's joint effort with UNICEF, the United Nations Children's Fund, in global monitoring of drinking water and sanitation.

The WHO/UNICEF team, called the Joint Monitoring Programme (JMP), collects information on access to drinking water and sanitation facilities from countries around the world, mainly from national statistical offices. Rick and the JMP team check the data against other data the team has already collected to produce estimates of national coverage, and they publish country, regional, and global estimates in semiannual reports. National coverage figures are used to track progress toward Millennium Development Goals (MDGs). Besides seeing if a country is on track to meet the MDG targets for water and sanitation, the JMP assesses disparities in access: between urban and rural areas, rich and poor, and other stratifiers of inequality. JMP reports are designed to be accessible to a wide range of readers, so they are very graphic-oriented with simple charts and graphs that show important trends or gaps in service.

The last few years have been exciting for Rick because the entire global water and sanitation sector has been working hard to reach the MDG targets by 2015. The report he is working on now will be the final assessment of progress made since the baseline year of 1990. He is even more excited to be a part of the planning process for the next round of global targets for water and sanitation, which will set the development agenda for 2015-2030. Setting these targets is an extremely political process, but it has to be underpinned by sound technical ideas—that is where Rick and the JMP team contributes. To contribute effectively, they have to bridge the gap between sector specialists who know what could and should be done on the ground, statistical organizations who monitor conditions, and political actors who set policies and allocate budgets.

The JMP reports on water and sanitation coverage are widely cited by governments, donors, and researchers. Donors use these figures to target funding, and researchers use them to investigate all types of questions related to water and sanitation (e.g., connections with health status, economic outcomes, human rights). The reports aim to highlight important progress that is being made but also to reveal areas that still have a long way to go. By showing data from all countries, the reports invite comparison and foster a positive competition among countries, especially within a region. For example, when Bangladesh improves its sanitation coverage faster than India, Indian politicians take note.

Rick's hope is that his contributions toward planning for the new global development targets will help push investments by national governments and international donors in directions that are beneficial for the sector and will improve the lives of people everywhere. For example, the 2015 MDG targets were fixed only for access to water and sanitation facilities in the home. The new targets, to which Rick and the JMP have contributed, expand these targets to include water quality, wastewater management, hand washing with soap, and access to water and sanitation in schools and health centers. It also calls for more explicit monitoring of access by disadvantaged groups. If JMP reports expand to monitor these more detailed indicators, people will find surprisingly poor numbers in many settings, which Rick hopes will motivate change.

Rick loves that his job is always changing, with new challenges arising all the time. He loves constantly learning new information about health, drinking-water regulation, and human rights. He is based at WHO headquarters in Switzerland, so he interacts every day with a variety of smart people in the field of public health—some in-house, but many passing through Geneva for a meeting or consultation. Rick dislikes that he does not have the time to

> Have an open mind, and listen to people. In my field like any other, you cannot support development if you do not understand the situation people are in and the reason they make the choices they do.

complete everything that needs to get done to the quality that he would like. Rick keeps his work fairly separate from his personal life. While he likes to socialize with his office-mates, they are all busy and live across the city from each other, so outside events are rare. Additionally, evenings and weekends are precious times to spend with his family.

Career Trajectory

Although Rick's specialty now is drinking-water quality in low-income settings, he started his career in the liberal arts with an undergraduate degree in French and history. After graduating, he went to Asia for three years, teaching English in Taiwan and backpacking through East Asia. This was a great experience that gave him time to think about future steps; he became increasingly interested in environmental issues and went back to the US to get a degree in the sciences. He started by taking a year of science courses at the University of Illinois and then by pursuing an MS in hydrogeology at the University of Wisconsin-Madison. He then switched into an MS program in environmental engineering at Johns Hopkins University.

After finishing his master's in groundwater contamination, he moved to Bangladesh because his wife was pursuing doctoral fieldwork there. By chance, he arrived just when it was discovered that many of the drinking-water wells there are contaminated with naturally occurring arsenic. He worked on measuring the extent of the problem and eventually on providing safe alternatives, first with a local NGO and later as a consultant with UNICEF. At UNICEF, Rick had the chance to work closely with government counterparts and to get practical experience in monitoring drinking-water quality at scale, in low-income settings with weak government capacity. When he returned to the US after three years, he started a PhD on arsenic removal and then returned to Bangladesh as a UNICEF staff member for five years. His experiences with UNICEF, combined with an academic orientation, led him to Switzerland to join Sandec, a research department within the Swiss Federal Institute of Technology (EAWAG) focusing on water and sanitation in developing countries. After nearly five years with them, a more exciting opportunity came up at WHO headquarters, and it has been a great fit.

Rick credits his success to good grades and test scores (to get into Hopkins), specific data management skills (at Hopkins he learned STATA, a statistical software package that he has used ever since), writing skills (from his liberal arts background), and a love of different cultures (traveling to France, Taiwan, and Bangladesh—he has always tried to learn about local cultures, study local languages, and listen to local music, which has helped him to make connections with people at personal and professional levels). It has also been essential for Rick to have strong professional networks: he got his first job with UNICEF in Bangladesh because he had been volunteering at an NGO, got to know some of the people working with the UNICEF office, and ended up serving as the official note-taker for a meeting that one of them was organizing. That meeting was not even in the water section, but it was a foot in the door that allowed Rick an opportunity to meet the water people and eventually work with them. Years later, one of the key experiences that introduced him to the WHO team was again serving as an official note-taker for a meeting! This time, the meeting was about water quality, but he had to understand where people were coming from, find a coherent way to present their arguments, and position all the different arguments in a convincing meeting report.

Rick's career decisions have all been made along with his wife, considering what was best for both of them and their children at each stage. His wife also has a career in public health, but she now works part-time to take care of their children. It has been difficult for them to manage two careers and balance family needs, but Rick is incredibly grateful for his wife's support and understanding and getting him to Bangladesh in the first place! Rick would like to stay with WHO, if they will keep him, for the rest of his career. He is excited to plan the next cycle of global development targets for 2030, after which he plans to retire—which is mandatory at age sixty-two in the UN. He likes working at headquarters but would love to return to a country office at some point. The work he does is varied and interesting enough that he is sure he can continue to grow and learn new things even after ten years in the office.

⌂ Shomik Mehndiratta, 44

World Bank
Lead Urban Transport Specialist, Latin America | Six figures

EMBA, INSEAD (2010)
PhD, University of California, Berkeley (1996)
B.Tech, Indian Institute of Technology (1991)

Job Description

In contrast to international development work conducted by the United Nations, international NGOs, and grass-roots activists, the World Bank distinguishes itself by loaning money to governments with the intent of creating a world free of poverty. The World Bank is a multilateral organization, meaning that it obtains its funding from multiple governments (in this case around 180). The Bank invests in specific country projects and additionally devotes funds to solutions to global issues. The World Bank borrows money from governments and bond markets before loaning it to the governments of other countries. In addition to loans guaranteed by countries (because the World Bank does not take on financial risk), the World Bank also gives policy and technical advice as needed. Twenty years ago, the World Bank was the only option for countries that needed money for large projects, such as infrastructure development projects. This was an undesirable situation because it allowed World Bank to have significant authority and power. Often, people's ideas were implemented without sound validation and larger support. Now, the World Bank is often part of an investment portfolio. For example, in China, the World Bank makes up less than 0.1% of their investment portfolio. The World Bank is competing with the country's own investments, capital markets, and other international finance institutions and development banks. Countries often come to the World Bank only when they need advice because their loans come with a lot of strings attached, and it is a slow, bureaucratic process to obtain them.

The World Bank has five internal organizations: International Bank for Reconstruction and Development (IBRD), International Development Association (IDA), International Finance Corporation (IFC), Multilateral Investment Guarantee Agency (MIGA), and International Centre for Settlement of Investment Disputes (ICSID). Within these internal units, there are sectoral focuses such as education, health, public administration, agriculture, and urban transportation. With urban migration becoming a major trend across the world, urban transportation is emerging as a large concern. One of the biggest problems for urban transport sustainability is public transport fares. If fares are too low, public transport becomes a political and inefficient process to improve. Fares need to remain at cost-recovery level, so cities usually impose high fares, which excludes the poor and leaves them with no option but to walk. Shomik Mehndiratta, lead urban transport specialist for the World Bank, seeks to solve such problems by combining financial support with policy and technical advice to help governments improve their urban transport infrastructure.

Shomik's job is to help cities function better by improving their transportation infrastructure. He finds that as cities grow, they often have to alter their conventional means of transport. For example, to accommodate more cars, Shomik advises governments to first take care of walking, cycling, and public transport. Also, he ensures that governments address the climate change implications of their actions. Most of his work entails convincing cities to adopt sustainable transportation solutions. Currently, his work is primarily with the governments of China and Latin America. His work involves core management of implementing and evaluating loans and making sure countries follow due process. He continually monitors projects to ensure they are moving forward and addresses hurdles as they emerge. For example, in China, he is helping leaders to be more responsive to using technology in ways that lower barriers for successful planning and management of transportation systems.

In order to make urban transport more affordable and accessible to the poor, Shomik created a project where he searched for a monetary trust fund to implement a study and a mayor willing to team with him on the project. The mayor of Bogotá, Colombia, aligned best with Shomik's vision, so he and other members of the World Bank met with him and told him they wanted to support his work. The mayor had campaigned for the vision of public service delivery for the poor, and he was excited to get started on a research study. The study aimed to figure out how to take advantage of social infrastructure to identify the poor and to figure out what was financially feasible to benefit them. He designed the study and hired consultants to implement it. After evaluating and sharing the positive results, many other cities have approached Shomik to conduct similar studies and implement context-appropriate programs.

Shomik loves that he gets to set his own agenda and prioritize his work. He focuses on sustainable urban mobility because he thinks it is important. Not many professionals have his level of independence and freedom; people who work in consulting have to report to clients, and entrepreneurs do not often have the money, credibility, and social capital that he has. The World Bank's combination of money and convening power afford Shomik significant work independence. On the other hand, he dislikes that he has to constantly respond to bureaucracy. As the World Bank responds to outside groups, it becomes less effective and more risk averse.

> Get hard technical training in whatever—math, engineering, political science, or economics. Do not just have an easy time. Train yourself hard, and then go out in the field.

Shomik's typical day includes a combination of international conference calls, mostly on contractual and substantial issues as he tries to navigate government bureaucracies. Most of his day is spent working on projects: creating projects, forming teams to handle them, financing them, creating agendas, making procurements and terms of reference, moving projects forward, and advising teams. He brings work home all the time, but having kids has been a transformative experience. Being a father has forced him to have a personal life because his kids are more important than anything else to him, and he wants to be there for them. He tries to leave work at a decent time and he minimizes travel.

Career Trajectory

Shomik grew up in India in a standard upper-middle-class setting where anybody smart and quantitative like him was encouraged to pursue medicine or engineering. His high school education taught him how to do things well but did not involve critical thinking. He had no idea what he wanted to do with his life, so he took his college-prep exam and went to the Indian Institute of Technology to study civil engineering, just like his dad. He hated it! It seemed very constricting, dull, and limited to him. However, he became interested in his coursework on the transport sector. It seemed to be the one thing that had to do with people and society and involved issues larger than formulas and buildings, and so he decided to pursue graduate school. Shomik did not quite know what he wanted to do, but he got into MIT and Berkeley for graduate work in transportation. Berkeley offered him some funding, and so he jumped on the offer. He came into the program knowing how to write and do math, and fell in love with the multidisciplinarity and flexibility afforded by it. After he completed the one-year master's program, he still did not know what he wanted to do, except that he wanted to do more problem solving. He again applied to MIT and Berkeley for a PhD and stuck with Berkeley—which he considers the best decision of his life. His doctoral education and research at Berkeley exposed him to the cutting edge of thought in the transportation realm. By the time he graduated, he had used every single library on campus and attended research seminars in many of the departments. He made the most of his time at Berkeley; it was a very exciting intellectual experience for him.

Upon graduation, Shomik decided to stay in the US and work for a consulting firm called Charles Rivers Associates (CRA). He wanted to do more multidisciplinary work on the boundary of economics, and CRA allowed him to work predominantly in transport. He was semi-interested in a career in academia, so he continued to publish his work. He has now published around twenty-five articles despite not being an academic. He was always interested in joining the World Bank, and after six years with CRA, a window opened when he coauthored a report with someone at the bank. Shomik applied for a position, and thanks to his connection, expertise, and experience, he was hired! He has been working at the World Bank for ten years now.

It was in his later years at Berkeley that he truly started his professional development. Mentors have been critical for him. He says, "Everything you are is a reflection of your mentors," and Shomik's academic advisors from Berkeley remain mentors for him. He visits them every year, and he continues to turn to them for advice on difficult decisions. He also has a mentor from his time at CRA who taught him management, discipline, integrity, and quality of work. Shomik continues to search for mentors in a manner that will help him build his personal brand.

In June 2015, Shomik accepted an offer from Uber to be their director of policy development for Asia Pacific. He now leverages his experience and network to make transportation greener and more accessible through this for-profit company.

🏠 Jason Lee, 30

International Finance Corporation
Investment Officer | ~$100,000

JD and MBA, University of Maryland (2010)
BS, Computer Engineering, University of Arizona (2005)

Job Description

Unemployment lies at the core of poverty. For many people in developing countries, gainful employment is the only asset they can use to improve their well-being. Therefore, creating productive employment opportunities is vital for reducing poverty and attaining sustainable socioeconomic development. Growth of the private sector in developing countries can provide many jobs, but starting a private business requires a significant amount of capital. Unfortunately, there is a lack of financing available to the private sector in developing countries, perpetuating the cycle of poverty. It is difficult for banks to operate in countries where poverty is prevalent because often the regulatory framework for doing business is unfriendly, and rampant corruption ultimately makes doing business costly, timely, and inefficient. This makes it difficult to predict the likelihood of a business venture succeeding and thus increases the risk for banks to provide loans. While global commercial banks like the HSBCs and Barclays of the world do operate in developing countries, and there are a growing number of homegrown banks that have started to emerge, local firms still often have difficulty accessing finance. As a result, access to finance, or lack thereof, remains a constraint on the growth of the private sector.

The International Finance Corporation (IFC) is an arm of the World Bank Group. The IFC has 184 country governments as shareholders and a mandate of facilitating economic development in its member countries. IFC also has a AAA credit rating, which enables it to raise capital inexpensively. Combined, these two aspects enable IFC to provide flexible financing with a longer-term view. IFC has three primary businesses: (1) Investment Services, which provides debt, equity, and quasi-equity financing to the private sector; (2) Advisory Services, which provides advice to the private sector as well as to governments to assist them in structuring public-private partnerships in infrastructure; and (3) Asset Management, in which IFC manages third-party equity to co-invest in IFC deals. Jason Lee works within the Advisory Services business of IFC, advising governments in structuring public-private partnerships (PPPs) or privatizing assets and assisting them in soliciting private sector investment. PPPs refer to transactions in which the government seeks to shift the provision of public services to the private sector with the aim of increasing efficiency, reducing cost, leveraging private sector finance, and/or ensuring agreed performance standards. PPPs are typically used in the context of infrastructure and are often used in the power, water, and transport sectors.

Jason's job entails providing advice to governments to structure public-private partnerships as well as advising on privatization. Jason works on a range of transactions, from instances where very little risk is transferred to the private sector, such as a management contract, to full transfer of risk to the private sector through asset sales or privatization. Part of Jason's work involves providing recommendations to governments on the most appropriate mode of private sector participation. In privatizations, Jason assists governments in selling assets. For example, Jason has advised governments in privatizing tea factories, electricity utilities, and hotels. In a privatization, the government has no further involvement with the object of the sale once the sale is complete. In this case, all risk is transferred to the private sector.

On the other side of the PPP spectrum, there are relationships where the government retains almost all control of the asset and simply hires the private sector to perform a specific function. For example, Jason's team recently advised the government of Liberia in identifying and selecting a private sector company to take over the management of the power distribution utility in the capital city of Monrovia. In this particular deal, the government of Liberia maintained ownership of all the infrastructure and retained responsibility for maintaining and upgrading the distribution network. In this case, the private sector was not required to invest any money and came in only to provide more efficient operations of the utility under a management contract. This is common in cases where the business is viewed as too risky and private sector financing is not available. In difficult countries or sectors, management contracts may be appropriate since it involves very little transfer of risk to the private sector party but still allows the government to benefit from private sector expertise. In Liberia—a country that only recently emerged from a civil conflict—it is difficult to attract the private sector, and the market's appetite for investing in such countries is usually quite small. Thus, in order to attract private sector participants, one must minimize the amount of risk to find ways to attract these private sector participants.

Jason's favorite part of his job is working with clients and providing them with innovative solutions to meet their infrastructure needs. He can see his social impact with the satisfaction of his clients at each closure of a deal and how this helps many people in developing countries. His least favorite part is the highly political and controversial nature of infrastructure development, which leads to long lead times to develop and close projects.

Career Trajectory

Jason's vision and passion for economic development began in earnest at the end of his undergraduate years. As he neared the end of college, he experienced a lot of uncertainty about his future and found himself struggling with the weighty concepts of purpose and legacy. He knew he wanted to pursue something worthwhile, but he felt that directly using his engineering degree was not going to satisfy that desire for him. He decided to take a year off after college to plan his next steps. He volunteered for various organizations, took random classes, and fortuitously stumbled onto an internship with Food for the Hungry. This internship proved to be a watershed moment for him. His days were spent teaching high school kids in the Kibera slum of Nairobi. He was not prepared for what he experienced that summer, in particular, the wealth inequality between and haves and have-nots. He decided that he wanted to return to Africa and find a way to battle social injustice in some small, personal way, and he promised himself that he would be better equipped next time around.

Jason was scheduled to begin law school the following fall and was fixated on the image of fighting social injustice at home and abroad. He was also flirting with the idea of getting involved in local politics and considered laying the foundation for a future in public service. This all started to change after his time in Kenya. Around that time, microfinance began to get a lot of attention, and he started reading Hernando de Soto, Muhammed Yunus, and others to better understand this movement of tying access to finance to the improvement of economic well-being. As he read about the ability to use economic empowerment as a tool for people around the world to lift themselves out of poverty, he became obsessed with learning more and decided to pursue a joint JD/MBA to gain a better grasp of business concepts with the aim of preparing himself for a future working overseas in the field of economic development.

During his MBA studies, Jason was engaged in a collaborative project with the Engineers Without Borders program in the college of engineering. The engineering team had designed a solar lighting system and planned to install these systems in several villages in Burkina Faso. The engineers found out about a World Bank grant competition that solicited proposals for sustainable, off-grid lighting solutions, and they approached the business school to assist them with a business plan to transform their technology project into a social business. The concept soon developed into a cooperative of sorts in which solar charging stations were initially provided to facilitate the switch from kerosene lamps to fluorescent lights. The proceeds of the charging stations were pooled and used to purchase additional charging stations with the idea that eventually entire villages could have access to reading light and phone charging stations. They started with eleven systems, and at Jason's last count, they had reached seventeen and were still going strong. This was an incredible moment for him as he realized the "power" of using the principles and creativity of business to provide a social benefit in a sustainable way.

Despite this incredible experience, common sense dictated to Jason that he apply for traditional jobs, so he accepted a summer associate position with a law firm in Washington, DC. This experience only pushed him further toward economic development. The size of the summer associate class that year was fifty people, and in order to facilitate the process of getting to know one another, Jason organized a basketball game. One of the gentlemen needed some prodding to play since he had not touched a basketball in years. After considerable effort on Jason's part, he reluctantly decided to join. Inevitably, after only a short period of time, he landed awkwardly and managed to break his leg. Jason spent the rest of the evening with him in the emergency room. Fortunately, the guy was quite a good sport about everything, and they became good friends through the experience. Through their friendship, he learned of Jason's experiences and interest in Africa, and he mentioned that he would be willing to pass along Jason's résumé to his father, who had long been involved with the International Finance Corporation. He took him up on this offer and ended up with an internship working for IFC. The rest is history.

♥ **Mark Henderson, 61**

UNICEF
Senior Specialist, Water, Sanitation, and Hygiene | ~$120,000

MS, Water Resources Management, UW-Madison (1983)
BS, Biology, Beloit College (1976)

Job Description

Over half the children in Mozambique lack access to an improved water supply, meaning a source that is likely to be protected from outside contamination due to its construction or active intervention. For example, pipes and hand pumps are considered active intervention, and filters are constructive interventions, which provide improved water sources. Rivers and traditional wells, on the other hand, are unprotected water sources. In the rural areas of Mozambique, only one in ten families have access to improved sanitation facilities. Over 90% of cases of diarrhea, a major cause of death for young children, are related to poor water and sanitation.

UNICEF, The United Nations Children's Fund, is a United Nations program that provides long-term humanitarian and developmental assistance to children and mothers in developing countries. UNICEF's focus areas are child protection and social inclusion, child survival, education, emergencies, and humanitarian action. To improve child survival in Mozambique, UNICEF has a Water, Sanitation, and Hygiene (WASH) program. While there are hundreds of organizations working to provide clean water and sanitation for the developing world, UNICEF can do a significant amount more than other organizations because of its strong credibility and financial resources. Mark Henderson is the senior specialist for WASH in Mozambique. After working with other international development organizations, Mark came to UNICEF to continue improving the human condition with better resources.

Mark and his team focus on improving living conditions for children and families with limited access to improved water supplies. They fund projects through partnerships with the government of Mozambique, donors, and the private sector. On the sanitation side, the WASH team encourages all families to build their own toilets so that they can avoid open defecation, which is practiced by 93% of the poorest societal segment. Mark learned several decades ago that trying to convince village elders who are set in their ways to improve water and sanitation conditions was silly. Instead, Mark focuses on educating children in schools to improve the learning environment and to establish good hygiene practices from an early age. Some children in school are already caregivers, heading families and caring for their younger siblings. Mark believes that focusing on children is the most effective way to make WASH behavioral changes.

Mark explains that even though Mozambique has plentiful fresh water resources, most are contaminated and/or far from rural areas. Groundwater is the best route to obtaining water at a low cost because it requires minimal treatment. Because of the increased need for water from agriculture, population growth, mining, and industry, Mozambique's ample water resources have to be properly managed. One thing that Mozambique now excels at is regional systems to manage dams and relations with neighboring upstream countries with early warning systems in case of floods. The system of dams and communication helped during the flood emergency in 2013. Unfortunately, flooding still displaces thousands of people in Mozambique every year. When floods are predicted, Mark actively prepares for them by making visits to at-risk areas and assessing stocks of pre-positioned emergency-response supplies. Once people are displaced from floods, Mark leads the emergency response WASH team, coordinating and managing information around a collaborative response. The WASH team provides families with buckets, water treatment products, soap, and construction materials for latrines. The WASH team also sets up camps where they organize trucked-in water and support the construction of latrines. After floods, Mark's focus shifts to disinfecting wells, fixing pumps, and helping families rebuild latrines.

Mark's emergency-response coordination must be a high-impact, efficient response that can be put in place quickly. WASH's coordination has improved over the years while at the same time Mozambique's government water sector has also progressed, establishing a semiautonomous body that manages urban water supply in all major towns and cities. Professionalizing the work in this manner has resulted in better service delivery and the ability to respond with preventive measures. One example of a collaborative, effective flood response was in Gava province in 2013. During the floods, the spread of disease was effectively averted in the worst-hit city of Chokwe, thanks to the quick reaction of UNICEF WASH and Mozambique's governmental authorities. Before the floodwaters hit, they removed pumps from the boreholes and sealed them, and they turned off the power supply to minimize the risk of damage. Once the waters receded, they went in, reinstalled the pumps, and got the system up and running. This was a huge improvement over the year 2000 when floods had a far more devastating effect. Mark knows there is a long way to go in making sure all children and their families in Mozambique have access to safe water and sanitation, but he also knows they will get there.

Mark loves his job because he gets to actively work with people to improve their daily lives through improving their water and sanitation. At the same time, his management role allows him to indirectly influence a myriad of teams and projects. Through his extensive work in developing countries to improve WASH, he has learned that best practices include targeting a small number of risk practices, targeting school children and caregivers specifically, identifying motives for changed behavior, and adapting methods to local context. Mark has overcome his challenges by working in partnership to leverage strengths; by increasing coherence of messages, effectiveness, and reach; and by understanding the role that children can play as messengers in different contexts.

Career Trajectory

Mark Henderson was born and raised in Angola to missionary parents, so Africa has always been familiar to him; he has spent most of his life there. Mark was mostly home-schooled (Calvert School correspondence course) but sometimes studied with other missionary children. For high school, he went with his brother to neighboring Congo to attend the American School of Kinshasa. In 1969, he returned to the US when his parents were forced out of Angola by Portuguese colonial authorities. Mark finished high school in New Jersey, which took a lot of adjustment. College was better for him, and he became very attached to Wisconsin. Nevertheless, Mark returned to Africa whenever he could, for backpacking and volunteering. After graduation, he joined the Peace Corps in Senegal, and his experience in a Sahel village has always stayed with him. He left to study water and identified the UW interdisciplinary water resources management program as the best fit for him; it has proved to be a perfect background for his career.

Mark then joined CARE, a leading global humanitarian organization, in war-torn Chad and then in Cameroon, working on irrigation projects and rural community water supply. His four years working with CARE were fascinating and deeply rewarding. Mark then joined his wife-to-be in North Carolina where she earned her MS in public health while he worked in environmental consulting as a hydrologist doing underground storage-tank site assessments and remediation. Mark enjoyed working as a hydrologist because he was involved in projects from start to end, and he traveled all over North Carolina. However, his heart was in Africa, and when the UN started a "corridors of peace" operation in war-torn Angola in 1991, Mark got an offer from UNICEF to be a team leader for a rural water-supply program in southern Angola. Living with a young family there was tough. After working there for one and a half years, the war broke out again, and Mark and his family were evacuated to Namibia. Mark was transferred to peaceful Zambia to start a water program there in response to their drought and then on to Mozambique and Zimbabwe—all in a ten-year period. During this time, Mark raised his family while he built his skills with UNICEF to develop water and sanitation programs in support of better government services, mostly in rural contexts.

Mark's career path changed somewhat in 2001 when he became a global WASH adviser at UNICEF's New York headquarters. His experience there opened up a whole world of new partnerships and interests. One of his responsibilities was ensuring UNICEF's response in emergencies. Therefore, he was sent to Banda Aceh just days after the tsunami. His work there led to him becoming the regional WASH adviser in the Bangkok office, which gave him the opportunity to travel and become familiar with fourteen countries across East Asia and the Pacific. Mark loved it! In 2010, when the earthquake in Haiti happened, Mark joined the initial response, and that led to the job of leading UNICEF's WASH response operation for two and a half years. That was a very intense experience, but it rewarded him with a great sense of accomplishment. Now, Mark is back in Mozambique where he worked fifteen years ago, and he is still with UNICEF, working with some of the same colleagues. For Mark, it feels like a good place to retire from his UN career.

MULTILATERAL

Shruthi Baskaran, 24

United Nations World Food Programme | Innovation Consultant
Boston Consulting Group | Senior Associate | ~$75,000

BS, Civil and Environmental Engineering, Penn State University (2012)

Job Description

How can a large, geographically dispersed organization with employees in around eighty countries operate, innovate, and stay focused on its goals? Large organizations, having operated a certain way for a long time, often struggle to build the momentum necessary to truly change and improve. Innovation cannot be an occasional word of the week for an organization, and it cannot be the job of a few. It needs to be part of the DNA of an organization with every employee embodying it, living it, and continually striving to find a better way to work. To encourage continuous innovation, employees need to be incentivized and recognized for their efforts. One organization that eats, sleeps, and breathes innovation is the World Food Programme (WFP), the largest humanitarian organization fighting to end hunger worldwide. Shruthi Baskaran is an innovation consultant, i.e., an overseer and curator of innovation, across WFP. Only a few years out of college, Shruthi was able to land this amazing position with WFP thanks to (1) her extensive portfolio from her undergraduate years where she demonstrated that she was already doing what WFP wanted her to do, and (2) the professional skills she obtained while working on diverse projects at the Boston Consulting Group.

The World Food Programme works to ensure that every person around the world has the food necessary to be healthy. WFP is part of the United Nations system and is voluntarily funded. Countries are not required to fund it, but more than sixty do. Increasingly, businesses and individuals are also making a vital contribution to WFP's mission. Around 15,000 people work for WFP, with about 3,000 NGOs acting as cooperating partners. Shruthi's role is to identify and help mainstream innovations from across WFP into their strategies and operations. In her time at WFP, she has curated the first-of-its-kind Innovation Challenge across the organization and created a "change agenda" for translating broader organizational priorities into actions. She also helped operationalize a conceptual "Value for Money" framework that helps WFP managers articulate how they optimized their initiatives and projects along the dimensions of economy, efficiency, and effectiveness at both the global and country office level. Shruthi thinks of her job as an application of her private sector skills from BCG to the public sector to improve the way WFP functions.

Shruthi's social innovation and impact come from identifying innovations from across the world and ensuring that the broader organization is moving in the right direction, aligned with their goal of ensuring "Zero Hunger" by 2030. Shruthi's work contributes positively toward enhancing WFP's delivery of life-transforming food assistance to 90 million beneficiaries in a more economic, efficient, and effective manner. Shruthi loves that she is working in an area that matters the most to her—food security. She also loves the fact that the work she does directly and indirectly translates into the betterment of lives and livelihoods for some of the most vulnerable populations in need. On the other hand, Shruthi dislikes the bureaucracy that comes with large organizations despite understanding that the protocols are in place for valid reasons.

Career Trajectory

Shruthi's passion for food security was spurred at a young age when she witnessed the poverty and food insecurity in her father's native village. She subsequently realized that while her family often expressed affection in terms of food, the food that she took for granted was not assured in everyone's life. While Shruthi pursued a bachelor's degree in civil and environmental engineering, she devoted a large part of her collegiate life to programs that focused on using engineering design to solve pressing problems in emerging economies. The Humanitarian Engineering and Social Entrepreneurship Program (HESE) helped her grow as a leader and taught her how to learn by doing. She traveled to Kenya and Rwanda with her HESE team and piloted food-security related projects, which have since expanded to several other regions in Africa. Through the Engineering Leadership Development Program, she was able to create tools that aid the delivery of clean water to developing world communities. These academic programs developed her ability to apply engineering skills to solve problems in developing world communities.

> Paul Polak (author of *Out of Poverty*) told me at an awardee dinner that social impact begins when you impact at least a million people. Until then, think of everything you do as community service, as building blocks, and do not stop till you achieve social impact. Do not measure your worth or success through other people's eyes, and accept that real impact takes time!

Upon graduating from college, Shruthi accepted a position at the Boston Consulting Group in their Houston office. Through a series of organizational and operational transformation projects, she helped corporate clients deconstruct their operations using business frameworks and maximize both shareholder value and employee engagement. Outside her regular job responsibilities, she gave back to the office by being part of the Green Team and the recruiting team. As the social and budget chair, she also oversaw social event organization for roughly thirty associates in the Texas system. Though these activities were not directly related to her passions, they helped her expand her leadership and networking abilities. Despite enjoying her work at BCG, her desire to return to working on food security was as strong as ever. In her second year at BCG, she was approved to pursue a competitive social impact sabbatical and accepted an offer to join the WFP, which is where she currently works.

Along the way, Shruthi has had several mentors who have coached and guided her, including the director of HESE, who was a huge inspiration in helping her realize that social impact and nonprofit do not have to be synonymous. Several mentors at BCG took her under their wings to help her gain a set of core professional skills that are translatable to a wide variety of jobs: the ability to analyze data to synthesize trends, to liaise with stakeholders of diverse backgrounds, and to prioritize her activities. Having worked "in the field" on small-scale projects, while thinking of taking a break from BCG, Shruthi wanted a role that would help her understand how large organizations scaled impact. The BCG network helped her identify a position that was conducive to her planned learning trajectory, and her next steps are returning to BCG shortly and pursuing an MBA from the Stanford Graduate School of Business for the next two years. After completing her graduate education, she plans to work at a large, international development-driven organization like the Gates Foundation or the Clinton Foundation. Eventually, she plans to transition to a social enterprise focused on addressing food production challenges in developing economies by streamlining every step of the food value chain.

Food, as a construct, has been a large driver of both personal and professional decisions in Shruthi's life. She integrates her work and personal life by carrying forward a love for cooking and food with her. Shruthi is informally trained in six types of cuisine and loves to cook for large groups of people. She has also used the opportunity to travel to different developing world regions as a means to really tap into their cultures and understand what it is, as humans, that makes us so different and alike in terms of using the resources we are bestowed with to improve our lives. If Shruthi had to start over again, the only thing she would do differently is learn French or Spanish in school so that she would be able to better converse with the people she seeks to empower.

⌂ Saurabh Mishra, 29

International Monetary Fund
Economist

MSc, Applied Economics and Finance, University of California, Santa Cruz (2008)
BA, Economics, University of California, Santa Cruz (2007)

Photo by Rashmi Ekka

Job Description

As part of the United Nations system, The International Monetary Fund (IMF) and the World Bank were established in 1944 with the goal of economic cooperation and development that would lead to a more stable and prosperous global economy. While this goal remains central to both institutions, their work is ever evolving in response to new economic developments and challenges. The World Bank provides long-term assistance, and IMF focuses on short-term assistance. To maintain stability and prevent crises in the international monetary system, the IMF promotes international monetary cooperation and provides policy advice and technical assistance to help countries build and maintain strong economies. The IMF also makes loans (funded mainly by the pool of contributions that its members provide) and helps countries design policy programs to solve balance-of-payments problems when sufficient financing on affordable terms cannot be obtained to meet net international payments. IMF is mostly made up of economists, including Saurabh Mishra who also has experience working for the World Bank.

If an individual is spending too much money buying more than they are earning or has too much debt financing their investments, it is not good for them when they go to continue with their natural course of expenditures; they have to turn to a lender. In the same way, if a country has international payments that it cannot make, they have to turn to the IMF as a lender of last resort. The IMF has been working on country-specific programs as well as research on broader issues of macroeconomic policy. When Saurabh first started at the World Bank, he was travelling significantly and working on the ground in emerging markets, but today he is engaged with research-based work. Some of Saurabh's research has explored what makes countries grow and what drives world trade. World trade has been evolving quickly over the past few decades from people trading simple commodities to a complex web of supply chains of service providers even within manufacturing products. Saurabh has worked on international capital markets, statistics, and economic methods to better understand changes in the world economy. This has provided avenues to study aspects including economic forecasts, public finance, unemployment, inequality, and inclusive growth. He tries to be interdisciplinary because if you are too specialized, it becomes hard to grasp the reality and complexity of some of the problems the world economy faces. His interests are broad and diverse, which keeps him personally and professionally driven and always trying to push for the frontier. Recent projects Saurabh has worked on include an international jobs report to capture the pulse of the world labor market as they have recovered from the 2008 financial crisis, an in-depth study on what exports can drive the next wave of growth in India, and tracking economic transformation in nonrenewable resource rich nations.

In addition to his services at the IMF, Saurabh is working toward his PhD in reliability engineering at the University of Maryland College Park. He pursues research interests both at work and through his degree where is working with mathematics, mechanical engineering, and computer science faculty in topics of probability theory, machine learning, and algorithm design. Additionally, he is an executive associate with Cellucci Associates engaged in private fundraising and equity investments in disruptive technologies. Saurabh has been designing new programs and opportunities in economic security in international markets. Most of his time through his various engagements is spent as a data scientist, writing, presenting, and interacting with people across disciplines and organizations.

Saurabh enjoys the ability to expand his network of innovators and increasingly through his work in international finance and technology to converge with building systems specific to addressing social and economic challenges. The most interesting part of Saurabh's work is the critical questions that are raised. Some of Saurabh's recent work explores the role design of technology systems that better help address information, government, and market coordination failures. Whenever all of his work gets to be too much, he goes into his recording studio and plays music, a great therapy for him.

Career Trajectory

While an undergraduate and graduate student, Saurabh took advantage of speaking with students and professors from various and different disciplines which helped him gain a more interdisciplinary education. He traveled and did some consulting work while still in school through an internship with the World Trade Organization in Geneva. These interactions enabled him to perform better later on. Saurabh earned his master's degree right when the 2008 financial crisis hit. The job market was tough, but he always wanted to work on economic policy and development, so he aimed for the stars for his first job out of college: the World Bank. He interviewed and was hired to join the Chief Economist Office in South Asia's poverty reduction and economic management network. He spent two years on various lending, operational, and technical assistance projects and in areas including Afghanistan, Bangladesh, Bhutan, India, Maldives, Nepal, Pakistan, and Sri Lanka. It was an enriching experience to go to some of these regions, interact with policy makers, and to lead and manage teams of international financial and development specialists.

> In order to offer a solution that addresses an important challenge, one must understand the challenge very deeply, and in order to do that, it is important to keep a very open mind and gain knowledge about these issues that young people might be very interested in. Bold new ventures that compete with oligopolies in the design of new markets is the way of economic change.

Saurabh went on to work for the International Trade Department, Chief Economists Office in Europe and Central Asia, as well as matters related to innovation and private sector development. Over time, he got more engaged in projects on how the World Bank could be relevant in terms of technology, transparency, and accountability in development projects by mapping them all over the world, getting citizen responses, and helping open up the vast amounts of knowledge at governments around the world. This is just a tip of the iceberg for bringing new technologies that can change the nature of economic development. After working with the World Bank for five years, he wanted to gain a deeper perspective on macroeconomic management through monetary and fiscal policy issues, so he switched over to the IMF. Saurabh's keys to success have been keeping an open mind and listening to everybody, and over time developing strong intuitive skills. He tries to keep an open mind in terms of what is happening with geopolitics, the economy, and technology.

In five to ten years, Saurabh would like to have successfully been directly engaged with a socially impactful and disruptive innovation that has a positive impact. He would like to develop new methods to increase the reach of the Internet and influence the way web-based businesses are developed. He would like to build these specific systems with great talent and thinkers from around the world. In the next twenty years, he would like to be engaged with building great ideas, more than just in one company, but with leveraging culture movements for the next wave of social and economic progress.

Photo by Mary Gardella

Jenn Gustetic, 33

White House Office of Science and Technology Policy
Assistant Director for Open Innovation | ~$140,000

SM, Technology Policy, MIT (2007)
BS, Aerospace Engineering, University of Florida (2005)

Job Description

How do you get organizations across the US to innovate? That is a tall order! The question that needs to be asked first is how does one get the US government, with so many agencies with limited communication between each other and burdened by bureaucracy, to innovate? One approach is Open Innovation, which entails opening up problems to be solved by people internal and external to the government. Open Innovation could be a "prize" offered by the government to the best solution offered for a specific problem. A "prize" is essentially a pay-for-performance-based approach that the US government is now using regularly to efficiently develop innovative technologies, products, and services with American tax dollars. Jenn Gustetic has led NASA's use of Open Innovation to transform how they solve technical, science, and behavioral problems, and she is now working with the entire federal government as the White House's assistant director for Open Innovation. She is shifting various problem-solving events out of a conference room of only subject-matter experts into an interdisciplinary, networked, and innovative global community. Jenn's education in both aerospace engineering at the University of Florida and technology policy at MIT have been vital to her ability to work across these diverse technical areas.

Jenn spends her days building a community of thousands of practitioners to scale the use of prizes, citizen science, and crowdsourcing methods in a wide range of fields, persuading late adopters of the relevance and importance of Open Innovation methods, designing incredibly complex technical prizes and crowdsourcing projects, and making it easier for the public to find opportunities to participate. Two examples of "grand challenges" for which Jenn has been a lead designer include the following: (1) NASA's first grand challenge to find all asteroid threats to human populations and to know what to do about them; prior to the grand challenge, this problem was being addressed largely only through the traditional scientific community and scattered amateur astronomers around the globe; (2) USAID's Fighting Ebola Grand Challenge; this sought to help health-care workers on the frontlines provide better care and stop the spread of Ebola during the height of the crisis in the fall of 2014. Jenn played a key role in designing several high-impact Open Innovation activities to posture these challenges for success. The Asteroid Data Hunter Challenge—an Open Innovation project in support of the asteroid grand challenge—has resulted in an algorithm that is 15% better than the current method of identifying asteroids in the main asteroid belt. USAID's Ebola grand challenge provided the first opportunity in over a decade to reinvent the personal protective equipment (PPE) that health-care workers use when treating infectious diseases. By structuring this part of the response as a challenge, USAID was able to quickly engage out-of-discipline experts, ranging from wedding-dress designers to athletic-apparel manufacturers to bioengineering researchers at Johns Hopkins to redesign a more practical, comfortable PPE while maintaining safety.

Jenn works on building up dozens of different hot spots for innovation that are at different levels of maturity and readiness every day. Her recent work has focused on scaling the use of Open Innovation tools within the federal government to enable the government to better tap into American ingenuity to solve complex problems. Open Innovation approaches include prizes, challenges, citizen science, and crowdsourcing. Jenn's work involves massive capacity building: identifying, training, and cultivating talent with real-world experience. It also involves evidence gathering, storytelling (reporting on results; making the subjective and objective case; persuading leaders, managers, and employees of the value), bringing down barriers, and providing top cover (identifying major legal obstacles and working to mitigate them). All her activities have one thing at the core of them: understanding people and relationships. One of the most compelling ways to convince someone to try using a new method of problem solving is through success stories of other Open Innovation projects. Therefore, Jenn shares compelling cases about success by focusing on the people that were part of Open Innovation projects: the winners that started new companies participating in an incentive prize or the federal employee who thought to approach problem solving in a way that got higher-quality solutions for less money.

Her education in aerospace engineering at the University of Florida and technology policy at MIT have been crucial to gaining credibility in the science and technology community. Her role requires her to be a science and technology generalist who knows how to ask the right questions of the experts rather than being an expert herself in every area. Jenn's roles require less "hands-on building," but her role is critical for enabling other people to build. Jenn loves the variety of content she gets to work on. She enjoys getting to work closely with the scientists, engineers, and technologists who are the best in the world on all the topics she encounters. Because of the nuances with goal setting and evaluation approaches involved in the prize design process, working with subject-matter experts is critical. The amount of work she does with other people is both the best part and sometimes the hardest part of her job. The more people you work with, the more likely you are to run into difficult personalities, but she has grown in experience and learned to deal with all types of personalities to get the job done.

> You can always remind yourself of a fact you forgot by Googling it, but skills reinforce themselves over time. Skills you should develop if you want to work in social innovation: identifying opportunities; pitching ideas; socializing ideas and getting buy-in; relationship development; compelling oral communication skills; networking; rubrics for making judgment calls and weighing options; leading teams; managing projects and programs (budget, cost, people, schedule); recognizing failure, brushing yourself off, and starting again; resolving conflict; handling stress; knowing when it is time to be humble or listen; building political capital; spending political capital.

Jenn's work is highly related to her personal life. Many of her friends have come from school and the various jobs she has had. It is difficult to completely separate work from personal life, but Jenn prioritizes health and fitness in her weekly routine by running, eating healthy, and spending time with friends outside work events. She loves to travel, so she occasionally goes home to Florida to visit her family, takes a long international vacation, and takes long weekends to go on yoga retreats.

Career Trajectory

Jenn was always highly involved in extracurricular activities. In high school, she was involved in theater, student government, varsity soccer, and even had a purse-making business for a while, through which she developed her teamwork and leadership skills. In college, she rushed the Zeta Tau Alpha sorority, was involved in student government, led a mentoring program, and had a part-time job at a career counseling center, all of which kept her balanced in very stressful academic programs. While at the University of Florida, an internship on Capitol Hill opened her eyes to the world of policy. Her time at MIT gave her frameworks to think about technology policy issues while increasing her confidence in her own intellect. After her first stint in government as a grants specialist at the Transportation Security Administration right after MIT, Jenn joined the consulting world for a few years. While working at a small consulting firm, Phase One Consulting Group, Jenn was afforded promotion and responsibilities that would have come much slower at a larger firm—accelerating her skill development in new areas and positioning her to come back to the federal government at a much higher level. Her role there also helped her develop relationships with the people who would ultimately hire her at NASA.

Jenn's time at NASA has been critical on many fronts: it is the first job where she worked on exclusively STEM topics; it afforded her the opportunity to interact with and learn from titans in the technology industry; it gave her the flexibility to build an innovation program with incredibly supportive leadership and brilliant colleagues; and it helped her develop relationships with the people that would ultimately pull her up to the White House. Jenn's time at the White House has expanded her view of science and technology beyond space and transportation topics. She is growing her network, knowledge, and movement creation skills that she is sure will be key to future opportunities. In the future, Jenn wants to work on science and technology topics through cross-sector innovation management and capacity building. That could take a number of different roles at a number of different organizations, but she wants to work on meaningful problems (not just squeezing five cents out of the cost per unit of a manufacturing pipeline) that are pushing the boundaries of what science and technology can do to improve life for people on earth (and beyond!).

Frances A. Colón, 38

US Department of State
Acting Science and Technology Adviser to the Secretary of State | ~$120,000

PhD, Neurobiology, Brandeis University (2004)
BS, Biology, University of Puerto Rico (1997)

Job Description

The Department of State (DoS) is in charge of international relations for the United States. It is a federal executive department led by the secretary of state, who is nominated by the president and confirmed by the Senate. The mission of the DoS is "to shape and sustain a peaceful, prosperous, just, and democratic world and foster conditions for stability and progress for the benefit of the American people and people everywhere." To carry out this mission, DoS conducts US diplomatic missions abroad and implements foreign policy. Science and technology are incredibly important in making decisions about the United States' international relations, so the secretary of state staffs someone to advise them in this area. A deputy science and technology adviser is a scientist that provides decision makers in the public-policy space with the best evidence-based assessment available to help the decision-making process. As the deputy adviser for the secretary of state, Frances Colon brings science, technology, and innovation resources and tools to the table when the secretary of state is engaging a country or set of countries on a given set of issues.

Frances promotes science, technology, and innovation dialogues; global advancement of women in science; science and technology policy fellowships; and public outreach as tools of science diplomacy. Frances's job sometimes entails building a science cooperation model from start to finish with partners around the world and involves outside technical agency partners. Other times, she is creatively solving a problem, such as how to build an innovation ecosystem from the ground up in parts of the world where failure and risk taking are not widely accepted. In such places, the government often has the right goals of "economic growth" or "prosperity of their people," but they need help from science policy officers like Frances to address regulatory reform and incentives to support their entrepreneurs. Part of Frances's work takes place overseas at meetings or negotiations with other countries, part of it takes place in Washington, DC, where she answers many emails, and part of it happens in other parts of the United States where she speaks at universities and meets with innovators. One university she visited recently was the University of Texas where she spoke about modern trends for scientists to collaborate internationally and the importance of broader scientific communication skills. She also recently visited El Salvador where she spoke with students about the importance of science and technology for the economic development of their country.

Every challenge the world faces needs science and technology as well as collaboration in order to be solved. Frances believes it is innovative to bring the best talent the United States has to tackle these challenges together with their counterparts from around the world as a central piece of the United States' diplomatic engagement. The social innovators of today want to move beyond the geopolitical and security conversation and infiltrate it with action on sustainable growth and education that will lift women. These conversations are the ones that will change the world. When Frances first took over her job as deputy science adviser three years ago, she felt her team was still "selling" the rest of the diplomatic apparatus on the benefits of science and technology for diplomacy. She is now at the point where her team cannot keep up with the requests they get, and the rest of her agency speaks more "science and technology" now than it ever did.

Frances loves that she can go anywhere in the world, and when she interacts with scientists, they are all speaking the same language and have the same end goal of changing the world. The part she likes least is that her work is incredibly fast-paced, so she has little time to reflect and plan long term. Strategizing is important, and sometimes the day is just too short, even with self-imposed twelve-hour workdays. Frances is always on the go. She serves on various boards and spearheaded a new initiative at the state department titled Networks of Diasporas in Engineering and Science (NODES) through which she and her team empower diasporas (communities of people settled in a new geographic location away from their ancestral homeland) to influence effective policies and take on development challenges in their countries of origin. She regularly participates in events to promote women and minorities in STEM fields, including the Latinas Think Big Innovation Summit. Frances's friends have started to believe that she does not actually sleep! The key for her is to find some time for herself every day, a moment to disconnect and reenergize. She also treasures and protects her time with family and friends; that time is set aside in her calendar to keep her sane and feed her soul.

> I think we need to do a better job of analyzing the lessons learned from social innovation efforts in the past and linking those results to new initiatives. There is not enough quantification of results and certainly not enough cross-talk between academia and the policy makers on this side. We should create more joint decision spaces where needs, expectations, progress, and results are worked on jointly.

Career Trajectory

Frances always knew she wanted to take her scientific background and use it for advocacy. While completing her PhD, she was involved in community activities such as science camps for minority youth and campaigns to elect officials friendly to scientific funding. She also wrote for local blogs in the Boston area focused on STEM and Hispanic issues, which helped her develop her own voice. Women's professional networks and support groups have been essential in building Frances's confidence and helping her fight back the classic impostor syndrome (feeling that you do not deserve your success, particularly common among high-achieving women). Leadership courses such as the National Hispana Leadership Institute, Executive Leadership Program, and fellowships like the US–Japan Leadership Program have helped Frances acquire skills she did not even know she needed and have helped her build a network of peers and mentors across cultures and sectors.

Upon earning her PhD, Frances left academia and joined the policy space through the American Association for the Advancement of Science (AAAS) Science & Technology Policy Fellowships. She started as a fellow at the state department working on Muslim–world outreach through K-12 math and science education programs. After her fellowship, she took a full-time position with the department as science and environment adviser for Western Hemisphere affairs. Here she designed and implemented a climate strategy for the Energy and Climate Partnership of the Americas. After three and a half years in that position, she was promoted to her current position as deputy science and technology adviser to the secretary of state.

If Frances could start all over, she would have dedicated much more time to internships and leadership activities during her college years. She discovered the amazing world of social innovation later in life, and now the ideas just keep coming. She wishes she had even more time to do it all! In five years, Frances would like to have been actively involved in the technology sector working toward a solution to a development or governance challenge in the world. In ten to twenty years, she would like to have run for office and brought her perspective as a minority woman scientist into that decision-making space to serve her community.

⌂ John Doe, 47

US Government | ~$115,000
Electrical Engineering Manager

MBA-MIS (Masters of Business Administration & Management Information Systems)
BS, Electrical Engineering

Job Description

While some people are satisfied with their day job, it is normal for humans to be multidimensional and seek to explore additional interests outside work. If you have the will and the way, you can moonlight with a secondary job or pursuit. It helps to work for an organization like the government that gives a lot of vacation time. John Doe is an electrical engineering manager for the government by day and a humanitarian engineering volunteer by night. Through his day job, he makes a stable living to provide for his family and accrues vacation days that he uses to make service trips. John's main responsibilities for the government are managerial; he leads projects and oversees other engineers. His team provides telephone, Internet, satellite, microwave, and other types of connections for military communications and ensures they are functioning properly. A typical project involves testing a new piece of communications equipment from a vendor. John and his team will test it, and after getting results, he will make a detailed scientific report for the customer. Sometimes the vendor will fix their equipment to meet the required higher expectations in order to be used for government networks.

Another interesting project is as chief engineer for remote locations. Working with a team of fifteen engineers under him, they fly to various locations around the world to fix problems in communications systems. The most common problems are bad grounding or bad power since these locations tend to be in the middle of nowhere. Many of these setups were originally a small grounding spike in the earth that would not ground, or their power would be running off a generator and the fuel would run out. John also goes beyond his full-time responsibilities to help in humanitarian activities. This is actually what he enjoys most because he loves helping people in need. For example, in response to hurricane Katrina, his organization sent a team to set up satellite and cellular communications for responders and those who were stranded. The best part of John's job has been the flexibility to go anywhere in the world. If you work hard, the government offers opportunities to see the world, meet people from all over, and learn about other cultures. When he has worked internationally, he has maximized his free time to get out and explore communities. His least favorite part is the paperwork that comes about naturally when working with a large bureaucratic organization.

John builds up enough vacation days to go on service trips about once every two years for two to five weeks at a time. The projects that he implements abroad are focused on humanitarian needs and instructing others. Most of his trips are faith-based initiatives, and they provide assistance to anybody who asks. While on these trips, John meets with two to three groups per day to find needs, usually shared by village elders, and to help as requested. On these trips, John travels constantly, digging wells, speaking to different groups, providing training or instruction, and providing direct assistance. Activities are usually focused on individual needs, civilian infrastructure, installing wells, or fixing buildings that have been destroyed. His experience as an engineer helps him with many of these tasks. The groups John works with do not charge for their services. Volunteers pay for all their expenses, and they use some donations for travel; empathy is the main driver for these people of faith to go abroad and help others. John has recently volunteered in Malawi and Mozambique.

Career Trajectory

John has been involved in service trips for many years but wishes he could have been involved even earlier. In college, he was a working student competing for athletic and scholastic scholarships and therefore did not have time for any other commitments. His major takeaway from all his volunteer and work experiences is that engineering is the science of doing better and more things with what little you have; you have to use ingenuity and innovate to make the most of what you have.

Right out of college, John interviewed with many companies but chose to work for the US government and has been with them ever since. His first few years he evaluated and installed upgrades to old systems to keep them in service. Then he was sent on a special project for a crisis in an unmanned vehicle program. They had crashed several unmanned vehicles, and it was John's team's responsibility to figure out what was wrong. Other projects include server consolidation programs, which means that he looked at server systems facilities and figured out how to consolidate them and make them more reliable. In recent years, he has moved up to a management position overseeing other engineers.

There are some who can forge their own path, marketing and making their own solution work; they should do this if they can follow this opportunity and pay the bills. If you cannot, do not overwhelm yourself with the needs of the day. Spend some of your resources to follow your passions while making money from your day job to pay the bills. Seize opportunities to do good, even if it is a small portion of your efforts.

Over time, John has found a way to balance his personal and professional life. He is committed to his job and service trips but is still a committed husband and father. He does the best he can to maximize all parts of his life, but it is a difficult balancing act for him. In the future, John believes he will continue with his current path, but his ideal career would be combining his volunteer and work activities. He would also prefer working directly in engineering and being in the field working on technical issues rather than having managerial responsibilities, so he is continually investigating other options and will evaluate opportunities as they come up.

🏠 Jennifer Schmeltzle, 28

United States Army Corps of Engineers
Project Engineer | ~$86,000

BS, Civil Engineering, Lehigh University (2007)

Job Description

Founded in 1802 with a mission to solve the nation's toughest engineering challenges, the US Army Corps of Engineers (USACE) has evolved to now deliver vital public and military engineering services in more than 110 countries. During peace and war, 33,000 USACE civilian employees and 800 soldiers work to deliver vital engineering solutions in collaboration with their partners to secure the United States, energize the US economy, and reduce risk from disaster. With environmental sustainability as its guiding principle, USACE has many responsibilities, including restoring, creating, and preserving tens of thousands of acres of wetlands annually; and researching and developing technologies to protect the environment and enhance the quality of life. After holding several positions with USACE, Jennifer Schmeltzle landed a position with them as project engineer and contracting officer's representative in the special projects section of the Europe district. Through this role, Jennifer has been involved in humanitarian-assistance projects in sub-Saharan Africa and eastern Europe. These projects have included construction and renovation of buildings such as schools, health clinics, and libraries. She is directly responsible for projects, from scope and design through completed construction and acceptance of the facilities.

Since the end of the Cold War, USACE has increasingly become involved in humanitarian-assistance projects funded by US, European, and African commands. The US Department of Defense Humanitarian Assistance Program administers a variety of activities funded by the Overseas Humanitarian, Disaster, and Civic Aid Appropriation (OHDACA). The USACE supports EUCOM and AFRICOM, humanitarian-assistance programs designed to assure support to friendly nations and allies of the US and to provide basic humanitarian aid and services to populations in need. Projects are identified by conducting needs assessments of villages where the DoD is interested in building good long-term relations.

Before starting each project, Jennifer coordinates with different stakeholders to create a project scope that adequately meets the needs of the customer and the end users. She acts as a liaison between US embassies in each country, contractors, customers (EUCOM and AFRICOM), and local end users. She reviews the designs, specifications, and safety plans of buildings to make sure they are constructible and does her best to anticipate problems. Throughout the entire preconstruction process, she also provides guidance and technical advice to other engineers. Additionally, she coordinates and executes meetings to ensure there is mutual understanding among all stakeholders before construction begins. During construction, Jennifer makes sure the builders are using reporting systems for construction management. She is ultimately responsible for all aspects of construction management, including the paperwork for making changes to the original plans, negotiating these modifications, processing requests for payment for materials and services, and answering requests for information on the project. To ensure that construction is completed according to the set timeline, she is also responsible for reviewing schedules and updates.

Jennifer has loved working in various countries in West Africa and the Balkans. In a little over a year, her team successfully completed six schools, six health facilities, a center for deaf children, a garbage-collection facility, a laboratory, and a library. It has been incredibly rewarding for her to work on these projects, from awarding a contract, to managing design and construction, to handing over brand-new facilities to communities that are in need. For many of these projects, the Army Corps' contractors hire locals for the construction teams and teach them how to safely construct new buildings using local materials. She is glad to be part of this capacity-building that further enhances the future of the community.

One of Jennifer's biggest challenges has been overcoming language barriers and cultural differences while working abroad. During preconstruction meetings, her discussion points are translated from English to French to the local language and then occasionally to another version of the local language. Communication often feels like a game of telephone, which sometimes results in misunderstandings that have to be resolved. Also, while she is proud to represent female engineers in areas where technical jobs are dominated by men, this comes with some challenges, including being proposed to by locals during site visits.

One way that Jennifer assesses the impact of her projects is from feedback gathered during site visits. Very often, the entire community attends site visits—everyone from village elders to the mayor or chief, to school teachers and students, to nurses and doctors. During these visits, she hears praise for the ongoing construction work, such as, "Future presidents will learn in this school," and "The library will increase students' knowledge and open their minds. Many thanks to the US government and the contractor." During several final inspections, she is repeatedly thanked for the generosity of the people of the United States of America. During a site visit at a health clinic, one of the head nurses took a wooden bracelet off her wrist and placed it on Jennifer's. Even though they did not speak the same language, Jennifer could see the woman's deep gratitude in her eyes. Touching moments like these have made Jennifer even more passionate about her work.

Career Trajectory

During Jennifer's senior year at Lehigh University, she attended a career fair specifically for civil engineers, and the US Army Corps of Engineers had a booth that caught her eye. The items that appealed the most to her were a thorough training program for new employees, the chance to participate in emergency management, and the opportunity to work anywhere in the world (the Corps has nine divisions and forty-three districts throughout the US and abroad). Jennifer took her engineer-in-training exam the month before graduating, which was a big help in finding her first job after college: an internship with the Army Corps. Her internship rotated her throughout several divisions, including construction, civil works, design management, geotechnical, planning, water resources, operations, public welfare, and emergency management. This was an incredible opportunity for her directly out of school, especially because she was not sure which path she wanted to take with civil engineering.

Getting the special projects position with the Corps took some luck on top of her qualifications. When she moved to Germany in 2010, she worked in a very remote office with one other coworker. In April 2011, she attended training in Denver, Colorado, where she met another colleague working in Germany; this ended up being a career-changing connection! In 2012, a big project of hers was quickly coming to an end, and she was not sure what would come next. Then she got a call from the colleague she met in Denver. He told her the special projects team was looking for a third engineer, and she was being considered for the job. Up until that point, she was not even aware of the Corps' work to support humanitarian assistance in Europe and Africa because it is a very small group of people. She is now so thankful to be a part of it!

Constantly being on an airplane and traveling to remote project sites has affected her personal life, but it has been an opportunity of a lifetime and worth every minute on the road for her. When she feels good about the work she is doing, there is not a huge disconnect between her work and personal life. She wants to be at work and feels like she is contributing to the world in some way, which is a very rewarding feeling. Had she known of the opportunities in humanitarian engineering, she would have focused on that from the beginning. However, overall she is very satisfied with her education and career path. With constant support from mentors and supervisors, she has been able to see and do things she did not know were possible. Within the next five to ten years, Jennifer hopes to move into a supervisory position overseeing special projects.

Photo by Jones Ngala

Farah Husain

United States Centers for Disease Control and Prevention
Epidemiologist

DMD, Tufts University
MPH, Harvard University
BSc, Anatomy and Cell Biology, McGill University

Job Description

Soon after natural and manmade disasters such as floods, civil wars, and earthquakes occur, public health emergencies follow. Chaos ensues when humanitarian relief organizations rush in to help thousands, or even millions, of displaced people left without food, water, shelter, and basic health care. Disaster relief camps are often overcrowded, thus increasing the risk of waterborne disease transmission and the potential for outbreaks of diseases such as cholera, polio, and jaundice. At such times, public health experts are needed to minimize the chances of disease spreading through disaster relief camps as well as disaster-ravaged communities. The Emergency Response and Recovery Branch within the US Centers for Disease Control and Prevention (CDC) is one of the first responders to disaster situations around the world. Their primary scope of work is to respond to, and conduct operational research related to, public health emergencies. The CDC works with United Nations agencies, nongovernmental organizations, ministries of health, and other partners that focus on displaced populations, including refugees and internally displaced persons.

Farah Husain is an epidemiologist at the CDC who focuses on communicable disease surveillance as well as water, sanitation, and hygiene (WASH) in emergencies. Communicable disease surveillance entails monitoring and tracking the health status of an affected population to prevent outbreaks in crowded settings. For example, in collaboration with international and local partners, Farah and her colleagues recently set up a communicable disease surveillance system in Northern Syria in response to the ongoing civil crisis. There was very limited health information coming from the opposition-controlled northern areas of Syria. She worked with a local partner to identify and train surveillance officers, map functioning health facilities and laboratories, and engage health partners working in northern Syria to submit standardized health data on key priority conditions on a weekly basis. These standardized health data were used to gauge trends and to estimate the burden of disease in order to identify critical gaps and implement control measures. She also helped to formulate a rapid response team to verify and investigate potential outbreaks. Currently, this system includes approximately 400 health facilities and covers seven million people. Farah and her colleagues did this all remotely from southern Turkey as the US government does not have access to Syria. The current polio outbreak in Syria was detected through this early warning system.

Farah also conducted an acceptability study of a novel hand-washing station among recently displaced Sudanese refugees in western Ethiopia. Hand washing with soap has been shown to have the highest disease impact when compared to other WASH measures. However, in the context of public health emergencies, access to water is inadequate, and soap supply is usually insufficient. To address this gap, Farah and her colleagues piloted an acceptability study of a simple collapsible ten-liter heavy-duty plastic hand-washing bag with a spigot and soap pouch at the household level. Randomly selected households were followed over a six-month period to assess durability, utility, and acceptability of the bag. The results revealed the hand-washing bag performed well during the early phase of the emergency when basic public health services were insufficient, and a longer-term study is planned to determine its effect on hand-washing behavior. In addition to projects abroad, Farah teaches courses on health and epidemiological methods in humanitarian emergencies to graduate students and partners working on emergencies overseas. When she is not traveling, she sees patients, one day a week, at the Veterans Affairs Medical Center in her hometown.

Farah sees her impact as ensuring the health and safety of vulnerable populations. In emergencies, systems are often not functioning, infrastructure is usually destroyed, and therefore, routine methods do not often apply. By implementing modified surveillance mechanisms, such as simplified disease reporting, Farah and her coworkers lay the groundwork needed to manage the spread of disease. By exploring different modalities, such as the hand-washing bag, they hope to facilitate basic health and hygiene behaviors that may be difficult in humanitarian emergencies. Since people are far more transient today than in the past, monitoring disease and facilitating behavior change overseas also helps ensure health and safety at home.

Farah's favorite part of her job is the immediate effect of interventions and response activities following an emergency. Her least favorite part is the bureaucracy and restrictions that can limit the access and response capacity.

 Keep it simple, but think outside the box. Keep the big picture in mind as you take small steps to get there.

The constant traveling, difficult living conditions, and stressful working environment can take a toll on Farah's physical and mental health; however, she makes sure to take time for herself and her family, especially immediately following a long response mission. The CDC does a good job of making resources available if Farah needs them. Communication and setting priorities with friends and family are important for her. The CDC's senior staff are very supportive of personal commitments because they believe that having a good work-life balance makes their employees better at what they do.

Career Trajectory

Farah always wanted to work in the field of public health. After completing her undergraduate degree, she applied to both the Peace Corps and dental school and got into both in the same week. She decided to pursue her dental degree, which would provide her with a skill set that she could then use in a public health setting. After dental school and residency, Farah was a National Health Scholarship Corps recipient and provided dental care to the underserved in Worcester, Massachusetts. She went on to get her master of public health (MPH) degree and worked at the Pan American Health Organization (PAHO) in Washington, DC. At PAHO, she was able to focus on population-based oral health care, writing the ten-year oral health strategy for the Americas as well as evaluating a three-year research project on a novel dental technique used in resource-poor settings. Farah was subsequently hired by the International Medical Corps (IMC) as a dental consultant to train local dentists in Kabul, Afghanistan, on the same technique. Following these activities, Farah realized her need for additional training in epidemiology as well as increased exposure to general public health areas outside oral health (since oral health programs are not standalone, but part of a broader public health strategy). That is when she applied to the Epidemic Intelligence Service, a two-year training fellowship in applied epidemiology at the CDC. She thought she would go back to PAHO or to an NGO after her two years were over, but she has been there ever since.

Farah sometimes thinks she took a circuitous road to get to where she is, but she believes the accumulation of all her previous experiences got her to her current position. It is an unconventional path for a dentist, and many of her former classmates still do not understand what she does. Farah believes that her academic training, international experiences, and supportive mentors encouraged her to pursue this path. Looking to the future, it is hard for Farah to say where she thinks she will be. She did not think she would still be at the CDC six years ago, but she truly enjoys what she does and is continuously challenged in her day-to-day activities. The world is getting smaller. Diseases in one part of the world can quickly spread to other parts of the world. We need to think of new, innovative strategies to mitigate these acute public health events.

Photo by USAID

⚙ Ticora V. Jones

United States Agency for International Development (USAID)
Division Chief of Higher Education Solutions Network | ~$100,000

PhD, Polymer Science and Engineering, University of Massachusetts, Amherst (2006)
BS, Material Science and Engineering, MIT (2000)

Job Description

What role can higher education play in ventures aimed at improving the human condition? The US Agency for International Development (USAID) finds that opportunities for collaboration are plenty. USAID partners to end extreme global poverty and enable resilient, democratic societies to realize their full potential. To reach these ambitious ends, game-changing approaches to international development are needed. Universities are one source of innovation, bringing together experts across many disciplines and pairing them with energetic, motivated students. In November 2012, USAID united eight development labs across seven universities to create the Higher Education Solutions Network (HESN). The network brings together 100 additional partner institutions in academia, civil society, and government across thirty-eight countries. Together, HESN harnesses the ingenuity and passion of university students and faculty to discover, develop, and implement new science and technology-based solutions to the world's most challenging development problems.

Leading this charge is Ticora Jones, division chief of HESN. Through her various roles with USAID, Ticora Jones has been supporting the reemergence of science, technology, innovation, and partnerships within the agency. Her team within USAID consists of thirteen grant and program management professionals that facilitate complex multidisciplinary agreements between USAID and the academic community. Ticora leads and coordinates strategic, operational, communication, budget, and programmatic elements of the HESN portfolio. She also plans, manages, and executes major events to facilitate the HESN network of academics, practitioners, innovators, entrepreneurs, and investors.

At the core of these responsibilities is relationship management. The HESN team not only facilitates communication among HESN development labs, but the team must also convey and tailor HESN's value-add to the rest of the agency and the broader development community. Therefore, Ticora's daily dose of meetings varies widely—sometimes it entails coordinating opportunities and events for the development labs to convene, while other times she is reviewing and providing feedback on their work from an agency perspective. At other times, she is attending management meetings at a variety of levels to ensure the success of her team, program, and larger organization. It is also on her plate to ask big-picture, strategic questions and get people to think differently about the agenda that they are undertaking. Outside her team, she is trying to collaborate with different divisions within USAID to determine the best resources and fit for her team.

The biggest challenge Ticora faces is time management; it has been a difficult lesson for her to learn that she cannot do everything and has to be comfortable delegating to her team and prioritizing what to keep and what to let go. She has learned through her experience with USAID how to best allocate her time to balance different projects. Her favorite part of her job is that she gets to build communities of awesome students and professors, create spaces for them to innovate, and empower them to connect and make impact. She is the person who finds the right individuals at universities to go on the ground to tackle issues and who connects them with opportunities to do so.

One of the HESN development labs is at the University of California Berkeley. Students and faculty there are working to establish a new field of development engineering and move many development solutions, such as low-cost, solar-powered vaccine refrigerators, through their pipeline of research, field evaluation, translation, and scaling. Another lab at the College of William and Mary is building a world-class research consortium of geographers, economists, epidemiologists, political scientists, computer scientists, and statisticians to collect, geo-code, and analyze data that enables USAID and developing country governments to make evidence-based decisions.

Academics, policy makers, and international development practitioners all tackle the same issues, but to reach sustainable results, mechanisms for interdisciplinary collaboration must exist. HESN and USAID adopt the role of convener, which is part of the reason Ticora enjoys working for a government agency. The government provides a fundamentally different type of view because she has the ability to frame conversations and invite people into them, ultimately building a community and ecosystem of innovation.

> Recognizing the skills that you have that are soft is incredibly important if you want to create social value. Technical will not do it all. The most important skills you can have are empathy, diplomacy, communication, passion, and appreciation of others in the community that you work in. At the end of the day, people matter. Make sure you can listen, engage, and empathize with your community.

Career Trajectory

From an early age, Ticora sought opportunities to advance in math and science, such as attending a STEM-focused high school and spending summers in university research labs. However, she also supplemented these technical abilities with activities such as tutoring, singing, acting, and volunteering with her church. Learning to balance hard and soft skills when she was young and continuing to grow those abilities has enabled her to develop strong leadership and communication skills. After high school, she earned her bachelor's degree from MIT in material science and engineering. At MIT, she cofounded a black woman's organization to create a community for support and understanding. During her college summers, she worked at a DuPont polymer processing plant (which produces ingredients, chemicals, and materials), a metallurgy lab in Sweden (which studies the physical and chemical behavior of metallic elements), and the IBM Almaden Research Center doing chemical research. Although Ticora always thought she would be a chemical engineer at a large manufacturing plant, a summer of hands-on experience in this setting convinced her otherwise. Her experience in Sweden was the first time she tuned into international collaboration.

After MIT, she was chosen to be a teaching fellow through the American Association for the Advancement of Science (AAAS), enabling her to go beyond the traditional lab experience and use her skills in another venue. She was sent to a middle school in Washington, DC, to support middle school teachers as they refreshed their science and math curriculum and to teach classes of sixth through eighth graders. After a year, she went back to school to earn her PhD in polymer science and engineering and then did a postdoc at Lawrence Livermore National Laboratory. September 11th occurred on Ticora's second week of grad school, and with a high awareness of the importance of global issues, she was further motivated to pursue a career that bridged academia and public policy. Thus, after her postdoc, she became a congressional legislative fellow for a year. She focused on energy and environment issues relevant to Wisconsin's constituents and to the Senate Foreign Relations Committee. It was through this opportunity that she started working on resource issues in Africa, clean energy, and learning about the legislative process. From there, Ticora was chosen to be an AAAS Science Policy Fellow at USAID and eventually helped establish what was formerly called the Office of Science and Technology.

Ticora is incredibly thankful for her supportive parents who have helped her get where she is today. Growing up in Colorado, her parents were great role models in an area that did not have many people of color to look up to. They encouraged her to explore her own decisions and set ambitious goals. Ticora has always wanted both a service and a technical side to her career. In her current position, she is thrilled that she can effectively marry those two concepts. Despite her highly technical degrees, she did not pursue a career in academia because she wanted an environment that rewarded public service. If she could start over, Ticora says she would have had more fun and questioned herself more often about what she was passionate about and what was possible. Regardless of where her career trajectory leads, Ticora would like to continue building community wherever she has the opportunity to do so.

⚙ Lara Allison Campbell, 47

United States National Science Foundation (NSF)
Program Director, Office of International Science & Engineering | ~$125,000

PhD, Chemistry, University of Texas at Austin (1998)
BA, Chemistry, Rice University (1991)

Job Description

The National Science Foundation (NSF) is a United States government agency that seeks "to promote the progress of science; to advance the national health, prosperity, and welfare; to secure the national defense." With an annual budget of $7.3 billion, NSF supports basic research and education in all nonmedical fields of science and engineering; its medical counterpart is the National Institutes of Health. NSF is the funding source for nearly a quarter of all federally supported basic research conducted by higher education institutions in the United States. Enabled by financial support from NSF, scientists around the country can pursue scientific research to improve the human condition and beyond. In order to secure funding, a major criterion for NSF is the broader impact of the research.

As program director for international science and engineering, Lara Campbell manages, develops, and supports international research cooperation between US scientists and their counterparts, especially in the Middle East and Africa. This requires working with colleagues across NSF and other federal agencies, counterparts in other international funding sources, and scientists around the world. Lara shares the NSF's goal of developing activities that have strong scientific merit and valuable broader impact for people and societies in the US and around the globe. An example of this is her work with Iran. Lara was contacted by an investigator who was curious if she could submit a proposal for work in Iran, given the US sanctions. Shortly thereafter, several NSF program officers also asked Lara about work with Iran. Some program officers assumed that it was not possible to even consider such proposals, and others were willing to fund projects that received good merit review but were unlikely to be legally implementable. Lara investigated the sanctions regime and spoke with colleagues at the Department of State and the Office of Foreign Assets Control about licenses for scientific work with Iran. She determined the parameters under which such projects could be funded and general guidelines for contingency plans. The principal investigator with the original query should soon receive a grant that includes fieldwork in Iran, and other grants for work in Iran are in the pipeline.

Since Lara's portfolio area is predominantly developing countries, the projects she works with tend to involve very smart people with limited resources. One major way she meets this challenge is by sending US personnel overseas because their international partners rarely have funds to travel to the US. She loves to see the benefits to the host countries, but arguably even more so to the US personnel—often students or junior staff—who are completely transformed by the experience. International collaboration opens up entirely new opportunities for everyone involved! Lara loves to see that her work is truly making the world a better place and promoting the spirit of global collaboration. Her biggest impact comes from helping smart people develop and implement excellent projects. Together, international groups can advance frontiers of knowledge, but the greatest personal value for Lara comes from seeing the relationships develop and collaboration improve the broader community and society.

Lara's favorite part of her job is dealing with scientists—hearing about their ideas for research projects, workshops, and new topics for collaborations. She also greatly enjoys dealing with colleagues in other agencies and her counterparts overseas as they discuss their challenges and envision cooperative success. In addition, she loves traveling to several regions where she gets to learn and see the value of many different projects—from astronomy to zoology (with a lot of engineering and innovation in the middle). The variety is key to enjoying her work. Amongst all that she loves about her job, she does get bored with some of the paperwork; writing up the umpteenth justification for funding is just not as fun as envisioning new collaborative projects.

Career Trajectory

Lara has been interested in the Middle East since she was an undergraduate where she took several religious studies and history courses on Islam and the region. In graduate school, she tried to take courses in Arabic and Middle Eastern studies, but the chemistry department at the time absolutely forbade any "outside" classes. Nevertheless, she read a lot, started teaching herself Arabic, went to cultural events, and found some connections to the region. After she finished her PhD, she took an adjunct faculty position at the University of Texas rather than move her family to a smaller city for a full-time faculty position.

Most of how I got here is probably serendipity, but serendipity only works if you are prepared and jump when you see an opportunity!

After teaching and doing postdoctoral research at UT for almost two years, Lara had saved up a fair amount of money but felt herself sliding into a rut. She quit her job, bought a ticket with a flexible, six-month return window, and left for the Middle East. She traveled (sometimes alone but also with family and friends) to Jordan, Syria, Lebanon, Turkey, Egypt, and Iran. While she was overseas, she applied for postdoctoral positions in cities that were likely to have interesting opportunities for her partner. While she was in Syria in an Internet café, she accepted a position as a postdoc at the National Institutes of Health.

While at NIH, Lara attended almost any event involving the Middle East that she could justify to her boss, from state department events to meetings organized by think tanks and professional societies. She also started taking night classes in Arabic. Finally, a friend passed along a job announcement for a position at the American Association for the Advancement of Science (AAAS). Lara had unsuccessfully applied twice to be a science policy fellow at AAAS, but landed the job in the Research Competitiveness Program. She loved the work! Her fellow staff respected her enthusiasm, language skills, and modicum of expertise on the Middle East, and that led to opportunities for international work, even though her position had no official international responsibilities. She organized conferences and workshops whenever she could on topics related to science and collaboration with the Middle East.

A few years later, the same friend who had connected her to the AAAS job mentioned Lara at her own interview for a company. That company ended up contacting Lara several months later and persuaded her to leave AAAS. She moved to CUBRC, a small nonprofit research and technical management organization with an office in Washington, DC, that managed cooperative threat reduction programs for the US government. The work there was mostly with countries of the former Soviet Union, but it involved tremendously interesting technical, political, and interpersonal challenges as well as great people and amazing travel. It was Lara's first explicitly international job, and she loved it! However, she continued to study Arabic and still yearned to work with the Middle East. After a few years, she applied for a Fulbright Scholar position to do a regional research project looking at innovation development. She won the Fulbright, and while she was overseas at CUBRC, she won a contract to support a USAID Middle East program. Lara moved directly into that work when she returned. She had managed to make herself into a Middle East "expert"!

After almost eight years at CUBRC and having moved up to become the director of their Center for International Science and Technology Advancement, Lara was feeling in a rut again. When another friend forwarded a job ad for a position at NSF, she thought it seemed perfect. She was right: it has turned out to be a great fit and a ton of fun! Early in Lara's career, she had no work-life balance. Graduate school is not conducive to a personal life or even interests outside the lab, although she had many. The same has been true for much of her time in Washington, DC. Having an amazing partner with much better work-life balance skills helped her stop working obsessively on weekends—there was always something fun to do together. Still, it was not until they had a child that she stopped working late into the evening far too often. Now, she has finally learned that whatever it is, it can almost always wait until tomorrow. She has also become more efficient during her working hours.

Lara could see herself staying at NSF for a long time, maybe even finishing her career there. On the other hand, she enjoys new challenges, so she could also move to another federal agency that has international offices, perhaps USAID or the Department of State, Energy, or Agriculture. She also might move back into work more focused on implementation than management, perhaps working for a government contractor in one of the aforementioned agencies. In the long run, she would like to be deputy director or director of an office that manages and implements international scientific activities.

Greg Lank, 36

Environmental Protection Agency
Mechanical Engineer and Project Officer, Office of Research
and Development | ~$95,000

MEng, Mechanical Engineering (Energy and the Environment),
University of Maryland (2010)
BS, Mechanical Engineering, Penn State University (2001)

Job Description

Ever since the 1970s, with the establishment of the Environmental Protection Agency (EPA), the United States government has worked increasingly hard to protect and maintain clean, healthy, natural environments for the American people. Today, the EPA is helping to tackle large-scale issues such as climate change, waste management, and green living. In an effort to educate the next generation on the principles of sustainability, the EPA's Office of Research and Development designed the P3 program: People, Prosperity, and the Planet. The P3 program is a unique competition through which college students can help people, promote prosperity, and protect the planet by designing solutions that move us toward a sustainable future.

Projects that compete in the P3 competition address challenges in categories such as water, energy, agriculture, built environment, materials, and chemicals that are found in both the Western and developing world. Some examples of former projects include an energy-saving technology for schools and other organizations, the nation's first floating wetlands classroom powered by renewable sources, and a company that converts carbon found in wastewater into high-performance biodegradable plastic. There are two phases of the competition: interdisciplinary teams first apply for $15,000 grants, and then chosen teams develop their projects further to compete at the National Sustainable Design Expo in Washington, DC. At this expo, P3 student projects are exhibited alongside EPA programs, other government agencies, nonprofit organizations, and businesses to showcase their achievements. Student designs that are awarded win grant funding of up to $90,000 for further testing and marketing of their project. Many of the winning teams go on to become companies that can expand and make an even larger impact after the competition. Proper management of this program ensures that the competition runs smoothly every year and that great ideas are constantly being submitted.

A mechanical engineer by training, Greg Lank is one member of the small, dedicated team that manages the P3 program. Greg has a variety of responsibilities, partially driven by the position requirements and partially driven by his personality and academic background. His job includes technical insight, grant management, outreach, and partnership development. His background in mechanical engineering affords him the technical insight necessary to understand the technologies, and his other responsibilities are key for the success of the competition each year. Managing the grants and funds for the program ensures that competitors receive their money, which is vital to the success of their ventures. Outreach and partnership development are important for the longevity of the program; having partners and support from outsiders ensures that the P3 program is held to high standards and is sustainable. Greg also helps plan the National Sustainable Design Expo for the P3 teams to showcase their projects.

In Greg's opinion, the P3 program works to further the agency's mission of protecting human health and the environment by funding the research of sustainability innovations. The impacts of the P3 program include small-scale development, education, and social entrepreneurship. Each of these impacts improves the world by helping people, promoting prosperity, and protecting the planet. In addition to his work with the P3 program, Greg is involved with the EPA's SBIR program: Small Business Innovation Research. For this program, he manages SBIR contracts for innovative environmental technology startup companies. This enables him to have further impact and gets him outside of working with universities.

Greg's least favorite parts of his job are his long commute into the office, being removed from the actual physical research, and the inevitable bureaucracy (excessively complicated administrative procedures) associated with federal research. However, his overall enjoyment for his job stems from great colleagues, innovative research funded by the program, and the fact that the mission of both the agency and the program add purpose to his career and personal life. His experiences with volunteering have shown him that it is important to pursue a career that makes his life more meaningful—through social impact.

Career Trajectory

Greg earned a bachelor of science degree in mechanical engineering from the Pennsylvania State University followed by a master's in mechanical engineering from the University of Maryland. Immediately after graduation, Greg worked as a non-nuclear propulsion engineer testing aircraft carrier propulsion plants, what he considers a dream mechanical engineering job. During his almost seven years with this job, he landed on and was launched off aircraft carriers in both the Atlantic and Pacific Oceans. He witnessed air shows offshore and experienced sea trials pushing ships to limits that "the navy itself will most likely never attempt." He also crawled inside reactor plants before they became too hot and ran tests in the control tower alongside the captain. While the job was exciting and provided amazing experiences, Greg yearned for a purpose he felt was of greater value.

> Diversification is the secret sauce to success: diversification in cultural and economic backgrounds, diversification in academic skill sets, and diversification in travel and associated experiences. I feel diversification adds to the tool box and provides the references people need to pull from to make better decisions.

Looking for adventure and the freedom to explore "both the world around and within us," Greg, his wife, and two dogs left the Hampton Roads area to take a sabbatical living on a twenty-seven-foot boat in the Bahamas. He had grand visions of living off the land and sea only to find that, even in the most remote islands, the seas were overfished, and the vast majority of the produce came from the US; those living in the outlying islands were completely dependent on ships to bring any and all supplies. The reality of the living conditions was far different from what he had previously imagined. This sabbatical provided Greg with an outsider's perspective on mainstream America, which made him realize the truly unsustainable nature of living in the US. He then vowed to return to a career with greater purpose.

Within a year of moving to the Washington, DC, metro area, Greg attended a college graduation ceremony where the dean spoke about Engineers Without Borders (EWB). This was his "aha" moment—he had finally found an avenue to apply his engineering skills to social issues. Within one more year, he traveled to South Africa with EWB and learned of the EPA's P3 program. Greg's travels exposed him to the severe needs in developing countries, which created a curiosity to learn more about these challenges. Through his volunteer work, he learned how to address social challenges using the tools obtained through scientific training. Upon his return from EWB, there was a position open with the P3 program. It took career dissatisfaction, a subsequent sabbatical, and overseas volunteer work for Greg to end up where he is now: facilitating innovative sustainability research. While the process appears very happenstance, the real framework stemmed from curiosity and a desire to improve the quality of life for other people in the world. Greg benefitted from extensive volunteer work with organizations such as the Chesapeake Bay Foundation, Reef Relief, and Chesapeake Regional Accessible Boating.

Having a family has meant that Greg has had to cut back on volunteering gigs. He recognizes the importance of giving back and balancing it with being there for his loved ones. Since Greg believes that many of the global injustices are due to ignorance of current issues, he stays informed and makes sure his family and friends are aware of social and environmental issues. If Greg could do one thing differently, he would have earned an MBA instead of a master's in engineering. While he likes understanding the technology, he truly enjoys the challenge and potential of helping to take social and environmental innovations to market. He thinks he would be better at marketing with an MBA in his toolbox. Greg believes his personality type supports business and entrepreneurial initiatives, coupled with life experiences and an education that drive him to try to address life's injustices. In the future, Greg sees himself working in product development and marketing social and environmental innovations.

⚙ Jay Goyal, 33

Ohio State Government
State Representative | ~$60,000 base + $10,000 – 20,000 bonus in a leadership position

MBA and MPP, Harvard Business School and Harvard Kennedy School of Government (2015)
BS, Industrial Engineering, Northwestern University (2003)

Job Description

In the United States, people are moving increasingly farther for jobs. People migrate to where opportunities are ample, leading to net migration out of some states and into others. States with mostly agrarian and manufacturing jobs tend to lose people while states with strong universities and high-tech corporations increase their populations. Ohio has had one of the highest levels of outmigration for the past few years with nearly 1,400 net outbound moves during 2014. How can states like Ohio create new jobs and attract smart people to grow their economy? To embrace the transition to a knowledge economy, states must inspire and foster innovation to bring about economic development. Governments must strive to create business environments that beckon the best and brightest innovators and entrepreneurs to build the companies of the future. Jay Goyal, a former Ohio state representative, applies his expertise in industrial engineering and experiences running a technology-based family business to foster economic development in his state.

Jay knew it would be an uphill battle running for office as a twenty-five-year-old, ethnic minority, Democratic candidate in a Republican area. However, he was elected and then re-elected twice. When in office, Jay focused on creating well-paying jobs in a manufacturing area where manufacturing jobs had been declining. He worked on a number of initiatives, the biggest of which was creating a $700 million fund to support entrepreneurial activities from research and development support, to technology commercialization support, to entrepreneurial support. The money from the fund is also being used for internship programs and a number of other programs in Ohio. In addition to this bill, Jay tackled the issue that while a lot of great research is being done at public colleges, there are still many barriers preventing that technology from being spun out into new companies to create jobs. Jay passed legislation to eliminate one of the barriers by allowing public colleges to take equity in startups. Jay also introduced a bill to publicly finance judicial elections in the state of Ohio because he saw that unless there are 100% publicly financed elections, there is no way around outside money in campaigns.

Aside from the legislation, Jay was able to improve the lives of constituents often through one-on-one cases. For example, he helped recently laid-off people navigate the unemployment bureaucracies so that they could collect their unemployment compensation. He also assisted churches that had been taxed improperly to ensure they were receiving their nonprofit status and collecting their tax refunds from the state as they should have. The most rewarding assistance he provided was working with the state department of health insurance as well as private insurers to make sure that a constituent whose son had cystic fibrosis received health insurance.

When he was in session in Columbus, Jay started his day with leadership meetings among the top leaders in the House and the Democrat caucus to discuss the bills that were going to be on the floor that day. Jay would then discuss the bills with other Democrats before proceeding into the session to vote on the bills. In addition, there were hearings where Jay would listen to people testify on different bills. Aside from the more formal parts of his job, Jay spent a lot of time meeting with stakeholders and constituents. Sometimes he spoke to student groups who were at the capitol building taking a tour. He also worked on legislation with his staff, experts, or stakeholders who were interested in the issue. Generally in the evening, he would attend receptions or other public events. Throughout Jay's day, he always tried to maximize the interactions he had in person, on the phone, and through email. Some of Jay's legislative work emerged from reading and talking to people to find good ideas. Then, to transform good ideas into bills, Jay worked with his staff. As they went through the process of drafting bills, Jay always made sure he included diverse stakeholders to get their feedback on what they thought of the latest drafts.

Some of the biggest challenges Jay faced in office involved the state budget. Particularly in the 2009 aftermath of the financial crisis, state revenues plunged, and as a result, the legislature had a significant budget gap to fill. At the time, the governor was a Democrat and the House was run by the Democrats, but the Senate was controlled by the Republicans. There was going to be an election in 2010, and thus, in the midst of the worst financial crisis since the Great Depression, Jay was also in a very critical election-year cycle. While the Ohio legislature managed to eventually pass the budget, it was a messy process. They ended up cobbling it together with only five Republicans in support, the bare minimum they needed in the Senate to get the majority to support it. Even through the chaos, the thing Jay liked most about his job was working on policy. He enjoyed taking a problem and thinking through ways to solve the problem positively from government and then working with stakeholders to craft specific solutions to come up with the best ideas, policies, and legislation.

> I think all routes to creating social value are equally valid. If someone were to think about the public service route and running for office, I would strongly advise them to be rooted into their community and understand the community that they want to represent. Also, many times it is helpful to have a private sector career before going into public service so that you will gain business experience and develop a network which you can then utilize when in the public sector. I think some of the people who have the most interesting and fulfilling careers are those who just do not choose one of those paths but try to take multiple paths.

Career Trajectory

Jay was very active as an undergraduate student in a number of social justice student groups on Northwestern's campus. As part of one of his clubs, he pressured the university administration to sign on to labor monitoring to ensure that none of the university apparel was being made in sweatshops. He ran for undergraduate student body president as a sophomore, and although he lost the election, the experience taught him how to run a campaign. Jay was also part of the Undergraduate Budget Priorities Committee where he researched student priorities and presented recommendations for directing university funds to the board of trustees. Through his extracurricular activities, he learned about different styles of leadership, group decision-making processes, and how to deal with the emotions of a public campaign.

Upon graduation, Jay joined his family business: a small manufacturing company. Jay wanted to have a wider impact on people, so he joined some community nonprofit boards and volunteered for political campaigns. Through these endeavors, he met a lot of people who encouraged him to run for office. At twenty-five, he took the plunge and got 62% of the vote. After Jay was elected, he realized that his Indian ethnicity did not affect him negatively in his campaign. However, while he was running, there were many people who were concerned about whether he could win with his ethnicity. He dealt with instances such as people saying he was "not even a real American." Jay characterizes what they said as ignorance more than racism because many people who said those things told him later that they were glad he talked to them so that they could have a better understanding of who he was and what he stood for. On the other hand, Jay feels that his age may have affected him negatively once he was elected because sometimes he would have to work harder to earn people's respect.

Getting into politics was not something Jay predicted. Because of his upbringing, Jay always assumed he would get an engineering degree and stay in the family business. His engineering degree was still useful because it helped him develop the mindset of a problem solver and systems thinker, which he applied not only to the manufacturing process, but also to the problems he had in his legislative office and dealing with constituent concerns. For example, he applied it to the process of creating well-paying jobs. His engineering degree made him comfortable with technology issues and meeting with people in the technology community across the state on the entrepreneurial as well as the research and development side. Jay's degree also boosted his credibility when trying to pass bills.

Jay sacrificed on the social end in order to fulfill his position as a public official. Attracting a lower salary than he would have as an engineer, Jay chose to go into public service because he cared about serving his community by affecting policy. Jay considered running for the United States Congress, but he decided he wanted to take a different route to solve social problems. He is now in graduate school figuring out how he wants to effect change next. He is not sure where he will go next, but he is interested in finding ways to use technology to solve public policy and social problems. Over his summers from grad school, he has worked for a startup as well as with a venture fund looking for technology companies that can help make government more efficient or effective.

GOVERNMENT » INDEPENDENT STATE AGENCY

Katherine Record, 30

Massachusetts Health Policy Commission
Senior Manager, Behavioral Health Integration | ~$90,000

MPH, Health Policy & Management, Harvard School of Public Health (2012)
MA, Health Psychology and JD, Health Law, Duke University (2010)
BA, Psychology & Sociology, Georgetown University (2006)

Job Description

Currently in the US, we largely rely on a system that waits on people with mental illnesses to have a crisis, including sometimes committing a crime, before considering need for treatment. Katherine is focused on integrating mental health and substance use disorder treatment services into the health-care system that has traditionally focused nearly exclusively on medical/surgical services. She is currently with the Health Policy Commission (HPC) of Massachusetts, an independent state agency established by Chapter 224 of the Acts of 2012, "an act improving the quality of health care and reducing costs through increased transparency, efficiency, and innovation." Her work promotes integration via pilots, investments, technical assistance, and provider certification programs.

More specifically, Katherine is charged with developing and implementing the behavioral health integration portion of certification programs, conducting research and advising on key barriers and accelerators of reform for integrating mental health and substance use disorder services into new care delivery and payment models, analyzing and evaluating these models and their impact on health-care expenditures, advising HPC staff tracking market performance on the impact of material changes in the market on access to behavioral health care, overseeing HPC investments in pilots and technical assistance that accelerate behavioral health integration (via care delivery or payment transformation), and advising the executive director and chief of staff on legislative proposals related to advancing behavioral health integration. These include portions of the Community Hospital Acceleration, Revitalization, and Transformation Investment Program (CHART), the Innovation Investment Fund, and portions of HPC's budget allocated to technical assistance.

Katherine is an instructor of public health law at the Harvard School of Public Health and a collaborating mentor with Boston's Children Hospital Strategic Training and Research Initiative on the Prevention of Eating Disorders. Prior to working at the HPC, Katherine was a clinical instructor at Harvard Law's Center for Health Policy and Innovation where she led work on mental health court design and standardization processes, privacy law, and implementation of the Affordable Care Act. She has also worked at the O'Neill Institute for National and Global Health Law at Georgetown University where she worked on mental health law and gun control, the use of antiretroviral drugs as preexposure prophylaxis, and public health law reform in low-income countries.

Career Trajectory

Through her education, Katherine pursued a combination of psychology and law. She wanted to be a public defender and worked with juvenile delinquents throughout her undergraduate career. She learned that she hated criminal law and the day-to-day work of a defense attorney, preferring academic and policy settings that allow for more creativity and more potential to enact change. Katherine's first job was in Washington, DC, at a policy institute that focuses on global health. Her main project was developing a public health policy reform book that contained laws that should be on the books to make the health arena run smoothly. She liked working in global health so much that she then got her master's in health psychology from Harvard School of Public Health. Her experiences have enabled her to meet people in the medical and health policy field who were not lawyers. Working with diverse people has brought her a broader perspective on how to go about different issues. Upon graduation, she stayed in Boston to work at a health clinic and eventually found herself back at Harvard as an instructor.

In the future, Katherine can see herself both inside and outside academia, balanced with time in government where the ideas generated in academia are put into place. If she could do it all over and time and money were not an object, Katherine would get a PhD in clinical psychology to get a better understanding of mental illness.

Do what you care about, not what looks good—that is how you meet people who share your passion and gets you where you want to be.

In the legal profession, one can play a role in social change because the laws have a bigger impact on day-to-day life more than most people realize at the granular level. Law affects the economy and incentives to do different things. With respect to everything, law is making things the way they are at least in part.

♥ Brinnon Garrett Mandel, 38

Jhpiego
Director of Innovations | ~$100,000 – $125,000

MBA and MPH, Johns Hopkins University (2004)
BA, International Political Economy & Biology, Colorado College (1999)

Job Description

Every year, over half a million women die from causes related to pregnancy and childbirth, and nearly four million newborns die within one month after birth. Almost all maternal and newborn mortality—99%—occurs in the developing world where more than 50% of women still deliver without the assistance of skilled health personnel. This is a complex, multilayered challenge with ground realities and possibilities varying significantly from region to region. Accordingly, a large cohort of organizations, from the Gates Foundation to UNICEF to Pathfinder to Jhpiego, are testing and employing a smorgasbord of approaches to improve maternal and newborn health. The Gates Foundation invests in high-risk, high-reward research; UNICEF works with governments around the world to develop home-based maternal and newborn care programs; and Pathfinder initiates programs in communities to train midwives that can facilitate safe pregnancies and deliveries.

Jhpiego prefers to work directly with community health workers who are at the forefront of health care in developing countries. They work closely with ministries of health, professional associations, and preservice (academic) institutions to develop a competent workforce, introduce new evidence-based guidelines, and lead innovative approaches to deliver high-impact interventions. Jhpiego develops innovative, low-cost, easy-to-use solutions and makes them available to populations in greatest need. For forty years, Jhpiego has been working in over 155 developing countries to improve public health conditions. How does a geographically dispersed organization of this magnitude become a dynamic innovative organization? In the past few years, in order to accelerate their impact and to work on solutions that can expand coverage, quality, and equity of life-saving interventions, Jhpiego formed the Innovations Program. Brinnon Garrett Mandel, the director of the Innovations Program, empowers a team of engineers, public health clinicians, researchers, and practitioners to work together to produce and implement a small portfolio of global health innovations.

Jhpiego is affiliated with Johns Hopkins University (JHU), which has arguably the best hospital and biomedical engineering program not only in the US, but in the world. Jhpiego is the vehicle to get JHU innovations to the people. Members of the Innovations Program take the latest knowledge in science and technology and apply it to develop practical, extremely affordable solutions and make them available from home to hospital, rural village to urban center. They train doctors, nurses, midwives, and community health workers with evidence-based skills and techniques to deliver quality health care. Jhpiego brings health services to people in remote communities who previously could not easily access services.

Although Jhpiego is a large, well-established organization, the Innovations Program is relatively new to Jhpiego and is doing things that are new to the organization in the areas of product development and engineering. In many ways Brinnon is running a startup and charting new territory to operationalize the vision and goal of the program. With a background in both public health and business, Brinnon has worked in various roles at Jhpiego with an interest in the intersection of global health, technology, and business. On any given day, she is working with engineers on understanding their product-development processes, writing proposals and grants, and doing some communications and advocacy (through guest lectures at colleges, appearances on radio shows, webinar series, and blog posts). She could also be balancing long-range portfolio planning, which means planning which new product developments they will fund to achieve their objectives. This involves Brinnon overseeing the products that her team members design and assessing their potential value. She hosts team meetings and leads discussions to determine which products will be most effective at improving maternal and newborn health. In addition to her main responsibilities, Brinnon often finds herself educating her peers and supervisors about what they are trying to do and why it is taking so long. There is a constant challenge in balancing the market factors that drive technology adoption with the global health needs, and how different types of investors view the viability of a solution in different ways.

Within the Innovations Program, Brinnon assesses the impact of her activities by making sure her team is asking the right questions, ensuring that they make progress on their projects, and figuring out how to "fail better" (earlier and faster). Brinnon loves the passion and commitment to global health that her colleagues bring to their work. She also loves the variety and the challenge of doing something new, different, and tough. What she likes least is that it is hard to measure and define success when so much of what she does is challenging and she is so far removed from the people whose lives she is trying to influence. There are several projects that she believes have the potential to save millions of lives, but getting them to the frontline health workers—and the women and babies who need them—is arduous.

> Be bold and tenacious. But also be rigorous and realistic. It is challenging, and we should view "failure" in a positive way so that we do it better, earlier, and cheaper and take what we learn and apply it to our next idea or partnerships. Partnerships are fundamental to success in getting a social innovation adopted and sustained. Bring partners and different perspectives into your thinking from Day 1.

Career Trajectory

Brinnon developed her international interests in college: international affairs and development and how that affects inequality in opportunity and human suffering. After college, she joined the Peace Corps to further explore these interests and became a health volunteer in Honduras. She learned more than what she contributed to her community, but it was a very transformative experience for her. Experiencing the good, bad, and ugly of development work and understanding the challenges in low-resource settings have stayed with her in everything she does. After returning, she struggled with what to do. She had been pre-med in college and was working in HIV and reproductive health in Honduras, so she gravitated toward health; however, she took a while to decide if she wanted to pursue a clinical degree or public health. She still considers that trade-off: the appeal of making systems better, improving health at the population level, and the magnitude of impact versus helping an individual get better and be healthy, and the immediate feedback of clinical work. Luckily, she had an opportunity to add an MBA to her MPH, which has turned out to be valuable for her career. Once she completed these degrees, she experimented with different types of jobs—in local public health, business consulting, and working at a university as a business liaison. Each of those was a great experience, and she thinks stepping outside global health for a bit helped her develop some other skills and appreciation for other approaches. However, she was drawn back to global health about four years ago.

There are days when Brinnon sees herself as a landscape architect because she likes to produce and be outside in nature. This desire may be the counterpart to being in front of a computer a lot and not always feeling productive in tangible ways. But she may stay in global development or do something local and focused. In any case, what is attractive to her is solving social problems and figuring out the tools and processes to do that successfully, which is why she is attracted to design thinking. She thinks there is a tendency to not be as holistic or creative as possible in mission-driven jobs, but they should be bold and risky.

If Brinnon could go back in time, she might pursue a clinical degree. She knows a lot of people who have clinical backgrounds or even a clinical practice who work in public health. It is appealing to her that with a clinical degree she could step into a room and directly help a person in front of her. She would also have taken additional difficult classes in finance, epidemiology, forecasting, modeling, and projections because she believes these courses are universally valuable. Work-life balance is very important to Brinnon to maintain relationships, be healthy and active, and be a good citizen. She struggles with it because to really excel at her job, she says she should travel a lot more than she wants to or can with her family life. Brinnon finds herself fortunate to work for an organization that is very flexible and generous with alternative work arrangements. She wishes she had this job and experience ten years ago when she had the energy and freedom to dedicate every ounce of herself to her job.

Photo by Wendy Jenkins

Bernhard H. Weigl, 48

PATH
Portfolio Leader, Diagnostics for Noncommunicable Diseases

PhD, Analytical Chemistry, Karl Franzens University (1993)
BS, Chemistry, University of Innsbruck (1987)

Job Description

While a woman in sub-Saharan Africa is unlikely to travel six hours and spend ten dollars on a doctor's visit for some concerning symptoms, she may be willing to spend twenty-five cents on a simple diagnostic test that she buys from a community health worker and uses in the privacy and comfort of her own home. By purchasing a diagnostic test, she can find out if a trip to the doctor would be worth the time and money. Low-cost, easy-to-use, and durable diagnostic tests have the potential to drastically improve how we measure a patient's health condition in low-resource conditions and get them to the right place quickly. These diagnostic tests use materials including paper, cell phone cameras, and syringes to keep costs low.

PATH is an international nonprofit organization that transforms global health through innovation. They take an entrepreneurial approach to developing and delivering high-impact, low-cost solutions—from lifesaving vaccines, drugs, and diagnostics to collaborative programs with communities. Through their work in more than seventy countries, PATH specializes in overcoming obstacles that can keep an innovation from reaching widespread impact—especially during steps including testing and refining, gaining approvals, commercializing a product, and introducing new approaches. Through experience, ingenuity, and persistence, they accelerate the speed at which innovations make it into the hands of the people who need them.

Bernhard Weigl is a portfolio leader for PATH's Noncommunicable Disease Diagnostics team. He oversees global health diagnostics programs funded by a variety of sources, such as NIAID and NIBIB, the Grand Challenges program of the Bill & Melinda Gates Foundation, USAID, and the PATH Health Innovation Portfolio. Diagnostic technologies under development at PATH include strip-based immunoassays, instrument-free molecular assays, and a variety of isothermal amplification assays. His focuses include diabetes, cardiovascular disease, and cancer screening, diagnostics, and management in low-resource settings; screening and diagnostics related to antenatal care; as well as instrument-free, isothermal approaches to nucleic acid amplification (NAAT) assays.

Bernhard is also an affiliate professor at the University of Washington in the Department of Bioengineering where he has taught the "Diagnostics for Global Health" summer courses for five years and serves on several PhD committees. Bernhard is interested in traditional and paper-based microfluidics as well as any diagnostic platforms that allow simplification and integration of previously complex assays. As chronic diseases, and especially diabetes, are emerging as a major health threat in developing countries, he is now also focusing on their diagnosis, screening, and treatment. He has led projects across the diagnostics value chain, from invention and proof of principle through product introduction and support.

During a typical day, Bernhard devotes most of his time toward reviewing and developing his current projects, writing grants, and holding meetings. Aside from his main projects, Bernhard also consults with colleagues and partners on a variety of projects related to his work and fulfills a teaching position at the University of Washington. Mentoring students, hosting visitors, and meeting with press round out his time. Bernhard also spends a significant amount of time traveling across the United States and abroad. He feels that his work contributes more indirectly to development in low-resource settings. Bernhard is no stranger to novel uses for products or indirect impact of new inventions; it often takes a new mind, even a competitor's, to take a product to its highest level of usefulness. The constant innovation is a thrill for Bernhard and one of the things he loves most about his profession. Although constantly chasing the next grant through different levels of bureaucracy can be a drag at times, the collaboration with brilliant minds across the country and around the world is more than worthwhile.

Career Trajectory

Bernhard discovered early on his passion for diagnostic research and development throughout his experience in academia and industry. He completed a PhD and postdoc in organic chemistry, has authored more than 100 scientific papers, and is an inventor on over eighty US patents and patent applications. For ten years after his postdoc, he served as a founding member, consultant, scientist, business manager, and ultimately director of Micronics, a microfluidics and nanotechnology medical startup. In the early stages, his work was similar to academia, balancing time on the bench with managing grants and intellectual property, working toward new innovative technologies in the field of diagnostics. As a director for Micronics, Bernhard oversaw a variety of projects in all stages of the pipeline as they related to microfluidics (the flow of small volumes of fluids), including projects such as cell separation, protein characterization, rapid blood typing, and nucleic acid analysis. Micronics ultimately grew to be so successful that the company was bought out by Sony, and Bernhard spent a short time with MicroPlumbers MicroSciences, another startup focused on fluid flow. Although Bernhard left MicroPlumbers MicroSciences after only a year, he still retains an ownership stake in the business.

> One idea, hatched in a lab somewhere, is extremely unlikely to change the world. Lots of work, creativity, people, and, yes, money are needed beyond that initial idea, or that initial bit of lab work, before a product can be introduced, and even more so, before something can be scaled to actually have wide impact.

Bernhard left MicroPlumbers MicroSciences for the opportunity to take on a leading role at PATH Diagnostics, an innovator in the field of diagnostics. Much of their work focuses on developing diagnostic tools for the developing world, to better combat HIV/AIDS, malaria, tuberculosis, and other diseases. Bernhard started at PATH as a group leader for the diagnostics team, coordinating a variety of experiments, interpreting data, and ensuring scientific credibility for the development team. He also takes an active role in the conclusion of experiments, reviewing manuscripts for publication and preparing progress reports for donors and collaborators. As group leader, Bernhard also spent significant time developing his own business acumen, networking with international, nongovernmental, and commercial partners for supply, development, manufacture, distribution, and testing of new products. In his role as group leader, Bernhard was also responsible for earning $20 million in grant money for PATH.

Bernhard quickly rose through the ranks at PATH to become the director of the Center to Advance Point-of-Care Diagnostics for Global Heath, a joint effort between PATH and the University of Washington and funded by the NIH. There, he directed efforts to improve the availability, accessibility, and affordability of essential diagnostic tools. Recently, Bernhard took on the role of senior technology officer and portfolio leader for NCD Technologies, a company that specializes in engineering diamond films to improve medical devices. There, he leads development teams in diagnostics and microfluidics for diabetes, breast cancer, proteinuria, preeclampsia, and many other projects. Bernhard uses his connections at PATH to ensure collaboration between NCD and PATH in key areas of chronic disease treatment development for global health.

Throughout his work, Bernhard relishes opportunities to attend conferences and lectures, connecting with other brilliant minds. Twice, he connected with excellent mentors: during his PhD work with Otto Wolfbeis and during is postdoctoral work with Paul Yager, both of whom provided him with great connections moving forward and lifelong collaboration opportunities. Looking toward the future, Bernhard is confident that he will still be working in global health and diagnostic development. He has found success with a variety of ventures and is open to new ones, whether private or academic, moving forward. Anywhere that he can take the time to go on a hike outdoors with his son or explore a new country with friends will feel right at home for Bernhard.

Bernhard Weigl accepted a position in May 2015 as senior platform manager and technical expert of flow based diagnostics at Intellectual Ventures/Global Good, an organization funded and led by Bill Gates, where he continues to lead the development of diagnostics for global health.

♥ Steve DeSandis, 26

Clinton Health Access Initiative
Cold Chain Technology and Innovation Analyst | ~$55,000
BS, Mechanical Engineering, Penn State University (2011)

Job Description

Vaccines are the most cost-effective preventive health interventions in the world. However, vaccines are also incredibly delicate biological cargo. In order to distribute vaccines safely from central stores to remote healthcare facilities, a refrigerated supply chain, known as a "cold chain," must be maintained and expanded to meet the needs of vaccination programs. Lower vaccine costs and increased funding for providing vaccines in remote world regions is driving the development of cold chains across Africa, Asia, and South America. The Clinton Health Access Initiative (CHAI) is working to ensure that the investments made in vaccines will gain returns in a well-immunized, healthy population. This is essential for development because reducing the disease burden in developing countries in the long term leads to dramatic improvement for economic prosperity of both people and their governments. Steve DeSandis's team at CHAI is focused on ensuring the best available cold-chain equipment for vaccines is available at the best prices to developing countries that are carrying out immunization programs for their children.

Within a dynamic team of entrepreneurs, financiers, and engineers, Steve's focus is on building relationships with manufacturers of cold-chain equipment, understanding their product offerings, and investigating emerging innovations that stand to improve the cold chain's reliability, efficiency, and safety. He acts as an advisor to these manufacturers, enabling them to develop, improve, and scale their products based on user and performance feedback from the field. Such feedback is collected through CHAI–sponsored pilot programs in Africa and Asia that evaluate technology on a small scale. In addition to providing product feedback to the manufacturers, the pilot results are used to provide guidance to governments on which equipment to purchase for expanding their cold chain. Some of these emerging technologies include battery-free solar refrigerators, freeze-prevention methods to keep vaccines safe and effective, and vaccine storage containers that can remain cold for weeks to over a month with a single load of ice. All the work done identifying and developing the best technologies is complemented by the other half of Steve's team that focuses on ensuring that this equipment is available at an affordable, sustainable price.

Steve's team includes professionals in diverse world regions, so he works from home and also travels extensively to CHAI focus countries and manufacturer locations. Most recently while working from his home office in Philadelphia, he has been collaborating with global health organizations and manufacturers to address the widespread problem of vaccine freezing in the cold chain. In order to reduce the vaccine efficacy loss caused by freezing, Steve has been researching different vaccine refrigeration methods, identifying design enhancements, verifying hypotheses through field and lab testing, and recommending ways for standardizing safer products. Steve's fieldwork includes traveling to meet with manufacturers to discuss field-testing updates, product-development ideas, and new equipment standards. This face-to-face time is critical for building relationships, checking out the product through inspection, walking down assembly lines, and directly collaborating to identify ways to enhance product offerings. Armed with this direct product knowledge from the manufacturers, Steve visits CHAI country teams across sub-Saharan Africa to discuss and evaluate products in the field. In these countries, his fieldwork includes demonstrating a prototype designed to protect vaccines from extreme temperatures during transport, inspecting ongoing field pilots, conducting solar refrigerator installations, and training local technicians to perform additional installations.

Steve loves the adventures that frequently emerge in his work. One such adventure occurred while working with CHAI colleagues in Tanzania to coordinate a pilot with new solar refrigerator technology. The equipment had already arrived in-country, but his team had not yet identified adequate training resources to educate the equipment installers. With deadlines looming, Steve got approval to lead a CHAI team to go out and train the installers. A few weeks later, having no experience with the technology other than speaking with the manufacturers, studying manuals, and possessing strong technical confidence, he found himself in the remote regions of southwestern Tanzania. He led classroom instruction on the basics of electricity, solar power, and refrigeration and successfully installed two different solar refrigerators in a step-by-step educational format. Steve was deeply satisfied with his work because he knew that his ability to think quickly, technically, and critically enabled him to empower local technicians to improve their own country's cold chain and in turn increase access to lifesaving vaccines.

Steve's current work can make striking a perfect work-life balance difficult. Gone for three weeks, home for two weeks, gone for two weeks, home for four weeks becomes exhausting. Fortunately, many of his colleagues have become his dear friends, so when traveling for weeks on end, they do their best to make time for local adventures, morning runs, or socializing after a long day of meetings. No matter the exotic destination, he always looks forward to returning home to Philadelphia where it is nice to spend time catching up and sharing his latest travel photos with friends and family.

Career Trajectory

Throughout college, Steve pursued opportunities in and out of line with the typical path of an aspiring mechanical engineer: traditional internships at ExxonMobil and Air Products and Chemicals and the unconventional pursuit of a minor in engineering leadership development at Penn State. Through this minor, Steve led a team that invented, developed, and built a baobab fruit processing machine for an agricultural cooperative in northwestern Benin. Less than twenty-four hours after receiving his diploma, Steve was boarding a flight for Benin to deliver and demonstrate the technology to their client. This innovative processing machine would enable the cooperative's workers to greatly improve their productivity, profitability, and ultimately their lives. This exhilarating engineering experience opened Steve's eyes to a world where problems abound and opportunities to make a difference lie in finding the right solutions.

After graduation, Steve followed the only path he knew and started a position with Siemens in a two-year, rotational leadership-development program. This program

> Network, stay curious, do not always accept the path most traveled, and most importantly, know WHY you want to do something in life. Knowing why to do something is critical in ensuring you are focused on the big goals in life. Often people get lost in the how: How will I ever realize my dream of creating social benefit for people in faraway places? How will I afford my school loans if I take a job with a nonprofit rather than a well-established company? If you know WHY to do things such as this, the 'how' will come through keeping a diligent work ethic, finding new ways to grow personal knowledge, leveraging relationships, and enjoying the process. Knowing WHY to do something will also prepare you to deal with the doubters or naysayers you are likely to confront on your path along a nontraditional career. When you find something you are truly passionate about, you need to rely on your own personal drive and not finding confirmation in others.

provided him the opportunity to rotate among various businesses within the massive engineering conglomerate and try his hand in a variety of roles, including strategic marketing, product development, technical support, and sales. The experience gave him a broad view of how large corporations operate and the drivers behind the business of engineering. Managing projects and networking with different business leaders were critical elements in his maturation from an eager engineering graduate into a young professional ready to take on growing levels of responsibility and leadership. After two years in the Siemens leadership program, he was tasked with finding a full-time position within a huge organization undergoing restructuring and strategic realignment. While his managers and peers were impressed by his work ethic and accomplishments, he struggled to find an opportunity that could match the excitement and interest he had found in his undergraduate work with the baobab processing machine.

After working with Siemens for another nine months, a good friend and engineer from Penn State sent Steve an email to gauge his interest in a position with his team at CHAI. Steve immediately saw this as an opportunity to return to the social impact work that he had previously found so satisfying. He graciously accepted the offer to apply for the position and, following a few rounds of interviews, was offered the position as cold-chain technology and innovation analyst at CHAI. Steve was absolutely thrilled to have the opportunity to join a team focused on technology for the developing world. However, the reality of leaving his job at Siemens as a young, high-potential employee was difficult. He felt strong loyalty toward the people who had helped him develop within Siemens throughout his early career. Through conversations with mentors, family, and friends, he realized that these tough career-altering decisions are difficult yet essential in the pursuit of personally and socially rewarding work. He ultimately decided to leave Siemens (and a nice paycheck) to follow what he felt could be a real opportunity to return to his passions for technology and development.

As a young, versatile technical person, Steve is prepared to recognize and seize opportunities as they arise. Looking forward to the next steps in his career, he is interested in pursuing roles where he can continue to act as a technology consultant or work directly on products and technologies that have the potential to positively affect people's lives. In order to continue growing the skills necessary to do this, he is weighing different opportunities, including higher-level education and/or a return to the private sector.

NONPROFIT » INTERNATIONAL NGO

Steve Dennis, 40

Corporate Social Responsibility Training Institute
East Africa Coordinator | Salary varies month to month
Formerly with Médecins Sans Frontières (MSF) International

MA, International Relations, University of Toronto (2010)
BASc, Civil Engineering, University of Toronto (1999)

Job Description

War, persecution, natural disasters, and poverty force millions of people from their homes every year. There are currently over 50 million internally displaced people (IDPs) and refugees worldwide. People from countries big and small, of all ages and many nationalities leave their homes for safety in other countries. Many organizations, including governments, the United Nations, the Red Cross, and intergovernmental and nonprofit charities build and run large camps to house and care for refugees.

What does it take to run a refugee camp? Refugees need shelter, food, clean water, sanitation, and health care. This means huge challenges in building shelters, providing sanitation, preventing illness, and getting fresh supplies to thousands of people. Médecins Sans Frontières (MSF), commonly known as Doctors Without Borders in the US, works in over seventy countries to provide this sort of aid to refugees and other vulnerable people. It is a neutral aid organization that works to support humanitarian rights and to offer second chances to millions of at-risk people. MSF hires many professionals, from doctors and nurses to public health specialists and engineers.

Steve has held a number of different roles within MSF in many diverse regions throughout Africa and beyond. Over his nine years with the organization, Steve started in Sri Lanka as a logistician and administrator, worked in South Sudan as a supply and technical logistician, as a project coordinator in the Ivory Coast, as an emergency team project coordinator in Sri Lanka, as a water and sanitation officer in Eastern Chad, as an emergency team project coordinator in Somalia, and as a logistics coordinator in Sri Lanka. He has worked on nutrition programs, sanitation systems, latrine building projects, supply efforts in insecure places, education of community leaders, new employee training, and much more. Steve believes that the role of an engineer is to be able to adapt and translate solutions into a global context: it is not enough to have technical solutions; someone has to adapt them to different situations abroad.

One particularly challenging project for Steve was when he was brought in to run a latrine program for internally displaced persons (IDPs) in Eastern Chad. They set up a clinic to help many of them with health issues and found there were many people sick with diarrheal diseases related to bad sanitation. Steve could not get steel into the area to make latrines because of insecure roads, so he pushed forward with what he could get—concrete—and directed MSF staff in making concrete dome slabs. This project required a good understanding of concrete and of the local situation. It took a very creative, experienced, and globally conscious engineer to pull it off! Beyond these technical issues, though, he also had to work on "softer" problems. Communities will not use toilets they do not trust! So he trained volunteers how to talk to community leaders, manage concerns, and hire local workers. He also had to clarify MSF's relationship within the community: MSF staff offered tools and training, but the community dug its own latrine holes. Steve had to make sure to include community leaders in the decision processes. The first latrine also had to be great so that people would have confidence in the project.

Another example of Steve's work was in 2009 in Sri Lanka. When the national army achieved its military victory over the rebel troops, approximately 200,000 people fled the area. He led the emergency logistic coordination of MSF's projects to start a feeding program (feeding 22,000 people per day) as well as supply and logistic support for two operating theaters servicing the hundreds of war wounded coming out of the frontline area. Steve's biggest takeaway from working for MSF is that it is worth it to slow down a little bit, listen, and observe what is going on around you. He learned through experience that he is more successful if he starts by asking questions and listening and then acting decisively with everybody's voice in mind. He loved his work with MSF but ended up leaving them for opportunities with other organizations doing similar work.

Career Trajectory

After graduating from the University of Toronto in 1999 as a civil engineer, Steve took an engineering position in Canada for two and a half years, working as a technical engineer, often being a liaison between clients and contractors and acting as cochair of the Joint Health and Safety Committee. Soon after, he made the drastic jump to working in Sri Lanka for MSF. After first being rejected, Steve asserted his motivation to work with MSF and rounded out his application with some overseas experience, therefore passing the application process the second time around. He was quickly sent to Sri Lanka, beginning his nine-year career with the world-renowned aid organization.

> When you go overseas, try not to get overwhelmed. Slow down and listen to what people are saying; get a broader perspective before taking action. Just like with firefighters, if you run, you can trip and slow down the operation. It is very important to do it right the first time.

During his first six or seven years on the job, Steve worked in South Sudan, the Ivory Coast (Côte d'Ivoire), Chad, Kenya, Somalia, and Sri Lanka. These experiences opened his eyes to diverse new worlds that he had yet to study and felt a bit unqualified to understand. Steve decided to pursue a master's degree in international relations to address this gap, which turned out to be surprisingly challenging for someone with an engineering background. He finished in 2010 and returned to fieldwork with MSF, again in South Sudan. About a year later, he took a position with the Norwegian Refugee Council, a good opportunity for him to gain new experiences and observe how other organizations operate.

In a challenging position as program manager in Eastern Kenya, Steve found himself tested in more ways than anyone expected or hoped. In June of 2012, Steve and three of his colleagues were abducted from the Dadaab refugee camps. Being shot and kidnapped forced clarity for him: some risks are not acceptable while others are worth taking, especially when you could be part of the efforts to save half a million people from probable death. He reflects now that what he likes most about his job is assisting people in their time of need, a dire time where you can give them a second chance. At times when Steve himself was vulnerable, people gave him a second chance by stepping up. On the other hand, the danger is a negative of this work, especially if you are not trained properly. Steve urges that safety and security training is essential!

In an attempt to balance personal life and work, Steve took breaks between foreign assignments, giving him time to spend with the people who provide him sanctuary: his friends and family. While on assignment, there are always too many high-priority jobs to do. You can be constantly working to push through emergencies, but doing it for too long will drain you and leave you burnt out. It is common among aid workers to feel that they have a responsibility to people they see in extreme suffering, and they do not take the rest they need. In 2013, Steve transitioned out of aid work and into consulting. He now works in East Africa for an organization called the Corporate Social Responsibility Training Institute. He trains and consults for organizations on how to engage everyone involved in projects, from locals to outside funders. He also facilitates lessons on safety, security, and operations for another organization.

Leslie Light, 43

International Development Enterprises (iDE)
Project Manager for Product Development | ~$500/day

MBA, Entrepreneurship, University of Pennsylvania (2000)
BS, Product Design Engineering, Stanford University (1993)

Job Description

It is rare that people start their career with their dream occupation; it often takes years of professional work for some to realize what their dream job is. That was certainly the case for Leslie Light who held eight jobs before realizing that she needed to make a big change to be happy. Without any sense of furthering a larger purpose in these eight jobs, she took a break from working to identify certain attributes her next position must have. She wanted a job where she had creative freedom, a supportive team, chances to travel, the ability to personally see and assess her social impact, and frequent use of her engineering skills. With this criteria in mind, she was able to recognize a perfect fit when she heard an acquaintance describe the company for which she is currently working, iDE (International Development Enterprises).

iDE's mission is to increase the income and livelihood opportunities for poor rural households. Many rural households in developing countries suffer from subsistence poverty, earning less money than is required to support physical health. Leslie and her coworkers design appropriate technologies to sell to farmers that will enable high-value crop yields during the dry season. The technologies they design will enable these impoverished farmers to feed their families year-round and earn the necessary additional income to permanently escape subsistence poverty.

iDE's Product Development Initiative, overseen by Leslie, was developed to identify and vet the best low-cost agricultural products available for the base-of-the-pyramid market that iDE serves. The initiative is making a more sophisticated decision-making model to determine which customers have what needs and which products are most applicable to these needs. In order to ensure that iDE's Product Development Initiative is providing a plethora of products desired by smallholder farmers at a price point they can afford, Leslie's job includes frequent trips to developing countries in Asia, Africa, and Latin America. There, she interviews and observes customers and establishes productive connections between iDE's in-country field staff and the Denver-based workshop efforts.

Leslie's main responsibility as a project manager in product development is to make sure her team is delivering on what they have promised to their various funders. This could involve determining when they need to adjust the course of their longer, multiyear projects. She is in contact with a large, committed network worldwide in order to assess her company's progress. Therefore, she is frequently emailing and video calling with coworkers in Asia, Africa, Europe, and Central America. Additionally, Leslie conducts budgetary oversight and decides how to reallocate funds if the situation calls for it. She pitches the vision of iDE directly to a myriad of foundations through grant writing. Leslie and her team work together, brainstorming ideas and crafting concise, compelling proposals. She also spends time in their workshop, which is separate from their office space. There, she and her team set up and execute product tests on inventions developed for base-of-pyramid farmers. She read and writes many summary reports of interesting field tests for new products, and also determines quality-control procedures for launched products being employed in the field.

Leslie enjoys working at a job where she can leverage her education, skills, and experiences to significantly improve others' lives. She can tangibly see and experience the fruits of her labor when she travels to the field and speaks with iDE's customers about their preferences, experiences, and hopes. She also loves that her company attracts genuinely fantastic people, and not just in a superficial sense. Some of her coworkers have lived in really rough conditions in the field and are committed to being part of the solution for developing regions. She finds it constantly uplifting and inspiring working with professionals who have persistence, creativity, and compassion.

As a market-based humanitarian organization, iDE often has to wait for customers' responses to make product iterations, at times causing work to be slow. Factors such as product performance, appearance, usability, accompanying services, and price all must line up in order for the more exciting, constructive steps to be taken. Also, iDE generally works with local manufacturers and other entities to make their solutions work for the long term. Given the stakes and importance their projects have, this can be disheartening at times. She also often experiences disconnect between the level of financial need and the willingness of her financial backers to provide sufficient support. This is a challenge, but her team works hard to continually close the all-too-common gap.

Career Trajectory

After graduating from Stanford, Leslie felt driven toward working on appropriate technology solutions. However, the international development organizations she contacted never got back to her, so she instead took a six-month opportunity in Pune, India, to redesign steam engine components. The job was not the most rewarding, but India was eye-opening, and working there was an amazing experience for her—so she found a fun engineering job and moved in with an Indian family. Her role was to develop unique designs for thermal flasks and insulated lunch boxes for a traditional Indian consumer-products company. This job was a hinge-pin in her career. The products were not overly complex, and she had plenty of latitude on making new forms, shapes, and concepts. At the same time, she had to learn to design for people different from herself. Leslie learned to have fun with it; she explored traditional Indian art forms and began to incorporate these into her designs. She was the only foreigner working in the plant and the only female engineer anyone there had ever worked with. She learned to sink in neck-deep with her colleagues and not be so concerned with their ideas of her limitations, but rather just focus on their common goals. After her time in India, Leslie worked in Silicon Valley in the product design field as a project manager and account liaison. She then decided she wanted to expand her horizons by attending business school.

> Hone your listening skills and powers of observation. Learn how to shed your assumptions and conceptual blocks. It is impossible to effectively help other people if you cannot clearly and fully understand the problems and issues at hand. Instead of adopting a judgmental mind frame, become open-minded, curious, and ask good questions.

For a year in business school, Leslie worked part-time at the Wharton Small Business Development Center where she helped local small businesses be more profitable and successful. She spent a summer in South Africa teaching a course to University of Cape Town students on "consulting to businesses of the informal sector," as well as advising two such small businesses. Leslie was recruited out of business school by a globally expanding company with a large population of nearly retired employees. She served in a variety of roles (project manager, parts pricing, business development) for nine years without much overseas action. Without any sense of furthering a larger purpose while also not seeing much of her husband and two young children, she decided it was time for something different. She did not have much time to look for a job while working, so she quit, determined to take her time finding the right kind of job in the right location.

Fortunately, her husband landed his perfect job in Golden, Colorado, transitioning out of being a house-husband and allowing her to be a house-wife for a while. During her sabbatical, she serendipitously ran into a long-time employee of iDE and recognized from her description that iDE fit most of her criteria for her next job. They agreed to stay in touch, and soon enough Leslie signed on as a contractor, pulling together their product catalog. It was the perfect arrangement for her at the time: she was able to continue her sabbatical while learning about iDE and better refining her ideas regarding her next career steps. She loved iDE, was soon asked to do more projects, and converted to a part-time employee a year after beginning her first project. Leslie credits her strong project management skills, ability to articulate her strengths, and knowing what she wanted in a job for finding this position.

If she could do something differently, Leslie says she would be more patient and less judgmental of herself. At some of her former companies, she often felt extremely stressed and out of place. However, in retrospect, the skills and experiences gained during difficult times have been very useful to her professional development. By the time she found her ideal job, those hard-won experiences enabled her to take on more responsibility and get more done. She would not change anything about her specific educational and professional path. Instead, she would have just been less concerned about where each place was taking her and enjoyed the present experience and her coworkers more. She is proud of the humor and fun she has brought to her workplaces and wishes she had done this a lot more over the years.

Photo by TWP

Sebastian Africano, 38

Trees, Water & People
International Director | ~$55,000

BS, International Business and Marketing, Penn State University (1999)

Job Description

Nearly half the world's population burns solid fuels (wood, charcoal, crop residues, and coal) in traditional cookstoves or open fires to cook their food and to stay warm. Unfortunately, this is a major contributor to indoor air pollution in developing countries, causing millions of people annually to get injured, fall ill, and prematurely die. Women are disproportionately impacted by the health burdens (emphysema, cataracts, cancer, heart disease) from traditional cookstoves because they breathe in harmful smoke while cooking. Further, indoor air pollution is the leading cause of death worldwide among children under five.

A wide range of organizations, from small foundations to the Environmental Protection Agency (EPA), are investing in creating better cookstoves not only to improve individual lives but also to reduce global pollution from dirty, inefficient fuel and carbon emissions. There are also many international nonprofits working in developing countries to disseminate clean cookstoves. This process of behavioral change is particularly difficult because people are used to cooking in certain ways, and it takes convincing for them to understand why they should use new cookstoves. Trees, Water & People (TWP) is a nonprofit that works collaboratively with large international nonprofits and serves as an implementer of improved cookstove programs. TWP's clean cookstoves include a chimney that vents smoke out of the home. Emissions testing conducted on their stoves indicates that the chimney, which removes the toxic smoke from the kitchen, reduces exposure to carbon monoxide and particulate matter by more than 80%. TWP is essentially a conduit between the clean cookstove donor community and the implementation community in Central America. TWP seeks funding and directs it to local nonprofit partners who implement the projects.

TWP is a seventeen-year-old organization founded by foresters, one of whom was in the Peace Corps and had worked in Central America, Guatemala, and Honduras. The founders wanted to form an organization to increase the supply and diversity of trees, to reduce disaster risk brought about by deforestation, and to regulate carbon emissions through forestry. They determined that one big driver of deforestation in the developing world was the harvesting of wood for cooking. Therefore, part of their repertoire became the design and construction of clean cookstoves to reduce the quantity of wood needed to cook everyday meals. Along the way, they hit upon the fact that clean cookstoves reduce indoor air pollution and thus reduced health risks for families. Cookstoves became the principal pillar of the organization, and TWP became a pioneer in that movement. They now operate in Guatemala, El Salvador, Honduras, Nicaragua, and Haiti, with strategic partnerships in Peru and Panama. Recently, TWP added solar lighting to their project portfolio.

TWP is donor funded, financed by private foundations, individual donors, grants from the government, and corporate sponsorships. In the past, TWP used a community-centered, village-based approach, but now they are dabbling in larger endeavors that have better ability to scale. This sometimes causes them to sacrifice quality and frequency of interaction as they grow because they do not have the capacity to provide the same quality to large numbers of beneficiaries, but in the end, they are helping more beneficiaries. As education and general awareness levels improve, lateral knowledge sharing becomes more pronounced, and that over time makes up for the lower level of interaction from TWP.

Sebastian Africano, international director for TWP, has traveled extensively over the past decade to oversee, evaluate, and monitor the impact of projects and report back to donors. That entails working with partners, visiting project sites and homes, validating and verifying the work, and feeding that information back to headquarters. He also does administrative work, which entails engaging with donors and funding organizations, trying to find out their interests and what they want to fund, and then talking with his international partners to see if they have a project in the pipeline that fits the donor's interests or if they can start a new one. He is no stranger to the field and knows the circumstances under which TWP's beneficiaries' live, which helps in designing coherent, culturally appropriate, and impactful programs.

TWP also acts as a marketing and communications company that serves as a conduit of information between donors, implementers, and beneficiaries. Therefore, a big part of Sebastian's role at TWP is keeping all stakeholders informed at the corporate, foundation, government, and individual levels. He tailors projects to meet the donor's goals, organizes players in their place, and puts resources where they need to be at the right time so that things happen and he can track them. On a day-to-day basis, Sebastian is a desk jockey, seeking new funding opportunities, reporting to existing funders, Skype calling with implementing partners or potential partners, and fleshing out new and old projects.

Get involved with a diverse set of people and activities and travel as much as possible early on to understand realities different from yours. There is so much you can learn by getting out in the world early and exposing yourself to unique experiences. Put yourself in uncomfortable situations outside your day-to-day life, or take a year after high school to do something nontraditional. Whatever it is, it will completely influence your worldview, your connections, and future opportunities.

If it is not for you, why waste time with it? Rather than have a list of what you want to do, make a list of what you do not want to do and cross stuff off from that.

Sebastian's favorite and least favorite part are the same—travel! He travels a significant amount but has slowly cut back from six months per year to two; Skype and improvements in mobile phone service abroad have helped. When he started with TWP as an intern in 2005, one of his principal goals was to travel for a living, but after being on the road for ten years and starting a family in the process, he feels it is time to develop new talent for this important role. While he has not lost his gusto for serving populations in high-risk areas, such as refugee camps or countries in civil conflict, his priorities have definitely been reshuffled by the addition of two young kids, and he feels it is an appropriate time to make a shift.

Career Trajectory

Sebastian graduated from Penn State in 1999 with his bachelor's degree in international business and marketing and moved to the Bay area less than two weeks after graduation. He took classes at San Francisco State University while volunteering and working for several nonprofits engaged in urban sustainability, education, and job training. He loved it so much that he decided he wanted to use his formal education and skills to work for a nonprofit with a mission to help the environment and society. He found a group in Oregon working on appropriate technology for the developing world and landed an internship with them. He learned all about business-to-business approaches to implementing those technologies in the developing world. He could not have articulated this as an undergrad, but this internship experience brought it all together and blew open doors for him—he was offered work with TWP as a marketing intern in Honduras. He stopped his studies and moved to Central America. After developing his own rural development consulting practice in Central America in 2006, he went on to provide support to organizations working on cookstove projects in fourteen countries, helping them with rural implementation, monitoring and evaluation, impact measurement, carbon finance, and carbon offsetting work. In 2009, he came back to TWP as deputy international director at the home office in Colorado.

Sebastian's personal life currently revolves around his wife and kids. He and his wife met while working on similar projects in Honduras, so their lives are inextricably linked to Latin America. His three-year-old son has already traveled to El Salvador and Chile, and he had the opportunity to eat different foods, speak different languages, and experience different realities—an important part of fomenting creativity and versatility. If he could start over again, Sebastian would pursue an engineering education. Having designed, tested, and implemented cookstoves for ten years, he has always felt like an engineer but with a rudimentary tool kit. Sebastian is in the process of starting a professional MBA to improve the hard skills in his tool kit. In five to ten years, he hopes to be supporting the social sector but traveling less. At some point, he wants to take his new skills from his MBA and move his family to Latin America so that he does not have to leave home to work there.

⚙ Timothy Carter, 28

Samaritan's Purse – International Relief
Deputy Country Director, South Sudan

MS, Civil and Environmental Engineering, Wayne State University (2011)
BSE, Mechanical Engineering, Hope College (2009)

Job Description

In a field where financial rewards are few, stress is high, job security may be low, and work is frequently difficult, strong motivators are needed to pursue a career in helping others. Tim Carter's motivation stems from his religion. He currently works for Samaritan's Purse (SP), an evangelical Christian humanitarian organization that provides aid to people in physical need as a key part of Christian missionary work. Since 1970, they have helped meet the needs of people who are victims of war, poverty, natural disasters, disease, and famine with the purpose of sharing their God's love. SP now works in more than 100 countries around the world and specializes in emergency relief, shelter, water and sanitation, food and nutrition, medical care and public health, HIV/AIDS, and community-based livestock and livelihood projects. Tim works to improve water, sanitation, and hygiene (WASH) in sub-Saharan Africa.

Tim splits his time between office work and fieldwork. His office work includes analyzing water quality and water-pump testing reports, performing engineering calculations for projects, developing proposals for new projects based on needs assessments and the latest social and technological innovations, and providing leadership and vision. Trips to the field are typically to provide supervision in order to ensure the projects are completed according to acceptable international technical standards. At times, Tim also participates in fieldwork when the project requires a high level of technical skill. For example, in order to ensure effectiveness and efficiency, Tim was personally involved in installing a solar-powered well that is now pumping water over one kilometer to a water storage tank at the center of the community. Tim has also overseen the installation of four additional solar-powered wells in the Yida Refugee Camp of South Sudan.

Tim employs the latest technologies in water resources in order to yield a lasting source of water for drought-affected communities. For example, when he rehabilitated a well with a hand pump for one community, he also modified the pump to pipe water to both a tap stand for human consumption and an animal trough for the livestock. The new arrangement is supporting their primary livelihood (pastoralist) and also providing a source of income to conduct maintenance (community members are charged for each goat that drinks the water). Another innovation includes equipping boreholes (narrow holes dug/drilled deep into the ground) with solar-powered pumps that can pump water closer to the communities without burning fuel. Every water project is done in conjunction with sanitation and hygiene. SP assists community members with the technical expertise to construct a latrine slab while the household provides materials and constructs the rest of the latrine. They also train community health workers on health and hygiene and conduct regular health and hygiene campaigns to raise awareness. All their projects are done with strong community support in order to promote sustainability. The communities must take ownership and contribute materials and labor for every project.

In order to assess the impact of project activities, Tim conducts both baseline and end-of-project surveys in the communities where programs are being implemented. The surveys reveal whether or not the projects had a positive effect in promoting behavioral change and improving health and quality of life in the communities. Tim personally justifies the impact of his role by the joy on the faces of community members. The hope and excitement expressed by the community reveals the impact and significance of the project and the work he is doing. Community leaders and members are constantly coming to his office to thank him.

Tim loves being able to wake up every morning and go to a job where he has the opportunity to serve other people and his God. Being able to bring water to a community that used to trek thirty-five kilometers roundtrip to fetch water during times of drought makes all the challenges he faced worthwhile. The most difficult part of his job is that he is constantly surrounded by immeasurable needs. With so much suffering, it is easy to get discouraged. However, Tim takes comfort in knowing that SP is doing everything they can to help as many people as possible. Tim has worked in a very remote region in Kenya and now serves in a remote region of South Sudan, so the isolation can contribute to the added stress of having only the basic necessities.

Career Trajectory

Tim's career path in relief and development began when he was pursuing a bachelor's degree in mechanical engineering at Hope College in Michigan. For the first three years of college, he had no idea what he was going to do with his life. He struggled immensely with the thought of getting an engineering job and making a lot of money. He felt his God was calling him to follow a different path. During his junior year in college, he finally discovered a career path that would allow him to leverage his education to positively change the world—he joined his college's chapter of Engineers Without Borders (EWB). Tim jumped on board by designing a diversion dam for the village of Nkuv, Cameroon, and at the end of his junior year, he traveled to the community. Tim was heavily involved in the construction of the diversion dam, which would serve as a water intake for a distribution system to bring water from the mountains to the community. He loved every single minute of his adventure and connected with the people of Cameroon.

> Engage in as many opportunities as possible while in school: Engineers Without Borders, Habitat for Humanity, mentoring local primary or high school students, volunteering at local soup kitchens, getting involved in spring break mission trips, etc. This experience will be critical when you graduate and start looking for a job. This kind of work, particularly in relief and development, is a highly competitive field, so any advantage coming in is extremely beneficial.

Over the next few months after returning from Cameroon, the words of a friend kept coming back to Tim: "Are engineering missions what you want to do with your life?" He had never even considered it before, but over the next several months he slowly began to realize that his God was calling him to follow this path. During Christmas vacation of his senior year, he began researching opportunities, such as the Peace Corps, to continue assisting developing communities around the world with WASH. At that time, he received an email from SP highlighting their work helping communities both spiritually and physically with their WASH needs, so he decided to apply for their internship program. By the grace of his God, he was one of ten interns selected out of hundreds.

Upon graduating, he first returned to Cameroon as a trip leader and project manager with EWB to construct the water distribution system that he had designed. Tim then began his internship in Kenya where he assisted with a biosand water-filter project, conducted water-source assessments, and did research and development on a method of desalination for remote, rural communities. During the internship, he realized that there was a lot he did not know about water resources, so he returned to Detroit to study civil and environmental engineering with a focus in water resources at Wayne State University. He also completed a graduate certificate in sustainable engineering. After the devastating earthquake struck Haiti in January 2010, he flew down as a representative of SP and designed and constructed latrines for a temporary shelter site that the organization had established for earthquake victims. He completed his master's degree and was then called by SP again to return to Kenya as a water engineer during the severe East African drought of 2011. Tim and coworkers installed water storage tanks in communities for the water-trucking program, including rainwater harvesting systems for when the drought ended.

Following the drought, Tim was asked to stay on with SP as the senior program manager as well as the WASH program manager. He built a team that worked to provide long-term, sustainable solutions for the affected communities, which would improve their resilience to future droughts. They constructed large rainwater catchment systems, rehabilitated wells, trained community water committees on how to manage their water sources, provided health and hygiene training, and distributed soap and jerry cans. Tim is now working in South Sudan where he has served in various management and technical roles, most recently as the deputy country director. In his role as deputy county director, Tim is managing the work of more than 500 field staff implementing programs in WASH, food security, nutrition, health, and Bible literacy; overseeing logistics and human resources; providing guidance for program development; and building relationships with the donor community.

Tim does not see his work as a job, but rather as a part of who he is. He believes that living a life in service to others is something that can be done regardless of one's career. Although he knows his God will lead him in the right direction, Tim is likely to stay involved in nonprofit work that is helping others in the future, likely in relief and development. Whether he ends up in a management role or a technical role, his technical background will be critical in his career because he has a passion for water, which requires a high level of technical expertise.

Photo by Larry Padget

Alison Padget, 39

World Hope International
Vice President of Programs | ~$100,000 – $145,000

PhD, Nutritional Sciences, The University of Texas at Austin
MBA, University of Massachusetts-Amherst
BS, Biology, Southwestern University

Job Description

In the ecosystem of organizations focused on social impact are small nonprofits to large consulting companies, all of them competing for funding from large donors. Organizations compete for grants from multilateral and bilateral agencies, private foundations, and individual donors. Earning grants is a competitive process, and donors are often looking for very specific projects. Grant writers serve as the conduit between grant applicants and the grant providers; their role is to put into writing the applicant's concepts and convey them in a way that the funding institution will support. Beyond strong writing skills, grant writers need to have a strong understanding of (1) the problems on the ground, ideally with experience operating projects and knowing what is doable; (2) current best practices on interventions; and (3) what donors are looking for and how to innovatively capture their desires in a grant proposal. Crafting a grant proposal is a specialized, time-consuming process, so grant proposal writers need to be selective when aiming for grants. Alison Padget, an expert at writing grant proposals, works for World Hope International (WHI), a faith-based organization.

As vice president of programs, Alison designs programs, develops grant proposals, and provides technical oversight to nutrition programs. The program design process starts one of two ways for Alison. Either WHI field staff in a developing country identify an opportunity or problem they would like to solve and ask for Alison's help to design a project and find funding, or the problem is identified by the donor and published in a request for proposals. If the donor-identified problem is a good match for the kind of work World Hope is doing, she will write the grant proposal. The proposal process covers all aspects of designing the program: identifying the problem, understanding the context, defining the goals, proposing an approach, bringing together the right partners and sometimes the right technology, determining the requirements for staffing and budget, and creating a work plan as well as a plan for evaluating the project's success. Alison's work does not end with writing the proposal; she is also responsible for overseeing the funded programs.

In a typical day, Alison works on more than one grant proposal at a time. She might be doing a literature review on one subject, like how to economically empower women through agricultural technology, while creating a budget for a different project, like one to bring solar-powered Internet access to remote locations. Alison is constantly looking for the right people and institutional partners to collaborate on projects and is always scanning to see what donors are interested in funding. Sometimes Alison will travel to a proposed project location to get a better sense of what is possible and to make the necessary personal connections. When she cannot be there in person, she relies heavily on Skype, conference calls, and email. In addition to writing grant proposals herself, she oversees two other grant writers.

The social innovation in Alison's career comes from using STEM skills to find creative solutions to really difficult problems in developing countries. For example, imagine a smallholder farmer in sub-Saharan Africa. The farmer has access to mangos that grow wild, but most of them end up rotting on the ground. Meanwhile, his country imports mango juice at great cost from other countries, and he can barely feed his family. The obvious solution would be for the farmer and his neighbors to go into the mango-juice business. However, without access to credit, information on how to harvest and transport mangos, transportation, good roads, electricity, and clean water, the mango-juice business is unlikely to succeed. Alison's job is to help World Hope look at situations like the farmer's, analyze where the obstacles are, and connect with the right people and technology to remove the obstacles.

Sometimes, assessing impact is easy. For example, Alison helped develop a mobile app that gives the public the ability to report suspected human trafficking directly to the authorities in Albania. Alison knows for a fact that her app helped to identify and remove children from the street that had been forced into begging. To her, that impact made the whole project worth it. However, development projects do not always work. Alison tries to avoid failure by carefully choosing the organizations she works with. Organizational culture makes a difference; delays and cost overruns should not be business as usual.

Alison loves the intellectual challenge of learning everything she can about different countries and different sectors and thinking creatively about how to use technology to solve problems. She also loves her interactions with staff in the field and all the people they bring together to imple-

 Do not expect quick wins in this business. Keep working on something long after others give up.

Above all, be kind. A mentor of mine once said, "I know a lot of smart people, but I do not know that many of them that I want to work with." Be the person other people want to work with.

ment a project. She meets many interesting people and travels to places far off the tourist track. On the other hand, the worst part of her job is the paperwork. Every donor has their preferred way to construct grant proposals and budgets. Alison spends a significant amount of time rewriting and reformatting the same information. Working across time zones and with field staff who have limited connectivity is also a challenge, particularly when they are working under a deadline.

Career Trajectory

While Alison does not explicitly use her undergraduate major and minor in biology and chemistry, she consistently uses the critical-thinking and writing skills that she learned through her degree. When Alison was working on her doctorate in nutrition, she discovered that she enjoyed the social science aspect of the field more than the natural sciences—she could not envision spending the rest of her life in a lab. After graduation, she did not want to relocate and landed a job in program evaluation for Mothers Against Drunk Driving (MADD); it combined her love for statistics with a social impact project. She later relocated to China where she worked with a nonprofit that provided rural orphans with nutrition and medical care. Her position in China was her first exposure to severe poverty and her first opportunity to manage a project in a developing country. She realized quickly that she needed to broaden her skills beyond nutrition in order to be successful in international development, so she started studying remotely for an MBA.

After China, Alison moved to Russia and worked for the United States Agency for International Development (USAID). Moving to Russia for the position was a key move because it gave her insight into the inner workings of a major international development donor. The experience and contacts she gained in Russia landed Alison her next job, managing a project in Russia for an information and communications technology (ICT)-focused USAID grantee in Washington, DC. Alison did not have an ICT background at all, so she faced her steepest learning curve with some of her work that was quite technical. She did a lot of studying on her own and asked a lot of questions.

Alison's key to success has been her flexibility and willingness to build skills outside her academic area. She does not approach projects through the lens of a single discipline. She understands the business side, the donor side, how to build monitoring and evaluation into project design, and also what it takes to implement a project in a difficult environment. She actively seeks the expertise of others to fill any gaps in her knowledge. She was an operations and finance manager for a nonprofit for a while. She not only learned that this was not something she wanted to do for a living (a valuable lesson), but she also learned some new skills, such as how to hire people and negotiate contracts. She has also benefited from collaborating with university students and professors on projects. It has been great for her to learn from people with a very deep knowledge base in a particular subject.

Alison's husband is in the foreign service, so they move internationally every two to three years. Moving so often has forced her to be creative and look for ways to build her career and skills in a more circuitous route. It has also opened up a world of interesting connections for her. She makes a point of attending events and hosting people because she truly enjoys meeting people, but also because a large network is very valuable. To integrate her work with her personal life, she takes full advantage of technology to telecommute. She lives in London, works for a Washington, DC–based organization, and develops projects all over the world. She makes her own hours for the most part, and although she works more Friday nights and holidays than she would like, it has been well worth it for her to work for flexible organizations. At some point, Alison would like to transition away from international work, put down some roots, and focus on the community where she lives, perhaps running a local nonprofit.

♥ Mary (Thomas) Nicholas

Kaiser Permanente's Center for Health Research
Director of Genomic Resources

PhD, Biochemistry, University of Illinois at Urbana-Champaign
BS, Biochemistry, Benedictine University

Job Description

Mary is currently the director for genomic resources at the Center for Health Research at Kaiser Permanente, a nonprofit integrated health organization that is focused on the health and well-being of its members and communities; Kaiser Permanente (KP) provides health-care services to more than 9.3 million people across the US through its progressive products, services, and advancements. KP also does scientific research and engages members from diverse communities to partner in a number of studies that can help improve the health and well-being of communities throughout the US.

Mary works together with a strong, interdisciplinary team located in various parts of the US to build a centralized KP research bank, a research asset that can be used by scientists who need access to high-quality biospecimens (e.g., blood, urine, saliva) and associated data to advance their research. These specimens and their associated data are unique collections consented by KP members, many of whom have been with KP for quite some time. This enables follow-up with research participants over their life course and helps researchers understand health and disease throughout the aging process. Mary develops strategy to keep members/participants of diverse backgrounds engaged in research studies that can advance our understanding of health disparities; at the same time she is also developing an access policy and process that maximizes the use of the resource while safeguarding the trust members have in KP.

What she enjoys most about her current role at KP is that there is an opportunity to find innovative ways to engage not just individuals but populations of diverse backgrounds to be involved in science. Another aspect that Mary loves about her job is in working with interdisciplinary colleagues (e.g., IT experts, data analysts, scientists, marketing, recruitment, bioethicists, health economists, physicians, health-care workers) with whom she can exchange knowledge. With these different perspectives, Mary can build a picture in her mind of how the research enterprise in a large organization works and how it integrates its research into the health delivery system to improve the health and well-being of communities.

Mary did not become a director by simply focusing on becoming a director in the earlier parts of her career; instead, she focused on doing what she loved, which was to work at the intersection of science, innovation, communities, and public policy. One great piece of advice she got was to not keep going back to school for more degrees, but to focus on getting firsthand experience in the work and having opportunities to grow in responsibilities.

The experience that launched Mary into this director position was acquired from working at the Bill & Melinda Gates Foundation as a program officer and Gates fellow. Mary entered the Gates Foundation through the Gates Fellows Program and AAAS (American Association for the Advancement of Science). In both programs, she connected with a global network of scientists and policy makers, who helped expedite her on-boarding experience at the Gates Foundation. At the foundation, Mary was embedded in the Grand Challenges team in the Global Health Division from 2012 to early 2015. One of Mary's main projects involved driving the launch of a program called Grand Challenges India where innovations and proposed solutions to pressing global health challenges would be led by Indian scientists who also had an in-depth awareness of the socioeconomic and cultural complexities of scaling up solutions in India. In developing the request for proposals (RFP), Mary consulted with experts within the foundation and with government partners so that the RFP would articulate exactly what funders were looking for from these applications. Before any funding decisions were made, Mary worked with a team to review applications and develop a short list, which was further reviewed by other experts, including a technical advisory group composed of international subject-matter experts. In other projects, Mary worked closely with grantees, making sure that they were meeting their deliverables and helping them communicate updates of their work with others in the foundation and/or other appropriate funding partners.

During her time at the Gates Foundation, Mary grew to appreciate the complexity of real-world challenges that innovators had to solve and the amount of resources and coordination it took to guide resources in their direction. She loved that she was part of the support ecosystem for global problem solvers. Every problem solver needs support, and through Mary's position with the Gates Foundation, she strove to direct resources to grantees to help accelerate their ideas into solutions that could change the world.

> Do not burn bridges once you cross them; help others get to where they need to go as well and work with the community to build new bridges for others.

Career Trajectory

A common question people (students, postdocs, midcareer professionals) ask Mary is how one can successfully jump from being a bench-side scientist in a laboratory to a director in a complex health-care organization. For Mary, it was not a single leap; it was and continues to be a journey. Starting from being an undergraduate, Mary chose a small university, Benedictine University in Lisle, Illinois, where the classroom sizes were small, which allowed her to get to know her professors—something that was very helpful when it was time to ask for references when she applied for summer internship positions at the University of Texas and for a part-time job working in a small company developing sensors.

Mary was constantly scanning the environment, from bulletin boards to websites, looking for opportunities and firsthand experiences in the lab that would help her understand the world of research, beyond the words and data buried in publications and textbooks. Mary went on to pursue her PhD in biochemistry at the University of Illinois in Urbana-Champaign where she worked in the laboratory of a new investigator who was focusing on the molecular basis of cancer. This was her first experience in seeing how competitive the funding environment was for basic science researchers and how publications in top-tiered journals were important to one's marketability, to being funded, and to getting a faculty position. She moved with her laboratory to Case Western Reserve University in Cleveland, Ohio, and continued her research until she published in a high-tier journal and eventually went on to earn a prestigious award for her dissertation work in cancer and human papillomaviruses.

Mary continued her research in cancer as a postdoc because continued specialization in a field was what she thought was the obvious next step as a scientist, but this time she did so in a very different research setting: St. Jude Children's Research Hospital where they treat children with cancer and other catastrophic diseases. The hospital had research and patient care under one roof. Seeing patients and their families placing their trust in doctors and researchers made a deep impression on Mary from day one; she could see the impact of science on saving lives or, at the very least, striving to improve the quality of life for children through medical research. In addition to research, Mary had the opportunity to participate in the Radio Cares for St. Jude's Kids fundraising program, an activity that energized her and enlightened her to how important public engagement was for the research enterprise.

After completing her postdoc, Mary joined the National Academies in Washington, DC, as a Christine Mirzayan Science & Technology Policy Fellow. She was placed on the Committee of Science, Engineering, and Public Policy where she learned how the academy gathered its evidence, convened experts, worked on pressing issues in science and technology, and how they advised the nation in various matters. She realized how important it was to have the right people from various communities advising and providing input. As a scientist, she also was able to infuse evidence-based thinking in the work she did for the academies and was able to further broaden her knowledge so that it went beyond technical scientific problems and into understanding how policy and programs were developed.

Mary became more aware about issues on allocation of resources when she worked for the NIH, first at the National Institute of Mental Health (NIMH) and then with the National Cancer Institute (NCI). At the NCI, Mary worked with a team on advancing programs to ensure that human specimens available for cancer research were of the highest quality, an experience that eventually became invaluable in her current role at KP. Another experience that continues to serve Mary well in her current role was when she worked as a science policy analyst at NIMH where she developed the analytic framework to support the analysis of the autism spectrum disorder portfolio.

Mary sees herself working in the health-care sector for many years to come. It is complex, dynamic, and fascinating to see innovations be better integrated in the health delivery system. It perfectly marries her experience in research, government, and in global health and development, helping her make better sense of how the world works and how she can make a difference in helping people thrive.

🍃 Peggy M. Shepard, 67

West Harlem Environmental Action (WE ACT) For Environmental Justice
Executive Director and Cofounder | ~$100,000

BA, English, Howard University (1967)

Job Description

Environmental justice is the fair treatment of all people regardless of race, national origin, or income with respect to the development, implementation, and enforcement of environmental laws, regulations, and policies. Unfortunately, many low-income communities and communities of color are disproportionately impacted by environmental hazards because of significant air pollution emitted from transportation, significant land pollution from old factories, and produce in grocery stores with significant pesticide residue. Peggy Sheppard has dedicated her life to fighting for environmental justice. This has required community mobilization and educating people in low-resource contexts. The fundamental problem is that since people in low-resource communities often have many struggles to deal with, from landing one of the limited numbers of jobs to staying safe from criminal activities, it can be difficult to show them the importance of an intangible issue such as environmental justice.

Peggy's nonprofit, WE ACT, was founded and incorporated in 1988 as one of the first environmental organizations in New York State to be headed by people of color. It has taken Peggy and her organization many years of education and advocacy to achieve their current level of development. Since her community members are worried about everyday struggles, they are not thinking about environmental issues, so Peggy's challenge has been to show them how environmental issues directly influence their health and quality of life. Peggy is proud of WE ACT because it has galvanized a grassroots voice into an institution that has built capacity within an underserved community to defend its quality of life, to improve its environmental health through community-based participatory research partnerships, to reform environmental policy, to increase environmental literacy among residents to make them more informed voters, and to support the national environmental justice movement.

The founding of WE ACT was a result of local community struggles around environmental threats and resulting health disparities created by institutionalized racism and lack of social and political capital. Events leading up to its founding include the siting and poor management of the North River Sewage Treatment Plant, the siting and operation of six diesel bus depots in Northern Manhattan, and the use of Northern Manhattan communities as Manhattan's dumping ground for a host of other polluting facilities. WE ACT combined grassroots organizing with policy reform, sustainable development, and corporate accountability to bring forth positive environmental and social change for the community. Today, WE ACT has sixteen full-time staff operating on an annual budget of $1.3 million, of which 90% is restricted to project funds. Peggy's time is involved in problem solving on ten individual projects, managing staff issues, speaking to university classes, attending meetings of various government and nonprofit advisory boards, leading conference calls for government work groups, testifying at the city council, maintaining communications with donors, and interacting with student teams on capstone-type projects.

One of WE ACT's many successful projects involved organizing hundreds of Harlem residents in a sustained five-year government accountability campaign utilizing direct action, civil disobedience, and negotiation to convince the City of New York to commit $55 million to abate environmental pollution from a newly constructed, "state-of-the-art" local sewage plant. WE ACT has developed a national reputation for its community-based participatory research partnerships to improve environmental health locally, to develop a national environmental health research agenda to address a broad array of community-based environmental exposures, and to translate research findings into reformed public policy. For example, WE ACT created and implemented an environmental health curriculum that has increased environmental literacy by training over 100 New York City community leaders to understand environmental health issues and to advocate for their concerns to be addressed.

To proactively plan for healthy, sustainable communities, WE ACT works to develop community planning processes, trainings, resources, and community benefits agreements with developers that empower residents to participate in democratic decision making that affects their health, safety, and quality of life. For example, WE ACT is developing a "green building" Environmental Justice Resource Center to demonstrate how the sustainable use of resources—e.g., alternative energy sources, energy efficiency, air quality, water conservation—can be achieved in a typical one-to-three family building in New York City, a model that can be followed by owners, developers, architects, and other building professionals.

What Peggy loves most about her job is the power, space, and authority to develop her ideas and vision and to implement it. This requires a significant level of creativity, patience, and persistence—sometimes over a period of years—to achieve the resources and the political environment that are needed to implement a specific idea, project, or vision. What she likes least is that her vision and effectiveness are hampered by a lack of resources (money, technology, and skilled staff). In the environmental advocacy field, studies document that organizations headed by people of color receive much less funding than the rest. Peggy and her team must spend significant time on fundraising rather than implementing innovative projects.

> I believe that one person makes a difference, especially if you can convince at least one other person to work with you. The job you may succeed in probably has no name at this time. All of us can constantly reinvent ourselves. Students should find their passion, and where they think they add value, and then take the risk of accepting opportunities when they come. Contributing to social value—having a sense of demonstrated agency—is why I work hard and enjoy it.

Career Trajectory

After college, Peggy began a ten-year career in newspapers, book publishing, and consumer magazines. This led her to be a newspaper reporter in Indianapolis followed by a researcher, home furnishings editor, and copy editor in New York City. When a new startup magazine for which she was editor did not publish, she took a job as a speechwriter in a state housing agency. In 1984, Peggy's government colleagues urged her to go to an organizing meeting for the New York City campaign of Jesse Jackson's run for the United States presidency. She left that meeting as the public relations director for the Manhattan campaign, and it set her on a path that would change her life, career, and aspirations. Through that campaign, Peggy used her writing skills, gained an important political mentor, interacted with key leaders around the state, and had the opportunity to gauge the disparity between communities in regard to the distribution of benefits and burdens. The Jackson campaign manager became her political mentor, and she became his go-to girl, accompanying him to high-level political meetings, writing speeches for candidate David Dinkins, and becoming his general assistant and confidante. Peggy began to observe and understand the different resources and activism some communities benefitted from, and others that were bereft of those dynamics. After Jackson lost the primary, Peggy was recruited into the Mondale-Ferraro campaign where she coordinated Women For Mondale-Ferraro.

After that failed campaign, Peggy was asked by her political mentor whether she wanted to work behind the scenes producing other people, or whether she was interested in being out front, such as running for office. Under the banner "Leadership For A Change," Peggy ran as an insurgent and was elected female Democratic district leader in a Harlem assembly. A trio of female senior citizens provided Peggy's insurgency and leadership position with an energized base of support, became her community-based political mentors, and told her that it was her generational turn to take over the organizing and community education to improve West Harlem's quality of life. That effort in 1985 to grow new, progressive political leadership in West Harlem became the foundation of the struggle for environmental justice in Northern Manhattan and New York City. Through strong organizing efforts, Peggy got the city to commit $55 million to fix the North River Plant and received a $1.1 million settlement of a lawsuit against the city. Eighteen years of advocacy have made the NYC Metropolitan Transportation Authority diesel bus fleet one of the cleanest in the nation, and there are many other such victories in communities around this country that were made dumping grounds for polluting facilities. The quality of life in Peggy's neighborhood is dependent upon decisions and policies made at the municipal and state levels, between and among government, civic groups, private developers, corporations, and large community-based institutions. To develop the capacity to work at this metropolitan/regional level is a challenge for any group, especially a community-based organization in an under-resourced community of color. To create the political will and opportunities to infuse these metropolitan and regional initiatives with procedural, distributive, and social equity, she realizes it is necessary and daunting, yet possible.

It is difficult for Peggy to separate work from her personal life while struggling to run a nonprofit. She enjoys her time off, but she firmly believes that to be successful requires thinking and envisioning constantly—especially if you are understaffed and advocating for people of color and low income who are not held in the highest regard. In five to ten years, Peggy hopes to be retired from WE ACT but active on many of the same issues. She will probably continue to speak at universities and hopefully have time to write a book. If Peggy could start all over again, she would have studied law, paid attention in biology and attempted chemistry, and gone to an Ivy League school. But all in all, if WE ACT could just get more resources, she would be happy with where she is and what she has accomplished.

⚙ Jakub Felkl, 33

Texas Foundation for Innovative Communities
Assistant Director | ~$75,000 – 100,000

PhD, Mechanical Engineering, The University of Texas at Austin (2013)
BS and MA, Physics, The University of Texas at Austin (2007)

Job Description

Innovation increases productivity and drives economic growth. Higher productivity results in more prosperity (e.g., better median wages, more jobs—direct and induced) and a higher standard of living. The focus on economic growth via innovation is not a zero-sum game; the more productive our economies become, the more—and better quality—services and products become available at lower costs to more people across the world. Austin, Texas, like most other parts of the country, felt the 2008 economic crisis with people losing jobs, spending less money, and perpetuating cycles of low economic activity. Because of its highly skilled workforce, history of technology entrepreneurship, and supportive environment, Austin entrepreneurs have been fighting back by starting their own businesses and thereby creating jobs. Many of these jobs fall under the innovation, high-value added, highly differentiated category that provides significant job multipliers (induced jobs) to the local economy.

Policy makers want to support entrepreneurship and innovation, an engine of the economy, but how can they do this? Entrepreneurship is extremely difficult, requires significant risk (an overwhelming majority of startups fail), often benefits from outside support, and requires the entrepreneur to make many new connections. Technology-based entrepreneurship is especially boosted in a well-functioning ecosystem. An ideal innovation ecosystem for entrepreneurs includes empowering and visionary long-term policies; accessible human and financial capital; an encouraging culture; large and small companies; a supportive research university; a supportive community and local government; and a variety of institutional and infrastructural supports. In addition, a well-functioning ecosystem reduces "social distance" between various players and thus reduces time to market for companies. Such an ecosystem takes a vision to build and is a long-term endeavor beyond any elected official's term. In central Texas and statewide, The Texas Foundation for Innovative Communities (TFIC), a nonprofit funded in part by the state and federal governments, strives to create and advance development of such ecosystems with some of their most recent efforts focused on rural communities that are often overlooked.

The way TFIC views an innovation ecosystem is in how effectively it can solve a series of about forty classes of problems that entrepreneurs face. To a large degree, if these are preaddressed in a particular cluster, the companies in that cluster located in the area can and will be more effective. On a micro-level, TFIC supports economic development in Texas by connecting individual local companies to the resources, talent, and capital that they need. TFIC also supports the larger state innovation ecosystem and strategy by working and partnering with incubators, chambers of commerce, local governments, service providers, and research universities, as well as other organizations across the state.

As the associate director of TFIC, Jakub Felkl coaches, provides feedback, reviews, and otherwise supports companies that apply for the state venture fund or companies that are at various stages in their technology and business development. In addition, he also works with partners to develop programs to support innovation and high-growth technology companies. Jakub and his team also provide training for entrepreneurs and facilitate investor-company showcases and meetings. On the ecosystem level, Jakub's team manages an organization dedicated to supporting comprehensive entrepreneurship infrastructure in the state: the Texas Association of Research Parks and Incubators (TARPI). Research topics within TARPI include creating innovation ecosystems, extracting working principles, and building self-contained and efficient innovation centers at research universities. Another topic of interest is bringing in entrepreneurs.

Jakub recently worked with one company that had a very differentiated, unique product and a limited market penetration. Because the founder considered this to be more of a personal/lifestyle business, little thought was given to scale and growth in the company's operations and plans. Jakub and his team helped the client company put the right resources in place, redefine part of the growth vision, open the potential to bring in additional capital, and show the path to scale effectively, quickly, and appropriately. The founder was extremely grateful for their advice and expressed how without their help, the company would have been stuck on a low-growth path or may have been ultimately unsuccessful. The last time Jakub checked with them, they were about to double their revenues since the prior year.

Jakub's days are filled with a healthy mix of meetings, research, and project work for clients. He fosters partnerships with other support organizations in Texas as well as with public officials, firms, universities, and nonprofit groups. Jakub frequently works with early-stage technology companies within the state-designated emerging technology industries. He often researches technological and economic topics applicable to these industries, regional economic and competitiveness drivers, and analyzes data on high-performance companies to determine how their developmental or competitive strategies could apply in Texas. Jakub also has a number of more eclectic duties, from working with a manufacturing organization to develop new client programs to helping individual companies apply for federal grants. Some days, Jakub helps client companies directly by educating, counseling, or recruiting talent for them. On other days, he focuses on advanced methodologies for developing competitive advantages and innovation ecosystems.

> Have a dream, follow your passion, know where you are going, and get a mentor. Just like in a successful business, you should think of the valuable differentiation, unique skill, or quality only you can provide. Think about building and advancing this expertise in which you are passionate while still being open to fortify it with ideas from all around. There is no recipe on life—you write your own code for life. Failure is good—pick up the pieces, learn, and keep moving forward. Appreciate small things in everyday life.

Jakub measures the impact of TFIC's work in the success of their clients, but also in some larger statewide metrics. One of these metrics is the increase in the attainment of federal Small Business Innovation Research (SBIR)/ Small Business Technology Transfer (STTR) grants, which have increased considerably due to TFIC's efforts. Typically, these larger macroeconomic indicators take a while (longer than a year) to show the impact, but median wages in an area, productivity (GDP/capita), or overall amount of early-stage risk capital invested in the state are quicker and reliable measures.

Jakub loves innovating and creating new ways to support TFIC's endeavors. He finds challenges, the necessary speed and flexibility, and working with entrepreneurs stimulating—no day is ever the same. Sometimes there are necessary tasks that need to be done, such as reporting to funding agencies or additional bureaucracy and educating legislators, which Jakub finds less exciting than day-to-day work with entrepreneurs and innovators. Because he likes working around entrepreneurs, Jakub's personal life overlaps significantly with his work life: many evening events involve both business networking and catching up with good friends he has developed over the course of the years in the tech-entrepreneurship arena. On weekends, Jakub likes to play sports, run, swim, hike, take short trips, and spend time outside since the weather in Austin (and Texas in general) is warm and sunny most of the year. On those "indoors" days, Jakub enjoys reading, working on side projects, fixing, repairing, or just tinkering and improving things.

Career Trajectory

Jakub has always been interested in innovation; he took entrepreneurship and innovation classes alongside business and engineering design courses at the university. Most of his twenties were spent pursuing a PhD in mechanical engineering at the University of Texas at Austin, which he views as a worthwhile investment that will bear interest in accelerated career growth. Outside his coursework and research, Jakub taught classes in science and technology commercialization and aided groups in the front end of innovation—early stages of product development, including ideation. He also ran the Global Idea to Product Program and took part in Three Day Startup, many Business Plan Competitions, and the Global Venture Labs Investment Competition—first as a participant and now as a mentor. After earning his PhD, he worked for the Austin Technology Incubator for a few months, mostly focusing on Clean Energy Incubator startups and writing grants. With his expertise, a recommendation from his mentor and supervisor, and a little bit of luck, Jakub landed his position with TFIC in 2014.

If Jakub could start over, he would have formed a better, longer-term career plan from the start and held true to it. He would have let fewer distractions sway him from pursuing his passions, even though he regrets none. Jakub now has a clear vision for the future. In five years, he will be working in an energy-tech startup (oil and gas), hopefully a well-established and funded one. In ten years, he will be working with energy again (electricity storage) on a different startup. Fifteen years down the road, his focus may shift to other parts of energy (generation and transmission) and angel investing; twenty will be biotechnology; and in twenty-five plus years, besides venture capital investing, he will be focused on startups of every boy's dreams—in transportation, space, and aerospace.

Divyesh Mehta, 38

The Recovery Center for Alcohol and Drug Services of Central Oklahoma
Corporate Compliance Officer | Six figures

MBA, Healthcare Administration, Oklahoma City University (2002)
MBBS, Medicine, MS University-Baroda Medical College (2000)

Job Description

Substance abuse has a debilitating effect on the health of individuals, their families, and their communities. While the United States government has criminalized the use of many drugs in an attempt to ban drug supply and eliminate drug abuse, such policies have been largely unsuccessful. Other solutions are critically needed. Looking at the overall socioeconomics contributing to the issue and improving the situation from the roots would be great, but in the meantime, drug users are patients in need of rehabilitation, not criminal records. State governments are interested in rehabilitation centers as a means of fostering socioeconomic development through the rehabilitation of citizens into healthy, productive members of society. Rehabilitation centers require experts to work with them, ensuring they comply with both local and national laws, while delivering the best care possible and preventing illegal, unethical, or improper conduct. Divyesh Mehta serves in this role for The Recovery Center for Alcohol and Drug Services of Central Oklahoma (TRC). Divyesh knows how to effectively and appropriately manage health facilities thanks to his experience as a medical doctor coupled with his MBA in health care administration.

TRC is one of the first organizations in the state of Oklahoma to be certified and licensed as a "Comprehensive Community Addiction Recovery Center." TRC is a private nonprofit business that specializes in medically supervised detoxification of patients that suffer from alcohol and other drug addictions. They also offer ambulatory detoxification; outpatient, family, and case management services; and aftercare planning. TRC can host forty-eight patients at a time, and their operational costs are funded by contracts with the state, insurance, and patients who pay privately without insurance coverage. Due to the progressive nature of chemical dependency, TRC strives to assist patients at the moment they reach out for help. TRC is available 24/7 to assess and admit as necessary users who need substance abuse services—publically provided for people that meet Oklahoma's state eligibility criteria and privately provided for those who do not.

As a corporate compliance officer, Divyesh serves as one of the head executives at TRC directly under the CEO. He serves as a liaison with their accrediting and certifying bodies, CARF (Commission on Accreditation of Rehabilitation Facilities) and ODMHSAS (Oklahoma Department of Mental Health and Substance Abuse Services), as well as other contract sources. His main responsibilities include developing, initiating, maintaining, and revising policies and procedures for the general operations of TRC and its programs, as well as their compliance program to ensure proper conduct. He acts as an independent review and evaluation body to ensure that compliance issues and concerns within the organization are being properly evaluated, investigated, and resolved. He also identifies potential areas of compliance vulnerability and risk, develops and implements corrective action plans for resolution of problematic issues, and provides general guidance on how to avoid or deal with similar situations in the future. At this time with financial scarcity and budget cuts, Divyesh is trying to keep TRC diversified by adding a variety of service delivery systems. At the end of the day, Divyesh is the person responsible for TRC operating efficiently, legally, and ethically. He loves the way he incorporates medical knowledge into health administration to make effective changes in the field of addiction treatment.

Career Trajectory

Divyesh graduated with his bachelor of medicine, bachelor of surgery (MBBS) degree from MS University (Baroda Medical College) in India after completing one year of clinical internships. MBBS is a baccalaureate degree in medicine awarded in several countries, especially those with historical or colonial linkages to England. Divyesh dreamed of studying abroad if he ever got the opportunity to do so, and his dream came true when he accepted a part-time scholarship for enrolling in an MBA in health care administration program at Oklahoma City University. After his graduation in 2003, he started interning at the Oklahoma Department of Mental Health and Substance Abuse Services (ODMHSAS) where he closely observed patients with addiction problems who

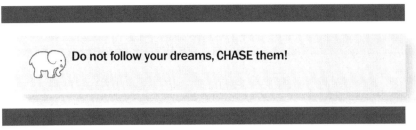

Do not follow your dreams, CHASE them!

were also facing mental health issues. He realized that treatment in such conditions can be much more effective if delivered in a highly individualized manner.

He was moved by the co-occurring treatment model of addiction treatment and substance abuse services, so he looked further and sought a position at ODMHSAS to continue working with this newly developed interest. He was selected to be an addiction specialist at one of the ODMHSAS facilities, called NADTC (Norman Alcohol and Drug Treatment Center). NADTC served sixty-two patients at a given time, each suffering from co-occurring disorders (coexisting substance abuse and mental health conditions). The center is an inpatient residential unit with an average patient stay between thirty and forty-five days. While working at NADTC, he was promoted to admissions director and later to executive management. He passionately enjoyed every day of working at NADTC from 2003 to 2010, learning a lot at every step. He quickly learned that just like other fields, addiction treatment is all about networking and collaboration. A holistic approach to treatment is what a substance abuser/mental health patient needs, and one organization cannot be a subject-matter expert on everything that each patient will require throughout the treatment process. Extending a helping hand, developing partnerships, and helping patients to benefit from all the services that are available can be achieved through a holistic approach. In 2010, Divyesh got an opportunity from TRC to be on their staff, enhancing their private services, performance, and quality improvement services. He accepted the challenge and helped the organization to achieve one of the best accreditation surveys in its history. He was promoted to become their corporate compliance officer, which helped him build upon his executive, administration, and management roles.

In five years, Divyesh wants to be working with a team to enhance TRC services to make it a self-sustaining and innovative organization. He would like to see TRC create significant positive impact on its patients, aid in reducing imprisonment and death rates due to alcohol and drug overdose, all while improving wellness and overall health throughout Oklahoma. In ten to fifteen years, he would like to see TRC get noticed on a national level for its determination to improve patient outcomes for those suffering with addiction through their unique treatment approach. Despite being a workaholic, Divyesh strongly believes in the phrase, "Do not count every hour in the day, make every hour in the day count," so he tries to efficiently and effectively use his entire day for his professional and personal life.

Photo by Iridescent

📖 Tara Chklovski, 37

Iridescent Learning
Founder and CEO | ~$90,000

PhD, Aerospace Engineering, University of Southern California (2007)
MS, Aerospace Engineering, Boston University (2003)
BSc, Physics, St. Stephen's College (1999)

Job Description

Scientific and technological innovations are becoming increasingly important as benefits and challenges arise from globalization and our knowledge-based economy. We need leaders in STEM fields to tackle the greatest challenges that the twenty-first century holds. Despite the high demand for skilled workers in STEM, not many young people are being inspired to pursue these fields. Additionally, there is a lack of gender and ethnic diversity of students entering STEM educational programs and careers. Women and minorities are often discouraged from pursuing STEM fields due to reasons including stereotypes about their abilities, lack of role models, and lack of support at lower grade levels. Supporting the underrepresented population in the STEM fields is essential for solving global challenges and for the greater economic success and equality of women and minorities. Iridescent is bringing STEM inspiration to young people in underserved communities all across the US and globally (with a footprint in more than sixty-four countries). CEO Tara Chklovski founded her nonprofit in 2006 to equip children from underserved communities—and girls—to become innovators because she knows that diverse teams converge on innovative solutions faster than homogeneous teams.

Iridescent has twenty-two employees and hundreds of volunteers. They teach STEM through hands-on lessons using engineering mentors and encouraging strong parental involvement. Iridescent runs two programs, "Curiosity Machine" and "Technovation Challenge." Through Curiosity Machine, engineers and scientists are trained to develop hands-on projects based on their work, following which they teach these projects to underserved K-5 students and their families. These engineers and scientists then continue to mentor the families via an online curriculum and mentoring platform. Through this online platform, parents can access videos to show their children the challenge and can then help their children design and create their solutions from household materials before posting a video of it online. A virtual, trained STEM mentor then provides feedback to give the child ideas to improve the design, encourage the child to persist through failure, and reinforce the science concepts behind the challenge.

Iridescent's other program is the Technovation Challenge, the world's largest technology entrepreneurship program for girls. Middle and high school girls work in teams through an intensive three-month, fifty-hour curriculum to design and create mobile apps and launch startups to solve local problems. Over the past five years, Technovation has engaged more than 5,000 girls in forty-five countries to address problems such as access to clean water, early marriage, health, safe transportation for women, school attendance tracking, traffic policing, and teen pregnancy. In addition, over 600 women tech professionals have served as mentors while developing their own project management and product development skills. Many women mentors have even gone on to launching their own startups after Technovation.

In order to make all of Iridescent's programs happen, Tara brainstorms ideas for new workshops for children and talks to her team to help them solve problems, such as how to logistically run a workshop or how to get a new university on board for engineering student mentors. About 70% of her time is spent problem solving in meetings and conversations and the other 30% is spent creating new things. She especially loves the creative aspects of her job when she gets to apply her physics and engineering background to artistic challenges. She also loves working with children and seeing the impact she has on their lives. As CEO, she is in charge of her entire company, but she makes sure she does not spend her days doing just her least favorite things: managing or being prompt-driven. Right now, she is working on developing a curriculum for a summer camp for preschoolers that will be completely in a forest. They will be looking at nature from a systems engineering point of view. She is also working on creating a book of hands-on experiments.

Tara collects data obsessively—at the minute. She ensures that her employees and volunteers track the number of participants they have reached through which program and the number of contact hours they have received. Iridescent is not in the business of short-term rewards, so Tara needs to follow participants over many years. She has two National Science Foundation awards to evaluate the impact of her programs on the same participants over five years.

Success for Tara is when families change behavior long term and pursue science as a hobby, tinkering each weekend and over many years. Success is also when children go on to become scientists, engineers, and inventors. So far, Tara has consistently and cost-effectively doubled Iridescent's impact every year by heavily relying on technology, synergistic partnerships, rigorous evaluation, and volunteers.

> If you have any idea that you want to try out, then build something fast, and try it with people—but then focus a lot of resources on LISTENING to what people are telling you. Then see past your ego and try to analyze what you are hearing and try and address the issues.

Career Trajectory

Going along with her company's design to have parents involved, parental influence was Tara's biggest driver and influencer. Her father is a former pilot in the Indian Air Force, and her mother is a doctor. Both of her parents treated her as they did her brother, giving her tremendous intellectual freedom and introducing her to engines, cars, sports, and other male-oriented fields. She went to an all-girls school for many formative years, which reinforced her confidence in her abilities as well as gave her opportunities to be a leader. Her family in India runs two schools, and this influence strongly shaped her decision to start Iridescent.

After college, Tara spent a year mountaineering in India while applying to universities in the US for a master's degree in aerospace engineering. Concurrently, she received a full scholarship to Boston University and an invitation to an expedition to Bhagirathi peak. It was a tough decision but she chose the former. Tara went on to pursue a PhD in aerospace engineering at the University of Southern California (USC). USC is a unique learning institution with its close proximity to high-need communities and high-crime areas. It reminded her of India where she was constantly surrounded by poverty. She decided to drop out of her PhD and go into education to solve bigger problems and gain a greater sense of meaning through her work rather than analyzing columns of data from a wind tunnel. Ideally, she would do both, and that is how she started Iridescent.

Tara reads like crazy. Her parents modeled self-directed learning for her repeatedly. She learned that she could teach herself anything from a book. She read *How to Start a Nonprofit in CA*, filed the paperwork for Iridescent, and it was accepted as a 501(c)(3). She even read a book to help her do the taxes the first three years. Tara is not afraid to ask for help. She has reached out to experts and asked them for help throughout the course of starting Iridescent. She sat in on a course at UCLA on science education, and one of the texts talked about a school in Utah (Open Classroom) where parents were required to volunteer three hours every week in the classroom—not cutting paper, but actually teaching. She spent a week at that school, and it blew her mind. She decided that she wanted to test that model in south central Los Angeles with parents. The core would be that engineers would show underserved families the coolest, most amazing aspects of science and engineering, thereby letting them see that a career in STEM could not only be a way out of poverty, but would be an extremely powerful career for their children.

Tara's PhD committee advisors Dr. Blackwelder and Dr. Browand were instrumental in believing in her vision of empowering university engineering students to teach local underserved families. They let her run her first "engineers as teachers" Iridescent workshop at their aerospace and mechanical engineering department where students received three units of technical elective credit for developing five open-ended engineering design challenges that they would then teach to local children and parents. Dr. Kassner, the former director of research at the Office of Naval Research, was an extremely innovative and visionary funder for Iridescent. He recommended that Iridescent receive a scale-up grant that enabled Tara to take her programs and models nationwide—and from there, global. Without his visionary support, Iridescent would not have been able to grow as fast as they did.

Tara works from home and has two little girls. It is hard for her to separate work and play because she really loves what she does, and it does blend into what she needs to do with her little ones as well. For instance, she is running a Little Engineers and Parents program and her three-year-old was her first subject. More recently, she ran a summer camp focused on nature and robotics for preschoolers. There are few programs that introduce such concepts to little ones, and it was awesome for Tara to see how receptive they are and how much they are capable of grasping. She strongly believes you have to be brave and take the plunge to do new things. Tara is very happy with her life and sees Iridescent's work as her life's work, something that fulfills her on a daily basis as well as holistically.

Photo by Laura Riley

❤ Imran Babar, 33

Rare Genomics Institute | Vice President of Scientific Affairs
OrbiMed Advisors | Private Equity and Venture Capital Senior Associate |
Six Figures

PhD, Molecular Biology, Yale University (2011)
BA, Biology, Carleton College (2004)

Job Description

Rare diseases affect approximately 250,000 people globally. A majority of the estimated 6,800 rare diseases do not have a name, let alone a cure. Rare-disease patients often slip through the cracks as researchers focus time, money, and effort studying more widely known diseases. Since many rare diseases are genetic in nature, genome sequencing can be a powerful tool to discover underlying mutations that cause or contribute to the condition. However, many families affected by rare diseases lack access to genome-sequencing technology. Additionally, beyond genome sequencing, research in general on rare diseases is limited since so little is known about them that researchers do not have a good place to start.

The Rare Genomics Institute (RG) is focused on bridging this gap by providing patients with access to genome sequencing and promoting post-sequencing research. The organization does this by (1) giving patients a micro-funding platform to raise funds for research, (2) providing access to top genomics researchers who can sequence patient genomes and analyze the data, (3) connecting patients with clinicians and genetic counselors who can help interpret and translate the individualized findings, (4) promoting research for rare diseases, and (5) educating patients and the broader research community about rare diseases.

Imran Babar cofounded RG in early 2011 with Dr. Jimmy Lin (currently president of the organization), and in recent years he has served as the vice president of scientific affairs. Imran knew Jimmy and other early members of RG from the Harvey Fellowship, which is awarded to Christians who are pursuing graduate work at top-rated institutions. During his time at RG, Imran has seen firsthand the impact that genome sequencing can have on patients' lives. While RG does not promise patients a cure, the organization aims to at least initiate the research process. Once in a while, sequencing results reveal a mutation in a gene that is targeted by currently available treatments, but this is not common. As RG moves forward, the organization hopes to not only research the causes but advance research into cures.

One project that Imran's team led is the beHEARD competition, which called for proposals from researchers investigating rare diseases around the world. His hope for the competition was to stimulate more research on rare diseases by linking donors with scientists who could use donated resources to advance their rare-disease research projects. RG first solicited donations from service providers and industry partners from around the globe, which amounted to nearly half a million dollars. These donations included reagents, supplies, research tools, consulting, animal models, and more from industry partners. Imran's team then assembled a group of experts to review the proposals and award the donations to the best proposals. Scientists who participated later noted how the program was instrumental in advancing their research for rare diseases.

Another project Imran has been involved with at RG is helping patients who have Hailey-Hailey Disease (HHD), a very painful blistering skin disease that currently does not have good treatments. Imran's team was approached by the HHD Global Support Network with evidence from patient experience that a particular generic drug could alleviate symptoms. Based on this evidence, support from the literature, and a plausible mechanism of action, Imran's team has worked with academic institutions to initiate a clinical trial to test this drug in patients. Additionally, the team is working on a publication that will summarize the data on the condition, including the scientific rationale for using the generic drug as a treatment.

Despite the excitement of his work at RG, he is only volunteer with them on nights and weekends. Imran spends most of his time at OrbiMed where he is a senior associate on the private equity team. OrbiMed is a leading investment firm dedicated to health care. Although OrbiMed has a few different strategies for investing in health-care companies, Imran specifically works on the private equity/venture capital team. The venture capital business has three main buckets. The first is to find interesting companies and source deals, many of which come from relationships with companies, academics, and other venture-capital firms. The second is to conduct due diligence on companies and evaluate if they would be a good investment for the firm. The last is to help manage portfolio companies after investing in them, for example by becoming a board member. OrbiMed team members may also provide portfolio companies with connections to consultants and other industry professionals who may be able to help create value for the companies.

> Be collaborative! Sometimes people are overly protective or competitive and keep everything to themselves for fear of getting scooped. But sometimes it can be beneficial to both sides if you are open and collaborative.

Imran describes his job as both relational and analytical. He notes that he uses analytic skills gained while doing his PhD on a daily basis. Additionally, he describes the business as being very relational because he is constantly working with other professionals in the industry. Imran loves the fact that he is constantly learning. Since there are many factors that go into evaluating a company for investment, he is regularly exposed to many different areas, including scientific, medical, intellectual property, regulatory, clinical development, market analysis, financial modeling, and more. Imran gets personal fulfillment from the social impact aspect of his efforts. One challenge with his career is that sometimes he can get incredibly busy and has to be very efficient with his time. He believes that to be successful and happy with a career, you need to find the best balance of (1) compensation, (2) work-life balance, and (3) content—a job you find interesting and challenging in a good way. He finds that many careers can give you two, but it is hard to get all three. While he finds his work-life balance to be a bit challenging at times, he believes his career strikes a great balance in all of these areas.

Career Trajectory

Growing up on a sheep farm in rural Minnesota, Imran always had a love for nature. He studied biology as an undergraduate at Carleton College, a small liberal arts school in Minnesota. Carleton encouraged students to get a well-rounded education and to consider nontraditional career paths, so pursuing a nontraditional career was engrained in Imran from early on. As an undergrad, he was given the opportunity to participate in a program through the Howard Hughes Medical Institute (HHMI) working with Dr. Tyler Jacks and Dr. Carla Kim at MIT on lung cancer for one summer. This exposure to high-level research convinced him to pursue a PhD in biology upon graduation.

Although he applied to graduate schools during his senior year in college, he decided to defer his enrollment for a year to do something nontraditional. Although he was accepted to nearly every graduate school to which he applied, Imran decided on Yale because its umbrella program gave him access to a lot of different areas of research. During his year off, he gained more exposure to cutting-edge research through a three-month internship at the Rocky Mountain Laboratory (RML, part of the National Institutes of Allergies and Infectious Diseases or NIAID) in rural Montana. While at RML, Imran worked with microarray technology and was able to coauthor two scientific articles. He recalls his mentors, Dr. Steve Porcella and Dr. Kimmo Virtaneva, as being particularly supportive and fun to work with. After his time at RML, he then spent some time with his family in Minnesota and worked as a restaurant dish boy and a gas station janitor. Finally, since he wanted to grow by spending time in another country, he volunteered in India for six months with a Christian nonprofit organization.

At Yale, Imran researched the role of microRNAs in cancer in Dr. Frank Slack's laboratory. A hallmark of his graduate school career is that he collaborated with researchers in many different departments. These collaborations ultimately resulted in numerous publications that he otherwise would not have gotten. When he started, his dream was to become a research professor because he was passionate about science and teaching. Plus, many of his advisors and mentors encouraged him down that career path. However, keeping with his tradition of being nontraditional, toward the end of graduate school, he explored other options. He considered working overseas and applying for a Fulbright Fellowship, but he decided he wanted to work closer to family in the long term.

Throughout his last year of grad school, he conducted informational interviews with many friends and alumni to learn about their jobs and consider what he would like to do. He eventually applied for a position as a biotechnology analyst with Cowen & Company. Although he did not know much about the career path at first, he thought the idea of applying analytical and science skills sounded interesting. He landed the position and was thankful to work with very bright, influential people, particularly Eric Schmidt and Phil Nadeau. He learned to evaluate science from the perspective of developing a product—how a company can bring a drug from preclinical development to the market. He also had to take a series of FINRA exams in order to become a licensed analyst, which helped him develop his financial acumen. After working at Cowen, Imran transitioned to the buy-side and joined OrbiMed's venture-capital team. Imran has worked with RG during both his time at Cowen and his time at OrbiMed.

117

Alyssa Grinberg, 35

Friends of the Arava Institute

Associate Director, Marketing and Communications | ~$55,000 – 70,000

MA, Sustainable International Development, Brandeis University (2014)
BA, Art History and The Visual Arts, Occidental College (2003)

Photo by Joshua Beckmann

Job Description

Scientific researchers at the forefront of their fields are making amazing discoveries every day. More than ever, people need some understanding of science, whether they are involved in decision making at a national or local level, in managing industries, in skilled or semiskilled employment, in voting as private citizens, or in making a wide range of personal decisions. However, who is going to read a twenty-page journal article about a very specific topic? How can important scientific information be communicated to the masses? Such communication requires somebody who understands the science and can make it more accessible to nonscientists—oftentimes across cultures.

One institution where amazing discoveries are happening is the Arava Institute for Environmental Studies, a leading environmental and academic institution in Israel, named one of the top 100 environmental think tanks in the world. The institute offers students and interns a once-in-a-lifetime opportunity to immerse themselves in a cross-cultural environment with others who are equally passionate about building a more sustainable and just future. No other program in the Middle East brings together students from such varied political, cultural, and religious backgrounds to live, study, and learn from one another for a semester or full academic year. The Friends of the Arava Institute (FAI) is a nonprofit organization with a mission to support the critical work of the Arava Institute for Environmental Studies in Israel through public awareness, student recruitment, alumni relations, and fund-raising campaigns.

As a marketing and communications specialist, Alyssa promotes the Arava Institute in the US to various constituents, including university faculty and staff, students, and supporters. Using their strongest assets and positive outcomes, she creates content to highlight the effective work being done at their sister organization in Israel. Whether through a film about biogas technology or a webinar about the remediation being done around the Evrona oil spill, Alyssa creates content that brings the work to life for people from around the world.

Throughout her career, Alyssa has developed and promoted innovative educational programming. It is through the students themselves, and what they go on to achieve as alumni, that she sees the most profound change. Alyssa knows that the academic programs that she has worked on over the years have helped to shape these young adults to be actively engaged, positive contributors to society. In her current position at the Friends of the Arava Institute, she is supporting the development of environmental activists and peace builders who are making great impacts in the Middle East and beyond. Working for a small nonprofit organization has afforded Alyssa the opportunity for a lot of creativity and innovation. Since FAI is small, they have the ability to move quickly on big ideas and put them into action. This benefit of being small is great, but it also presents some challenges as there are limits in resources (from a financial and personnel perspective), so they cannot implement all the things they desire. They must prioritize and adjust according to what is realistic.

Alyssa always brings her work home, but she does not necessarily recommend this! Alyssa believes in the importance of peace and creating a more environmentally sustainable way of life. In her personal life, she always strives toward having positive, peaceful interactions with people, even with those who do not seem to hold the same beliefs. She tries to make decisions in her life that take the environment into consideration: she has not owned a car since 2005, she is careful about what she buys (and minimizes as much as possible), and stays politically active on a number of different environmental issues. Being politically engaged and writing to your representatives are important, even if it sometimes feels like there is little progress. Having a voice is essential, and she is reminded every day that there are people all over the world who do not have that and do not have the luxury of the myriad of choices she is afforded each day.

Career Trajectory

Raised by an architect and an artist, Alyssa has always been drawn to the visual arts and various forms of creative expression. From a very young age, she also developed a strong desire to give back and to fight toward a more just and sustainable world. She was likely influenced by a long line of Quaker heritage—her ancestors were abolitionists and women's rights activists—as well as an older sister who lead the way in her dedication toward helping those in underserved communities through her career and personal life. A semester of studying abroad with the International Honors Program (IHP) in India, South Africa, and Brazil, further solidified her strong desire to make the world a better place in any way she could. She has experienced

> With social value creation, I am reminded that these concepts of balancing social good and profits are not mutually exclusive. We can make a difference in the world and live comfortably. To do social good, you do not need to be a martyr, and to be financially driven, you do not need to be a demon. We can create innovative solutions to our world's problems and still afford that vacation in Bali.

firsthand the powerful impact that education and exposure to different cultures can have. It led her to live in a more conscientious manner, especially when it comes to consumption and the ways in which we interact with our environment. As an undergraduate student, she studied film production, but her career in international and experiential education postgraduation took her on a different path.

After working for a couple wonderful organizations over the course of five years, Alyssa was given the opportunity to live on a sailboat for a year, which she seized and found her way to the Dominican Republic from Boston. It was dream, but it ended abruptly, and she found herself without a home, money, or a job. Luckily, she had amazing friends and family who supported her through this very difficult situation and the fortune to land a newly established job at Brandeis University. In this position, she was able to work with faculty across different departments, such as computer science and environmental studies. She was also able to take courses at the Heller School for Social Policy and Management. Originally, she had planned to apply for a master's degree in sustainable development in Amsterdam, but by chance, she fell in love with the Heller School and their degree in sustainable international development. She had incredible mentors, and as part of the program, she completed a practicum working for UN-Habitat on their cities and climate-change initiative.

She would have never predicted that she would come back to filmmaking and use this skill to communicate pressing issues such as climate change and access to water and sanitation. After working as a filmmaker for UN-Habitat, she realized that she could merge her love of transformative education, environmental sustainability, and peace building with her skills in communications, marketing, and filmmaking into a career. All it took was one question: "Can you still make films?" Her answer was, "Yes." Sometimes, all it takes is a "yes" and the confidence that what you do not know you are capable of learning. Alyssa went on to make four short films for UN-Habit, a handful of promotional videos with other agencies, and most recently a short film about a biogas project with the Arava Institute for Environmental Studies.

The activity that has helped Alyssa the most during her career is her continued pursuit of knowledge. Her curiosity continues to drive her, and she will never stop learning; whether that is from a book or a conversation, intellectual pursuit fuels her. Keeping a healthy balance in life is also incredibly important and is essential for a healthy mind and a successful career; therefore, Alyssa does yoga, sails, hikes, runs, and dances as much as she can. Laughing is also key, especially when dealing with really challenging global issues—she has to keep a sense of humor. Alyssa has always tried to foster positive relationships in her life, whether with colleagues or other acquaintances. She genuinely enjoys helping and connecting people. She has found that her genuine nature has likewise helped her a tremendous amount, and these relationships that she has cultivated over the years have come back to aid her in many ways. Alyssa's career outlook is positive, but she cannot say with certainty where she will be in five, ten, fifteen years, and beyond. She knows, though, that she will always be mission-driven and striving to make a positive impact on the world.

NONPROFIT » SMALL, UGANDA FOCUS

Chris Ategeka, 30

Rides for Lives
Founder and CEO

BS and MS, Mechanical Engineering, University of California, Berkeley (2012)

Job Description

The "last mile" challenge of connecting rural dispersed communities and urban slums in developing countries to the public health-care infrastructure is one of the biggest opportunities for growth of our times. Particularly in rural areas, people cannot afford the time or money required for a several-day trip to the local urban center to see a physician. While community health-worker programs have been implemented and are improving health in developing countries around the world, these mobile health workers do not have any level of specialty close to a physician's and cannot give treatment. There is a critical need to simply, affordably, and quickly connect trained medical attention to people in rural areas who are facing a complicated birth, illness, or injury. Rides for Lives manufactures locally sourced mobile health clinics that combine pharmacy, general practice, and lab tech services, and provide ambulance services to hospitals to complete the last connection for access to health care in East Africa. Rides for Lives operations are based in Uganda where about 88% of people live rurally, and on average, only one in ten people seek medical treatment when ill.

Chris Ategeka founded Rides for Lives in 2011 and continues to serve as CEO for the company. Rides for Lives maintains offices in San Francisco, California, and Kampala, Uganda. Rides for Lives currently operates a fleet of medical vehicles outfitted to bring the amenities of an urban physician's practice to the countryside. Their flagship vehicle was a refitted bus containing a World Health Organization (WHO)-standard fully stocked pharmacy with a full-time pharmacist; a general practitioner's office with a full-time physician; and a medical lab with staff who perform tests for infectious and chronic diseases, offer family-planning services, and provide preventative care. The units can provide care in rural communities and also act as ambulances to bring people from rural areas to hospitals for more intense care. In addition to buses, they also have an adaptive motorcycle with health services, and they are currently designing repurposed drones to provide medical care to areas without easy ground access. The drones are an exciting project for Chris; he has helped design them to carry five pounds of medicine, supplies, and test kits from a centralized hospital out to mobile health units.

In the past, Rides for Lives was a charity that primarily used donations and competition winnings to give away bike and motorcycle ambulances to Ugandan hospitals, NGOs, and government clinics. In 2014, they changed their business model to be self-sustainable by selling mobile health units where the health workers running them charge their own fees for services, slowly repaying the price of the unit. Owing to his technical background, Chris spends a significant amount of time designing and manufacturing the repurposed medical vehicles, as well as developing new strategies for health-care delivery. He is also a lead salesman and fundraiser and attends conferences to present his work. He spends much of his time writing grant proposals and attending meetings with foundations, work that he admits can be tedious at times. However, seeing a baby born on one of his mobile health units or a patient leaving smiling and happy reminds him it is well worth his efforts. Chris visits Uganda regularly to check in on the program. His impact extends beyond improving health in rural communities. Because people who are treated by Rides for Lives health workers spend less time being sick, they have more time to pursue economic activities. Additionally, Rides for Lives provides better access to economic opportunities by creating microbusinesses and entrepreneurs. Their mobile health units are a stable source of income for their operators.

Although Rides for Lives is his main focus, Chris is also the cofounder of Privail, a company dedicated to creating innovative health-care devices to track and detect diseases such as HIV. With the assistance of cutting-edge nanotechnology, Privail aims to provide simple and affordable in-home tests to both developing and developed nations.

Career Trajectory

Living in Uganda, Chris was orphaned around the age of seven by parents who had HIV/AIDS. He soon became the head of his household and caretaker to his four siblings, an experience he credits for his leadership abilities. He constructed a mud hut for them to live in and worked in gardens weeding, harvesting, and grazing animals in exchange for food and money to support his family. One horrible day, one of Chris's younger brothers fell very ill. Chris and his other siblings tried to carry him to the closest hospital, which was many miles away. He died in their arms as they struggled to get him to a doctor who could have saved his life. This was the sad moment when the seed for Rides for Lives was planted in Chris's mind.

> It is all about passion. I honestly believe that passion is what you need to be really successful in anything you do. You have got to find out that thing you really, really love.

When Chris was around twelve, he was sent to live with his uncle, a farmer who decided to make use of his nephew as a human scarecrow. Chris stood for hours in a crop field as dawn broke, throwing rocks at predatory birds, chimpanzees, and baboons until it was time for him to set out, barefoot, on his hours' long walk to school. One day when he was about fifteen, Chris ran away to Fort Portal to talk to Y.E.S. Uganda, a youth encouragement program, who he heard could help him pursue further education. After helping him get better schooling in Uganda, two benefactors of Y.E.S. supported him to attend a small college in California and then UC Berkeley for his undergraduate education. While still an undergraduate, Chris won a $25,000 award for undergraduate research and used the money to found Rides for Lives. He went on to pursue a PhD in mechanical engineering from Berkeley, but he is currently on a leave of absence to devote all his time to Rides for Lives.

Chris believes talent is universal, but opportunities are not. He has met equally intelligent people in New York and Uganda, but those in Uganda simply did not have the resources and opportunities available to them to make use of their talents. In the future, Chris hopes to pay forward the opportunity he was given by connecting talented people with opportunities otherwise outside their reach. His professor at Berkeley served as a mentor for his dreams, and Chris hopes to mentor similarly in his life. Chris's work is deeply integrated with his personal life: his passion is his work. Chris believes in an X-Y-Z axis of brain, heart, and work and describes Rides for Lives as the intersection of those three axes. He would not describe his job as work, but rather as passionate service for others. It is easy for him to be answering emails at 3:00 a.m. because he lets his passion for Rides for Lives flow.

Looking to the future, Rides for Lives will continue to have a very important, central role in Chris's life. He has learned invaluable lessons from mistakes and successes and is constantly looking for the next challenge. Developing mobile air health units is an innovative step that will require Chris's passion to succeed. And while he loves his home country of Uganda, Chris recognizes the global nature of the problems he faces. Through it all, he has kept an open mind. Life is not flat to Chris, but rather a series of ups and downs—and both are necessary to innovate, learn, and succeed.

⚙ Arjav Chakravarti, 34

Dasra
Associate Director | ~$55,000 – 65,000

PhD, Computer and Information Science, Ohio State University (2004)
BE, Electronics Engineering, University of Mumbai (2001)

Job Description

India is a country on the move. Life has improved significantly for millions of people, but there are millions of others who have yet to see the trickle-down effect. Social change that impacts the lives of 1.2 billion people takes a while to spread. India has a long history of philanthropy and social work, but even with the best of intentions, most social organizations struggle to grow and have a larger impact. To fill this need, there has been a rise in catalyst organizations: ones that take a small social venture with a dedicated corps and endow them with connections, information, awareness, training, and capital that they would be otherwise unable to find. Catalyst organizations rapidly speed up the development of social ventures by creating positive, powerful ecosystems for growth. Moreover, they provide avenues for funders to direct capital and effort toward credible organizations that will create sustainable social change, thus avoiding potential pitfalls like internal bureaucracy, external corruption, or long-term insolvency.

Dasra, one such catalyst organization, empowers social ventures by building partnerships between diverse stakeholders in the social sector of India. Stakeholders in India's social sector include philanthropists and corporations that fund good causes, nonprofits and social businesses that work in a variety of sectors, various levels of government, and a media that provides coverage of critical issues. Dasra builds partnerships among a range of stakeholders to bring together knowledge, funding, and people to catalyze social change.

Arjav Chakravarti plays a critical role within Dasra: he oversees impact assessment, systems, and operations. Impact assessment is the method by which Dasra both sets its bar and achieves its goals. Dasra constantly helps other organizations build short- and long-term strategies to tackle the issues being faced, as well as metrics and tools that help gauge progress and ultimately success along those strategies. Arjav's role in impact assessment is not limited to extrospection either. Dasra frequently uses similar practices internally, setting their own ambitious goals and established criteria for achieving them. Dasra must be ambitious with their goals as they work in a country where 800 million people live on less than two dollars a day. The role of technology is critical to Dasra's and its partners' ability to achieve scale, which is why Dasra's technology systems and operations are a significant area of focus.

Dasra's ambitious goals and meaningful impact are what attracts Arjav to the line of work. Being surrounded by dedicated, highly committed people from all walks of life with deep experience of both the corporate and the social sectors is one of the most satisfying rewards. The downside of working on impact assessment is being far from the frontlines of social work, but Arjav relishes the opportunity to connect with his colleagues and experience their stories. The work is demanding, but that does not dim the excitement of facing up to the challenge.

Career Trajectory

After earning his bachelor's degree in electronics engineering in India, Arjav came to the United States and earned his PhD in computer science from Ohio State. Arjav started his work in the information sector at MathWorks, a leading developer of software for data analysis and simulation. He worked for them as a software engineer and then as a marketing manager. While working for MathWorks in Boston, he became involved in the local chapter of the Association for India's Development, a not-for-profit development organization dedicated to his home country. After a few months, Arjav discovered his passion both for social development and his home country. In 2011, after ten years in the United States, he returned to India to earn an MBA, specializing in social entrepreneurship. Shortly after graduating in 2012, Arjav joined Dasra and has not looked back.

Volunteer work helped Arjav appreciate how challenging the social sector could be, that there were several inspiring leaders already creating change, and that with some support they could achieve so much more. Arjav credits his volunteer work as the impetus for his career and discovery of his passion; he only wishes he would have started sooner. He is excited to apply his passion and expertise to his work at Dasra. The social sector benefits from professionals that have honed their skills in academics, government, and corporate sectors. Arjav's skills have been instrumental in addressing challenges for each of the organizations with which he has worked. While Arjav's skills and experience have made it possible for him to gain credibility despite switching midcareer to the social sector, he credits the connections that he made over time with helping him move forward in his life's passion. Advice from peers has proved invaluable to gaining the confidence to take risks without being foolhardy, risks that have had incredibly rewarding experiences as their payoff.

Looking twenty years into the future, Arjav is sure he will remain in the social sector, possibly doing the same work he is today or something completely different. He wants to be part of an innovative organization, building teams and relationships with others in the sector. Beyond that, he will let the dynamism of the social sector help him determine at different points in time where and how he should spend his professional life.

> Think about what you want to do and then take the plunge into the social sector with eyes open. Even if you do something completely different later on in your career, you will be enriched by what you gain in humility and the ability to achieve more with less, all of which will shape you into a better professional.

♥ Vineeth Vijayaraghavan

Solarillion Foundation | Director of Research and Outreach
Panchabuta | Founding Editor

MS, Electrical Engineering, Ohio State University (2003)
BE, Electronics and Communications Engineering,
University of Madras (1998)

Job Description

The information technology (IT) industry has transformed India's image from a slow-moving bureaucratic economy in the late twentieth century to a nation of engineers and entrepreneurs in the early twenty-first century. The IT sector in India now generates 2.5 million direct employment jobs, and all the major players in the international IT sector are present in the country. What can India learn from the success of the IT revolution and apply to other industries? Will biotechnology be the next industry to take off in India? Data informatics?

Vineeth Vijayaraghavan believes solar energy is the next frontier because of advances in sensor-based technology, development, and the availability of low-cost hardware, energy-efficient and low-power portable computing technologies, and the emergence of microgrids. These advances have opened up many exciting research opportunities and Vineeth knows that in order to make solar energy take off, he needs to bring together technical knowledge of solar energy, regulatory regimes, and socioeconomic challenges. Therefore, he founded Panchabuta in 2010 and the Solarillion Foundation in 2012. Panchabuta is a website that is now one of India's leading sources of information on renewable energy. Solarillion Foundation is a nonprofit research, outreach, and education organization supported by Panchabuta that seeks to enable a wide spectrum of individuals and reputed organizations to take solar energy and its awareness to college students. Solarillion encourages and mentors highly motivated undergraduate students interested in research in the emerging areas of renewable energy and sustainable engineering.

As the editor of Panchabuta, Vineeth covers the sector with the intent to bring news, insightful analysis, and commentary to local and global audiences. As an independent online resource, Panchabuta also focuses on policy making in the clean-tech and renewable energy space in India and provides valuable inputs to various organizations and stakeholders in the ecosystem. As the director of research and outreach for the Solarillion Foundation, Vineeth encourages and mentors highly motivated university students, individuals, entrepreneurs, and organizations interested in research in the emerging areas of renewable energy and sustainable engineering. He leads a small research team that has conducted policy research for state governments, looking at the impact of solar power on agriculture and microgrids for alternative power management, distribution, and improved energy-consumption tracking.

Vineeth also mentors student teams, such as a team of five undergraduate students investigating a proof-of-concept prepaid energy meter. The cost of hardware and service on power meters make them unviable on a large scale for resource-constrained contexts, and Vineeth's student teams have met incredible success: the power-meter team submitted and won best poster at MIT's International Conference on the Internet of Things 2014. Another project Vineeth mentored was a hybrid battery charging system using solar photovoltaics and a utility grid. For this project, Vineeth guided a group of university students and partners through developing and implementing a hybrid design of a battery charging system. The system was designed based on a novel algorithm to couple existing solar PV charging and utility supply charging systems. Vineeth made sure the system was designed to suit a typical Indian scenario where there is intermittent power supply due to power shortages.

Vineeth seeks out students from local universities and partners them with local businesses as a professional development opportunity and research experience for both sides. Though much of the work is currently volunteer-based and lacks proper funding, there is still an exploding number of applicants each year: 450 last year and 550 this year. Much of his work and the projects he oversees are devoted to local nonprofits and social organizations that bring research into the social impact and development sector. Vineeth is highly motivated by his opportunity to just continue learning from a variety of valuable stakeholders with a diversity of opinions and skills. The wide variety of teams enables Vineeth to tackle difficult social problems.

Currently, government subsidies and research contracts fund much of Vineeth's work. He has narrowed down earning funding to a science—highlighting his team's mastery of technical skills, regulatory compliance, and social impact. However, relying on government grants is something he realizes may not be scalable. Much of Vineeth's time is devoted to investigating new, scalable business models with growing numbers of people; he is particularly interested in scale by replication. Because there is so much room to grow, Vineeth enjoys a tremendous amount of freedom in his work on both the business and technology side. Occasionally, because of limited funding, they cannot follow through with their ventures to completion; therefore, the social impact is limited. The constant innovation, however, drives Vineeth forward. While Vineeth spends almost ninety hours per week building Solarillion, he does not see it as difficult or overwhelming because of the variation in his work.

Career Trajectory

Although his academic focus was in engineering with an MS in electrical engineering from Ohio State and a bachelor's degree in engineering in electronics and communications from the University of Madras, Vineeth made sure to carve out time to audit business classes. In his business classes, he learned from key business mentors to grow his venture from just a small research firm to a consultancy with the potential to connect students, government leaders, and business visionaries to tackle new challenges in energy. Vineeth graduated from Ohio State in 2003 and soon after took notice of the entrepreneurial boom in solar energy. Vineeth saw the success of the IT industry and wanted to replicate it for the renewable energy sector. He also wanted to deeply integrate students and revolutionize the curriculum, leading him to decide upon creating a bridge between academics and research careers.

To maintain an income, he worked for several companies after graduate school. After moving back to India in November 2004, Vineeth worked for a product startup company called Synaptris Decisions, starting out as a business development manager and then moving on to become a product manager, overseeing the product road map and owning the outbound product management role while working with key customers during that period. The product that was developed was an online reporting and business analytics product developed for business users.

However, on the side he explored a number of opportunities leading up to 2011, when he attended a conference for young innovators working on clean energy that was sponsored by a bipartisan group of politicians working to understand the impact of clean energy. Vineeth was the only outside expert to attend the ten-day program in Washington, DC; Ohio; and California; learning the context of different environments and the needs of different engineers. He recognized the need for an independent organization without ties to companies or governments and therefore founded Solarillion in India in 2012.

Vineeth often works on the weekends because that is when his students are most available. He then takes his "weekend" on Monday and Tuesday, which gives him valuable time to get Panchabuta work done. Balancing work with personal life depends on how his work is going; he often works eighty to ninety hours per week, but part of that time is spent meeting people, developing relationships, and learning—none of which he considers work. If Vineeth had to start over again, he thinks he would have enjoyed completing his undergraduate degree in the US where there is more room to innovate. Then he would have skipped his master's and gotten right to his current work. In the future, Vineeth hopes to continue growing his mentorship for students and professionals interested in social entrepreneurship and renewable energy.

Willow Brugh, 31

Geeks Without Bounds
Executive Director

BS, Sociology, Indiana University (2007)

Job Description

Self-declared geeks, nerds, and dorks, do not fret—the real world has a place for you, and you can find it. Seeking your role in service to the unheard needs of others can help you find your niche in the field of social innovation. By being original, exploring, taking random opportunities, and constantly reflecting in order to learn quickly, you can excel and find your way to empowering otherwise marginalized communities. One successful self-declared geek out there used her computer, community-building, and communication skills to co-run a business that helps others develop their own social ventures! She cares about developing tools to help improve the human condition and gathers other geeks together to help develop and implement them in the field. This innovator is Willow Brugh, cofounder of Geeks Without Bounds (GWOB).

Willow, along with Johnny "Diggz" Higgins, started GWOB to provide ways for geeks to also do some good in the world. During her tenure as the executive director at GWOB, from 2010 to mid-2014, she described her role as "traveling the world teaching geeks how to use their powers to make the world suck less." In other words, at GWOB she made speeches to talented people with technical skills, organized and facilitated collaborative events to gather them and come up with great ideas for social issues, and mentored them to turn these ideas into real solutions. One type of event she continues to organize is hackathons, twenty-four– to forty-eight–hour events where end users explain a humanitarian problem to a diverse group, and then everybody there works together to develop prototypes to help first responders and others directly involved envision the role of technology in changing their work. While other organizations similarly organize hackathons and these types of events, many do not go anywhere after the event; this is where GWOB continues to have their niche.

Twice a year, GWOB takes a group of promising projects (those they believe have the potential for greatest impact) from hackathons and brings their creators into a six-month mentoring program to turn these ideas into reality. The six months of mentorship include field experience, connection to existing organizations to reduce redundancy, technical development, help with security and human rights awareness, business development and legal container formation, and pitch refinement to better explain ideas to people who might become partners or investors. Over the course of the six months, project teams start a business (often a nonprofit or benefit corporation), get hired as a team by an existing organization, or sell their project onward. In most cases, graduates of the six-month, intensive mentorship continue to be active in the GWOB community, both getting support and providing mentorship to other teams.

Past GWOB Accelerator participants include Taarifa, a FLO infrastructure tracking platform used in Tanzania; My Results, a collaboration between Sexual Health Innovations and the Baltimore City Health Department to create an open-source platform to deliver STD test results online and by phone via an automated voice-response system; Bachchao, a distress beacon, sexual assault map, and police accountability tool in Bangalore; and Red Cross Disaster Incident Content Management System, a streamlined incident reporting framework for the American Red Cross of Greater Chicago. For the Red Cross project, through digital forms for paperless processing, a database storing the information, and a web application to visualize that information, the goal is to give the Red Cross a greater ability to analyze their internal operations; forecast, plan, and predict incident occurrence; and educate the public about their services and how the public can help assist in their operations.

Willow's day-to-day life includes giving speeches, traveling, and working with the groups that GWOB mentors via email. Each group receives support virtually through video conferences and email where the team's designated mentor advises them, encourages them, holds them to delivering on their amazing ideas, and connects them with the global community of responders who can aid in tool learning, maintenance, and further development. With Lisha Sterling now acting as executive director of GWOB, Willow continues her work through the Center for Civic Media at MIT, the Berkman Center for Internet and Society at Harvard, and as a professor of practice at Brown University. GWOB has been supported by organizations such as Tropo, Splunk, HP, and Netsuite, who commission subject-specific hackathons and provide funding to help run the business in return for high partner visibility and being plugged into cutting-edge, responsible, digital humanitarian efforts and summits.

> Everything you create and do has some effect on the social fabric. Being cognizant of and intentional in that effect means you can do beautiful things.

GWOB's social innovation is done by expecting people with technical skills to deliver tools that close technological gaps instead of increasing them. That means GWOB expects them to listen to and uplift the populations they aim to serve through solidarity, rather than charity; they also expect everyone involved to be able to support themselves from the outputs because philanthropy is not sustainable for the philanthropist and can be undignified for the "beneficiary." GWOB assesses the impact of projects by the ease of interaction in desperate situations and how many more people can be the architects of their own fate. Willow's favorite part of her work, both at GWOB and at Aspiration, is when people are truly able to listen to another person's needs and to put their skills in service to that need. The thing she dislikes the most is when "it is just policy" blocks necessary work from getting done.

Career Trajectory

Willow loved school. She took a variety of classes that she found fascinating, always seeing an expression of a skill through any topic. She considers herself lucky that her interests eventually combined into a "degree-shaped transcript." As an undergrad, she used to run a dark dance night with friend and roommate Libby Bulloff. That, along with a monthly transhumanist discussion group, taught her about event organization and facilitation, a skill she uses on a daily basis and often for pay. Working through school was important for her. "It is essential to me to remember what reality is like, to have calluses on my hands and a proverbial hanky in my pocket." Additionally, she got involved in hackerspaces/makerspaces because she wanted to start building a future and not just talk about it. She cofounded a makerspace in Seattle in 2009 to teach people how to get involved in building their own futures and to share her love of education, science, and technology. Hackerspaces and makerspaces are essentially creative, do-it-together community workshops where people can gather to create, invent, and learn. These community interactions gave her reason and direction for her passion for learning. It also honed her organization and facilitation skills from a monthly instance to an everyday reality.

In 2010, Willow wanted to attend Chris Pirillo's conference, Gnomedex, but she could not afford it. She tried to get a volunteer spot, but there were none left. Instead she was offered a spot as a speaker about "Transhumanism 101." She missed the speech after hers because she was catching up on questions. Over lunch, she caught up with that speaker, and that was the first time she met Diggz. He described to her his idea for Geeks Without Bounds, and she asked how he was going to make it happen. When he said he did not know, Willow told him how she would do it, and he offered to hire her. She says this sort of thing has happened for her several times. Life is always a strange series of fortunate events. Willow has been encouraged along her career journey by her incredible family, who completely support her desire to learn about things and take strange paths. She considers herself privileged that she has been able to go down non-lucrative paths that connect her brain and heart because her family is a safety net. She has also been able to live with not much money in the past because she has incredibly supportive personal networks to which she contributes and which support her. She is thrilled to now be in a spot to add threads to that same safety net.

On her career outlook, Willow says, "I still have no idea what it is I am doing." She sees the sorts of changes that need to happen in the world, and she finally has a shared language and framing to work from through Complex Systems Science. In this, both the grassroots communities she inhabits and the libraries and institutions she loves have come together in a continuum, rather than in tension. Willow used to bemoan that she mostly relates to people around projects rather than outside work; now she kind of loves it. She finds joy in all the things she does. Sometimes she goes completely off-grid, but she says she feels like she is just living, not balancing work and life. Being consistently, fully present has been a challenge for her, but one she is glad to partake in, regardless of context. The healthiest thing she has done to separate her professional and personal lives has been removing email and her laptop from the space she is sleeping in that night.

In January 2015, Willow became a community leadership strategist at Aspiration. She continues to be an affiliate at Center for Civic Media at MIT Media Lab and a fellow at Harvard's Berkman Center for Internet and Society.

Kate Chapman, 36

Humanitarian OpenStreetMap Team
Executive Director | ~$70,000 – $90,000

BA, Geography, George Mason University (2003)

Job Description

Humanitarian responders want to be efficient, so they need to know how to quickly get to people who need them. Getting around in an unfamiliar area can be confusing, especially when a disaster such as a flood or earthquake has struck, leaving streets and landmarks either moved or covered. Google Earth is a powerful innovation, but it can fall short of delivering free, collaborative, rapidly updating, and highly detailed maps of developing communities. With the help of hundreds of volunteers, Humanitarian OpenStreetMap Team is working to develop up-to-date maps for humanitarian response. Volunteers contribute to OpenStreetMap's open-source project by surveying with global positioning systems (GPS), acquiring digital photos of regions, and unifying existing public records of geographic data.

Just a few hours after the 2010 Haiti earthquake, the OpenStreetMap community began tracing roads from previously available imagery and continued to add in as new high-resolution imagery became available. Within the first month, over 600 volunteers added information to OpenStreetMap in Haiti, including data on transportation, education, health, water, and sanitation facilities. This provided the default base map for responding organizations, such as search and rescue teams, humanitarian mapping NGOs, the United Nations, and the World Bank. More recently, the Humanitarian OpenStreetMap Team (HOT) has assisted aid organizations in eastern Africa responding to the Ebola outbreak. It is crucial for aid response work to drive rapidly through the territory and quickly locate those infected. Detailed, accurate maps of the region are vital, which is why organizations such as Doctors Without Borders and the Red Cross are working closely with the Humanitarian OpenStreetMap Team to coordinate mapping and deliver maps to fieldworkers.

Kate Chapman oversees all of Humanitarian OpenStreetMap Team's operations as the executive director. Like many coordinating executives, she does not have a typical day but rather performs what needs to be done, such as managing staff and contractors directly, leading grant proposal writing and financial budgeting, fundraising, and delivering keynotes at conferences. HOT's board of directors sets HOT's overall goals, and it is Kate's main responsibility to lead the accomplishment of those goals. This includes managing the work plans, budgeting, and fundraising so that the organization is able to fulfill its mission. Kate would not immediately say that she is a social innovator or impact maker. Instead, she is simply following her passions—teaching technology, working on international teams, and studying geography—and letting that drive her social impact. She does realize the social capital that she is generating by observing the people who use her work; she is a part of the decisions they make and the influence they have on their community. For example, the government in Jakarta turns to maps produced by OpenStreetMap during times of flooding crises, and Kate takes enormous pride in her results. Kate is most proud of introducing people through public speaking to ideas around open source and open data who might otherwise not be aware of those ideas. Of course, traveling the world and meeting new people at every turn is also a reward for Kate.

Career Trajectory

After initially dropping out of high school, Kate pursued a computer science degree at a community college. She left school a second time because she devoted most of her time and energy to "side projects" with friends who were unemployed due to the 2001 tech bubble burst rather than to her coursework. To keep up with expenses while taking a break from school, she got a job with a mosquito control company, but on the first day realized she was allergic to pesticides. Rather than firing her, the company asked her to learn GIS (geographic information system) software to make maps for the field staff. She loved GIS so much that she switched to majoring in geography when she returned to school. Discovering this interest in mapping was key to her career, but having spent time in computer science gave her a firm programming basis, which was also important later on.

For her professional development, attending meet-ups and participating in open-source work have been key for her. After applying to work at FortiusOne and

> Do not be afraid to take risks. One of the phrases that I have the most difficultly with is when people say, "I have never done that before." Take the risk. Figure it out.

not hearing back, she made it a point to attend meet-ups where their staff would be. Finally, she met up with their team at a conference and landed a job with them. Being persistent and making sure to meet the right people have continued to be key. She never again depended on an anonymous application; instead, she seeks to make personal connections through meet-ups and social media. She met her cofounders for Humanitarian OpenStreetMap Team through an unconference and online mailing lists! These cofounders are now her good friends, and thanks to that and her dedication to her job, she has very little division between her personal life and work.

Looking toward the future, Kate has developed a love for nonprofit work as well as the challenges of managing a fledgling startup. The Humanitarian OpenStreetMap Team has benefitted immeasurably from her leadership, but Kate feels her future is not tied down to just one venture. Five or ten years down the line, Kate hopes to transform her experience into a consulting practice where she can participate in and advise a variety of ventures from all sub-disciplines of nonprofit work. She considers herself an open-technology generalist, always using her skills and directing her passions to the next project.

⚙ Alexander Nicholas, 39

The Lemelson Foundation
Program Officer

PhD, Neuroscience, Florida State University

Job Description

Jerome Lemelson was one of the most prolific inventors of the twentieth century. Jerome and his wife, Dorothy, believed that "invention and innovation were essential to economic success and vitality," and as a result, founded a nonprofit organization to promote that vision. Based in Portland, Oregon, the Lemelson Foundation seeks to strengthen the US economy and stimulate emerging economies by using the power of invention to inspire and educate new generations of inventors and support the launch of invention-based enterprises. To do so, it works with key partners to build, support, and enhance the invention and innovation ecosystem dreamed about by its founders. In order to maximize its impact, the foundation needs champions who are able to recognize global trends and strategically decide where and with which partners to invest. Alexander Nicholas, a program officer for the Lemelson Foundation, plays just that role.

Alexander designs and invests in programs that inspire inventors and entrepreneurs to launch products and businesses that strengthen the economy in the US and address the needs of the poor in developing countries. His responsibilities include finding opportunities to support the organization's strategic priorities, working with colleagues across functional teams, establishing and maintaining high-quality relationships with grantees in the field, and monitoring and assessing the impacts of each investment. For his role in building new partnerships, he represents the foundation at various meetings and conferences, which causes him to spend some of his time traveling. The ventures that emerge from Alexander's investments make an impact through the products and services they offer, and the programs he designs equip entrepreneurs with the skills, tools, and finances needed to take their businesses to scale.

Strengthening the invention ecosystem requires equipping inventors with world-class science and engineering knowledge, as well as the skills to create new solutions and translate those inventions into businesses that serve the needs of customers living in poverty. To this end, the foundation's approach is to support the creation of hands-on educational activities that equip students with the "inventor's tool kit": (1) the capacity to think critically and to identify solutions to real-world problems in the users' context through questioning, empathy, idea generation, and design process thinking; (2) a strong base of knowledge in skills necessary to invent; and (3) the ability to turn ideas into solutions through creating designs, fabricating prototypes, and incorporating entrepreneurial thinking. The foundation seeks to create the environments that spur local invention, innovation, and entrepreneurship.

One project Alex is supporting is in partnership with Rice University, University of Malawi Polytechnic, and Queen Elizabeth Central Hospital (QECH). Together, these organizations have proposed to establish an international, interinstitutional program to improve health care through invention. A key part of this program will focus on creating and implementing the "Nursery of the Future" at a target cost of $5,000 per district hospital. Students will be trained on how to invent technology solutions to outfit a neonatal unit in low-resource settings. The objectives of the program are to: (1) develop people through educational programs that give students the technical knowledge, entrepreneurial skills, and compassion to become global health inventors; (2) develop a sustainable process to generate and deploy new, high-impact global health technologies for low-resource settings; and (3) develop novel products to improve neonatal care in low-resource district hospitals in Africa.

The kind of social innovation that Alexander promotes falls at the edge of the mainstream because resource-constrained communities have needs that are not adequately addressed through traditional nonprofit approaches and emerging market channels. He and his colleagues constantly ask themselves how they can facilitate social change; this motivates them to think about how they can build the capacities and ecosystems innovators need to address the needs of the poor. Capacity building can be difficult to measure, but Alexander believes there is a growing recognition of value in an ecosystem that supports invention and innovation. The foundation is making an impact by creating those ecosystems, and he is able to see success through the products invented by the students, companies, and organizations that he works with. In addition to interacting with the foundation's direct beneficiaries, Alexander loves meeting the partners that make his work possible. Meeting these people is both gratifying and educational, and it is also his primary opportunity to learn how to more effectively identify what the real issues affecting social change are.

In addition to his work with invention-based businesses, Alexander manages a portfolio of grants, contracts, and partnerships with other organizations. He invests in all facets of the "invention pipeline," which begins from stimulating college students' interest in creative projects, research, helping innovative businesses get off the ground, and publicizing the careers of successful inventors. This means that he directs funds to the invention process from start to finish: inventions, inventors, and the organizations employing them (specifically, universities and hospitals). Alexander manages investments in higher education in the US and in student-led invention-based businesses in the US, Indonesia, Malawi, and India. One major partnership involves VentureWell, a higher-education network that cultivates revolutionary ideas and

> I would connect with more students from other disciplines. Early in my career, I interacted mostly with other scientists and engineers. If I could do something differently, I would reach out to others students and mentors in the business, public health, and other departments because I have grown to realize that great inventions and technologies alone are not enough to make a difference in the lives of the poor. A business perspective allows scientists and engineers to create more appropriate scalable solutions for the poor.

promising inventions. Supported through their partnership with VentureWell, the Lemelson Foundation provides emerging student startups with early-stage funding; helps collegiate teams with business strategy development, mentoring, and investment; and supports professors with funding for programs in tech entrepreneurship, opportunities for recognition, and entrepreneurship education, training, and networking.

Many innovations do not reach scale because they fail to account for the complexities of implementing a new technology in the developing world. To address this gap, the Lemelson Foundation and the Bill & Melinda Gates Foundation are partnering to provide venture development support to catalyze the creation of socially beneficial, scalable ventures for Grand Challenges Explorations (GCE) grantees as they develop their highly innovative solutions to grand challenges in health and development. This initiative leverages the BMGF's commitment to encourage scientists worldwide to expand the pipeline of ideas and to move forward promising candidate interventions; the Lemelson Foundation's history of nurturing ideas into inventions with the potential to reach people who can use them the most; and the VentureWell's substantial experience in training inventors to turn their ideas into self-sustaining enterprises.

Career Trajectory

Alexander received a PhD in neuroscience from Florida State University and then conducted postdoctoral research at Harvard Medical School and Beth Israel Medical Center. During that time, he served on the Harvard Postdoctoral Association Governing Board and was an active member of Harvard Biotechnology Club. For him, the social sector was not something he had envisioned for himself; he did not thoroughly understand how the skills and training as a scientist were applicable to social problems. He believes that participating in groups with a development focus as well as in science and technology clubs such as the Biotechnology Club and Consulting Club helped him get to where he is today. Engagement with these groups opened his eyes to opportunities to make a difference in both the local and international communities.

After his postdoc research, he went on to complete an American Association for the Advancement of Science (AAAS) Science & Technology Policy Fellowship. As an AAAS fellow, he worked on graduate education, industrial partnerships, and national innovation policies at the National Science Foundation. He also managed the work of the National Advisory Council on Innovation and Entrepreneurship's subcommittee on collaboration, which advises the White House and the secretary of commerce on innovation policy, and he co-managed the i6 Green Technology Commercialization Program. Prior to joining the Lemelson Foundation in early 2012, he served as a senior policy advisor in the Office of Innovation and Entrepreneurship at the US Department of Commerce. In the near term, Alexander is building a portfolio of investments that contribute to the strategic direction of the Lemelson Foundation. Ultimately, his goal is to support the development of inventions and innovations in low-resource settings around the world.

Alexander firmly believes he would not be where he is today without the guidance of mentors he had as both a student and research scientist as well as a professional in Washington, DC. In his words, "It is difficult to overstate the value of having effective and active mentors when you are a young professional." As an example, when in Washington, DC, he was fortunate to have mentors who were senior in their careers and took an interest in his professional development. More importantly, though, he had mentors that shared their time, providing feedback on his ideas and identifying other professional development opportunities suited for him. Alexander's wife also works in the social sector, which means both of their careers focus on making valuable contributions to the lives of some of the poorest populations in the world. The line between his personal and professional life is blurred for the better as they often share lessons learned over Sunday coffee and point each other to resources that help with their work. Both Alexander and his wife consider themselves fortunate to have careers exciting enough to integrate into their personal lives.

NONPROFIT » FOUNDATION

❤ Rebekah Neal

Bill & Melinda Gates Foundation
Program Officer, Global Health and Translational Sciences, Grand Challenges Team

PhD, Biomedical Engineering, University of Virginia (2010)
BS, Biomedical Engineering, Georgia Institute of Technology (2005)

Job Description

The Bill & Melinda Gates Foundation believes that all lives, no matter where they are lived, have equal value. To help realize this mission, the foundation focuses on the areas of greatest need in global health, development, and US education, as well as where the foundation's funds and advocacy efforts can bring the most value. Much of the foundation's efforts are aimed at people in developing countries who live on less than two dollars a day. In addition, the foundation seeks to improve the lives of the over one billion people in developing countries who suffer from infectious diseases that attract little donor funding, mainly because those diseases are rare in wealthier countries. The foundation's work targets many underserved populations, including those infected with tuberculosis, malaria, guinea worm disease, elephantiasis, and other neglected diseases. While some investors will invest only in what they know will succeed, the Gates Foundation has the opportunity to fund high-risk, high-reward ideas.

In the Global Health program, the Discovery & Translational Sciences team identifies, supports, and shapes scientific research and innovation that can have the most impact and that can accelerate the translation of scientific discoveries into solutions that improve people's health and save lives. Within the Discovery team, the Grand Challenges initiative provides an opportunity for innovators from around the world to bring their ideas to bear against the toughest global health and development challenges. Much of the Grand Challenges work at the foundation is done with partners, including government agencies and other donor institutions, by defining areas of urgent need, fostering collaboration among researchers, and building a global network of research initiatives and funders.

As a program officer on the Global Health Discovery & Translational Sciences team, Rebekah's work focuses mainly on the Grand Challenges program, a family of initiatives fostering innovation to solve key global health and development problems. Rebekah focuses much of her work on the innovation-focused small-grants initiative called Grand Challenges Explorations (GCE), which funds high-risk, high-reward ideas in the foundation's priority areas. She seeks challenges well-suited for the GCE program, gathers key stakeholder input about those challenges, collects teams of experts to review proposals, and works with partner organizations to build a success-oriented network. To support the Grand Challenges grant programs, Rebekah helps to build the innovation ecosystem that supports solutions for global public health and development. While much of her team's work and funding supports early-stage research and discovery that may be many years from changing or saving lives, they also fund projects on the delivery end, work that is much closer to impact. Regardless of the timeline, Rebekah celebrates successes with grantees and partners as well as encourages the innovators to fail early and often in their path to transformational change. She supports innovators and partners on projects ranging from basic science research to translational clinical studies to last-mile delivery challenges. At all stages, her work fills the pipeline with creative, exciting, novel ideas to change the lives of those at the bottom of the pyramid.

Most of the roles at the foundation are specialist roles, which require deep subject-matter expertise in malaria, TB, HIV, and other foundation focus areas. Rebekah's role is a bit unique in that she has the opportunity to work across many of the teams rather than focusing on a specific disease or platform technology area, providing her the opportunity to continue to learn a diversity of topics from some of the most intelligent and passionate scientists, engineers, and innovators in the field. The Gates Foundation's mission states, "All lives, wherever they are lived, have equal value." While Rebekah admits the cliché of that sentiment, she also deeply appreciates its true meaning. Even the smallest tasks she completes every day can ripple into life-changing developments for those living in poverty and suffering from the diseases that disproportionately affect the poor. Rebekah works hard to keep her work and personal lives separate (which sometimes results in long hours at work), but she finds that her home and family life is happier and more relaxing if the work stays at work.

132

Career Trajectory

While pursuing her PhD, Rebekah sought to learn everything she could about the different career options open to her, attending all the "alternative career" days and lectures that were offered and following up with connections she made there. She pursued an internship at a biotech startup through the NIH Biotechnology Training Program; there she tested out how she might fit in at a small research company while learning about the industry and academic opportunities in a new city. She worked there translating materials patented through her doctoral research into marketable products for stem cell research. During her postdoc, she continued to attend seminars and lectures in and outside her department that highlighted people with interesting career trajectories. In fact, one of her former colleagues at the foundation gave a talk about the Grand Challenges program to the department where she was a postdoc. Rebekah followed up with her after the talk and then looked her up when she moved to Seattle. The colleague helped introduce Rebekah to many of her contacts in Seattle in academia, in the biotech industry, and at the foundation.

> Learn as often as you can. Social innovation is a quickly growing field and is not really something you can read about in a textbook. Attend talks and networking events to meet people who are doing what you think you want to do and then nurture a few of those connections as advisors and mentors.

Rebekah attributes much of her success in her career to an openness to new opportunities and to knowing when to accept opportunities. Once she moved to Seattle, she quickly immersed herself in the biotechnology industry, from private companies to academic departments to nonprofits. Coffee conversations slowly turned to career discussions, which eventually matured into job opportunities. A strong technical background in biomedical engineering, with focus on problem-solving, design, and biomedical science, ultimately led her to a career at the Gates Foundation. Beyond gaining expertise in biomedical engineering, her academic background required Rebekah to communicate well with clinicians, scientists, engineers, and potential patients. Those communication skills and the breadth of her scientific background have served her well in her role on a cross-disciplinary team that works on a variety of problems and challenges in global health and development. Despite her good preparation for the Gates Foundation, it was quite an adjustment to transition from being a bench scientist to a desk job. In her academic years, Rebekah spent much of her time at the bench, working on tissue engineering and biomaterials solutions in the nervous and cardiovascular systems. Her transition to the foundation was a big shift in subject matter, from bioengineering to global health, and a big shift in day-to-day activities, from the lab to the desk and conference room.

A welcome transition, though, was the move closer to impact. Her projects in academic research were years, even decades, from translation to practice, and while much of her work at the Gates Foundation is focused on early-stage innovation and discovery, many of the projects she supports are much closer to making a difference in the field. From both perspectives, though, there is a real need for researchers, engineers, and innovators on the frontlines of global health and development. Like most, Rebekah is not sure exactly where her career will take her or whether she will continue to be on the funding side, or at some point make the switch back to benchtop science. She knows, however, that she would like to remain close to those making impact, either empowering them or working side by side with them. Looking back on her career thus far, Rebekah understands the experiential education was much more valuable than the coursework and degree requirements. The mission of the Gates Foundation is well aligned with her own passions, but she knows she arrived there partly by serendipity and good networking. Networking has brought her to where she is now, and confidence in her abilities has turned that network into opportunity. Openness to opportunity has brought her to her current career and discovering her passion. She will continue to be open to new opportunities throughout her career.

Steve Downs, 51

Robert Wood Johnson Foundation
Chief Technology and Information Officer | Six figures

SM, Technology and Policy, MIT (1992)
BS, Physics and Applied Physics, Yale University (1986)

Job Description

How do you get people to stop smoking? Smoking does not only harm the voluntary smokers but also harms the involuntary bystanders through secondary smoke. For example, at the individual level, you could distribute Nicorette gum and patches to smokers or start support groups. The Robert Wood Johnson Foundation (RWJF) seeks to effect country-wide change to improve health. Consequently, when they took on the challenge to lower smoking rates, they focused on system-wide measures, including advocating for policies such as clean indoor air laws and higher taxes on cigarettes. "We live in a vast world and a vast country, and if you really want to make meaningful change on large numbers of people, you have to think at a systems level and think about what levers you can pull to make the biggest difference," explains Steve Downs, chief technology and information officer for Robert Wood Johnson Foundation (RWJF). Robert Wood Johnson II built the family firm of Johnson & Johnson into the world's largest health products maker and established RWJF at his death with his shares of the company's stock. Now, RWJF is the third-largest foundation in the US.

Steve's role at RWJF is to decide how to use technology to do all the things that RWJF has to fundamentally do as a foundation: make good decisions, build networks, grow networks, exert influence, and spread ideas. Steve has a dual-track career at the foundation: he has done programming, which entails grant making and social change strategy on one side and management on the other. He continues to do both today but has a very clear management day job. Within management, his role is split between managing how they use technology and working with the senior management team to run RWJF. Steve's primary responsibility is to make sure that RWJF aligns its technology use with the organization's mission and what they are trying to accomplish. Practically, this means that he runs an IT department with over twenty people where he mostly gives them broad directions and challenges on how they want to steer the technology ship as opposed to getting into details of specific projects.

From an organizational perspective, Steve's role is figuring out how RWJF as a whole can bring more data into the decision-making process. America's business culture has historically been very collaborative-consensus driven, i.e., people get together for meetings often and make decisions at those meetings. In the past, the information that people have had at the time they made their decisions was limited to meeting agendas or background material; however, after that, decisions have mostly been based on what is in the heads of the people around the table. With Steve's improvement in technology, the team can look up on the web what a specific project is doing, what comments are being made about it, what they are saying they have accomplished on their website, if there are other efforts out there doing the same thing, and if an evaluation has been done on the project before. They can make an informed decision on whether, and how, they should support the project further. Steve's actions translate to larger social impact because by improving the technology that enables people to access more information at the time of a decision, RWJF overall can make better decisions about what to invest in.

Steve loves working for an organization that is dedicated to improving the health of people in the US and has a good track record of making a difference on some of those issues. RWJF, as the largest philanthropy focused on health in the US, can do things on a large scale, which generally has national repercussions. There is such a variation in the amount of impact philanthropy can have, so knowing that you can always do so much better than you are doing is a real motivator for Steve to continuously improve. He is a generalist by nature and by training, so he also loves being able to get involved in a wide variety of interesting problems and challenges that utilize his different skill sets. One day, he is figuring out a strategy for introducing an internal social network and how to roll it out in a thoughtful way that maximizes its uptake. On another day, he is trying to figure out on a national scale how to make research on self-tracking data a viable enterprise. Some of the challenges are big and have social impact, and some are very micro and focused on how they do their work at the foundation. Steve's least favorite part of his job is the speed. Social change is hard and takes time, so he feels like he has been working on some issues for an extremely long time and wishes they would progress faster.

Career Trajectory

Despite having a really rough freshman year in physics, Steve did not give up. He was planning on studying electrical engineering but was struggling in physics. He stuck it out and earned his engineering degree. Steve got a couple professional summer jobs during his last two years in college, and the job he had before his senior year at a telecommunications company connected him with a company that had an engineering management development program for new graduates. Steve spent a couple years at different locations learning their business, learning different business units, and getting some experience. He then went to grad school for a technology policy program at MIT. He chose a technology policy degree because telecommunications (telecom) was a technology area that interested him greatly.

> If you do what you love, you are good at it, and you are working on important things, the money will take care of itself over time. Remember that you are going to be spending half to most of your waking hours doing work, and it better not make you miserable.
>
> Really focus on things like culture and anthropology and emotional intelligence. That stuff is so important. It is the difference between a contributing engineer and a senior executive.

A few months after graduating, Steve's MIT academic advisor invited Steve to a lunch meeting in Washington, DC, where Steve met somebody at the US Department of Health and Human Services (HHS). Through this meeting, Steve made a connection that landed him a two-year fellowship at HHS in Washington, DC. Then the Clinton administration came in and wanted to ramp up telecom. During a brief internship with a congressional subcommittee, Steve had worked with someone who encouraged the new head of the commerce department's National Telecommunications and Information Administration (NTIA) to take a look at Steve's résumé. NTIA was launching a grant program around the Internet and various nonprofit social service application areas, including health. Steve was hired to run the health aspect of their grant program. After a couple years, Steve became the director of the program. After eight years at NTIA, a mentor of his who had run the office where Steve had worked at HHS recruited him to work with him at RWJF. Once he got to RWJF, he realized that the organization was able to find spots for people who contribute value in different ways. Steve finds himself lucky to have had a bunch of different opportunities and to grow through the management ranks while at the same time being able to do the programming that he loves.

While working for the two US government departments, Steve found that there was a challenge around mistake avoidance. Due to the scrutiny often associated with federal programs, it was very important that he and his team did not "mess up." Additionally, the federal grant-making process can be fairly rigid, and it was difficult to invest funds strategically, except for designing a process that would lead to strategic outcomes. The program Steve was in was political from the get-go because support for it was a partisan issue. Political pressures lead to being safe rather than being bold. In contrast, at RWJF, his hands are less tied, and he has much more freedom to be creative in how he works with others to catalyze social change. He has a much wider range of tools to bring about social change than government grant making. Also, at RWJF, he feels in many ways you can be recognized for your creativity, boldness, and vision. When he shifted to RWJF, Steve felt, as one of his colleagues had predicted, like a bird being let out of a cage.

Steve enjoys the freedom of being able to do something personal while he is at work and deal with work while at home. Steve thinks this integration happened particularly due to smart phones since now you can reengage in work for a minute or ten minutes instead of going into work for three hours. Steve wishes he would have spent more time in communities that he is now trying to help in order to deeply dive into challenges and how things work. However, his wife, who is a social worker, has been a tremendous help, and she has always grounded him when his visions have started to stray from the realities on the ground. While Steve does not often have an exact plan for his next steps in his career, he knows he wants to be at the intersection of technology and social change. Throughout his career, he has always viewed new opportunities through that lens.

❤ Aydogan Ozcan, 36

University of California, Los Angeles
Professor | ~$175,000

PhD, Electrical Engineering, Stanford University
BS, Electrical and Electronics Engineering, Bilkent University

Job Description

Professors work on the frontlines of research, creating and disseminating new knowledge while educating the next generation of innovators. While traditionally professors stayed in their ivory towers teaching in classrooms and doing research in a lab, their role has now evolved to reach out more into the real world. Globalization has led to better awareness of global concerns as well as more research being conducted to address these challenges. Professors are often at the forefront of solutions to global challenges because they have the academic freedom to explore with their research and be innovative with relatively few constraints. An extra spark for professors to take on global challenges and be innovative was provided by the Bayh-Dole Act of 1980, which allows them to own patents for their inventions. Dr. Aydogan Ozcan, owner of twenty-seven issued patents and over twenty pending patent applications, embodies the innovative spirit of professors as the chancellor's professor at the University of California, Los Angeles (UCLA), and an HHMI professor with the Howard Hughes Medical Institute.

Dr. Ozcan has observed that great social innovation often happens when the technological trends of the developed world intersect critical needs of the developing world, such as with the fields of telemedicine and mobile health. The cost of cellular phone technology has reduced significantly over the last decade, and as a result, cell phones are now commonly used in the remotest corners of the world. The technical capabilities of cell phones are rapidly improving, and almost anyone can access a technological platform with significant computational power and the ability to run various applications. As an expert in the fields of design and biomedical device physics, Dr. Ozcan sees the rise in cell phone access as an incredible opportunity to create technological solutions to global health problems. By devising ways to transform cell phones into point-of-care diagnostic tools, sensors, and microscopic imaging applications, he can ensure health-care professionals have new ways to fight infectious-disease epidemics, such as HIV/AIDS, tuberculosis, and malaria.

As a professor at UCLA, Dr. Ozcan teaches classes, conducts research, and makes his findings publically available as an author on several manuscripts for various journals and conferences. In three undergraduate courses—electromagnetics, engineering physics, and lasers in biomedical applications—he has encouraged students to participate in interdisciplinary research and to obtain diverse backgrounds in STEM fields. He is also the author of a book, coauthor of more than 350 peer-reviewed research articles, and has received many awards for his innovative scientific achievements. He also writes proposals to secure funding for his groundbreaking projects and meets with students, scholars, and administration to gather support.

The Ozcan Research Group has made several breakthroughs in telemedicine and global health. Members of this research lab share a vision for creating new imaging and sensing architectures by using novel theories and numerical algorithms to simplify optical components. They create simple, functional imaging tools that are capable of addressing immediate needs and requirements within the realm of global health. The group's current portfolio of inventions includes a cell phone camera-enabled sensor that can detect allergens in food products, a smart phone attachment that can conduct common kidney tests, and a fluorescent microscope that can transform a cell phone's camera into a device powerful enough to detect nanoparticles or a single virus. This last invention has received critical acclaim from global health professionals and has particular value for the developing world where medical technology lags and facilities are extremely limited.

Research labs exist in academic institutions, nonprofits, government, and industry. At the head of every lab is a principal investigator (PI); Dr. Ozcan is the PI of his lab. Under him, he currently has nine postdoctoral scholars (a.k.a.: postdocs), then nine PhD students, one MS student, two research engineers, and thirty-three undergraduate students. Sometimes, he will also have visiting research scientists (from industry, museums, international labs, etc.) and/or lab technicians. Research labs typically meet as a whole weekly or biweekly to collaborate with each other on projects, provide feedback to each other, practice presentations for conferences, and/or discuss current scientific literature. Dr. Ozcan is in charge of advising everybody in his lab and guiding their research. Often, MS students, PhD students, and postdocs conduct their own research while undergraduates assist them. The PI can be very involved in the work of those in his or her lab or can take a more hands-off approach; likewise, PIs have varying expectations for each level of researcher in the lab. Many PIs have very high expectations of their postdocs because they are very close to becoming PIs. Dr. Ozcan even has high expectations for his undergraduate researchers; many of them have authored journal articles, presented research at conferences, and received prestigious awards.

> The depth and impact of what you technically do is extremely important; however, it is mostly wasted if you cannot present or write your results well.
>
> Impact comes with absolute academic and financial freedom.
>
> To cope with those moments of disappointment and failure, one has to balance passion with patience.

It is important for universities to share knowledge outside the institutional walls in order to educate a broader audience and improve communities. UCLA's mission is to create, disseminate, preserve, and apply knowledge for the betterment of society. Therefore, at times Dr. Ozcan's influence and responsibilities reach outside UCLA and can take him all over the world. For example, he was one of the speakers chosen to deliver a talk at TEDxBigApple, a TED Talk event hosted in New York City in 2012. In total, he travels around 200,000 miles every year to deliver guest lectures and seminars.

Dr. Ozcan loves the academic freedom and flexibility that his position at UCLA provides. This is a professional feature he deems to be truly priceless and is one of the biggest perks of his job. Additionally, he sees his research and field of study as having "the potential of creating a revolution," which is a massive motivating factor and driving force behind his efforts. His professional efforts are somewhat of a hobby in terms of how he treats it. It is difficult for him to draw boundaries between his personal life and work since they are highly integrated, and he finds entertainment through his academic pursuits.

Conversely, Dr. Ozcan dislikes the mentality of most of modern academia. He feels that the status quo tends to promote and defend mediocrity in various taboo formats. For example, the process for a professor to gain tenure at many universities is based solely on teaching and publishing; therefore, many professors, at least in some institutions, are neither encouraged nor rewarded for doing professional service or earning patents even though these are also very important. A mentality that is fine with how things are is detrimental when it comes to this important, emerging field. He sees these drawbacks as regrettable and unfortunate, but ultimately as a manageable part of the job. As long as he remains excited, passionate, and curious about his field of study, he is confident he will enjoy his time doing cutting-edge work.

Career Trajectory

Dr. Ozcan is quick to reference his educational background as the foundation for his current position in his own professional journey. A science high school in Istanbul for specially selected students, a private technical university (Bilkent) in Ankara, and graduate studies at Stanford School of Engineering provided and defined his core technical strengths in engineering. A postdoctoral research experience at Harvard Medical School gave him the touch for sensing and understanding important health-related applications and global needs. All of these experiences complement each other, and they together define who he is today, professionally, and drive his academic interests.

Outside his engineering skill set, Dr. Ozcan credits his development of technical presentation and writing skills as essential to excelling in his career. Also, federal agencies, such as the National Institutes of Health, National Science Foundation, Army Research Office, and Office of Naval Research, as well as nonfederal institutions such as the Howard Hughes Medical Institute provide unique funding mechanisms to support and protect young, junior faculty who have bold, risky ideas. They protect young innovators from other senior and well-established investigators and researchers, giving these junior scientists the financial means to pursue their research initiatives. Dr. Ozcan considers himself very fortunate to receive funds from these federal and non-federal organizations to find all the resources that he needed to test, implement and mature his ideas.

❤ Nigam Shah, 38

Stanford University

Assistant Professor of Medicine (Biomedical Informatics) | ~$150,000

PhD, Biosciences, Molecular Medicine, Penn State University (2005)
MBBS, Medicine, Maharaja Sayajirao University (1999)

Job Description

When you go to the doctor with a new symptom, the doctor decides upon treatment by drawing upon their knowledge from medical school, results of clinical trials, and what they have seen in their patients. What if the doctor could also draw upon what hundreds of other doctors have seen and learned? Even better, what if they could do this by clicking a few buttons? With the right algorithm, Nigam Shah argues that sifting through electronic health records (EHRs) can become a learning system for one doctor, an entire hospital, or a nationwide health-care system. To make such learning possible, his research focuses on combining machine learning and text-mining with knowledge encoded in EHRs to learn practice-based evidence from unstructured clinical data. The research that has come out of his lab has shown that by using unstructured data, it is possible to monitor for adverse drug events, learn drug-drug interactions, identify off-label drug usage, generate practice-based evidence for difficult-to-test clinical hypotheses, and identify new medical insights. Nigam and his team have also founded a company, Kyron, to create a search engine for doctors to explore the best treatment options right at the point of care. The idea for Kyron came out of Nigam's day job as a professor of biomedical informatics at Stanford University.

One example of an application of his research involves identifying eye inflammation in children. Children with juvenile idiopathic arthritis not only have inflamed joints, but often get eye inflammation. Unfortunately, the inflammation may not be identified in a reasonable time because symptoms may not show, children may not share that something is wrong, or they may not visit an ophthalmologist often enough. Nigam teamed up with a faculty member in rheumatology to search for risk factors that might provide early warning cues in a group of young arthritis patients. They applied automated methods and a customized algorithm to search over one million EHRs specifically prepared for research use at Stanford. They discovered that if the child also had allergies, their odds of eye inflammation were two and a half times higher than young arthritis patients without allergies. Nigam's published research on eye inflammation may help medical teams identify which patients are in critical need of keeping up with their eye exams.

In addition to his research, Nigam teaches a graduate class on data-driven medicine, mentors students in his lab, gives invited talks, and attends faculty committee meetings and conferences. With his plethora of responsibilities, Nigam keeps his work structured. He spends Mondays in his lab meeting with his students, removing obstacles for their research and helping set their research trajectories. He currently has seven postdocs, eight PhD students, three medical students, and then several undergraduates and affiliates. Nigam tries to keep all his meetings (faculty committees and invited talks) to Tuesdays and Thursdays. Then, on Wednesdays and Fridays, he engages in research work on what he is interested in—developing new ideas for using aggregate patient data at point of care, reading up on advances in the field, and devising new experiments to assess the reliability of inferences made using EHR data. He cannot always stick to this schedule because of the high demands on professors, but he does his best to keep his work structured.

Nigam's impact is focused mostly on making better medical decisions using big data. He hopes to measure his impact based on how many patients' treatments are altered because doctors could use data on similar patients. While publications and citations are the academic measure of his impact and could get him promoted, he cares deeply about improving medical decisions in practice. Nigam most loves his freedom of exploration in academia. At Stanford, if a professor has an idea, they can get money to try it out. If it is successful, they will teach you how to take it further. Exploration is encouraged, and they will let you try anything. Unfortunately, Nigam dislikes that United States academia has turned research into a business. Nigam is expected to cover the majority of his salary on research projects, but he has to do so much outside it (teaching, mentoring, speeches, conferences, and the list goes on) in roughly "5%" of his time. He loves his job but feels that the expectations on faculty members to do a lot of work for which they are not paid, or rewarded, is an ongoing problem. To combat the problem, Nigam keeps his ratio of the number of hours spent on his goals versus someone else's goals as high as possible.

Career Trajectory

Upon earning his medical degree, Nigam was planning to pursue a specialization in orthopedics. However, a family friend convinced him to apply for PhD research programs in the US, and Nigam ended up attending Penn State for a molecular medicine program. He brought a wealth of expertise in medicine to the table but did not know how to type when he came to the US—his first term paper for an immunology class was handwritten. Nigam quickly got up to speed, and in the year 2000, the human genome program hit popular press. Nigam got excited about the emerging game changer for medicine and lobbied his grad program community to let him do informatics research. Little did he know, Penn State was already creating an informatics program behind the scenes. Nina Fedoroff, a plant biologist, took on Nigam as her advisee and brought him into the new program. After several years of classes, two summers interning with IBM, and completing a thesis that evolved from analyzing data to reasoning about biological processes, Nigam graduated with a PhD in biosciences. Nina connected Nigam with people doing informatics in medicine at Stanford and gave up her invited speaker slot to him. This one introduction got his name out there to people at Stanford who ended up offering him a postdoctoral position in biomedical informatics.

> Do not take no for an answer—if anybody says no, ask why!
>
> Spend at least a year or two trying out different things after college—then take action when your desire to do something different consumes you.
>
> Find a mentor—you can find one by working for people you admire, whether that be as their intern or chief of staff or whatever, and find a person that will let you explore. In order to maximize your potential to find these people, you should to go to events at universities.
>
> Do not be afraid to ask for help—if you go to people you admire with well-formed requests, people are quite generous.

After his postdoctoral work, Nigam was not sure if he wanted to stay in academia, so he took a staff scientist position with the Stanford University School of Medicine. He conducted research on improving the success rate of in-vitro fertilization, figuring out if variants in the embryo could signal disease and should therefore not be implanted. He was one of the early members of the team at a company that is now called Natera. This work solidified his interest in clinical informatics, and after a few years, he and his wife decided it was time to settle down; they had their first child, bought a house, and Nigam landed a faculty position at Stanford. Nigam found himself with the right expertise at the right time with his varied experience in informatics and the nationwide discussion on health care. He saw that doctors could learn something new from big data that they would not learn from one patient at a time.

Nigam has an intertwined work and personal life. He makes sure to be home at least four times per week before bedtime for his kids. One day every weekend, his family has a "no electronics day" where they go to the park or go for a hike. If he could redo his career, the only thing he would change is he would learn to code earlier on. In the future, Nigam sees himself continuing to work on analyzing EHR data but is also keenly interested in working out a better business model for academia.

Photo by Carnegie Mellon University

Bruce Krogh, 62

Carnegie Mellon University, Rwanda
Professor and Director

PhD, Electrical Engineering, University of Illinois (1982)
BS, Mathematics and Physics, Wheaton College (1975)

Job Description

The American university system is arguably the best in the world. Half the world's top one hundred universities are located in the US. These universities are increasingly growing their global footprint with the interconnected goals of providing their students a more global education and educating students in other corners of the world. While study-abroad programs, summer programs, and short-term faculty-led international programs are extremely common, there is another movement underway. Universities are establishing centers, or even sister campuses, abroad. Since developed countries already have well-established universities, US universities are increasingly focusing on developing countries. Texas A&M University has a campus in Qatar, American University in Cairo, NYU in Shanghai, and Temple University in Japan. Carnegie Mellon University, one of the most prestigious universities for technology education, has established programs in Porto, Portugal; Doha, Qatar; Adelaide, Australia; Guangzhou, China; and Kigali, Rwanda. This affords faculty to educate the best of the best students throughout the world where the graduates will play prominent roles in the future.

Africa has several of the fastest-growing national economies in the world, and large international players such as Microsoft, Nokia, Visa, Samsung, General Electric, and IBM have launched major initiatives across the continent. The government of Rwanda has made substantial investments in information and communication technology (ICT) to position itself as an attractive hub for companies to anchor their initiatives in East Africa. In 2007, the International Telecommunication Union, the United Nations agency for information and communication technologies, recommended establishing Centers of Excellence throughout Africa to cultivate the science and technological skills required for developing an IT workforce and expertise in Africa. Motivated to elevate global intellectual and economic vitality, Carnegie Mellon University became the first major US research university to offer master's degree programs taught by its own full-time faculty resident in Africa. The Center of Excellence benefits from the combination of Rwanda's bold ICT strategy and CMU's culture of innovation to provide a platform for students to become technology thought leaders in emerging markets.

As a location of Carnegie Mellon's College of Engineering, CMU-Rwanda now offers two professional master's programs in Kigali, the master of science in information technology and the master of science in electrical and computer engineering. Only about the top 5% of applicants are accepted. Students complete these degrees in two or three semesters in Rwanda, with a small number of students offered the opportunity to spend one semester at CMU's main campus in Pittsburgh, Pennsylvania. With an interdisciplinary environment and a focus on hands-on experience solving real-world problems, graduates from CMU-Rwanda enter the workplace with the experience and skills required to pursue creative, productive careers in Africa. CMU-Rwanda offers a stimulating and unique opportunity to study with faculty, researchers, and other MS students in East Africa, one of the world's most rapidly developing economic regions. In addition to selecting from a full set of courses in Rwanda, students can enroll in a number of technology enhanced, distance courses from CMU's Pittsburgh and Silicon Valley campuses. The curricula at CMU-Rwanda are strong in telecommunications, wireless networks, software engineering, mobile computing, data analytics, and energy systems, with a special emphasis on emerging ICT innovations and applications in Africa.

To ensure that Carnegie Mellon University's research and curriculum in Rwanda remain relevant to Africa, the faculty and students engage with local companies and multinational corporations on a continual basis. Companies that have recruited Carnegie Mellon University students for internships in East Africa include General Electric, IBM, Marriott, Microsoft, and VISA. Bruce Krogh, the director of CMU-Rwanda, believes that being present in East Africa is the only way to understand the region's technology needs and opportunities. Creating a long-term educational program is critical because it gives students time to analyze problems and develop solutions in the context in which they occur. In addition, Bruce says that it is important that students stay in East Africa instead of studying in the US or elsewhere. If Africa's best students leave to study abroad for two years, they become disconnected from the markets in which they want to work. At CMU-Rwanda, students remain plugged in to the region's rapidly evolving technical and business networks.

As director of CMU-Rwanda, Bruce Krogh oversees the academic programs and coordinates the collaborations with CMU's programs in Pittsburgh and Silicon Valley as well as with the government of Rwanda and regional companies and universities. On a daily basis, Bruce works with the faculty to help them deliver the best possible educational experience for the students and helps cultivate relationships with industry partners who sponsor internships and practicum projects, and who ultimately hire graduates from the master's programs. In addition to running the program in Kigali, Bruce teaches classes and conducts research as a professor for the university. His research focuses on the synthesis and verification of embedded control software, discrete event and hybrid dynamic systems, optimization of energy systems, and wireless sensor networks. In Rwanda, Bruce is focusing on energy systems research with an emphasis on smart-grid technologies for new off-grid and on-grid electrification. He has found that the absence of legacy power systems in Africa presents a particularly compelling opportunity to leverage the power of IT to realize energy systems that are truly agile, resilient, and both economically and environmentally sustainable.

Bruce's favorite part of his job is working with the students from East Africa. He is inspired by their enthusiasm and desire to develop their knowledge and skills so that they can be Africa's future innovators and leaders. His least favorite part is taking care of administrative details that take time away from direct involvement in teaching students and collaborating with other faculty members on research projects. Bruce's work-life balance has not been easy because starting CMU-Rwanda has been more than a full-time job. But his wife and he have thoroughly enjoyed exploring Rwanda, which is a beautiful country with near-perfect weather and remarkable variety, from the famous mountain gorillas in the Virunga Volcanoes National Park, to the Nyungwe Mountain Rain Forest, to the Akagera Game Reserve.

We all have some very busy and demanding weeks ahead of us, and there will be times it will seem there is no way to do everything that needs to be done. But I want to encourage you with two observations. First, it is only for a fixed period of time that in retrospect, after it is all over, is likely to seem like a brief time (really!). Second, in my thirty-two years as a professor at Carnegie Mellon, although I have known many students and colleagues who have found the load almost unbearable, no one has ever said to me that it was not worth it. That is pretty remarkable, but it is true. Being at Carnegie Mellon is a very special experience that stretches you to achieve and learn far beyond anything you ever thought was possible. So press on through those difficult times, and enjoy the camaraderie with your colleagues who are going through it with you. Many of them will be part of your professional network and personal friends for life.

Career Trajectory

In college, Bruce pursued a liberal arts degree, focusing on the things that came most easily for him. After earning a BS in mathematics and physics, he pursued an MS and PhD in electrical engineering, focusing on control theory with applications to power systems. Between his MS and PhD, he worked as an engineer in the Energy Systems Division of Westinghouse Electric Corporation where he designed and implemented software for utility energy control centers. Upon completing his PhD, he became a professor of electrical and computer engineering at Carnegie Mellon University. Early in his professional career, he received the Presidential Young Investigator Award from the US National Science Foundation and the Senior US Scientist Award from the Alexander von Humboldt Foundation. These awards recognized his commitment to research and encouraged him to forge ahead. Throughout his career, he has enjoyed the flexibility offered by being an expert in control theory, which is applicable to such a wide range of problems. His research and publications include applications in power systems, mobile robots, semiconductor manufacturing processes, automotive power trains, and aircraft control. In 2012, he became the director of CMU-Rwanda and has now been a professor for thirty-two years.

♥ Douglas Postels, 52

Michigan State University
Associate Professor of Pediatric Neurology | ~$160,000

MS, Epidemiology, Michigan State University (2015)
MD, Loyola University (1988)
BS, Microbiology, Indiana University (1984)

Job Description

In the US, the ratio of physicians to patients is approximately four hundred to one. In Africa, the ratio is one per five thousand patients. In low- and middle-income countries, large physical distances and poor public transportation and infrastructure are additional impediments to medical care access. While the presence of community health workers and new technologies such as mobile phone devices (sending pictures of ailments to far away physicians) are helping, increased numbers of qualified doctors are needed to improve the physician-to-patient ratio. Creating medical expertise is an enormous undertaking, and while considerable progress is being made, only so many health-care workers can be trained each year. Educating specialists is even more challenging. Where can a mother in rural Kenya take her daughter for severe epilepsy? Primary-care doctors do not have expertise in complex neurological disorders. Training programs for specialists are rare, and those trained abroad may not return to their homelands because of greater opportunities and better facilities abroad. Research expertise and infrastructure are rare in low- and middle-income countries, which may lead to a paucity of investigations into diseases most prevalent in these areas.

Douglas Postels is a pediatric neurologist who wants to have a larger impact on the health-care challenges of underserved communities. In 2010, Doug quit his day job running a successful neurology practice and accepted an appointment at Michigan State University. He spends five months abroad each year conducting research and practicing medicine. During his time at Michigan State University, Doug teaches clinical tropical medicine and pediatric neurology. He writes grants, authors papers, and mentors undergraduate, graduate, and international students. Doug's research interests are in the epidemiology and clinical care of nervous system disorders of children in sub-Saharan Africa. One of his current research studies is investigating the neurologic effects of malaria in African children. As a practicing pediatric neurologist, Doug's clinical work is with disorders of the nervous system affecting children. The most common of these include epilepsy, headaches, movement disorders, developmental abnormalities, and disorders of metabolism that affect the nervous system.

His work abroad is split between Uganda, Ghana, and Malawi. While in Malawi, Doug works in the largest public hospital in the country in a research unit focusing on uncovering the underlying causes and discovering new treatments for African children in coma. As a medical doctor, he does not perform surgeries, but he treats neurologic disease through medication, rehabilitation, and physical therapy. A typical day in Malawi begins by making rounds to check up on his pediatric patients. He spends much of the remainder of the day working on multiple research projects and scientific manuscripts, all at different stages of development. His research in Africa is funded by the US National Institutes of Health and Michigan State University. Others in his research group receive funding through the Wellcome Trust (the largest private medical funder in the world aside from the Bill & Melinda Gates Foundation). He teaches residents and college students at the University of Malawi College of Medicine, training the next generation of health-care workers. To him, the best part of his work is that it enables him to make a small difference for the children of Africa. He feels the research he works on may help children in the future, children he will never meet.

Career Trajectory

Doug's medical training includes an undergraduate degree in microbiology, four years of medical school, three years of residency in pediatrics, and three years as a postdoctoral fellow in pediatric neurology. His first experience in Africa came in 2002 when he took a year off to travel there. This was a very valuable experience, and he learned that he is okay living in less than ideal conditions. Doug went back to practicing pediatric neurology in the US until 2009, returning to Africa once as a visiting professor at the University of Malawi. In 2009, he left his permanent job in the US, joined Doctors Without Borders, and moved to the Democratic Republic of Congo. This experience was transformative, and Doug was hooked! During his time in the DR Congo, he was recruited by Michigan State University to join their faculty and become a patient-oriented researcher. While continuing his work at MSU, Doug is also completing his master's in epidemiology. He began the program in 2010 and plans to finish it in 2015.

Doug is very thankful for his supportive family. He explains that you need a supportive family to do this work, either a partner that is understanding of prolonged absences or one that enjoys travelling abroad. If Doug had to start his professional career over again, he would have begun his current professional life immediately after the completion of residency training, not after spending twelve years in private practice in the US. In the future, he hopes that his epidemiological and clinical research skills will translate into the ability to prevent and intervene more effectively in neurological disorders affecting African children. Though he has begun on a small scale, he sees huge opportunities to test more innovative strategies for improving the neurologic health of African children. He believes that this is a neglected area of study, and to his knowledge he is one of only two US–based pediatric neurologists working in Africa. Doug's wishes that pediatric neurologists will aspire to work in the developing world.

🛡 **Andy Vidan, 34**

Massachusetts Institute of Technology Lincoln Laboratory
Associate Technology Officer | Six Figures

PhD, Applied Physics, Harvard University (2006)
BS, Applied and Engineering Physics, Cornell University (2001)

Photo by MIT Lincoln Laboratory

Job Description

Humanitarian response to disasters such as Hurricane Katrina in 2005, the earthquake in Haiti in 2010, and the typhoon in the Philippines in 2013 can be very complicated. Hundreds of different humanitarian organizations scramble to provide food, water, and basic health care on a time-critical basis. With so many organizations working separately, they can overlap, providing services to the same areas while missing other areas completely. There needs to be a system for coordinating across these organizations to achieve the mission of helping people recover from these disasters as quickly as possible. This is one of the complex systems challenges that US national research labs try to address. One such lab is MIT Lincoln Laboratory where scientists and engineers are working to figure out how to best facilitate communication among responders during disaster-relief operations and solving other problems critical to national security.

A Department of Defense federally funded center, MIT Lincoln Laboratory has a focused commitment to building prototypes and demonstrating operational systems under live test conditions that meet real-world requirements. Unique from other research and development labs, the MIT Lincoln Laboratory takes its projects through their full cycle: from initial concept stage through simulation and analysis, design and prototyping, and finally field demonstration. With experts on subjects including cyber security, information technology, and physics working together in the lab, somebody needs to bring the technologies, people, social context, and disaster context all together. At the MIT Lincoln Laboratory, this person is Andy Vidan, associate technology officer.

When Andy first joined the laboratory in 2006, he began developing mathematical and physical models for homeland defense problems. This included calculating the rate of spread of infectious agents through buildings and transportation systems and developing sensor simulations to guide the development of novel chemical and biological sensors. He then transitioned to managing small teams of computational scientists, analysts, and engineers on several Department of Homeland Security programs. Andy subsequently served as the program manager and technical lead for the Distributed Disaster Response program and developed a cloud-based enterprise information system for professional emergency responders that is highly robust, reliable, adaptable, and affordable. The California Department of Forestry and Fire Protection (CAL FIRE) in Riverside and San Diego counties were the first to use the system in August 2009. A number of emergency response organizations across the nation have adopted this enterprise information system, as the Next-Generation Incident Command System (NICS), using it to coordinate small- to large-scale response activities. NICS is a web-based command and control environment for incidents that facilitates collaboration across federal, tribal, military, state, county, and local levels of preparedness, planning, response, and recovery.

According to Andy, no day is "typical" at MIT Lincoln Laboratory since they constantly work on new and innovative programs supporting a range of government sponsors and communities. He is excited to be able to work in a laboratory setting where the mission has real impact. After the September 11th terrorist attack and the subsequent anthrax attacks, MIT Lincoln Laboratory became involved in supporting the Department of Homeland Security on a variety of efforts to protect and defend the homeland. One early project Andy worked on was modeling a simulation of a biological terrorist attack on an urban area and developing the technology requirements necessary to support early medical response to such an attack. Andy served on the US Southern Command assessment team that responded to the Haiti earthquake for Operation Unified Response. Working in twelve-hour shifts around the clock, they provided the commanding general a daily comprehensive assessment of ongoing operations. Andy's specific duties included building a general framework to assess if operational objectives were being met through a formulation of indicators, measures of effectiveness, and measures of performance. Being embedded in an operational environment was an extremely unique experience that helped him bridge the gap between science, engineering, and operations.

144

Andy loves many aspects of his job, and having supportive management that encourages intellectual freedom is at the top of his list. He was fortunate to always have technical managers and supervisors that allowed him to define his own research path. Also, working in a true meritocracy where technical integrity is core to the culture has provided him an excellent work environment. Finally, he has truly enjoyed working in a "rapid development cycle," in tightly knit technical teams on full end-to-end engineering, designing, building, and demonstrating hardware and software prototypes. Unfortunately for Andy, along with the broader research and development ecosystem across the nation, risk tolerance (by the public) is fairly low, and therefore new, innovative, high-impact, but high-risk approaches are sometimes avoided.

> Get involved in as many hands-on projects as you can. Commit to going out to the field to gather data, directly interact with communities, and field test your concepts or solutions.

Career Trajectory

Andy powered through school for nine years, earning his BS degree in engineering physics from Cornell and then his SM and PhD in applied physics from Harvard. He was very dedicated to his studies and looks back wishing he had participated in organizations like Engineers Without Borders to get direct experience in humanitarian assistance and international development work. However, his dedication to his Ivy League education has paid off in landing him in his current job. Having a rigorous technical engineering background has enabled him to become a broad "problem solver." In the final year of his PhD, Andy worked as a research physicist at the US Army Natick Soldier Research, Development, and Engineering Center. From there, he was hired into the MIT Lincoln Laboratory and has loved it for the past eight years.

Andy Vidan learned firsthand the extremely complex, chaotic nature of humanitarian assistance and disaster-relief operations during rapidly evolving, catastrophic events in 2010 through responding to major wildfires in southern California, the Haiti earthquake, and the Deepwater Horizon oil spill disaster. These operations required coordination and command of thousands of responders from hundreds of agencies. Andy observed that these responders had inadequate communication capabilities and lacked real-time information and situational awareness (e.g., limited understanding of the location of incidents and widely dispersed crew, the location and spread of fire or oil, etc.). Responders were constantly losing time and put in potentially life-threatening situations because they needed to have frequent face-to-face meetings with each other in order to communicate. Sharing information quickly and effectively translates to saving lives, reducing loss of property and resources, and protecting the environment.

Observing these major disasters happening around the world served as a pivot point in Andy's career. Following the series of disasters in 2010, he transitioned to work on a new MIT Lincoln Laboratory program area in disaster-response technologies. More specifically, he looked to develop advanced technology solutions in support of large-scale crisis response and management. The program quickly partnered with professional first-response agencies across the country, and Andy participated in training and response operations to understand where the technical challenges are and to define end-user requirements for technology solutions. Andy enjoys developing advanced technology solutions that have a global impact, but he still enjoys an excellent work-life balance and spends time with his wife and kids playing sports, mountain biking, and exploring New England. In the future, he hopes to continue defining new concepts and strategic visions for a variety of problems.

Lina Nilsson, 34

University of California, Berkeley
Innovation Director, Blum Center for Developing Economies

Dr Sc, Engineering, Swiss Federal Institute of Technology
MS, Biomedical Engineering, University of Washington
BS, Chemical Engineering, Illinois Institute of Technology

Job Description

Interdisciplinary collaboration can catalyze meaningful social innovation. People with diverse perspectives, experiences, and skills must work together in order to understand—and design promising solutions to—complex global challenges in environment, health, or poverty. The Blum Center for Developing Economies is an interdisciplinary "think and do tank" that was founded in 2006 to create this multidisciplinary ecosystem at the University of California Berkeley. Every year, faculty and students from across more than eighty departments take part in the center's various programs with the goal of understanding and acting on global poverty and inequality. The programs also engage hundreds of community members, government and social sector leaders, and startup and industry experts.

This emphasis on cross-disciplinary collaboration informs all of Blum Center's flagship programs, including the Global Poverty & Practice Minor, one of the most popular undergraduate minors at UC Berkeley; the Development Impact Lab, a collaboration with USAID to more effectively spin out university technologies for "global good"; Big Ideas@Berkeley, one of the nation's oldest and largest student social innovation competitions; and new programs like development engineering, a PhD curriculum in technology design for social impact. As innovation director for the center, Lina Nilsson helps design and implement new components of these Blum Center programs and creates new initiatives that train and support the next generation of inclusive innovators.

In a typical week, Lina advances Blum Center strategy and programs. To gain insights that underpin this work, she also teaches and does her own research. For example, she helped launch the center's Development Impact Lab, a $25 million initiative that aims to make the design of science and technology solutions for global development quicker, more reliable, and more responsive to the needs and challenges of developing communities. In order to come up with new methods and best practices for the lab, Lina and her Blum Center colleagues work with over ninety teams of faculty and students with projects in thirty countries. The center supports these innovators along the entire arc of technology creation, from ideation to manufacturing and scale-up. The work ranges from developing new approaches for revealing user demands and needs to generating models for financial and environmental sustainability. In addition to working with specific project teams, Lina helps create programs that have broad reach: funding competitions, workshops, consulting hours, discussion salons, and other programs that ensure that development engineers across UC Berkeley have the training, research, and networks necessary to design, scale, and launch truly impactful projects.

The projects in the Blum Center's innovation portfolio target a variety of humanitarian challenges and include CellScope, a smart phone–based medical device that can be used to automatically detect tuberculosis and other deadly diseases; WE CARE Solar, which equips off-grid medical clinics in over thirty countries with lighting and electricity for lifesaving medical devices and mobile communication; and NextDrop, which was started by UC Berkeley students to provide timely information about water utility distribution and delays in cities with intermittent water supply. Toward the end of project life cycles at the Blum Center, successful initiatives are spun out of the university. For example, Endaga, which helps remote rural communities install independent, profitable cellular networks, has raised a $1.2 million in external investment and is now a for-profit serving multiple countries. Lina and the Blum Center's emphasis on connecting university innovators to relevant external networks helps facilitate such transitions from research to real-world impact.

Lina views her largest impact as rigorously preparing students to become the next generation of social entrepreneurs and development engineers. To facilitate these efforts, Lina launched "The Social Innovator OnRamp" to support student innovators and bridge the gap between idea development and off-campus impact. To identify best practices, tools, and networks, she first interviewed students, staff at incubators and accelerators, and technology and international development professionals. These interviews uncovered what kinds of skills and resources student innovators need and identified gaps in existing programs and services. Based on these insights, she developed a series of complementary pilot programs: a Social Innovator OnRamp class, an online resource guide, and a series of standalone workshops. She is now expanding these resources into a multiyear program, incorporating lessons learned from the pilots. This iterative process is typical of Lina's program creation at the Blum Center.

Another critical component of Lina's work is communicating the center's vision, programs, and research findings to an external audience. Her talks and publications have reached academic and professional audiences through peer-reviewed journals and conferences. She also reaches general audiences through forums such as *The Washington Post* and *The New York Times*, radio shows, and Science@Cal lectures. By working within both academic and nonacademic media, Lina is able to ensure that the center's work is relevant for a broad swath of stakeholders in the engineering and international development communities.

 Do not be too timid to reach out to experts. It could change your life.

Above all, whatever you do, do not fall into passively absorbing information: engage actively, practice critical reflection, and begin to develop your own path. As one small example, I challenge myself at every talk to know the answer to these four questions: (1) If I had to ask the speaker a question right now, what would it be? (2) If I could ask the speaker for help, what would I ask? (3) If I would offer the speaker help, what would I offer to do? (4) Where do I agree and disagree with the speaker, and why?

One of the things Lina likes most about her job is working with a talented, supportive team. Like the broader community of innovators with whom they work, the Blum Center team has a very diverse skill set; they are engineers, lawyers, international development practitioners, economists, anthropologists, and public policy specialists. This is great for each team member's intellectual growth and enables the team to achieve more complex goals—a must for social mission goals. For Lina, this diversity means that she must have a clear and nuanced understanding of the language and academic norms of a variety of disciplines so that she is able to effectively work with her team and communicate cross-disciplinary concepts to a broader audience.

Career Trajectory

Lina's PhD was squarely in the basic sciences and traditional academic engineering. Her thesis was on computer simulations of nonequilibrium protein structures. Even though she seldom uses the content of her dissertation anymore, she makes use of her broader engineering expertise every day. She also relies on approaches to problem scoping, quantitative critical thinking, and project execution that she developed during her PhD studies. After her PhD defense, she took one year to travel throughout Asia and South America on a Bonderman Fellowship. While she did not do any engineering, this time turned out to be an important turning point in her life that allowed her to think more critically about the role of engineering in society and the direction of her career. Sometimes, she realized, what you are good at (e.g., computer modeling) is not what you want to spend your career doing.

After this break, it took Lina several years of exploration—and hard work—to make the transition to her current field. She taught high school and took a lot of time to read up on topics across the social sciences and humanities that she had previously neglected. As she began to narrow in on her new interests around global social mission tech, she started to write and, eventually, get published across a variety of platforms. She collaborated with US engineers and Vietnamese medical doctors to develop a novel medical diagnostic tool. She also founded a tech initiative for building DIY science lab equipment using locally available supplies, for which she was recognized as a global innovator by *MIT Tech Review*. Eventually, all of these experiences coalesced into a permanent career pivot made possible by being undaunted by false starts (being a high school teacher), creating her own opportunities (writing articles, starting an organization), and frequently asking for support and advice from mentors.

Lina strongly believes in the Louis Pasteur quote "Chance favors the prepared mind." She therefore strives to meet at least one new person every week (e.g., someone from an interesting organization or a passionate student), regularly reads a number of diverse magazines and journals (e.g., *The Economist, Stanford Social Innovation Review, Science,* and *Nature*), and schedules one event every week that is not an immediate job requirement (e.g., an interesting lecture, a discussion group, or a meet-up). Lina also believes that a balanced, multifaceted life is a resilient, sustainable, rewarding life. She runs, bikes, skis, and for the last few years, she has led multi-week backpacking trips in remote wilderness regions of Alaska. She does not always succeed in an integrated balance between her professional and personal life, but when she does, she often finds that this is when she is the most creative and truly productive. Still, Lina does not know where she will be in twenty years. Snufkin, a cartoon character in the popular Finnish cartoon Moomin, has a few words of wisdom that she has taken to heart: "Everything is very uncertain, and that is exactly what calms me."

Photo by Penn State Photography

NONPROFIT » ACADEMIA

❤ Meg Small, 48

Penn State Prevention Research Center | Assistant Director | ~$100,000
Live It | Chief Social Science Officer

PhD, Community and Public Health, University of Maryland (1993)
MS, Community Health, University of Alabama (1989)
BS, Health and Human Development, Penn State University (1988)

Job Description

What do public health researchers (PHRs) do? PHRs use the scientific process to reduce disease burden and improve health. PHRs are generally cross-trained in life science, behavioral science, and quantitative methods. Since public health research is closely tied to public health practice, it almost always has a practical application. In practice, the application can take the shape of policies (mandated seat-belt use), campaigns (Strive for Five), programs (Life Skills Training Drug Prevention), or clinical guidelines (vaccination). PHRs work on a vast array of topics and in many different settings. As health behavior and impact become increasingly important to corporations, PHRs are expanding their roles in industry. At the end of the day, PHRs use science and technology to do as much as they can, for as many as they can, with the fewest possible resources. There is an emerging cadre of innovators who are leveraging insights in public health to develop and launch entrepreneurial ventures to take more direct action. You can have policies and campaigns and programs, but only a fraction of people will align with, comply with, or benefit from them. Meg Small is a leader of this cadre as a PHR at Penn State University.

Meg's work focuses on the prevention of health problems, including obesity and substance abuse, as well as the promotion of healthy development for children and adolescents. Meg is motivated to expand efforts to scale up and have real public health impact. To tackle these problems, Meg applies design thinking methods. The Prevention Innovation Lab that Meg directs hosts a team of undergraduate and graduate students that develop and redesign empirically grounded programs and practices. Meg and her team design products and services that improve the user experience for preventive interventions and enable public-private partnerships to increase efficiency and impact of resources. Current efforts include a platform designed to increase college student engagement in out-of-class experiences that advance personal and career goals. The team works problems through empathic inquiry (observation and interviews with the end user), ideation (generate, prototype, and test new ideas), and implementation (deploying innovations in context). Meg's team uses multiple methods to evaluate their impact. They try to get as close to behavioral indicators as possible (how did people use this) versus self-reported attitudes (what do people think of this).

So what does a public health entrepreneurial venture look like? Meg's work with the Bennett-Pierce Prevention Research Center has led to the creation of a spin-out technology company: Live It. Live It promotes an engaged lifestyle using venues and events throughout Penn State's broader region. Live It has an app that lists university talks, live music nights, cooking classes, sporting events, yoga classes, and other events happening in the broader Penn State community. While a lot goes on, many people either do not know about it or are overwhelmed by their options. Live It provides the platform for people to learn about and evaluate their options on how to spend their leisure time. It also promotes local businesses by listing their events and selling their gift cards through the app, which are a great way for parents to support their kids in pursuing nonalcoholic activities and which provide a profit for Live It to function. In Meg's technology startup, iterating quickly, identifying new opportunities, and deploying features with strong market potential are critical. The speed at which Meg's team moves through these cycles is much faster than in the academic setting. The outcomes are tangible success (revenue) or failure (no sales or investment).

Meg loves the flexibility and institutional support for innovation at Penn State. Her best days are spent collaboratively working a problem with her energetic team. Meg is also passionate about helping graduate students identify their interests and supporting them as they break new ground. She loves the pace at which they move at Live It and the creative ways they pursue opportunities. There is no bureaucracy, so ideas can be implemented and tested quickly. Seeing the impact of their solutions and collecting real-time data is very motivating to her. Although Meg acknowledges that embracing failure is a critical part of innovation, it takes her a very long time to get comfortable with and even longer to embrace the wisdom that comes from each failure. She also dislikes the major challenge of persuading others to invest time, money, or social capital because it is often difficult to secure traditional lines of funding (e.g., NIH). Often, her proposals are rejected by the scientific status quo because currently, new science is highly valued while the application of old science to solve a new problem in an entrepreneurial way is still making its way to mainstream popularity.

Career Trajectory

Straight out of graduate school, Meg became a behavioral scientist at Centers for Disease Control and Prevention (CDC). She analyzed large surveillance datasets and even oversaw the design and implementation of one. Her biostatistics work gave her great insight into how data and research could inform policy, funding, and the programs that are delivered in schools and communities. Meg was then asked to serve as a liaison in Washington, DC, where she infused data into government decision making. Her work in Washington, DC, gave her insight into how impactful government programs could be. She also saw the limitations—namely sustaining high-quality implementation after initial funding. Meg began interacting with people in other fields, such as business and engineering, to learn the methods they use to scale and sustain innovative solutions.

It was at that point that Penn State's Prevention Research Center was founded. After learning the Center's focus would be innovation and impact, Meg accepted a position there. Meg's major inflection point came during her first year working for Penn State when she entered an online executive education program at Stanford to learn the techniques of design thinking. Her coursework gave her a framework to apply her research, teaching, and entrepreneurial work. Letting go of traditional markers of success (e.g., grant funding) was the hardest and yet most liberating aspect of her trajectory.

Engage in as much science-based training as early as you can in your academic career. It is difficult (though not impossible) to get this training "on the job." Many of the world's problems and solutions have a scientific basis. Being well trained in one of these disciplines and in behavioral science for their application will be useful.

Take initiative. Do not hold back your ideas. Put them forward with a plan for testing them. Be open to feedback that is not 100% positive. Learn how to create space in difficult situations without detaching or devaluing the process. Take care of your physical, mental, and emotional health. Trust your instincts and intuition as often as you trust your analytical skills.

Thanks to her statistics expertise, Meg can represent many problems mathematically, particularly complex relationships between concepts. Her exposure to the arts was a surprise benefit of her life at Penn State. Creating experience challenges for Live It (for example, "Go to the museum and take a selfie with a painting!") have forced Meg to attend exhibits and performances. Meg has learned how to connect her artistic experiences to many aspects of innovation and design. Professionally, formal training in design thinking, participation in professional organizations such as the Society for Prevention Research, and conferences outside her field have also helped her career. In addition, her doctoral advisor who held a dual degree in computer science and public health showed her the benefit of interdisciplinary work. Her funding for dissertation research from a private foundation helped her understand the benefits of public-private partnerships to advance health in underserved communities.

It is hard for Meg to say where she will be in twenty years, but she has embraced the journey thus far. She believes she will still be working to innovatively solve public health problems and would love to continue to mentor the next generation of researchers. She would like to create a prevention designer career in public health. She sees herself mixing academic and startup worlds and always having a living laboratory to work within. She would like to increase the number and scope of public-private partnerships in which universities engage to advance research. Meg believes that her personal and work lives integrate. She establishes and commits to a set of priorities that guide decisions about her time. She is married with two teenage children, and maintaining her relationships with friends and family is a top priority. She often extends travel for work so that she can visit a friend or bring a child along for an interesting adventure. As for her personal health, she exercises regularly, spends as much time outdoors as she can, and has developed a regular mindfulness meditation practice. Her healthy habits lay the foundation for her full engagement at work. She loves that she works in an organization that values health and well-being and that she (mostly) has control over her flexible schedule. She works at staying open to new opportunities while integrating her work, social, and family life.

Photo by Harpreet Singh

Brian Bell, 28

Acara Institute, University of Minnesota
Assistant Director | ~$62,000

MS, Environmental Sciences (Sustainable Development), Utrecht University (2011)
BS, Civil Engineering, University of Minnesota (2009)

Job Description

Entrepreneurship programs focused on social impact are becoming increasingly popular at American universities. These programs teach students how to develop innovative ventures that tackle grand challenges for society, often in developing countries. Acara is one such program at the University of Minnesota's Institute on the Environment. Started in 2008, Acara has more than seventy to ninety UMN students and 100 to 150 non–UMN students participate in the program each year. Students have the opportunity to take several different courses within Acara, mainly focused on challenges in Minnesota, India, and Uganda. In these courses, students develop market-centric solutions to address social or environmental challenges facing large numbers of people. Brian Bell serves as assistant program director with Acara where his primary responsibility is to ensure that the program meets its educational and impact missions.

With Acara, Brian co-leads impact entrepreneurship courses in the US, India, and East Africa. Much of the time spent preparing for courses involves writing syllabi, identifying and reviewing background materials, meeting and talking with entrepreneurs and enterprise service providers in order to learn about their ventures/services, and developing strong relationships with entrepreneurs who will participate as guest speakers, venture mentors, and experiential learning partners. Acara's programs focus on water, agriculture, waste, energy, or health. In the classroom, Brian works closely with the venture teams to help turn their understanding of a challenge and market need into a financially viable venture with defined revenue streams, distribution channels, and partner organizations. Teams must summarize these different aspects into a coherent business plan and pitch. Brian loves the opportunity to work with bright, passionate change makers designing businesses with strong financial and social value propositions to address wicked problems, while at the same time traveling to Asia and Africa regularly.

The classroom portion of this program develops venture teams and educates students on ideation and design thinking, business model generation, and financial models, along with cultural context. But this encompasses only half of Brian's work. He also facilitates and provides seed funding to student teams piloting and launching new venture. He spends a lot of time working closely with venture teams, tracking progress, helping to define needs and next steps, distributing and monitoring seed funding, and providing guidance and connections. With some technically focused ventures, such as MyRain, a distributor of drip irrigation products in India, he is able to leverage his engineering knowledge to provide technical guidance alongside business support.

Through education and impact, Brian believes he and his team changes the world in two ways. First, he helps students become globally aware entrepreneurs prepared to work on multidisciplinary teams to develop innovative solutions. Secondly, he and his colleagues incubate venture teams interested in launching enterprises in the US and abroad to address important challenges, such as electricity shortage, waste management problems, inefficient water usage, and malnutrition. His team measures the true impact of their activities by quantifying outputs such as the number of students taught, the number of ventures launched during the program, and the number of students who launch or work for social ventures after graduating.

As key vessel for both education and impact, Brian also has administrative responsibilities with Acara. He supports organizational strategy, program management, and financial management. He and his team plan and execute several venture competitions throughout each school year. These competitions offer students opportunities to pitch their ventures and convince others that their ideas are worth funding, which teaches valuable communication and business skills. While most of Brian's time is spent with Acara, he is also involved with several other organizations. He works with IMNPACT Angels, Minnesota's first impact angel investing network, which makes investments in companies, organizations, and funds with the intention of generating measurable social and environmental impacts along with a financial return. Brian is an active member of the Minneapolis Hub of Global Shapers, an initiative of the World Economic Forum. Over the past few years he has also been involved advising development engineering projects with Engineers Without Borders in rural Uganda and with Kounkuey Design Initiative in Kibera, Kenya. Brian appreciates any opportunities to support socially driven entrepreneurs and engineers in the US and abroad.

Career Trajectory

Brian's journey started at the University of Minnesota when, while obtaining a civil-environmental engineering bachelor's degree with an architecture minor, he actively sought a bit of adventure and real-world project experience. He started by joining the University of Minnesota chapter of Engineers Without Borders in the spring of 2007, within which he quickly became a leader. As president and project manager with EWB-UMN, he led teams planning, fundraising for, and implementing water, sanitation, and waste projects based in Uganda with Uganda Rural Fund and in Haiti with Sustainable Organic Integrated Livelihoods (SOIL). In summer 2008, he led a team of eight engineers to implement a 100,000-liter rainwater system and then returned a year later leading a team of sixteen engineers to implement a solar-powered groundwater system with a 190-foot bore well.

> **Know yourself.** Spend time reflecting on your motivations, capabilities, strengths, and weaknesses, and take steps to improve in order to be prepared to be an effective leader.
>
> **Get started.** Often we have great ideas but do not start because the idea is too big, too expensive, too challenging. Find ways to start small. Think, "What if ...?" and go from there.

On this experience, Brian remarks, "For my Engineers Without Borders team, it was an adventure. For the students at Hope Integrated Academy, a school for AIDS-affected kids in rural Uganda, it was a daily reality. They NEVER before had a clean water supply. These are the extracurricular experiences that lit my fire more than any other research project or engineering internship I had before." As an undergraduate, Brian also had the opportunity to participate in the first Acara Challenge venture design program at the University of Minnesota in 2009. Specifically, his team developed ReachOut Water Solutions, a community-managed water venture to address issues of water quantity, quality, access, and management in the slums of Mumbai. After his team won the challenge, they traveled to Mumbai for three weeks to conduct a business feasibility study and meet with community leaders, residents, and municipal engineers. Working with Acara helped develop his interests in utilizing business tools commonly applied in corporate and startup environments to address development challenges in emerging economies.

Brian's experiences with EWB and Acara opened many new doors and guided his interests in engineering and also in governance, economic development, and business development. After graduation he served as the US delegate to UNESCO's 2009 General Conference Youth Forum in Paris. Brian then pursued grad school in Nepal, India, and the Netherlands over a span of two years while obtaining a master's in environmental sciences-sustainable development from Utrecht University, funded by the generous Huygen's scholarship from the Dutch government. While in Nepal and India, he conducted graduate research internships evaluating rural water/sanitation programs with UN-HABITAT Nepal and the Government of India. This master's program offered the opportunity to gain an education through practical experience with large multilateral and government organizations focused on water and sanitation solutions in South Asia, which ultimately guided his professional work on topics related to environment, infrastructure, and health. Following grad school, Brian was an engineering intern with Kounkuey Design Initiative, working closely with communities in Kibera, Kenya, to design "productive public spaces," including public parks and playgrounds, water and sanitation services, and structures to house microenterprise and community-based activities.

These early multifaceted experiences guided his interests in bringing together engineering, sustainable development, impact entrepreneurship, and investing. In the future, Brian plans to pursue a joint-degree program including an MBA and MS in engineering at a top university. Ultimately, he believes these academic experiences will prepare him to lead a successful company providing market-based water and energy solutions to address important challenges in the US and abroad, and later an impact investing firm that is focused on clean tech in emerging economies.

Blake Angelo, 29

Colorado State University
Project Manager, Office of Community & Economic Development |
~$50,000

MPH, Health Systems, Management and Policy, Colorado School
of Public Health (2014)
BA, Ecology and Evolutionary Biology, University of Colorado-Boulder (2008)

Job Description

The average distance food travels from farm to plate in the United States is 4,200 miles. This average is driven up by elaborate global supply chains which, paradoxically, results in areas called "food deserts," which lack ready access to fresh, healthy, affordable food. The long trip for trucks and trains to bring food to people contributes not only to heavy carbon-dioxide emissions but also to nutritional challenges for many urban and rural residents with low to moderate incomes. Rather than supermarkets, fast-food restaurants and convenience stores may serve as the only source of food for many residents of food deserts. The food available at these locations tends to be notably high in sodium, sugar, and fats and equally low in crucial nutrients for health and vitality. Relatedly, we see rising levels of obesity and other diet-related diseases in most cities due to the excessive intake of such calories, coupled with limited physical activity.

If urban areas could attract and retain farmers, they could improve access to better nutrition. Unfortunately, urban farmers often struggle to make a profit because of the high cost of living in the city, lack of open space, substantial municipal restrictions, and lack of knowledge on how to maximize employee labor and crop yields. To attract farmers, urban farming has to be made more profitable. Who can help farmers help cities? Private companies? Nonprofits? Many land-grant universities are by definition located in rural areas, but with urban migration, they are increasingly getting involved in urban areas. One such university is Colorado State University (CSU), which runs programs for farmers in cities like Denver.

Blake Angelo, a native of the city of Denver, is helping urban farmers through CSU's Office of Community and Economic Development. His expertise is in nonprofit management and government, and he uses his experience to support the passions of urban farmers by sharing his business knowledge with them. For example, he reviews their business plans and advises them on improving their financial statements, labor strategies, and market niche. He guides them through the regulations that affect farming in cities, including restrictions on noise, odor, and waste. He also advises farmers about insurance and other measures to protect their assets from lawsuits. Blake believes that making a profit will turn urban farming from a short-term trend into a long-standing movement. In addition to talking with farmers, he also speaks with local and national media, politicians, and policy makers to teach about the plight that both urban farmers and the urban poor face and to advocate for food and agricultural policy that will help them.

Another part of Blake's job is project management. In order for CSU to carry out all their projects in the community, he must carefully plan time and money allotted to each project. One example of a project he managed was an eight-week program for farmers to teach them about developing a budget plan, marketing their products, and maximizing efficiency of their resources, such as water and employees. For this project, he first met with the farmers interested in the program to gain a better understanding of their needs. Then Blake planned who from CSU should be part of the program and what they would be responsible for completing and delivering to the farmers. Then he arranged those deliverables into a timeline so that everybody involved in the program knew what had to be done by when. Lastly, he estimated how much time and resources it would take each person at CSU to complete their part and came up with an estimate of the total cost to run the program.

As a part of a large, land-grant university, Blake sees himself as an "intrapreneur," someone working to develop entrepreneurial solutions to social needs within the apparatus of a large, bureaucratic organization. It is both exciting and overwhelming to be in a university with 2,000 other professionals, but the extraordinary amount of expertise, knowledge, and passion that CSU has throughout the state makes it a perfect partner for systemic change. Blake's favorite part of his job is, by far, working with the community to solve real-world urban agricultural problems. His least favorite part of his job happens when the university's partners have misaligned incentives or conflicting values. He has found that most tensions and conflicts among partners can be resolved, but conflicts about values and/or incentives are not often solvable. That being said, these conflicts can sometimes lead to the most brilliant solutions as the group is forced to think far outside the current constraints to create a truly innovative solution.

Career Trajectory

When Blake was an undergraduate, he received important advice from a mentor: he recommended taking an extra $5,000 loan to travel for a few months before working. He explained that most loans do not need to be paid for the first six months after graduation, so Blake could travel for three months and then work hard in the next three months to pay back the full amount without interest. The trip Blake took changed the trajectory of his life. By traveling without a specific destination in mind, he discovered many passions, such as urban agricultural issues, that had been buried in his education, and he explored them. After returning home, Blake took the only job he could find, delivering salad during the week and wedding cakes on the weekends, and he paid back his debt on time.

> With strong relationships, social entrepreneurs can quickly and easily convene groups of change makers, which would otherwise require months or years of coalition building.

Meanwhile, Blake spent as many hours he could networking through friends and volunteering with causes he felt passionate about. These efforts paid off quickly and he landed an internship with the Beanstalk Foundation, a social change nonprofit based on helping local social entrepreneurs increase their capacity to fundraise and manage their organization. At first, he made only $12.50 per hour and worked twenty hours per week, so he had to keep delivering salads. There were even times where he was assembling salads for delivery while he was on a conference call for Beanstalk. After about two months, he was offered a full-time position with Beanstalk as a project manager, and he jumped at the chance to leave his delivery days behind. Shortly thereafter, the director of Beanstalk resigned, and Blake became the sole employee. Working at Beanstalk was like drinking from a firehose, but over the next few years, he learned a lot about managing a nonprofit foundation and eventually become the director. It was an amazing opportunity to quickly learn about the tax, legal, IT, human resources, board development, fundraising, and many other components of nonprofit management. While working with Beanstalk, he continued volunteering and networking with organizations that shared his passion for social change.

Because of his relationships in the community, he was recruited by an employee at CSU Extension for a new position they were starting focused on urban agriculture and business development. This position was in perfect alignment with his passions, but it required a major financial risk: there was only a starting budget of $25,000, and after that was gone, he would have to generate all his own income from grants, contracts, etc. Given the opportunity's alignment with his passions, he decided to take the risk, and thanks to generous partnerships with faculty and the community, he extended that $25,000 into a full-time job for well over two years. Based in part on his successes with Extension, he was offered his current full-time, permanent position with the CSU Office of Community and Economic Development.

While in school, one of the most enjoyable clubs for Blake was a think tank of college students where they each took turns preparing a mock TED Talk on a public issue and then engaged the think tank in solving the problem. He also participated in a president's leadership class, which taught him a number of critical interpersonal and leadership skills as well as exposed him to other highly motivated individuals who were exceptionally talented in a diverse range of skills. This group of peers has continued to provide professional opportunities and lifelong friendships with like-minded and like-hearted individuals, people who truly understand the challenging life of leading social change.

After completing school, Blake served on the advisory board for a local food organization, recruited speakers for his local TEDx event, and served on mayoral commissions to address critical local issues. Such affiliations allowed him to connect to his community and build an essential professional and personal network. Blake has developed a cadre of mentors and advisors who help him navigate critical leadership, legal, and other challenges. Looking back, Blake sometimes thinks he would have preferred to follow an academic track with more practical skills (e.g., engineering, business, or architecture), as it would have made him more immediately employable after graduating though he recognizes that some of those tracks may have required him to explore other topics of interest (like food!) outside the required set of classes. Looking to the future, Blake sees himself working toward a position in private sector management with a socially motivated company.

♥ Toral Zaveri, 32

Penn State University
Postdoctoral Scholar | ~$44,000

PhD, Biomedical Engineering, University of Florida (2011)
BE, Biomedical Engineering, Mumbai University (2005)

Job Description

In the United States, women represent 20% of those infected with HIV; in sub-Saharan Africa, women make up 59% of the HIV population. Due to gender inequality and socioeconomic dependence on their partners, women are not always in a position to negotiate condom use with their partner. Younger women are even more vulnerable when they are in relationships with older men. How can women protect themselves without relying on men? Microbicides—in the form of vaginal gels, intravaginal rings, creams, foams, sponges, films, and tablets containing antiretroviral drugs—have become a prime focus for women-controlled HIV prevention strategies. There is no commercial product in the market right now because while such products hold great promise scientifically, they are not yet widely accepted by women. Since microbicide products are inserted vaginally and used during sex, several factors—such as sexual and cultural practices, partner awareness, and product feel—affect women's choice to use the product as directed. Biologically efficacious products may fail to show value in the market because of lack of use as shown by investigations in clinical trials. Toral Zaveri is tackling this challenge as a postdoctoral researcher at Penn State University.

Considering the intimate nature of these products, several sexual and cultural factors need to be considered in the product design process. Toral and her team are currently working on a semisoft vaginal suppository as a novel form of microbicide delivery mechanism. The product is currently in the preclinical stages of development. In the lab, Toral formulates suppositories using biopolymers such as carrageenan and starch to make suppositories of varying sizes, shapes, and textures. She characterizes the physical properties of what she creates and studies the release of the drug from the suppositories over time in a simulated vaginal environment. Her main focus, however, is on ensuring the product is one that women like and would be willing to use. Therefore, the largest and most interesting part of the job for her is gathering feedback from women. Toral is in charge of the sensory evaluation of the suppositories, so she has designed tests where women come and evaluate the suppositories in their hands in individual booths and provide feedback on the product design. Toral and her team have also conducted focus groups and Internet-based surveys to gather a wide array of opinions. In addition to designing suppositories and conducting studies herself, she supervises undergraduate students and other project staff on other aspects of the project for them to gain this experience as well.

Toral is constantly integrating women's opinions into the next iteration of the suppository design to optimize it. Several good products fail in the field because the developers do not consider the context of the product in a particular setting. For example, Toral learned during fieldwork that the desired lubrication during intercourse varies across different cultures and countries; in countries where dry sex is preferred, the resulting lubrication from the vaginal suppositories would be a critical design feature. Toral has received favorable feedback on her products prepared with carrageenan. Usually, suppositories are made with gelatin. However, carrageenan is a plant-based material, so it is favorable for vegetarians and does not melt at high temperatures, making it suitable to be transported and used in tropical climates. Based on their current optimization efforts, women are 70% likely to try the product.

While you may think Toral is in the life science arena, she is actually based in food science! Sensory science has traditionally evolved in the realm of food science to provide guidance to product developers in areas ranging from innovating the next flavor for potato chips, to replacing the vanilla extract in ice cream, to optimizing spice levels for salsa. Over the past several decades, sensory evaluation techniques have been applied in optimization of personal care products such as skin creams and cosmetics and now to the field of drug delivery products. Additionally, carrageenan is a common food additive, and studying its properties in the context of this drug delivery product is a food science problem.

As a postdoctoral scholar, Toral has more autonomy on the microbicide project as compared to graduate students; she is expected to ensure that the project deadlines are met with minimal intervention from her advisors, Dr. Gregory Ziegler and Dr. John Hayes. Toral has presented her findings at national conferences and written several publications regarding preferences for vaginal products as the findings are not only useful to the field of microbicides but to the field of vaginal products as a whole. Toral loves that she can get relatively quick feedback from consumer tests so that she can avoid investing months in a design that many women dislike. She enjoys the flexibility of having an academic job over other industry jobs because it allows her to better balance her work and personal life—she has

> Follow your passions. Focus on problems that matter to you. Do not constrain yourself to your field of study. If something you find interesting comes up in a different field, just do it. You may excel at it, and if not, learn something new. Foremost, create time for yourself and your loved ones. You live only once, and time is a one-way street.

an overactive two-year-old and a hyperactive husband who travels over 200 days of the year. On the other hand, Toral dislikes that her project is in its preclinical design phase, and she is unable to conduct studies with animal and human subjects. She is extremely passionate about championing this project forward so that it can reach women faster and help them prevent HIV infections.

Career Trajectory

As a high school student enthralled with biology, Toral thought she would go to medical school. However, her extended family advised her parents against it considering the overnight shifts and long hours expected from medical professionals. Like many other top-ranking high school students excelling in math and science in India, she joined an engineering college to major in electrical engineering. A month into her studies, she knew something was amiss but was hesitant to switch paths because she did not want to have wasted her time in electrical engineering. However, she took a chance and applied to another engineering college's biomedical engineering program. Thanks to her great grades and a spot opening up serendipitously, Toral was accepted! She was really excited because biomedical engineering allowed her to bridge her two passions, medicine and engineering. She interned at a reputed hospital in Mumbai as a biomedical engineering trainee, which allowed her to work with several medical instruments whose circuit diagrams she had only seen in textbooks. She majored in medical instrumentation for her undergraduate degree and decided to pursue graduate studies in biomedical engineering at the University of Florida.

While working on her master's, she attended a seminar by Dr. Benjamin Keselowsky on his work on immune response to biomaterials and ways to mitigate it. His work greatly intrigued her, so she joined his lab and switched over to a PhD program. She worked on a project to improve the functional life of implanted joints that help restore mobility and alleviate pain for people with knee injuries or those suffering from arthritis. The project had a two-pronged approach, looking at both surface modifications for biomaterial implants as well as mitigating the attack from the body's immune response. It was a truly multidisciplinary project integrating principles of immunology, material science, and drug delivery techniques. During two of her summers in graduate school, Toral supervised high school students in lab research and also taught a course on medical instrumentation. Upon earning her PhD, Toral wanted to pursue opportunities as a research scientist in pharmaceutical companies. She knew she wanted to work on something more applied and translational than her PhD research.

A few months before graduation, her husband, who worked at Penn State and was rooting for her to move closer to him, met a faculty member from the food science department. They struck up a conversation regarding a grant Dr. Gregory Ziegler and Dr. John Hayes had just received to study a novel drug delivery product for HIV prevention. Toral's husband mentioned her experience with drug delivery and landed her an interview for a postdoctoral scholar they were looking for to run the project. This project was a great next step in her career as it allowed her to use her knowledge of biomaterials and drug delivery while working on a product that could eventually reach the market. Toral was particularly excited about the potential of the project to address one of the biggest health-care challenges in the world—the HIV/AIDS epidemic.

Toral had no formal training in sensory science prior to joining Penn State, but after working in Dr. Hayes's lab for three and a half years and having a keen interest in the field, she picked up the tricks of the trade. She even got an opportunity to manage projects for Penn State's Sensory Evaluation Center, a state-of-the-art, fee-based sensory testing facility handling several industry projects. In the future, Toral wants to apply her expertise in biomaterials and sensory science in the pharmaceutical or personal care product industry. She wants to design products that reduce human suffering, are context appropriate, and are well received by customers.

Sintana E. Vergara, 32

University of California, Berkeley
Postdoctoral Scientist | ~$60,000

PhD, Energy and Resources, University of California, Berkeley (2011)
MS, Civil and Environmental Engineering, University of California, Berkeley (2009)
BS, Biological and Environmental Engineering, Cornell University (2004)

Job Description

Worldwide, the largest fraction of municipal solid waste (the fancy phrase for garbage) is organic waste. When organic waste is mixed with other garbage, its value is negligible. But if that waste is separated, it is a resource rich with nutrients and energy. The latest International Panel on Climate Change report concluded that climate change is irreversible unless we can find a way to sequester carbon from the atmosphere. It turns out that compost has the potential to do that while providing other ancillary benefits (e.g., improving water retention in soils, recycling nutrients, minimizing the need for waste disposal). Composting, an age-old practice, is the source of tremendous environmental benefits, and Sintana Vergara studies it in order to improve humans' ability to recycle and reuse our waste and lighten our footprint on the Earth that sustains us. Sintana Vergara is motivated to catalyze the use of waste as a resource.

Sintana is a postdoctoral scientist at the University of California Berkeley where she is currently conducting research on greenhouse gas emissions from compost, seeking to understand what factors control the emission of methane, nitrous oxide, and carbon dioxide—all important greenhouse gases. Her days are delightfully varied. She is currently in the startup phase of her compost project, so she is reading many papers to learn about different methods to measure emissions (particularly in micrometeorology) and to develop her own innovative way to measure emissions from compost (has not been done before). She spends time thinking about the instrumentation she needs to make these measurements, and soon she will be in the field, building both compost piles and the instrumentation around them. Once the experiment is up and running, she will spend many days in the field, collecting data and fixing things when they go wrong. Sintana will also be conducting statistical analyses on the data she collects and writing papers about the results.

After working for three years at the World Bank in cities that mostly lacked formal waste management systems and whose waste was mostly organic, Sintana chose to zoom in on the potential resource of organic waste, and she aims to understand how to improve the composting process. In doing so, she is answering some basic science questions: What are the conditions under which we get nitrous oxide emissions? When do we get methane emissions, or oxidation? At the same time, the research will help inform best management practices for communities and cities aiming to use their organic waste as a soil amendment. Sintana is working under UC Berkeley Professor Whendee Silver, whose lab conducts the scientific research that drives The Marin Carbon Project, a multidisciplinary collaboration among scientists, farmers, and policy makers that aims to understand how land-use practices can increase soil carbon sequestration. Research thus far has demonstrated that the one-time addition of compost to rangeland soils in California leads to significant carbon sequestration in the soils. This is potentially a game changer.

Sintana enjoys being a scientist because her work is driven by the quest for knowledge. She enjoys the rigor associated with conducting academic research, and she is humbled to be surrounded by world-class scientists, who are generous with their time. She also enjoys the varied nature of her days; they oscillate among reading papers, meeting with other researchers, turning compost piles, and analyzing data. While studying for her PhD oral exams, Sintana learned an important lesson about balancing work and life: work would fill as much space as she gave it. Therefore, she set time limits moving forward: she would work only between nine and five each day. Sintana has found that it makes her more productive during the day and allows her to enjoy many other things that she values in life: athletics, cooking, and spending time with friends.

Career Trajectory

A child of a chemical engineer and a literature professor, Sintana was encouraged to pursue academics and was told she could do anything. When she was six years old, her family took a trip to the Amazon rainforest, and they spent a week floating on a river that seemed to her to be as large as an ocean. The magnificent forest extended to the horizon, and for the first time, Sintana realized how small she was on a large planet. Through this trip and other adventures, Sintana's family instilled in her a love of science, observation, and discovery. Her brother would often take her on trips to their local creek, lake, and forest, and he showed her how to catch frogs and go camping—but he also taught her to care for those creatures. When they were both very young, she asked him why she should care about the birds flying overhead, and he said, "Because they have families too." As a woman scientist, Sintana looks backs and realizes that this early, consistent encouragement from her family and all her teachers was a key factor in her success. She now aims to be a voice of encouragement for other girls and boys interested in science.

Hold yourself to the highest moral standard. Know that what you do, even if it is small, matters. How you treat people on a day-to-day basis, as well as what you put your time or money into, has a big impact. Imagine if we all viewed our choices as a vote for the world we wanted to live in! The world would be a better place.

A wise professor of mine, the late Alex Farrell, gave my class some advice that stuck with me: "Find something you are interested in, and pick the hardest question you can find. Try to answer it." By doing something difficult, you are bound to learn a lot. By doing something meaningful, you are likely to feel fulfilled.

In college, Sintana pursued engineering because it was a rigorous way to focus on what she found the most interesting: the environment. She was interested in many subjects and passionate about doing something to improve how humans tread on the Earth. Her path was guided by a class she took in her final semester called "Garbage" (technically "Solid Waste Engineering"). Her life was changed, and she began to look at all objects as having long lives of their own. Studying engineering (and playing sports), a field in which she often worked in teams to conquer problem sets, taught her how to work effectively in teams.

In graduate school, she was fortunate to find a program, the Energy and Resources Group at UC Berkeley, that encouraged interdisciplinary approaches to solving environmental problems. Finding opportunities for applied research during her undergraduate and graduate studies gave her good real-world experience and also taught her that the world is huge and filled with opportunities. For her master's research, she studied the ability of small-scale water-treatment technologies to improve access to safe drinking water in Bangladesh and Mexico, and for her PhD research, she studied the environmental benefits from reuse-oriented waste management strategies with a case study on the climate-change benefits from informal recycling in Bogota, Colombia.

As Sintana was finishing her PhD at UC Berkeley, she got a job offer from the World Bank to work on precisely what she most wanted to work: to improve how waste is managed in developing cities. She worked in the urban development group as the only American and one of the few engineers/scientists. Since most of the World Bank's employees were economists, engineers and scientists were in relatively high demand, so she had the opportunity to do a variety of technical and analytical work in the solid-waste field. She conducted analytic work—for example, advising the government of Romania on what options they had for treating their organic solid waste—as well as project-based work on solid-waste projects in developing cities. She worked mostly on projects in the Middle East (but also Southeast Asia) and aimed to help cities implement new solid-waste management plans. She traveled regularly to check on the status of her projects (infrastructure, environmental protection, and social safeguards) and also to provide direct assistance to cities to help them overcome any obstacles. She was fortunate to have a boss who believed that their main purpose was to give her clients the tools they needed so that the project could be entirely run by them and would no longer need assistance from the World Bank.

After three years with the World Bank, Sintana decided to return to California and to academia to get back into science, to learn new skills, and to zoom in on a key waste management problem: what to do with organic waste. All along the way, Sintana has found that her technical background has enabled her to pursue different topics and wear many different hats. If she could start all over, Sintana would take advantage of more opportunities around her, especially as an undergraduate: join new clubs, learn new skills, take classes in wholly unfamiliar fields, join a lab group early on, do research, and practice presenting results early too. In the future, Sintana would like to still be pursuing applied environmental research, learning new things, and hopefully making an impact with her work. She sees herself becoming a staff scientist for a university or nongovernmental organization.

Photo by Scholar Academies

Julia Wittig Silvasy, 29

Scholar Academies
External Relations Manager | ~$60,000

MEd, Urban Education, University of Pennsylvania (2011)
BS, Biobehavioral Health, Penn State University (2009)

Job Description

Urban schools in the United States are struggling; standardized test scores are low while dropout rates are high. Millions of students growing up in poverty, often concentrated in urban areas, lack quality education to bring them to their full potential. There is a nationwide focus on closing the achievement gap between students from low and high economic backgrounds and eradicating inequity in urban education. Scholar Academies is a network of high-performing schools in Washington, DC; Trenton; and Philadelphia that provide traditionally underserved, urban students with a meaningful, high-quality education. Scholar Academies believes that every child is capable of academic achievement. Therefore, they make no excuses and do whatever it takes to drive results for their students and employ a talented, driven, and aligned team of teachers and leaders to achieve their vision: to drive social change in cities through education.

As manager of external relations for Scholar Academies, Julia Silvasy is the primary liaison for fundraising, event management, and board of trustee development in Philadelphia and Trenton. The root of her job is to influence people to take action that will help students thrive. At the same time, she investigates opportunities for the organization to be more effective at project implementation and scaling up. It is important that she has a strong understanding of science and education so that she can fully convince others of its importance. She also needs a strong understanding of administration so that she can take this knowledge of how it is actually possible to implement and scale up projects for students and work effectively with people internal and external to Scholar Academies to make it happen.

A typical day for Julia might include meeting with a board member to discuss the subcommittee they are forming to increase parental engagement on their board. Then, a few hours could be spent strategizing how to increase the funds raised in their signature event from $125,000 to $250,000 by exploring questions such as "What sponsors can we attract?" and "How do we dramatically increase ticket sales?" Team meetings are also a daily activity: Julia and her team of three others discuss strategy concerning prospective audiences and crafting the narrative of their organization both internally and externally, based on the recent academic results they have received from their schools. Sometimes she will give prospective donors a tour of the schools in the program and help them understand the added value they could bring as a future donor. Finally, she might conclude her day by meeting with teachers about their science programs and offering advice for how to better engage students through hands-on activities that will help build their interest in STEM fields. Overall, Julia explains that the year will ebb and flow with the size of projects, but there are always many balls to juggle on any given day.

Scholar Academies cannot sustain itself or grow without Julia's innovative fundraising efforts. She is ultimately securing the salaries of individuals and enabling the students in her specifically assigned schools to have the best learning environment possible. Sometimes assessing the impact of her activities is simple. By collecting data on fiscal targets, attendance at events, number of donors, types of gifts, reoccurrence of gifts, and engagement of board members, she is able to qualitatively evaluate the positive impacts. However, she likes to think of herself as more of a grassroots organizer and advocate. If she does her job well, the students have access to a higher-quality education, thereby giving them the opportunity to attend the best high schools and colleges. However, performing well does not come without challenges. Julia says it is difficult for her that her day-to-day activities are removed from the larger outcome, especially having come from jobs where she had everyday interaction with students, families, and teachers. It is also easy to get caught up in pieces that feel like they may not matter, such as what types of flowers are on the middle of the lunch tables with potential donors. She has to be intentional about carving out the time to stay connected and to prioritize her time in a way that she never gets too far away from what is real and really important.

Julia enjoys spending time in the schools and classrooms. "When I get to interact with our students and teachers, that is what makes it real; that is what makes it matter." Her favorite part is helping to develop the strategy for her organization and asking questions such as "How do you get maximum output with minimum input?" She uses her background in science to help teachers make the most of their resources to engage students in active learning. It is special for her to see hard work come to fruition: seeing the playground erected after a successful fundraising event, watching the students take a trip to a science museum funded by a board member, or having a building outfitted with air conditioning based on a grant received. "Those are big moments," says Julia.

Career Trajectory

Julia received a bachelor of applied science degree in biobehavioral health with a minor in women's studies through the Schreyer Honors College at Penn State. Biobehavioral health coupled with women's studies enabled her to explore a world in which equity, justice, and social good were the foundation. During her junior year, she enrolled in a class that enabled her to travel to Tanzania over the summer for a service-learning project. Through this course, she was introduced to and began working with students in the Humanitarian Engineering and Social Entrepreneurship program. Her team founded Mashavu: Networked Health Solutions, a telemedicine system aimed at improving preprimary care in rural areas of Kenya. Mashavu now has seven full-time employees and is a sustainable, cash-positive organization.

Working on this project forced her to collaborate with people she would probably never have crossed paths with otherwise, gaining skills in team work,

> Do not be satisfied with the status quo if it feels unsettling to you. More concretely, do not be afraid to surround yourself with different people or take a gamble on a class that sounds outside your norm.
>
> Be humble. Humility is something I have learned the hard way at points in my career. Listen first, speak second—your user/champion/recipient has more to teach you than you do them.

leadership, and communication. This work forced her to practice time management; while her peers were doing any number of things outside class, she was traveling to conferences, working extra hours in a lab, or writing grant reports. Finally, this work showed her that it is truly possibly to combine passions with work. Some of Julia's closest connections from college are professors. She considers herself lucky to have developed relationships with mentors that helped to nurture her passions, develop her skill sets, and push her to think beyond the conventional boundaries that are often placed upon college students or recent college grads.

After graduation, Julia joined Teach For America, a program that trains and places high-achieving college graduates into high-need/low-resource classrooms around the country for a two-year period. Specifically, she was placed in Philadelphia and taught high school science at a charter school for youth in foster care. While teaching, she was also studying for her master's in urban education from the University of Pennsylvania with a focus on health in schools. The summer between her first and second year of teaching, she traveled to East Africa (Kenya and Tanzania) to train teachers on an innovative science curriculum to use with their students. Joining Teach For America sent her career down a path she did not expect, and it taught her that you do not have to know the next five steps in order to take one; she learned to make choices that feel authentic and exciting.

This experience led Julia to decide that she wanted to try something outside the classroom but remain in science education. She joined the Teach For America staff as a manager of teacher leadership development where she managed a cohort of thirty-five teachers in twelve schools in Philadelphia and Camden, motivating them to strive for ambitious student outcomes. From there, she decided to take her current role in order to help develop a new skill set and broaden her perspective of what it means to work in the nonprofit sector. Julia is a fierce defender of balancing the personal and professional. As a working mother of two young children, Julia knows that an unbalanced life is not sustainable, especially with a family to answer to at the end of the day. Therefore, she is constantly learning how to prioritize tasks and reflect on how she is working in order to highlight inefficiencies. Her roles as a wife and mother have also emphasized the value in doing work she believes in because work takes her away from her family.

She once heard someone say, "The way to get to where you want to be is to become the best at what you are currently doing." It was the best professional advice she received; it helped to ground her in understanding that careers are an ever-evolving process. In the future, Julia hopes to return to school to earn a PhD with a long-term goal of ending up in academia while at the same time returning to science education projects in sub-Saharan Africa.

Photo by Steven Waite

Sarah Peterson, 26

Nathan Hale High School, Tulsa Public Schools
Teacher and Department Head | ~$40,000

BS, Immunology and Infectious Disease, Penn State University

Job Description

Of course STEM professionals can play a larger role in social innovation and sustainable development, but how do we make sure we have enough of such individuals? We need to produce a steady stream of high school graduates who pursue STEM fields, and we need them to be representative of the larger demographic. Unfortunately, many colleges of education are producing math and science teachers in the single digits each year, and teachers often leave the profession within five years. Programs like Teach For America, UTeach, and 100Kin10 are trying to address this challenge, and yet cannot catch up with the number of STEM professionals graduating every year in India and China. If we are going to continue to thrive as a world leader, we need to continue to be a leader in STEM; however, without enough qualified teachers to inspire tomorrow's STEM leaders, it is not going to happen. We need more teachers who are committed and innovative and can educate students about how the STEM professions play an extremely important role in society. Creative thinking is needed to approach the needs of students and schools, especially in an urban setting. Teachers have a huge impact on how much students learn. If a student has a teacher that is set up to be successful, then they are likely going to graduate with a higher reading level, higher test scores, and a higher likelihood of graduating from a four-year school as opposed to their counterparts with a teacher who does not have the same support for success.

Sarah Peterson is a science teacher who brings innovation into her high school classroom in Tulsa, Oklahoma. Most of Sarah's day is spent in front of students leading them through subject materials through a variety of reading, writing, lecturing, and application-based learning. Her goal is for every student to be able to access material, regardless of his or her learning style or level of comprehension. Before and after the standard school day, her time is spent tutoring individuals or small groups of students who need additional time to access the material. Outside the teaching aspect of her job are the very important components of forming new and innovative lessons and constantly improving herself as an educator so that she knows that her students are always offered the best education possible. Efforts to improve herself include pursuing advanced degrees, professional development, and dedication to reading scientific articles. The final major component of her job involves assessing student data to understand where learning is occurring and where it is not. This can include grading essays, exams, exit tickets, or class activities and tracking the data to determine where students are struggling and where they are excelling.

Sarah loves the young people that she works with who share her excitement in science and the learning process. Every day she gets to work with them and discuss topics that are pertinent to the world and their success in it. While there are obviously frustrations some days, most are filled with starry-eyed young people looking to chart bright futures for themselves. Sarah's biggest frustration with her career has been seeing the process of the education system producing distinct winners and losers. It pays large financial dividends to have some top-notch schools in your district, rather than a large number of "average" schools. This means that, in order to get the recognition and wanted funding, it is incentivized for districts to put more money and special projects into certain schools. Sarah is frustrated that students' education is radically different according to whether they go to one school or another. Having spent time studying the system, Sarah does not fault the people involved because she has come to understand that everyone just wants what is best for his or her group of people. However, the overall system makes it so that there are winners and losers, and as a society that prides ourselves on being one of the best in the world, it is unacceptable to have winners and losers in the system that educates our future generations.

Sarah is still working on the concept of a work-life balance. She tends to approach challenges head-on and does not back off until she is satisfied with the results. Effective teaching is a constantly evolving challenge on which she could work one hundred hours a week for ten years, and she would likely still not be satisfied with the results.

This has led to her finding friendships and personal joy within the spectrum of her job. Her coworkers are her biggest support network in Tulsa, and they are most of her closest friends. She coaches cross-country with her boyfriend, which allows them to spend time together while spreading their love for running.

Career Trajectory

After spending four years studying immunology and infectious disease at Penn State, Sarah was offered a fellowship in the National Institutes of Health working in a lab studying hematopoiesis (the formation of blood cellular components). However, in the budget crisis of 2011, the program funding was cut. That all came to a head on a Monday, and on a Thursday, she was accepted into Teach For America. Prior to that, she had thought about teaching but was not sure if it was for her and thought it was too late for her since she was not an education major.

One mentor, her high school science teacher, was particularly influential on her decision to do Teach For America and later to stay on as a faculty member at her placement school. When she first got into the program, Sarah called to ask him for advice. He replied, "Simple. Do not do it." His reasoning was that problems in urban education are not going to be fixed by people looking to serve for two years to make themselves feel good. He told her that she would likely not start pulling her full weight at the school site until at least her third year of teaching, well after the completion of her contract with Teach For America. This advice changed the way Sarah looked at the program and her decision to join it. She was not joining for a two-year experience to make her résumé look nicer. She made the ultimate decision to join because she deeply believed that problems that she saw in society could be fixed through education, and she wanted to be a part of that change.

> Look for the good everywhere and capitalize on that. When you appreciate the good things that are already happening, it allows you to build on it rather than focusing on all of the frustrations in your path.

The keys to her success have been adaptability and facing every challenge head-on. This has involved trusting that things will always turn out the way they should and committing to making every opportunity the best it can possibly be. While things have not always turned out the way she thought they would, it has always led to great things. Academically, she is thankful that she opted for a science major that interested her because she constantly uses her knowledge and passion for immunology and infectious disease to fuel conversations with students and shape lesson plans. It also encourages her to keep reading and learning because she is so invested in the current research in the field. She also encourages students in her class to find an area of interest in the realm of science. Professionally, she has made it her mission to attend every meeting and conference that she possibly can. Sometimes this is in science, sometimes in education, sometimes in classroom literacy or other topics that may not be direct related to her field. This has enabled her to improve her practice and meet incredible people doing amazing things.

Sarah's career outlook has changed quite a bit in the past few years. While Sarah still loves medicine and would love to someday involve it more in her career, she also believes that, as a teacher, she has the highest possible influence on her students' health. Through the sciences that they discover in the classroom, discussions of a public health nature constantly happen. As of now, Sarah sees herself staying in the classroom because she believes she is making the best impact where she is. If that feeling changes, then she will move according to where she could make a larger impact. This could be creating science curriculum for a district, moving into an administrative role, or something that does not even exist yet.

Sarah is currently pursuing a master's degree in chemical and life sciences from the University of Maryland. She chose this degree because she finds it critically important for teachers to constantly evolve and improve in their craft. The master's program enables her to improve her knowledge in science while also facilitating curriculum-building skills to put the new knowledge into practice in the classroom. She hopes to use this to continue to improve her skills in the classroom and beyond.

Photo by Cassie Thiel

⚙ Alexander Dale, 27

Engineers for a Sustainable World
Executive Director | ~$40,000

PhD, Civil and Environmental Engineering, University of Pittsburgh (2013)
BS, Engineering Physics, University of Pittsburgh (2009)

Job Description

A sustainable world needs a robust ecosystem, a lasting and equitable society, and a stable economy. Engineers for a Sustainable World (ESW) is a chapter-based network that has crafted their mission around this vision, rallying support from corporate sponsors, individuals, and college students from across North America. ESW focuses on technical design projects, member education, and building a shared community of technically minded individuals to address some of society's most pressing challenges. A growing number of students are entering college with a hunger to change the world. ESW draws on this hunger to create impact domestically and abroad. The vast majority of ESW chapters are university affiliated and student run. They form locally and have significant autonomy in project selection, allowing for adaptation to local contexts, needs, and interests. ESW-National serves as a critical connection between universities and private sector contributors to provide the visionary leadership needed to foster cross-sectoral collaborations to create a generation of technical professionals who can engage with sustainability and complex global challenges. A key player in providing this leadership is Alexander Dale, executive director of ESW-National.

Alexander has been working with ESW-National for five years on top of his two-year involvement with the ESW chapter at the University of Pittsburgh. Through his various roles with the organization, he has led the expansion of ESW-National into an independent legal entity that serves thirty-seven college-based and three professional chapters. He now leads the ESW-National team and works with universities across the country. His goal is to be a guiding force in ESW and to find new resources (often people) to create and strengthen their network of chapters, partners, and sponsors to accelerate impact. ESW is leading change in the sustainability sector by developing ventures to solve problems at various levels, from campus-specific problems to global challenges.

One example of a campus project is Tiny House, ESW-Northwestern's 128-square-foot, off-the-grid home used to demonstrate a person's footprint on the environment. On the other end of the spectrum, in terms of global relevance, is ESW-Purdue's Global Irrigation Simulator, used to determine the most economically, socially, and environmentally sustainable option for irrigation in a given scenario. On the more applied side are ESW-University of Iowa's campus rain gardens. ESW-UI partnered with several university offices and departments to develop a sustainable storm management plan for the campus. The team mitigated the effects of increasing storm-water runoff from impervious surfaces through the design and installation of rainwater gardens. Students identified and evaluated potential rain-garden sites, designed gardens specific to each site, constructed them, and also developed maintenance plans. Through activities like these, ESW members learn how to select and implement sustainability projects that are pertinent to their communities and to work with partners to build the skill sets they need to carry them out.

In addition to network building, Alexander's responsibilities include blending research (designing new studies, gathering data, and writing technical papers) with administration. He spends upwards of 25% of his time meeting with the ESW-National team to build consensus on new initiatives, develop action plans, and identify next steps for day-to-day activities. About 10% of his time in any given week is spent firefighting—managing a sudden crisis around an event or ESW's website. The rest of his time is spent presenting at conferences, reaching out to companies or individuals, and writing grant proposals. As an administrator rather than a project implementer, these aspects are critical to his efforts to increase ESW's visibility and revenue. Alexander measures the impact of ESW at the most basic level by counting increases in the number of chapters established, members they reached, and attendance at seminars and webinars. Digging deeper into measuring ESW's complex role in making real impact, he looks at new partnerships, projects, and ideas, as well as at what ESW members are doing after graduation. Alumni go on to work in the renewable electricity sector, develop new biofuels, conduct environmental research, and hold positions outside engineering.

Alexander also serves as an adjunct professor at the University of Pittsburgh. He has designed, and now teaches, two multidisciplinary courses. The first one, "Social Entrepreneurship: Engineering for Humanity," focuses on creating social enterprises in the context of sustainability and complex problems. For this course, students must come up with a business plan to address a specific problem, with additional feedback provided by experts in the problem area through ESW's Wicked Problems in Sustainability Initiative (WPSI). The other course is "Energy: Science, Society, and Communication," which is a collaboration among Pitt, Carnegie Mellon, and the NAS/NAE Science and Engineering Ambassadors program. Through this course, students interact with energy-related researchers and professional engineers and discuss societal impacts of energy as well as how to communicate this information. As a final assignment, groups of students work with a community partner to do an outreach event involving an energy topic to a public audience.

> I stand by Woody Allen, who said, "80 percent of success is showing up." That has been my key for years—show up to events, be involved and engaged, follow interesting information sources, and be ready to say yes to new interesting things.

At times, Alexander's work melds with his personal life, an aspect of the job that he enjoys. He travels to interesting places and meets new people, causing carbon emissions that he would find hard to justify without the work component. His wife shares these experiences with him since her PhD work (in environmental impacts of nanoparticles) also allows her to travel. There are other times when he takes a hard break from work to relax or do something completely different. However, he finds that the topics of sustainability, energy policy, and big questions are what he is intensely passionate about, so pursuing these topics during personal time makes sense. The communities that he enjoys hanging out with are often involved with ESW or related groups, so discussions flow between "shop talk" and the standard arbitrary set of topics.

Career Trajectory

From a young age, Alexander knew he would be an engineer. He enjoyed building things, taking them apart, and learning how they worked. His mother instilled a concern for the environment in him and taught him about conservation before it was a topic on a national scale. His father, too, was a major influence in his life and encouraged him to be independent and to create his own opportunities. At the University of Pittsburgh, Alexander was not initially involved in any engineering clubs. Instead, he was involved with the Student Honors Activities Council, which provided experience with basic strategic planning and program formulation. He also was a tour guide for Pitt's Nationality Rooms where he was exposed to new cultures and became an excellent communicator, both through giving tours and eventually training other guides. He became involved with ESW-Pitt during his third year of studies and became the president of the chapter during his senior year. He took engineering classes focused on sustainability as well as nuclear engineering, both of which were new focus areas in Pitt's engineering course offerings.

In graduate school at Pitt, Alexander spent a year and a half working on a life-cycle analysis of the Marcellus Shale, talking to industry professionals and the activist community. A life-cycle assessment is a technique used to assess environmental aspects and potential impacts associated with all the stages of a product from cradle to grave (i.e., from raw material extraction through materials processing, manufacture, distribution, use, repair and maintenance, and disposal or recycling). His analysis of the Marcellus Shale involved quantifying impacts, including greenhouse gas emissions and water contamination. Talking to a variety of people to perform this life-cycle analysis taught him a lot about differences in language and provided some experience going between different value sets. Also while in graduate school, he initiated a TEDx series at Pitt and ran three successful events with around 100 attendees each, with talks focused on exemplary student and community speakers sharing creative ideas for the future.

Alex's overall doctoral work focused on the life-cycle impacts of future energy and water scenarios for specific regions. The Marcellus Shale work was important for scenarios in Pennsylvania while existing data was used for most sources around groundwater replacement in Arizona. Alex also spent four months in Rio de Janeiro, Brazil, which resulted in a collaborative paper on future electricity scenarios, a new ESW website, and a broader cultural viewpoint. Throughout graduate school, Alex was involved in ESW at the national level, first as the director of communications and technology (2009-2012) and then as education director (2012-2013), both on a volunteer basis of five to ten hours per week. He was involved in restructuring the organization, rebuilding the website, and building up the volunteer team. Following the 2012 ESW-National Conference, he was chosen to be the new executive director, a role he gladly accepted.

In five years, Alexander would like to be working in planning and policy at a local or national level. In between, he plans to work for ESW for two (or more) years and then potentially apply for various policy fellowships in Washington, DC. He is likely to become a professor in the long run, hopefully teaching multidisciplinary courses that encourage discussion and project-based learning. Alternatively, he might run for office, contributing his engineering and sustainability background to the political scene.

Photo by Matt Dixon

Aurora Sharrard, 35

Green Building Alliance
Vice President of Innovation | ~$83,000

PhD, Civil and Environmental Engineering, Carnegie Mellon University (2007)
BS, Civil Engineering, Tulane University (2001)

Job Description

Aurora Sharrard is a quintessential example of an individual who dreams, lives, breathes, and works for her passions. For Aurora, these passions include sustainability, environmental accountability, and engineering. As the vice president (VP) of innovation at Green Building Alliance (GBA), Aurora leads the DASH (Database for Analyzing Sustainable and High Performing Places project) and Pittsburgh's 2030 District team. DASH is a web tool that provides building-industry professionals with building performance information. Building performance is essentially a measure of how energy-efficient, water-efficient, and healthy a building is to live, work, or learn in. The goal of DASH is to get real-world measures as opposed to a building's designed performance in order to make better decisions about building design, construction, operations, and maintenance across the triple bottom line. Aurora's other project, the Pittsburgh 2030 Districts, is a collaborative, local effort to create a community of high-performance buildings in two Pittsburgh neighborhoods: Downtown and Oakland. These two projects have different approaches for impact (information and decision making with DASH versus engagement and action with Pittsburgh 2030 Districts). Aurora likes this variety and believes that both approaches are imperative to change not just how people act, but how they think about what is possible today and in the future.

The Green Building Alliance was founded in 1993 and is headquartered in Pittsburgh. It is one of the oldest regional green building organizations in the United States; its impact is tangible and visible around western Pennsylvania in the form of the sustainable building projects and programs they advise and support. GBA acts as a catalyst for sustainability in building design, construction, and operation. Aurora acts as a spark in the organization and entices people to make inspirational commitments to creating a healthier and higher performing western Pennsylvania. Through the process of empowering people, Aurora enjoys her variety of activities at GBA: hosting engaging educational events, scoping interesting building tours, quantifying building performance, evolving organizations' cultures through sustainability decisions, and just answering "green" questions. Aurora never has the same day twice. She usually has a mix of internal and external meetings related to one of her programs or GBA in general. These meetings can be with a partner, funder, potential sponsor or collaborator, or just someone doing something interesting. Given the long-term timeline and vision of the building industry and its sustainability focus, her best days include the culmination of a project she has been working on for a long time. This includes ribbon cuttings, building occupancy, certification, meeting an energy performance goal, as well as the initiation of new ideas and activities toward future progress.

Aurora's biggest challenge at work is that it can be frustrating when people want to consider only how much a building or renovation costs and the financial payback of that decision instead of more broadly incorporating function, quality, people, sustainability, and resiliency. Her favorite thing about working at GBA is that she has never had to "justify" the impact of her activities to herself. She can see and touch many of GBA's older accomplishments because they are tangible places. However, GBA's true impact is their community of stakeholders in whom she has had the opportunity to see and hear positive change over time. Oftentimes, these people-focused impacts are hard to quantify, but given the many "Top 10" lists Pittsburgh is on for being a wonderful place to live, work, and play, Aurora has no doubt that GBA's work in creating healthy, high-performing places has paid off in droves by helping create a community that espouses those ideals. It has been wonderful for Aurora to have a hand in making that happen.

Aurora maintains her certification as a LEED accredited professional in building design and construction. For this, she is required to take continuing education courses on a regular basis. Aurora likes such opportunities as she is extremely interested in learning about and connecting new ideas, people, practices, and technologies. She serves on a variety of committees at the local and national levels. At her house, she does her best to be sustainable; she owns a 1905 house in Pittsburgh, so there is a lot that can be done to improve it from its original state. At the house level, she has weatherized, upgraded lighting (CFLs and LEDs), installed smart surge protectors, replaced windows with double- and triple-paned versions, blown in insulation, and installed carpet tiles with 80%+ post-consumer recycled content! On a personal level, she does not buy what she does not need or will not use. Aurora buys used furniture and clothes when possible; is a community-supported agriculture (CSA) member year-round; buys local, sustainable, and/or organic; gardens; composts; has a rain barrel; bikes to work when she can; and rides the bus. Most importantly, she lives in the city and will send her children to public school. All of this has been made possible with the support of her husband, who has always been an essential supporter of Aurora doing what she loves.

Career Trajectory

Playing team sports throughout high school was where Aurora learned many life skills that she uses daily. After her junior year in high school, she attended a weeklong paid engineering program at the University of Nebraska-Lincoln, which convinced her to major in engineering. As an undergraduate, Aurora got involved with student chapters of the American Society of Civil Engineers (ASCE) and Society of Women Engineers (SWE). This early engagement with professional associations helped her become familiar with other engineering students, figure out her desired career path, and even meet her future employer.

Upon completing her bachelor's in civil engineering, Aurora practiced as a geotechnical engineer in Greater New Orleans. She did a mix of office and fieldwork but realized quickly that there were many things that could be improved on construction sites to reduce environmental impact. She was drawn to sustainability because she knew there had to be a better way to create buildings and infrastructure. From there, Aurora describes her career path as "short and straight forward." She spent four years as a research assistant and doctoral candidate in the Department of Civil and Environmental Engineering at Carnegie Mellon University and then seven years (and counting) at Green Building Alliance in Pittsburgh, moving up from research manager to director of innovation to her current position as VP of innovation.

Throughout her career path, Aurora has struggled to find a mentor since she has very few others with parallel careers in the building industry or small nonprofits. When she was working on her graduate degrees, Aurora searched for a mentor who exemplified what she wanted to become (a female engineering PhD not in

Take the leap. Even if you have to start out taking a job that you think just pays the bills, do not give up your dream and do what you know you need to do. Do not be too stringent on your criteria for your dream job. Even though the job might not have the title of "sustainability coordinator" or "director of innovation," if you are working for a company that you believe in—or, even more importantly, a company that believes in you—then you are in the right place.

You do not know if you do not ask. There are so many things in this world that you might assume the answer is "No," but you do not know if you do not ask. This could apply to doing an independent study, negotiating your salary, or asking someone to commit to something big. Ask the question; do not assume the answer.

Leverage your network. Through your family, friends, fellow students, and friends of friends, you have a great network that probably stretches around the globe. If you are not already reaching out to people in that network to find out more about them, what they do, how they might be able to help you take your next step, or how they might be a good future collaborator, you are not doing yourself or them justice.

Get out of your box. For some students, this might just mean get off campus and experience the wonderful things your city has to offer! For others, it might mean get out of your comfort zone and do something different or expose yourself to new ideas. Do not let your perceived boundaries box you in. It is only by being exposed to new and different ideas that you even know where and how you can best create value for others.

Get firsthand experience. In the world of sustainability, if you cannot back up your recommendations with some real knowledge of how something works at a technical level, then you are not effecting the change you expect to see in the world. The best way to get that technical knowledge is to do it yourself and learn firsthand.

academia). Although such people do exist and she knows people today who represent aspects of that mentor in her life, she found it very frustrating for a planner like herself to plot out a career path when there was no map. As a result, Aurora does her best to be an example of that opportunity for others. Aurora does not have any regrets about her career path and believes that people can avoid regret by putting tremendous commitment behind their convictions. She has made very deliberate decisions with her life and is extremely happy with the outcomes.

Iana Aranda, 35

**American Society of Mechanical Engineers:
Engineering for Global Development**
Senior Program Manager | ~$80,000–$100,000

BASc, Mechanical Engineering, University of Toronto (2003)

Job Description

Millions of people across the world live on less than two dollars a day. The institutional, environmental, and social challenges they face require innovative and multidisciplinary solutions. One organization promoting the development of appropriate technology for underserved communities is the American Society of Mechanical Engineers (ASME). ASME is a not-for-profit organization that enables collaboration, knowledge sharing, career enrichment, and skills development across all engineering disciplines toward a goal of helping the global engineering community develop solutions that improve lives and livelihoods. One sector of ASME, Engineering for Global Development, serves designers of technology-based solutions for disadvantaged communities. The goal is to ensure that evidence-based engineering knowledge is infused effectively into global development efforts in order to create more sustainable and effective methods and solutions. Iana Aranda is the senior program manager of engineering for global development and the origination editor of *DEMAND* magazine.

Each day, Iana plays multiple roles as a project manager, business analyst, editor, designer, and curator. The bulk of her day is devoted to program design and execution, knowledge synthesis, and collaboration with a variety of teams. She is responsible for developing and deploying new technical programs to meet the demands of engineers in global development. To launch each new program, Iana must first outline a strategy and determine what success will look like. Once the goals are set, she is responsible for the creation of a sustainable business model for the new product or service. This business model includes the entire project life cycle, from definition of requirements to implementation. Finally, to execute, she assembles and manages matrix teams comprised of staff, volunteers, and subject-matter experts and facilitates collaboration among technical subject-matter experts, nonprofit organizations, and industry. Iana's work can be challenging since she is the lead program architect for many different projects; however, she sees the payoff through the social impact of her work.

Iana has launched many programs and projects. Some of her creations include a publication, a webinar series, and an online platform supporting knowledge exchange. She is the origination editor of ASME's *DEMAND* Magazine, a publication that was launched to meet the needs of individuals and organizations working at the intersection of technology and global development. *DEMAND* showcases a mix of case studies, stories, and original reports representing the diverse challenges and solutions emerging in the space. Their unique stories and information focus on integrating existing technology and engineering solutions into systems that meet the needs of the developing world. *DEMAND*'s information is high quality, easily accessible for anyone, and most importantly, up-to-date on current technologies and challenges.

Iana sees the social impact of her work immediately through Engineering for Change, a global alliance that facilitates the development of technology-based solutions to improve the quality of life in underserved communities worldwide. This platform now reaches a global community of more than 700,000 people, including engineers, technologists, representatives from NGOs, and social scientists. Their work encompasses a broad range of issues and solutions for water contamination, alternative energy, infrastructure for agricultural growth, disaster relief shelters, sanitation, and access to health care. The exponential growth of the community since its launch in 2011 validates that it is truly filling a market need and making a valuable impact.

ASME's *DEMAND* magazine showcases and builds upon much of Engineering for Change's work; it is an essential resource for engineers who want to make a difference. The magazine has a webinar series that showcases leading practitioners of sustainable design, a solutions library with appropriate solutions to on-the-ground practical challenges, and constant updates on the world of engineering for global development. Working on many different ventures at once requires a constant awareness of emerging concepts and technologies, knowledge exchange platforms, and targeted engineering areas related to ASME's mission. As the origination editor of *DEMAND* and lead program architect for Engineering for Change, it is particularly important that Iana is up-to-date on socio-environmental trends and technological developments alike. Iana devotes part of each day to the review of key publications and engagement in social media forums.

The resources provided through Iana's initiatives are supporting the work of numerous social enterprises, nonprofits, and academic programs. She is constantly encouraged by positive feedback from members of various organizations. Her

> Do not constrain yourself with a singular definition of social value creation. This pursuit can take many forms even in the most conventional circumstances, but practice will prepare you to identify the right opportunity.

favorite part of the job is the opportunity to work beyond the company borders on projects that improve quality of life for the underserved. She works with teams comprised of passionate, leading-edge professionals, students, and academics that share a commitment to humanity. "The opportunity is unmatched and thoroughly rewarding." The most challenging aspect of Iana's work is that her career trajectory is largely self-defined, which is exciting because it gives her the opportunity to pursue what she is passionate about, but it can often be isolating and difficult.

Career Trajectory

Iana received a bachelor's degree in applied science in engineering from the University of Toronto. She went on to obtain a certificate in global affairs from New York University. Through pursuing her certificate, she gained a broader understanding of the economic and political forces influencing global development. Her love of physics and technology led her to pursue an engineering degree, but her belief in social justice drove her to dive deeply into volunteering. She volunteered with Engineers Without Borders-USA to pursue her passion for global development. That experience, combined with her existing knowledge and scientific background, further convinced her that "the intersection of technology and global development was the space [she] wanted to occupy professionally."

Following graduation, Iana worked as a biomedical instrumentation design engineer in a cancer research lab in New York for nearly five years. This work provided her with a training platform in multidisciplinary collaboration and human-centered design, as well as a background with hands-on engineering work within the sciences. Iana considers this experience as pivotal in shaping her approach to problem solving and her understanding of incorporating user needs into her work. Iana's engagement with EWB-USA since graduation laid the foundation for her career in engineering for global development.

Iana believes that "luck is the intersection of preparation and opportunity." EWB-USA enabled her to explore her passion for global work and to make connections. In committing to her very first EWB-USA project, she connected with a network of people who inspired her and supported her in global development pursuits. Serendipitously, it was from a fruitful meeting at a social event with a stranger, who is now her colleague, where Iana learned about her current position at ASME. Within the next few years, Iana hopes to have the necessary experience and skills to amplify her impact in the global development space and continue to have the privilege of designing her career.

⚙ David Fields, 31

National Peace Corps Association
Program Director, All Resource Connect | ~$60,000

BS, Biology, Marshall University (2008)

Job Description

The US government's Peace Corps Agency currently has around 7,000 individuals tackling the pressing needs of people in sixty-nine countries. How does the Peace Corps strengthen itself over time? Over 220,000 individuals have served in the Peace Corps since 1961. Serving in the Corps provided them all with a phenomenal personal and professional development experience that fundamentally affected their lives, their careers, and their way of relating to the world. How can this energy be leveraged, and on the other side of the coin, how can these Returned Peace Corps Volunteers (RPCVs) be supported? Many of these RPCVs continue working in the development community far after their end of service, and many want to help the currently serving volunteers. The combination of current and past volunteers makes up the "Peace Corps community." The National Peace Corps Association (NPCA), a thirty-five-year-old nonprofit, is dedicated to connecting and supporting the Peace Corps community for the betterment of all.

The idea is simple: bring together a group of remarkable people in the Peace Corps community and see if they can become something more, see if they can use their individual talents and the STEM resources we have raised collectively to solve global development challenges and make the Peace Corps the best that it can be. The Peace Corps community has tens of thousands of teachers, dozens of ambassadors, and hundreds of leaders in both the public and private sectors, but perhaps their largest resource is that they have an unparalleled connection to the rural and hard-to-reach communities in the developing world. There is a need for intrapreneurs within NPCA to innovate on ways to engage the prominent social entrepreneurs of the community and to best leverage the energy of the whole community.

David Fields is one of these people who invented his own position at NPCA. Officially, he is the director of the All Resource Connect (ARC) Program at NPCA. The ARC Program is an effort to aggregate and merge various STEM resources with both the Peace Corps community and the international communities they currently serve or served in the past. On a daily basis, David gets to work on a variety of problems in a variety of places—hence his nickname "Chief of Stuff." The community is far larger and more powerful than the ARC program can contain, and ultimately, the community decides the direction of David's work each week. David's work hours will fluctuate constantly since the community has projects in almost every time zone— 2:00 a.m. Sunday morning conference calls are fair game for him. The primary focus of David's work comes from two simple guidelines, and anything that can be fit into one or both of those categories is fair game: (1) Does this program add value to the Peace Corps community as well as the host country communities within the Peace Corps network? (2) Does this program utilize the experience and cultural expertise of the Peace Corps community to improve the development practices of outside organizations?

An example week of David's work includes connecting an engineering team from Arizona with a RPCV starting a community benefit energy company in West Africa, preparing a scouting trip for an engineering team from Michigan, and working on a textbook for Peace Corps prep students to highlight the types of obstacles they may face once they ship out. It also includes connecting a current volunteer with resources to expand a portable water system in Ghana and finalizing a deal with an RPCV-founded but locally owned and operated last-mile distributor so that they can bring their successful innovations to markets in various developing countries. During this time, David is also supporting twenty-five requests from volunteers in thirteen countries who need technical assistance to solve a problem they have isolated or need guidance to find the best practices they can replicate to solve a local problem.

The biggest perk of David's job is seeing how his work is rippling through the Peace Corps community: volunteers are undertaking projects never done before, and they are engaging with partners they have never worked with before. He is seeing more and more positive change at the community level, and he thinks when people look back on what is working in the developing world, they will see the fingerprints of the Peace Corps community all over it. David's least favorite part of his job is the red tape (excessive adherence to rules and formalities) he has to navigate with the Peace Corps Agency and, even more so, universities. Fortunately, NPCA has partnerships with individuals within academia to help him navigate university policies. David struggles to integrate his work with his personal life. It takes passion to create something new, and it is impossible to leave that passion at the office. He has found that the more encompassed he is by work, the more his work associates become social friends, and he has to be careful to not let the one aspect of his life affect the other.

> Never stop learning new things. I did not learn to code until I was twenty-nine. In my college years I took up Photoshop as a hobby. Neither of these are essential to what I do now, but I use those skills a lot more than I thought I would. With such diverse programs, we are constantly trying to find people with specific skill sets.

Career Trajectory

While taking graduate-level courses in soil science, David founded Grounds for Growth, a small houseplant fertilizer company that sold used coffee grounds collected from various coffee shops in the area and donated proceeds to support Peace Corps Partnership Programs. David decided to leave graduate school early to join the Peace Corps in Ghana to work on water sanitation and food security projects. While abroad, David found a problem he wanted to solve: why are so many resources being used on solutions for communities they do not understand? After living in a rural community in Ghana for two years, he began seeing development projects from the Western world the way local communities see them, and that perspective was not always pretty. Teams bring innovations that are designed with little or no understanding of the local culture, the local resources available, even basic understandings of why these developing communities do things the way they do them. To David, it seemed as if the Peace Corps community had a never-ending list of real developing-world problems that needed to be solved. He also saw that universities have a nearly unlimited number of bright emerging professionals that want to solve problems, so he wondered: why do I see so many promising development innovations in academia, and why do I not see those innovations being used in the field by locals? Coming from the Peace Corps community where so many people are trying to bring positive change to their community, he simply could not understand why these innovations he would read about never made it to the people the projects were designed to support. It was not long until all David wanted to do was solve these problems.

Upon return from Ghana, David decided that he wanted to become an intrapreneur instead of an entrepreneur. He wanted to work with the Peace Corps Agency as well as the National Peace Corps Association; but instead of filling out an application to work with them, he met with NPCA to convince them that they should have a department that solves the problems David wanted to solve and that they should hire him to run that program. Fortunately, the concept was well received by both the Peace Corps Agency as well as the National Peace Corps Association. However, neither organization had the resources or extra room in the budget to start a new program, so David went out and raised money for the NPCA so that they could bring this program under their umbrella. By making his way into an existing organization, he avoided many of the traditional problems that he would have faced as an entrepreneur in a startup. Now, he had the clout of a thirty-five-year-old nonprofit and an established pipeline into the bigger Peace Corps community. David was able to organize his program that has now become All Resource Connect with a donation from an angel investor. In his second year, he transitioned to being a consultant for NPCA, and now his salary comes completely from the National Peace Corps Association. David sees himself with NPCA long term; he hopes to be there for many more years as the Peace Corps community becomes more robust and connected more with the private sector and other large development agencies.

⚙ Saurabh Lall, 32

The Aspen Institute
Research Director, Aspen Network of Development Entrepreneurs |
~$70,000 – $80,000

PhD, Public Policy and Public Administration, George Washington
University (2015)
MPP, George Washington University (2007)
BEng, Electronics, University of Mumbai (2004)

Job Description

International development researchers need help from people living in communities of interest to understand the challenges they face and identify research questions. Researchers seek to publish their findings to build their portfolio while simultaneously helping the communities they worked with. Does all research help the communities? Not necessarily. In the past, umpteen researchers have produced academic knowledge that was out of touch with the realities of the people's lives. Communities have sometimes been left without follow-up from research studies, leaving them feeling used. Over time, researchers have come to understand the importance of sharing lessons learned with communities and helping them integrate the findings into their ways of working. There is now an understanding that knowledge transfer is a two-way street between community members and researchers at universities, research labs, and corporations. There is knowledge created by communities around the world that is specific to certain contexts; researchers need to respect this indigenous knowledge and share it. The idea is to meld indigenous knowledge with academic knowledge to find practical, innovative, and sustainable solutions. The Aspen Network of Development Entrepreneurs (ANDE) knows this all too well because they propel entrepreneurship in emerging markets.

As ANDE's research director, Saurabh Lall coordinates and facilitates research on the impact of small and growing businesses in emerging markets and developing countries, as well as effective approaches to support them. ANDE is a network of organizations that supports entrepreneurship in emerging markets with the broader vision of contributing to poverty alleviation. Saurabh works with academics and practitioners to facilitate collaboration and drive more research that can address key, practitioner-relevant questions on small business development in developing countries. The bulk of his work at ANDE is developing sector-level strategies for research on various topics (such as poverty measurement, impact of business acceleration services, and effective data collection approaches). For example, over the past four years, he facilitated several collaborations between academics and practitioners, and published a report on social enterprise accelerators. Overall, his role is to cross-pollinate ideas he identifies from different sources and help connect people and organizations that would not normally be connected. One example of this work is a report on assessing entrepreneurial ecosystems, published by ANDE in 2013. This report synthesizes various frameworks and approaches on the topic produced by academics (such as the Babson Entrepreneurial Ecosystem Project and George Mason's Global Entrepreneurship and Development Index) in a practitioner-friendly format. The report is being used by NGOs to assess local ecosystems in Mexico, Pakistan, Kenya, and Central America.

To work most effectively, Saurabh tries to schedule his week so that he has two to three days of meetings and two to three days of open time for thinking, strategizing, reading, and writing. In practice, this is harder to do since unexpected deliverables and meetings come up all the time. Saurabh's work at ANDE is a few steps removed from the actual social impact he is making on the ground. Since Saurabh does not directly work with the entrepreneurs, it is difficult for him to see his impact directly. However, his work provides him with a great overview of the broader landscape on small business development at a global level, which is a unique opportunity to get this "30,000-foot perspective" on an emerging development paradigm. In the short time that Saurabh has been working in the field of enterprise development, he has seen the sector mature and evolve to a considerable extent with the emergence of industry standards, mainstream attention, and most importantly in his opinion, a greater focus on measuring the impact of activities in more rigorous ways. The social enterprise investing sector still has a long way to go before they can definitively determine what works and what does not, but Saurabh thinks they are moving in the right direction.

Saurabh loves that he gets to meet people doing incredibly innovative things to support entrepreneurs around the world. It is fascinating for him, as a researcher, to compare various approaches from Latin America to Southeast Asia and to see common elements. Saurabh finds that identifying and prioritizing projects that he works on is quite challenging, given the wide range of opportunities that align with his interests. He has had to drop many interesting projects that he would have loved to work on simply due to lack of time.

Career Trajectory

Saurabh was about two and a half years into his undergraduate engineering program when he realized he did not want to be an engineer. He had always been more interested in the application of technology to solve specific problems than actually developing the technology. Saurabh's aunt and uncle were both development economists, and he had always found their work on rural development fascinating. In 2005, Saurabh's uncle offered him a position developing a database for a rural water and sanitation development project in north India. However, before creating the database, the data had to be collected. Saurabh's uncle called to ask if he would be interested in conducting household surveys in the Indian state of Haryana. Saurabh jumped at the opportunity and spent a week conducting surveys on water and sanitation. A similar data collection effort later that year in Leh and Kargil turned out to be the most challenging field research experience Saurabh ever had. These experiences taught him to be flexible and to recognize that field research was rarely as clean and straightforward as desk research. Once the research team was not able to conduct surveys because of heavy snowfall in the region. They had to adapt the sampling design to ensure that they could still collect relevant data for the project.

> Always think about how you are actually going to measure social value creation. It is not easy, but it is essential for us to have any credibility, as a sector.

In 2006, Saurabh began a master's of public policy at George Washington University. At GWU, Saurabh became more interested in the intersection of the public and private sectors and the use of market-based approaches for development. He interned at the National Council for Public-Private Partnerships and worked as a research assistant for the Government Performance Project, developing skills in evaluation and performance measurement that he uses in his current job. He also became aware of the nascent field of social entrepreneurship and concepts such as "base of the pyramid," inclusive business, and market-based approaches to development, which led him to apply for a job at the World Resources Institute's New Ventures program, which focused on supporting environmental entrepreneurship in developing countries.

When Saurabh joined New Ventures in 2008, the world of impact investing and social enterprise was just starting to coalesce around the ideas of industry associations and standards and the need for greater cooperation and coordination. Saurabh's balance of technical skills, understanding various renewable energy technologies, and a policy degree was helpful in his work at New Ventures where he did research on key sectors (such as energy service companies in India and the role of social enterprises in energy access and rural electrification). Both topics have gained a lot of attention in recent years, and he is happy to say that his research reports were some of the few early studies on those topics. Saurabh continued to do field research on environmentally focused social enterprises in India, Cambodia, and Bangladesh while he was with New Ventures.

During this time, Saurabh realized that his true passion was doing research, and his research interests were more practically oriented than purely scientific endeavors. Therefore, he decided to go back to GWU and start working on their PhD program in public policy on a part-time basis with a focus on evaluation and performance management. His research interests focused on the evaluation and performance management of social enterprises. When Saurabh saw the open position for research director at Aspen Network of Development Entrepreneurs (ANDE), the overlap with his academic interests was so strong that he jumped to apply for the position. He joined ANDE with the primary goal of setting up a research initiative that would drive more rigorous, academic-quality research on the impact of small and growing businesses (including social enterprise), as well as more effective ways to support them.

Saurabh's training in evaluation methodologies and performance measurement has been the most effective in helping him get to his current position. From his engineering background, the exposure to calculus and statistics and coursework on renewable energy technology have been most relevant. With New Ventures, Saurabh saw the social sector from the bottom up, but he also saw it mature and become more formalized. At ANDE, he gets a great overview of the whole sector, and he gets to see all the different connections and how they work (or sometimes do not work) together. Saurabh is sure that further down his career he will still be working in the social sector and producing actionable research for practitioners. Saurabh thanks his understanding wife for helping him integrate his work with his personal life. He tries to develop hobbies that are completely unrelated to his work, such as photography, which satisfies both his artistic and geeky sides. He also loves to travel, and travelling for work or pleasure is a great opportunity to practice photography.

Photo by Ranjith Krishnan

Paul Belknap, 33

Villgro Innovations Foundation
Investment Manager – Health Portfolio | ~$22,000 – 30,000

MBA, Penn State University (2013)
BS, Mechanical Engineering, Gonzaga University (2005)

Job Description

Entrepreneurs need advisors to check on their project and business design to identify potential hurdles as well as opportunities for growth. Advisors are all the more important for technology entrepreneurs in developing countries due to the larger gaps in the ecosystem that make the commercialization process harder. Paul, an engineer with an MBA, works with Villgro, an organization operating in India that strives to enable innovations to impact the poor through social enterprise. Paul finds the best ideas from early-stage entrepreneurs and provides mentoring support across the venture life cycle—from product design to manufacturing to distribution to after-sales support. Paul's work centers around two primary responsibilities: sourcing new entrepreneurs to support and then actually providing them that support once he decides to bring them into Villgro's incubation programs. The sourcing role starts with speaking with potential entrepreneurs on a regular basis and, through fairly brief phone calls or meetings, gauging the strength of both the business model and the entrepreneur. The ones that show promise move to more detailed due diligence, where Paul researches the proposed venture by speaking with people knowledgeable about the sector, including competitors, sector experts, and other investors. If the entrepreneurs pass that test, the real work begins as Paul helps accelerate the growth of those companies.

Paul's work centers around helping entrepreneurs fix concerns in their business models by thinking through various alternatives. Tools such as the "Customer Empathy Map" and "A Day in the Life Of" help entrepreneurs understand their customers better and identify their assumptions. Once the assumptions are articulated, entrepreneurs use lean experiments and human-centered design techniques to validate things like the highest potential customer segment, product requirements, and an appropriate pricing strategy. Paul relies heavily on senior mentors to guide the entrepreneurs through the development process, so Paul's role is to complement the mentors' work and connect entrepreneurs to additional resources. As the entrepreneurs address the largest risks and are ready to raise more funds, Paul connects them with the right investors and helps them prepare to pitch their ventures so that they can access capital that will fuel their next phase of growth.

The social entrepreneurs that Villgro works with are all focused on solving problems for the base of the pyramid (i.e., the largest, but poorest socioeconomic group in society) in India. Villgro has a fairly rigorous definition of social impact, which is an important criteria Paul considers when vetting an enterprise. The social impact that Paul is creating comes from helping those entrepreneurs scale faster and serve more people. Paul truly believes that if he does good work, he can help entrepreneurs solve big problems, and it is his job to make sure they do not make avoidable mistakes that will limit their growth and ability to make impact at scale. Paul's favorite part of his job is working with the entrepreneurs, both at the deal-sourcing stage and the support stage. Paul works with a bunch of really passionate, brilliant people on a constant stream of fresh challenges, which means that his job never gets boring. Helping them solve those challenges is really exciting and interesting for him. Paul's least favorite part of his job is reporting (recording his work metrics), but thankfully Villgro's reporting processes are pretty lean, so he does not need to spend a lot of time on it.

Career Trajectory

Paul's journey began at adventure camps for six summers during high school and college. He joined the staff when the camp was a startup, and having that as his first job is probably what "ruined him for the corporate world." It was during that time, being surrounded by a lot of passionate, forward-thinking people, that his social conscience developed. That time, combined with the Jesuit education he received at Gonzaga University, made it inevitable that he would eventually migrate to working in the social entrepreneurship space.

After Paul graduated from college, he worked for five years as a mechanical engineer designing industrial equipment for the paper industry at a world-class machinery company in his hometown. His experience through his first job honed his problem-solving skills and attention to detail. Working on side projects in process improvement was what got him interested in business and what made him consider getting an MBA. He ultimately decided that he wanted to pursue a career in social enterprise and decided that he wanted a strong business tool kit, so he went back to get his MBA at the Smeal College of Business at Penn State. Going into school, he knew that he wanted to work with social enterprise and that he wanted to work in an emerging market; those goals became more focused as he worked his way through his MBA. By the time he graduated, he knew that he did not have that one idea that he wanted to take the leap and start a company around, so he searched for roles to support entrepreneurs or to work at an early-stage startup. After graduating, Paul landed a role with MBAs Without Borders, supporting a company called Sustaintech in South India.

Working for MBAs Without Borders was an excellent opportunity. Getting your first international role in the social enterprise sector can be really tough because international work experience is often a key hiring criteria for international assignments, which means that you need experience to get experience. Paul's role working as an adviser to Sustaintech gave him that crucial international experience and ultimately led to his current role with Villgro. Villgro was incubating Sustaintech, so he was presenting the results of his work to the Villgro people working with Sustaintech, and they were ultimately impressed enough with what they saw that they offered Paul a position working with Villgro when his assignment with Sustaintech was over. Not only was the MBAs Without Borders role a key stepping-stone to the role with Villgro, but it also gave him a lot of eye-opening experience as he took a deep dive into a successful social enterprise. He believes the lessons he learned there in a short, intense assignment will serve him well in the years to come.

Paul's MBA from Penn State prepared him very well for the work that he is doing today. The business fundamentals are the same in a for-profit social enterprise as they are for a regular business, and the MBA program gave him the flexibility to put together a really strong set of general business skills from the courses offered. Most of the companies he works with are young enough that they need guidance in most areas of their business, so having the ability to help them think through challenges from human resources to finance is beneficial. Paul did a market research project with Penn State's Humanitarian Engineering and Social Entrepreneurship (HESE) program that gave him an introduction to how different market research can be for a social enterprise when compared with the multinational corporations that are the core of an MBA curriculum. Paul first discovered the lack of availability of good market data during his HESE project, and he has continued to see it in his other work. Finally, being president of the Smeal Net Impact chapter gave Paul great exposure to the broader impact space, helped him develop some good connections, and gave him some great program management experience that helped him get to where he is today.

Paul leverages his mechanical engineering background frequently since most of his work involves technology in some form. His undergraduate degree from Gonzaga gave him a sound foundation that helps in understanding technology-based products that Villgro is supporting in areas such as health care, energy, and agriculture, even if the products are not purely mechanical in nature. He has recently transitioned to leading Villgro's health-care incubation work, which means that the vast majority of the enterprises he is supporting are science and technology-based. As Paul's career progresses, he is hoping to stay in the impact investing and incubation space. In the next five to ten years, he sees himself moving downstream into a social venture capital firm, working with later-stage companies and larger investments than he is currently involved with. Paul's work and personal life blend more now than they have in the past. His schedule tends to be very fluid with a lot of work happening outside core work time, but also a lot of flexibility in terms of when he is in the office. His balancing act, along with the opportunity to travel extensively throughout India on work, keeps him fresh. He is currently acting as an alumni advisor for MBAs Without Borders, which is a great learning experience and an important way to pay it forward.

Ross Baird, 30

Village Capital
Executive Director | ~$110,000

MPhil, Comparative Government, University of Oxford (2009)
BA, Government and Foreign Affairs, University of Virginia (2007)

Job Description

Traditional thinking is that the only way to solve social challenges is through government and charity and that the only purpose of business and investing is to make money. However, successes like microfinance and for-profit social ventures have proven that business can produce profits alongside a social return. Impact investors recognize that for-profit investment can be both a socially responsible and economically effective way to address social and environmental challenges. Therefore, they invest their money in organizations in order to generate a measurable social or environmental impact as well as a financial return. Village Capital is a nonprofit organization that works with early-stage ventures solving major global problems in agriculture, education, energy, financial inclusion, and health. They run programs for groups of such ventures to train them on developing their business models, creating and managing a team, interacting with potential customers, and connecting with investors. At the end of their programs, the group votes on which two ventures most deserve to be funded, and Village Capital's affiliated for-profit investment fund, VilCap Investments, LLC invests around $50,000 in those top peer-selected companies.

Examples of Village Capital's programs include one focused for "edupreneurs," reducing the education gap in India, and another geared toward reducing greenhouse gas emissions through clean technology in energy and agriculture in the agricultural region of Louisville, Kentucky. Village Capital's programs generally consist of three four-day workshops over a three-month period led by leading entrepreneurs, investors, industry experts, and the Village Capital teams. In between each in-person session, teams continue to collaborate remotely and receive training through biweekly webinars. The curriculum has been designed to give entrepreneurs both an insight into their own enterprises "through the lens of the investor," as well as a focus on the customer through forums designed to accelerate customer validation. Village Capital has had 450 entrepreneurs come through nearly thirty-five programs, and their companies have created more than 7,000 jobs and raised $110 million in follow-on capital to scale their businesses and impact.

As the founder and executive director of Village Capital, Ross Baird spends most of his time building strategic partnerships, fundraising, meeting entrepreneurs, and developing Village Capital's long-term strategic vision. His organization has grown rapidly over the last fifteen months (they had five team members at the beginning of 2014 and twenty-three by mid-2015), so Ross has spent a large amount of his time recently dealing with issues related to building a team to reach scale. Ross's impact through Village Capital first of all comes from redefining entrepreneurship to mean problem solving. Too many talented entrepreneurs are founding businesses that make the lives of middle- and upper-class Americans easier, instead of taking on the biggest problems facing our world. Village Capital's impact also comes from fundamentally changing the way people and organizations allocate and invest capital in businesses around the world. At the end of each of their programs, the participating entrepreneurs choose which of their peers receive seed capital from their investment fund. Over the last five years, they have made nearly forty investments, and peer selection is proving to be a far more inclusive process than mainstream venture capital. For instance, 40% of their portfolio companies are women-led, compared to just 8% of a traditional portfolio. Also, 27% of their companies are run by minority entrepreneurs, compared to 2% of a traditional portfolio.

The best part of Ross's job is the opportunity to support all the amazing entrepreneurs he works with from around the world. It is inspiring to be able to help them along their journey to solve major societal problems. Facilitating Village Capital's workshops with cohorts of entrepreneurs is consistently a reinvigorating experience. Ross's least favorite part of his job is navigating his email inbox every day. He gets hundreds of emails daily, and it is nearly impossible to respond to all of them while keeping up with his other responsibilities. Alongside Village Capital, Ross teaches courses in entrepreneurship and impact investing at the University of Virginia. Ross also helped start two training programs that he continues to work closely with to help professionals align their careers with their values: Impact Business Leaders and Frontier Market Scouts. Village Capital has been an enormous part of Ross's life for the last five years. He is incredibly thankful for his wonderful wife who is willing to put up with all the time he spends on the organization. Ross travels about 75% of the time and works fourteen- to sixteen-hour days, but he is excited about his work, so it does not feel overwhelming (for the most part).

Career Trajectory

Ross graduated from the University of Virginia, where he was introduced to the notion of the "academical village," which refers to Thomas Jefferson's idea that learning is a lifelong pursuit and a shared process for all members of a learning community; students and professors alike. That idea is at the foundation of Village Capital's peer learning model. While an undergraduate, he became class president and raised the most money from a class giving campaign in university history.

Ross has always been an entrepreneur. Before launching Village Capital, he was involved in the founding and development of four education-related startup ventures. The first one, where he was the assistant director for a short time, was the National College Advising Corps in Chapel Hill, North Carolina, a nationwide nonprofit that places recent college graduates in high schools with low college attendance. Then Ross became a research consultant for the Indian School Finance Company in Hyderabad, India, where he conducted market research for a startup finance company providing affordable loans to low-cost independent schools in slum areas of India. Ross visited over one hundred schools across the country and did a market assessment of five major urban areas, recommending expansion opportunities. Ross also was involved in the development of two ventures using technology to promote civic participation.

> For students interested in starting a business that also makes a social impact, I think it is key to recognize that you do not have to choose between profits and impact. There is a false prevailing narrative that suggests so-called "social entrepreneurs" cannot compete with traditional business, and that is a dangerous notion to embrace. At Village Capital, we see counterexamples every day in businesses that are tackling some of the biggest problems in our world related to agriculture, energy, education, financial technology, and health, and they are doing it to make an impact while creating a massive business.
>
> Albert Einstein once said, "If I had an hour to solve a problem, I would spend fifty-five minutes thinking about the problem and five minutes thinking about solutions." That is a crucial lesson for entrepreneurs everywhere, and universities are positioned to help understand major problems and their causes. Professors of entrepreneurship in particular should be emphasizing how new innovations can solve world challenges, not just make the lives of the upper-middle class incrementally more convenient.

In addition to his startup experience, he worked on the investment side of the industry for First Light Ventures, a seed-stage venture fund aimed at high-impact businesses. The genesis of Village Capital came from that experience; Ross learned the entrepreneur-investor dynamic was extremely skewed, leading to poor results for both parties, and the cost of diligence was too high to make a high number of investments despite an abundance of quality companies. Ross's boss and mentor at First Light Ventures has been instrumental in helping Ross to this point; he invested in one of Ross's earliest ventures and has been a supporter ever since. This mentor, Bob Pattillo, helped develop the Village Capital concept while Ross worked at First Light and encouraged him to bring this idea to scale. Ross hopes to still be running Village Capital long into the future. He is hopeful that the next twenty years will bring new, exciting challenges for his organization to tackle, and he feels like they are just getting started on making an impact.

Photo by Todd Stark

🍃 Miguel Zamora, 38

Coffee Gente LLC | President | ~$85,000
UTZ Certified | North America Business Developer

MS, Agricultural Economics, Michigan State University (2004)
BS, Agronomy and Agribusiness, Zamorano University (2001)

Job Description

Coffee is a globally traded commodity, most of which is produced in the developing world. Many small-scale coffee farmers live in remote locations and lack access to the supply chains needed to directly sell their product in the global marketplace at competitive rates. Hence they typically sell their coffee to middlemen who offer them instant cash at rates far lower than the market value. Several organizations have emerged to support small-scale farmers by bringing them together, engaging in value-addition activities, and facilitating market linkages. This has become its own organized social movement that aims to help agricultural producers in developing countries create improved trading conditions while promoting sustainability. This movement includes several certifying organizations that champion higher payment to marginalized producers as well as higher social and environmental standards for all stakeholders.

Miguel Zamora supports one of these organizations, UTZ Certified, the leading third-party certifier of sustainable coffee, cocoa, and tea in the world. As a company, they enable socially aware people in the US to make a difference with their dollars while providing farmers in developing nations the tools to thrive in this complex international business. Instead of creating dependency on foreign aid, UTZ Certified uses a farmer-centric and market-based approach that gives farmers better management tools, creates safer condition for workers, and supports entire communities to create healthier and more sustainable livelihoods. Miguel works with coffee, cocoa, and tea companies, smallholder farmers, and farm workers all over the world to create opportunities for farmers to access better markets for their products. He also helps workers to achieve better working conditions, communities to access premiums to improve their situations, and companies to build sustainable supply chains and find the great quality and sustainable coffees they need.

In order to improve the sustainability of coffee supply chains, Miguel identifies potential opportunities for collaboration between stockholders. Specifically, by helping coffee farmers prepare for receiving sustainable certification, he helps them improve their management practices, improve their yields, decrease costs of production, and receive above-market value for their goods. Once they are certified, Miguel connects farmers with buyers through sustainable supply chains supported by buyers themselves. Buyers also receive information about how their purchases improve farming communities. Buyers share this information with their customers and coffee consumers so that everyone is part of this journey that benefits farmers and workers all over the world. Miguel is proud of all the matchmaking he has accomplished between farmers and buyers and finds it rewarding to see the net impact of all of those initial connections and capacity-building experiences.

For Miguel, the social impact is much more than words on a page. For example, let us consider a family-owned coffee farm in Nicaragua that Miguel worked with in his previous job. The farm was certified after satisfying their rigorous standards. Just by meeting this standard, the Nicaraguan farm was required to improve their working conditions for better worker safety, such as using adequate protective equipment in the fields. On the other end, coffee buyers pay above-market value for the coffee bearing this prestigious certification. The certification ensures access to coffee that is produced sustainably, for both the environment and workers. In this case, the above-market premium was distributed to the workers via a small committee of workers, appointed by the workers themselves; this committee decided how the capital should be reinvested in the community. The workers decided to use the funds to provide workers and their families something they had never received before: access to clean latrines and medical care. This was the first time some community members had a functional latrine in their homes and purchased eyeglasses! In essence, coffee farmers and workers improve their communities, and coffee buyers build stronger and more sustainable supply chains for the future.

From his role representing UTZ Certified in North America, Miguel explores how UTZ Certified can evolve to create more value for companies and farmers, reach farther, and increase impact—specifically, how UTZ Certified can help companies in North America to build more sustainable supply chains through the use of traceability systems, stronger measurement & evaluation (M&E) and sustainability standards that help farmers to become more profitable and workers to work in safer conditions; and improve access to health care, clean water, and education. He is constantly leveraging his knowledge and background in agronomy and his experience in agribusiness to identify ways to improve the efficiency of his work and that of his company. To understand and further quantify this, in his previous role, Miguel's team, along with other nonprofit organizations, farmers, farm workers, and coffee companies, designed an impact assessment system. This system captures and illustrates the impact of Miguel's work on coffee farms using face-to-face surveys, workshops, and cell phone technology. It enables Miguel and his company to understand, directly from farmers and workers, how their work needs to improve and what impact they are truly creating.

Miguel is on the road for several months each year, visiting coffee- and cocoa-growing communities in countries including Brazil, Colombia, Honduras, and his home country, Ecuador. He also travels across the US and Canada supporting coffee, cocoa, and tea companies to strengthen their sustainable supply chains. His background helps him to relate with farmers and workers in a more direct, technical way. He listens to their stories, meets their families, learns about their work, and finds out how sustainable trade makes, or could make, a meaningful difference in their daily lives. Miguel knows that the things he learns on these visits are vital to determining best practices for innovation and exploring more sustainable models. Fortunately, the one hundred employees of UTZ Certified and many businesses, nongovernmental organizations, co-op leaders, farm workers, and conscious consumers stand firmly behind the idea that sustainable farming should be the norm and that all farmers, workers, and their families deserve a better future. UTZ Certified is committed to creating more opportunities for sustainability for farmers, workers, and North American companies, and has increased its team in North America explore new opportunities. Miguel is excited to lead this work for North America.

Career Trajectory

Miguel left his native country, Ecuador, when he was seventeen. He studied agriculture in Honduras because it was a great university and also because he wanted to see what else was out there. Back then, Miguel was not particularly interested in agriculture but wanted to see the world, and this was a great opportunity to begin doing that. Once he began working with rural communities, it became clear how important agriculture was for the well-being of millions living in rural communities. He met people who did not have enough food to eat. Witnessing little children working in agricultural fields and workers being sprayed with dangerous pesticides without wearing proper protection proved to be an important experience for Miguel. The reality of the agricultural sector in Latin America was crude and eye-opening. It impacted him tremendously, and he saw an opportunity to do something with his life by working in solidarity with those rural communities he loved so much.

Miguel has tried to learn from every step of his career in agriculture, from working on fruit production in Ecuador, to working on development projects that assisted and trained small-scale farmers in Honduras. He likes working on initiatives that clearly create value for farmers and farm workers, that are flexible enough to continue improving and adapting to changing realities, and that are innovative. Miguel believes that his experiences serving on boards and participating in committees have helped him get to where he is today. Miguel is currently a member of the Specialty Coffee Association of America Sustainability Council and a board member of an NGO working on food-security issues in Latin America called Food 4 Farmers. Miguel enjoys working with like-minded professionals in similar or different fields to shape the future of these exciting programs. Miguel's work is a part of his personal life. As someone whose profession reflects his values and passions, it is difficult to truly separate the two. Miguel's wife is just as passionate as him about Fair Trade, which certainly makes things easier. Miguel sometimes wishes he had taken more risks early in his professional career. However, overall Miguel is happy with where his journey has taken him and excited about the prospects for his future.

Photo by Dawn Nixon

Steve Garguilo, 27

Johnson & Johnson
Senior Manager, Creative Engagement and Curator,
TEDxJNJ | ~$140,000

BS, Information Sciences & Technology, Penn State (2009)

Job Description

When thinking about large multinational corporations like Johnson & Johnson (J&J), images of cubicle farms and men in suits often come to mind. While this is true of many jobs at such workplaces, there are also important, impactful innovations being advanced by passionate individuals at these companies. With the global market reach of J&J (the world's largest, broadly based health-care company), potential profits are massive, but social responsibility is also important. J&J recognizes this and has a positive social and environmental track record, from engagement on key global health issues like providing critical access to medications that address intestinal worms, TB, HIV, and Ebola worldwide to an incredible commitment to sustainability and environmentally friendly practices, from the sourcing of materials to the design of packages. As it grows, J&J is increasingly engaging in emerging markets such as Africa and the Middle East, but there is so much more to do as populations in these regions continue to grow. Steve Garguilo believes that companies grow by innovation, and innovation starts when employees share their ideas with others.

Steve is currently senior manager, creative engagement and curator, TEDxJNJ for J&J, a company that impacts billions of people's health-care decisions. This position enables him to work on his true passion: social impact. When Steve started with J&J, he worked in IT, but he quickly started volunteering for projects focused on emerging markets, which soon turned into his full-time job. For nearly three years, his responsibility was for the distribution of consumer products in rural communities throughout Europe, the Middle East, and Africa. This involved answering a lot of emails and talking on the phone as well as travel to these markets to implement and oversee his projects. Steve worked on the ground in Kenya to implement a mobile commerce solution that optimized route management for J&J's distributors, enabling more products to get out into communities that need them. Additionally, Steve worked in partnership with ColaLife, a nonprofit organization that allows for companies like J&J to piggyback on the supply chain of Coca-Cola by adding consumer health-care products to the Coca-Cola crates.

Alongside completing these tasks, Steve adopted a new approach to social innovation by starting the first corporate TEDx program to help people pick themselves and make their ideas happen. After starting this as a grassroots movement, he again created a new full-time job and now serves as the curator of the company's global TEDxJNJ program, leading a team of over 300 people and building a community to create a space for ideas within J&J. By offering employees permission and an opportunity to discuss new ideas and concepts, Steve has brought about tremendous change, driving a culture of innovation at J&J. TEDxJNJ events have been held in thirty-eight countries and over seventy-four J&J locations. Many ideas have gone from being presented at TEDxJNJ to becoming real J&J initiatives, such as a telemedicine project that they are launching in Colombia to help patients in rural areas. In addition to TEDxJNJ event programming, Steve now leads training programs, a leadership development program, a digital platform, and a host of other offerings to help instigate a culture of innovation at the company.

By helping people to approach work differently and work more creatively, Steve is seeing a lot of people question existing processes and approaches and make new ideas happen. Many of these ideas impact the developing world as J&J continues to work to best meet the needs of people across the globe. Steve has been fortunate enough to create his own position multiple times within a large corporation. As a result, some of the best aspects of his job are the freedom and leeway he enjoys in his created role. In addition to this freedom, Steve also maintains the high level of job security that a corporation such as Johnson & Johnson is able to provide. Because of the global nature of his job at J&J, Steve has lived in both Switzerland and New York City and has traveled to over ninety other countries.

However, working in such a large company can have its drawbacks as well. Steve says that along with the security provided within a large company, employees also have to navigate a convoluted bureaucratic corporate framework, which can be quite frustrating. He finds that being open and honest when interacting with others builds his credibility. This can be challenging at a large company, but it has worked out well for Steve.

Career Trajectory

Steve Garguilo started his journey with an education in information sciences and technology at Penn State. Following graduation, he felt pressured to pursue a career with one of the large corporations that sponsored his college. Steve followed this popular track, but chose a company whose mission he strongly believed in, Johnson & Johnson. After spending a year building credibility within the company by consistently delivering for Johnson & Johnson, Steve leveraged this credibility into acquiring a position where he could work on what he truly cared most about, social impact. He decided to become a maverick within the company and push for a more socially aware agenda. He was pleased to find there was a huge appetite for this within the corporation, and he experienced a genuine desire to see his career succeed. Through showing passion and articulating his ideas well, Steve tailored a position to fit his desired role. Two years after joining the company, Steve moved to Switzerland and was the emerging-markets business lead for three years. Since then, he has moved back to the US but now with enterprise-wide responsibility for instigating a culture of innovation.

> Do not feel pressured by high schools, colleges, or universities to follow a certain typical path. Rather, look to those who are actually working in social value creation, like those profiled in this book. Many successful social entrepreneurs took a lot of time to build up the confidence to actually do what they felt passionate about. Skip this step, take the plunge, and go after the impact you want to see happen. The best time for you to go all-in on social innovation is now.
>
> You have to work tirelessly toward what you believe in. Otherwise, why are you here?

Steve credits his tenacious approach to his career and profession as one of the most important characteristics that has helped him be successful. He believes that tenacity is the most under-recognized attribute to being successful. Those who make an impact tend to have a vision and exhibit the impressive work ethic necessary to achieve that vision. Constantly being open-minded and having a desire to try new things have helped Steve develop a creative thought process and approach, which has also proven to be a huge professional advantage. After beginning his career in information technology, Steve began to channel his skill set toward a commercial business development role and now to a creative, human resources role.

An important inflection point for Steve was recognizing what he was passionate about and how he used his free time. He then began to take constructive steps toward integrating these passions into his occupation. As a student, leadership opportunities, whether in the Penn State Blue Band or student government, were very important to his professional development and success. Additionally, Steve claims that his most valuable academic experiences were international experiences in Rick Schuhmann's engineering leadership development minor courses and Khanjan Mehta's Humanitarian Engineering and Social Entrepreneurship Program. Steve holds these experiences in highest esteem because they provided him with exposure to diverse teams, the opportunity to travel abroad, as well as eye-opening experiences, challenges, and opportunities in the developing world. Before Penn State, Steve had traveled in only six US states. Steve left Penn State a global citizen committed to positively impacting the world.

Steve finds it difficult to see his work and personal life as separate. Instead, he finds his personal life and work life integrated into each other. Steve believes that those who need to balance personal and work life tend to not enjoy their work and hence need an escape in the form of their personal life. Steve finds himself lucky that he thoroughly enjoys what he does for a living, and his personal life is more of a complement than a separate entity. Many of his connections and mentors have come from the TED community. Steve believes his experiences with TED are a tremendous testament to the benefits of pursuing your passions and interests. As an undergrad Steve was on Facebook and saw that someone at Carnegie Mellon was hosting a TEDxCMU and thought, "We should do that at Penn State." So Steve put a committed team together who worked on TEDxPSU in their spare time. Little did he know that this experience would come full circle and eventually help him start the first corporate TEDx event, TEDxJNJ.

Rather than establishing a detailed long-term plan, Steve prefers to have a general compass that guides his professional decisions and to periodically reevaluate and adjust these parameters. He has found that several times since undergrad graduation, this compass has changed course significantly, so instead of being bogged down by a rigid plan, Steve prefers flexibility. One of the consistent parameters Steve uses is the amount of measurable impact he produces through his work. He intends to continue to increase this impact over the course of his career.

John Tran, 27

Campbell Soup Company
Procurement Corporate Social Responsibility and Sustainability
Lead | ~$70,000 – 80,000

BSE, Material Science Engineering, University of Pennsylvania

Job Description

Palm oil is a globally traded agricultural commodity found in roughly half the packaged goods sold in grocery stores, including chips, cookies, bread, pizza, chocolate, margarine, instant noodles, and soap. Production of palm oil by food companies doubled in the 2000s and is expected to double again by 2020. Palm oil comes mostly from developing countries because it grows in tropical climates that coincide with sub-Saharan Africa, Southeast Asia, and northern South America. Unfortunately, palm oil procurement can cause deforestation, forced labor, and violations of forest-dependent communities' rights—mostly in developing countries. The establishment of palm oil plantations is often promoted as a way of bringing development to poor, rural regions of Southeast Asia. However, palm oil plantations can potentially have devastating impacts on the people in these areas.

Companies are increasingly realizing the value that social and environmental projects can play for their stakeholders. Collectively, large food companies that use palm oil can have a large impact by improving their practices. Developing regulations for palm oil production requires an understanding of the complexity of the issues surrounding it, from the aforementioned environmental and social problems to the dependence of people in developing countries on palm oil for their income and survival. Some corporations taking action to commit to their social responsibility, not only in terms of palm oil, have formed Corporate Social Responsibility (CSR) programs. CSR programs employ people specifically to ensure that their company is contributing positively to the world, socially and environmentally. One company with such a program is Campbell Soup Company where John Tran works as a sustainability procurement senior analyst.

John's role is to make Campbell's supply chain more environmentally sustainable and socially responsible. Supply-chain management includes the oversight of materials, information, and finances as they move in a process from supplier to manufacturer to wholesaler to retailer to consumer. John's projects to improve Campbell's CSR program revolve around four key areas: relationship management, telling the company's CSR story, capacity building, and policy and tool development. For relationship management, John is constantly speaking to, meeting with, and communicating with various internal and external stakeholders. These stakeholders include suppliers, customers (such as Walmart), cross-functional teams within Campbell, and shareholders. They discuss current projects that are in progress as well as initiatives to be rolled out in the future. Keeping stakeholders engaged is very essential to John's role. As a sustainability professional, it is his responsibility to keep them informed and make sure they are aligned in their goals. In order to keep stakeholders engaged, a big part is telling a holistic CSR story. John works closely with the CSR program office to answer questions related to sustainability and social responsibility. These questions come from customers, investors, and industry surveys and questionnaires. He also works closely with the communications department to develop and write articles that celebrate wins in CSR. His articles are sent across their supply chain and company through the annual CSR report, external newsletters, and other communication tools, such as presentations for conferences and industry forums.

For capacity building in his job, John explains there are many nuances to supply chains that take a lifetime to master and understand. To expedite the process, John is always challenging himself to continuously improve and understand the impact of sustainability on the categories that he manages. These categories include ingredients for products, packaging materials, and indirect purchases (such as IT services, marketing, and consumer packaged goods). In order to do so, he will attend conferences, participate in industry trade shows, and listen to webinars to improve his knowledge and understanding of CSR issues in the supply chain. Networking and partnerships with NGOs also help him. Finally, for development of tools and policies, John will work on tools and initiatives that improve their reporting process. The tools help to develop a policy around specific emerging issues that in turn improve their transparency as a good corporate citizen. He will research metrics and scorecards that benchmark their performances in CSR.

Looking at the social innovation and impact in his job, John explains that it comes from their supply chain. The projects he creates, the policies and statements he writes, and the initiatives that he works on influence and engage the entire supply chain. Every decision he makes will have an impact on their suppliers, which directly affects the quality of their products and the satisfaction of their consumers. He knows he needs to "move a big needle" when it comes to food and corporate social responsibility. He feels that if he can influence the one or two key suppliers in a specific industry, it will trickle down the supply chain to the farms in which they source. John loves the versatility of his position. Every day, he is working with various departments and cross-functional teams to promote their program. One day, he is working with the communications team to tell their CSR story, and the next day, he is working with buyers to engage their supplier base. He also enjoys getting to work on a wide spectrum of projects, especially since CSR covers so many topics.

> STEM: Pursue it. The learning helps you understand situations from a critical view and solve problems by considering various factors. Many professionals here at Campbell's in social value creation did not start out specializing in their roles. They learned other technical trades and leveraged their personal brand as social ambassadors, letting their brand speak for itself. If you are inclined, pursue social value creation opportunities as extracurricular activities. Everything will fall into place if you network correctly and develop your personal brand well.

Recently, John worked on an interesting project where he engaged and collaborated with an NGO to make sure that animals within their supply chain are treated more humanely. Specifically, for this project, he was able to make a public commitment to stop sourcing from suppliers who use gestation crates to house pigs. These crates are inhumane, and to be a better corporate steward, Campbell is committed to eliminating them from their supply base. Another interesting project focused on conflict minerals (e.g., tungsten, tantalum, tin, and gold that are mined in conditions of armed conflict and human rights abuses, most notably in the Democratic Republic of the Congo). The profits from conflict-minerals sales continue to fuel violence and strife in these areas. John made sure that Campbell is investigating and mapping their tin sourcing to ensure that they do not support any continuation of exploitation or war by way of conflict-mineral mining from suppliers. One last interesting project focused on palm oil and deforestation. John has recently written a policy statement on Campbell's commitment against deforestation and their commitment to source only 100% sustainable palm that does not harm forest or peat lands, does not invade indigenous species or people, and is sustainable.

Career Trajectory

John majored in material science engineering, and after graduating from undergrad, he took on a job as an engineer for a food company. The company, a supplier to major Quick Service Restaurants around the world, was committed to social responsibility and developing its CSR program. As an engineer, his role began to revolve around environmental sustainability engineering. As a manufacturing organization, the company believed that engineers and operations managers were essential to improve the company's overall environmental performance. As the role progressed, social responsibility and community outreach also became part of his job. Getting his foot in the door through engineering helped him to establish himself. But once he was established in his role, he began to take more interest and jumped on opportunities for making social impact whenever they presented themselves. He was vocal about his interest and savored any opportunity to be part of extracurricular work opportunities. Eventually, the social responsibility aspects began to present themselves rather than him seeking them.

His extracurricular work activities revolved around advocating for human rights and marriage equality. Participating in various affinity groups external to his job has added to his credentials and his network. He genuinely believes that having a STEM degree helped him leverage his skills in social engineering and value creation by affording him skills in critical thinking. He also believes that mentorships and connections were the main drivers to starting his career. Like John, his mentors also followed in the philosophy that one should pursue STEM degrees and can transfer that knowledge and critical-thinking aspect to solve social issues and problems. Making those connections was what really propelled him.

In the upcoming years, John sees himself still within a corporate function but with greater responsibility and influencing change. He would like to pursue more philanthropic ventures in the longer term where he not only influences decisions, but also makes decisions. He would like to continue to build his network base and eventually establish his own nonprofit. John lives how he works. For example, sustainability does not stop at 5:00 p.m. when he walks out of the office. When he goes shopping, he is socially conscious regarding the items he buys. He is also pragmatic about what issues he takes on. For him, it is about setting a good example and living his personal life with the same integrity as his professional role. If he could start his career over again, John would have taken on more responsibility and leadership roles at an earlier age. He would also take on mentors and career coaches much earlier.

FOR-PROFIT » LARGE CORPORATION

❤ Sue Burriss, 55

Major Pharmaceutical Company
Clinical Development Scientist | ~$100,000 – 200,000

MS, Quality Assurance and Regulatory Affairs, Temple University
School of Pharmacy
BS, Nursing, DePauw University

Photo by Sue Burriss

Job Description

How do pharmaceutical companies actually confirm that their drugs work without considerable side effects? Before a doctor can prescribe a drug to treat you, the new medicine must demonstrate that its benefits outweigh any potential risks. The medicine needs to go through a significant amount of clinical research prior to approval by the Food and Drug Administration (FDA) and other entities. It is important to get better treatments out there for burgeoning diseases, but most medicines must be tested on several thousands of patients in clinical trials before they can be approved for treatment. Drugs, vaccines, and other treatments that have made it through clinical trials have, in some cases, nearly eradicated diseases such as polio and measles. Unfortunately, in developing countries, places in high need of these treatments, the regulatory process can be even more complicated because of additional research requirements to rule out biological differences in patients' reactions to medicines, more regulatory agencies, and additional legal and ethical challenges. Sue Burriss, a clinical development scientist at an international pharmaceutical company, works with a large team to get quality research done globally that supports the best treatments for the people that need them. Without her expertise, and professionals like her, who work in clinical research in the pharmaceutical industry, great medicines might not make it into the global marketplace.

Sue's role is to manage large international studies going on around the world. She strongly believes in having a good understanding of the cultures she and her team members work in. In many cultures, relationship building and professional courtesies are expected before the team can get down to business. Communication is always the largest challenge she faces in her day-to-day work. Sue has worked with physician experts from around the world to develop protocols that can answer not only global clinical questions but regional ones as well. She also implements key clinical trials to support existing drugs or to get a new indication for that drug.

One of the trials she is working on now is a drug for lupus. The drug is already approved for lupus but further research was requested by regulatory agencies on how people of African heritage reacted to the drug, so they are conducting a study with this minority population. Many patients with lupus (mostly young women) develop kidney disease. Therefore, she is also managing a trial, which if positive, will help expand the use of the approved drug for lupus for patients who have a certain type of kidney disease. These studies take a long time to conduct, often many years from protocol design to completion.

Sue was privileged to be part of a team working on a clinical study needed to get approval for a pediatric pneumococcal vaccine in Latin America. The licensing of the vaccine has changed the face of pediatric infections globally because without it, pneumococcal disease kills children. She has worked on several other research programs, one in rheumatoid arthritis, which expanded the indication and has been proven to stop the progression of this disabling disease. Rheumatoid arthritis used to lead to confinement to a wheelchair. Sue knew the impact this drug would have on patients suffering with rheumatoid arthritis since her maternal grandmother was very disabled due to this autoimmune disease. While Sue had a direct one-on-one impact on patients in her days as a nurse, she now impacts patients around the world by working in research for various pharmaceutical companies.

Issue management is a big priority for Sue because she is responsible for the operations of the trials around the world. She has a contract research group on the ground for all trials, and they follow good clinical practices to ensure patient safety and quality data; however, she and her team have ultimate accountability for what is going on. As part of all studies, there is a quality plan that includes audits done internally and externally to make sure good clinical practices are being followed. She works as part of a professional team and redirects clinical/safety issues on the study to others on the team, including physician medical monitors. She personally answers questions on organizational strategies, such as, "What do patients need to know to feel comfortable about consenting to participate in, understand, enroll in, and stay in the trial?"

Sue loves having a team-focused role where they are looking for creative solutions to global medical problems; historically, the pharmaceutical industry was the second-most regulated industry after the airlines. She also loves going out to visit clinical-trial sites and interacting with the investigators who occasionally update her with personal stories about the life-changing effect some of the drugs she has worked on have had on their patients. She dislikes doing mundane tasks like paying invoices and gets frustrated because working for a company so large, she cannot move quickly—decisions take a long time.

> You do not need a medical background to go into the pharmaceutical industry. This career would be good for people interested in working internationally, with many different cultures, who have an interest in medicine and world health. There is a nice financial component; the pharmaceutical industry historically pays well.
>
> If you want to work in the pharmaceutical industry, start with a big company and then go to a smaller one. You can learn the regulations, systems, and processes from the larger company and bring your knowledge to the smaller one.

Career Trajectory

Sue decided she wanted to be a nurse when she was sixteen because her grandfather, who lived with her, had Alzheimer's, and she enjoyed caring for him. In college and during her years of nursing, she took one-month trips every year to Latin America to provide medical care and fell in love with working in developing countries. At one point, she lived in Peru to set up a local education network for health-care providers. She stopped traveling abroad annually when she had kids and started up again when they were older. Had she not decided to marry her high school sweetheart, she thinks she would probably have stayed working in Latin America as a nurse full-time.

As a nurse, she worked in a hospital and an outpatient family medicine clinic. After working as a nurse in a hospital for nearly two decades, Sue started looking for changes in her career because she was spending less time interacting with patients and more time keeping records. She knew she was not going to be able to keep going financially with hospital nursing (college educations in the near future for three) or physically as she aged. She always had an interest in law, so she got a job with a medical malpractice defense firm. She reviewed chart records, reviewed standard of care for what should have happened to the patient, and found medical experts to defend cases and decide on whether or not malpractice occurred. While working for the firm, she became a nationally certified legal nurse consultant and was one of the first 800 nurses to pass the board exam.

When her law firm was having challenges, she decided to get a job with a large pharmaceutical company. She began doing clinical research in pediatric studies in early 2000 as part of the medical affairs organization. Sue recognized that while there was a growing need for research in emerging markets, there was a lack of consistency in the way research was being conducted. Sue was able to convince the company's management team that they needed operational support for emerging markets. The company responded by creating an operations group in medical affairs for the Asia Pacific and Latin America and put Sue in charge of it. There was a need to improve consistency with standard procedures and make sure employees in emerging countries were kept in the loop as to what was important in terms of research, what research they would fund, and what would advance the understanding of the drug scientifically around the world.

People often tell Sue she needs more of a work-life balance, but she loves her work, and it is part of who she is. To help with her personal life, she had au pairs to help raise her children when she traveled significantly for work. She is proud to have three very accomplished children who have learned to be independent. The diversity of her work has made her family grow, and she has brought all her kids with her on foreign trips to give them a better understanding of the world. In the pharmaceutical industry, she has had a more flexible schedule; she has her weekends and holidays off. However, work is never really done. She often checks her emails at night or when she is on holiday in comparison to when she was a nurse and had to work weekends and holidays but could clock out after her designated shifts, knowing that other nurses would care for her patients. Sue could be content doing what she is doing for the rest of career if the company continues to direct challenging trials her way. She would really like to combat significant diseases in developing countries. She has a set of skills, which might interest a smaller startup company that needs an executive leader of operations, so she might leverage her experience and do that.

♥ Joanna Sickler, 34

Roche Molecular Diagnostics
Scientific Affairs Lead, Point of Care | ~$200,000 – $300,000

MBA and MPH, University of California, Berkeley
BA, American Studies and Cultural Anthropology, Wesleyan University

Job Description

Health disparities persist around the world, impacting the quality and duration of peoples' lives. A child born in Malawi has the life expectancy of forty-seven years while a child born in Japan has a life expectancy of eighty-three years. These disparities exist within countries as well. In the US, infants born to African American women are one and a half to three times more likely to die than infants born to women of other races/ethnicities. However, new health-care technologies have the potential to improve peoples' lives and contribute to closing the health disparities gap. Joanna Sickler's passion is developing such technologies and making them accessible to the patients who need them most. She defines technology broadly: diagnostic tests, new pharmaceuticals, and online analytic tools that support the successful implementation of diagnostics and pharmaceuticals; at the core, they are all novel developments to help patients.

As the scientific affairs lead for point of care, Joanna is focused on Roche Molecular Diagnostics' expansion into new markets and their development of new point-of-care (POC) tests. POC testing includes any screening or diagnostic test that is performed outside a main hospital or laboratory and near a patient. Over the last decade, the trend toward greater POC testing has been driven by faster results positively impacting clinical decision making. In resource-limited settings like countries in East Africa, many areas lack the infrastructure to support clinical laboratories (no consistent electricity, appropriate facilities, etc.). POC tests can bridge the gap, providing critical diagnostic testing in rural and other remote geographies. Prior to joining Roche, Joanna worked with nongovernmental organizations, global funders, national governments, and private companies to improve access to diagnostics and treatment for HIV to patients in Africa.

The focus of her career has been using business acumen to create social impact in health care. She has worked with national governments, private companies, and global health funders to lower the prices of technologies through pooling volumes to allow a large price reduction. Her work can also include collaborating with guidelines committees and global health stakeholders to align purchasing across countries, again increasing volumes and lowering prices.

Joanna's day-to-day activities involve constant qualitative and quantitative analysis, conversing with physicians and patients to understand their medical needs, developing forecasts, sizing markets, and considering how to make money for health care stretch as far as possible to improve public health. She works significantly on relationship management: listening to different stakeholders and understanding their concerns, developing compelling presentations and documents, and speaking publically to present ideas and answer questions. She works with leading clinicians, laboratory professionals, and public health experts to have them evaluate different products and develop independent publications on their effectiveness. To stay up-to-date in her field, Joanna attends conferences, presents at them, and follows the latest innovations through reading academic articles and news media. Interacting with brilliant innovators and interesting people around the globe is what Joanna loves about her job. The biggest downside is that finding a work-life balance can be a challenge.

In her prior role as vice president of commercial operations at Zyomyx, Joanna's team was responsible for defining the product requirements for the POC test that the company was developing for use in HIV programs in Africa. The original version of the instrument was electricity-free, using a manual crank to power the test. While at face value this seemed like a huge benefit for a test to be used in places with limited and inconsistent access to electricity, it also had many downsides. It made the instruments more expensive and less durable, increasing the price per test. It required additional time and labor from the health-care worker operating the test, who generally would be the only staff person at the clinic.

Joanna was tasked with determining whether the final version should be powered by the manual crank or electricity. Her team conducted market research in Africa, speaking to purchasers and operators of the test. Joanna ran a market segmentation analysis looking at the testing needs at different levels of the health-care system in Africa, which identified that the largest unmet need (highest number of tests that could *not* be done today) was in health-care centers that generally had inconsistent access to electricity. The market research in Africa provided data that it was only a small percentage of sites that could provide

> Success is a combination of passion and skills. Really think about what you are good at, and focus on developing those skills. Passion alone is not enough.

treatment for HIV but did not have any access to electricity. It also indicated that operators did not want to have to manually crank twenty to thirty times a day to run the test. As a result, Joanna made the recommendation to switch to a long-lasting rechargeable battery to lower the cost, increase the durability, and enable testing to continue even when the power was out. The new version was positively received, with all but one national HIV program in Africa preferring the new battery-powered version.

Joanna feels strongly that large, for-profit corporations can have tremendous innovation and social impact. It is important to assess and judge every company and NGO based on their conduct, not the label of "nonprofit" or "private." Assessing real impact is a challenging endeavor. Joanna believes it is critical for individuals and organizations to be introspective and constantly self-auditing.

Career Trajectory:

Joanna has worked across health-care sectors, beginning with social science research at the University of California, San Francisco (UCSF), though she quickly realized she did not want to be an academic. She moved away from a PhD path toward an MBA and MPH so that she could improve her management and analytical skills and play a more active role in implementation and affecting change. At UCSF, she was exposed to how stigmatization impacts public health, and she has focused on technologies that could tackle the problem of disparities in health care for people because of their race, economic status, or sexual orientation.

After graduate school she joined Gilead, an American biotechnology firm, developing drugs to combat infectious diseases such as HIV and hepatitis B. At Gilead, she played a key role in launching a drug to treat hepatitis B (HBV). Her passion for global health took over, and she left Gilead for a resource-constrained setting, working with the Clinton Health Access Initiative (CHAI) in India. While there, she worked on reducing the cost of drugs to treat HIV and improving health accessibility. Working for CHAI introduced her to the impact of point-of-care diagnostic testing to improve public HIV treatment programs in Africa. Therefore, she went on to join a small biotechnology firm developing a point-of-care test for HIV programs in resource-constrained settings. Unfortunately, the company was unable to raise the funds to bring the product to market, primarily because of a lack of funding available to support companies launching products in lower-income markets.

Joanna came to believe that the resources a large company could bring to support implementation are critical for the success of innovative POC diagnostics, so she looked for a job with a macro-level impact and found her new home at Roche Molecular Diagnostics. She credits her success to frequent introspection and honesty with herself paired with a desire to work from different vantage points in the health-care system to gain a unique perspective. Additionally, she always followed her passion despite what other people thought. For example, she took a 70% pay cut when she joined the Clinton Health Access Initiative but jumped at the opportunity because she had always been interested in global health and wanted to work abroad. All along her career path, she balanced listening to her gut and to her mentors.

Joanna finds it difficult to integrate her work with her personal life because she has traveled significantly in her career; during one period, she was living outside the country for 50% of the time. There are only so many hours in each day, and it is all about prioritizing. Those priorities can shift, and right now, Joanna is trying to work on bringing more balance to her life. Looking back, Joanna would like to have taken many more science classes; she now feels like she is playing catch-up. Joanna wants to continue working on projects that excite her and continue to increase her responsibility level to have more influence. Right now, she is interested in working in new types of roles to further expand her understanding of how the health-care system works in different countries. Focusing on what excites her has served her well, instead of focusing on a step-by-step path to reach a certain destination.

Nigel Snoad, 42

Google
Product Manager, Crisis Response and Civic Innovation

PhD, Computer Science/ Biology/Engineering, Australian National University (2000)
BSc, Physics/Mathematics/Evolutionary Biology, Australian National University (1993)

Job Description

From times of excitement to times of crisis, people everywhere turn to the Internet for up-to-date information. The Internet is an essential tool for humanitarian response. Not only do affected people and first responders use the Internet to search for the latest information on their location and status of roads, weather, friends, and family, but people elsewhere use the Internet to search for ways to help. Disaster response can be extremely chaotic, so improved access and speed of information can be of vital help. Who ensures the right information is on the Internet and readily accessible for people in times of need? Google's crisis response team builds tools to collect and share emergency information and supports first responders in using technology to help improve emergency response and save lives.

Nigel Snoad is a product manager in Google's social impact team focusing on crisis response. Most of his job revolves around what keeps people safer, so he is constantly thinking about how aid, information, risk, and crisis management all come together and how crowds, networks, design, tools, systems, experience, and being thoughtful about complexity can help. Google has been responding to natural disasters since Hurricane Katrina in 2005 by preparing information including storm paths, shelter locations, emergency numbers, and donation opportunities in a way that is easily accessible. First responders can use Google's services to streamline their internal operations and share information with the public rapidly, broadly, and efficiently. Google partners with government agencies, NGOs, and commercial organizations to improve their services and ultimately aid the right people working together at the right time.

Nigel's team is also changing how citizens engage and become effective and active participants in their societies, particularly during times of crisis, social change, or moments of civic engagement. The teams provide information and tools to help the public become more effective participants in their societies, build resilient communities, and collaborate during emergencies. For example, in response to the Nepal earthquake, his team launched Person Finder, a missing-persons tool enabling people to search for and report on the status of their loved ones after a disaster. They also collected and made available satellite imagery and supported local response teams.

Career Trajectory

After completing his PhD in computer science and complex adaptive systems at Australian National University, Nigel worked for a small company called Nuix. Nuix was made up of engineers who had a vision of making possible an online marketplace for complex goods and services. This was Nigel's first taste of the product skills that he would eventually apply to humanitarian work through Google. Nigel managed Nuix's research and development as well as product design and specification.

Desiring to apply his knowledge and background in search and rescue to the social sector, Nigel became an analyst for UNICEF (United Nations Children's Fund), his first job in the United States. For a year, he analyzed statistics on HIV/AIDS and orphans around the world and wrote up reports of policy advice to improve the statistics. Nigel was then moved to the field to work as the de facto chief information officer (CIO) of the United Nations Joint Logistics Centre (UNJLC). He was responsible for providing information, technology, and field support for UNJLC missions in conflict and disaster areas. He managed a distributed team of geographic information system, web, and information communication technology officers who produced and analyzed information about logistics and general situational awareness in complex emergencies, conflict areas, and natural disasters. At the UNJLC, his biggest projects included working as the logistics coordinator for the international humanitarian response to the 2004 Indonesian tsunami and as deputy head of the mission for UNJLC Iraq in 2003.

Returning to the US, Nigel next worked for the United Nations System Influenza Coordinator. He developed planning methodologies and contingency plans to enable the United Nations system to respond effectively to pandemics while continuing to serve others in need. The team conducted the first-ever system-wide planning exercise for over 200,000 staff worldwide. He then designed and ran training programs and simulation exercises for UN offices worldwide and correspondingly evaluated these plans. Moving away from the UN system for a while, Nigel worked for a few years as a program manager at Microsoft leading humanitarian systems research and development for Ray Ozzie, the CTO and chief software architect.

Nigel returned to the UN system for a few months as information management strategy advisor at the UN Office for the Coordination of Humanitarian Affairs before coming to Google. On the side of his "day jobs," Nigel has been an adjunct faculty member teaching courses in design strategy and humanitarian design, a core team member for Random Hacks of Kindness (http://www.rhokaustralia.org), and a board member for several non-profits including the Humanitarian Innovation Fund. All his side activities have helped him gain and share the expertise he brings to Google.

⚙ Janeen Uzzell, 47

GE Global Research
Global Director of External Affairs and Technology Programs | Six figures

MBA, Management and International Business, Farleigh Dickinson University (2002)
BS, Mechanical Engineering, North Carolina Agricultural and Technical State University (1991)

Job Description

Large corporations are particularly adept at identifying trends and then designing products and business strategies to address customer needs. Making jet engines more fuel-efficient and MRI machines capture sharper images are essential and are important sources of revenue. However, it is just as important for large corporations to explore new markets—finding technologies in their portfolios that can address unmet needs at scale and then identifying partners who bring complementary resources to solve the problem. There is a need for intersectional innovation to bring new products and services to life. Can companies profit from such projects? As a public company, GE is committed to making a profit for its shareholders. However, some projects with social returns present different kinds of opportunities that align with GE's commitment to better health for all people.

Working on socially beneficial projects helps GE with its brand, ethos, and purpose. Therefore, GE does have some leeway to use its significant resources to create social impact across the world. How does GE decide what projects to work on? How does such a large organization get them done? Such endeavors involve an incredible amount of applied research and development with murky timelines since the end product is not always well defined. Like many other large corporations, GE has its own Global Research and Development Center that leverages expertise in fields from electronics to chemistry, biosciences to computing, and materials to imaging to tackle big societal challenges. During her tenure as the director for healthy imagination GE Africa, Janeen Uzzell and her uniquely designed team supported the company in their global efforts to use technology to improve the human condition. She has recently repatriated to the US and is leveraging the lessons learned to launch innovative technology programs and partnerships in her new role as global director of External Affairs and Technology Programs for GE Global Research.

Janeen leads a team of scientists who are also business development leaders. They focus on developing and designing programs for the GE Global Research Center that are funded by the government, global partners, and customers. These research programs focus on leveraging technology that GE has as a part of its core portfolio and integrating that technology into various contexts. In addition to working with technologies and products that GE has already designed, Janeen's team identifies global technological trends and develops a strategy around them. The team then focuses efforts on shaping the program and finding the funding resources for these projects. Last year, her team funded over $100 million of research programs at the center.

As the head of the team, Janeen works closely with the business and technology leaders to set the strategy and to help to shape partnerships with other external organizations. The team is responsible for designing programs. One of their projects is helping solve the global challenge of malaria. Janeen knows that the Gates Foundation has several malaria initiatives and that GE has technology that can help bring about a faster eradication of the disease. Janeen reached out to the Gates Foundation to build an impactful partnership. A business development leader on her team followed up and shared GE's diagnostic technologies with the Gates Foundation so as to accelerate its dissemination in the field. Through such partnerships with diverse organizations, GE can play a pivotal role in fighting malaria.

Janeen believes that when working in an area considered nontraditional, the most important thing that you can do every day is educate the leadership around you about (1) why the work they are doing is critical, (2) the outcomes you are expecting, (3) how it will help the business grow, and (4) why it is important to be in that business. One project she worked on was determining GE's position in rural health and how to best address the pain points that impact the world. She led her team in building a solution around GE products that could be affordable and could be made accessible. They also considered who could be trained to operate and maintain them and the kinds of partnerships that would facilitate long-term sustainability of the product. Her team concluded that maternal and infant care was the best fit for GE and went on to create a business case proposing a playbook for action over the next five years.

To assess the impact of her activities, Janeen has goals and objectives that she has to meet, such as design a research study for the continued care of ultrasound and training, or design a public-private business partnership with an international NGO. GE then has to assess if meeting those goals and objectives translates to incremental growth and money made for the business. Janeen is driven by passion, but at the end of the day, she has to make sure GE's stakeholders are benefitting. Occasionally there are projects that come across her desk that she reluctantly turns down because they are not the right fit for the company. Driven by purposeful work, Janeen seeks to help others find solutions, even if they are outside GE's capacity, by leveraging her contacts to find other partners that could support impactful work that she is unable to focus on at GE. Janeen appreciates that her company can deliver social impact in the global space and is not held back by the lack of resources like many nonprofits are. However, she is challenged by partners that presume that GE does not carry a mission of caring as a part of its cause.

> It is so important to consider a role overseas to gain experience in the global space, even if it means that you are volunteering your time. But you need to get connected to a group that will get you the proper exposure. You have got to see it, taste it, and touch it because it is going to drive you further. After your experience you can determine if it is for you or not. Either way, you gain an incredible experience, and the people who you meet along the way can become your mentors.

Career Trajectory

Janeen knew that she wanted to be in health care even before she went to college. She was heavily influenced by her elder sister, a nurse who was strongly driven by the ethos of helping others. Janeen was drawn to global health because she was interested in diseases and trauma that were not part of regular discussions in the US. Janeen's older cousin pushed her to pursue an engineering degree because he believed it would be great for her as a woman of color to stand out with her technical knowledge. She did not have an awareness of the public health discipline and did not want to study medicine, so Janeen set out to understand how someone in engineering could help solve health-care problems. Obtaining an engineering degree gave Janeen a capacity to study, to push through hard work, and to hold her own in an environment where she was different.

After college, Janeen began working on the manufacturing floor at the Ethicon business of Johnson and Johnson (J&J). Janeen experienced downsizing when her manufacturing unit was moved offshore, and she was transitioned into a number of misplaced roles. While studying toward a master's in engineering, Janeen's manager and now long-time mentor pointed out that the company would be willing to fund her further education. He also challenged her to reconsider if she truly wanted to work as an engineer, and whether it was her core strength. He suggested that she had great potential as a team leader because she had the unique ability to comprehend technology and business challenges, and she had more personality than most engineers. He encouraged her to pursue an MBA, which she did while still continuing her coding job. While completing her MBA, she worked on case studies for GE and decided that she wanted to work for the company. She was hired at GE Healthcare prior to completing her MBA and has been with the company for fourteen years. She joined as a director of service with then GE Medical Services. During her time on the service team, GE began implementing special programs in hospitals in New York—Janeen's coverage area. They sponsored the Hip Hop Stroke program with Harlem Hospital, and Janeen became an advocate for such programs for low-income areas in the US.

Janeen continued to work her way up the ranks, working with technology but also with marketing and research, transitioning with GE to focus more on global health challenges. Janeen become an ambassador for the Developing Health Globally program launched through the GE Foundation where they donated over $35 million worth of products to Africa. GE insisted that company donations should not be delivered without sustainable maintenance, so she became responsible for building partnerships with organizations that could service their products and ensure that the biomedical products worked well in developing countries. Now, Janeen works for GE's Corporate Research and Development Center, charged with leveraging global expertise and experience with technology to assess the landscape and identify trends and needs to build global, government, and commercial partnerships, and ensure optimal alignment with internal GE business partners. Janeen has a strong commitment to take the knowledge and exposure she has gained at GE and use it to advance a world-changing cause.

Photo by Brendan

Brendan Kissane, 40

The Hershey Company
Senior Director of Responsible Sourcing | Six figures

MBA, Georgetown University (2002)
BASc, Chemical Engineering, Rutgers University (1997)

Job Description

All the world's cocoa is grown in the region ten degrees above and below the equator: 70% is grown in West Africa, with 50% grown in Ghana and the Ivory Coast. Most cocoa is grown on smallholder farms, which are often family plots that are two to five hectares. These smallholder farmers depend on cocoa for their livelihood, yet at the same time they often do not take a longer-term view to follow agricultural practices that sustain cocoa production over time. This question of a sustained supply chain for cocoa is of great interest to chocolate companies around the world. They have come to realize that their destinies are directly intertwined with the destinies of these smallholder farmers, so in the long term, they need to ensure the farmers are well trained in good agricultural practices. The Hershey Company provides farmers with support and education to sustainably increase their cocoa yields. However, with four million farmers and no easy way to reach them, the chocolate industry faces a significant challenge in dissipating information to make growing cocoa more profitable and sustainable for the farmers.

Hershey is a founding member of CocoaAction, which helps to enhance and accelerate cocoa sustainability through cross-industry collaboration. By 2020, CocoaAction aims to train and deliver improved planting material and fertilizer to 300,000 cocoa farmers and empower communities through education, child labor monitoring, and women's empowerment. In October 2012, Hershey announced that all cocoa sourced globally would be certified sustainable by a third party by 2020. As one of the largest cocoa buyers in the world, this has put a lot of pressure on Hershey's commodities purchasing group to organize cocoa sustainability work. In order to meet this goal, Hershey has launched the Learn to Grow program, targeting 60,000 farmers by 2019. One tool Hershey uses to communicate with farmers is CocoaLink, which has enrolled more than 45,000 farmers in Ghana. GPS mapping through the CocoaLink program enables farmers to understand the size of their farm and to use optimal amounts of fertilizer. The program also provides text messaging to farmers with tips on pruning, weeding, good fertilizer use, crop protection, and pest and disease control. To further increase yields, Hershey plans to distribute one million high-yielding cocoa trees in West Africa. Hershey also works to improve the overall communities where cocoa is grown by improving access to education, good nutrition, and clean water.

Brendan Kissane, senior director of responsible sourcing, is part of Hershey's responsible sourcing group of four people, and his role is to work with Hershey's cocoa buyers and suppliers to ensure Hershey is responsibly sourcing cocoa. He loves working with suppliers who work on the ground in-country and who understand the subtleties of the issues they are working with and the best way to address them. Brendan helps set Hershey's standards for suppliers to meet, which requires a lot of time communicating as well as traveling to West Africa around twice a year. He educates the buyers based on what he learns from suppliers and gets the buyers to factor in the responsible sourcing aspect of buying.

His job can be both rewarding and frustrating. It is rewarding to see students in Ghana connect with students at the Milton Hershey School using video conferencing, as is done through Hershey's distance-learning program. It is also satisfying to sit in a farmer field school and watch lead farmers train their neighbors in the best agricultural practices. Yet the issues surrounding sustainably sourced ingredients are complex, and affecting large-scale change is difficult. Working with Hershey' suppliers to train 60,000 farmers feels like an enormous accomplishment, but Brendan has to keep in mind that millions of other smallholder farmers need similar training. That is why partnering with suppliers and competitors through CocoaAction is so important.

Brendan's metrics of success for his work are numbers of farmers touched, average increase in yield per farm, and premium paid to the farmers. Sourcing, and specifically sourcing cocoa, is very satisfying for him because it is a relatively small crop, and there is a small community of people involved in cocoa trading and buying. He calls it a romantic crop, and visiting the places where it is grown is wonderful. People are emotionally attached to cocoa, and being a part of continuing that is satisfying. Cocoa was not touched by the green revolution (research and development initiatives around the 1950s that increased agricultural production worldwide), so while yields of other agricultural products have gone up at a 45-degree angle, cocoa yields have not changed at all. Being a part of kick-starting that improvement in yield is an amazing opportunity!

Career Trajectory

Brendan earned his undergraduate degree in chemical engineering and then worked at a paper-processing mill for three years. The paper industry was very specific, and he did not want to get stuck in something so focused. In order to move into a position with more of a business perspective, he earned his MBA. Soon after, he landed his first position at Hershey in the industrial engineering department. Half his job involved new product development, and the other half involved in-plant engineering (making lines more efficient, addressing problems on the lines, and new product backings). For example, he could solve the problem of there being an improper number of almonds in a chocolate bar.

Throughout his first few years, he moved around and met many people at Hershey; the company is very diverse and therefore offers a wide range of opportunities. Brendan eventually found an internal job posting for the position of cocoa buyer in the commodities department, and sure enough, he got the job. All his previous work experience revolved around solving internal problems; in this new position, he solved externally facing issues. As a cocoa buyer, he traveled around the world to see cocoa-producing regions. Throughout his six years on Hershey's cocoa-sourcing team, the questions and concerns about cocoa sustainability increased. Hershey recognized this need and created the responsible sourcing group. Brendan left his job as a cocoa buyer and began leading the responsible sourcing team, which addresses many sustainability issues outside cocoa, like palm oil sourcing.

If you want a position like mine, get a job in West Africa working for cocoa-sourcing companies first. This will give you a base of knowledge and allow you to speak from a point of authority for the rest of your career. If you do not like how a company sources their product, get as close to the problem as possible for a couple years—it does not have to be social impact work. You can get a job sourcing coffee in Central America, and you will understand the issues of sourcing, and at the end of a year or two, you can apply the knowledge in the next thirty years of your career.

Put more thought into what doing the right thing is—you do not need to work for a nonprofit to make a difference. Large companies like Hershey have the size to make a positive social impact while still making a profit for their investors.

There are many opportunities in a large company, so Brendan has gotten to move around and find a position that truly suits his passions. The paper mill he started out at had no opportunities; you have to look at the big picture and give yourself room to move and grow. Brendan sees a long-term future for himself with Hershey—in one of many different roles—but he definitely wants to continue working on the sourcing side. If he could go back, he would get in-country experience instead of working for a paper mill.

⚡ **Alakesh Chetia, 48**

SunEdison
President, Social Innovations | Six figures

MSEE, Computer Engineering, Michigan Technological University (1992)
BE, Electrical & Electronics Engineering, National Institute of Technology
Karnataka (1989)

Job Description

Life is not a straight line. After graduating with a bachelor's degree in electrical (power) and electronics engineering, Alakesh spent twenty years in electronics-related businesses before coming to SunEdison, a renewable electrical power generation (energy) company. SunEdison is the world's largest renewable energy development company, currently managing over five gigawatts of solar and wind assets worldwide. They operate in thirty-five countries around the world, primarily focusing on building large solar farms that feed electricity into the grid. They finance, install, own, and operate solar and wind power plants, enabling them to provide predictably priced electricity to residential, commercial, government, and utility customers.

After spending a year in India as the managing director of rural electrification, Alakesh led the formation of SunEdison's Social Innovations business unit, seeking to bring energy access to the 1.3 billion people in the developing world without access to electricity by solving the technical and financial equations while understanding the social and cultural contexts. The business unit was formed by combining SunEdison Foundation and the for-profit rural electrification business, using the foundation as a strategic charity for testing sustainable business models for rural electrification besides contributing for disaster relief and other charitable causes. As president of SunEdison Social Innovations, Alakesh leads the unit in creating appropriate business models that incorporate local culture and social context to bring electricity to developing countries. He recognizes that besides the technological and financial part of the solution, his team needs to understand and innovate on the social aspects for long-term sustainability of the solution.

One of the beneficiary groups that the Social Innovations unit supported was salt farmers in Little Rann of Kutch in the state of Gujarat in India, who use diesel pumps to extract brine from the ground to make salt—a livelihood for generations that was initiated by Mahatma Gandhi's Salt Satyagraha against British rule more than eighty years ago. The income of these salt farmers, estimated to be nearly 20,000 in number, had been dwindling over the years with the rising cost of diesel as the Indian government removes subsidies to diesel. While solar water pumps would be cheaper in the long term as they involve no fuel cost, these subsistence farmers could not afford the relatively larger up-front cost nor could they qualify for bank loans. Working with SEWA (Self-Employed Women's Association), one of the renowned Indian NGOs that count these salt farmers among their members, Alakesh created a revolving fund through SunEdison Foundation through which the salt farmers were given solar water pumps, which they would pay for over a period of four to five years. The salt farmers saw an increase in income of 20–30% immediately, even after installment payments for the solar water pumps. Their income is expected to double after the solar water pumps are fully paid off, helping them to break out of the cycle of poverty by being able to send their children to school and higher education.

On a daily basis, Alakesh spends his time meeting potential partners for technological solutions, finding funding, and visiting rural communities in countries such as India, Nepal, Bangladesh, Myanmar, and the Philippines. This breaks down into many calls and meetings where he is heavily engaged with partners and customers and traveling a significant amount as he goes out to see things for himself. Alakesh's favorite part of his job is being able to use his business skill set to develop solutions for underprivileged communities and seeing the potential to break their cycle of poverty. On the other hand, he dislikes when he encounters people who negatively view the problems that he works on as unsolvable or "just the way they are" and therefore create additional hurdles.

SunEdison measures their impact directly from their work in terms of the number of people they are serving, and they have set targets and end goals. They target to serve one million people by the end of 2015 and twenty million by the end of 2020. In terms of personal impact, Alakesh is grateful for the opportunity to serve but finds it humbling that even serving 20 million people—which would be fantastic—is a fraction of the 1.3 billion without energy access. Alakesh's work is highly integrated with his personal life because the work he is doing is out of choice and is how he wants to live his life on a daily basis regardless of it being part of his job.

Career Trajectory

During the recession years of 1991–92, Silicon Valley companies did not see a need to fly in new college graduates for interviews from across the country. So, after graduating with his master's degree in electrical engineering (with a computer major), Alakesh packed his belongings into his Honda hatchback and drove 2,500 miles in three days from Upper Michigan to Silicon Valley. He landed a design engineer job at a large computer manufacturer within days of arriving in Silicon Valley and worked there for five years before going on to found a couple startup technology companies, followed by the creation of a new business within a billion-dollar public semiconductor company.

What does one do when one gets fired as the vice president and general manager of a $100M business he helped create? Faced with that situation, Alakesh spent a year and a half soul-searching and getting into the mindfulness practice of Vipassana, which ultimately led to his current mission to serve the underprivileged. Because renewable energy in developing countries was a completely new area for him, Alakesh turned to networking and improving his knowledge in the subject matter. Unfortunately, all his contacts at the time were in the high-tech computer industry, so he had to build a new network of people. He read an incredible amount about the solar industry and became a member of solar organizations in person and on LinkedIn. He joined SunEdison as advisor to the CEO and quickly moved up to the position of managing director of rural electrification in India and then president of SunEdison Social Innovations. Alakesh has now been working for SunEdison for two and a half years. In the future, he wants to apply his skill set and abilities to make a difference around the world, having a larger impact as he gets older. He hopes SunEdison will have served twenty million people in five years, and one hundred million in ten years, and five hundred million in twenty years.

> Align yourself with what you want from within your own heart and what you are passionate about; ask why it matters to you. If it resolves to love and compassion for others—whether be it for your loved ones, friends, or the general masses—go find that work. When we look deeply inside ourselves, we find that love is what makes us go round, so work in service of others can be very fulfilling.
>
> It is about aligning the heart with the work, but it is also important to understand the critical thinking necessary to be able to see problems the way they are and to be able to find solutions. Having both intuition and the analytical skills to be able to dissect the problem into pieces that can be solved is very important.
>
> Charity alone is not sufficient. Charity is okay in some cases, but we cannot give enough. For the solutions we think of to have a large impact, they must be commercially sustainable. That means that it pays for the goods, it pays for the services, and it pays for some profit for the people involved. It will keep the people motivated and wanting to solve those problems.

FOR-PROFIT » LARGE CORPORATION

⚡ Frank Bergh, 29

SoCore Energy, an Edison International Company
Director of Engineering Operations | ~$100,000

BS, Electrical Engineering, Washington University in St. Louis (2008)

Job Description

Solar energy is at a tipping point, along with other renewable distributed generation technologies that are shifting the way we think about electricity supply in the US and around the world. While many companies are focused on selling to environmentally conscious homeowners, one company, SoCore Energy, is focusing on selling solar energy to multisite retail and industrial companies who have substantial ecological footprints, reducing carbon-dioxide emissions with onsite rooftop solar energy. SoCore has the creativity of a small solar energy startup and the stability of a Fortune 500 balance sheet since being acquired in 2013 by Edison International, one of the largest electricity companies in the US. The rooftop solar energy systems are installed and interconnected to the electric grid at no cost to the customer; SoCore then sells the solar electricity to the customer from their own rooftop, reducing their electric bills.

As director of engineering for SoCore Energy, Frank Bergh is responsible for setting the strategic direction of their engineering team, as well as overseeing the design and installation of hundreds of solar energy systems annually, including their successful interconnection to the electric grid. In his first year at SoCore, he doubled the headcount within the engineering department while improving teamwork, efficiency, and design quality to keep pace with 800% growth in total sales from four megawatts in 2013 to more than thirty megawatts in 2014. Along the way, he has worked with policy makers and utilities to enable increased solar energy penetration, including community solar gardens and virtual net metering. Frank also works closely with his clients in developing innovative business models that blend the benefits of distributed renewable energy generation with energy storage, energy efficiency, building optimization, and ancillary utility services. On a typical day, Frank will review potential solar energy sites, evaluate new solar energy technology vendors, address technical inquiries from utility companies, meet with clients to discuss integrated energy solutions, and facilitate collaboration within the engineering team and other SoCore departments.

By developing solar energy on a portfolio basis (building many sites simultaneously for the same client) SoCore Energy enables large-scale adoption of renewable energy, saving their clients money on day one, without any up-front cost. Meanwhile, they are shifting the paradigm of how large retail and industrial clients use electricity and educating them on the benefits of solar, both ecologically and economically. Frank's favorite part of his job with SoCore is that he is on the right side of history, advancing a renewable energy revolution. His least favorite part is the number of barriers and obstacles created by the industry's status quo.

In addition to his responsibilities at SoCore, Frank is an active volunteer and leader within Engineers Without Borders USA. He is also a contributing editor for the blog *Engineering for Change*, a collaboration of engineering organizations and societies pioneering new and innovative coverage of appropriate technology in the developing world. He regularly writes articles for the news section and blog on topics ranging from appropriate technology to community engagement in engineering design. As an instructor for Village Earth, a grassroots network supporting marginalized indigenous communities to have greater control over the decisions that shape their lives, Frank teaches an online course that covers the principles of implementing technology effectively in community-based development.

Career Trajectory

As a sophomore in college, underwhelmed by prerequisites, Frank nearly transferred out of his engineering major because he perceived his coursework was preventing him from building and deepening relationships that could change the world. To merge his interest in engineering with his desire to build a more just and peaceful world, he cofounded the Engineers Without Borders (EWB-USA) chapter at Washington University in St. Louis. Engineering is dedicated to improving the quality of life, which means that engineers must address the real challenges of real people. Under his leadership, the Washington University chapter of EWB-USA pursued projects in El Salvador, Guatemala, and

Malawi. His involvement in EWB-USA is ultimately what made him decide to become an engineer, and it continues to inspire his professional ambitions to this day.

His first job after college was a consulting position, helping electric utility companies plan for the future. At that time, in 2008, many utilities were grappling with the implications of large-scale renewable energy for the first time. Nevertheless, his first assignment was to study an interconnection request for what he later learned was a tar sands facility in Northern Alberta, Canada, and a precursor to the Keystone XL Pipeline. Despite being only two weeks on the job, he mustered enough courage to pull his boss aside and explain his ethical concerns with this line of work. He felt that despite the consequences, he needed to let his boss know where he stood as a pacifist and an environmentalist in a firm that worked in defense contracts and fossil-fuel interests. Ultimately, taking a stand paid off, and several weeks later, Frank's manager pulled him aside and offered him the opportunity to strengthen the firm's consulting practice in utility-scale wind energy. Over the next two and a half years, Frank was involved in over fifty wind farms, with clients ranging from large utilities to small upstart wind-energy developers.

> You do not have to compromise between your values and your profession. If you do not like war, do not design weapons. Your engineering practice, your career, is a radical act. Design what the world needs most right now—do not settle for anything less.
>
> Engineering is about improving the quality of life, and therefore it is a service-driven profession, not a profit-driven profession. We must recognize our responsibility for developing solutions based on greatest human need, and not greatest net worth.

Despite the ability to work primarily on renewable-energy projects, Frank felt a cognitive dissonance working as a consultant. Ultimately, he felt he was a brain for rent to the highest bidder—for now wind energy was booming, but sooner or later he would end up on projects that did not reflect his values. He was not satisfied by confining his professional impact within the narrow partitions of a cubicle. In his evenings, he would serve food at a local soup kitchen or babysit children at a nearby shelter. He organized numerous volunteer projects for friends and coworkers through an organization called Project Change Kansas City. In one instance, he even left work over his lunch hour to join a protest at a nuclear weapons factory that was actually a client of his own firm! As time went on, it became clear that Frank wanted to pursue a profession more closely aligned with his values.

Frank left the consulting firm in 2010 to join Nordex, a German wind-turbine manufacturer, at their North American headquarters in Chicago. During his three years at Nordex, Frank was the lead engineer for grid interconnection of wind farms in North and South America. He participated in market research, project development, engineering design, and construction. After experiencing the rapid growth of the wind industry in the US from an environmental aspiration to the number one source of new power plants on the electric grid in only a few short years, Frank soon had the opportunity to bring wind farms to developing countries. He was making frequent trips to Chile, Uruguay, and Honduras, leading negotiations with utility companies in Spanish, and continuing to develop his knowledge of large-scale renewable energy integration. Nevertheless, Frank began to wonder if the scale of wind farms was out of pace with the needs of developing nations.

While working full-time at Nordex, he accepted a part-time role as the chief technology officer of a small renewable-energy startup company called Light Up Africa (LUA). This company's mission was to create culturally appropriate distribution channels for generating, selling, and buying clean electricity while displacing the need for kerosene fuel and its detrimental health impacts in rural Kenya. Frank spearheaded the design and prototyping of a "handheld power plant," for the conversion of kinetic energy (shaking and vibrations of everyday activities) into electricity stored on a battery for use in flashlights and cell phone chargers. The experience of working in a startup gave him an appreciation for the human scale of engineering technology. Frank's involvement in LUA and his experiences with Nordex in Latin America led him to believe that solar energy is ultimately a more applicable technology for humanitarian development projects. Frank's recent transition to SoCore has given him the opportunity to innovate and evolve the way large retail and industrial consumers conceive of their energy supply, "the implications of which are fundamentally disruptive and even revolutionary to the dirty, inefficient, and wasteful energy paradigm in the US."

Frank has continued to work with oppressed communities in Chicago as he did in Kansas City, eventually cofounding The Emmaus House in the historic North Lawndale neighborhood on the west side. Frank often reminds his colleagues in Engineers Without Borders that sustainable community development does not require airfare, and he is eager to partner with developing communities both at home and abroad. In the future, he sees himself continuing to pave the way for renewable energy in the US as well as in developing countries, where he believes affordable and ecological electricity is an absolute engineering and ecological imperative and one of the defining challenges of his generation.

FOR-PROFIT » MID-SIZED FIRM

📖 Andreina Parisi-Amon, 30

Coursera
Course Success and Research Specialist | ~$100,000

PhD, Bioengineering, Stanford University (2013)
BSE, Biomedical Engineering, Duke University (2006)

Job Description

Education is a major catalyst for human development. Receiving a good education can give a person a better sense of right and wrong, help them understand the world we live in without superstitions, give them a better chance to contribute more to society, get a better job and make more money, and teach them how to take better care of their health. With the shift over the past few decades from an agrarian to an industrial to a knowledge economy, education is more important than ever. A college degree is quickly becoming a minimum requirement in the United States to get a decent job, but what about the rest of the world? How can education be scaled to be accessible and affordable even in developing countries? Building schools is not scalable, and training good teachers is a difficult, long process. As 3G and 4G networks emerge across developing countries, one good teacher teaching thousands of people through the Internet could be the key to taking education to the masses.

Coursera.org is leading the way with hundreds of massive open online courses (MOOCs) and a mission to provide universal access to the world's best education. They do this by partnering with the top institutions around the world and working to reach as many learners in all types of life situations as possible. They believe everyone should have access to high-quality education, whether you are an eighteen-year-old in India who aspires to become an engineer or a mother who wants to learn calculus along with her children. Coursera offers ambitious, motivated people of all ages the opportunity to learn for free and earn verified certificates for a fee from world-class educational institutions. Over twelve million learners from around the globe have come to Coursera to take courses offered by their partners, more than 100 of the world's top institutions.

Through developing courses that help those who engage with the platform open the doors they care about and make the changes they want in their lives, Andreina Parisi-Amon is changing the world: one empowered person at a time. She is part of Coursera's Course Success team, which is focused on helping educational partners create learning experiences that enable learners to achieve their goals. To assess her impact, Andreina looks at a large amount of data to understand the effectiveness of the courses and the platform at engaging, retaining, and teaching learners. She also interacts directly with professors, teaching teams, and instructional designers and gets feedback about how her aid and interventions assist in course creation and iteration, both directly through what they tell her and indirectly through the actions they take in their courses after they talk. One of Coursera's guiding principles is "Learners First," and by far, their learners' stories about how finding and taking courses on Coursera have changed their lives are the clearest signals of the impact Coursera has.

Andreina's days at work are ever evolving. Her team and her role are like a startup within a startup, so they are still figuring out what the highest leverage touch points are within the company and with their partners. The first major component of Andreina's role is course creation assistance. This entails developing and disseminating best practices in MOOC creation to instructors and teaching teams through their Making MOOCs 101 course, written documents, and virtual and in-person meetings and workshops. The second component is interfacing with product teams where she is able to inform the development and design of Coursera products from a pedagogical perspective. This is both for the learner experience—what type of assignments should they make available, what is the ideal flow through a course, what should the role of grades be—as well as the instructor experience—how do we help them thoughtfully build their course? The final major component of her job is developing Coursera's research community. Andreina's team believes highly in the power and importance of research, and part of her role is to help build out the researcher community among partners so that they can better connect and collaborate and so that they can all better understand how learners learn.

Andreina loves the course-creation process. Coursera's learners are different from typical on-campus university students, so she enjoys helping the professors identify their target audience and all the different ways of teaching afforded to them by the platform. Andreina also loves to "nerd out" on Coursera's data and enjoys thinking about how she can understand more about how people learn and use that to inform how the Coursera platform is built and how courses are created. The least favorite part of her job is convincing others in the company of the importance of developing pedagogically sound courses, since it is not always clearly connected to increases in company revenues or profits. Not only is it important that her team execute well, but also that they are able to represent successes with metrics that are relevant to the whole company, so as to show the continued value of the team.

> Find the right mission for you. What really gets you excited and driven to make a change? Caring deeply about what you are doing provides the needed motivation to make it happen.

It is difficult for Andreina to integrate her work with her personal life because she cares deeply about Coursera's mission. At a startup, there is always more to be done than there are people to do it, but now that Coursera is bigger, more structured, and more focused on pushing toward the long haul than when Andreina started, it is clear that they need to be working at a level of sustainable urgency. She appreciates the flexibility that a Silicon Valley tech job provides. At least one day per week, she works from home instead of the office, and vacation is unlimited. However, she still needs to be conscientious and deliberate about not letting her work be her life. To maintain her personal relationships, Andreina marks Tuesdays and Thursdays on her calendar for going home earlier to make dinner with her fiancée and early Friday mornings for bike riding with close girlfriends.

Career Trajectory

Making the tough, scary decision to change her long-held plan to become a doctor, Andreina decided to study biomedical engineering. She loved the combination of math and biology and appreciated applying both under the umbrella of engineering where she worked toward solving novel and difficult problems. Teaching has also always been fun for Andreina, so she sought it out wherever she could. Tutoring and teaching in high school and college helped her hone her skills and motivated her to take education courses along the way, building both theory and practical experience. After earning her undergraduate degree, she considered going straight into teaching at the high school level, but she was not ready to fully commit. Instead, she followed her dream to live in Italy where her father had grown up. She worked for Bombardier Transportation in the Health, Safety, and Environment Office of their locomotive factory. She learned about a new industry, made amazing friends, and traveled a ton. While in Italy, she decided to go back to school for her PhD, excited about the potential of both making an impact on students through teaching and making an impact on patients through novel research.

While in grad school, Andreina attended a Saturday workshop where she met the founder of Miss CEO. She talked with the founder about her shared interest in empowering young girls through leadership and her experience with different levels of course and curriculum development; this eventually led to Andreina becoming the VP of programs. At Miss CEO, she developed leadership curriculum at the late elementary and high school levels, started an annual summer leadership academy, taught some of her curricula internationally through partnerships with the Department of State, and prepared others to teach these curricula to new audiences in Mexico. This work demonstrated her passion for education and helping others via education, both of which were important when she applied to work at Coursera. Andreina's continues to stay involved with Miss CEO.

Andreina cast her net wide as she searched for opportunities after earning her PhD, looking into teaching, K-12 STEM programs, university STEM development programs, and educational technology. Coursera, the biggest name in the educational technology world, got her excited but she was not sure that they would want someone like her, given that her background was most specifically in science, not in partner relations, teaching, or coding. She intentionally attended a panel about online education where a person in the role she wanted to apply for was speaking. After she attended the event, she connected with that person, which led to an informational interview and eventually to Andreina being hired and working happily at Coursera. As the Course Success team grows, she could see herself continuing to grow with the team, perhaps moving into a management position. She could also see herself returning to a university environment, working even more closely with instructors as they create online courses, diving into the educational research possible through the huge data sets that education online provides, and perhaps even going into teaching directly.

⚡ **Mark Brill, 30**

Blue Oak Energy
Business Development Engineer | $80,000 – 120,000

BS, Mechanical Engineering, Penn State University

Job Description

The US has expanded its solar energy capacity over 400% from 2010 to 2014. Over these four years, the cost of solar energy has dropped significantly because of technological improvements in photovoltaic (PV) panels, dramatic increases in overseas manufacturing capacity, and government tax credits and rebates for homeowners and businesses to adopt PV panels. Additionally, solar energy companies have scaled up from small local installers to Wall Street corporations; financial institutions, large energy companies, land developers, and major equipment manufacturers currently dominate the solar PV industry. Collectively, solar energy initiatives have the potential to have a step change effect in our energy sources and lead to a more sustainable energy future. While large organizations are selling solar energy, they need design and construction services to size and install systems. Blue Oak Energy is a fifty-person, privately owned design and construction firm that provides technical services solely to the PV industry. Blue Oak designs and installs commercial systems ranging from a 100 kilowatt system on top of a retailer to a thirty-seven megawatt solar farm with its own substation. Blue Oak employs drafters as well as electrical, civil, and structural engineers, and construction professionals and project managers.

Blue Oak's mission is to deliver real-world energy solutions today to build a sustainable tomorrow. Mark Brill, a business development engineer, wants to provide meaningful change to society through engineering. Having an ecological impact through his work is important for him. Mark provides clients with preliminary design, pricing, and energy modeling support in the early stages of their projects, often while clients are trying to win the right to build a project. Mark has to have a strong understanding of all the aspects of PV design and installation, and he must work on large projects for a short time just to get the project started successfully. On any given day, Mark may have meetings with clients to understand their needs, help them make equipment selections, create site layouts and single line diagrams in CAD, provide energy models, and estimate the cost of a design or full construction. He also visits construction sites or potential sites relatively often to determine project feasibility, collect data, and perform field inspections and commissioning.

While other people are doing the same thing as Blue Oak, this competition is driving down the cost of PV significantly (by about 50% or 60% since Mark got into the industry eight years ago). This is leading to an explosion of clean renewable energy, an acceptance by big energy companies that PV is economically viable and that it will be a part of the future energy portfolio—and less carbon in the air! Because of Blue Oak's competition with many other solar installers, he often wonders if Blue Oak is making an impact—if he did not install a particular farm, someone else would. However, he reminds himself that every time his company wins a job, that means they are doing it better or cheaper than it would have been done without him, and that means he is pushing PV forward.

Mark strongly believes companies should adopt a triple bottom line, meaning their actions should have positive ecological and societal implications and have a successful financial model to remain a sustainable enterprise. Considering that the industry is dominated by such large companies, Mark is glad that at the very least his work satisfies two of the three principals: it provides energy with much less environmental impact than traditional sources, and it is economically viable. He does not see spending the majority of his life at work to simply collect a paycheck as a worthwhile use of his time on Earth. Mark's favorite part of his job is solving many unique problems with solar projects every day, but he does not like it when clients do not keep their PV projects in perspective.

Career Trajectory

While an undergraduate student, Mark led a project to install a windmill in rural Kenya. This gave him the drive to pursue sustainable engineering. Practically, it gave him many leadership and problem-solving examples that he was able to use in interviews, which showed he had experience above what he had learned in books. Mark believes he got to where he is now foremost by taking any job he could to get into renewable energy. He worked in manufacturing solar to start, and with the tasks he was completing, for all he knew, he could have been making washing machines. He took this job with an eye on working his way up to a more hands-on role implementing projects. He made connections, and when there was an opening at the right time with his company, he made the switch. He was assigned to be the lead project engineer for the owner on what was at the time the largest roof mount PV array in the country as well as what still is the largest ground mount array on the East Coast.

I remember when I was starting out, I would at times pretend I knew what everyone was talking about. I was afraid to ask questions because I felt I needed to hide my inexperience because I already looked very young. Just this week I stood in a silent electrical room looking at closed-up electrical cabinets with several electricians and the client, unable to sort out in my head how it tied together. Some would have been embarrassed, but I asked, "What is going on here?" We all got a good laugh out of it because everyone admitted they could not make heads or tails of the situation. Ultimately we figured it out as a team. I now know to ask questions all the time, and I learn a lot. Do not be afraid to ask questions!

This was truly a pivotal moment in Mark's career. He had the good fortune to be mentored by a highly respected expert in the field. Mark believes that he was able to earn his mentor's respect by demonstrating that he was a studious engineer and willing to work hard, which were qualities his mentor shared. It was scary for him to basically learn PV as he went, but he credits his mentor for letting Mark find the answers on his own first and then providing feedback only after the problem's nooks and crannies were fully explored. This enabled him to come up to speed very quickly. He is very happy to have taken his first job in manufacturing and working his way up from there so that he can now see the fruits of his labor firsthand.

Mark completely consumes himself in his work for ten hours per day, but not outside that time. He currently spends time outside work doing many outdoor activities, watching baseball, and preparing to start a family. He would love to return to not-for-profit engineering enterprises on the side. Mark does not know exactly where he will head in the future. Right now, he defines his career by his wife's geographical requirements. Geographical restriction often happens when two professionals are married, and Mark is worried about it getting more complicated once they have children. The problem does not bother Mark, but it makes planning out his future nebulous at the moment.

✒ Stefano Concari, 41

Tropical Food Machinery
Managing Director of Italian Branch & Overall Technical Chief |
~$60,000 + Bonus

BS, Mechanical Engineering, Parma University (1999)

Job Description

Food security is a top priority among the Millennium Development Goals (MDGs). Many countries are making great progress toward achieving the MDG target to halve, between 1990 and 2015, the percentage of people who suffer from hunger. However, developing countries are struggling to make progress due to challenges including rapid population growth, climate change cutting crop yields, and land being depleted at unprecedented rates. Despite these challenges, many believe Africa could become the breadbasket of the world. In addition to large areas of fertile land, significant water resources, and plentiful farmers, there are currently few farms that are irrigated or treated with fertilizer. While farmers on other continents have mostly plateaued their crop yields, there is a large potential for developing more farmland and increasing crop yields in Africa. With improved efficiency of farming, African countries can develop export markets for food where they can further advance their societies while feeding the world, a win-win for development. To serve export markets, farming needs to operate on larger scales, way beyond the current widespread practice of subsistence farming. This requires sophisticated yet context-appropriate machinery that is easy to maintain and operate. Tropical Fruit Machinery (TFM) is a company that designs fruit-processing equipment in developing countries to add value to the raw materials available there.

Stefano Concari is currently managing director of the Italian branch of Tropical Food Machinery (TFM) as well as technical chief of the overall TFM company. The company has twenty employees in Italy and forty-five in Brazil. TFM builds fruit-processing plants in developing countries that each offer direct employment (fifty to one hundred people per plant). On a bigger scale, each plant has an effect on indirect employment in agriculture, transport activities, and services (hotels, food, accommodation, and maintenance services). Stefano estimates that this indirect employment equates to at least 500 to 1,000 people for each small project in Africa, and even more if the project becomes bigger. Plants often create a local spark in farming activities and bring more money to rural people. With this increase in fruit availability, the factories normally grow and invest money back in more equipment, creating a positive spiral of economic growth for the area.

On a day-to-day basis, Stefano checks in on project managers to make sure they are delivering on their projects. He acts as a project manager for TFM's most critical projects. Additionally, he develops new fruit-processing machines as well as provides support to the sales department if they need high-level technical support in dealing with customers. His work requires him to travel seven to ten days every month, mainly to Central and South America as well as Africa. A typical day for Stefano starts at 7:00 a.m., revising his personal emails and then checking the ongoing work in TFM's technical department and workshop. From 9:00 a.m. to 5:00 p.m., he opens his connection to all departments of TFM and customers to offer guidance, look over progress, and answer any questions. Then, from 5:00 p.m. to 7:30 p.m., he follows his personal projects, which include developing equipment and designing factory layouts.

In designing a factory layout, Stefano must account for all aspects of processing fruit. The most common fruits that TFM processes are tomatoes, pineapples, oranges, and mangos. They turn these fruits into many products, including canned fruit, oils, juices, and sauces. The process to make these products requires washing the fruit, sterilizing it, extracting juices, removing residuals, and refining and concentrating juices and sauces. This requires a lot of equipment that Stefano designs and lays out in factories.

Stefano's background in mechanical engineering not only helps him design and lay out this equipment in the best manner, but it also ensures the best quality food products. He must understand the ideal degree of ripening for each fruit and design a system of machinery that will control the ripening and stocking of the fruit. This requires a scientific assessment of the fruit-ripening process, the role of each machine, each machine's placement in the factory, and the timing of the fruit moving through each machine. Stefano enjoys the challenge his work provides him—with his competitors and with himself. He strives to fully use what he knows and to put all his creativity, strength, and experience into every project he works on.

 Believe in yourself; be patient sometimes to wait for the best opportunity, but do not be patient throughout your whole life.

Career Trajectory

Immediately out of college, Stefano moved into his family business. He started in the technical department of TFM following workshop activities and low-level development of equipment. After two years, he started to go abroad to learn to follow the assembly, start up, and commissioning of plants. Five years later, he started to be responsible for new projects and also increased his activity as a high-level designer of equipment. Then, more and more, he has increased his responsibility, taking charge of technical matters with each plant and ensuring the company's financial success in emerging markets.

Stefano has always traveled a lot and speaks five languages. Feeling like he is part of the world as a whole has opened his mind to the opportunities that are all around. He believes that the borders defining different parts of the world are present only in our heads. Despite being a global citizen, he still loves being a part of the small village he came from. Stefano has always been very dedicated to his job, leaving very little time for extra activities outside it. He tries to keep some time for his family first and then for his friends, but this has become more and more difficult for him each year. Looking back, he regrets not spending more time over summer holidays in English–, French–, and Spanish–speaking countries in order to be more fluent in these languages. In the future, he sees himself staying in the same position throughout the rest of his life while continuously growing his company.

Adele Peters, 35

Fast Company's Co.Exist Website
Staff Writer

MSc, Strategic Leadership towards Sustainability, Blekinge Institute of Technology
BA, Journalism, University of Iowa

Job Description

Innovators are working on all kinds of exciting things, such as creating a twenty-six–story passive apartment building in New York City, developing an app that can help farmers save water, and turning major streets in downtown Dublin into car-free plazas. Who is going to know about the new plate that graphically illustrates a balanced meal, the new park design that minimizes noise pollution, the new program that turns decommissioned buses into portable showers for the homeless, or the new sneakers knit entirely from ocean trash? The innovators behind these projects need their stories told so that they can get access to resources, new partners, and customers. On the other side, you have people who love to learn about new innovations that can improve the human condition. They turn to outlets such as Fast Company's Co.Exist website to learn about the latest and greatest with the environment, energy, technology, food, health, transportation, and more.

Fast Company is the world's leading progressive business media brand with a unique editorial focus on innovation in technology, ethonomics (ethical economics), leadership, and design. As a staff writer for Fast Company, Adele writes stories about social and environmental impact. Each day, she identifies people working on solutions that can address large societal challenges. She tracks each person down—not always an easy challenge—and talks to them about their work at length. On a typical day, she might get up early to make a call to Amsterdam or London and talk to others in Australia or Japan in the afternoon. In an interview, she strives to make the person comfortable enough to speak honestly about their challenges and successes. After they talk, Adele makes sense of the details, sketches out a story, and starts writing. Part of her job is digging into how their work connects with others trying to solve similar challenges and understanding the role the new project or company can play.

Adele writes three articles every day, which keeps her stimulated and always learning something new. The articles help emerging projects get more attention, more connections, and move forward more quickly. It is not uncommon for people to tell Adele they have gotten new funding or new partners after a story comes out, or that they have been flooded with emails or sales. For small social enterprises, this coverage can make a difference. Few mainstream media sources focus exclusively on social impact, so Fast Company provides Adele and social innovators a unique platform.

Adele's favorite thing about her job is talking to people who are smart, passionate, and taking clever new approaches to long-term challenges. She has the chance to talk with astronauts, politicians, artists, and brilliant urban hackers. She loves the variety—she will be learning about e-waste recycling in Ghana one day and Danish fiscal policy the next. It is never boring. Each day, though, she wishes she had more time. Because she writes so many stories, she rarely has time to dive into any particular story in as much depth as she would like. Adele works from home, so she tries to be conscious of maintaining work-life balance and not letting work bleed over into the evening hours. However, her job is genuinely interesting to her, so it is not uncommon for conversations at parties to veer to things that she has been learning about or things that she might want to write about; she is always thinking about these things.

Career Trajectory

Adele has followed a circuitous path: she started out studying journalism as an undergrad, but her first job was in business. She convinced an apparel company to hire her to work on sustainability challenges and dove into the world of organic cotton and fair labor. Since then, she has worked at nonprofits, in academia helping researchers find commercial paths for sustainable products, and at a startup social enterprise that has since quintupled in size. At each point in her career, she has learned about sustainability from a new perspective. All of that experience has been valuable, but she is happiest where she is now, sharing stories.

Adele's undergraduate degree in journalism was helpful—though not necessary. It did help her get her last job at a magazine and taught her the basics of the craft. Her graduate degree, from a university in Sweden, focused on sustainable development and gave her a different perspective on the field; living in Sweden (and near Copenhagen, a city she loves) helped her see what life could be like in a place that has focused policy on sustainability issues for decades.

This is a great path to choose because it is easier to stay motivated than if you take a job that is just about money or recognition. You are always working for something larger than yourself. At the same time, it is important to keep that larger goal in mind. Whether you are starting a new business or working inside a larger corporation, there will be times when it is tempting to make decisions that are not necessarily aligned with social good. Stay strong. Because sustainability and social impact can be fuzzy concepts, I also think it is useful to build hard skills separately, whether that is in coding or finance, and then build sustainability into whatever work you do.

Adele is always reading. This, of course, helps her with her job, but she also just loves to read and learn—it never stopped after school. Living in the Bay Area, Adele constantly meets new people working on social impact and sustainability-related projects. She has a great network of friends in this field, and she has met hundreds of motivated, talented people through work. She has had the chance to go to unique events, such as the Greenermind Summit, which is basically a sustainability summer camp for adults up in a redwood forest. It seems that every night in San Francisco there is a lecture or party or hackathon or something else related to social impact.

Adele keeps writing about the future of robots taking over jobs, so who knows how long she will be penning articles. There are also longstanding rumors about journalism being a doomed field. Luckily, Adele is comfortable with change. She can imagine herself going back into the business world at some point and helping companies find new approaches for sustainability challenges.

Chris Hsiung, 38

Hidden Story Productions
Independent Owner | ~$70,000

BS, Electrical Engineering, University of Calgary (1999)

Job Description

Stories are the way people make meaning of life; the stories an individual carries are of critical importance to how they see and understand life. Stories can turn us into consumers who believe more is always better, or they can enlarge our compassion for humanity and life. Before any helpful action there lies an inspired, well-informed, compassionate mind. Chris Hsiung is the independent owner of Hidden Story Productions (HSP), which aims to educate minds by telling the story of human achievements and failures through film and video. He helps clients use video as a tool to educate, engage, or advocate for social issues through short documentary stories or creative projects. He partners with people and organizations to conceptualize messaging and education projects, conduct research and field investigations, produce the video, and ultimately, distribute it.

Chris's most recent production is a feature documentary exploring First Nations culture and history called *Elder in the Making*. Chris is a first-generation Chinese Canadian who grew up on Treaty 7 Territory knowing little about the treaty signed for the territory nor how many promises made in it have been broken. In his film, Chris and a Blackfoot man revisit the circumstances surrounding the signing of the treaty. Chris hopes to educate people across North America about the modern implications of treaties signed with Native Americans over 100 years ago. Chris believes that what makes his company unique is an understanding of development issues and how they fit into the context of the global environment and humanity. Chris wants to develop the collective narrative to produce a more compassionate, intelligent society. Each video project HSP takes on requires preproduction, which may include fundraising, research, location scouting, storyboarding, recruiting contractors, as well as scheduling and logistics. Once the video footage is captured, the far more time-consuming process begins with logging and transcribing the footage, and then editing the scenes together in such a way as to effectively tell the story to a specific audience. When the editing is done (or the time is up), the next phase is marketing and promoting the film.

Outside his direct work with film, one of the most important activities Chris does each day is read. He reads books, articles, and news to feed his sense and understanding of the world in which we live; no discipline or field is off-limits. One day he may be reading about the effect of prescriptive regulations on individual judgment, and the next, he will explore the history of a treaty signed with aboriginals. According to Chris, without this broad understanding of the world, he would not be able to decide which stories need to be heard and told and where he can make a difference.

Chris tries to stay connected with communities attempting to make a difference globally and locally. This may involve volunteering or organizing events. Two of his largest involvements are with the Human Venture Institute, an organization studying the achievements and failures of humankind, and with TEDxCalgary, a local independently run TED group for which he is the creative production director. It is through this network that he is hired for a variety of video production services. Projects can range from something as simple as a live-event capture at a conference to a full documentary production in a foreign country. For example, he was recently commissioned to go to Kathmandu, Nepal, for four weeks by an international development agency. While abroad, his goal was to produce, in collaboration with Nepalese youth, an educational resource that would connect youth in Canada with youth in Nepal.

Equally as important as the videos he is commissioned to create are his personal projects where he pursues key stories he feels are important to tell. Recently, a tip from a friend led him to the nearby city of Vernon, the historical site of one of Canada's east European internment camps. From this visit, he produced a story about human-rights abuses there. A rewarding experience came one evening when Chris showed one of his films projected on to the side of a wall at night in front of a captive audience. It was his first documentary, which was about a girl who built a bike-powered generator as a way to engage people with energy issues. According to Chris, "It was really neat to give people a year's worth of experience in fifteen minutes. None of us live long enough to experience all the lessons of life, but with films, you can learn from a hundred lifetimes, and that can really affect how you live your life."

Another rewarding moment Chris had was when, sometime after showing one of his films at a festival, a man sent him a note saying that his son wanted to donate his birthday present to a nearby drop-in center. His mother asked him why, and he told her it was because of Chris's documentary on homelessness at the film festival. Chris loves to see the good change in people that his films contribute to. He remarks, "Youth teaching youth through their investigation of a story can be powerful!" Chris firmly believes the video camera is just a tool used to accomplish his larger purpose of educating people's imaginations, not making films. Therefore, in

There is a saying in martial arts: "How you train is how you live." Does one stop doing good, living well, or thinking deeply when one stops work? When work is not contributing to my sense of life purpose, then I try to change it.

Keys to success: prepare, read, learn, do, fail, and try again. One of the most liberating aspects of making your own path is that you get to explore. Part of the fun of exploring is finding dead-ends, promising paths, rough patches, and stunning moments.

addition to owning Hidden Story Production, Chris runs a program called Reel World Youth Documentaries, which spends a few months taking youths through the making of a documentary. Each group of youth take on the challenge of selecting a topic they are interested in, then investigating it, holding interviews, filming it, and finally sharing their film at a film festival. While his goal was never to turn students into filmmakers, he was still surprised by how working on a long-term project taught the students lessons, such as how to approach adults, get organized, work as a team, take responsibility for their own work, and face setbacks.

The biggest privilege of being a documentary filmmaker is that the camera serves as a passport to all sorts of experiences and locations for Chris. Whether it is living with a wheelchair-bound person or participating in activism with Nepalese youth or being welcomed on the aboriginal reserve, the camera is his way in. While sometimes he has to choose projects not by topic but by economic gain, he tries to keep the perspective that each project can teach him something, and as long as it does not actively take away from his purpose, he can be proud of the work he does.

Career Trajectory

It began with a book, *Shake Hands with the Devil*, and a meeting with the author Lt. Romeo Dallaire. The stories of child soldiers hit Chris in a way that made him question what he was contributing, if anything, to the broader human journey. In the beginning, Chris enjoyed the relative independence and freedom of being a software designer for almost eight years. It afforded a great lifestyle, and the work was interesting and challenging. Nevertheless, his engagements with the community were taking up more and more time and thought. It ended up being that reading and trying to understand the human situation did more to change his life than any specific volunteer activity. Ultimately, somehow climbing the corporate ladder, living in a big home, and luxury vacations became more and more irrelevant.

So Chris began to shift his path and priorities. Financially, he downsized and increased his savings. Socially, his relationships incorporated those seeking to improve the world. He also started a side consulting business to learn the ropes of going independent and began working with a business/life coach to create space for reflecting on his priorities. Hidden Story Productions started as the side business to his consulting practice. He borrowed money to invest in some equipment and started with any video job where he could learn the basics while at the same time taking courses from local film group workshops at large conferences.

As one can gather, most of skill sets Chris uses now were acquired in extracurricular activities. His engineering experiences were not all wasted, however. His project management skills he learned through engineering have often come in handy. He also had many opportunities to exercise planning and analytical abilities and, as a result, approach art, social pursuits, and business in a relatively pragmatic way. His minor in English helped expose him to the structures of stories. However, he did find it unfortunate that most engineering courses he took did not teach anything about initiative, creative problem solving, risk taking, failure, and society.

Nevertheless, Chris is excited to be where he is today to say the least. In the future he would like to see HSP tackle bigger stories that help people learn from the failings and inspiration of humanity. Specifically, that means doing longer-form documentaries or collaborating with other groups to use films as one tool in a larger effort to create change.

Photo by TechShop Pittsburgh LLC

⚙ Matt Verlinich, 28

TechShop Pittsburgh
General Manager | ~$50,000 + Quarterly Performance Bonus

MS, Engineering Science, Penn State University (2009)
BS, Engineering Science and Mechanics, Penn State University (2008)

Job Description

Entrepreneurship is becoming an ever-increasing aspect of popular culture. Households around America are hooked on *Shark Tank*, a show where innovators pitch their new product ideas to potential investors. Students are rushing into academic entrepreneurship programs and research labs to invent new products with faculty collaborators. A pivotal part of the entrepreneurial journey is the design, development, and field-testing of product prototypes. Nothing conveys the form and value of a product more than a physical prototype that potential customers, collaborators, and investors can see, touch, and play with. Most innovators do not have easy access to the tools and equipment needed to quickly and inexpensively fabricate product prototypes. TechShop is a for-profit, membership-based, fabrication and prototyping studio, hacker space, and learning center that fills this critical gap in the entrepreneurial ecosystem.

TechShop, whose motto is "Build Your Dreams Here," provides access to over $1 million worth of professional prototyping equipment and software. Each studio is equipped with state-of-the-art technology, including laser cutters, 3-D printers, plastics and electronics labs, a machine shop, a wood shop, a metal-working shop, a textiles department, welding stations, and a water-jet cutter. In addition, they each have a retail shop where members can purchase basic hardware, such as pliers and safety equipment. For a monthly or annual fee, members have access to machines, project areas with large worktables, conference rooms with projectors, wireless Internet, professional software (Autodesk, Adobe, and National Instruments), and free coffee and popcorn. In addition to membership, TechShop also offers a wide variety of workshops, community events, and safety and basic use (SBU) classes for each of the in-house machines. The captain and general manager of this progressive innovation space, Matthew Verlinich, is instrumental to the success of inventors in the Pittsburgh area.

Matt is responsible for every detail of shop operation, maintenance, financial performance, customer service, quality assurance, sales, and marketing. In order to accomplish all of this, he has to rely on a dedicated team of twenty-three people who work for him. Matt spends most of his time communicating objectives or more specific action items to his leads: lead dream consultant (DC), front desk (FD) lead, event coordinator, education coordinator, and senior account manager. Lead DC manages a team of DCs who are responsible for inspiring and empowering their members to build their dreams; FD lead manages the staff of FD inceptionists who are responsible for all transactions that occur in the shop, including selling memberships and classes; event coordinator promotes, manages, and executes on paid and promotional events (like school field trips and corporate team-building events); education coordinator manages their team of part-time contractor instructors; and senior accounts manager is the point of contact for all group sales of memberships, classes, and events.

Matt follows up with his leads to make sure things are proceeding according to plan. Some of the leads take care of the action items directly while others are supervisors of additional employees or contractors. As a result, his main functions include hosting meetings, sending emails, putting things on calendars, managing to-do lists, making budgets, and checking budgets. The most important parts of Matt's job are managing the profit-and-loss statement (P&L), a.k.a. the financial performance of his shop, and improving the TechShop Pittsburgh experience. P&L boils down to striking a balance between managing expenses and driving sales. Matt claims this is the nice, simple, black-and-white side of his job.

The colorful, creative, and intangible side of his job comes from being the ambassador of the TechShop Pittsburgh experience. Matt leads by example while getting people to work together to elaborate and execute on ideas that emerge during brainstorming. He has to be friendly and inspiring to members in order to keep their creative juices flowing. For example, Matt recently collaborated with TechShop members to create Boxzy, an all-in-one 3-D printer, computer numerical control (CNC) mill, and laser engraver. Boxzy takes 3-D printing to the next level, allowing for serious and multi-material manufacturing. Matt helped them learn industrial design skills, complete multiple iterations and tests of their design, and produce a creative video for marketing the product. Without Matt's guidance and the ability for fast prototyping through the TechShop workplace, Boxzy may never have become a reality.

Matt believes that for-profit businesses often get a bad reputation in socially oriented circles. If TechShop was really a cutthroat, for-profit company, they would have pivoted a long time ago and figured out a way to take equity in all the busi-

> Do not think about it as "social value creation." Endeavor to do good and be sustainable. Doing good without being sustainable is charity. Being sustainable without being good is socially pointless. In accomplishing those two things together, you will create something socially valuable.

nesses that have generated millions of dollars since the start of the company. However, he firmly believes that TechShop has stayed true to its commitment to provide open access to anyone with a dream, not just those people whose dreams might benefit TechShop. Therefore, it is easiest to assess the impact of the business's activities by the connections Matt has made with his members; social impact can be seen through the designs he has helped make a reality, the workshops and presentations that have shared knowledge with so many, and the rave reviews he receives about the shop. Matt considers the best part of his job to be the people. Many of his days have been elevated to the highest highs by seeing and sharing in the success of his staff and members.

Career Trajectory

Matt was a member of the Schreyer Honors College at Penn State where he majored in engineering science and mechanics. Matt believes his education prepared him for this job because he got great exposure to different technical disciplines while at the same time being afforded the flexibility to pursue new ones that interested him. When he was looking for undergraduate research opportunities, his interest was piqued by a PhD student working on biodiesel reactors. That summer, Matt traveled across six different countries while studying photography and architecture in Rome. When he arrived back on campus, he dived right into the biodiesel project and carved out his honors thesis from it. From then on, Matt and the PhD student worked hand in hand with a startup company for the next two and a half years developing bigger and better biodiesel reactors. Matt graduated from the integrated BS-MS program and took on an entry-level mechanical engineer position with Westinghouse Electric Company. The research and teaching assistantship he held in graduate school sharpened the educational, customer service, and leadership aspects of his current position.

Westinghouse was a big change from the startup/research community he had been accustomed to. With this first job, he had opportunities to see nuclear facilities, do inspections, get training, and attend industrial conferences. However, at the end of the day, he wanted to be more creative, faster, and freer to build his own dreams than this position allowed. While stewing at home over Christmas because a trip to India fell through, a friend mentioned TechShop was opening in Pittsburgh. He immediately applied because, after considering so many options, this one was the first that felt right; it felt like it fit not just because of the difference in day-to-day responsibilities, but the limitless potential for where it might lead and who he might come across in this brand-new community.

Matt has been told he is a person of extremes, something he illustrated while applying for the job at TechShop. He did everything he could to get this job: he tailored his résumé and cover letter, did research, put together a plan of how he could help the business succeed, and created a portfolio of everything he had physical proof of ever making. He stayed up late every night for a week putting many hours of work into thinking of every reason why he was the best person to work at TechShop. After multiple long and unconventional interviews, the work paid off, and he was hired. Reflecting on the path he took to get where he is today, Matt realized it was important that he set himself up at every turn for a safe, comfortable existence while waiting patiently for something to excite his passion. "Every time I saw an opportunity that excited me and felt right, I did everything I possibly could to seize the opportunity with both hands."

Matt sums up his entire journey by stating: "There are those who like to gamble, dive in headfirst, and experience the highest highs and the lowest lows within weeks; and then there are those who like to slowly and methodically pursue their goals over time, exploiting delayed gratification and building a strong foundation to grow on. At the end of the day, I got a master's degree learning exactly what I wanted to, paid off my loans without any assistance, gained valuable industrial experience, saved up more money than I know what to do with, and now I have a job I love and a reason to wake up." In the future, Matt hopes to still be working at TechShop but at a higher level, taking over a position with more responsibility and more say in the overall strategy of the company. Ultimately, he sees himself owning multiple successful companies and doing what he loves the most: teaching.

⚙️ Mark Randall, 55

Worldstudio
Principal and Creative Director | ~$100,000/year
BFA, University of Washington

Job Description

Believe it or not, you are constantly being told what to do. Media is designed to influence your behavior, so would it not be great if design made people behave better and contribute positively to society? Graphic designers have a significant role to play in the social impact space—not only influencing behavior, but also figuring out ways to communicate messages for socially relevant causes. Mark Randall heads Worldstudio, a design studio that seeks out projects to drive positive social change. Worldstudio operates in two ways: a for-profit side provides design and communication services to clients; a nonprofit side, Worldstudio Foundation, creates socially minded projects that use creativity to impact positive social change.

Four employees in total comprise Worldstudio: Mark as principal, two designers, and a program coordinator to manage the foundation. As a small organization, they rely on a range of professional, corporate, and foundation partners to support them in executing their nonprofit work. The for-profit side of the business has a focus on civic and nonprofit clients; for example, they do a lot of work for civic organizations, such as the Times Square Alliance (the agency that manages Times Square) and the Garment District Alliance—creating identity programs, brochures, websites, and print collateral. The for-profit side of the business generates the income for Mark's and the designers' salaries through client work. The nonprofit side generates ideas for the projects Worldstudio wants to execute, and then they find partners to make them happen. Financial partners cover the salary of the program coordinator.

The Urban Forest Project is a great example of an initiative that bridged the gap between the for-profit and nonprofit sides of Worldstudio. The for-profit client, Times Square Alliance, wanted a public art project using the banners that hang from light posts in the district, so they came to Mark for ideas. He started brainstorming on how he could use the project to make a social statement. Mark chose to promote sustainability and thought a tree was a good symbol for the notion: an urban forest of trees in Times Square. Mark and his project partners, Times Square Alliance and the New York Chapter of AIGA, recruited 185 artists and designers from around the world to create banner artwork, which used the tree to make a compelling visual statement.

The banners hung in Times Square for three months, gaining them great visibility. To support the concept of sustainability, instead of tossing the banners in a landfill after they were taken down, the accessories designer, Jack Spade, turned them into stylish tote bags. The bags were then auctioned off to raise money for scholarship and mentoring programs for young people interested in art and design. This was another expression of the idea of sustainability, sustaining and supporting the next generation of creative talent. Worldstudio then received unsolicited requests from cities across the country who wanted to expand the project to their communities. The requests came from city officials who wanted to use the project as a platform to promote their own local forestry and sustainability initiatives. The project launched in eight cities, and Mark loved how each city adapted the project to their needs, engaging local artists and designers.

Adobe Foundation heard about the Urban Forest Project and reached out to Mark to see how they could work together. At that point, the Worldstudio team was beginning to incubate the idea of Design Ignites Change, a showcase of social design talent and projects in high schools and colleges across the country to encourage students to get involved in important issues, encourage universities to include it in their curriculum, and honor the work with award money. Inspiring young artists and designers is an area that Worldstudio has always focused on in their nonprofit work; the partnership with Adobe provided sustained support for five years that allowed his team to create a robust program that continues to grow.

On the for-profit side, Worldstudio is currently working on a tool kit for affordable housing units in dense urban areas to better prepare for a disaster such as Hurricane Sandy, which struck New York City several years ago and caused widespread devastation. Worldstudio's nonprofit client, a leading developer of affordable housing units in the United States, created a very complex, dense tool kit comprised of guides, worksheets, and short video content—over sixty documents. Worldstudio's main task was to turn this massive amount of content into accessible, easy-to-understand information for staff and residents of affordable housing units. Mark and his team started by thinking about ways to structure the content: What form is this information going to take? What are some visual devices that could help to clarify and guide people through the content?

> Many equate social design with pro bono work where you donate your services for the benefit of a nonprofit project. While this is admirable, it is not sustainable in the long term as pro bono does not pay the bills. I believe that designers should get paid for the socially minded work they do. It is your challenge to be creative about how you do that. One way to do it is to always be engaged and curious about the world. You never know what opportunities may arise.

In his daily activities for the for-profit side of the business, Mark works on a mix of strategy, creative direction, and business administration. On the nonprofit side, he works closely with the program coordinator on strategy, planning, and partnership building. The majority of Mark's time is delegated to for-profit projects because that is the engine that keeps things going. He has to make sure that the cash is coming in. Mark loves the process of the work he does; to him, process is primary to the end result. The journey is the destination! The aspect of his job he likes the least is the ongoing struggle to find the money and resources to implement the social initiatives they develop. The work of Worldstudio is unusual and somewhat complicated to explain, so Mark's biggest challenge is that people do not always clearly understand what they do. He feels that if they get better at explaining to people what they do, they might find more opportunities to do it. Currently Worldstudio is revamping its website and social media presence to tell a more compelling, cohesive story to their potential clients and partners.

Career Trajectory

Mark originally went to college to study music at the University of Washington in Seattle; at the time, he did not even know what graphic design was. After his first year, he realized that he did not want to play the French horn for the rest of his life. He started flipping through the course catalog and took a disparate range of classes that sounded interesting to him. One was a basic introduction to design. He learned through the instructor that his school had a highly regarded graphic design program that was difficult to get into. At the beginning of the year, the entry process started with over 100 applicants; over the course of a year of vetting through required design classes, Mark was one of twenty finally accepted into the program. After graduation from undergrad, Mark worked for a small design studio in New York City for two years and then for Vignelli Associates, a leading international studio, for another two years. After his stint at Vignelli, he was not sure what to do next, so he worked freelance for about four years.

Through his freelance work, he met the noted graphic designer David Sterling, who at the time was a partner in the firm Doublespace. David hired him to design a logo for a new kind of design studio he wanted to launch, a studio that blended traditional client services with self-generated work that had positive social impact—this was in the mid-1990s when nobody was talking about social impact design. David and Mark really hit it off, and through the course of working on the identity program for what was to eventually become Worldstudio, David invited Mark to be his business partner. In 2003 David left Worldstudio to start a new business venture in Mexico, and Mark has maintained the business ever since.

At Worldstudio, Mark firmly believes everybody has to have a life outside work, so his company is loosely structured. People can come and go as they please, but there is an expectation about what they need to get done and how many hours they need to work in a day. Outside Worldstudio Mark has a variety of activities that he enjoys doing, from beekeeping and baking to kickboxing. These are important aspects of his life and help to keep him going. Mark is always thinking about what is next—what kind of impact he wants Worldstudio to have and how he can create a sustainable business model to support the nonprofit side of the business in a more robust way. In the future, he would like to create larger social programs that have a more populist and mainstream appeal to demonstrate how design and creativity can impact pressing social issues.

FOR-PROFIT » STARTUP

Andrea Spillmann-Gajek, 30

Captricity
Vice President of Customer Success

MPH, University of California, Berkeley (2011)
BA, History and Science, Harvard University (2007)

Job Description

Data on transportation, education, and especially health is incredibly important in developing countries. Health data can be used to decrease costs, improve service quality, and collect feedback about a program, all of which is valuable to the many organizations and governments working on limited budgets. Collecting, aggregating, and digitizing data for analysis can be difficult for small companies with low resources who could face challenges such as lapses in power access or miscommunication because of language barriers.

Captricity makes the process of digitizing data easier with a technical system they created to extract digital data from paper documents. Captricity's founder created this system while he was doing his PhD research in Tanzania and Uganda. It is the first web service that can read human handwriting at 99.9%+ level of accuracy. With quickly digitized data, doctors have faster access to electronic medical records and can track trends such as health-worker performance or the number of births happening at home (which are much more dangerous than births at a clinic).

Many organizations in both the public and private sectors are fighting expensive, time-consuming, and ineffective paper processes and resulting backlogs while struggling to make better use of their customer data. Therefore, many organizations outsource their data digitization to Captricity. These organizations drive Captricity's business; Captricity can succeed only if its customers from different countries and cultures succeed. Therefore, Captricity's success comes down to the person who is in charge of customer success. This person needs to understand diverse customer problems and work with them to be successful. Andrea Spillmann, vice president of customer success, oversees a team that manages all interactions with customers.

Upon learning about Captricity's technology, Andrea was excited about its potential to have a major impact on global health. She saw that by giving health-care workers around the world faster access to data, she could help them analyze trends, make improvements, and inform policy. Andrea jumped at the chance to work for Captricity where, in the startup stage of the company, she started by writing the first business plan. Now, along with managing customer interactions, Andrea manages Captricity's support teams and the company's community program (Captricity.org).

Through the community program, projects that cannot afford Captricity's services are provided access at or below cost. Captricity therefore can work with social enterprises and NGOs who badly need digitized data but might not be able to afford enterprise-level solutions. Through their community program and Captricity's normal business, Andrea works with many individuals and organizations, including Jhpiego, Poverty Action, Grameen Bank, New York Life, and the Federal Election Commission. These customers need their data digitized quickly to analyze it and provide the best quality health products and services to people around the world. They choose Captricity thanks to their unique ability to read handwriting with great accuracy, their speed of service, their community program, and the dedicated attention that Andrea's team offers to every customer.

Many of these global health organizations are collecting data on health conditions in rural communities. Several developing countries have community health worker (CHW) programs where volunteers collect health data from members of their own communities. CHWs can report their data to the formal health-care system or the government for use in studies. In any case, it must be digitized to stay organized and travel far. Andrea's background in public health helps Captricity because she can understand health data, decide how to best use and digitize it, and make recommendations for the CHWs collecting the data. Her knowledge of the sciences also enables her to have high-level discussions with Captricity's engineers and technical staff. She additionally can quickly understand new ideas and projects that clients are working on in the health domain.

Andrea's days are often filled with meetings, including calls with customers and status meetings with her growing team. She works directly with project managers at client organizations in order to ensure they are getting everything they want out of Captricity's product. As a member of the executive committee at Captricity, she gives input about the direction of the company and other major issues they face. She enjoys the excitement that comes with a startup and seeing it grow. Many of the projects and processes they implement are being done for the first time, and she knows how crucial it is to learn from everything they do, even failures. Working at a startup, it can be difficult for Andrea to separate her work and personal lives. Some days she finds herself in the office long after normal working hours, but because she loves her work, long days fly by. She also tries to balance out long working hours by taking time off on the weekends.

Career Trajectory

Although Andrea went to college to study bioethics, she quickly found that neither biology nor philosophy was what she was truly interested in. Thankfully, a friend pointed her toward public health and history of science, and as someone who always loved science, Andrea decided to pursue both fields. She majored in history of science while getting minors in both Latin American studies and public health. She lived in Argentina and Chile as an undergrad and completed her undergraduate thesis on the health-care system in Chile. Her international experiences sparked a broader interest in global health, and following graduation, she decided to work with this topic from the US to be close to her family.

Through an internship with the University of California, San Francisco, she worked with medical researchers to create a survivorship program for breast-cancer patients. Andrea experienced how universities and hospitals approached large health problems. Living in the startup culture of San Francisco, she wanted to know how Silicon Valley could create solutions for global health issues. She joined a startup creating the "Wikipedia of medical knowledge" and after a year, returned to school to pursue a master's of public health at UC-Berkeley. While pursuing this degree, she met the founder of Captricity and worked on early versions of Captricity's technology with him. To some people, the problem they were solving, data entry, sounded boring, but Andrea looked past this and saw its great potential to improve global health.

As an actress in theater clubs from age eight through college, Andrea had to put herself into someone else's shoes and empathize with each character she played. The ability to see things through different eyes has been helpful in her role at Captricity. Being on a stage in front of a thousand people also forced her to be conscious of how she stands, what she says, and how she behaves—all crucial skills she uses now when talking to customers. When she was an undergrad student, Andrea had no information about the types of careers that were available in her area of interest. When she finished her bachelor's degree, few startups could call themselves social enterprises. Despite not even knowing what startups were at that time, Andrea now finds herself in a high-level position at one.

Andrea often sees her impact in the form of conversations with clients where they excitedly tell her about the amazing things they can do with the data digitized by Captricity. After several years of working in the field, she is seeing firsthand the value of data. Andrea and Captricity value putting data out there so that it can get into the hands of organizations doing work on the ground; they have plans to explore this area further in the coming years.

Photo by Cat Laine

FOR-PROFIT » STARTUP

Peter Haas, 39

XactSense | Chief Operating Officer
Former Executive Director of Appropriate Infrastructure
Development Group

BS, Philosophy and Psychology, Yale University (1998)

Job Description

"Appropriate technologies" refer to simple technology solutions that aim to improve the lives and incomes of people in developing countries. Appropriate technology projects include solar-powered lightbulbs, pot-in-pot refrigerators, bike-powered water pumps, and the LifeStraw water filter. The appropriate technology movement started to gain popularity in the 1970s as an alternative to foreign aid. In 2004, Peter Haas was inspired by his travels to developing countries to create a new, more sustainable type of aid organization. He wanted to help people by using market forces and embracing local production and innovation in emerging markets. Instead of "appropriate technologies" to help individuals at a very low cost, he aimed for larger, scalable projects to involve more people in a business. Intermediate technologies help you play in larger economies and leverage market forces—for example, a large solar food dryer that a group of entrepreneurs can invest in so that they can buy fruit from farmers and dry it to make a larger profit.

Peter cofounded the Appropriate Infrastructure Development Group (AIDG), a business-development charity that provided access to environmentally friendly infrastructure in impoverished communities via a combination of business incubation, education, and direct outreach. Over a ten-year span, AIDG helped launch new services that have helped over 200,000 people. AIDG worked with university teams and private inventors to design products for the developing world and test them in communities; developed renewable-energy, water and sanitation, and cookstove systems; created a mason training program to improve the safety of new buildings following the 2010 Haiti earthquake; helped Guatemalan enterprises by providing seed financing and technical support; and much more.

At AIDG, Peter did everything from managing invention charrettes (intense periods of design activity) and trainings, to meeting with donors, to getting his hands dirty in villages shoveling pig excrement into biodigestors. While many would argue that an executive is best suited focusing on the high-level function of their organization, Peter prefers the hands-on approach advocated by Paul Farmer, a public health specialist and pioneer. Peter believes that if you can see from the bottom-up how your company is functioning, you are better informed to make solid executive decisions about the direction of the company. Without experiencing the small details in client interaction, one can lose touch with the end, and this can have disastrous results.

AIDG helped companies and independent inventors working on products to solve rural infrastructure problems. Peter and his coworkers measured impact through the number of families served by their new products, which totals in the tens of thousands. In 2014, Peter shut down AIDG to become COO of XactSense. The funding for the charitable model of AIDG was increasingly detached from results. Peter was frustrated by seeing impact go up and funding go down, so he decided to shift to do something for-profit, where performance and income were better tied together.

At XactSense, he primarily works with drones that are revolutionizing the way we see and measure the world in terms of power lines, telecommunications, mining, rooftops, oil and gas pipelines, and bridges. Following the April 2015 earthquake in Nepal, XactSense sent drones there to assess the damage and survey unreachable areas to assist other organizations with on-the-ground response. Just like at the beginning of AIDG, Peter wears many hats at XactSense because it is a startup. Peter can be doing mechanical engineering work, talking to an investor, or making sales, depending on the day. It is all about removing barriers to get a product to market and to improve the customer experience. He feels like he is stuck inside the book *The Way Things Work*, getting to play with new mechanical, electrical, electronic, and social systems. He thinks this is a great way to live and that he could not handle a job where he did the same thing for twenty years.

Career Trajectory

During his college years at Yale, kung fu was the most important activity for Peter. It taught him how to be observant before being reactive and to respond to issues only after they have entered his circle of influence. Kung fu also emphasizes exerting the minimum required effort to resolve a problem, and this is something Peter is still working on mastering in his day-to-day life. After college, he worked on a horse ranch and then joined a startup that enabled him to pay off his student loans and save enough money to travel around the world volunteering for nonprofits. Getting out there into different cultures and different organizations helped him to learn a lot about what works in international development and what does not. Peter advises to never underestimate the importance of taking time to learn from what is being done. One of the greatest failings of social enterprises is a constant reinvention of the wheel without capturing the learning from what has gone before. This leads each new generation to make many of the same mistakes when confronted with the challenges of addressing issues like poverty.

> Make money while doing good. The old model of donation-based charity will never solve the problems of the world at the scale needed. Charitable work can be good for a proof of concept, but if you really want true scale in the hundreds of millions, you need to be making a profit. A good example of this is how Grameen Phone pioneered the prepaid cell phone in the nineties, and demonstrated that people who were poor could afford cell phones. Grameen Phone had a great proof of concept, but it was not until other for-profit cellular startups jumped in that you saw phone service for people making a few dollars a day balloon into hundreds of millions of subscribers.

To push his career forward, Peter took advantage of social media. He realized he did not need to be "sales-y" or self-promoting, but he did need to reach out to people. Peter and his team got on National Public Radio (NPR) because of a tweet and originally got into the TED community through a single blog post. Being yourself and having genuinely interesting content can go a long way. On the work side, Peter is heavily involved in hackathons and believes it is the best way to play with new technology without commitment. Attending hackathons gives him a break and enables him to dabble in a variety of projects. Recently, Peter got involved with a laser-scanning project and a disaster-response network project at a hackathon. Neither of these projects directly related to his work at XactSense, but he was able to draw parallels. "It is important to let yourself think about other things every once in a while if you want to make breakthroughs. The great physicist Richard Feynman once made one of his greatest breakthroughs after messing around trying to calculate the spin of the logo on a Frisbee." Hackathon projects have taught Peter not to get caught in the rut of trying to solve problems only for work.

For many years, Peter maintained a poor work-life balance, letting work dominate his personal life. This was a problem because he worked with his wife and partner. He made great efforts trying to reclaim a balance; he went to retreats and talked with monks and coaches, but he was not able to fix it. He would always let that one more thing on his to-do list creep up on his agenda. One day, Peter woke up and found out he was not as young and indestructible as he thought; some health issues caught up to him, and he could not manage the long hours anymore. Now, he tries to prioritize physical fitness, works on projects well in advance of deadlines, and finishes working at the end of a normal day.

If Peter had to start his education over, he would have pursued a computer science or engineering degree—it was ridiculous how many times early in his career that he had to explain away his philosophy degree. Even though he is skilled and had worked on complicated software projects, the credentials help. Also, before starting his social enterprise, Peter would have saved up a lot more money. Startups usually require an amount of personal runway where you do not make much money and need to find other means to support yourself. Being able to save for that time to give yourself the time you need to launch your next company is important. In the future, Peter hopes to become more like the people he admires most in this world—i.e., people that have made large-scale impacts, not only by outworking the other guy, but by looking at future trends, searching for that leverage point that will cause a major shift, and persisting on that point to make great change. Peter hopes in the next ten years he will be able to start working on that type of leverage-point project, specifically to do something about impending social issues involved with increased automation and artificial intelligence.

FOR-PROFIT » STARTUP

❤ Matthew Callaghan, 40

OneBreath | Cofounder and Chief Medical Officer
Stanford University | Physician

MD, SUNY Downstate College of Medicine in Brooklyn
BFA and BA, Product Design and Biology, Carnegie-Mellon University

Job Description

Doctors are already improving and saving lives on a daily basis, which is more than enough to be proud of. However, a doctor's job does not have to be limited to working with patients. Doctors have the best understanding of health problems, the context of use, and most importantly, the stakeholders (doctors, nurses, and patients) associated with life-saving technologies. They understand what the stakeholders will and will not do, so is it not natural for them to identify opportunities for technological innovations for products or processes to improve the health-care system? Surgeries and treatments for diseases and ailments are improving every year because of innovations. While some doctors may not see themselves as inventors and technological innovators, Matthew Callaghan certainly does.

When Matt was a surgery intern, the medical world was concerned about the prospect of a global flu pandemic. If one were to occur, the US would not have nearly enough ventilators to keep everybody alive because hospitals cannot afford to stockpile them for emergencies at $3,000 up to $40,000 apiece. With expertise in both product design and medicine, Matt developed the simple, low-cost ventilator, OneBreath. OneBreath runs on a twelve-volt battery for six to twelve hours at a time and is small and lightweight for easy transport and deployment wherever it is needed. While originally designed for the US, Matt's company now operates mostly in India because of the number of new hospitals emerging.

Building on his creation of OneBreath, Matt started a medical device company to launch other products. In addition to creating new projects, his company works on contending with consumer product approval as well as regulatory approval and documentation in order to be certified by the Food and Drug Administration (FDA) and the European Medicines Agency (EMEA). The process of approval adds a significant amount of time to product development. Right now, they are deep into their product development and approval phase. While the architecture of his company is done and the design of OneBreath is also complete, Matt is preparing for regulatory provisions and is writing software code, hoping to be approved in the summer of 2015. Then the company will transition from research and development into sales.

With all his responsibilities for his company, you would think that it was his whole life. However, Matt holds a faculty position at Stanford and sees patients once a week on top of that! Matt's days are never the same, but he always begins working very early because of the time differences between California and India. He usually takes a few hours to Skype with his team members in India and then performs his physician and faculty duties during the day. Because he is the founder of his company, he has to attend several meetings and phone calls with investors every day. Working as a traditional physician is comforting to him because interacting directly with his patients reminds him of why he went into medicine. Matt realizes his crazy busy schedule cannot go on forever. OneBreath is his first entrepreneurial venture, so he would like to see it through, but on future projects, he would like to take a step back and have a less relevant role. He would like to get back into more clinical practices and at some point take what he has learned from starting his company and work in a biomedical engineering lab, but that is far in the future. For right now, starting up this company has been a time-consuming endeavor.

Career Trajectory

During Matt's undergraduate career, he interned in the medical robotics laboratory of the Robotics Institute. When Matt graduated with degrees in product design and biology, he had no plans to go to medical school. He moved from Pittsburgh to San Francisco right after undergrad and worked as a designer for a biomedical product design company and then a biotechnology company for a few years before he moved to New York City, his home city, for medical school. He knew at that point that he somehow wanted to get back into engineering and devices later on in his career. Between his third and fourth years of medical school, he became a research fellow at NYU focused on wound healing and vascular biology. After med school, he went to the University of California-San Francisco to do some training in general surgery and then became a postdoctoral fellow in Stanford University's biodesign program. It was in the biodesign program that OneBreath was born. The program gave him freedom that he did not have while practicing medicine to think about some of the critical problems he had seen, and it also gave him the resources to think about how to solve them.

> Make a little company at the undergrad level—I think that is one of the best things you can do. Or offer your time to a small company that is just starting out. That will give you insight on how to organize that chaos and how to execute your ideas. Do it in a sheltered university type of way before you really get out there.
>
> If you want to go to grad school and do something entrepreneurial at the same time, it is very hard, but you can do it. Make sure you carve out dedicated time for your venture but still complete your degree—you will never feel right if you do not. Make sure you find a university that has a program with a history of entrepreneurial endeavors at the graduate level.

His idea for OneBreath did not start with an emerging-market or low-income market focus. Matt and his team started it as a research project with grant money to solve the need for ventilation during a mass-casualty event in developed countries. It was after they developed the product that they realized it was innovative and could be very beneficial elsewhere. Focusing on the emergency cases for a market strategy was not a good idea, so they decided to expand their target market. Some of Matt's mentors and investors told him that there would be a real market for OneBreath in India and places that were building hospitals. They could not just switch their project over, so they validated what they thought was the right market for ventilators in a low-income hospital. They evaluated India, Southeast Asia, South America, Africa, and other emerging markets. Unfortunately, neither Matt nor any of his team members had local experience in any developing country. They ended up choosing India as their entry market because the country has a good democracy and court system, which enabled them to have more confidence in the stability of working there.

Throughout the whole process of building his medical device company, he held a faculty position at Stanford and saw patients to pay his bills. He has a lot of respect for other entrepreneurs' appetite for financial risk that he does not have. Matt gave himself six months to cut back on his credible work, focus on OneBreath, and see if could make a company out of it. It took a little longer to get the company going, but he took that risk because there are very few people who are going to want to work on a project for free. Matt and his two team members worked on the company for a while and paid themselves very little until they started making some money and picked up investors.

Matt finds it very hard to integrate his work and personal life. He is used to not having an integration because of his experience being on call for general surgery. However, with a startup, it can be even worse because you are on call 24/7, not for specific hours. Matt deals with the challenge by living close to work in an exciting community. In his town of Palo Alto, it is common to be part of a startup, so his friends are understanding of his work demands.

Riana Lynn, 29

FoodTrace
CEO | ~$90,000 – 110,000

Master of Public Policy and Administration, Northwestern University (2012)
BS, Biology, University of North Carolina at Chapel Hill (2008)

Job Description

Thanks to Rachel Carson's book *Silent Spring*, which revealed the hazards of pesticides in 1962; several food safety scares concerning salmonella, E. coli, and mad cow disease in the early 2000s; and the documentary *Food Inc.*, which revealed the operations of the food industry in 2008, many Americans have been paying more attention to where their food comes from. While many Americans have continued business as usual, diets including gluten-free, vegan and vegetarian, organic, whole food, and low glycemic index have been gaining popularity. Another common trend is concerned with eating local foods, getting to know your farmer and butcher, and/or buying products certified as fair trade to ensure the people farming their food are fairly compensated. How can one trace where their food comes from? Starting in the Chicago area, FoodTrace is enhancing communication of data throughout the supply chain while building stronger restaurants, artisans, grocers, and farmers.

FoodTrace is bringing daily operations and communications solutions to the multibillion-dollar US food-distribution and food-service industries. FoodTrace is a powerful software platform providing food businesses with tools for next-level sourcing management. They help farmers and artisans sell more and buyers buy better. The platform has been built on proven solutions for businesses to mapify and build new customers, utilize data as insights and food trends for better strategy, and increase revenue with sharing tools for the value-added marketability of quality sourcing. There is tremendous opportunity for disruption in food technology, so as owners and farmers become less digitally divided and the growing industry searches for answers, FoodTrace will continue to use their partnerships, such as with Google, to build value and ubiquity of features and need.

Riana Lynn, CEO of the young venture FoodTrace, starts her days early, sometimes answering emails as early as 4:30 a.m. After breakfast and a morning workout, the day really begins at the office where she will map out weekly agendas for her team; make headway on some tricky code with developers; meet with customers, investors, or partners; and then debrief her team in the early evening. Other days, she never makes it into the office; farm visits or restaurant tours are frequent as the venture continues to expand. As CEO, Riana is selling FoodTrace at conferences and traveling to development workshops. Riana also keeps her mind on the future, looking at how FoodTrace's growth statistics match up with the competition and where the sector is headed as a whole.

Riana meets with big investors who are looking to build a foundation in the next big thing, with farmers worried or excited about bringing a product to a new distributor, and with coders who need advice on how to keep websites and apps effective but fun for the average user. Tying all of these facets together is how FoodTrace forms its social impact. There are millions of food companies in the United States alone trying to feed some 300 million people, and the process can always be optimized. Riana especially focuses on smaller companies or single farmers who bring their food to open markets where unsold product often turns into waste at the end of the day. From seed to distribution, around 45% of food is wasted—almost 1,400 calories per person in the United States. When Riana is able to improve efficiency of coordination between producers, distributors, and consumers, less food and time get wasted. Simply growing the number of food companies in FoodTrace's communication network improves their social impact.

One of Riana's greatest satisfactions is knowing that less viable food is ending up wasted in a trash can at the end of the day. Unfortunately, work at a budding startup takes much of Riana's time, and progress in the long run can still be slow. She does, however, manage to find time for herself on occasion, stepping back and relaxing to keep herself sharp and happy. In her free time, Riana serves on panels about being a woman in technology, gives business development advice, and works with initiatives for minorities in technology. Her business development consulting primarily consists of mentoring students or young entrepreneurs who have a great product idea but little else. Riana sits down with them to give advice on how to create a website, how to establish a target audience, and how to transform their idea into a sustainable business.

Career Trajectory

Riana's interest in technology started at the University of North Carolina. A pre-medicine student athlete, Riana vividly recalls watching a newscast about Hurricane Katrina during her sophomore year and feeling a profound respect for the anthropologist being interviewed about their work in community health. Something clicked, and she began to focus more and more on the impact of food access in social settings. She shifted gears academically toward research in the natural and social sciences and graduated with a bachelor of science degree in biology and a double major in African American studies and a minor in chemistry.

Her first job brought her into clinical trial research coordination, as well as website design and coding for a research team at the Durham Department of Veterans Affairs Medical Center and Duke University. She then went on to work for the University of Chicago and observed that every community health project she worked on had underlying issues with food access and food quality issues, so she started biting more into the questions of how food deserts, food access, and food quality affect all our health and chronic diseases. She brainstormed with friends and family on how to bring more fresh fruit options into Chicago and ended up jumping into building a juice bar, which quickly grew in one year from just one place to over three and more than thirty employees.

> Learn coding through YouTube, blogs, Khan Academy, and coding manuals. Overall, every career is going to be impacted by technology in some way, and the more you understand it, the easier it is going to be for you no matter what field you are working in. ... Finding someone who has done it before is the first step, and sharing your idea is the next step.

Riana has a master's of public health and pursued her master's in public policy and administration at Northwestern University. During her graduate years, she was a public health fellow through the US Department of Health and Human Services and an intern at the White House. During her time at the White House, she worked for the Office of Public Engagement where she learned to connect small businesses across the country to government initiatives that could improve their social impact and profit margin simultaneously. While working in government, she witnessed firsthand many initiatives for women in STEM and food programs championed by the First Lady. She saw how entrepreneurship was a powerful force and how small businesses served as the backbone not only of the economy, but also of change in the social sector.

One of her biggest challenges throughout her varied experiences was communicating with a diverse group of business owners about growing their food and distributing their products. Therefore, she began consulting for food companies and started a firm that ultimately grew into FoodTrace. Business development is far from easy, making it difficult to work on several fronts at once, but Riana's focus is on developing easy-to-use tools that do the work for her. FoodTrace has developed a new software platform for a next-level two-sided food sourcing marketplace, which she likens to Alibaba and LinkedIn for food business owners. These owners can advertise their products and be connected with other buyers and sellers through analytic algorithms that advise what should be grown next, what can be sourced elsewhere, and how to connect with hotels, restaurants, and cafeterias to ultimately get their food onto a plate. All of Riana's hard work is paying off; groups such as Google for Entrepreneurs are noticing FoodTrace.

Riana credits much of her success to a blend of industry and academic experience. She worked for only one year following her undergraduate studies before returning to academia to pursue an advanced degree. During graduate school, she ultimately chose a master's program to blend her desire to research new solutions with the goal of having real, tangible impact. While picking up web design coding on the side, she was invited to meetings and seminars where she connected with a Chicago native focused on community nutrition and genetics. The ability he had to blend public service and private work together into one passionate career helped Riana to discover her passion. Riana loves traveling and wants to continue visiting farms and trying dishes over the next five years. Looking farther into the future, Riana has ambitions to be an expert leader in the intersection of food, technology, and data, someone who is called upon to speak across the country. Her only regret is not choosing a graduate school in California, closer to all the cutting-edge technology development epicenters.

Justin Kosoris, 32

Chemonics International
Agriculture Practice Manager | ~$70,000 – $80,000

MPA, The University of Texas at Austin (2010)
BA, International Studies, Johns Hopkins University (2005)

Job Description

The USAID is the primary US government agency that works to end extreme global poverty and empower resilient, democratic societies. USAID invests in ideas that improve the lives of millions of men, women, and children. They announce challenges publicly around areas such as increasing agricultural productivity, combating deadly diseases, providing assistance following a disaster, promoting human rights, and fostering sustainable economic growth. Nonprofit and for-profit companies respond with proposals of their solutions to the challenge, and the company with the best proposal is awarded funding to carry out the project. For example, one challenge for which USAID recently put out a request for proposals is "Improving Food Security and Resilience through Agricultural Disaster Risk Reduction Programs in Guatemala" where they are seeking to provide funding to organizations that have grand ideas to (1) build resilience to cyclical droughts and floods, (2) reduce the likelihood of food insecurity during drought events, and (3) provide humanitarian assistance through mitigation programming.

Chemonics is a for-profit, employee-owned consulting company that applies for funding from USAID to implement their international development projects. Chemonics helps governments, businesses, civil society groups, and communities promote meaningful change so that people can live healthier, more productive, and more independent lives. In Africa, they manage projects that are increasing food security and promoting economic growth, agricultural productivity, and health and education services; in Asia, they are improving health services, enterprise growth, agricultural productivity, and environmental resource management; and in Latin America and the Caribbean, they are building local partnerships to protect natural resources and promote economic growth. They also work on projects in Europe, Eurasia, and the Middle East around good governance, improved education systems, civic engagement, and enterprise competitiveness. Overall, they have experience in over 150 countries and are organized regionally to respond quickly and effectively to local and client demands. Their technical practices range from agriculture and private sector development to health and education, and their services include program design and implementation, measuring and evaluation, and knowledge management and communications.

A former Peace Corps volunteer with significant experience in agricultural fieldwork and environmental technical work, Justin Kosoris is well equipped to lead Chemonics's agriculture technical practice and coordinate its overall agricultural programming and knowledge-sharing strategy. Justin has conducted technical research as well as managed projects for agricultural development. Chemonics has a significant commitment to agricultural projects and encourages technical practices to serve both as avenues for research and also warehouses for knowledge. In his current role, Justin meets with potential partner organizations, conducts brainstorming sessions with teams, drafts technical proposals, and prepares and presents work externally. Justin serves as the bridge between the technical agriculture information and the resource-driven business proposals and is expected to speak the language of experts on both sides. As part of his work with Chemonics, Justin also has the opportunity to travel frequently to conferences and job sites; in the past year, he has traveled to Mali, Cote d'Ivoire, Haiti, Sweden, Indonesia, Zambia, and Abu Dhabi.

As the leader of a technical team, Justin constantly works to foster an environment for inventiveness, then promotes those new technologies on a larger scale. One of the great benefits of Justin's job is seeing projects eventually reach maturity, particularly those projects he has personally nurtured. One of his key design targets for any project is sustainability. The whole development community is becoming more adamant about evaluating sustainability as a key metric of success. One of Justin's former projects involved installing solar street lights in Haiti; he recalls clearly the meetings with community leaders about the best places to install lights not only for an environmentally sustainable impact, but also for social sustainability. Justin also connected them with the installation company to fix issues after the end of his involvement. Justin's recent switch to technical research is where he derives most of his passion for this career: the varied nature of problems, both in subject area and geographic area. His personal expertise is climate-smart agriculture in West Africa, but his passion is for learning about various development projects all around the world.

Working for a larger firm that provides services to the United States government and other donors can be challenging. Much of Justin's time when he first started at Chemonics was spent learning the rules and regulations that govern everything the company does. While knowing all the policies is not the sexiest part of the job, he has seen the consequences when projects are done without proper oversight. For example, he managed many construction projects in Haiti for which he held local engineering firms to the highest standards and was 100% strict about any defects. In this way, he was able to provide functional electricity in one of Haiti's largest hospitals, among other successful infrastructure works. In one of their partner communities, another donor had completed a project that did not follow the same standards, and the roof collapsed during construction. Justin was on his construction sites daily and often made his local partners redo defective work even if it was minor. They learned to do it right the first time to avoid increased costs, and the communities benefited from a lasting public work as a result. Failure has taught Justin what projects look like when key details are not well looked after. Seeing the ultimate success of a grand venture, and being able to pinpoint his specific (and well-functioning) place in that machine, is the ultimate reward and incentive for Justin to start tackling the next project.

> There is a lot of opportunity, but it needs to be hedged with realistic expectations of what these ventures can accomplish. Be patient, prove yourself capable of doing even the smallest tasks correctly and efficiently, and you will be rewarded.

Career Trajectory

Justin was first exposed to the development world working for the US Peace Corps in Senegal. No other agency provides the same opportunity to live, work, and, most importantly, learn in a different culture for over two years. It was in the Peace Corps that Justin found his passion for development. Upon returning to the US, he quickly enrolled in a graduate program that would help him succeed. Throughout graduate school, he worked for several nonprofits on organizing environmental campaigns, researching grant opportunities, analyzing US development efforts abroad, and writing research articles on sustainability. The expertise developed from graduate-level coursework and independent projects is a key tool to his success that he still uses daily. The Peace Corps also helped narrow Justin's focus to environmental issues, particularly in sustainable agriculture. Justin believes that you never know what the next door will lead to, but you should walk through it if it is open. Justin's first door was a two-week assignment in Haiti to cover for someone on vacation, and his success in that assignment led to additional assignments and eventually a long-term position in Haiti. Through that work, he proved himself to Chemonics, and the future is now wide open for him.

At Chemonics, graduate work directly related to science is valuable; but graduate scientists are even more valued if they have management experience and expertise. Justin, with his educational background in public affairs and experience with the Peace Corps, fits this mold well. Working in Haiti specifically, he very quickly came up to speed on basic engineering, construction, and sustainability thanks to his training in environmental compliance in graduate school and the tutelage of amazing engineering colleagues. Coupling technical disciplines with the leadership to manage a team has opened doors for Justin and set him apart from the field in international development. Being able to speak local languages has been of significant additional help (he is fluent in French and Fulani and speaks a decent amount of Italian and Haitian Creole). Justin also credits his success to his graduate-school mentors who helped him articulate what he wanted to do after school as well as influential people he has worked to prove himself to in order to gain their guidance.

Justin works hard to make sure he has proper separation of work and life. He has observed that people who get their work done efficiently and leave at 5:00 p.m. are more valued than those that do not and leave at 8:00 p.m. Good managers know the difference and will encourage their employees to have a life. Justin lives in Washington, DC, where there are always things going on but where there is also too much work discussion outside work. Justin copes by associating with people who also know how to separate the two. He finds that playing team sports is the best way to get away from work discussions. Justin does not know where he will be in the future as part of his passion is shifting gears and learning new trades. Technical expertise is a newfound drive, especially in agriculture and climate studies. Travel has also become a reward for Justin, and he has only just begun to see what the world offers. He hopes to maintain a balance of time in the United States and developing countries in the future.

FOR-PROFIT » DEVELOPMENT CONTRACTOR

Vishalini Lawrence

Development Alternatives Inc. (DAI)
Chief of Party, USAID's Transition Initiative for Stabilization (Somalia)

MA, International Studies, Ohio University (1997)
BA, International Relations and Affairs, Ferrum College (1996)

Job Description

Over the past few decades, much of Somalia has been torn apart by conflict between rival clans, continued attacks by the terrorist group Al-Shabaab, and violent power struggles amplifying humanitarian disasters such as refugee crises, famine, and poverty. While millions of dollars in international aid have been used to rebuild the country, there have been mixed results, and many Somalis believe that the well-intentioned assistance has amplified conflict and increased corruption. In response, the US Agency for International Development (USAID) Transition Initiatives for Stabilization (TIS) has developed a program that is welcomed by Somali communities and government. The localized program design brings together communities and local government to prioritize projects in the communities where they will be implemented, with planning sessions facilitated in the Somali language. They then design projects—such as the construction of roads, schools, health clinics, stadiums, and markets—to benefit the whole community and promote peace and stability.

TIS is being implemented by DAI, a private sector international development consulting firm that has worked in more than 150 countries on implementing solutions for economic growth, environment and energy, governance, health, information and communication technology for development, and stability. TIS is addressing what Somalis say are their root causes of instability: lack of inclusivity, transparency, and ownership in the process of decision making. To promote inclusiveness and transparency, TIS Stabilization Planning Sessions are held in a neutral, local space and bring together government staff, businesspeople, and community members including elders, religious leaders, women, youth, and minority clans. This approach helps build Somali ownership over both the process of program design and helps ensure sustainability of the end products.

The leader of USAID's project team, called a "chief of party," provides leadership in the overall management of large projects by designing program strategy and being responsible for delivering program results. Vishalini Lawrence is the chief of party for DAI's TIS project in Somalia. The overall goal of the TIS project is to promote peace and development through increased social cohesion and to enhance trust and confidence between citizens and their government. Examples of projects that TIS has implemented include construction of a sports stadium for young people to improve relationships between youth from different social groups (a popular sport in Somalia is football/soccer) and construction of social or community halls where elders from different social groups or clans could come together if there had been a conflict to mediate and facilitate peacebuilding. Community halls are also venues for cultural events, such as dances and art festivals. Finally, they wanted a symbolic building or place to meet with the governmental administration. Most TIS projects are infrastructure related, but there has also been programming related to government capacity building on governance, social reconciliation, youth sport, and promotion of Somalian arts and culture. Other projects include building new roads to bring products to markets, equipment for the local trades (e.g., fishing, farming, etc.), training for youth, and vocational education.

When DAI first started the TIS program in 2011, the focus was only Somaliland because a large portion of South Central Somalia was controlled by Al-Shabaab, and they did not allow any humanitarian assistance or international development programs. Gradually, through the support of the Somali government and AMISOM (African allied force of peacekeeping), more places were cleared of Al-Shabaab control and brought back under the control of the federal government. During her time on the TIS program so far, Vishalini has seen conditions drastically improve. In some instances there have been some setbacks, but Vishalini is very optimistic about the prospect for lasting peace and stability in Somalia. There is a great entrepreneurial spirit and an appetite to try new things in Somalia despite unstable conditions. Through mobile phones and the Internet, Somali youth have been using social media to condemn acts of violence. It has been empowering for them to share that information amongst one another and dream of a better future. Vishalini has also seen the power of mobile phones grow for banking as well as conflict warning and response. Additionally, solar lights have provided a measure of security for communities.

Vishalini often works crazy hours, but because she has two young children, she tries to be home before they go to bed—finishing up her workdays at home. She does not find the long hours too stressful though because she loves her job and the team she leads. She has made conscious decisions on the projects she accepts for work based on her family. Some projects allow her to take her family with her, so she accepts

🐘 There is no substitute for honesty, integrity, hard work, and humility. Seize opportunities, take risks, and put your heart and soul into whatever career path you choose to pursue.

those once in a while. Her husband also travels significantly for his work, so they try not to be away from home at the same time. It is a fine balancing act, and sometimes it is not balanced; because of this, she sometimes likes to unwind by going on weeklong vacations with her family and completely unplug from work. She needs these opportunities to completely unplug and recharge because it is easy to always have an adrenaline rush over her work, but luckily, her husband helps her set boundaries. She takes care of her health by making sure to de-stress through yoga and by making time for friends and family wherever she can.

Career Trajectory

Despite never traveling to either East Africa or Southeast Asia, Vishalini became fascinated with them when she was young. Thus, she chose to major in international studies for both undergraduate and graduate school. Soon after graduate school, she landed an entry-level position with DAI helping a project in the Philippines. She learned quickly and moved up the ladder to become a business manager after just four years in the Economic and Agricultural Group. Then an opportunity came up to work in Indonesia on a small grants program. Vishalini went to Indonesia, did some intense evaluations, and learned the language so well that she was able to do these monitoring evaluations all over and conduct interviews. It was an interesting learning experience for her. Then, because of that position, she was able to land her next job in Kenya as the program manager on a conflict mitigation and response program.

Next, she wanted a change, doing something completely different, so she found a position in Cambodia on the USAID funded Micro, Small, Medium Enterprise (MSME) project. She was always interested in private sector development that helped with poverty elimination, so she worked on a DAI project where she worked on ten different value chains on all sorts of things such as water supply, non-timber forest products, sanitation marketing, and agriculture. The Cambodia MSME project worked with business associations in those value chains to help them lobby for their cause and with the Cambodian government at the policy level to improve the business enabling environment. After four years in Cambodia, Vishalini took her current position to manage TIS. Altogether, Vishalini has worked for DAI for seventeen years and plans to continue working in the exciting field of international development.

Sally Atalla

Accenture Development Partnerships Global Programs
Senior Manager, Client Account Lead, and Program Director

BASc, Mechanical Engineering, University of Toronto (1998)

Job Description

Organizations sometimes need external help, such as bringing in specific expertise or a fresh perspective. In such situations, these organizations may reach out to consulting companies to work with their employees to solve a problem. Some consulting companies that have traditionally consulted for only large private and public sector organizations are increasingly offering services or creating their own internal units to meet the needs of nonprofit organizations, donors, and other players in the social sector. This offers a great advantage, as the non-profit organizations benefit from the lessons and industry practices by working with consulting companies experienced in many sectors." Accenture is one of the world's leading companies providing management consulting, technology, and outsourcing services, and it has an impact-focused group called Accenture Development Partnerships. Sally Atalla is one of the global programs senior managers within this group.

Sally works with international nongovernmental organizations (NGOs) and donor clients. These clients are serving in areas such as global public health, nutrition, education, livelihoods, and emergency preparedness and response. She helps them as a project manager or program director with activities such as managing system and vendor selection, process improvements or redesign, project definition and planning, business case development and partner identification, and feasibility studies for geographic expansion or other strategic initiatives. Sally asks clients questions, analyzes the information available, presents options to them, and facilitates the team to help them to the next stage. This enables them to be part of all stages of the process and own the decision.

For example, one nonprofit client wanted to expand into ten countries within a decade. They asked for help with studying countries of interest to look at the feasibility of launch and need of their services. They also needed assistance with the business case to obtain funding for the creation of the new regional hub location for these countries. Sally led a small team for the expansion study of two countries and business case, proposing one country as a regional hub. The work achieved several results. The client received commitment from a donor for five years of funding and opened doors within six months of the study. The study, business case, and implementation plan approach were also the foundation repeated for future studies and movement into additional countries over the years that followed.

In another case, a client needed help with a holistic view as well as more agility to strategize and operate their donor and beneficiary activities and information. They needed a new centralized system, so Sally's team was asked to help them find a product that would be the technical foundation for this. She started with the business foundation first. The client team was brought together to align their organizational thinking and creativity in workshops. This was important to get everyone in agreement about how they wanted to improve the way they serve donors and beneficiaries. Once the business's foundational goals were understood, she facilitated the procurement process of selecting a system by studying the products, introducing them to technical vendors, and helping them evaluate their options to make their own decision. (It is important to make sure the client decides what is best for their own organization.)

Accenture Development Partnerships collaborates with organizations working in the international development sector by delivering innovative solutions that truly change the way people work and live. This group provides assistance in organizational strengthening and in program innovation and delivery and partnership services. The mission is to have a significant impact on global development challenges by (1) providing development sector organizations with access to Accenture's top people, knowledge, assets and global network; (2) teaming with clients to help them become high-performance organizations and applying Accenture's business and technology capabilities to help them maximize their impact; (3) advancing market-based solutions to development challenges that are scalable, sustainable, and outcome-oriented; and (4) fostering collaboration and partnerships between the public, private, and nonprofit sectors in order to address global development challenges. This group also helps companies targeting emerging markets for growth to develop the kind of social development projects that are essential to build traction in these regions.

The program's award-winning business model enables Accenture's core capabilities—its best people and strategic business, technology, and project management expertise—to be made available to clients in the international development sector on a not-for-profit basis. Other organizations offer pro bono work, but they are typically capped on a monetary or time contribution that limits how much they can do. Accenture Development Partnerships offers reduced rates for their non-profit clients in international development to make services more attainable and affordable. There is a three-way contribution model shared by Accenture, Accenture employees on the projects, and the client. The model is not-for-profit, but also not-for-loss, so all the contributors have a stake in the initiative or project.

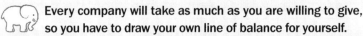

Every company will take as much as you are willing to give, so you have to draw your own line of balance for yourself.

Take opportunities as you see them to be interesting, even when you do not fully know what is involved. It is good to give different things a try. You will never know everything or how it will turn out, but following your gut will often prove to be worth it.

Over the past decade, Accenture Development Partnerships has made a positive impact in finding solutions to global development challenges—working in over seventy countries worldwide and deploying more than 1,000 Accenture employees, completing over 640 projects for more than 140 clients as of 2013. The core team is made up of a small team of permanently assigned staff, but Accenture employees from other parts of the organization offer their commitment to projects, amounting now to 250–300 people on projects annually.

The core team members generally have a similar social philosophy and enjoy working in an entrepreneurial way within a large organization. It is sometimes frustrating encountering project challenges that are new or different from the standard work. Because the work this team does is sometimes atypical or in complex locations, the team has extra work or diligence on important areas such as project team security and tax or legal matters. When working long hours, Sally is motivated by what her clients are pursuing socially and remembers that they themselves are resource constrained. She likes the autonomy she has in leading certain activities, as well as working with a lot of like-minded, kind, smart individuals.

Career Trajectory

Between her third and fourth years of undergraduate study, Sally took on a sixteen-month engineering internship with an aerospace company. After graduation, there were not many engineering opportunities, and she heard about management consulting companies interested in engineers' problem-solving capabilities. Accenture initially offered her a position in computer programming, which she accepted knowing it was not her long-term interest or strength. It is a very large organization, so she took steps to learn about other topics and multiple industries within Accenture over time.

Sally decided to specialize in an industry instead of technology and chose a sector with a social aspect: health care. She then contacted Accenture's Development Partnerships to try a project for a client in the international development sector. She took her first development assignment based in South Africa, Kenya, and Tanzania; returned to Canada; and took a second assignment in Switzerland. There was a period of back-and-forth time between international social sector assignments and traditional assignments in Canada. After performing well and showing strong interest on her international assignments, Sally received an offer to join the global Accenture Development Partnerships team full-time. Since then, she has worked on projects in Haiti and in client headquarters locations in the US.

Sally is always looking for opportunities to work on projects for clients where she is interested in their cause, can offer help, and can learn something new in the sector. Overall, her career has shifted more from the initial core technology and process work to broader and strategic project management, business development, and client relationship work. Sally's work-life balance changes over time. If she is going to travel for work, she prefers it is for a good reason and likes to select the opportunity based on learning a new part of the industry or something about a particular region.

Photo by Brendle Group

Becky Fedak, 34

Brendle Group | Sustainability Engineer | ~$70,000
Running Water International | Technical Director

MBA, Global Social and Sustainable Enterprise, Colorado State University
BS, Environmental Engineering, University of Wisconsin Platteville

Job Description

One out of every eight people worldwide does not currently have access to safe drinking water, and one out of every three does not have adequate sanitation. Around the world, water and sanitation issues impact all aspects of life, from agriculture to health care, climate change to the economy, security to education. As the world's population continues to increase, sustainable management of natural resources, including water, becomes ever more critical and deserving of acute attention. In the United States and abroad, there is an increasing need for professionals like Becky Fedak. Becky uses her expertise in environmental engineering and sustainability to make sustainable water and sanitation solutions affordable and accessible to all.

Becky Fedak pursues a dual career as an engineer at Brendle Group and as a technical advisor for Running Water International. The Brendle Group is an engineering and sustainability consulting firm based in Colorado that works with a variety of groups, including cities, schools, and private businesses, to address their sustainability needs. Many times these organizations do not have the experience or expertise in-house to tackle specific topics like sustainability, so they hire a consulting firm like the Brendle Group to provide the technical knowledge, experience, and lessons learned from past projects to most efficiently and effectively provide the most appropriate solutions.

Becky's primary responsibilities for Brendle Group are determined on a project-to-project basis and vary tremendously because of her extensive experience as a water resources engineer with a business background. One example is Becky's role as program manager and technical lead for the Net Zero Water (NZW) Planning Toolkit. In coordination with members of the Colorado Water Innovation Cluster and other Fort Collins companies, Brendle Group is leading this initiative, centered on a sustainable water management approach, using only as much water as is available and reducing water quality impacts within a defined site boundary. The NZW Planning Toolkit includes a user-friendly analysis tool and a companion guidebook. It is designed to help people define their water footprint and identify, test, and plan for water quantity and quality management strategies that will help them move toward their water goals. For other projects where Brendle Group was hired as a consultant, Becky's responsibilities have included greenhouse gas inventories, climate and sustainability planning, large-scale water resources planning and design, business plan development, and gathering input and ideas from the community. Her main priority in her position is to exemplify Brendle Group's objective, which is to meet people where they are along the sustainability spectrum and find suitable solutions to meet their needs.

In addition to her day job, Becky advises Running Water International (RWI), an organization she helped to found. RWI is a nonprofit organization based in Kenya that sells water and sanitation solutions to communities throughout the country. As a technical advisor, she addresses any questions related to the technical aspects of the company, which can range from approaches for designing a community-scale water collection and treatment facility to reviewing a research proposal for water quality sampling to test the efficacy of filters already installed. She also supports the director in Kenya in the identification of new project contacts, connecting him with individuals or groups in the US who are interested in integrating clean water and sanitation into their work in Kenya.

Becky considers her work at Brendle Group and RWI similar when it comes to creating social impact. She has to consider economic drivers when addressing environmental and social challenges for both roles. At Brendle Group, the focus is on finding the business case for sustainability—making it about more than the environmental or social good but really focusing on how sustainable solutions can help organizations make or save funds. Becky believes that triple bottom line solutions with clear economic, social, and environmental benefits are necessary to mainstream sustainability. Along those lines, at RWI they are moving beyond the traditional philanthropic model, which is difficult to sustain over the long run, to a business model that addresses the water and sanitation needs in Kenya. With so many people throughout the developing world still lacking access to safe water and sanitation facilities, utilizing business-based solutions that ensure financial sustainability and help to more quickly scale up solutions will be necessary. Additionally, with both organizations, she emphasizes the importance of partnerships, recognizing that it will take many players to address the world's environmental and social challenges.

> Keep thinking big. Always ask the question "What sucks?" and then try to find a way to fix it. Know what you are passionate about and go for it.

Whether it is working for Brendle Group in the community or finding the next viable partner for RWI, Becky loves what she does because it actually makes a difference in people's lives. Sometimes it can be frustrating because working for an organization that is on the leading edge involves constantly coming up with new innovations with limited time to develop the solutions. However, knowing she is positively making a difference in the global community motivates her to get out of bed each morning and work with her team to solve the problem at hand.

Career Trajectory

Becky has always had a passion for environmental issues and performed well in math and science. Therefore, she decided to get her undergraduate degree in environmental engineering from the University of Wisconsin, Platteville. Her first job out of college was with a large civil engineering firm modeling large-scale water resources projects in California. While she enjoyed the experience and the challenges it offered, Becky still aspired to work internationally in underdeveloped regions where her knowledge and skills could have a larger impact.

Luckily, when working in California, she got involved with Engineers Without Borders, which provided her an opportunity to participate in developing-world projects and fueled the fire for future endeavors. She chose to pursue Colorado State University's MBA program in global social and sustainable enterprise. This program teaches students about how to network and become a global social entrepreneur with a focus on the triple bottom line of people, planet, and profit. The core of the program is working in teams on a venture domestically or abroad; many of these teams continue on as social enterprises after graduation, including Running Water International.

Becky attributes much of her success to time-management skills learned through academic and extracurricular activities as well as her initiative and networking skills. She believes she also benefited from opportunities to learn about others working in this space because partnerships and collaboration are such an important part of social innovation. She always finds time to calibrate against like-minded organizations and learn from them. Moving forward, Becky would like to link her work with Brendle Group and RWI. Specifically, she is currently working to develop and implement a business plan to translate the work Brendle Group does for communities in the US to communities in the developing world.

✿ Mahad Ibrahim, 39

Gobee Group
Managing Partner | Six figures

PhD, Information Management & Systems, University of California, Berkeley (2009)
BS, Applied Economics and Management, Cornell (1998)

Job Description

While external consultants can help organizations determine strategic direction, utilize limited funds effectively, and expand their sphere of influence, their recommendations are seldom fully implemented. The constraints on a given challenge often rapidly change as projects move from the planning phase to implementation, yet few consultancies guide their clients through the dynamic, chaotic aspects of bringing projects into fruition. The Gobee Group is a social innovation design consultancy. They partner with clients in the private, public, and social sectors to create products, services, and organizations for impact. Most often, they work at the interface of sectors and organizations as translators, and in fact "Gobee" is derived from "go between."

Mahad Ibrahim is the managing partner of Gobee Group. He spends his time in diverse ways: meeting with partners, drafting proposals, advising his team, and building products. He is always having conversations, but over the years, the conversations have changed because Gobee has its own products now, along with consultancy services. Gobee has four partners who loosely work in different areas; each partner has a set of relationships they maintain. Mahad, due to his broad expertise, manages projects related to health care, data analytics, technology, and creative storytelling. Gobee is fluid; there are always two partners working on each project (one leading and one supporting). Mahad loves that no two projects are the same; he gets to solve many unique social challenges, learning more each time. He does get worn out by all the traveling, however.

Within Gobee's first year, Mahad received a call from a woman at the Clinton Health Action Initiative who got his name through a mutually known colleague. Since funding for HIV prevention was strained by the financial crisis, they were seeking innovative ways to ensure drug access. Though the partnership between the Clinton Health Action Initiative, Gobee, and Google started out as a conversation, it quickly became clear to Mahad that the problem's framing was limited—CHAI wanted a technology solution but did not have a clear path. Mahad utilized his honed systematic process asking questions akin to the follow: (1) What does the marketplace look like, not just for antivirals, but for broader HIV treatments? (2) What areas could benefit from the use of technology? and (3) What would that mean specifically around the area of optimization? In a working meeting, Mahad led the organization in determining clear problem areas, one of which is aligning their efforts to global guidelines. The World Health Organization issues guidelines around the standard of care (e.g., which drugs should be distributed to patients). For governments with limited time, resources, and capacity, it can be difficult to understand how guideline changes affect their drug procurement and distribution processes. To address this, and a slew of other challenges, Gobee and CHAI built a platform that organizes supplier, drug, and guideline information as well as enables users to compare drug prices with global benchmarks and to optimize procurement. The platform, OptimizeARV, consists of an extensive data structure as well as several apps that facilitate improved decision making.

In the future, Gobee is looking to grow although this is a controversial topic because current employees enjoy the flexible culture and working directly with partners; growth may threaten that. Revenue has grown every year, but now Gobee is more selective about what they take on as they build infrastructure to support clients and themselves. The Gobee team holds yearly retreats to get feedback on how every member would like to move forward. Mahad foresees growth in expanding to the East Coast and building a team there, as currently most of company is based in Oakland, California. No matter what, Gobee is changing because it has invested in other companies strategically, owning a piece of several products and working to incubate them. For example, one of those companies, CellEd, has developed a mobile education product with Gobee that uses SMS and voice to teach adults literacy through mini courses. Gobee also codeveloped a medical app that facilitates knowledge sharing among doctors. Doctors can post pictures of ailments tagged with 140 characters straight into the cloud and organize patient information.

Career Trajectory

Mahad's career path started with graduate school as he was looking for a place where he could use his multidisciplinary background to create impactful change. He did not want to go to business school or policy school, but he eventually discovered a program at Berkeley that intrigued him. He went on to earn his master's in information management and systems with the specific purpose of landing a job in a corporation to do work in technology and information strategy. The students and professors at Berkeley introduced him to the world of research and convinced him to pursue a PhD. While in his doctoral studies, his primary research focused on security and privacy with a secondary focus on technology and society. During his PhD, he also worked at a law, public policy, and technology clinic looking at privacy protocols and searching for intersections.

> If you want a PhD but do not want to stay in academia, do not keep it a secret. You need a supportive PhD committee, and while contributing one or two publications a year to the body of knowledge in your field, you can also work with companies on the side.

What catalyzed Mahad's career path was a United Nations Industrial Development Organization (UNIDO) sponsored program. He received a stipend while working on his PhD to do research on the Aravind eye care system, studying how they leveraged reducing their manufacturing arm so that they could make their services affordable and whether or not such a model could be extended to other medical devices (specifically hearing aids). He was working with students from mechanical engineering and public health and found it exciting to approach problems from multiple angles.

After completing the fellowship, Mahad wanted to find ways to use technology to make a societal impact. He met another PhD student (a later cofounder of Gobee) who had similar interests. They collaborated on a project with HP on a shared platform that they were marketing in Asia and Africa. This was the first time he noticed that industries were interested in doing social impact work—he was hooked and started doing more consulting with Microsoft and Intel on emerging markets projects. He took their existing platforms and found ways to adapt or use them within health and education sectors. One of his biggest projects was with Microsoft where he participated in the creation of the Information and Communication Technology (ICT) for Development Academy. The academy facilitated interaction between private and public sectors, but utilizing hardware and software effectively remained a challenge for NGOs. To address this, Mahad created a curriculum and resource guide for ICT in education, health, and government. Creating the infrastructure took nearly two years and led Mahad to interact with nearly 500 organizations. During this time, he came up with the idea for Gobee, and he invited close colleagues from different disciplines to join him. To get Gobee's first clients, he reached out to past classmates and contacts now working in industry. A major break for Gobee came when their names were passed to the World Bank, and they were fortunate to get some big clients to build their network.

⚙ Srik Gopal, 37

Foundation Strategy Group (FSG)
Director | ~$150,000

MBA, University of Michigan
B.Tech., Mechanical Engineering, Indian Institute of Technology

Job Description

In 2008, the global economy took a downturn, resulting in greater social need and declining resources for vulnerable populations. While this was largely a negative trend that severely compromised livelihoods and retirement accounts, the silver lining was the increased attention, efforts, and investments dedicated to finding better ways to solve social problems. Since then, in tandem with this increased social investment, technological innovation has expanded the sector's capacity for understanding and addressing social problems. As we design and implement innovative solutions to social challenges, how do we find out what is working and what is not? How do we define progress, and how do we evaluate whether we are actually making progress? As social problems increase and resources to address them decrease, evaluation becomes an increasingly important driver of engagement and investment strategy. Evaluation of organizations' efforts and impact is crucial for them to measure their progress and most effectively direct their future efforts.

One organization dedicated to evaluation, as part of its mission to find better ways to solve social problems, is FSG. FSG is a nonprofit consulting firm with employees who strongly believe that solving the world's most challenging societal problems requires new ways of thinking, acting, and partnering. In order to do this, FSG has identified four key ideas critical to encouraging large-scale change: catalytic philanthropy, collective impact, shared value, and strategic evaluation. FSG achieves large-scale impact through consulting services, field and grant-funded research, partnerships, events, communities of practice, and published work.

Srik Gopal is the director of FSG's strategic evaluation approach area, and a key part of the firm's leadership group. His role spans consulting, intellectual capital, firm development and leadership, and business development. He is usually involved in a range of evaluation consulting projects, including formative and summative evaluations, developmental evaluations, and shared measurement. For example, Srik and his team helped create a set of shared measures for the "100Kin10" STEM teaching initiative. 100Kin10 is a network of partners from foundations, nonprofits, universities, school systems, and corporations working together to build up and support the supply of exceptional STEM teachers. With so many organizations involved, FSG was brought in to design a set of shared measures to keep everybody working toward a common goal and to be able to measure progress toward the goal. Srik and his team worked closely with the network of partners to codesign the set of shared measures.

In addition, Srik leads FSG's intellectual capital development around what "Next Generation Evaluation" would look like. In other words, how would evaluation as we know it evolve and expand in order to continue to be relevant, timely, and useful in an age of complexity, connectivity, and rapid change? As far as firm development and leadership, his responsibilities include mentoring and supervising staff, leading internal meetings and projects, hiring new staff, and contributing to the thinking on the firm's growth and strategic direction. Lastly, he engages in business development by cultivating clients, writing proposals, and attending conferences and networking events.

As part of FSG, Srik provides consulting to organizations to implement systematic evaluations, as well as to help them come up with a coherent and comprehensive strategy for evaluation. For example, Srik leads the evaluation of the "Challenge Scholars" project with partners in Grand Rapids, Michigan. Srik participated in a gathering with students, parents, and community members from the town in mid-2014 to celebrate the first generation of Challenge Scholars, i.e., sixth graders who would go through a new program designed to help them successfully prepare for college or other postsecondary career training. Many of the students in the program would be the first in their family to go to college; only 34% of adults possess even a two-year degree in Grand Rapids. Many partners are involved in the Challenge Scholars initiative, including higher education institutions, community-based organizations, faith-based organizations, and local businesses. Srik and his team developed an evaluation process for the program to ensure the program keeps all the partners on the same page and tracks the progress of each generation of Challenge Scholars as they move from sixty grade all the way through higher education.

To evaluate their social impact, FSG carries out regular systematic assessments of their work. Client interviews and surveys are carried out by a third-party researcher, following up at the end of the project and again a year later. Srik appreciates that his work stretches him in multiple ways, never leaving a dull moment. On any given day, he could be solving a complex problem on a case, brainstorming with colleagues about an upcoming meeting, thinking up a provocative blog post to write (triggered often by the cases he is working on), or mentoring a junior colleague on how to navigate a tough client situation. He has learned it is important to do things that give you energy in your personal life and that provide renewal from the daily stresses of work. Thanks to the fellow "foodie" and travel companion he has in his wife, Srik has a fulfilling personal life, which helps him deal with and tackle the challenges in the many aspects of his work.

> Find something that combines your passion with where you can add value as a unique individual. I know it can be hard and might take a few years, but try to consciously reflect on your experiences and projects and seek that "sweet spot." The field of social value creation is growing and definitely here to stay; however, the more you define your own niche and how you can add value, the easier it is for you to find the right opportunity and to stay fulfilled.

Career Trajectory

Srik started his career as an engineer but decided to go to business school to get a broader perspective about career options. In between his two years of business school, he applied for an internship with the Ball Foundation in the Chicago area that supported long-term systems change in school districts. Inspired by his mom, who had served as an administrator at a school in India, and his time spent mentoring children after school during college, Srik was intrigued by the field of education but skeptical he would be hired because of his engineering and business background. Fortunately, the foundation found his qualifications attractive. As an engineer, he had run a grassroots innovation campaign around product quality that required crosspollination of ideas and best practices among multiple company sites. The foundation was seeking to do the same across school districts they worked in, and so he was hired.

This internship was a life-changing experience for Srik. He realized he could use his analytical skills in a different way to benefit society, and he tremendously enjoyed working in a complementary way with people that brought decades of knowledge and experience about the education sector. Staff at the Ball Foundation taught Srik about systems thinking and what it means to truly affect social change. Therefore, when the executive director of the Ball Foundation eventually offered him a full-time position, he knew he had found his calling.

Srik started working with them full-time the following summer. Given his analytical background, he was charged with the task of setting up the evaluation function within the foundation. This required him to stretch in new ways—going out in the field and learning more about evaluation and about what other foundations were doing. He attended conferences and workshops and learned a lot more about the field. Eventually he was able to successfully coordinate several rounds of evaluations in the school districts that the foundation worked in, as well as lead organizational learning processes at the foundation. After seven years at the Ball Foundation, Srik took up a role heading the evaluation function at a national education nonprofit called The New Teacher Center. As their chief impact and learning officer, he set up frameworks for impact measurement as well as systems and processes for data-driven learning and improvement. Once he started working in the social sector, specifically in the area of philanthropic evaluation, he found it helpful to attend industry conferences and be part of professional networks, such as the American Evaluation Association (AEA).

In early 2012, a colleague and mentor in the evaluation field reached out to Srik regarding an opening within the FSG firm. He had been following FSG's work in the field for several years and knew the organization to be a pioneer when it came to discovering and implementing innovative solutions to some of the social sector's toughest problems. After several conversations with multiple FSG staff members, he was thrilled to receive an offer to be a director in the firm's San Francisco office. When considering his future, Srik tends to think less in terms of a specific position or firm and more in terms of the impact he wants to have on the world. His personal mission is to shift the way meaning is made in the social sector. In the next five to ten years, he sees himself continuing to make a personal impact by leading, consulting, writing, and speaking about innovative ways to strategically evaluate and learn in the social sector.

⚙ Liesbet Peeters, 37

D. Capital Partners (Dalberg Group)
Managing Partner | Six figures

MBA, MIT (2005)
Master's Degree, Commercial Engineering, Katholieke Universiteit
Leuven (2000)

Job Description

While foundations, Fortune 500 companies, and independent donors want to donate money to make social impact in the developing world, they often do not know where or to whom to donate. At the same time, many organizations are working on the ground in the developing world, but money can be a major hold up for their success. There is a need for matchmakers who can get to know all parties, connect donating and receiving organizations, and thus create value for both sides. Dalberg is a strategic consulting firm that works exclusively to raise living standards in developing countries and address global issues such as climate change and public health. They are for-profit, but they do not seek to maximize their profits; they instead seek to maximize their social impact and therefore only take on projects that will advance their mission. Dalberg's work helps governments, foundations, international agencies, NGOs, and Fortune 500 companies to make sustainable improvements in the lives of disadvantaged people around the world. They bring expertise gained in the private sector to address topics including access to finance, energy policy, public health, and human rights.

In 2010, Liesbet Peeters joined Dalberg as the managing and founding partner of a new business unit, D. Capital Partners, focused on facilitating the flow of impact capital to social causes. Her business unit is still in its startup phase today with close to fifteen employees, but it benefits from being attached to the larger strategy consulting firm addressing the same issues. On any given day, Liesbet could be in an office in London; Washington, DC; Johannesburg; or Nairobi. She advises foundations, development institutions, and private individuals on impact investments in emerging markets. Impact investments are made into companies, organizations, and funds with the intention to generate a measurable, beneficial social and environmental impact alongside a financial return. Her friends call her a "glorified matchmaker" because she matches those interested in putting funding into development with the right opportunities. The investors she works with want to know more about where they can actually make a difference in putting their money to work. Liesbet discusses with them opportunities and challenges of investing in different businesses. She tries to be as creative as possible in looking for opportunities that have not been looked at yet; she looks for gaps between people's expectations and objectives and attempts to match these gaps with reality. Of the work she does, 99% is with investments, not charity. Investors vary in the returns they expect, from capital preservation to commercial returns. D. Capital gets paid by the investors to find them a match.

One example of an investment facilitated by D. Capital is the Malaria Bond. Liesbet matched the need for more effective funding in malaria prevention and cure with the desire of the private sector to play a role in global health. She created a private sector–based pay-for-performance system where the local companies and organizations that benefited from malaria medication paid for materials through their cost savings once their results were being achieved; in the meantime, she matched them with socially minded investors that would come in and provide funding up front for malaria medication.

To ensure that she and her company have social impact, whenever she chooses a partner to work with, Liesbet confirms that what they do is impactful. Everybody at D. Capital holds each other accountable, and they ensure the impact is happening by following up with the businesses she matches with funding. Liesbet gets requests from both ends, investors and those who need funding. She typically receives requests directly by email to D. Capital. Her favorite part of her job is reading these emails and looking into these requests. She loves that she has been able to expand her own horizons because of all the places her job takes her to. She also enjoys trying to figure out how to solve problems in a creative manner and translate that back into the boardroom. On the other hand, her least favorite part of her job is when politics gets in the way of getting things done. This often happens because making a difference is subjective, and it is difficult for people to leave personal interests behind when making these investments. Liesbet is happy to be working at Dalberg because they are a partner-organized, mission-driven, sustainable company, and they drive the firm based on their values. At Dalberg, everybody is encouraged to think outside the box to solve problems, implement solutions, and work through entire life cycles, not just making matches, to make sure they are working out.

Career Trajectory

After graduating from college in Belgium with a degree in commercial engineering at the age of twenty-two, Liesbet moved to London on her own. She worked for two companies in financial analyst positions for four years. Her time in London was hard for her, being so removed from her family and working long hours. To enhance her skills, she came to America and earned her MBA from MIT. While she was there, she was told that she would only realize the true value of her degree five to ten years down the line, which she eventually realized to be true. The rigor, discipline, and exposure to a whole set of managerial issues and leadership potential have really helped her in the long run. During a summer at MIT, she came to sub-Saharan Africa for the first time to do a pro bono internship. After working with a nongovernmental organization to set up a microfinance program (financial services for entrepreneurs and small businesses lacking access to banking and related services) in the Ivory Coast of Africa, Liesbet knew that she wanted a career in development finance. However, with business school loans looming over her, she was torn between following her dream and pursuing a well-paying job in finance. When Liesbet was chosen as a Siebel Scholar, her decision was made clear: she could now take her dream job in international development. Liesbet spent several years at the World Bank's Grassroots Business Initiative, assisting with microenterprise development projects in Burkina Faso, Mali, and Nigeria. In addition to spending over 80% of her time in the field on these projects, she also helped her clients in Cambodia, India, and Nepal to develop income-generating activities for survivors of human trafficking. Working for the World Bank taught her about the fundamental issues they are trying to solve, and she became even more passionate about her potential to reach the two billion poorest people by applying her economics and business skills.

> A lot of young people want to be in a certain place. Remember it is not about what you become but who you become; be the person you want to be.
>
> Whenever you make a decision, make sure you think about what that decision will look like five to ten years down the line and make sure you will not regret it then.

From there, she started an independent advisory practice at thirty-three, working with a number of families and foundations by herself called Lapiluz Advisory Services. Many of her clients came from her World Bank connections. Being an independent consultant, she liked the freedom but also found it lonely. She learned a long, hard lesson from her early entrepreneurial adventure: she had to change from being a perfectionist to being an optimalist; in addition, failure, trial and error, and knowing how to sell your skills are all part of being an entrepreneur. After eighteen months working on her own, she joined Dalberg and has been happy there for the past five years.

Along her career journey, Liesbet has received support from her wonderful group of friends who have known her for a long time and will always be honest with her. She says that they keep her honest with herself in terms of personality and character traits. Liesbet feels that her professional and personal lives are often intertwined. The line between the two is blurred because she is able to pursue her passion as a job. She loves the traveling and being confronted by people with completely different backgrounds, cultures, and customs; she enjoys learning about those cultures and interacting with these people.

Looking back, Liesbet would have maybe taken more engineering classes in her undergraduate career and gotten more in depth, rather than economics, in which she would later get another degree. She believes engineering classes would have helped her have more details, rigor, and exposure to some things. The most valuable things Liesbet has taken away from her engineering degree are that she (1) should never take no for an answer and always make sure she understands all aspects before agreeing on something, and (2) has the ability to think in a multitude of degrees and variables and optimize across those systems. In the future, she will keep the entrepreneurial spirit she has nurtured, but she wants to do something more operational and concrete. She could see herself inspiring people as a leader rather than a manager and maybe spending a few years somewhere in Africa building up her own franchise.

FOR-PROFIT » CONSULTANT NETWORK, EMERGENCY RESPONSE EXPERTISE

Sarah Williamson, 39

Protect the People
Founder and Managing Director | Percentage of Protect the People's Annual Revenue

MA, Forced Migration, Oxford University
BA, International Relations and French, Gordon College

Job Description

Disasters—both natural, such as tornadoes, earthquakes, and hurricanes; and man-made, such as wars and epidemics—can happen anytime, anywhere. People can lose their homes, jobs, or even family members, and they may need clean water, toilets, sanitation, food, and health care to survive the aftermath. Organizations including the Red Cross, the World Food Programme, Doctors Without Borders, Samaritan's Purse, and many more provide short-term direct humanitarian relief. They all rush in to provide aid following any disaster, but some organizations lack the expertise to design the larger logistics of humanitarian aid. This is where Protect the People (PTP)—a network of humanitarian consultants working to protect people in conflict and disaster—comes in. PTP is a network of fifty consultants that have worked in eighty countries and speak over eighteen languages.

Sarah Williamson founded PTP in 2012 to bring a variety of expertise to humanitarian aid. PTP serves clients by building partnerships between corporations and humanitarian agencies, conducting civil-military training on peacekeeping and humanitarian operations, and supporting United Nations agencies and nongovernmental organizations (NGO). Some of PTP's projects for corporate clients include doing an analysis of the water and sanitation equipment used by relief agencies after a disaster to determine what innovations could make water purification faster and more reliable. Sarah recently worked with a company making personal protective equipment (PPE) for the Ebola response to ensure that feedback from medical personal treating patients was part of designing better protective clothing. Sarah also worked with a company that produces flares to see if peacekeeping forces could use them as warning signals for communities under threat where there is no cell phone connectivity.

In terms of their civil-military training, Sarah worked with the North Atlantic Treaty Organization (NATO) to develop a virtual game on complex humanitarian operations, creating simulations to teach the military how humanitarian workers make decisions and do their jobs. Sarah has worked with US Army battalions on field training exercises to train them on coordinating with humanitarian workers on food distributions, medical evacuations, and diffusing ethnic conflict. For their work supporting United Nations agencies and NGOs, Sarah is advising groups in Somalia about protecting women from sexual violence in internally displaced people (IDP) camps, and she is working with farmers in Haiti on ways to increase their income and learn from US farming techniques. PTP conducts research on all kinds of issues and countries, depending on the priorities of agencies that come to them for help.

Most of Sarah's day is spent figuring out how PTP can make a greater impact. She ensures that each project has consultants working to achieve specific objectives and that PTP administrative and finance procedures are accountable for the resources provided to do the job, and her team members respond to requests for proposals (RFPs) for new work and collaborations. What Sarah loves most about her job is the opportunity for invention. PTP has a unique model that lets them work with any type of client. Many NGOs will not work with the military, but PTP builds a bridge between the humanitarian space and the security sector. Most UN agencies just want monetary donations from corporations, while PTP can help them partner in a more meaningful way. What she likes the least about her job depends on the day; some days managing people and money can be a challenge. At the end of the day, she is responsible for the outcome of the work or product being delivered, signing checks to vendors, and making payments to consultants. Ensuring the accuracy of the work can be demanding.

Career Trajectory

Sarah Williamson grew up in Maine but was born in a small village in Eastern Kenya. She returned to her birth country when she was fifteen years old to build an elementary school. Unbeknownst to her was the fact that when she got involved, that experience would spark her lifelong passion. When Sarah went to college, she wanted to get further involved in politics and international affairs, so she directed a club called the Society for New Politics. Through the club, she traveled to the United Nations headquarters, met with world leaders, and held forums bringing local congressmen to campus to discuss current events. She also traveled to many conferences in Washington, DC, including the Interaction Forum Conference where she met the leaders of international NGOs and learned about what they were doing.

Go to industry forums and meetings, and hand out a business card with your name and contact information, as well as your degree program and the date when you anticipate completing your degree. This can help you get internships with organizations you may want to work in someday. Internships are a great way to understand how different offices function and to understand what skills you are good at in the workplace.

During her junior year, Sarah held an internship abroad with an organization addressing human-rights issues in Mauritanian refugee camps along the Senegal-Mauritania border. Sarah worked with camp leaders on a census to document how many people remained displaced in the area. Working with these refugees gave Sarah an appreciation for the difficulty of solving the problem of displacement. After college, Sarah's first job was with Senator Olympia Snowe at her congressional office in Washington, DC. She was a front-office assistant for a while until one day, as she was leading a tour, gunshots rang out. She kept her tour group safe, and the next day, Sarah was on the front page of the paper for keeping everyone calm in the midst of crisis and was instantly promoted to legislative correspondent. Writing about government policy enabled Sarah to hone her writing skills, and soon she was writing media releases, public speeches, and hearing testimony for the senator, which diversified her portfolio.

After working on Capitol Hill, Sarah returned to working overseas with the help of a mentor whom she met during her junior year abroad in Senegal. She worked for World Vision International in South Africa with a team responsible for crisis response. She built databases of lessons learned in World Vision crisis response programs and conducted trainings to build up the response capacity of regions around the world. She also developed materials for key sectors of the response, including human resources, finance, food aid programs, and child protection initiatives, and eventually moved up to World Vision headquarters to develop more material on crisis response. While the experience with World Vision was amazing, she learned that she needed to specialize in a certain area of work in order to more clearly define what she could offer in the field.

Sarah went to graduate school and earned her master's in forced migration at the Refugee Studies Center at Oxford University. During academic breaks, Sarah began working on a project to document Vietnamese refugees in the Philippines who had lost their identity papers. Because the refugees could not travel without papers, many had been separated from family members for years. Sarah worked in a large slum in Manila where a number of the refugees lived, documenting their identities and getting papers for them to travel. Upon earning her master's, she published her dissertation on *Refugee Return and State Reconstruction* in Afghanistan and Rwanda in a United Nations High Commissioner for Refugees (UNHCR) paper series. Her publication caught the World Bank's attention, and they hired her for several short-term paid assignments to write historical briefs on the movement of refugees.

After completing graduate school at Oxford, she was offered the position of program manager with the International Catholic Migration Commission (ICMC) to manage a United Nations High Commissioner for Refugees (UNHCR) project in Afghanistan focused on the protection of IDPs. Sarah worked in camps of displaced people throughout the region. She identified especially vulnerable individuals, such as female-headed households and handicapped people, who may need special assistance. Soon after the Iraq war began in 2003, Sarah found out that a colleague with the International Committee for the Red Cross (ICRC) who was a water and sanitation engineer had been executed by Al Qaeda and Taliban fighters while checking on wells he dug for local communities. Sarah returned to Washington, DC, sooner than she had hoped, but luckily, a friend from Oxford asked her to work with him on resettling the Vietnamese refugees in the Philippines to the United States. When a crisis would erupt, Sarah used her response background to identify local NGO partners who needed resources to help their communities. Sarah formed partnerships with Burmese refugees along the Thailand border after the Southeast Asian tsunami, worked alongside marginalized groups in Hurricane Katrina in the US, and supported Haitian organizations after the devastating earthquake.

The simple pleasures of life make the weight of the world lighter for Sarah. She has a supportive husband who encourages her in everything she does. Sarah does not think about what she will do in five years anymore; she is happy with what she has done and wants to do more of it on a larger scale. She would like to see PTP making a greater impact in the lives of vulnerable people overseas. If she had to start her career over again, she would get a law or business degree because she views the two degrees as the most versatile for whatever you want to do with your career.

Andrew Means, 29

The Impact Lab | Cofounder | ~$60,000
University of Chicago | Associate Director of Center for
Data Science & Public Policy

MPP, The University of Chicago (2011)
BA, Communications, University of Hartford (2007)

Job Description

Today, more data is collected every minute than has been collected in most of human history. The world is full of nonobvious causal relationships; for example, why do children in schools with fluorescent lighting get fewer cavities than those in incandescent-lit schools? Analyzing "big data," large or complex data sets with the potential to be mined for information using traditional processing applications, can provide researchers with insights on health care, education, energy, transportation, and more. Big data can be useful in many applications to create social impact. For example, food shortages can be predicted from mining a data set on past market prices, droughts, migrations, regional production, and seasonal variations. Another example is mining social media data and other online sources to identify individuals excluded from financial systems.

One organization jumping on this opportunity to have a positive social impact with big data is The Impact Lab, a data, research, and strategy firm that works with a wide range of social sector organizations. They excel at helping organizations make better decisions and improving their programs and operations by providing a wide range of research and analytical services. Andrew Means, a cofounder of The Impact Lab, has years of experience working inside social organizations and understands the unique constraints that many of them face. At The Impact Lab, Andrew's primary focus is on business development: meeting new clients, determining how to catalyze their ventures and who to connect them with, and even helping to develop new products within the framework of their venture. The majority of Andrew's clients are philanthropic organizations or nonprofits particularly focused in global public health and humanitarian development. One of Andrew's more interesting and early challenges was working for a workforce development organization. The Impact Lab was tapped to develop an algorithm to predict turnover rates and reasons for leaving; the workforce organization was looking for ways to fight quick turnover by providing unique support. The Impact Lab provided consulting expertise, allowing Andrew to discover his passion early on; business development was what excited him most.

Andrew has recently worked for the Center for Data Science and Public Policy at the University of Chicago where he had a similar role with an academic twist. While at the university, Andrew worked to build relationships, bring new ventures into the center, and write grants to support the center and their ventures. One of the center's best-known projects was a partnership with the Chicago Department of Public Health to determine safety of housing, particularly with respect to lead poisoning, and how to turn that information into an operation. The Department of Public Health approached the center with several questions, including how to reach out to people and what could be the source of the lead poisoning. Projects like this one inspire Andrew: it is a clear problem that he can tackle immediately, effect change, and have fun working on.

In both jobs, Andrew views his impact as a piece of the success of the organizations he advises. Andrew particularly enjoys seeing customers at The Impact Lab return again for more advice; they are genuinely being helped, seeing their ventures succeed, and relaying the impact back to Andrew. He knows that social endeavors and nonprofits will achieve their goals and create larger impacts because of consultancy groups such as his. The constant interaction with passionate, intelligent, driven people is what brings Andrew incredible satisfaction from his job. The bookkeeping and phone keeping can be draining at times, but delivering for his colleagues is both a motivator and a fulfiller.

Career Trajectory

Andrew was first exposed to problems in the developing world in high school during several mission trips. His experience abroad inspired him to read about developmental economics, and he found that the "economics way of thinking" resonated deeply with him. He went to college for communications and worked through his undergraduate years as a youth pastor, thinking he would continue on a religious professional path. When he graduated, he worked for a large church in Chicago where he ran large-scale programs, managed a sizeable budget, and spoke in front of many people, all of which gave him great experience and shaped his leadership skills.

> Figure out what you are really good at first. Do not worry about the typical jobs that people in nonprofits have. Figure out what you are really good at and *then* figure out how that helps people in some sort of way.

Through his work with the church, he became further interested in social justice and social change. Andrew realized that there were very few people who could fully commit to why and how they are making change. Therefore, he went to graduate school for a master in public policy and poured himself into academics, learning the ins and outs of the trade and building a framework for developing, nurturing, and growing organizations to their full potential. Looking back, Andrew regrets not taking quite as many technical courses, especially now that his work is in data science. Pushing himself academically during graduate school and afterwards was rewarding and gave him the skills he puts to use every day at the center and at The Impact Lab.

Toward the end of his graduate years, he started working for 5812 Group where he helped people on his team think through how they could use analytic goals and quantitative thinking to solve the social problem of affordable housing in the US. This experience enabled him to try out addressing a social problem using quantitative analytical thinking. He was hooked and took a job as an analyst at the YMCA, quickly advancing to director of research and analytics. He helped the YMCA of Chicago move toward a data-driven culture where they use data analytics to not just evaluate their programs but to actually improve the way their programs are operating. For a few months he worked for Groupon, helping them to think through their impact on local communities, what that means, and how it looks. Afterwards, he moved to the Center for Data Science and Public Policy at the University of Chicago. Andrew jumped through positions relatively quickly because he always wanted to maximize his potential for growth and do something interesting. He has a great ability to be passionate about a lot of ideas and projects, making it easy for him to shift from one thing to another.

Andrew left the University of Chicago in May 2015 to focus full-time on The Impact Lab. For the foreseeable future, Andrew will be focused on growing The Impact Lab's products and services. He is already building a strong team there, clients are being added with regularity, and they have launched two products. Within ten or twenty years, Andrew hopes to see The Impact Lab as the market leader in providing data services and products to the social sector market.

⚙ Tyler Valiquette, 35

Independent Designer and Social Impact Consultant | Dynamic Salary

BS, Mechanical Engineering, University of Idaho (2002)

Job Description

Many organizations around the world develop products and services intended to encourage positive social change. In order to succeed, they require a deep understanding of their target end users' culture and context; otherwise, the offered solutions could fail to produce the desired impact. However, these organizations frequently do not have the expertise and experience necessary to create context-appropriate products; hence, they hire specialized design companies to help them at any point in the development process. Such work-for-hire design companies range from large organizations such as iDE, IDEO, or Frog Design to small firms and independent consultants like Tyler Valiquette. Tyler is a social impact designer with significant experience creating products ranging from water purifiers to farming tools to improved cookstoves.

As a designer focused on social impact, Tyler works with clients to develop innovative offerings that are human-centered, mindful of society, and considerate of the planet. He prefers to work collaboratively and often leads cross-disciplinary design teams comprised of people with varied skills, including industrial design, anthropology, engineering, graphic design, international development, and business. Tyler relishes the endless variety of projects, working directly with people and organizations who are changing the world, and the creative possibilities that each project brings. Tyler sees his role as a liaison between a product's or service's end users and the organization providing it. The end users want to improve their quality of life in tangible ways that are meaningful given their personal contexts and perspectives; the organization wants the end users to change their behavior in specific ways that they believe will produce positive impact for both the end users and society. Ensuring that the voices of the end users are considered and that their desires align with the goals of the organization is a major undertaking that requires a nuanced understanding of both perspectives.

Take, for example, the case of a water-purifier project. The drinking water available to target end users was often contaminated with disease-causing pathogens. The for-profit organization wanted to help these end users avoid disease by providing a water purifier that treated their drinking water (the only way to accomplish their goal of improved health). However, the end users had limited income and struggled to meet the daily life demands that competed for their time and energy; water purifiers rarely reached the top of their purchasing priorities. In response, Tyler's team focused on the two occasions when the end users were already inclined to purchase a purifier: (1) they had disposable income and wanted a status symbol, and (2) it was recommended by a doctor for an ongoing health concern. The resulting design was aesthetically sophisticated (appealing to status-minded users), highly effective (appealing to users concerned with health), low cost (ensuring affordability), and easy to use (resulting in consistent and sustained use). The last point was critical; it was only by creating a highly convenient product that integrated seamlessly with the end users' existing water habits that they were able to incentivize regular purifier use and thus improved health.

Tyler has led social impact design projects like the one above for over eight years. In order to find these projects, he relies on his personal network, which ranges from small social enterprises to large development organizations, such as the Peace Corps and the World Bank. He also devotes a significant portion of his time to networking and new business development (attending conferences, meeting with colleagues or potential clients, writing exploratory emails, or crafting in-depth proposals). In order to keep his business running smoothly, he reads news related to his industry, publishes a blog, manages client relationships, keeps an eye on cash flow, and leads the design activities of teams that he assembles as needed on a per-project basis.

It is by getting deeply involved in projects that Tyler is able to do the design work he enjoys most: technical research, business model and strategy consulting, in-context user research (often involving international travel), concept brainstorming, design iteration (taking concepts from rough initial sketches through to refined designs), prototype fabrication, lab and field testing, and liaising with manufacturers. For example, on a recent project funded by a grant from the Gates Foundation that he coauthored, he co-led a team of students from Drexel University on a two-week trip to Thailand. While in-country, the team interviewed end users, built and tested prototypes, assembled a machine shop in a remote village, and taught local Thai farmers how to fabricate an innovative rice-planting tool developed by the students with guidance from Tyler and their professor Dr. Alexander Moseson.

Tyler stresses that this work is not without its many challenges, first of which is a lack of control. He works at the behest of his clients and does not have final say over the direction of the project or over what is done with his work once his contribution is made. To balance the uncertainty, Tyler strives to work with clients he believes in and chooses to focus on the integrity of his work and the possibility of positive impact.

Figure out yourself, your motivations, and your interests. This is not a path for the faint of heart, those attached to their comforts, or for those without a true and deep connection to *why* they are doing what they are doing. Are you interested in this path because you want to be a "do gooder," you are searching for meaning, or you feel guilty for your life of privilege? Or are you acting out of real connection to the issue and strong convictions about how and why it should be different?

Career Trajectory

As an undergraduate, Tyler gained a great technical background in mechanical engineering from his classes and excellent communication skills from competing on the debate team. After graduating, he was not certain what he wanted to do with his education, but knew he needed a job, so he turned to his university's career center. He applied to the first interesting position he found and was soon hired as a refinery engineer for Chevron. However, he quickly realized that being "a small cog in the massive machine of Big Oil" was not for him.

Uncertain what to do next, he decided to travel and spent two years exploring and teaching English in Latin America. This experience provided him with a more global perspective and tons of personal motivation. During his journeys, he came to realize that many communities were struggling to meet basic needs that nevertheless had an existing technical solution. Tyler returned to the US motivated to discover how he could apply his technical skills to the field of international development. While searching for graduate programs and job openings with aid agencies, he started volunteering at Engineers Without Borders (EWB-USA). That's where he connected with like-minded people who introduced him to "design thinking." He was inspired by the emphasis that the discipline places on human connection, contextual understanding, and a messy prototype-test-prototype approach to problem solving. Working with this group, he discovered the niche he had been looking for—designing consumer products to help people in developing countries meet their basic needs.

Building on this experience, he cofounded Catapult Design, a nonprofit design firm, and became the chief operations officer. During the two years it took to get Catapult established, Tyler worked a second job and received no salary from the startup. All told, he co-led Catapult for nearly six years through its conceptualization, startup, and initial growth. The rich experience provided many personal opportunities; he dove deeply into the discipline of human-centered design, became an expert in an emerging industry, developed an extensive network, and built valuable skills. When he left, Catapult was a successful firm focused on leveraging modern technology and design methods to serve the world's most disadvantaged populations. After thinking deeply about design for social impact, he realized that the approach he helped pioneer at Catapult could just as easily be applied to any socioeconomic context, not just the developing world. With that as his mission, he started his own independent consulting practice.

Tyler's personal and professional lives are inseparable, with his interests, beliefs, and ethics as the starting point for his career activities. He believes it takes a healthy, balanced, diverse person to have the presence and compassion his work requires. Therefore, he strives to work sane hours, practices mindfulness meditation, and prioritizes his personal relationships and interests. Looking to the future, Tyler will continue exploring his primary career interest—the intersection of creativity, technology, business, and social/environmental justice. In the course of things, he aims to create products and services that meaningfully improve lives and to constructively add to the ongoing human conversation of how we evolve toward a more just, healthy, and peaceful planet.

Kosta Grammatis, 29

Oluvus
Founder and CEO | ~$50,000 – 70,000

BA, Liberal Studies, California State University, Channel Islands (2007)

Job Description

The Internet is like magic—it opens up so many opportunities for people: from education through Coursera and Khan Academy to employment through Upwork and Elance to help with health issues through WebMD to a forum to amplify your voice through blogs and social media. The Internet is quickly becoming the most fundamental building block of economies! Many believe that it is becoming a new human right! With that said, still over four billion people in the world do not have reliable access to the Internet. How can this problem be solved? Back in 2009, Kosta Grammatis took making the Internet more accessible for all as his personal mission. He believes that access to education and therefore access to the Internet is one of the most important things we can do for humanity: making information, knowledge, and the exchange of knowledge available to as many people as possible. In 2009, he started striving toward his mission by founding a nonprofit, A Human Right.

Through a few years of improving Internet access with technology in some areas of the world and sharing stories of why the Internet matters through documentaries, Kosta learned that he was trying to solve a problem much more complicated than a technology one—he had to change the way people think about the Internet. Kosta learned early on that two big reasons that Internet access does not cover the whole world are monopolistic telecommunications companies and policies surrounding access. He was often running into battles with telecommunication companies, governments, and people who did not want the Internet to be brought to certain communities because of inappropriate websites, having a forum for negative speech, and a variety of other reasons.

Realizing a nonprofit was not the most efficient route for him, he switched over and started Oluvus, a company still dedicated to making the Internet more accessible for all, but as a public benefit corporation. Kosta decided to make Oluvus a public benefit corporation because he wanted to build the values of the company into its structure, and he wanted to take on investors, which he could not do through his nonprofit. Oluvus's strategy is to give free Internet access through wireless and mobile hotspots in developed countries, including the United States, and when people run out of the free bandwidth, they can pay for more, which will help support connectivity projects in developing countries. Kosta's role as CEO of Oluvus is to find opportunities with telecommunication companies, design products (or find other people to do so), and promote his company through speaking about its mission.

In addition to his "day job," Kosta is a correspondent for Al Jazeera, covering science, technology, and its human impact for the TV show *TechKnow*; an advisor to the Thiel Fellowship; and a speaker for audiences around the world on topics surrounding his science and technology projects he has completed so far in his career. These outside engagements help Kosta make a decent living and propel Oluvus forward without pulling a salary from it. Because of the variety of his commitments, Kosta could one day be sent to Tennessee to conduct an interview for Al Jazeera, the next day to the United Nations in New York to talk about why Internet access for all matters, and the next day recovering from all of his travel! He has a great amount of work to get done, and it could look drastically different from day to day, but he makes sure he is working toward his personal mission the best he can each day.

Kosta measures not only how people are getting connected to the Internet but also what they are doing with it. Kosta's mission with Oluvus is to bring education to the world through Internet access, but he knows that some places are resistant to the Internet because of what else it brings. For example, when talking with First Nation people in Canada, he learned that they got rid of their Internet access because they saw it only for its bad qualities (e.g., adults-only sites they did not want their children visiting). Therefore, Kosta aims to couple bringing the Internet to places with bringing new job programs, new tech centers, or centers for gender equality (e.g., a women-only cyber café in Afghanistan).

Career Trajectory

Kosta did not have a traditional start on his pathway to success—he almost failed out of high school. With a little bit of luck, he made it into a brand-new college with professors that were open to new ways of thinking about education. From there, he searched for and jumped on every opportunity to work on interesting and important projects. He took his time in college to "play and experiment," and although his school had no engineering program, he forged his own way into engineering. The college was surrounded by strawberry fields that were regularly sprayed with a strong pesticide, and to make sure the college's residents were safe, Kosta built a balloon-based sensor system to detect pesticide levels in the air around the college. With the help of a $14,000 grant from the school, several professors, the Internet, and two years of hard work, Kosta's project ended up beating California's top-tier engineering universities in undergraduate research competitions. This was the start of Kosta falling in love with using invention and technology in service of the greater good—and realizing how helpful the Internet was for teaching himself.

> Be kind and empathize with everyone you meet. You never know what journey they are on and how your journeys may align. This is part of what has allowed me to move between disciplines so seamlessly. School was important, but the Internet plus kindness and empathy have been even more important for my career.

Seeing graduation day quickly approaching, Kosta went on a quest to find interesting people working for exciting engineering companies, and he emailed them all. After SpaceX rejected Kosta twice for an internship, one of his emails helped him land an in-person interview with the company and get an offer for a full-time job! Kosta turned down an offer from Accenture and started with SpaceX right out of college. Kosta was thrilled that he could get offers from such prestigious engineering companies despite his nontraditional education. SpaceX saw a spark in Kosta and brought him in to gain a different perspective on the problems they were trying to solve. One challenge he was given was determining if SpaceX could lower their costs for communications with spacecraft. Learning a ton from the Internet, Kosta and his team designed a specialized experimental satellite that helped SpaceX prove they could control spacecraft through preexisting satellite networks.

Upon the end of his one-year appointment with SpaceX, Kosta decided to spend some time exploring the world outside his southern California region where he had spent his whole life. Amidst his travels, he read a magazine article about a filmmaker named Rob Spence who dreamed of filling his empty eye socket with a tiny video camera. He was asking the world for some help, and so Kosta wrote to him that he would build it for him. Rob housed and fed Kosta for several months in Toronto while Kosta worked on this project for him. Armed with experience dismembering electronics as a child for amusement and, of course, the Internet, Kosta formed a team, forged his way through building several failed prototypes, and in under a year developed a successful camera called Eyeborg for Rob's eye. The camera was named one of *Time* magazine's best inventions for the year.

After finishing up Eyeborg, Kosta moved to Berlin to work in an innovation think-and-do tank for T-Mobile with thirty other people. Tori Hogan, the eventual author of *Beyond Good Intentions*, taught Kosta about the aid industry and the struggles it faced. Kosta began his Internet search and quickly found that five of the seven billion people in the world did not have reliable Internet access. Kosta was in shock because one of his keys to success thus far had been his ability to search the Internet for information. From that moment on, Kosta's career path became self-driven with the mission to get as much of the world Internet access as possible. He gave a speech to his fellow think-tankers, formed a team, and attempted to start solving the problem from an engineering perspective: could they build a satellite network to cover the world with free Internet? Over the next six years, he would continue to learn through trial and error a great deal about global politics, financing, corruption, and the difficulty of bringing technology to people at that scale.

Kosta is now figuring out his role in solving the world's Internet-access problem as the landscape continues to change. Over the past few years, huge names have taken on this problem—Mark Zuckerberg is building drones, satellites, and low-bandwidth apps through Internet.org; Elon Musk is building a global satellite project through SpaceX; Internet Society is championing public policies that enable open access and bringing people together to share opinions; and The Alliance for Affordable Internet is partnering with governments, companies, and nonprofits to shift policies and regulations. Kosta would love to see everybody working more collaboratively, so he hopes to join others to further this collective mission and increase impact.

Photo by Acumen

Ghoncheh Jafarpisheh, 32

ZanaAfrica
Head of Manufacturing and Operations | ~$45,000
BS, Electrical Engineering, University of Illinois, Chicago (2005)

Job Description

It is 2015, the year we are reevaluating Millennium Development Goals. While we have made great strides in improving gender equality in primary education, gender equality in secondary education is still a distant dream. While there are several reasons for this gap, three of them are lack of access to feminine hygiene products, lack of access to private toilets, and the lower perceived value of educating girls compared to boys around the world. Without sanitary napkins, girls and women miss a total of five years of school. Girls and women living on two dollars or less per day cannot afford feminine hygiene products. Many organizations have emerged to create and sell low-cost sanitary pads. For example, Arunachalam Muruganantham in India created a machine that could manufacture low-cost sanitary pads for less than a third of the cost of commercial pads, and MIT and Sustainable Health Enterprises worked together to produce a machine that produces low-cost banana leaf–based sanitary pads. ZanaAfrica is a similar startup, based in Nairobi, that makes affordable sanitary pads, delivers health education, and informs policy. It was founded in 2006 and has reached over 5,000 women and girls to date.

As opposed to multinational companies with large factories dominating the global market, ZanaAfrica creates local jobs while improving gender equity in secondary education by locally manufacturing low-cost sanitary napkins. ZanaAfrica realizes that poor people expect products to work just as well as their wealthier counterparts, so they compare their product to similar offerings from large multinationals. How then does a small company like ZanaAfrica manufacture products at a good price point without sacrificing quality? Ghoncheh Jafarpisheh, head of manufacturing and operations, brings her engineering, development, and private sector expertise to ZanaAfrica to design and manufacture low-cost sanitary napkins. Ghoncheh is especially vital to ZanaAfrica because of her experience working in developing countries as well as designing high-quality, low-cost diapers and similar products for Proctor & Gamble. She understands the importance of quality control, accessibility, and affordability, all of which are essential for setting up manufacturing and operations.

Ghoncheh researches ways to set up onsite gear and contract manufacturers locally, and she also tests out products and new materials. Ghoncheh is developing a sanitary pad that is low cost but still attractive and good quality so that it embraces the dignity of women. She wants women to want to buy this product without shame and hence she strives to develop a product she would want to use herself. She is spearheading this effort in Kenya while working with a team in the US on research and development. In addition to creating this product, her other goal is to create local jobs. Ghoncheh is motivated by its potential to bring about gender equality in Kenya. Ghoncheh's favorite part is that she gets to create something from scratch—something that has been overlooked but is still very important. She also loves that she gets to do technical work that leverages her engineering background. Her least favorite part is that with any development work, one sometimes gets disillusioned and jaded. There are so many issues and so much corruption; it is hard to get anything done because of the umpteen barriers.

Challenges that ZanaAfrica already faces are that it is very new and the founder is American. Luckily, the founder has lived in Kenya for ten years and has built a network of connections. Additionally, it is difficult for ZanaAfrica to get funding; although they do not want to be at the mercy of philanthropists and donors, they have to be as a startup. It is also a challenge for Ghoncheh to decide whether they should manufacture locally or contract out. The easy way out is to source manufacturing out from China or India, but Ghoncheh chose to work with ZanaAfrica not only because they have a model to provide sanitary pads and education to girls but also to provide jobs.

Career Trajectory

After finishing her undergraduate degree, Ghoncheh immediately started grad school but was not very passionate about it because she did not know what to do with her degree and was quite worn out from school. When she got a job offer from Proctor & Gamble (P&G), she left grad school and accepted the offer. Through this position, Ghoncheh manufactured tampons in Maine and learned a lot about manufacturing and operations. She then went on to work in P&G's world headquarters in Ohio. While creating a whole new diaper for the company, she strengthened her project management skills by managing a $100 million project. P&G put confidence in her as a new employee, and this motivated her to succeed. After around four years, Ghoncheh chose to leave because she felt she was getting "too comfortable"; since she was making good money, she did not want to be drawn in by material things— she wanted to do something more.

> We need a lot of engineers for technology development for problems in developing countries. When graduating, focus on innovating on different projects that can improve the lives of other people. Do not focus on getting a really good job. There is another world out there—you can work in an awesome place like Kenya and learn about different cultures. Go out and get experiences to broaden your horizons. Study-abroad programs in developing countries can really change the way you think about engineering and innovation.

In 2008, on the side of her P&G work, Ghoncheh cofounded ROCK: Reaching Out with Compassion in Kibera. Because of the lack of a universal secondary schooling system in Kenya, many kids in slum areas cannot attend secondary education, which ultimately leads many to turn to crime or substance abuse. ROCK responds by providing a support system and academic assistance to at-risk youth in the slums of Kibera through a scholarship program to send more kids to secondary school, a tutoring program to assist students with homework, and a support network to discuss issues experienced at school and home and to reinforce the importance of making the right choices. Ghoncheh has continued to work with ROCK as executive director alongside her other jobs. Working for ROCK has been a big part of her life and has taught her how to best set up an organization.

Ghoncheh is very close with her family in Iran and passionate about social issues there. After the 2009 election, she moved back to Iran and tried to start a rural school with her connections there. Unfortunately, it did not work out, but to rebound from this failure, Ghoncheh applied for the Acumen Global Fellows Program even though she did not think she would get it. Sure enough, she was chosen and placed in Kenya! She also worked with Sproxil, a mobile product authentication app, to verify prescription drugs to make sure they are not counterfeit. This app already had a heavy presence in West Africa, and her job was to bring it into Kenya. Unfortunately, no pharmaceutical companies wanted to sign on first, and many were corrupted by drug counterfeiters. In retrospect, Ghoncheh realized that Sproxil should have diversified beyond pharmaceutical products early on. She also learned that just because a business model works in one market does not mean it will work elsewhere. Her best takeaways from her time with Sproxil and the Acumen Fund were using storytelling to get the message out in a dignified, honest way and completely empathizing with and understanding an issue before tackling it. From there, she landed happily in her current position with ZanaAfrica.

Ghoncheh's parents have been very helpful to her by instilling good values in her: to share and to have empathy and compassion. Engineering school also shaped who she is today; it made her put her guard down and let her explore things she was good at. Ghoncheh likes to blend her work and personal life. When she visits her friends and family in the US, she tries to teach her friends what she has learned about removing herself from consumerism and materialism as well as the benefits of volunteering. She often brings her work home with her, and her boyfriend does not mind because he is also engaged in similar work. He is actually another person profiles in this book—Jason Lee from the International Finance Corporation. Sharing passions for this type of work helps drive them both further.

In October 2014, Ghoncheh left ZanaAfrica to work on a startup with two other partners. They are setting up a peer-to-peer lending platform in Kenya for Kenyans. In the future, Ghoncheh would like to continue her education and start a school to make women stronger. Ghoncheh already helps run a Montessori school with her mom in Chicago and would like to start a new one in the US, Iran, or Kenya. If she could start over, Ghoncheh would probably go into public policy and international development work and get a master's degree. She believes shaping policy is important because you have to understand the core of government even though there is corruption. While you can learn other things along the way, Ghoncheh feels having a background in public policy would be a good foundation.

Steven D. Grudda, 26

Africa Felix Juice LLP
CEO | ~$60,000

BA, International Relations, Houghton College (2010)

Photo by Intermotion Media

Job Description

Sierra Leone is a small country in West Africa with a population of six million people. It has the second-highest rainfall on the African continent, and it is rich in diamonds, iron ore, and gold. While that sounds like a land of abundance, Sierra Leone also has some of the highest infant mortality rates and recently had a civil war that killed over 50,000 people. How does a country that has such amazing resources improve its lives and livelihoods? Trade with the outside world is one way to do it. Ultimately for countries to develop, bringing in external resources and trading with the outside world is more important than money changing hands within the community. How can Sierra Leone's natural resources be exploited to effect large-scale change? A great place to start is with mangoes—they grow on trees and require no action from farmers! While a few mangoes feed the population, the majority of them are left rotting. What if these mangoes could be collected and juiced and the concentrate sold on the international market? Development is not a zero-sum game; by collecting mangoes that would otherwise rot, juicing them, and selling the concentrate on the international market, Africa Felix Juice (AFJ) is increasing the incomes of thousands of people in Sierra Leone.

AFJ purchases fruit from around 3,000 farmers and provides jobs for over seventy employees in its processing facility. In addition to minimizing post-harvest losses, AFJ improves yields by importing pineapple suckers (little plantlets that grow between the leaves of the mature pineapple) and distributing them to farmers in tandem with training in cultivation and off-take agreements for the fruit. "I do whatever it takes," says CEO Steven Grudda, whose typical day at AFJ includes refining AFJ's data management system, forecasting cash flow for the week, inspecting the factory premises and machinery, and reviewing expense requests from each department. It could also include training his staff on a new mango procurement plan or questioning senior staff members to make sure they are thinking ahead. Steven also meets with local government officials to build good rapport; confronts service providers who try to rip him off; has international phone calls with board members, mechanical experts, or sales reps; or hosts visitors from the World Bank, Millennium Challenge Corporation, or members of the press.

Sometimes, the cell phone network goes down, so Steven climbs on the roof and uses his other phone to find a connection and make calls. As needed, he travels to remote areas of the country to meet with farmers, into Freetown to meet with bankers, or to the shipment port to supervise the release and transportation of expensive equipment. Sometimes he is out of the office all day; others, he is pouring over spreadsheets until 10:00 p.m. To Steven's surprise, a lot of his job has been figuring out how manufacturing equipment works. He never expected engineering to be such an important part of management, but it penetrates almost every aspect of his business. As a manager, he needs to ensure the company has adequate maintenance plans so that production is not interrupted by breakdowns. He needs to figure out how to improve efficiency as it relates to equipment performance and procurement.

Steven has seen young men move from the city back to their village to manage the family farm. One woman stopped performing female genital mutilation (FGM) when she gained the opportunity to replace the income earned from that activity with income earned from the sale of fruit. Steven is pioneering new business practices and promoting better lifestyles in Sierra Leone while also reshaping the international perception of the country. When some of AFJ's first containers arrived in Rotterdam, Dutch customs officials thought the shipping documents were falsified to smuggle in contraband. Today, AFJ exports to Europe regularly. The government of Sierra Leone hailed AFJ's products as the first value-added exports since before the country's civil war. Steven considers one of his key contributions to be restoring trust among Sierra Leoneans.

Steve loves how practical and "rubber hits the road" his work is. While he spends a significant amount of time doing analysis and calculations, he also gets to see his plans come to life—for better or for worse. If his plans do not work, then he learns from the failure and changes his strategy. Since AFJ's kind of business has not been done in Sierra Leone before, they are building from scratch. Every decision Steven makes shapes business process, personal relationships, and sometimes government procedure. Steven is "defining the undefined and building something real." Despite his passion for his job, he is sometimes brought down by the personal sacrifices he makes for it. The job requires Steven to live far away from his family and friends and work long hours in lower living standards. It also takes a toll on his health; he has spent several nights in Sierra Leonean hospitals recovering from various sicknesses. One time, Steven was medically evacuated and spent a week in intensive care in Paris before returning to the US for medical leave.

> Two things: (1) fail quickly but (2) do not quit. There is usually more than one solution to a problem. If your solution fails, recognize it as a failure and try a new one. Failing is part of growth. Leaders fail. Cowards quit.

Career Trajectory

During college, Steven threw himself heavily into leadership responsibilities. He was class president, varsity soccer team captain, upper-class men's housing resident assistant, and then co-resident director in his senior year. He also taught Sunday school, worked three jobs (off and on), and traveled abroad in Africa every summer (for service projects and research). Steven first came to Sierra Leone on a research trip as a college student where he studied how a business could mobilize a supply chain among mango farmers and submitted his research to World Hope International (WHI). The strain of all his college responsibilities helped prepare him for his job today.

His first job after graduating was an assistant logistics coordinator for an international move management and auditing company based in Waterville, Maine. The company serves mostly Fortune 500 companies and Steve's experience with them gave him a global perspective of corporate activity as well as a practical sense of international shipping and logistics. He was interested in getting more involved in foreign policy, so he applied for an internship with the Africa Program at the Center for Strategic and International Studies (CSIS) in Washington, DC. He issued a cold application online because he did not know anyone who worked there, but he was accepted and moved to Washington, DC. Part of the internship was participation in CSIS's leadership academy within which he chose to develop his debate skills. The former debate coach at West Point trained him, and he competed against interns at other think tanks around the city. That job exposed him to interactions among experts and senior decision makers and gave him insight into how informed decisions are debated and made. It also improved his professionalism and made him bolder and more confident.

Thanks to his research submitted to WHI in college, he was asked to return to Sierra Leone to lead the implementation of a project that would put his research proposal into practice. Steven spent eight months in Sierra Leone setting it up under the auspices of WHI. After a year in the US, Steven was asked to move back to Sierra Leone to serve as operations manager of First Step Economic Opportunity Zone. A year into that assignment, AFJ ran into some management troubles, and Steven was assigned to manage the company through a recovery effort. Initially, he served as chief operations officer for AFJ and then was promoted to CEO—at the age of twenty-six!

Steven sees himself working on agribusiness development in West Africa for the next twenty years. He would like to be based more in the US as he gets older. He wants to earn an MBA at some point and after that would consider consulting for a few years before coming back to project management and development. He would love to start, buy, and sell a series of agribusiness companies in West Africa throughout his career. He would also consider a position with a large multinational agribusiness company in the region at some point, but he would need to feel confident of their social impact. If Steve could start his career over again, he would study more business and engineering.

Currently, Steven puts aside his personal life to put his work first. He has made a lot of sacrifices in his personal life to be successful on the job, but he has also benefitted from developing good relationships through work. He enjoys spending time with his colleagues and believes rest is as important as work. Steven left AFJ in July 2014 to spend more time with family in the US. Ebola swept the country shortly after his departure, and operations at AFJ remain minimal as a result. Steven is now an associate at Endsight Consulting where he advises clients on agribusiness in Africa.

⚙ Spud Marshall, 27

co.space
CEO and Chief Catalyst | ~$35,000

MS, Strategic Leadership towards Sustainability, Blekinge Institute of Technology (2010)
BS, Mechanical Engineering, Penn State (2008)

Job Description:

Innovation happens when people from different walks of life—disciplines, cultures, mindsets—come together. In our world today, 65% of millennials hope to make a positive impact in the world, and 92% believe the world must undergo real change. Yet over half of all millennials, approximately 40 million people, admit to feeling powerless in the face of the world's problems. Without an infrastructure and culture that empowers innovators, this generation will not make a meaningful impact. Spud Marshall is an entrepreneur who developed the co.space and cofounded the New Leaf Initiative in order to address this challenge.

The co.space is a global network of co-living spaces for people who want to change the world. The co.space serves two key groups: undergraduate students by giving them real-world experience and mentorship, and social entrepreneurs by providing them with housing and connections in order to realize their ventures. So far, the co.space has one flagship home for passionate students in State College, Pennsylvania, and intends to establish these co-living environments in university cities around the world. The ultimate goal is to network these homes together and build a borderless community of young social innovators. Spud wants this network to partner with higher education institutions and local communities to bridge the positive efforts already occurring through collaborative communities of change makers.

As the chief catalyst of the co.space, Spud is his own boss and is free to pursue all his ideas to advance his initiative. This can prove challenging at times as he must constantly search for money to support the work that he loves. While the freedom to pursue many ideas is liberating, it can easily be distracting from his work. However, the co.space now provides a consistent source of income, which allows him to focus on his core business. Another challenge is developing strong relationships with universities and convincing them to relinquish full control of finances and operations when they support off-campus living communities like the co.space. This proved to be an initial challenge at Penn State, and Spud hopes to show through the first pilot home how other forms of partnerships can be developed through alumni relations, community outreach, and visiting professor housing.

Since Spud works with only one other entrepreneur, he is responsible for all logistics, programming, business models, and building up his company on a local level. Currently, Spud manages logistics for the co.space, meeting with business partners and coordinating projects. He is responsible for coordinating who lives in the co.space, advertising to the Penn State community, working with future partners to scale the co.space to other cities, and ensuring that the business model remains intact.

Career Trajectory

After graduating from Penn State with a bachelor's in mechanical engineering, Spud worked for the university for a year, creating education materials on community assessment for engineering students, developing the site layout for a community of handicapped individuals in Jamaica, developing zero-energy home curriculum for middle school teachers, and assisting in the overall management of AESEDA (The Alliance for Earth Sciences, Engineering, and Development in Africa) research and education projects. From there, he pursued a master's in strategic leadership towards sustainability (MSLS) degree in Sweden which allowed him to give companies a perspective of sustainability and innovation through consulting.

Spud's first entrepreneurial venture was through a socially minded talent agency in New York City where he worked with his partner Christian Baum and learned what it took to pursue his own startup. While this venture ultimately failed, this experience played a key role in the formation of the co.space. On this experience Spud notes,

"Whenever diverse people live together, challenges are inevitable. But when they are handled with humility, understanding, and sincerity, these challenges provide the richest ground for lifelong transformations." After this pursuit failed, Spud and Christian started the New Leaf Initiative in State College.

As an incubator, New Leaf provides a space and community for people to pitch ideas and network with others to turn them into a reality. New Leaf serves as a central portal in Pennsylvania to bring in a diverse audience—mission-driven entrepreneurs, passionate community organizers, engaged business leaders, motivated students, and determined local government—from the surrounding innovation ecosystem to collaborate. In addition to connecting individuals, New Leaf nurtures transformational ideas from conception to implementation and connects those ideas with the right resources in the community. With a larger team and more freedom to work with, Spud realized the need for the co.space after working with thousands of students and community members through New Leaf.

It is okay to make mistakes. As long as you approach it humbly, you will find yourself getting in the thick of things and learning at an amazing speed.

The value of a university is not in a degree, but in the community that a university can offer.

"Diving right in" helped Spud get to where he is today. He was greatly influenced by a professor in Jamaica, Neil Brown, who enabled him to experiment and fail on international projects, giving him confidence to start the co.space and New Leaf. In addition, Spud says that his MSLS degree in Sweden was critical in helping him get where he is, and he continues to make good connections with other MSLS graduates. Spud has found significant value in connecting with like-minded people across many different disciplines.

He fondly remembers first meeting some of his business partners through a chance encounter while traveling: "I am a connector, so for me it all has to do with the people that I lean on and who I am always hoping to support in some way. I was in Washington, DC, meeting with some friends, and as we were eating lunch, I noticed that the building we were in was also the head office of Ashoka, a global organization that identifies and invests in leading social entrepreneurs. I decided to randomly drop in and introduce myself. When I walked in, I was politely escorted back out into the hallway. Confused, I walked back in, and they said they do not take solicitations. Apparently I looked like an Apple salesman, and they thought I was trying to sell them an iPad. When I cleared up the situation, they laughed and admitted that no stranger had ever just wandered in off the street to say 'Hi.' Unsure what to do, they introduced me to some of the heads of a few programs, and after talking with them for a few minutes, we hit it off right away. From that moment, I found myself in an inner circle of disruptive change makers in higher education. The next few years were a whirlwind of new introductions, and after twelve months, I had met all my new business partners and fellow dreamers who have gotten me to this point."

In addition to networking and maintaining personal relationships, Spud recognizes the importance of balancing his work and personal life. He describes his work and personal lives: "They are one and the same, which is a good and a bad thing." He sets time aside for things like kayaking, rock climbing, and ultimate Frisbee, and though it is hard for him to pull away from work, he sees the value in taking breaks. Spud plans to run the co.space in the future and to continue to seek out new projects simultaneously. His focus will be on catalyzing and accelerating social entrepreneurs.

Roland Fomundam, 33

GreenHouse Ventures Ltd
Founder and CEO

MS, Technological Entrepreneurship, Northeastern University (2010)
BS, Business Administration and Biology, Northeastern University (2009)

Job Description

Cameroonian citizens, especially small-scale farmers, are unable to grow crops year-round. There is technology for indoor farming in most developing countries, but introducing them requires patience, persistence, and capital, which most farmers and social entrepreneurs lack. Not being able to farm during the off-season leads to loss of income and productivity as well as a hike in market prices for seasonal crops. Farmers tend to overproduce during the growing seasons, but the lack of affordable preservation mechanisms deepens their losses. They are unable to meet market demands and incur losses in the supply chain, which further exacerbates their socioeconomic standards. Roland Fomundam's company counters the hurdles faced by the farmers and the general population.

Roland is a Cameroonian native with education and experience in the US. The decision to move back to Cameroon was one that he made after his first year in America. Being a Westernized African willing to go back to Africa gives him a financial and educational advantage many do not have. Always an entrepreneur, he saw the problem of food insecurity in his home country and discovered a prime opportunity for a solution in greenhouse technology from Penn State. The Penn State Humanitarian Engineering and Social Entrepreneurship (HESE) program had developed affordable greenhouse technology that Roland licensed and now uses to build an enterprise that empowers farmers to make more money while improving food security in Cameroon. Roland is the CEO of GreenHouse Ventures Ltd, a one-stop shop that develops, deploys, and markets the technology to multiple users while training participants in the process. In so doing, his company has emerged as the only sustainable agriculture company with a goal to empower local citizens, giving them the unique ability to grow crops year-round. The business is backed by a market platform that packages and channels harvests to target markets.

Roland's licensed and customized greenhouse technology is the first of its kind in Cameroon. Coupled with a business model that ensures affordability and sustainability, GreenHouse Ventures has emerged as a leader in the agricultural sector. There is no other company in Cameroon doing what they do. His company develops and deploys the technology, thereby introducing Cameroon into a new era of green agriculture, a key aspect in the president's goal for the country's emergence by the year 2035. It minimizes the hurdles faced by farmers, encourages citizens—especially youths—to be involved in agriculture, and it curbs the high unemployment rates in the country. Acquiring the technology presents a good opportunity for investment especially in rural areas where one in three families own at least a hectare of land. Roland believes this approach is instrumental in uplifting the standards of living in these areas and reversing the trend of rural to urban migration. Farmers will be able to grow crops year-round using fewer resources, making it an economically viable venture. Seasonality will have no effect on production, farmers will keep up with demand, and market prices will be stabilized.

Today, Roland lives between Cameroon and the United States, and his priorities vary based on where he is. When in the United States, he does more thinking, strategizing, and brainstorming about how to improve his business in terms of helping more people become successful agro entrepreneurs. He also carries out consultancy services while seeking new leads for his businesses and also delegating duties to his employees on the ground. When in Cameroon, he implements and executes on any work needed to run the business, such as project planning, carrying out market studies, monitoring and evaluations, making revisions based on customer feedback, and sending his team members out to build greenhouses. He spends a lot of time connecting with his team to share his thoughts and perceptions so that they see his vision; this is one way he has kept this team motivated and working hard. Roland has become a source of inspiration and motivation, with many Cameroonians looking up to him as a mentor and leader for tomorrow.

Career Trajectory

Growing up, Roland was always trying to do what no one else was doing in his town in Cameroon. After high school, at a time in Cameroon when cell phones had just gotten into the country, Roland started a mobile phone repair shop. Roland had no knowledge about the technology, but he understood there was a market for people who wanted to buy the phones and therefore they would need repairs and maintenance. A year and half later, he played and won the American Diversity Lottery visa. He was excited about leaving Cameroon because he, like most Cameroonians at the time, had the perceived notion that there were more opportunities and resources out there than in Cameroon. Traveling to the US broadened his mind and gave him the independence to think and exercise his entrepreneurial mindset. Roland quickly learned that the American dream of wealth did not automatically come to you, but you could easily acquire the tools and resources in America and make wealth in Cameroon and Africa.

> Once you have the courage and can make the necessary sacrifice, then you have the preliminary tools of igniting change or creating social value. Thrive on intuition rather than intelligence. Listen to your inner calling and make the necessary sacrifice.

Roland had a turnaround moment in 2006 when he felt he cheated death and rose up from his hospital bed after a ghastly accident. This was not just a miracle for him but serendipity. From then on, the more he learned to satisfy others' needs, the more he learned about himself. That year, he graduated from community college and transferred to Northeastern University where he pursued a degree in biology. By working part-time as an on-campus tutor and lab assistant as well as with the help of scholarships, grants, and loans, he was able to fund his way through school. He had chosen biology to become a pharmacist but quickly realized that there was more he could do with his life besides spending days behind a pharmacy counter, so he added another major, business administration.

It all clicked when he met with Dr. William Tita, a business mogul and professor of entrepreneurship at Northeastern University. Roland envied his life, and together they went to Cameroon to establish a microfinance program to support a farm group in 2006. The trip was very inspirational, and upon returning from Cameroon, Roland started Youth Action for Rural Africa (YARA) with a mission to alleviate poverty through access to education and resources. The idea for YARA came to him as he realized that most Cameroonians were leaving Cameroon for education and resource-driven purposes. He realized that if he found a way to make these things available in the country, then most people would spend the little money they have to make tangible investments back at home, which in the long run would be more sustainable.

There are many Cameroonians whose parents spend their last savings and even sell their last properties just to send their children abroad. When the children arrive abroad, they are faced with the pressure of making a living while trying to meet family expectations back home. Most Cameroonians come to places like the US and have to do odd jobs just to make a living. Odd jobs also go along with a minimum education and minimum wages, which leaves them in a cycle of living paycheck to paycheck. More than 70% of Cameroonians who live in the US today end up spending over twenty years in the US; they acrue debts, remain undocumented, and cannot go back home, hence remaining stuck in the system. Everything Roland does is an attempt to find the right solution to achieve the vision of living an American life in Cameroon.

Starting in 2007, Roland went on a journey to find the right people to improve the quality of life in Cameroon. One of them is the former president of Botswana who told Roland that agriculture will be a major employer in the future. Roland graduated with a master of science in technology entrepreneurship in 2010, a degree he chose because he knew that any business success in Africa would have to include a culturally compatible technology and a mastery of the business acumen to deploy it. In 2010, Roland met with the Cameroonian Minister of Mines and Energy, who stressed the need for sustainable innovations in the country. While in search of an applicable technology, Roland stumbled on a solar dehydrator, which had been developed and tested in Uganda by a student. Roland contacted the team and requested that they work together in developing the technology. In 2011, Roland took a prototype to Cameroon where it was tested and sent to a lab for further improvements. Unfortunately, some shortcomings in JolaVenture made him go back to the drawing board; that was when he discovered HESE's greenhouse technology and decided to pursue its commercialization in Cameroon. In the future, Roland wants to expand his company to other West African countries and add a restaurant and supermarket chain, a school of technology development, numerous franchise locations, and cooperative centers. He also wants to become a motivational speaker, consultant, and professor, and he also wants to be involved in the politics of his country.

Photo by Angaza Design, Inc

⚡ Lesley Marincola, 29

Angaza Design
Founder and CEO | Modest Salary

MS, Mechanical Engineering, Stanford University (2009)
BS, Product Design, Stanford University (2008)

Job Description

Over a billion people in the world still have to burn kerosene to light their homes at night. The smoke from this is the equivalent of smoking two packs of cigarettes every night. These families are "off the grid" electrically and spend up to 20% of their income on kerosene. One alternative to this expensive, dangerous practice is solar energy, which is cheaper than kerosene over time but has a huge up-front cost for these families: around $50 USD for a typical three-watt multifunction solar lamp. This is unreachable for many families with low incomes and no bank accounts. But if we can find a way to spread out the up-front cost over time—a small initial investment and then remaining payments collected later—solar lighting can be much more financially accessible.

This is Angaza's proposition: Angaza Design is a Pay-As-You-Go solar technology development company. They license an embedded technology design to solar product manufacturers that meters a product's energy output and enables it to send information to and from Angaza's cloud-based software platform. Pay-As-You-Go product distributors then use this software platform to manage recurring energy payments from end users. For example, one of Angaza's manufacturing partners produces a very low-cost lamp called a "study light." It would normally cost about $15, an up-front price point that is prohibitively expensive to the majority of low-income, off-grid families. But, Angaza's Pay-As-You-Go technology enables distributors to sell this study lamp for only $1.50 up front with the remaining payments then spread out over about eight weeks. This Pay-As-You-Go study light has transformed many kerosene burners into first-time solar customers.

Lesley is the founder and CEO of Angaza. She wears many different hats in this role, but she works a lot on making sure the company has the right people and resources to effectively grow. Angaza consists of hardware and software engineers in San Francisco and an operations team in Nairobi, Kenya, that manages distribution partnerships and responds to user feedback. Lesley also plays a large role in fundraising for the company, which can be a full-time job in itself. Occasionally, she even still does some of the mechanical and graphic design work. Although Lesley's time spent on engineering activities is minimal, she could not run the strategic operations of this company without her engineering background. She would not understand the type of team it takes, how to facilitate the product development process, and how to focus and integrate customer feedback into their design work. In fact, she uses her engineering background every day.

On Lesley's most boring day, she will be answering emails, Skyping with manufacturers in India and China and distributors in East Africa, and calling investors. Her most exciting day involves getting out into the field in India or Africa to see their technology being used by families. She loves interacting with her customers, from their manufacturing and distribution partners to the families who benefit from their technology. Her least favorite part of her work is that as a startup, Angaza never has enough resources to execute on all their ideas.

The technology that Angaza licenses to product manufacturers allows the products to connect to the cloud wirelessly to communicate both usage and diagnostic information back to the cloud. When a customer makes an energy payment for the week, Angaza's software platform enables or disables the customer's product based on the status of their payment. Angaza's software interface, the Energy Hub, enables distributors to track customer information from the people they sold the product to and process payment information. The pricing is completely flexible for the users; if they do not have money for a whole week of energy, they can buy it for one or two days at a time. Some of the distributors will sell these products on a rent-to-own basis where, after a customer reaches a certain price point, the product permanently unlocks and no more payments are needed or required.

The Energy Hub also enables full insight into how a customer uses a product and how the product is performing. Before Pay-As-You-Go technology, a distributor might send a technician out to a customer to troubleshoot the malfunctioning product in person. Now, with Pay-As-You-Go technology, distributors can gather product diagnostic information remotely and avoid an expensive after-sales service trip, especially if the customer has just installed the solar panel incorrectly. By giving that kind of information back to the distributor automatically, they do not have to travel all the way to the village; they can just call the customer and tell them to make sure they are charging the lantern outside in the sun all day.

> Social innovation does not always equal starting your own company. If you have a great idea in a social innovation field and want to see it come to life, it is sometimes best to partner with existing companies to make the idea a reality.

Angaza is starting to do analytics work so that they can evaluate a customer's usage of the product, such as the number of hours of light a family uses per night, to predict expected repayment behavior. These analytics help distributors understand when some customers might be paying more slowly. Angaza operates at the intersection of microfinance and solar energy by enabling manufacturers and distributors to offer solar product loans with high repayment on those loans.

Career Trajectory

When Lesley was in high school, she barely knew what engineering was but had always liked math and science. She was also interested in international development and spent every summer in high school living in developing countries. After being accepted to Stanford, she was invited to a diversity-in-engineering summer session. That summer session changed her life because it exposed her to all the different types of engineering and guided her toward what she liked best. Lesley loves making products of her own, so mechanical engineering and product design were obvious choices. She also really liked product design because it focuses so heavily on the human experience. The human-centered design process was appealing because she wanted to create products that would truly address people's needs.

After earning her bachelor's, Lesley decided to stay at Stanford to complete her master's in mechanical engineering so that she could absorb more in-depth engineering knowledge. During that year, she jumped on the opportunity to take a class called "Entrepreneurial Design for Extreme Affordability." The class applied human-centered design principles to the design of products for the developing world where operating constraints are much different from the US context. The experience provided Lesley with a valuable perspective that enabled her to merge the product design and international development worlds. It was in this class that Lesley realized she would use her product design skills to benefit the world.

Lesley also worked with a corporate partner in this class, an off-grid solar manufacturer that got her looking at off-grid energy opportunities. She started to understand that if we can solve energy poverty around the world, we can enable other positive impacts on education, health, and income generation. Following her master's, Lesley spent a summer living in rural Tanzania with a host family to understand what it is like to really be reliant on just kerosene. Upon return to the US, she took a job as a design consultant for D2M near San Francisco and, for a year and a half, designed consumer products, medical devices, and more.

Lesley's work is very integrated with her personal life; she has stopped striving for separation between them because she loves her work so much. At the same time, she knows it is very important to take care of herself. Being an entrepreneur is incredibly stressful and demanding, so it is hard to remember to step back sometimes. Little things help her, such as standing during meetings, walking around, and scheduling meetings outside the office. She also joins her team for happy hours, holiday parties, and community service projects. In the future, Lesley wants to merge Angaza with a larger company and continue to prove that you can have both social and financial returns. She will probably keep working for internationally focused companies and might eventually become a social impact investor to help mentor and finance other startups.

⚡ Jona Raphael, 28

Lumeter Networks
Cofounder and Vice President of Product | ~$60,000

MSME, Mechanical Engineering, Boston University (2012)
BSME, Mechanical Engineering, Olin College of Engineering (2009)

Job Description

To tackle the energy poverty challenge in developing countries, many companies have recognized the need to help customers get over the financial barrier of renewable-energy up-front costs and the need of renewable-energy providers to consistently get paid for their services. For example, one company has helped a community organization in Haiti to develop a store to supply clean-energy technologies, education, and training to clean-energy entrepreneurs. Another company sells a rugged smart battery system to charge electronics via a solar panel, all of which can be paid for using existing cell phone systems via a rent-to-own model. With their own unique technology, Lumeter Networks works with many existing renewable-energy providers to integrate their prepaid off-grid electricity meter and cloud accounting software into their offerings. They seek to work with other entities already working on energy poverty and to bring their web of financing and other partners to the ecosystem to solve the problem.

Lumeter's technology enables customers to pay as they go while making sure energy companies are providing them with power only when they pay for it, thereby reducing the risk of investment in off-grid renewables for banks and private investors and making energy more accessible to more people. What makes them especially different is the fundamental flexibility of their technology, which accommodates countless business models, enabling the setup of novel energy businesses that can diverge from tradition and hopefully disrupt the field. It also gives other social entrepreneurs the electrical resources to do their jobs more efficiently, reliably, and cheaply. This means Lumeter can support local investors and inventors from afar—they do not need to keep reinventing the wheel in order to help hundreds of thousands of their underserved customers.

Jona cofounded Lumeter Networks two and a half years ago, and now he leads development for all their technology's user-facing aspects as well as their manufacturing chain from start to finish. Jona embraces the intense work and skill sets one needs for life in a startup company. He highly values communication skills because it is common that within a few hours of work, he has spanned several continents through conference calls alone. From managing manufacturing chains overseas, to dealing with client questions, to troubleshooting existing deployments, his attention must be able to dance among topics and immediately concentrate with laser focus. And finally there is creativity: some days it is making digital models of packaging designs; other days it is laying out a new product's circuit board. Some of Jona's personal time also includes design projects: from an ultra-efficient electric vehicle to a two-ton, six-legged ridable robot capable of delivering aid across disaster zones.

As for what sort of impact they are making, Lumeter Networks is still too young to have meaningful analytics. At this point, Jona measures success by unconventional metrics: for instance, the width of the grin he is offered along with the cold beverage from a town's first-ever refrigerator. Change is embodied by little girls dancing in their living rooms as music and light spill from their doorway on the first night their village has electricity. Impact is reaped when the small business owner on the corner selling goods out of a window can stay open long into the evening and ensure a better future for her infant. Improvement is tangible when the poorest villagers pay one dollar per week for some electricity: a level of poverty that precludes access to any other energy solution. Personally, Jona judges the value of a problem by how unsolvable it seems. In turn, he judges the value of a solution by how tractable it makes that problem. Technology that enables pay-as-you-go financing for utilities is the sort of solution that can bring basic services to even the most destitute communities.

Jona also loves the freedom and flexibility that comes with his startup's distributed workspace. He can program and hold conference calls from the beach or tinker and solder from his living room. He thinks that building his own company is a great way to always feel "in over your head," which happens to be the environment in which he works best. On the other hand, Jona does not truly have time of his own. Every minute of every day is fair game when it comes to putting out fires or hammering out a product before a deadline. Entire weeks can go by without a break; thus, seeking a work-life balance becomes a challenging chore.

Career Trajectory

Jona's parents instilled in him a passion for traveling from a very young age, and he has never stopped. He earned a degree in mechanical engineering from Olin College, a new school that is trying to change the way engineering is taught. Education there is centered on projects, not departments, and Jona thinks this taught him how to effectively interpret problems and apply creative solutions from other disciplines. Most importantly, he believes that his experiences at Olin College taught him how to fail and fail often. Every project was a moonshot, and yet every project resulted in a valuable deliverable, even if it was not the original vision. Throughout his education, it was extremely valuable to have a strong balance between technical internships and international internships (through sources such as idealist.org). At several points in both his educational and professional careers, he has taken extended leaves of absence in order to take advantage of some international or unique opportunity—and has never regretted doing so.

> Seek out those who are smarter than you. Frequently start projects that originate from passion or curiosity. Finish a few of them. Join others' projects until you do not have time left for sleep. Keep a list of the biggest problems you can think of, and stay in contact with anyone you meet working on them.

After college, Jona had a few jobs that did not advance his technical career. At one point, he had to move back home and clean houses for a living while continuing to search for a job in a struggling economy. When he did eventually find an engineering job designing skyscrapers, he quickly automated all the boring tasks and was able to concentrate on creative thinking. This still was not personally fulfilling though, so he went back to school to earn a master's degree from Boston University. His master's is in robotic and controls engineering and culminated in a whimsical submission of his master's thesis on robot dinosaurs. Throughout his time at BU, Jona made sure to surround himself with peers that he deemed smarter than himself, who would push and work creatively with him.

After attaining his master's, Jona moved to San Francisco, found some dream jobs, and applied to them—again and again. In the meantime, he sought out like-minded communities at the intersection of technology, international development, and sustainability. It seemed like a good strategy to build up a personal network, and he spent plenty of time attending mixers with curious eyes and ears. At one such event, he met Mitra Ardron, who told him a little about his idea for Lumeter Networks. Jona was hooked immediately.

If Jona had to start over, he would take more introductory courses in more fields, but he would also take the harder, more technical opportunity for a given option. He would document his ideas more extensively and seek feedback on them more often. Five years from now, Jona sees himself working on another startup. He already has a few ideas but is always eager to work on other people's projects if they can capture his imagination. Ten years from now, he hopes to be deep into a startup that has survived. His strategy will be to just keep going until something sticks or until he crosses paths with something that seems worth sticking to. Twenty years from now, he hopes to be consulting part-time for other companies attempting to revolutionize different markets around the world in order to pass on his future tricks of the trade.

⚡ **Mike Lin, 34**

Fenix International
Founder and CEO

MS, Mechanical Engineering, Stanford University (2006)
BS, Mechanical Engineering/Product Design, Stanford University (2003)

Job Description

The One Laptop per Child (OLPC) project aimed to provide each of the world's poorest children with a laptop in order to empower them through education. Along with the challenges of distributing and funding the laptops, OLPC faced the challenge of getting children access to energy to power their laptops. As a founding member of Potenco, the off-grid energy startup to power OLPC, Mike Lin gained an understanding of how great the energy challenge is in developing countries. Not only is it hard for students to power their laptops, but it is hard for their parents to light homes for their children to study at night. Mike saw that the majority of people did not have access to electricity at all, and others had very unreliable access, mostly based on the unhealthy burning of kerosene. Mike's background creating products led him to the opportunity to design a product that would power many devices using clean energy. He decided to turn that opportunity into a for-profit startup that would focus on technology for social change—and do it without having to rely on continuous donations.

Mike's company is called Fenix International, and their main product is the ReadySet, a smart battery system designed to withstand harsh conditions (high temperature, overloads, and short circuits). It can power lights, mobile phones, radios, and even televisions once it is charged via the included solar panel. Fenix also addresses the financial barriers to off-grid energy. Customers can lease to own ReadySet solar systems via ReadyPay, a mobile-enabled payment plan. ReadyPay uses existing wireless networks in sub-Saharan Africa that enable users to transfer money via cell phone. Once you make your payment, you are texted a code that unlocks the ReadySet until your next payment is due.

When Mike created his startup, he spent a lot of time traveling in East Africa to understand the technical and financial challenges he was tackling. He still travels today (six years later), but now it is more about fundraising—and sometimes he gets to test his products with real customers in Uganda. His travel is split between working with farmers that live on just a few dollars a day, to working in the machine shop to try to find ways to address their needs, to working with manufacturers in Asia to produce those products, to meeting with investors to raise venture capital in Silicon Valley, Wall Street, and Europe. Fenix is actively tracking numerous positive social and environmental impacts from how many watts of power they are generating, how much carbon dioxide they are diverting, and how many jobs they are creating for men versus women and young versus old. This is important because you should not set goals that you cannot measure!

Mike has seen firsthand how ReadyPay has improved lives. For a shop owner along the river in Uganda, he saw business boom as the store became brighter later at night to attract incoming fishermen. He has seen many happy mothers light their homes at night and feel safe knowing their children will not get hurt like they could have with kerosene lamps or fires. Mike's favorite part of his job is that it has so much meaning; there is never a day he dreads going to work. He might be jet-lagged and exhausted, but it is all worth it, and he is giving it all that he has got. His least favorite part is that, as with all startups, they are resource constrained and underfunded. Finding investors that fit well with any business—with the same goals and methods and enough capital to invest—is a daunting challenge.

Career Trajectory

After earning his bachelor's in mechanical engineering and product design, Mike went to Yale to take courses that were unrelated to his degree: gender studies, energy systems, industrial ecology, and social entrepreneurship. He had the opportunity to work as a research assistant and then began to teach. This period was pivotal in forming the way he thinks about the world and his approach to problem solving. Mike loved that he was able to take classes in an unstructured, non-degree fashion that allowed him to learn whatever he wanted while in a new environment with new faculty and people. Mike felt incredibly lucky and fortunate to get to know a specific professor who had a master's in art and a PhD in engineering and combined the arts and sciences for social change. One issue Mike and she worked on together was the challenge of getting people to be passionate about engineering. They designed a robot dog that was outfitted with environment sensors to measure pollutant concentrations at a park that was transformed from a landfill. After a year at Yale, Mike returned to Stanford to complete his master's in mechanical engineering.

Take time to understand yourself and gauge what you truly want to do. You might need to travel; you might need to work. There is no silver bullet and there is no right or wrong way to do it. For me, I was really fortunate to be able to spend a year taking courses at Yale before returning to Stanford for my master's degree. Figure out what you are passionate about and your risk profile. Once you know this, you can then pursue your passion in a manner that fits your personality and needs. For some people, that is founding a startup; for others, that is working within government, and for others, that is joining an existing venture which could range from early stage to post-IPO. Once you know yourself, your risk tolerance, and what you are passionate about, you can hopefully then pursue your dreams with the most relentless, persistent, unreasonable energy possible.

During grad school, Mike started his first company, a multidisciplinary web, interaction, and ecodesign consulting firm to help new ventures striving for social, environmental, and economic impact. Starting the company while in grad school was beneficial because it meant he was not giving up a stable, full-time job. He made a website, hired a handful of students, and marketed his sustainable engineering resources at a cost much lower than many competitors. He ended up with clients such as Nike and North Face! After his master's, Mike worked for Apple for a year as an environmental engineer addressing their carbon footprint, green materials, and environmental impact. Then Mike joined Potenco as their first employee and started designing power systems for the One Laptop per Child initiative. After two years, he founded Fenix. He bootstrapped Fenix with $100,000 in credit-card debt and deferred legal fees. He started earning a salary again once they raised their first million dollars in funding.

Mike's work is highly integrated with his personal life, so he is very happy to have a friend as his cofounder. They get through all the all-nighters and other rough times of the startup together. Looking back, he wishes he would have asked for help earlier, surrounded himself with mentors, and taken advantage of all the resources available to him while at school (office hours, guest speakers, and seminars). In five years, Mike wants Fenix to make a real dent in the global energy poverty issue; his metric is growing from 25,000 total systems to one million. In ten years, he hopes to impact fifty million households and in twenty, he hopes to be sharing what he has learned and inspiring people, probably at a university because he has really enjoyed teaching sustainable development at Stanford.

Dhairya Pujara, 27

Ycenter
Founder and CEO | ~$15,000 – $30,000

MS, Biomedical Engineering, Drexel University (2012)
BE, Instrumentation Engineering, University of Mumbai (2010)

Job Description

Despite the best intentions, traditional models of donations and charity do not create an impact if there is no capacity building within the community. For example, the medical equipment that is donated to hospitals in developing countries is often unused because of lack of training, and laptops donated to children in schools are never used because there is no stable power supply. Projects need to be inclusive, making sure the community is highly involved in the creation and that their actual needs and wants are what drive the project. This ensures that there is strong accountability and ownership for these projects.

Many students in the US are interested in improving communities abroad, but learning about global issues in a classroom setting is not enough to create real-world, impactful solutions. Students need to back it up with on-the-field learning experiences that provide cultural awareness, language learning, and empathy. To fill this need, there has been huge growth in academic programs that bring students abroad and engage them in rigorous fieldwork, working shoulder to shoulder with community members on health, finance, and other projects to improve lives. Such programs include the Humanitarian Engineering and Social Entrepreneurship program at Penn State, GlobalResolve at Arizona State, D-Lab at MIT, DukeEngage at Duke University, Humanitarian Engineering at Oregon State University, and Dartmouth Humanitarian Engineering at Dartmouth College. Such programs tend to be highly selective and demanding, and there are students who do not want to participate in courses but rather just engage in fieldwork.

There has also been growth in nonacademic programs to provide students with this fieldwork experience, including organizations separate from universities such as ThinkImpact, Cross-Cultural Solutions, and GlobeMed; and entities that partner with universities through student groups such as Global Brigades, Engineers Without Borders, and Engineers for a Sustainable World. Similarly, Ycenter's mission is to create community projects in Africa and India to improve social conditions through better health care and education while offering these projects as three-month experiential learning programs for US students and young professionals. In addition to having the communities drive their projects, Ycenter also builds capabilities in these communities to take these projects forward and make them sustainable.

For the founder and CEO of Ycenter, Dhairya Pujara, every day is a roller coaster. While in the United States, Dhairya's major tasks include reaching out to universities and planning Ycenter workshops for college students to help them understand the importance of immersing themselves in communities and breaking the barriers of traditional classroom walls. He juggles his time working out of his co-working office space in Philadelphia downtown and meeting university directors and international program officers in the tristate area. Dhairya also spends time in Mozambique, working on the ground with community members on their projects. While he makes sure Ycenter participants are directly implementing their projects in health care, he invests his time heavily in building relationships with local agencies and ministries to create a support network for Ycenter's projects in Mozambique.

For a long time, many malaria programs in Mozambique focused on distributing mosquito nets, antimalarial drugs, and rapid diagnostic kits; all of that is pointless, however, if people do not go to the hospital to get the tests done, or if the drugs are not available in remote places where the need is highest. Ycenter's main project in Mozambique is a low-cost electronic reporting tool called "Ola Health," which enables near real-time monitoring of essential data on certain diseases, starting with malaria. This tool enables community health workers (CHWs) to report test results on the go, along with other information from testing kits and the drug information for the patient. This creates a direct communication pathway between CHWs and central hospitals, which acts as a main terminal for monitoring trends and key indicators.

Data collected using Ycenter's software helps NGOs and public health agencies to make intelligent distribution models and provide care based on quantitative and qualitative information. To assess their impact, Ycenter uses basic tools such as listening to the community health workers and patients who use their tool and monitoring shifts in trends that are created because of their project. Dhairya is personally encouraged to continue with his Ycenter work because of all the local community members that tell him that he has made their lives simpler in the fight against deadly, curable diseases. Ycenter's other projects include developing solar-powered cell phone chargers, implementing medical device training in Mozambique, and creating innovative curriculum and pedagogy for students in public schools in Mumbai, India.

Dhairya's favorite part of his job is that he can try new things without fear of losing his job for doing so because he is the CEO. While he loves traveling most of the time, it is his least favorite part because it

> You should start in high school and college working in your own backyard before jumping out to save the world. When you work for yourself, you are accountable and responsible for everything. And when your work deals with social value creation, you are accountable and responsible for others' actions too. Students should start training themselves to be community leaders and responsible team players.

takes him away from friends and family for significant periods of time. Because Dhairya runs his own company, the line gets blurred sometimes between his work and personal life. However, over the past few years, he has realized that should not be the case. Therefore, he takes timely breaks from his work in order to come back again fully charged with refreshed, creative brain cells.

Career Trajectory

Dhairya's educational training as a biomedical engineer and taking subjects like health-care management and medical device development as a student helped him craft the Ycenter health-care projects in Mozambique. Participating in business plan competitions, organizing conferences like TEDx, and attending other such conferences also helped him expand his network and connect with some brilliant minds in the industry. Also, reading books on international aid and development such as *Dead Aid* by Dambisa Moyo provided poignant insights required for doing his job today.

After quitting a conventional corporate job on his first day, Dhairya chose to work in a rural hospital in Mozambique for five months. After three years of running a for-profit Internet startup in India and his time in Mozambique, Dhairya was ready to plunge into creating Ycenter. One year into trying to start Ycenter, Dhairya was at his lowest point and did not know what to do next, having exhausted all his savings. He participated in a community organizing and storytelling event organized by a social organization in partnership with *The Huffington Post*. Out of the fifty people who attended this workshop event over the weekend, six of them, including Dhairya, were selected to share their story and vision in the form of a six-minute talk with Philly's press and top influencers in the social innovation field. After Dhairya did his talk, he was approached by two local magazines and a news website to publish his interview and story. The founder of the co-working/incubation space in Philadelphia who offered Dhairya his support to launch and grow Ycenter read this story and tweeted with a hashtag #keeppujarainPHL. A few months later, Dhairya registered Ycenter in Philadelphia and has not looked back.

The key points in the last three years for Ycenter's advancement have included forming an advisory board with members from the United Nations and Twitchange in 2013, winning the Philly Dogooder award in 2014, receiving a special category visa approval from American immigration in 2015, and partnering with the Ministry of Science and Technology in Mozambique for running a youth social innovation program. Dhairya's key to success has been grit and ignoring skeptics. Public speaking on international development and blogging for *The Huffington Post* Impact has helped him reach a wider audience and spread awareness about Ycenter and its mission globally. Being part of groups like Founders Club at Wharton and Drexel, mentoring at a nonprofit where he taught millennials the principles of social innovation and entrepreneurship, and becoming part of World Economic Forum's Global Shaper community have helped him develop his personality in dealing with people from diverse fields and also learning things that he never did sitting in classroom lectures.

Dhairya believes that the best way to teach students to be social innovators is to get them in the field, living in the communities, getting a wider perspective, and possibly failing a few times before creating "the solution." Ycenter does exactly that, and in a few years, Dhairya hopes he can lead his enterprise to a point where they foster the growth of young social innovators globally and influence higher education institutions to form best practices to give real-world experience to students. In this process, he hopes to bring down the malaria infant mortality rate through their projects, improve access to basic health care in Mozambique and India, and be a thought leader for international development policies.

Diana Jue, 28

Essmart
Cofounder and Chief Operating Officer | ~$40,000

MCP, Urban Studies and Planning, International Development, MIT (2012)
SB, Economics, Urban Studies and Planning, MIT (2009)

Job Description

How do organizations designing products to improve lives in the developing world get their products in the hands of the people who need them? There is no Amazon Prime or Walmart in developing countries, and current rural supply chains are inefficient and fragmented. While millions of people have essential needs and there are hundreds of existing technologies to meet those needs, Diana Jue never once saw any of the product being used by the people who needed them during her graduate fieldwork in southern India. Hence, Diana cofounded a company, Essmart, in southern India to get technologies such as smokeless cooking stoves, solar lanterns, and water filters to the people. Essmart works through existing shops in urban and rural areas; they have a catalog of products that people can look through and order through the shop. When somebody orders a product, an Essmart employee brings the product from the closest of its six distribution centers and delivers it to that store where the customer can pick it up. Essmart's delivery method works well because many people in rural areas do not have addresses but already use these shops.

As COO and cofounder, Diana's work revolves around making sure that her company's supply chains are working efficiently; this includes checking that her managers are meeting due dates, her warehouses are stocked, and her customers and shopkeepers are happy. Her most recent project involved creating an online marketplace for urban areas (they have thus far relied on paper-copy magazines in shops). She is also working on developing the best way to test prototypes; they want to put products in stores and see if their customers will buy them, at what price, and for what reasons. She lives in Bangalore where she meets with suppliers and potential partners, including people who can provide financial support, people who have new technologies that they want to source, or people who have a new product that might help them with their operations. To grow her business, Diana builds domestic partnerships to expand Essmart's range of products, geographic reach, and international partnerships to source lower-cost products and potentially expand Essmart's reach outside India.

Essmart's catalog currently has about sixty products from over thirty manufacturers. They get ideas from different sources. When suppliers or manufacturers approach Diana with a product they wish to distribute, Essmart tests the product to confirm that it works as advertised. Sales executives take the product to stores to see if the shopkeepers think it would sell and to villages to see if it is of interest to potential customers. If the product passes the sales executive's testing, it is included in Essmart's catalog. Other product ideas come directly from the customers. For example, Diana is currently looking for a good headlamp because their customers wish to use both hands and see while in the dark. Diana's team searches to see what is already available in the villages, online, and in camping stores. They look for products that meet customer needs, fall within a certain price range, and are good quality. The catalog gets printed on a quarterly basis and contains pictures and prices. The catalogs are put in stores so that people can browse them, see what they want, and order from the shopkeeper. Shopkeepers then place the order through Essmart. It is similar to online shopping, but they operate out of a store because most customers do not have Internet access and houses do not have an address. All products have warranties, so customers can return them if they do not work. Essmart primarily functions as a distributor but also facilitates sales and demonstrates the products in the shops and villages.

To assess Essmart's social impact, Diana's team measures the number of products they sell and then estimates the number of people they reach by taking that number and multiplying it by the number of the average size of families that they currently work with. They also measure social impact by the number of retailers that they work with, which indicates the points of distribution that they have to get products to the end users as well as how many small businesses are improving by working with them because retailers make money for every Essmart product they sell. Their third social impact indicator is the number of distribution centers that they have, which shows how many geographic regions they reach.

Diana loves building her team, spending time with them, and watching them grow. One of her favorite times was bringing employees together for a company retreat. They discussed what Essmart is, what their values are, and showed the team the company culture. Diana and her management team made fools out of themselves doing skits and made their employees more comfortable around them. The atmosphere was unusual for their workers who grew up in Indian culture and expected to be quizzed during the retreat. Diana least likes doing all the tasks that nobody else wants to do such as managing expenses, checking invoices, and pointing out mistakes to people.

> Keep an eye out for the problems that frustrate people that nobody else is solving. You do not necessarily have to start up—there are so many great organizations out there. If they are solving a problem the way you feel like it should be done, then you should go join them because they need great talent like yours. But if there is nobody solving the problem the right way and you believe you have something in your hands that would work and nobody else is going to do it, then you start up and you do it and commit to it. It will be hard, but it will be worth it.

Career Trajectory

Diana became interested in international development during a study-abroad program during her undergraduate years at MIT. In college, Diana took a course called D-Lab where students design technologies for development. She was one of the few nonengineering students in the course. For the class, she traveled to western China and saw firsthand the challenge of distributing the technologies her classmates were designing. Her interest in the problem of dissemination fueled her master's research and thesis on social impact technology dissemination in India. She took a year off from her master's program to visit NGOs, microfinance institutions, and self-help groups around southern India to see how people were trying to disseminate social impact technologies and looking at models that were not working. When she returned to MIT the following year, her thesis reader put her in touch with Jackie Stenson, her eventual Essmart cofounder. Jackie's life was very parallel to Diana's, including writing a thesis very similar to Diana's but focused on Africa. They met up for lunch and ended up brainstorming Essmart in a classroom for several hours.

Jackie and Diana were enthusiastic about working to solve the problem of dissemination. They began by writing a business plan and building a student team. During winter break of her final year in graduate school, Diana ran Essmart's first pilot in India with her current Essmart colleague, Prashanth. They travelled to Pollachi, interviewed 200 shop owners, and put items in a store to see if they would sell. Sure enough, they did. When Diana came back, she, Jackie, and a team of students entered university competitions to gain grant money and publicity; their first big break was a win at the MIT Global Challenge and then the Dell Social Innovation Challenge.

After graduation, Diana moved to India and started building Essmart's team. The startup days were interesting because they did not know exactly what they were doing. They tested what products their shops liked for several months until they were officially set up and able to buy and sell as a company. They slowly expanded and hired a director of India operations and more sales executives. They also created distribution centers in other parts of southern India. They now have six distribution centers and have been operating for about three years. As they grow, strengthening company culture and communication have become increasingly challenging.

Diana has a personal life outside Essmart. Some people say that a work-life balance does not exist and that it is more of an integration, but Diana likes having her work during the week and fun on the weekends. She is friends with her colleagues, but they have their own separate social lives. She has many other friends around her age in Bangalore, where she lives, and keeps relationships with her friends and family strong using Skype. Diana is happy to have chosen to major in economics and city planning, but she wishes she would have learned more programming on the side. In high school, Diana was a pretty good programmer but gave it up in college to focus on her research and travels. In the future, Diana sees Essmart expanding all over India and into other countries in South Asia and Africa. Research is her passion, so hopefully this will become her major role. She loves asking questions to better understand markets and customers. It is her hope that with this new understanding, companies can better serve the needs of the people.

part four

Professional Preparation

FIVE STEPS TO ESTABLISHING GOOD OUTCOMES

Christina Garcia

Christina Garcia is a senior program officer for youth at The James Irvine Foundation where she works to increase the number of low-income young people who complete high school on time and earn a postsecondary credential by age twenty-five. The Foundation's mission is to expand opportunity for the people of California to participate in a vibrant, successful and inclusive society.

Getting clear on your goals, charting your course or evaluating options, setting milestones, assessing progress and adapting are reoccurring necessities both professionally and personally.

Are you considering what internship or job offer to take, what project to pursue? You may have a long-term career or life goal—a specific role, impact, or accomplishment you want to achieve. How will your choice in the near term contribute to your long-term goal or help clarify what it is? Or are you just trying to figure out how to have the greatest vacation on the lowest budget?

While there are volumes of literature and guides on setting goals and measuring impact, still the question of how to set good goals and metrics arises frequently, no . . . always. And what is the difference between inputs, outputs, and outcomes anyway?

The theory is straightforward.

- Inputs are what you need to do the work.
- Activities are what you do.
- Outputs are deliverables or products that are created.
- Outcomes are what we hope to achieve and are categorized as short, medium, and long term. Long-term outcomes are often called impacts and can be categorized separately from outcomes.

The challenge is in applying the theory to practice.

We typically have direct control over inputs, activities, and initial outputs because they have finite parameters. You have a certain number of resources (inputs) to work with; with those resources there is a specific amount of work (activities) that can be done, and that work will produce a quantifiable result or reach (output) that can be reasonably forecasted. Inputs, activities, and outputs are what we plan, budget, and implement, and they are the easiest results to measure by counting. But delineating between outputs and outcomes and identifying the right metrics for each is where practical application of the theory starts to get blurry. A logic model provides a systematic way of doing this and can be applied to any situation, from professional projects to planning a vacation to evaluating your work or that of others. Whatever the question (or problem), a logic model provides an objective framework for decision making and mapping and assessing the results. Simply put, a logic model helps us connect the dots between what we want to have happen and what we do.

Follow the following five-step process to make sure your measures will get you to your intended results.

#1 Use a Logic Model

A logic model, also called a logic framework or theory of change, is used to link planning, action, and evaluation and creates a picture of how your project will work. Developing a logic model is the foundation of a good project plan. It enhances the usefulness of evaluation as a management and learning tool by offering better documentation of outcomes and shared knowledge about what works and why.[22]

The visual design of a logic model enables you to develop and analyze your understanding of the relationship between your proposed solution (inputs and activities) and the intended results (outputs and outcomes). Its simple

---

[22] W.K. Kellogg Foundation Logic Model Development Guide: smartgivers.org/uploads/logicmodelguidepdf.pdf.

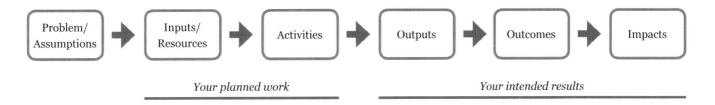

Your planned work   *Your intended results*

design creates an accessible presentation of the project plan that can be shared with others to get input and to cultivate buy-in. During project implementation and evaluation, the logic model is the primary reference point for assessing progress, success, and learning.

#2 Ensure Your Problem Identification Is Culturally Competent

Problem identification is the first step in any design process. Before you can develop a project plan, solution, and expected results, you must first understand the problem you are trying to solve and the environmental conditions or assumptions at play—both the limits and opportunities.

In the social entrepreneurship sector, a core element that must be included in the problem-identification process is culture. Proposed activities and results must be culturally competent to achieve success. During the problem-identification observation process, include the beneficiary community's cultural context as part of the project's assumptions by using a human-centered design approach.

#3 Know Your Goal and Work Backwards

Start with your ultimate dream or vision first. When all is said and done, what do you want to change long term? This is your long-term outcome or impact (seven to ten years, depending on the project), your Big Hairy Audacious Goal (BHAG).[23] Your goal should be concise and compelling, a motivator for you and everyone working on and benefiting from the project.

Fundamentally, the impact or ultimate goal is about comparison. Something is different (better) than it was before—a simpler solution, more efficient, less costly, more sustainable, etc. This is your beacon; every output and short- and medium-term outcome should flow out of and drive toward your ultimate goal or impact. And, your ultimate goal should sustainably address the problem.

The goal of the farm is to improve the health of its local community. Its BHAG is that every family (1,000) in the community has access to healthy, nutrient-dense, affordable food.

#4 Take It One Step at a Time

It is a little harder than it looks. A basic logic model, once completed, lays out a linear progression and relationship of problem/assumptions, inputs, activities, outputs, outcomes, and impacts. The process of completing a logic model is not linear. Getting to a true understanding of your goal (what you hope to achieve) and determining if (and how) it is measurable is often an iterative process. Make sure to build in time for drafting and reviewing goals and metrics before they need to be finalized.

Once you have your logic model "bookends"—the problem/assumptions and the ultimate goal—start by adding in your fixed inputs, the resources (money, time, staff, etc.) that you know you have at your disposal.

Next are the big questions of "what" and "how" your project will reach its intended results.

Counting effort:

- Activities: In order to solve the problem (reach your goal) using your resources (inputs), *what* activities will you implement?
- Outputs: Delivering the activities will produce *what* evidence that will be available to demonstrate the activities were executed?

---

[23] The term Big Hairy Audacious Goal was proposed by James Collins and Jerry Porras in their 1994 book entitled *Built to Last: Successful Habits of Visionary Companies.*

In one year, the one fully stocked and staffed farm (inputs) can grow, harvest, and deliver (activities) 200 meals and 200 food boxes that can feed six low-income families for four months (output).

Measuring change:

- Outcomes: By delivering the activities, *how* will your project lead to the change and intended results in the short and medium term?
- Impacts: By delivering the activities, *how* will your project lead to the long-term change or reach the BHAG?

Every year, the farm provides food to six families for four months (output) that improves the families' nutrition during that same period (outcome) and permanently changes the families' approach to nutrition and diet, increasing their long-term health (impact).

#5 Question, Refine, and Revise

The challenge of measuring change lies in both identifying the metrics you will use to demonstrate progress toward the outcomes and collecting the data. Not everything that counts can be counted, and not everything that can be counted counts (coined by William Bruce Cameron in *Informal Sociology*). The advantage of a logic model is that is provides a clear, objective basis for evaluating if the metrics identified sufficiently link to the outcome and if it is feasible to collect the data with the available resources.

How does food access contribute to community health? How will the farm know it is improving the nutrition and health of the family? What metrics can the farm use? Where will the data come from, and how will it be collected?

A logic model also offers a framework for considering if there are sufficient inputs and activities to reach the ultimate goal.

In order for the farm to achieve its long-term goal in a decade, what changes will be needed? How can the farm increase its inputs, outputs, and outcomes to achieve its long-term goal? If this is not feasible, does the farm need to revise its impact goal?

Once you have your logic model and related metrics, the best way to know if your metrics and outcomes drive toward your goal is to solicit external input, including that of the beneficiaries you are trying to serve. A completed logic model should be easy to explain and easily understood by others. Pay attention to the reactions and feedback of external reviewers: where do people get confused, excited, concerned, and why? Look for ways to simplify and clarify the problem/assumptions, the goals, and the related metrics. Refine your planned activities as needed to get closer to your intended results.

DECIDING WHICH OPPORTUNITIES TO JUMP ON

Editorial Team

Before you decide to engage in a professional activity, research what you are getting yourself into and if it is the right fit for you. What are you putting into the program, why, and for how long? What do you want to get out of it, and how? This chapter lists common educational and professional development programs and questions to consider through the decision-making process. Before you accept a major job opportunity, you will also want to refer to the salary and compensation brief in this book.

Types of Opportunities

#1 Internship

An internship is a full-time or part-time work assignment for one academic term, most often completed over the summer. It might be paid or unpaid; it is all up to the career field and the employer. For instance, the US Agency for International Development offers both paid and unpaid internships across many of their offices. Interns might work on monitoring programs in global health, or staffing an office abroad, or researching federal legislation in Washington, DC. Government agencies, nonprofits, and companies all use internships to "test drive" and train prospective full-time hires.

#2 Cooperatives

A cooperative is a full-time paid job with one employer, usually over multiple academic terms. Students typically alternate between work terms and school terms, often resulting in a five-year degree program. Many schools offer these programs, and majors at some universities even require co-op experiences. For instance, Drexel University heavily incorporates cooperative education into their curricula, and most students use a five-year degree path that results in three six-month terms of employment usually with a single employer. This means that while co-ops and internships can start out very similarly, long-term co-op students often end up with more pay and experience and in more senior positions that transition directly into entry-level hiring.

#3 Apprenticeship

An apprenticeship is a full-time, paid position under the supervision of a tradesperson or professional. It could include a combination of on-the-job training and related classroom instruction that covers both the practical and theoretical aspects of an occupation. Apprenticeships can take place after secondary education, after undergraduate university, or even after graduate school; the key point is that the apprentice is working directly toward a qualification and has qualified mentor(s) with experience in the job. For instance, World Vision offers postcollege apprenticeships in sectors ranging from peace building to childhood spirituality. Precollege apprenticeships are more popular in Europe, where many organizations sponsor them, including a few international aid organizations.

#4 Volunteering

A volunteer position is an agreed-upon time commitment to contribute to a task or cause, either for free or in exchange for payment other than money. Many people take volunteer opportunities that allow them to continue their current life and career, such as building houses for Habitat for Humanity or volunteering to manage a food bank. Other volunteer opportunities involve domestic relocation or international travel, and these typically do involve money because they do not enable another full-time job. Volunteers may have to cover these costs themselves or may receive a scholarship. For instance, WorldTeach programs place volunteers in schools from China to Costa Rica by charging some money up front and returning it throughout the volunteer year as a living stipend. Some of these programs also include scholarships or are completely funded by the host nation's government.

#5 Service Program

A position in a service program is typically a full-time, low-paid position for nonprofit or public sector organizations. The normal focus is on improving the quality of life for underserved communities. These programs blend into full-time volunteer opportunities but designate programs that do not have significant up-front costs to volunteers. For instance, the Peace Corps is run by the US government which directly provides a living wage to volunteer teachers and development professionals. Teach for America is a similar nonprofit that relocates volunteers to teach in underserved schools within the US. These schools determine volunteers' salaries as well as health and retirement benefits.

#6 Fellowship in the Field

Fellowship in the field is a short- or long-term, full-time appointment usually offered by a specific sponsoring organization to graduate students. It is likely to focus on the professional development and leadership experience in the given field and typically includes a stipend. This makes fellowship programs more targeted than unpaid overseas volunteer roles. For instance, fellows with the Acumen Fund receive intensive leadership training and work directly with the senior management of their partner organizations.

#7 Professional Association

A position with a professional association is typically a part-time, optional commitment to an organization aligned with a particular profession. The opportunity would be for a specific position within the organization as it works to further the related profession, the interests of individuals engaged in that profession, and the public interest. For instance, in college you might be the programming chair of Engineers Without Borders and travel abroad to prototype agricultural devices. During your professional career, you might serve a few terms as the treasurer of your local American Society of Mechanical Engineers.

#1 Outputs and Outcomes from the Opportunity

Congratulations! You have received one or more of the above offers! Now you need to decide which opportunity to take or which one will benefit your future the most. Assessing an offer can be stressful and should never be taken lightly. Whether you will be working for a particular employer for a few months or a few years, we have broadly classified important factors to consider: (1) outputs and outcomes from the opportunity, (2) alignment with values and goals, (3) finances, (4) workplace environment, and (5) personal factors. In addition, each type of opportunity has its own considerations.

Before you start looking deeper into an opportunity, consider what value it could add to your life or career.

- How will this opportunity help you grow professionally and personally?
- How will this opportunity improve your résumé? Does it open doors to other opportunities?
- Does the program have any licensing, board, or certification requirements? Is it reasonable and worthwhile for you to meet them?
- What tangible outputs will you walk away with (publications, certificates, etc.)?
- What technical and/or professional skills will you gain?
- Will this opportunity help you network with like-minded people? What reputation does the organization have?
- Can you get a new, valuable mentor from this opportunity?
- How did alumni of this opportunity continue in their careers afterwards? What jobs did they get, and what paths did they follow?
- Can you speak with anyone who has been through this opportunity? How was their experience? How do they answer these questions about it now? What do they wish they had known beforehand?

#2 Alignment with Values and Goals

Before you commit to any organization, you will want to understand its goals. Even if you are only a small part of its big picture, make sure it is a part in a picture that you want to play.

- Do your opportunity's core mission, vision, and values match up with your personal values and goals?
- Do the opportunity's ethics align with your sense of right and wrong? What is the culture of the organization like?
- What skills can you offer to this organization? Does this position make good use of your skills?
- Are you passionate about the work you could do? Will you be proud of it?
- Will this opportunity challenge you? Will it let you be creative and give you a sense of accomplishment?
- Do you believe you will enjoy the day-to-day duties of this job? Are there ancillary duties that are not in the main job description but are still required?
- Do you think you will be an overall good fit with the company?

#3 Finances

Remember that money is one of the more difficult practical considerations for any opportunity. Your time and energy are limited. Do not overcommit to the point where you cannot pay your bills!

- Is this opportunity paid? What is the salary and benefits package?
- Is funding contingent on something? Will you need to write your own grants?
- Is the proposed salary and benefits package acceptable for your specific skill set and goals? What are the specific terms of any proposed contract?
- How much money do you need to live at your expected lifestyle?
- What is the cost of living in the area? Is there affordable housing nearby? Are you willing to commute? How far?
- Is there potential for promotions or raises within this opportunity?
- Are this opportunity's products or services positioned to survive an economic downturn?
- What type of expenses are required out of pocket?

#4 Workplace Environment

Consider that even if the outcomes and organization are the best you could hope for, remember that you do have to work in this place every day (or as often as you are committing). Also consult the travel section in the salary and compensation brief if you will be living abroad.

- Do you feel comfortable with the workplace environment? What is the dress code? What does your office space look like?
- Where is the opportunity located? Is it an urban or rural environment? How do you feel about the living conditions?
- Will there be international travel?
  - Have you considered that you may not like all aspects of a host culture?
  - Have you considered that international development might not be as glamourous as you may perceive it to be?
  - Are you prepared to work with people who speak only the native language?
  - Can you handle living in an area with scarce sanitation? Are you aware of the high possibility of sickness?
- Do you feel comfortable around the coworkers and supervisors you met onsite?
- What type of time commitment can you make? Is there any necessary prejob training? Are you willing to undergo this training, particularly if the position is unpaid or part-time?
- How long are the workdays? Are the hours flexible or rigidly structured?
- How big is the organization? How is it structured, and are you comfortable with the level or lack of hierarchy?

#5 Personal Factors

Consider what else is important in your life, and try to assess these facets against your answers above.

- To what degree do the above factors (outputs, values, finances, work environment) matter to you? How would you weight each of them?
- How does this opportunity affect your personal relationships? Do you want to be close to family and/or a significant other?
- What do other people say about this opportunity?
- How do you like to work, and how do you best perform? Do you like working in teams or alone, with rigid schedules or creative milestones? Do you work well without clearly defined direction?

Summary

No job, organization, or employer is perfect. Consider your answers to all of these questions, but in the end it is up to you to weigh what is most important in your life and career and make the trade-offs. Jump on the opportunities you decide to, but remember to periodically ask yourself these questions as your career and each opportunity continues to develop. Good luck with whatever decision you make!

OVERVIEW OF FORMAL DEGREE PROGRAMS

Sarah Ritter and Dustin Ritter

Both Sarah and Dustin Ritter received their BS and PhD in biomedical engineering. After completing his postdoctoral training in the Department of Chemistry at Penn State, Dustin joined BioMagnetic Solutions, LLC as a senior scientist. Sarah is an assistant professor in the School of Engineering Design, Technology, and Professional Programs at Penn State and recently spent time in Zambia with the Humanitarian Engineering and Social Entrepreneurship Program. While they spent most of their time during graduate school in the lab conducting research, Sarah and Dustin did escape to Rwanda for a summer where they worked in the country's largest teaching hospital.

Successful social innovation and international development will require close collaboration of individuals with different backgrounds and various education levels. Certain career paths may require a minimum level of education (e.g., master's degree or doctorate for academia) while others may be less restrictive (e.g., entrepreneurship). Some of the more common degrees associated with social innovation and international development are provided below, along with a brief description of the educational experience, the average cost and time required, the skills that are acquired, and possible career paths.

#1 Bachelor's Degrees

The bachelor of science (BS) and bachelor of arts (BA) degrees are the most commonly granted degrees and typically require three to five years of full-time study to complete. Some universities also offer bachelor of applied science (BASc) degrees. Commonly, these degrees are the minimum expected for careers in social innovation and sustainable development. The average annual cost of attendance at public institutions can range from $20,000 (in state) to $33,000 (out of state), while private universities are significantly more costly (averaging $43,000). However, financial assistance is quite common, with most full-time undergraduate students receiving some aid. The purpose of a bachelor's degree is to focus on a major field of study while gaining introductory knowledge in a variety of subjects. Many undergraduate students will study abroad where they can build cultural competency and learn how to work in uncomfortable and/or resource-constrained environments. After obtaining a BS or BA, one should possess broadly applicable skills (e.g., written/verbal communication) to prepare them for the next step, whether it be entering the workforce or continuing on to pursue an advanced degree. Aside from technical positions in industry, those with a bachelor's degree may work in business, sales, or management consulting. This education level is also appropriate for those seeking fieldwork positions; for instance, 90% of volunteer positions within the Peace Corps require a bachelor's degree. However, for some programs, a higher degree might be required (e.g., USAID Global Health Fellows Program).

#2 Master's Degrees

The one- to two-year master of engineering (MEng) degree is focused on coursework and application of technical knowledge as well as development of leadership and management skills to prepare students for industry and fieldwork positions. Because the MEng degree does not require research or completion of a thesis, it is not well suited for continuing on to a doctorate. Graduating with an MEng could lead to job opportunities such as those in management consulting, technical consulting, information technology, and within engineering or medical device firms.

The master of science (MS) degree is a two- to three-year degree comprising coursework and research that can either serve as a stepping stone to a doctorate or as a terminal degree. Annually, one could expect to pay an average of $10,000 at a public institution and $23,000 at a private institution; however, a number of funding sources are available, including fellowships and assistantships. MS students acquire skills such as designing and carrying out experiments, technical writing of scientific papers, public speaking, time management, dealing with failure, and working within a budget—skills that are very relevant for careers in social innovation and international development. Graduates with an MS can expect similar job prospects as those with an MEng, but with a focus more toward the research and development aspects of industry, as well as opportunities to enter academia.

A master of public health (MPH) degree is typically a two-year, full-time program that focuses on areas such as biostatistics, epidemiology, environmental health, health policy and education, and social and behavioral sciences. Programs typically require students to complete a practicum experience, providing an opportunity to apply classroom knowledge to a real-world setting. Graduates with an MPH may seek positions in research, health education, or disease surveillance within nonprofit or for-profit organizations, hospitals, and academic settings.

Although a master of public policy (MPP) and a master of public administration (MPA) have many similarities (e.g., both are two-year, full-time programs), the MPP focuses on the analysis and evaluation of public policies while the MPA focuses on the implementation of these policies. Graduates with an MPP or MPA are well suited for careers as policy or budget analysts, program coordinators, researchers, and managers in government, industry, or nonprofits.

If pursued full-time, a master of business administration (MBA) is a two-year degree that focuses on developing the skills necessary for business and management careers. For the highest-ranked business schools, the cost of tuition alone can range from $50,000 to $60,000 per year. Fortunately, financial aid is available, and some companies may even cover some or all the costs for employees seeking an MBA. Individuals with an MBA are well qualified for executive and senior-level management positions, entrepreneurial ventures, and consulting.

#3 Doctorates

Earning a doctor of philosophy (PhD) requires completion of both coursework and original research to develop expertise in a particular field. On average, a PhD requires five to seven years postbaccalaureate, although this is highly dependent upon the course of the research and whether a master's degree is obtained first in a related field (not always required). Annual expenses for tuition and fees are the same as for the MS, though funding prospects tend to be better for those pursuing a PhD. One must develop and execute a research plan, disseminate findings (in scientific journals, at conferences, and ultimately as a dissertation), and defend his or her work as a novel contribution to the field. In addition to further developing the skills obtained in the MS, PhD students are usually involved in mentoring junior researchers, writing grant proposals, and in general, learning how to gain expertise in an area to solve a complex problem. While obtaining a PhD has traditionally been associated with joining the faculty at a university, the percentage of those who pursue this path is on the decline, especially in STEM fields. However, other career opportunities certainly exist and include research scientist positions in industry, national labs, or academia; technical consultants; positions within nonprofits and government (research or policy); a writer or reviewer of patent applications; and upper-level management positions.

For those with professorial aspirations, additional postdoctoral training is becoming widely accepted as the intermediate step required to transition into academia after obtaining a doctorate. This temporary position—commonly referred to as a "postdoc"—enables one to obtain additional training in a specialty area, typically under the supervision of a more senior researcher or advisor. Compared with a PhD student, a postdoctoral scholar is expected to perform more independent research, produce more scholarly publications, and often take a more active role in the grant-writing process. These appointments typically last for one to two years and pay an average annual salary of roughly $43,000. It is important to note that no degree is granted upon completion of one's postdoctoral training.

Having obtained a bachelor's degree, one may attend medical school for four years to obtain a doctor of medicine (MD) degree, the first of a number of steps to become a medical doctor. On average, the total cost of an MD degree is over $225,000 at public institutions and nearly $300,000 at private institutions. Medical school is then followed by three to seven years of residency (varies by specialty) under a senior physician and an optional one- to three-year fellowship to gain additional experience in a subspecialty. One must then become licensed in the state in which one wishes to practice medicine. Aside from traditional clinical practice, an MD may work in public policy (e.g., nutrition or health-care financing), nonprofits (e.g., Doctors Without Borders), medical informatics, research and development (e.g., pharmaceuticals), hospital administration, teaching, and consulting (e.g., for government, medical device manufacturers, or biotech and pharmaceutical companies).

After obtaining a bachelor's degree, one may pursue a juris doctor (JD), or law degree. A JD is a three-year degree and costs on average between $23,000 and $42,000 per year. Aside from learning the "ins and outs" of the law, other skills acquired during law school include written and oral communication, negotiation strategies, and the ability to research, teach, and counsel. Similar to practicing medicine, it is required that one pass the bar exam in the state in which one would like to practice law. With a JD, one may enter into private practice, academia, administration, financial planning, consultancy, or politics, as well as work for the government or nonprofit agencies.

#4 Joint Programs

It is worth mentioning that some programs allow two degrees to be obtained concurrently, which can endow one with very unique qualifications to set oneself apart. As an added benefit, the combined programs can often shorten the time to receive the degrees while allowing one to diversify his or her specialties. Some popular examples include an MD/PhD, PhD/MPH, MD/MPH, MBA/PhD, and MBA/MPP. Additionally, a JD could be combined with an MBA, MPP, or PhD. With any set of degrees, the recipient could choose to continue on to a career in either one of the specialties or within a niche field that combines the two.

ESSENTIAL LIBERAL ARTS COMPETENCIES

Susan Knell

Susan Knell is the director of Penn State's College of the Liberal Arts Career Enrichment Network, with the mission to enable liberal arts students to live a fulfilling life by enriching their education and connecting them to resources that expand their career opportunities. Prior to her current role, she served as director of Penn State's Science Career & International Education Office, connecting science majors to a range of global and professional opportunities.

An interest in social innovation and international development is not enough to ensure professional success; preparation and a focus on building your skill set should start long before you enter the field. In addition to your STEM education, here are ten liberal arts competencies you need to develop as you are considering careers in this field:

#1 Communication Skills

The ability to write clearly, speak articulately, and interact effectively with people from a wide range of cultures and backgrounds will be critical to your success. There are a variety of ways to develop these skills, ranging from specific courses focused on communication to involvement in extracurricular activities and professional organizations that allow you to develop and hone these abilities.

#2 Language Skills

Language includes many cultural values and norms; it is not just a matter of learning new vocabulary and pronunciation. This is true even in English where different English–speaking countries use different words to capture the same idea. Embracing a new language will provide you with insight that will not be available to you if you conduct all your interactions in English. Whether you choose to pursue a minor, take advantage of online language-learning resources, or connect with a native speaker to learn and practice a new language, the benefits will be well worth the time and effort invested.

#3 Global Competence

How do you know you want to work in international development if you have no global experience? Study abroad, participate in international service-learning opportunities, and/or volunteer with organizations working in the region of the world that interests you. Direct, hands-on experience in a global setting will give you a perspective that would be difficult to achieve through any other means. Learn how to travel lightly and connect with your host country and culture in a meaningful way.

#4 Professional Work Experience

Gain experience and develop your skill set through a range of professional work experiences. Learn how to work with colleagues in an office setting. This could be with nonprofits, government entities, or the private sector. It does not matter if your title is *intern*, *co-op*, or *volunteer*; the most important factor is to identify the skills you want to develop and then match that with an opportunity. At a minimum, you need to gain experience working in a professional office environment, both as part of a team and leading independent projects. Gain exposure and experience with office dynamics and various types of organizational structures and supervisory styles. Want to develop stronger business skills? Then maybe an internship or co-op in the private sector could help you with that. Interested in gaining exposure to nonprofits? Then seek out agencies working in areas that are meaningful to you, and ask about volunteer opportunities. Be intentional about your experience; consider what you have to offer and what you want to learn, and be clear with prospective employers about your interests.

#5 Empathy

You want to help people, but to do so, it helps to be able to relate to their feelings and put yourself in their position. Understanding another's perspective will help immeasurably in determining the type of support or assistance you can provide. One way to develop your ability to put yourself in another's shoes is through reading, discussing, and attempting to gain an understanding of the human condition from a multitude of perspectives. This could be accomplished through courses in sociology, psychology, area studies, languages, or literature where you have the opportunity to consider the perspective of another and how that perspective can affect interactions.

#6 Entrepreneurial Mindset

Every job deals with finances in some way. Whether you are involved in making money, raising money, or spending it, having an appreciation for the ways in which financial processes work and money is tracked will be useful. That does not mean a business major is required, but completing a minor or even elective courses in accounting, management, and/or marketing can provide you with a good foundation for considering how to develop, track, and position your projects with external constituents.

#7 Contextual Understanding

An understanding of the environment, the cultural norms and mores, and the history of a place can be critical to the development and success of a project. This understanding can be achieved through the study of history, anthropology, sociology, or languages and area studies. This could be as a major, minor, or simply through fulfilling general education requirements.

#8 Ethical Decision Making

Develop the ability to identify a problem, closely examine the facts in the case, identify possible options, and then test, review, and decide on a course of action. Ethical decision making means taking into consideration professional standards, your ability to defend your decision, and whether or not your choice does less harm than other possible alternatives. Consider the effects of the decision with all relevant facts and possible consequences in mind in a methodical way, rather than rushing to the decision-making phase without all the necessary factual information or consideration of potential consequences for those involved.

#9 Resilience and Adaptability

Engage in experiences that force you to stretch outside your comfort zone and learn how to not only succeed but thrive when things do not go as expected. This could include serving in a leadership role in a student organization, working on an entrepreneurial project, or just being involved in team-based projects. When things do not go as planned, be conscious of your ability to come up with other possible ways of tackling the problem. What other possible solutions could you apply that will get you the result you are seeking? Put yourself in new situations and embrace the unexpected things that happen as a result.

#10 Teamwork

It might be tempting to complete class group projects on your own because you can control the timeline and quality of work. To be most successful though, you need to learn to work as a member of a team, communicating expectations and timelines in a professional manner, being accountable and holding others accountable for the quality and quantity of work. From class group assignments to student organizations to sports teams, seek a variety of team activities and learn how to work through some of the common hurdles experienced in team settings.

Closing Comments

These competencies can be developed throughout your undergraduate educational experience by challenging yourself to complement your educational experience with a range of academic minors or by choosing to pursue multiple majors in diverse academic areas. Choose your general education courses strategically to gain exposure to different ways of thinking and to improve your communication skills. Pursue language learning, either independently or in combination with a study-abroad or global experience, which often can help you to complete a language minor. Get involved in campus and/or volunteer activities that develop your entrepreneurial mindset. Seek opportunities to connect with people from diverse backgrounds through clubs, student organizations, or even in classes. Ask questions, listen to their answers, respond thoughtfully, and try to put yourself in their shoes. Look for classes that combine more than one of these skills—a course that includes some entrepreneurial activity in a very team-focused learning environment, for example.

Not sure where these kinds of opportunities might be? Then ask your academic adviser, your career services office, your faculty members, and your fellow students, in addition to using the Internet to identify campus resources that meet your needs and interests.

Finally, self-reflection is an important skill to master as well, so spend time thinking about what you have done, ways in which it might have been done more effectively, and the values and biases that may have impacted the outcome. Develop your professional presence, which includes the way you present yourself physically (i.e., dress and personal grooming) and your interactions with people. For example, small things like a firm handshake, an email signature line, and respectfully crafted communications say a lot about you as a professional. Fellow professionals with more extensive knowledge will respond positively to you as you share your knowledge gained from research and coursework and consider how to apply that knowledge in practical ways. Application is not the final stop though; careful evaluation, assessment, and refining of the process indicate a true professional. Knowledge of yourself—your abilities and shortcomings, your strengths and areas for development—will mark you as a successful, competent professional in the field.

GRADUATE SCHOOL: LAUNCHPAD FOR AN IMPACTFUL CAREER

Kunal Parikh

Kunal Parikh is an NSF fellow and Roche scholar working at the interface of science and translation within the Center for Nanomedicine and the Center for Bioengineering Innovation and Design at Johns Hopkins University. He has founded companies in tech and biotech and also built and served as the executive director of the Social Innovation Lab at Johns Hopkins University where he developed global partnerships and advised dozens of mission-driven entrepreneurs.

At its best, graduate school can be a launching pad, providing you with an opportunity to immerse yourself in your passion, develop new skills, cultivate a wide network of advocates and colleagues, and build the foundation for the rest of your career. At its worst, graduate school is an exchange of several years of your prime and hundreds of thousands of dollars in expenses and lost wages for a few additional letters next to your name and entry into a stagnant job market. Below are some tips to help you make the most of your time in graduate school.

#1 Develop and Abide by Your Own Personal Inventory

The key to success in graduate school is focus. However, this may never be more difficult for you to achieve than while in a university setting where you will continually discover new people, opportunities, and interests. Avoid decision paralysis and maintain your focus by creating your own personal inventory: a collection of your life mission and passions, strengths, and weaknesses, and a unique set of filters. If an opportunity pushes you closer to your ultimate objectives, leverages your core competencies, and fulfills your own personal criteria (e.g., improves public welfare in your hometown, lies within your moral compass, allows you to work with people whose company you enjoy, etc.), then continue to investigate. Otherwise, forward the opportunity to a colleague who might find it suitable. Reevaluate your personal inventory every six to twelve months as you gain additional experience and insights.

#2 Build and Protect Your Reputation

While earning your professional degree, you will be surrounded by some of the most talented individuals in the country. How do you separate yourself from those with better grades or more experience? With your reputation—the quality of the work you produce and manner in which you behave and communicate. In every interaction, develop your reputation for speed, dependability, integrity, curiosity, and generosity. Most importantly, develop a reputation for following up and following through. Keep your promises and commitments. This will immediately distinguish you and provide you with more flexibility and greater access to opportunities.

#3 Know the End before You Begin

Through the first two decades of your life, you are given problems and expected to work through to the answers. Seek to change this paradigm whenever possible during graduate school and into your career. Always start with the expectations or ultimate objectives (answers) in mind and then work backwards to develop a plan of action. If the expectation is for you to publish three peer-reviewed journal articles and a book, choose your projects and activities accordingly. If your ultimate objective is to become a tenure-track faculty member at a top-tier research university, learn what these universities look for and about the path of successful candidates. Leverage this knowledge to set your own trajectory.

#4 Remain Cognizant of Needs and Motivations

Maintain constant vigilance regarding the driving forces present in your environment. What is guiding your partners, your advisors, or your department or college? Everyone has problems and internal motivations. Solving their problems will make you indispensable; being aware of their motivations will prevent you from working with the wrong people, falling into traps, and wasting your time.

#5 Apply "Lean Startup" to Explore Opportunities

When potential interests arise, apply "lean" principles to efficiently conduct due diligence and fully validate the opportunity. Time is your most important resource, and it must be protected at all costs. Prior to committing to a new activity, field of research, or career path, think about the quickest and cheapest way to obtain the knowledge or experience you need, whether it means reading a book, conducting interviews, interning with a potential employer, or starting a company. Apply 110% of your effort. If you uncover gold, continue to push forward. If you find dirt, pivot immediately.

#6 Form Deep Relationships at Every Level

It is absolutely critical that you spend time developing a number of diverse relationships while earning your degree. Find higher-level advocates who may not be able to spend much time with you, but who can vouch for you, make introductions, and recommend opportunities. Pick and build relationships with mentors who have succeeded or failed at the sorts of things you would ultimately like to do and that truly care about you as a person. When you are ready to undertake projects and build something, find partners who are talented, have integrity, and whose motivations are aligned with yours. Curate a network of supportive peers with whom you can share and learn. Pay it forward by sharing your knowledge and expertise with your own group of mentees. Ultimately, this may be the most important lesson and the greatest driving force behind your success both in graduate school and in your career.

#7 Build Something

You will learn more from building something, whether it is a medical device, a student organization, or even a cleaning company, than from any textbook or lecture. Experiencing the ins and outs and growing pains of building something will provide you with invaluable experience that you can leverage in any career. Regardless of what it is, make sure that you obtain hands-on experience building something on your own or while leading a team.

#8 Leverage Every Possible Resource

When you have found something you truly want to build, investigate every possible avenue to fuel it and to make it successful: human capital, funding, resources, intellectual capital, etc. Universities, their surrounding communities, and their alumni networks have everything. Never hesitate to ask for help or to cold call for something you believe in.

#9 Be Patient

Your career is a marathon, and so is your graduate-school tenure. Play the long game when it comes to your classes, your research, your relationships, and your projects. Pass on opportunities that are not a fit, invest in your growth, and build habits for long-term success.

#10 Keep Your Core Strong

If you enrolled in graduate school to obtain a degree, make sure you earn one. Everything else you do is unimportant if you are unable to meet your degree milestones. The most successful students are those that excel at what they are supposed to do while leveraging the remainder of their time and resources to build capabilities and opportunities for the future.

SHOULD YOU GET A PHD?

Toby Cumberbatch and Pritpal Singh

Toby Cumberbatch is a professor of electrical engineering at the Cooper Union in New York City. His principal interests are developing engineering practices to address the real needs of people in remote, rural communities through Engineering for the Middle of Nowhere.

Pritpal Singh is professor and chair of the electrical and computer engineering department at Villanova University. His research has ranged from solar-cell materials development to battery state-of-charge and state-of-health determination. Over his thirty-year career in academia, Professor Singh has been involved in many international development projects, including the design and implementation of a solar water-pumping system in the Dominican Republic, running a solar business in India, and the development of a tele-health project in Nicaragua.

You are at a crossroads, trying to decide whether to pursue your PhD or to start your professional career right away. Let us assume you have a technical background and are considering graduate programs in the US with tuition being waived and receiving a monthly stipend. Typical PhD programs start with one to two years of classes, followed by two to four years of research. Doctoral programs are a long-term commitment that can have a significant impact on your career trajectory. Hence, you must think deeply about this decision.

A PhD program teaches you how to define an original problem and gives you time to think about how to develop an original solution. It provides you with opportunities to acquire extra skill sets, such as programming and data science, that you may not have acquired during your undergraduate education. Most importantly, a doctoral degree teaches you how to work independently and persist in the face of political, technical, and institutional obstacles. After publishing their dissertations, new PhDs emerge with a strong work ethic, a confidence to be able to persist through challenging problems, and extensive experience in integrating information, subjects, and disciplines. This preparation provides PhD graduates with a strong foundation to embark on careers in international development and social enterprise.

Five Reasons to Get a PhD:

#1 To Become a Subject-Matter Expert

Undertaking a PhD gives you the chance to spend roughly five years focused on studying your favorite subject in great depth while devoting a substantial amount of your time to original research. You will not have either the time or the money to do much else, so you need to really love your subject. It is a fantastic experience to touch the absolute frontier of human knowledge in your one small area. The skills acquired are highly transferable and valuable when seeking opportunities for innovation, both in comprehending problems and in developing well-researched, well-tested, sustainable solutions.

#2 To Learn in a Focused, Dedicated, Disciplined Manner

Because PhDs spend a lot of time working independently, and often in isolation, you need to be able to motivate and organize yourself and bounce back from the inevitable setbacks. The appealing aspect of working autonomously is the feeling of achievement following a research breakthrough, thorough comprehension of a topic, or delivering an outstanding dissertation presentation. Earning a PhD is developing a set of skills to *produce* knowledge—to iterate on the scientific process and engage with the scientific community. This includes conducting in-depth literature reviews, developing innovative data-collection methods, designing statistically sound experiments, finding or creating metrics, communicating results, managing personalities, and sufficiently addressing a need within a field of research. There will be technological, academic, personal, and professor-based setbacks over the course of your PhD educational journey. Successfully navigating this process will be challenging, tiring, and at times deeply frustrating— but ultimately rewarding when success is achieved.

#3 To Meet Requirements for Certain Jobs

Rightly or wrongly, a PhD has become the de facto qualification for some careers. Engineers can start practicing and innovating with a BS (increasingly an MS is required), but in the natural sciences, it is common to require a PhD and one or more postdoctoral appointments to qualify for scientific research positions. If you want to teach at a university, in most cases a PhD is required. Many senior staff at large bilateral and multilateral organizations have doctorates, and the number is increasing.

#4 To Get on the Fast Track

A PhD gives credibility that helps you gain access to resources and be fast-tracked to more senior posts with overall better prospects in all kinds of organizations. To put it another way, obtaining a PhD is a little like taking out an insurance policy—it can give you a lot more freedom in career choice. You do not necessarily need it, but it is good to have it, and it does not make you overqualified for a position that you might want.

#5 To Build Your Network

Universities, particularly those with strong brand recognition, are amazing connectors of people and resources from diverse disciplines. As a PhD student you will enter an intellectually stimulating forum. You will have the opportunity to attend research seminars, national and international conferences, and in the process, meet many interesting people. You should take advantage of these opportunities to learn about new topics (they could stimulate new ideas for your own research) and to connect with the people that you meet. This network of contacts can provide you with new friendships, respected colleagues with whom you can dialogue about your ideas, and contacts for job opportunities.

Five Reasons Not to get a PhD:

#1 Because You Have Nothing Else to Do

Just because you are academically talented and always enjoyed school and your subject matter does not make you a good fit for a PhD. Embarking on a graduate program just because you want to keep studying is not a good reason to undertake a PhD. If you are uncertain, get a job outside academe when you graduate. This will help you think through your reasons for investing four to five years of your prime in earning a PhD.

#2 Because You Want to Become an Entrepreneur

You do not need a PhD if you want to be an entrepreneur, though it might help you get access to resources. Look no further than Steve Jobs or Bill Gates. Go back in history and look at a majority of the giants of industry. Two of the best known, Tesla and Ford, had no advanced degrees. Completing a PhD will certainly help you acquire the skills already mentioned, but the degree itself is not a prerequisite to being a successful entrepreneur. For that you need a brilliant idea, passion, and tenacity.

#3 To Be Well Compensated (Financially or Academically) for Your Work

Although you do get a stipend that enables you to eat and have some sort of housing, you will not be making income to put away and save. Furthermore, funding is typically tied to grants or academic semesters and therefore can be inconsistent and unreliable. It may be difficult to know that most of your undergraduate classmates are working for an income, buying houses, or going out on the town while you spend at least four more years in school. Further, while others are climbing the corporate ladder and gaining positions where they are better compensated for their work, you will continue to be treated as a student, learning and gaining knowledge on behalf of your advisor and university. Many of the roadblocks within the PhD will have little to do with your actual research work. Further, it is important to manage your ego throughout the process as your work will not be perfectly correlated to the credit you receive. However, if you choose a field of research that you intend to work in upon graduation, the knowledge, networking, and thesis will significantly elevate your credibility throughout the course of your career—but that seldom applies to your salary. To be highly compensated, you might want to join a financial institution, as many PhDs do.

#4 To Get Three Letters after Your Name/To Be Called a "Doctor"

This is probably the worst possible reason! You must be passionate about the learning that accompanies a PhD. Without a genuine interest in the material and the process, you are wasting your time and that of everyone else. You have to be interested in building a set of skills and expertise to challenge important problems in your field. The PhD letters might help with credibility when forging new relationships and applying for grants, but the true value of the PhD is the expertise, the academic networking, the results of the project that you spent several years spearheading, and the passion you developed for the subject.

#5 Because You Have In-Demand Technical Skills or Are Already an Expert

If you already have strong technical skills that meet the needs of a desired position, then you probably do not need a PhD. A PhD is much more than a high-level technical training course. It requires you to complete intellectually demanding research. If you only want to sharpen technical skills, you may be frustrated by the amount of literature review, writing, communication, and synthesis expected by a doctoral program.

In short, if you want to pursue a PhD, you must do so because you have an intellectual thirst for learning and knowledge—a desire to answer a question that no one else has answered and the tenacity to pursue this in the face of extreme adversity. You must do this knowing that the financial reward is tenuous at best, and the only satisfaction you might receive is a standing ovation at a conference or a frequently cited paper. Your major source of satisfaction is knowing that you had a degree of success and that, through this success, you grew as an individual and gained skills that will serve you well in your chosen career.

HOW TO EVALUATE AND SELECT A GRADUATE PROGRAM

Rachel Dzombak and Steve Suffian

Rachel Dzombak is currently pursuing a PhD in civil engineering at the University of California, Berkeley. Her research focuses on mechanisms of sustainable development and design of scalable systems.

Stephen Suffian is currently pursuing a PhD in electrical and computer engineering at Villanova University, Villanova. He is researching information-driven flexibility options for electricity grids with high penetration of variable and uncertain renewable energy sources.

When deciding to pursue a graduate degree, most people face three nagging questions: (1) What degree should I get? (2) What specific area should I focus on for coursework and research? (3) How do I go about finding the right program and university? Graduate school is a significant investment of time, money, and energy; you want to be sure your decision will advance your career! This chapter outlines ten things to consider when choosing a graduate program. Fair warning: we repeatedly nudge you to email or call people to ask questions. We cannot stress this enough. Grad school is the time for you to get proactive about your education. Find opportunities for yourself and dive right in because no one is going to do it for you.

#1 What Is My Passion?

Remember when you were a kid and people asked you, "What do you want to be when you grow up?" Well, it is likely you are still asking yourself that question if you are in college and will continue to do so during, and after, grad school. If you get a graduate degree, it ought to be in something that (1) you are passionate about, and (2) will land you in a career you want. Grad school is an investment and comes with substantial costs. You will be back in school. That means homework on nights and weekends, team projects with incompetent partners, and plenty of additional academic hoops. You will not have much money to travel. You will have to live where the school is located. Is your passion working on information and communication technologies for development (ICT4D) with a focus on East Africa? Before those warm Kenyan nights, you may have to spend two to three years battling winter storms in Ann Arbor, Michigan—so you should be sure before you commit.

Relative to undergraduate education though, you will be happy to find that there is far less time spent on work outside your field of interest. Master of public health programs do not need some basic meteorology class just to fulfill a science requirement. Instead you will spend your time deeply immersing yourself in your chosen field. So if you do truly love what you are doing, graduate school is an exciting step toward that endeavor. Ask yourself again and again, "What do I want to do?" Your answer will most certainly evolve over time, but it will help you decide whether you should make the commitment to graduate school.

#2 How Long Do I Want to Be in School?

Depending on what qualifications you already have and the type of program you are looking into, you could be in school for anywhere from a year to almost a decade. One-year master's programs have recently been on the rise. While these programs can be a good value, they are often quite intense, cramming the content of a two-year program into one. Dual-degree programs are also on the rise (e.g., a joint degree in public health and urban planning), and those programs typically last three years. For professional programs, MBA programs are a standard two years, law school lasts three years, and medical school is four years followed by a four- to six-year residency. Consider how long you want to be in school, what training you will still need after school (such as medical residencies, postdocs, or clerkships), what flexibility you want while enrolled, and whether you want summers off to pursue internships or work experiences. That said, attending graduate school will require some lifestyle changes. You may have to take out loans to pay for the program. If you are lucky enough to get paid to attend school, you still will not have a lot of personal income. Your friends working in the "real world" will make more than you. Period. They also will not have homework. Reflect on how these sacrifices will affect your life and how long you can tolerate them before you commit to a program.

#3 How Does Your Undergraduate Education Align with Graduate School Aspirations?

Graduate programs typically have very specific application requirements, with some requiring certain undergraduate degrees and many others requiring the completion of certain prerequisite coursework. If you are looking into graduate programs that closely align with your undergraduate work, these requirements will have been naturally met. However, if you are hoping to pivot your career aspirations or are looking into interdisciplinary programs, you must pay very close attention. For example, say you were in the humanities and now want to go to business school. Some programs require you to complete a college-level calculus class and a course in microeconomics. If you do not have these on your transcript, you may have to enroll in a local community college to get the credits you need. Every program is different, so it is important to make sure that you qualify before spending the time on an application. You do not want your application to be denied or acceptance to be revoked at the last minute simply because you are missing one class.

#4 What Classes Do I Want to Take?

Classes again. Depending on the program you enter, they are either incredibly significant or a nonfactor in your decision. If you are pursuing a PhD, you may think classes are simply an obstacle to overcome before diving into your research. However, if you are entering a professional or master's program, your classes and professors are much more important. First, you can always look online to see what classes a university offers. Normally, they are found at schedule.<school>.edu. If that does not work, just Google "[School Name] Schedule Fall 2017" or whenever you will be starting. Look through what is offered and check to see whether the classes you want to take actually count toward program requirements. This is sometimes difficult to figure out and can change from year to year, so do not be afraid to call the department and explicitly ask about which classes count. Does the program allow you or (better yet) encourage you to take classes from other useful disciplines? Then check out those classes, too. Make a list of the classes that sound the best to you, and then email current students or the professors to ask for more information. Read through syllabi and course descriptions. Will you love every class you have to take in your program? Probably not. But you should enjoy and be interested in most of them. Remember—you are pursuing your passion! It is not about going to school just for the sake of getting a degree. Unlike what many say about undergraduate studies, the skills you acquire will most likely be directly applicable in your day-to-day job post-graduation.

Additionally, many grad students get the opportunity to work as a teaching assistant (TA) or graduate student instructor (GSI). While the thought of teaching may cause some of you to panic, others find the prospect exciting. Teaching allows you to share knowledge of your favorite subjects with younger learners and gives you the opportunity to hone your communication skills and prove how well you understand the content. It can also be a chance to connect with a faculty member you admire, and it may help cover part of your tuition or other costs. When considering graduate programs, look for what undergraduate courses you could see yourself teaching in addition to what graduate courses you want to take. If teaching is something you definitely want to do in graduate school, ask current students whether or not the option is available. If it is not, that is one more program you may be able to cross off your list!

#5 With Whom Will I Be Working?

It is important to think about this question from multiple perspectives. You want to find people who not only share your interests, but who also have complementary working styles and are pursuing similar career paths—or at least agree that the program would help someone on such a path. The level of control that you have regarding your peers and advisor is dependent on the type of program that you are looking into. This question as a deciding factor is most applicable for master's, PhD, and other programs that include research advisors or collaboration with students outside your graduating class.

You should choose a program because of an advisor, not the other way around. Your advisor will be your primary point of contact into the broader academic, administrative, and in some cases employment world; sometimes, they may even become a lifelong mentor. It is critical to find an advisor who is interested in your personal success, whether that be academia or industry. Prior to applying to schools, prospective applicants should contact potential advisors by phone, email, or personal meeting. Look at professors who have recently published research in your domain. Read their papers. Are you interested in writing similar publications? Pursuing similar interests? Following a similar career path? Really spend time analyzing what the day-to-day work would look like. Do research well beyond a professor's website. Two professors may both work in a similar field, have the same "research interests," and maybe even attend the same conferences. However, their work could vary greatly in terms of theory versus practicality, data analysis versus conceptual analysis, or whether their students end up in academia or industry. While you will have some leeway in your research topic, the closer it aligns to the interests and direction of your advisor, the simpler the process will be. Knowing their research will also give you a great starting point when you contact professors.

If at all possible, talk to the current students of prospective advisors. This will enable you to learn about the professor's working style, the successes of past students, the career goals of current students, and the typical opportunities in the lab, such as conferences and publications. You can also see what the day-to-day work might be like there. Try to gain a more realistic expectation as to what your experience will be.

#6 With Whom Do I Want to Surround Myself?

Every program has a culture. For MBAs, there are the case studies, networking events, and weekend parties. In engineering programs, it is solitude and homework, followed by labs and conversations about research. Design programs are known for long hours in the studio, real-world project work, and critique sessions. When you are selecting a program, go to the visitation days that are available, but also look for other opportunities to experience the school. Talk to the students currently in the program. See if you can crash on their couch for a night. Email them as many follow-up questions as you have. Some important questions you can ask students include:

1. What do you really like about this program? What do you not like about this program? What do you wish you could change about the program?

2. Do the students hang out outside classes? Are people game for grabbing a beer on Friday, or does everyone do their own thing?

3. How often do you meet with professors? Are they accessible?

4. From where do most students enter the program? Industry? Straight from undergrad? Peace Corps?

5. How much flexibility do you have in tailoring the program to your interests?

Also think about the location of the program and the general community that you will join. You will be in school for several years, so you want to live in a place where you can grow both academically and personally. Would you prefer a rural or urban setting? What weather do you prefer or despise? What activities should be accessible for you to do when you need to chill out after a marathon of lab work? A graduate program can be extremely stressful, and at times you will need to fall back on friends, hobbies, and your personal interests outside school in order to stay sane. However, at the end of the day, you are going to school. Do not blind yourself to the faults and red flags of a program simply because it is in a desirable location.

#7 What Resources Does the University Offer?

Grad school is an opportunity to dive into a program and the larger campus ecosystem. You will have fewer distractions than you did in undergrad and more time to devote to building your professional identity. What opportunities in and around the school you attend will help you do this? Ask lots of questions, but remember that the program officers are trying to recruit you to their school. Make sure you talk with current students—they often have more honest insights! Some important things to look for are:

1. Events and resources on campus: Often programs or departments will have a weekly seminar. Are the speakers faculty members from the school or other institutions? Do people from local industries come on campus? (What local industries exist?) Look up the website for the school's career services office. Does it seem to focus on undergraduate job placement, or do they have resources for graduate students as well?

2. Multiple disciplines: Does the school specialize in a given field? Or does it have diverse strengths? For instance, I was looking to attend graduate school in engineering, but I still wanted to take MBA, law, and policy classes. When visiting schools, I was sure to ask how easy it was to enroll in courses from other disciplines and whether or not they would count toward my degree.

3. Ecosystem opportunities: What ecosystems exist on campus that you can plug into? Some programs may have a history of research turning into startups, others may be closely attached to large corporations, and still others may be focused on placing students into internships with the government. Some schools have easily accessible funding for conferences and travel. If you are interested in conducting research in developing countries or jump-starting ventures there, travel funding is an extremely important factor. Think about what you may want to do and how the school can help you to achieve it.

#8 What Career Paths Do Graduates of the Program Pursue?

It may be difficult to think about your graduation already, but it is important to remember that the purpose of your graduate degree is to prepare you for your career. Schools have different levels of relationships with corporations, nonprofits, multilaterals, and other organizations. Say you are passionate about tech entrepreneurship. Is there going to be a mountain of Silicon Valley firms recruiting at a large state school in the Midwest? Probably not. Alternatively, will you have many nonprofits focused on agriculture recruiting at an urban liberal arts school? Also no. School programs will often tend to be focused around their local academic, industrial, and government opportunities. After that, look more specifically at the strengths of the schools you are applying to. Ask the program director if you can be connected with successful alumni or how often companies come to campus and what networking opportunities the school sets up. It is your career after all. And as previously stated, grad school is an investment. It is up to you to make it a good investment.

#9 How Will I Pay for the Program?

Financing your graduate degree will depend on what degree you pursue and where you pursue it. If you want to get a PhD in engineering at a private, well-endowed school—yes, you will get paid to go there without having to look for your own funding. If you want to go to medical school, you will probably need to take out a lot of loans. Exceptions exist. For almost every discipline there exist options to get your degree paid for if you commit to serving low-income communities for a period of time. While we cannot provide a comprehensive overview of every scholarship out there, we can give tips about how to improve your chances of securing fellowships and scholarships.

1. Show your interest: Schools want to reward students who want to be there. If you are really passionate about a program, make sure the admissions officers know that! Visit the school and set up times to meet with the fellowships office. Write them an email and tell them exactly why you are a perfect fit for that program. Prep ahead of time for meetings and ask really great questions. Half of success is just showing up. Most people will take opportunities for granted. If you enthusiastically show your interest level, you will be ahead of the curve. At the same time, if you know you are not interested in a program and have no intention to attend the school—tell them that. There is no point stringing anyone along.

2. Write a good essay: I cannot stress this enough. No matter how stellar your college GPA or GRE scores were or whether you have done wildly impressive things, you will be judged again and again based on essays. This is true both for applications to schools themselves and to fellowships. And the thing is, everyone procrastinates and writes their essays at the last minute. Last year I had a friend ask me for advice about applying for a major graduate student fellowship. I told her to start early and have as many people as possible read her essays. In the weeks leading up to the due date, I kept offering to read her essays and provide feedback. She finally sent me her draft the night before it was due. At that point, you cannot help too much. The goal of your essay is to tell a good story. Anybody should be able to read your essay and understand the value of it. Therefore, give it to multiple people (your mom, a professor, your boss, or a good friend) to read and critique. Each reader will have different insights and will strengthen your chances of producing a great essay.

3. Have your act together: Applications to grad school and fellowship opportunities require a lot of logistical planning. You have to get test scores and letters of recommendation sent, get transcripts from institutions you maybe have not attended in five years, and fill out the same biographical information multiple times. It is tedious. There is a lot of room for mistakes. Successful applicants have all their information to the intended recipient by the deadline if not well before. You do not want to be discounted for a major scholarship just because you forgot to remind a former professor to get their letter of recommendation in on time. You may feel like you are harping on people, but you have to play the game, and they know that.

#10 What Is the Brand Recognition of the Program?

Graduate school is your last degree. Unless you are going to get multiple master's degrees (which probably is not as useful as it sounds, except in certain cases) your graduate degree is what will stand on your résumé as your final education record. Therefore, it should mean something. Think about the alumni network of the school and the brand recognition. When you say, "I got my master's *here*," are people going to respond by saying, (1) "Wow! That is a great program," or (2) "Hmm, I have never heard of that school"? Global or national brand recognition may not matter as much if you want to work in the location or specialty near the school, but you still want to be recognizable in that community. And if you are pursuing a global career with a large corporation or multilateral agency, or if you want to build credibility as an entrepreneur, you may want a compelling degree from a prestigious school.

SHOULD YOU GET A MASTER'S IN BUSINESS ADMINISTRATION (MBA)?

Stuart Merkel and Dave Lenze

Stuart Merkel is the director of corporate and foundation partnerships at Jhpiego, an international, nonprofit health organization affiliated with Johns Hopkins University that is dedicated to improving the health of women and families. Stuart is committed to designing and delivering innovative programs in low-resource countries targeting issues such as maternal health, malaria, HIV, and family planning. He got his MBA while working at Jhpiego and has worked and traveled throughout Africa, Asia, and Latin America with a particular emphasis on urban health in Africa.

David Lenze is director of the Applied Professional Experience Program at Penn State's Smeal College of Business. He works in the area of engaged scholarship with a particular focus on the development and implementation of experiential learning opportunities for graduate and undergraduate students. Originally trained as an architectural engineer, Mr. Lenze has over twenty years of corporate and consulting experience in the areas of project delivery, program management, strategic planning, and business strategy

A master of business administration (MBA) is a widely recognized and respected, practical, vocational degree that prepares individuals with the knowledge and skills needed to effectively manage a business. MBA programs often specialize in one area (e.g. finance), but a core set of topics includes corporate finance, regulation/tax, marketing, personnel management, business communication, leadership, and strategy. Many of these areas can prove extremely useful for STEM professionals. This is particularly true if they are interested in a management position within a traditional STEM company or in diversifying their experience to make a social impact either domestically or internationally. Nearly all the knowledge and skills one acquires in an MBA can be useful within a social enterprise. Net Impact highlights programs that offer an MBA with an emphasis on social impact.[24]

Ten reasons you might consider an MBA degree:

#1 To Accelerate Your Current Career

Early career success for many STEM professionals is driven by their technical abilities, but as they move up in their careers, many find that they lack leadership and management skills they need to excel. Successful professionals acquire these skills as they move from being a team leader to project leader to program leader and beyond. However, an MBA can accelerate this acquisition while serving as a visible credential that indicates leadership potential and ambition. The MBA credential and the skills it represents set you apart from your competition, both within your company and when applying for a new job.

#2 To Change Your Career Path

Unlike most graduate degree programs that enable students to go deeper into a specific area of study, an MBA is typically designed to provide students with broadly applicable knowledge and skills that can be applied to a wide variety of fields and disciplines. For example, a person who is working as a medical device design engineer can use an MBA degree as a means to move into business development in the biomedical device industry. Alternatively, they might make a larger change and move into financial services or strategic consulting. However, as with anything, an MBA is just a building block and does not replace experience. STEM professionals should not see an MBA as a wholesale "ticket" into international development or social impact.

#3 To Earn More Money

MBA programs (particularly full-time ones) can be very expensive. At the same time, MBA graduates significantly increase their earnings. The 2013 Graduate Management Admissions Council (GMAC) Alumni Perspectives Survey

---

[24] Net Impact's list of top social impact schools: netimpact.org/business-as-unusual/top-50-social-impact.

indicated that MBAs recouped an average of one-third of their financial investment immediately and managed a 100% return after four years. However, it is important to note that "typical" post-MBA career options (e.g., investment banking) pay significantly more than jobs in the social impact and sustainable development arena.

#4 To Gain More Job Security

Holders of advanced degrees have significantly lower risks of unemployment. According to the US Bureau of Labor Statistics (as of April 2015), the unemployment rate among holders of professional degrees (business school, law school, and medical school) aged twenty-five and older was the lowest of all categories at 1.9%. Holders of doctoral-level degrees were next at 2.1%, with the nonprofessional master level at 2.8% and bachelor level at 3.5%. This is in large part because the MBA teaches practical aspects of business management and is seen as a strong credential for business professionals. While an MBA by itself does not provide more job security, with the right complementary experiences and connections, an MBA can be an important differentiator for securing or retaining a job in the sustainable development arena.

#5 To Obtain Leadership Skills and Perspective

Strong MBA programs are designed to help their students develop as business leaders (as opposed to developing as technical specialists). Key points include learning about different leadership styles, consciously developing your own leadership style and leadership skills, and embracing an enterprise or organizational perspective. These strengths become particularly important when individuals move into organizational leadership roles and fully transition from a technical expert to a business leader. This is also important in large nonprofits and other organizations that have adopted business cultures and operations.

#6 To Learn Business Fundamentals That Are Important in All Companies

Many STEM professionals work in roles dealing with the business issues of their firms. They are asked to balance return on investment, technology adoption, organizational efficiency, change management, and supply chain optimization into their work. Yet most lack formal training in these areas. MBA programs typically have a set of core courses designed to provide their students with business fundamentals in the areas of finance, accounting, marketing, supply chain, and management. These business tools enable STEM professionals to more effectively engage with the "business side of the house" even when they are in primarily technical roles.

#7 To Add Value to Efforts Addressing Social Challenges

One of the most important barriers to advancing health and other social outcomes is successfully introducing and mainstreaming low-cost products that can benefit the poor. New technologies require a mix of people and skill sets to succeed: technical excellence as well as business modeling, market analysis, financial planning, execution planning, and general business savvy. A STEM education with an MBA and experience in the social sector can be a tremendous value-add to the team.

#8 To Facilitate Cross-Sector Partnerships

Particularly in international development, the way of the future to addressing poverty is partnerships among sectors—businesses and nonprofits, governments and businesses, and so on. Understanding and speaking the language of business is critical to making real advancements in social outcomes. A STEM professional with a social impact background may find that an MBA helps them "translate" between/among people who may not otherwise understand each other. This in and of itself is not enough to justify getting an MBA, but it is a benefit to explore.

#9 To Access Networking Skills and the Business School Network

Building a network of professional relationships is critical for career advancement. Strong MBA programs teach their students how to effectively develop, foster, and utilize professional networks. Moreover, MBA holders often cite the relationships made during the program and their connections to alumni and faculty as being instrumental to their career success. This can be particularly important for individuals who wish to start their own business or nonprofit. Additionally, knowing people who will eventually become leaders in their respective sectors—marketing, finance, and strategy—will help you advance your own career and social mission in the future.

#10 An Inherent Bonus of an MBA Is to Learn about Personal Finance

Regardless of your career, an MBA will force you to understand the world of finance, which can be very powerful for your personal financial outlook. There are many other (cheaper) avenues to learn about personal finance, and an MBA should not be seen as a personal finance course. But if you are interested in other aspects of an MBA, you have the added benefit of grounding yourself with a solid understanding of finance—how money works, and how you can make money work for you.

Potential pitfalls for a STEM professional considering an MBA degree:

#1 You Can Get Lost if You Do Not Know Where You Are Trying to Go

For individuals looking for a career change, an MBA can be a great tool. However, it is important for a person to start business school with a reasonably clear idea of what they want from the experience and where they want their career to go. For people "looking to find themselves," the pace of the academic experience along with the breadth of opportunity can be overwhelming. As with any educational experience, an MBA is a stepping-stone to other things. If you do not know where you are trying to go, it is hard to pick the right stepping-stones that will get you there.

Think carefully about what you intend to achieve. For some, a technical master's degree (e.g., master of public health) can establish excellent credibility in your intended field and might be more helpful than an MBA. Talk to people in the field you want to go into to gauge their reaction to the value-add of an MBA in their field. Some parameters to consider:

1. If you want to be an entrepreneur, a good starting point is to assess your ability to learn and adapt as you go. Experience—including failure—can be an excellent teacher. An MBA will give you a great head start on some aspects of entrepreneurship (at a huge expense) and maybe a little more credibility if you are seeking external funding for your new business/venture. Many entrepreneurs hire MBAs to run the businesses for the ideas they have.

2. If you want to work for a large organization focused on social impact or international development, an MBA will likely give you skills to help your organization grow. However, success will happen only with the right accompanying experience. A STEM career plus an MBA does not 100% prepare you for success in a large organization in international development.

3. If you want to work for a small startup or a small nonprofit, an MBA may be extremely valuable in that it could give you wide exposure to the operational aspects of the business. This can be a handy complement to your technical (STEM) background, and depending on the nonprofit, your value-add to the business side may be enough to warrant having you "learn on the job" in the social impact arena.

4. Is it about building a network only? While an MBA is certainly a great path to a network of friends and potential colleagues and advisors, you do not need an MBA to build a network. Depending on what you want to achieve, simply making a point to find venues in your area/city can be very effective in building up a network. You have many options: become active in your community, join young professionals groups, join clubs of unlike minds via Meetup.com, seek events targeting startups, etc.

#2 You Can End Up in the Wrong Program Very Easily

There are many options in the MBA marketplace: full-time residential programs, online programs, part-time programs, executive programs, and programs that combine multiple aspects. MBA programs vary widely by general reputation and ranking, strength in specific niche fields or industries, curricular structure, and selectivity. The experiences and the cost (in terms of money, time, and forgone income) can also vary widely. It is therefore important to invest the time to decide what you want and then research your options carefully. An MBA program with a stellar reputation can be a wonderful opportunity for some, but if it is not a good enabler of your career goals, it would be a major mistake to enroll in it.

#3 An MBA Is Not a "Ticket" into International Development

An MBA can be *part of a plan* to move a STEM professional into social impact or international development. The credential can itself be a strong entry point to having your résumé reviewed. However, international development organizations (as with other sectors) often place heavy emphasis on experience within the sector. In many cases, your experience will matter much more than your degree after working for a couple years. Therefore, STEM professionals should not see an MBA as a "ticket" into international development. Rather it is one building block that needs complementary experience, networking, and passion.

SO YOU ARE THINKING ABOUT BUSINESS SCHOOL?

Jailan Adly

Jailan Adly is the director of MBAs Without Borders at PYXERA Global. In addition, she has managed various corporate global pro bono programs for companies including IBM, FedEx, John Deere, Medtronic, SAP, and Novartis. Prior to joining PYXERA Global, Jailan was the deputy director of Rising Sun Energy Center, a workforce development organization in California, and she has extensive experience creating, facilitating, and managing workforce and leadership training programs. Jailan has an MA in tourism and a BA in international affairs from The George Washington University. Twitter: @PYXERAGlobal, @MBAsWB, @jaiadly

Business school is not cheap. If you are contemplating a career in social impact, your road out of debt is going to be far longer than those of your peers who are heading to Wall Street. Business school is a major investment. Before signing on the dotted line, consider these six things when choosing a school.

#1 How Strong Is the Alumni Network?

Most MBAs will tell you that the most valuable thing that came out of their B-school experience was the network. If you want to improve or gain skills in accounting or finance, there are less expensive ways to do so than going to business school. The experience is an investment. So if you are going to spend money, do so wisely. Invest in a network that will help you achieve your goals.

When you are considering schools, find out how engaged their alumni are. How accessible are alumni to current students? Are most of their alumni investment bankers, or do they have diverse backgrounds and networks that you can tap into after you graduate?

#2 How Diverse Is the School's Faculty?

It is important to have faculty who come from different backgrounds to enrich how you think about business. The diversity of faculty experience is critical. What is the ratio of faculty who come from a strictly academic background versus those who have real-life, practical experience? Theory is phenomenal, but when it comes to business, learning from those who have been in the trenches is just as—or even more—valuable.

Does the school enlist faculty who have started their own business? Business professionals who have failed themselves bring wisdom that comes from experience. Do professors showcase only the multinational corporate lens, or do they have experience working with small and/or social enterprises? Are they well versed in understanding how business develops and succeeds across various countries around the world, including emerging and frontier markets? Do they recognize the importance of behavior economics when exploring how to serve base-of-the-pyramid consumers?

#3 Does the School Encourage Design Thinking?

Often people mistake "design thinking" for the idea of making a product beautiful, but design thinking is much more than that. In the social impact sector in particular, there has been a recent shift toward using human-centered design to successfully create products and services for base-of-pyramid consumers. From sanitation and water-filtration products to agriculture and health-care distribution systems, human-centered design is showing positive results when compared to traditional development models. Forming a deep understanding of the user and their needs enables businesses to design products and services that truly meet their needs. Understanding design thinking is becoming a coveted skill by employers.

#4 Are Experiential-Learning and Global-Immersion Experiences Built into the Curriculum?

The truth is no classroom experience will ever teach you as much as tangible work experience. The practice of summer internships is commonplace, but most top business schools have taken this a step further by including experiential learning in their curriculum.

Business schools at Stanford University, University of California Berkeley Haas, and The George Washington University all offer consulting practicum courses in which students work with a company or organization in a consulting capacity. Haas's flagship global management consulting program provides students with the opportunity to work with organizations around the world and to work in person with their clients for up to one month. Four years ago, Harvard Business School launched one of the most ambitious programs to date in which all 900 first-year students participated in a global-immersion experience.

Global-immersion programs are increasing among leading business schools. However, if you graduate from a school without this offering, many organizations, including MBAs Without Borders, a program that I lead at PYXERA Global, offer direct experiential-learning assignments. MBAs Without Borders matches talented business professionals to skill-based consulting assignments in emerging and frontier markets. MBAs Without Borders advisors gain an experience that delivers a skill set and level of cultural understanding that cannot be acquired in a classroom.

#5 What Will Your Classmates Bring to the Table?

The diversity of experiences and backgrounds of your classmates are just as—if not more—important than those of the school's faculty and alumni. Most of your assignments will be team-based. The depth of your education will not come from textbooks, but rather from what you learn from and with your peers. You want to work with people who see the world through a different lens and who will expose you to different perspectives. You want to surround yourself with people who push and challenge you. Business school can be a great place to meet a potential business partner, especially if you are looking to use your time there to launch or refine a business plan.

#6 Research the Research Centers

Research centers are like your great-grandma's family recipe. It is a school's special sauce. They enable business schools to take a deep dive into specialized topics and to distinguish their thought leadership from other schools. Social entrepreneurship, global startups, impact investing, or corporate responsibility? Take the time to identify the schools that have robust research centers in the topics that interest you most.

While these considerations are specific to business school, they are not far from considerations one should explore before jumping into any kind of graduate program. Graduate school is a major investment that will not necessarily mean more money or a shortcut to your dream job. As with all decisions, what may be right for one person may not be for another. Take the time to talk to other social impact professionals, learn about their path, and then ultimately choose the one that is right for you.

SHOULD YOU GET A MASTER'S IN PUBLIC HEALTH (MPH)?

Anoop Jain

Anoop Jain is the founding director of Sanitation and Health Rights in India (SHRI). SHRI fights alongside communities to eliminate open defecation as a key step in the struggle for health equity and economic and social justice. Anoop Jain is an Echoing Green fellow and won the Global Citizen Award in 2014. He received his MPH from Tulane University School of Public Health and Tropical Medicine in 2013.

The twentieth century saw tremendous improvements in population-based health outcomes. Scientists developed vaccines that led to the worldwide eradication of smallpox. Family-planning efforts in the United States helped women achieve desired birth spacing while decreasing child mortality. Laws were enacted to improve workplace safety, which now prevent occupational hazards that were responsible for death and disease.

Unfortunately, billions of people still endure the undue burden of health disparities. Over 600 million Indians defecate in the open because they have no toilet, exposing the public to 100,000 tons of untreated, disease-spreading fecal waste. The 2014 Ebola outbreak in West Africa killed over 10,000 people. The obesity epidemic in America rages on as many inner-city residents live in food deserts without access to healthy, nutritious meals.

By pursuing a master's in public health (MPH), you will be on the frontlines of the effort to alleviate health disparities that account for so many unnecessary deaths and maladies every year. You will gain knowledge needed to help design health-care systems that can directly prevent outbreaks such as the one witnessed in West Africa. You will be able to design interventions that not only build toilets in rural India, but also motivate communities to use them. An MPH will arm you with the tools to fight for global health equity.

An MPH takes a minimum of one academic year to complete, but many students finish over two school years. You will pick your own concentration based upon your interests. For example, you could elect to concentrate in a field such as biostatistics, epidemiology, community health, environmental health, health policy management, or maternal and child health.

Four Reasons to Get an MPH:

#1 Learn the Hard Skills You Need to Pursue Health Equity and Social Justice

Many social ventures, NGOs, and multilaterals are trying to solve the world's most pressing health challenges. Mobile-health startups help doctors connect with patients living in last-mile villages. Sanitation organizations help prevent water-borne illnesses by improving access to toilets. International multilaterals such as UNICEF improve child health by promoting carefully crafted health-education curriculums. Funders are willing to support game changers in any corner of the Earth. But these funders are looking for leaders with the hard skills needed to drive real change.

An MPH will help you gain these invaluable skills. Courses in epidemiology will train you to understand the burden of disease in a particular location. This will help you communicate the need for services more effectively. Courses in biostatistics and impact evaluation will help you quantify the change your intervention is making. Classes in community and behavioral health will help you understand the best way to motivate people to use the services you are offering. Combining all of these skills will enable you to drive the change you so passionately believe in.

#2 Understanding the Root Causes of Disease

MPH degrees are uniquely designed to help students understand the root causes of disease. For example, India's sanitation crisis is predicated on landlessness, corruption, endemic poverty, and pathetic behavior change efforts. This is counter to widely held—and misguided—beliefs that people in India continue defecating in the open because of a simple lack of toilet infrastructure.

Understanding these social determinants of health is critical to successfully operating a social venture that hopes to change key health outcomes. This information will inform how you approach a particular health problem. It also enables social entrepreneurs to be more responsible in their efforts. Too much of today's development work takes the form of one-off solutions that do not fit into a nation's or community's broader health planning. By understanding the root causes of disease, we are able to design interventions that truly prevent the onset or furtherance of morbidity. This understanding will enable you to attack the root social, political, and economic causes for illness. Additionally, that big-picture understanding will train you to engage with communities. Instead of simply pushing a new medical device onto a market, you will be able to facilitate community-based change that also targets these root problems. That collaboration will be essential to your work.

#3 Gain Cultural Competency

Let us face it. The reason so many of us are able to even embark on journeys of affecting social change is because of our privileged backgrounds. Our incredible support networks make the journey so much easier. A local villager concerned with feeding her family does not have the luxury of serving others. Unfortunately, our good intentions are often devoid of the local perspective so desperately needed to change health and social outcomes.

Attending an MPH program will help you gain access to a diverse world of students of all ethnicities and backgrounds. Doctors from Ghana, nurses from Egypt, community health workers from Indonesia, and directors of non-profits working in America's troubled inner cities all matriculate at MPH programs. These people will be your colleagues and thought partners. They will provide you a lens to look through, enabling you to understand what solutions work where. If a solution is not culturally appropriate, it will fail. Use your time at an MPH program to learn how to best tailor interventions so that they fit the needs of the communities you support.

#4 An Opportunity to Network

One of the most understated benefits of attending an MPH program is the fact that so many midcareer professionals come back to earn this degree. This offers young students the opportunity to understand what it takes to be an effective change leader. These midcareer professionals will be your friends and project partners, but relationships can last long after you have walked across the graduation stage. Many midcareer professionals will go back to their jobs at the World Health Organization, UNICEF, the World Bank, and the Gates Foundation. Nurturing your network with these individuals can offer entry to the world of multilateral funders and other vital resources for your work.

This networking opportunity also applies across many other colleges and programs in your university. For instance, if your university has social entrepreneurship curricula, you will have access to training and guidance for starting your own social ventures. You will also be able to apply for funding opportunities that are not available to nonstudents. Additionally, you will be connected to thousands of students in all different disciplines. Students from the medical school will help you understand whether doctors could actually use your medical device. Business school students will help you design your business plan and understand the financial viability of your proposed intervention. Engineers will help you design your intervention so that it best fits local needs. The best part about all of this is that these resources are free!

Three Reasons Not to get an MPH:

#1 Disasters Need Doctors and Nurses

Masters of Public Health are rarely first-line responders during emergencies. The skills acquired in this degree mean that you will likely watch a disaster unfold from the sidelines as doctors and nurses treat the sick. This was the case in the 2014 Ebola outbreak. As the number of patients continued to grow out of control, doctors and nurses from around the world assembled in West Africa to provide patients and victims with the treatment they so desperately needed.

The lack of frontline applicability is a frustrating reality for many with an MPH degree. While you will belong to the community of global health workers, your skills will be most useful after the storm has passed. It is then that you can assist governments in building robust health-care systems to prevent similar outbreaks from occurring in the future. You can help identify what caused the outbreak in the first place. And you can help build community resiliency through health education so that communities do not need to rely on foreign aid. Consider what you really want to contribute as a global health professional.

#2 An MPH Is Very Expensive

Most graduate programs in the United States are extremely expensive. Many students have to take out tens of thousands of dollars in loans to help pay for their advanced degrees. In the case of business school, medical school, and even law school, this can be worth it because postgraduation salaries in those fields are quite high. This is not the case for public health workers. You will likely be working for a state or government agency that relies on fickle grant funding. Or you might work for an NGO, again with a limited budget, which will not be able to pay you anywhere near what you might earn as a doctor or lawyer. This makes the burden of taking out loans for an MPH that much more daunting. You will have to come to terms with the fact that being a public health worker is a thankless job. But if this is the profession you want, never let the meager compensation cause you to doubt the saliency of what you are doing.

#3 Your Faculty Have Different Challenges and Motivations

MPH candidates go into their programs bright-eyed, believing that they have finally stumbled on a field of academia that will couple their passion for health equity with the skills needed to effect social change. While this is not untrue, your advisors may make you question this. Public health professors are no different from professors in other fields; they must publish research to maintain their jobs. They will conduct thorough studies on how corruption in India is inextricably tied to poor child health outcomes. They will use robust research methods, employing randomized control trials to substantiate their findings. These methods are resource intensive and require community participation. Unfortunately, there is no guarantee that a researcher will translate findings into action. The publishing of a paper often means that a researcher can just move on to the next issue or topic, without committing to act on what she found. This is an incredibly discouraging truth about the field of public health. As an MPH candidate, your advisor will likely be this kind of professor. Do not go get your MPH if you think you are going to find a mentor who is equally passionate about translating research into action. The pressure of needing to publish to keep a job is far too pressing. Make it your job to use their work for real social change!

SHOULD YOU GET A MASTER'S IN PUBLIC ADMINISTRATION (MPA)?

Francisco Noguera

Francisco Noguera leads the Social Innovation Lab at Compartamos con Colombia (CCC). CCC is a nonprofit organization based in Bogota, whose mission is to strengthen social ventures and initiatives through sound business and management practices. The Social Innovation Lab mobilizes and facilitates collective efforts to address some of Colombia's pressing social and environmental challenges. Before CCC, Francisco worked with the World Resources Institute in Washington, DC. He holds a BA in industrial engineering from Universidad de los Andes and an MPA from Columbia University's School of International and Public Affairs.

So you are now a college graduate, maybe with a STEM degree or maybe not. You might have some work experience, or you might be looking to start your professional career. What you are sure of is that you want to make a broader impact, see the bigger picture, and maybe move past the profit concentration of a degree like master of business administration (MBA). There is another, newer choice: a master of public administration (MPA). The MPA is essentially the public sector equivalent of the MBA, covering policy making as well as economics and management. Moreover, top-rated programs, such as UCLA, Chicago, and Columbia, offer concentrations in a wide variety of humanitarian issues. MPA graduates with concentrations in health policy, urban poverty, education, or international affairs go on to serve as managers at many levels of government in the US and abroad. Alternatively, you might use your MPA (or master of public policy as it is sometimes called) to work in a nongovernmental organization, other nonprofit, or even a for-profit with a social mission.

Like many of you reading this piece, I studied engineering. After graduating, I started on a conventional business career path. My quantitative skills served me well, first in investment banking and then in management consulting. I worked on challenging projects with large corporations and built a solid professional network in my home country, Colombia. However, as I worked with more and more corporations, I began wondering whether my engineering and business background could have larger, more profound application. In particular, I started wondering whether there was anything I could do to improve the quality of life of the many low-income families in Colombia and Latin America.

I was able to switch tracks and join a research institution in the United States, which opened my eyes to the larger field of international and sustainable development. In the realm of social entrepreneurship and social innovation, I found a sweet spot right between my background and my future aspirations to make a social contribution. However, a point came when I felt that my academic background could be balanced with a deeper, more structured understanding of the institutions and rationale behind international and sustainable development efforts. That is when I decided to pursue a master's in public administration (MPA). In the next few paragraphs, I will share with you three key reflections related to that choice.

#1 The World Desperately Needs Systems Thinkers

STEM education gives us the tools and concepts we need to make sense of and tap into forces that govern our natural systems. But there is a bigger picture even than this, a larger field with increasing demand: systems thinking. Put succinctly, systems thinking relates to the ability to identify the nodes (components of a complex system) and the nature of the connections among them. This applies to both natural and social systems and is critical in the world of sustainable development and social innovation. Just like engineering gives you tools to understand the parts of a natural system and the laws that govern them, an MPA will help you understand the institutions and approaches that govern poverty-alleviation efforts. As a result, you will be better equipped to tackle and change these systems from the inside.

#2 The World Needs System Entrepreneurs, Not Only Social Entrepreneurs

Engineers and social entrepreneurs have delivered countless innovations for underserved communities in sustainable and even profitable ways. Electrical engineering drives solar-lighting ventures, and computer science builds Kenya's mobile money system. But social entrepreneurship is just one piece of the puzzle and must be accompanied by a new breed of entrepreneurs—system entrepreneurs. These are the people who are able to affect the existing relationships among key social innovation stakeholders and institutions. An MPA enables a system entrepreneur to not just support solar-lighting ventures, but to navigate the complex regulations and actors in the energy sector as a whole. I believe that the combination of engineering and institutional thinking—provided by an MPA—makes the perfect match to act and be successful in this new arena, understanding both the technical aspects and the institutions that govern solutions.

#3 The World Is Facing Wicked Problems that Require a New Way of Thinking

Engineering gives you the tools to tackle complex technical problems, like how to put a man on Mars. This problem is highly complex, but it can be solved through a rigorous technical process. Climate change, on the other hand, is an example of a wicked problem, which is caused by the complex and ever-changing interactions of multiple stakeholders—citizens, governments, industries, nature itself—none of which can be made solely accountable for its solution. Moreover, these wicked problems are often framed by complex institutions; for instance, climate-change policy is influenced by many NGOs and intergovernmental groups. My humble prediction is that we will be seeing more and more wicked, complex problems in a scale that has been unknown to us until now. They will likely be problems without a single solution, but rather an iterative, collective approach that allows us to solve them progressively rather than definitively. We will need a sound understanding of our natural systems, as well as a clear understanding of the role that institutions play in addressing societal issues. An MPA can equip engineers, the best solvers of our technical problems, with the larger view and understanding needed to tackle these emerging, complex, wicked problems.

Now, if all of this sounds too positive, here is one reason you might not want to pursue an MPA: It may take you far from the fun, practical world of problem solving and drive you to the work of larger institutions, which is often bureaucratic. That said, I think the combination of an MPA with an engineering degree will give you the satisfaction and ability to be effective in both realms.

FULBRIGHT SCHOLAR PROGRAM

Ruth Mendum, Michael Henry, and Shayne Bement

Ruth Mendum is the director of the University Fellowships Office and an instructor in the Departments of Women's Studies and Agricultural Economics, Sociology and Education. She works with students applying to the Fulbright and many other prestigious scholarships and teaches in the area of gender and international development.

Michael Henry completed a Fulbright in Tanzania in 2013–2014, studying novel methods for species determination of malaria vector mosquitoes. He is currently a medical student at Columbia University and hopes to pursue a career studying infectious disease epidemiology and surveillance systems.

Shayne Bement completed his Fulbright experience in 2014–2015, working with the University of Bamenda in Cameroon and accomplishing a variety of technical projects including an advanced method of processing and preserving fresh maize, as well as making improvements to the university farmland irrigation system. He is currently exploring the job market and the possibility of graduate school studying mechanical engineering to further his career in international development.

What is Fulbright?

The US Student Fulbright Program is funded by the US Department of State to support undergraduates, recent graduates, and graduate students. Administered by the Institute for International Education in New York City, Fulbright supports students doing a wide range of independent projects or research endeavors, those who study for master's degrees, and graduate students who are engaged in thesis or dissertation research. Not all program options are available in all countries, and the type of programing available changes and expands each year. There are two designated types of Fulbright applications: the full grant for research and study and the English teaching-assistant grant.

Full Grants

Full grants are the most diverse. Options can range from support for one-year taught master's degree programs in the UK to self-designed independent research projects under the supervision of a local university professor. Countries that offer specifically designated graduate-degree support beyond the UK include Finland, Iceland, the Netherlands, Taiwan, and Australia. Not all of these opportunities include explicit STEM training but may, for example, be in public policy, which can be relevant to some STEM students. STEM students may choose to apply for support to engage in laboratory research in a foreign lab or fieldwork at a specific location abroad.

Three countries have specific opportunities for STEM students. The Netherlands sponsors one student to do research in pediatric oncology. Indonesia's FIRST awards target STEM-qualified individuals in priority areas who want to spend a year doing research, teaching, or projects. Canada has the Canada STEM program, which provides three years of doctoral support for students pursuing a PhD at designated institutions throughout the country.

The Fulbright-Fogarty scholarships support students with medical or veterinary training who work at NIH-designated centers in a select number of low-income countries. Students interested in this program should contact the individual research sites to acquaint themselves with the particular projects as these are ongoing research institutes.

English Teaching Assistantships

STEM students tend not to think of themselves as good candidates for this type of grant, but in fact, the program may be a good fit under certain circumstances. ETAs supplement a local responsible teacher or university professor who teaches English or English as a second language pedagogy. As with any other Fulbright grant, individual countries have varying requirements. Some are happy to support STEM graduates who are interested in supplementing their English instruction with specialized scientific vocabulary lessons. For STEMs headed to graduate school, ETAs offer a chance to practice outreach and broader impact skills as well as to support the internationalization of science. Some countries offer the chance to do small-scale, independent research projects although one should not expect to have access to laboratory equipment.

Application Process

The application process as well as pay and benefits can change from year to year. Currently, enrolled students must apply through their designated Fulbright program assistant at their university if such a person has been designated. Alumni may, at some institutions, also be allowed to seek support from their alma mater and should do so if possible. The application process currently involves an online application where one must write a statement of grant purpose and a one-page personal statement, as well as answer several questions. Three letters of recommendation are required. Project-based grants require an in-country affiliate, and in some instances, proof of language competence may be mandatory.[25]

Support and Expectations

Depending on the country, a Fulbright grant can last from nine months to a full year. Participants are granted a stipend, travel assistance, health insurance, and sometimes tuition waivers. In return, the Fulbright program has one central expectation: that participants truly intend to engage fully with their host country both formally and informally. One should expect to spend a certain percentage of one's time (I always recommend 25%) interacting in a multitude of informal settings beyond the institutional alliances one may have. Fulbright is ultimately about bringing the world together and establishing long-term relationships.

Because of the emphasis on connecting with a variety of people in-country, potential Fulbrighters who are planning to engage in research, especially at the graduate level, should discuss with their research advisors the civic-engagement/outreach aspects of the program. One should not expect, nor be expected, to spend evenings and weekends in the lab or the field to the exclusion of social interactions with locals, including those outside one's field.

On a related issue, many Fulbright countries have language requirements although some can be much more flexible for STEM applicants. Even if one is expecting to work in a primarily English–speaking context, one should make every possible effort to learn the local language for hospitality purposes. One need not, nor always be able to, access formal language education before one leaves the US, but there now exists a wide range of online and distance language-learning options, and one should systematically take advantage of these opportunities as soon as one is certain that one wants to work in a particular country. Some countries provide language training prior to the beginning of the grant period, which enables students to enhance their language skills in-country.

Examples of Fulbright Awards

1. Public Health in Botswana – The Center for HIV/AIDS at University of Botswana and Department of Allied Health Sciences at Botho University are looking for applicants to teach undergraduate or graduate courses in the public health field with topics such as disease coding, medical transcription, epidemiology, and health ethics. Developing curriculum, courses, and training manuals while conducting research is all part of this grant that lasts for nine to ten months.

2. Science and Technology in Rwanda – The College of Science and Technology at University of Rwanda is looking for applicants to teach undergraduate courses in mechanical engineering, industrial or atmospheric chemistry, programming, and software and linear programming in information sciences. Assisting in curriculum, staff development, and conducting research are part of this grant that lasts for six to ten months.

3. Engineering in Italy – The Department of Civil, Environmental and Mechanical Engineering at the University of Trento is looking for applicants to carry out research and to give lectures to master's and doctoral students in atmospheric physics and chemistry, meteorology, environmental protection and management, and energy and materials sciences. Thesis advising and providing support to international students are other duties that will be asked of the candidate during this six-month grant.

Five Reasons to Serve with Fulbright:

(#1 and #2 apply to full grants only. ETAs and graduate programs have much less autonomy; grad programs typically have very clear expectations.)

---

[25] Details for Fulbright applicants: us.fulbrightonline.org/applicants.

#1 You Are Autonomous and Efficient Working without Guidance

The subject of your research, your work partners, and where you choose to live are all completely up to you. It takes a confident, independent person to select a research topic, locate and approach motivated counterparts, and develop a work plan without any outside guidance or preset structure. You will get the opportunity to improve your skills in project management.

#2 You Are Personally Motivated and Committed to a Successful Project

There is no set work schedule, no one giving orders, and no one watching to ensure that goals have been accomplished. It is easy to let a week pass and realize that no significant advances have been made to the research project. And, since Fulbright is a relatively short-term commitment, it is important to stay on task to make the most of the nine-month duration. Additionally, it is not just personal drive that may cause delays, but a plethora of circumstances that can bring any project to a grinding halt. Weddings, funerals, births, traffic, and a thousand other things will arise, postponing valuable work and leaving a Fulbright scholar sitting on their hands. It is their own personal commitment that will continue driving the project forward.

#3 You Are Curious to Explore and Willing to Make Mistakes

For a truly meaningful experience, a Fulbright participant should have a thirst for the world around them. Explore. Talk to people. Ask questions. Take aimless walks. Sit and drink a local beverage at the local bar. Share stories about your life experiences. By cultivating curiosity and treating every day and every encounter as a mini adventure, you will gain small insights toward understanding the culture, its people, and the global human experience. Not only will fostering this kind of understanding help give you perspective in your research, it will undoubtedly result in some meaningful, lifelong friendships and help to cultivate peace and understanding across cultures. The core of the Fulbright program strives to accomplish the "promotion of international goodwill through the exchange of students in the fields of education, culture, and science." It does not matter where your Fulbright might take you or what your project aims to achieve, it is essential that every Fulbrighter be willing to walk out on a limb and experience life in a new way.

#4 You Are Passionate about a Program at a Particular Host Organization

Many things can become frustrating in the course of your extended time abroad, and knowing what to expect will help immeasurably. Not only will a familiarity of your country, research group, and topic make your Fulbright experience go more smoothly, it will make you a more competitive applicant. Having a research affiliation with a group that has many ongoing projects can also help you discover new interests and broaden your horizons, especially if your project is at a standstill. Finally, you may not want to do research on a topic completely new to you during your Fulbright. Not only will you be less productive as a researcher, you may not know how much you enjoy the project you plan on working on.

#5 You Are Seeking a Mentor in Your Field

You will want to establish a relationship with at least one mentor in your research organization; when the inevitable roadblocks pop up in your project, they will help you over them or will give you ideas on new paths to follow. It can help you create valuable connections; you may meet other Fulbrighters who may become colleagues or friends in the future, and you will be able to network with a vast array of government-employed professionals based in your host country if you take advantage of the embassy-access privileges that Fulbrighters have. Your status as an alumni of the Fulbright program will open innumerable doors for you as you have proven yourself to be a committed, independent, curious, adventurous young researcher. You will find upon your return that senior researchers will be excited to talk with you about your experiences and work with you on projects in the future. Few things will give your career a boost as quickly as a Fulbright fellowship, and your professional growth will surely mirror your personal growth.

Five Reasons Not to Serve with Fulbright:

#1 You Do Not Do Well with Navigating New, Uncomfortable Situations

Even arranging housing is a task that is entirely unguided; a daunting task in the Western world, it becomes even more of a challenge in a different country. Navigating the good neighborhoods from the bad, negotiating rent (in a different language), figuring out how to carry furniture from Point A to Point B using unconventional modes of transportation—these are just a taste of the responsibilities of a Fulbright scholar, and on top of everything else, you are still required to develop and complete a meaningful research project while in-country.

#2 You Want Success Right Away

Even when a project is moving forward successfully, two weeks of intense work could result in a dead end, requiring a scholar to retrace their steps and start fresh with the same drive and intensity. While no one may be monitoring how much time and effort goes into the work, it *will* be measured in the success of the project, the state of the relationships between a scholar and their counterparts, and the personal fulfillment of the grantee.

#3 You Are Unwilling to Learn a New Language or Culture

You may find certain customs difficult to deal with in a certain country, or you might discover that it is nearly impossible to function without knowing a certain language. These are challenges that you might not be able to predict unless you have either done significant research on the country or have been there previously.

#4 You Are Unsure You Will Enjoy Working in the Field for a Year

Leaving your life in the US can be harder for some people than others. Doing a Fulbright is a commitment of uprooting your life and what you are used to and culturally immersing yourself abroad while doing challenging work. If you are at all unsure and feel like your commitment is lacking, reevaluate why you want to do a Fulbright in the first place. Although it can be a scary experience, the relationships created with colleagues are lasting and worth the risk of initial discomfort.

#5 You Are Doing It to Pad Your Résumé

The US Fulbright Scholar Program has been operating for the past sixty years and has some unbelievably accomplished alumni. The Fulbright Program has a name that is well known around the world, but you should not do a Fulbright unless it is a good fit for you personally and professionally. One year is a long time if you do not think you will enjoy it since the work tends to fully consume you.

PEACE CORPS

Eric Obeysekare and Liz Ewaskio

Eric Obeysekare is a PhD student at Penn State studying information sciences and technology with a focus on technology use in developing countries. Prior to beginning his graduate studies, Eric served in Peace Corps as an information and communication technologies education volunteer in Cameroon, West Africa, where he taught computer science at a local high school.

Liz Ewaskio served as a Peace Corps volunteer in the Kyrgyz Republic where she taught English in a rural high school on Lake Issyk Kol. In the United States, Liz has worked with Russian–speaking refugees, taught Russian language at the university level, and now works as the Peace Corps representative at Penn State. Liz received her bachelor's degree from Carleton College in Minnesota and her master's degree in Russian from Middlebury College in Vermont.

What is Peace Corps?

Peace Corps is a federal agency that promotes sustainable development and global understanding to countries around the world by sending American citizens to live and work at the community level with peoples of other nations. Volunteers serve overseas for two years in education, health, youth in development, community economic development, environment, and agriculture. Peace Corps provides volunteers with three months of intensive training prior to the two-year service, for a total of twenty-seven months in the country of service. There are currently nearly 7,000 volunteers serving in more than sixty countries around the world. We are recruiting people who have a history of volunteer experience, a desire for adventure, and passion to serve humanity.

Application Process

To be a Peace Corps volunteer, you must be at least eighteen years old and a US citizen. The application process as well as pay and benefits can change from year to year. The application process currently involves an online application, a health history form, choosing locations and projects, and an interview.[26]

Pay and Benefits

Peace Corps is a life-defining leadership experience you will draw upon throughout your life. The most significant accomplishment will be the contribution you make to improve the lives of others. There are also tangible benefits for you personally and professionally.[27]

#1 Living Allowance

During service, the Peace Corps provides volunteers with a living allowance that enables them to live in a manner similar to the local people in their community. The Peace Corps also provides complete medical and dental care and covers the cost of transportation to and from your country of service.

#2 Transition Assistance

When volunteers return to the US, the Peace Corps Office of Third Goal and Returned Volunteer Services provides them with transition assistance related to jobs and education.

---

[26] Official Peace Corps program and application information: peacecorps.gov.
[27] Tangible benefits of the Peace Corps Volunteer Program: peacecorps.gov/learn/whyvol.

#3 Language Skills

Fluency in foreign languages, international experience, and cross-cultural understanding are highly sought assets in today's global economy. The Peace Corps provides you with up to three months of intensive training before service begins and offers continued training throughout your service.

#4 Transition Funds

The Peace Corps recognizes that returning from overseas requires some adjustment, so when you complete your twenty-seven months of service, it provides some funding to help with the transition to life back home. This money is yours to use as you wish.

#5 Federal Employment Benefits

Volunteers who complete two years of service receive one year of noncompetitive eligibility for employment in the federal government. This means that at the hiring agency's discretion, if a volunteer meets the minimum qualifications for a position, he or she can be hired without going through the standard competitive process. Those who are employed by the federal government after their Peace Corps service can receive credit toward retirement for those years of volunteer service.

#6 Loan Forgiveness

Peace Corps Volunteer Service is considered "qualifying employment" for the Department of Education's Public Service Loan Forgiveness Program. Details, instructions, and frequently asked questions can be found at the Department of Education's website for PSLF information and question 19 of the Department of Education's FAQ on PSLF.

#7 Educational Opportunities

Does the idea of Peace Corps service interest you, but you want to go to graduate school soon? You can do both with Master's International. As a Master's International student, you have an unparalleled opportunity to live and work abroad while completing a master's degree in your field of interest. To become a Master's International student, apply to one of the graduate school partners, and then, within a year of your desired departure date, apply to the Peace Corps. You must be accepted to both programs.[28]

Returned Peace Corps Volunteers can receive financial aid to pursue a master's degree or doctorate in a wide variety of subject areas at more than ninety universities through the Paul D. Coverdell Fellows Program. Returned volunteers have lifetime eligibility for the programs and may choose to participate immediately after service or anytime thereafter.[29]

Examples of Peace Corps Projects

In addition to their Primary Assignments (in education, health, youth in development, community economic development, environment, and agriculture), most volunteers are involved with secondary projects during their service. As these are projects that volunteers identify and customize based on their own experience and their community's need, there is no typical project! Examples of projects include school renovation projects, leading community exercise groups, training inner-city youth to become rock-climbing guides, running Girls Leading Our World Camps, alternative energy projects, and malaria-prevention programs.

Five Reasons to Serve in Peace Corps:

#1 You Want to Gain International Work Experience while Making a Positive Difference in the World

As a Peace Corps volunteer you will have the opportunity to work alongside extremely diverse individuals in a dynamic work environment. As a volunteer you will be assigned to work with an organization. This could be a high school, an NGO, a local business, a government agency, or something else entirely. During your service you will have the opportunity to collaborate on projects with people working at that organization as well as other organizations around your community. You may also choose to undertake a project together with fellow Peace Corps volunteers

---

[29] Master's International, including individual school programs and specific details: peacecorps.gov/masters.
[29] Peace Corps Fellows Program, including a complete list of schools and programs peacecorps.gov/fellows.

where you can learn from older volunteers, show new volunteers the ropes, or just work on projects with your close friends. This valuable, real-world experience will teach you a lot about getting things done in a foreign country while transferring skills to your coworkers that will make them better workers themselves.

#2 You Want to Become a Part of a Community Overseas

As a Peace Corps volunteer you will become an integrated member of your local community. Your neighbors and friends will probably be host-country nationals. The relationships you develop with these people will be extremely strong, and you will quickly become one of the community. You may even live with a host family and have the opportunity to introduce your mother to your host mother. Many people in your community will know who you are and will always be looking out for your well-being. The relationships you build during this time will be long-lasting—I talk to friends from my service today and get updates about the local news and things going on in the community. You will also form strong relationships with your fellow volunteers. These other volunteers will become an important support structure that can continue even after you return to the US. Strength of community is one of the most impactful things I took away from my service.

#3 To Learn More about Yourself and Your Own Culture(s) as well as Another Culture

Living in another culture is an extremely unique, gratifying experience. The host-country national friends you make while serving will be eager to explain their culture to you. This is a great opportunity to see how others live and experience the things that are important to them. Being taken to my friends' home villages to see where they grew up are some of the more memorable experiences from my service. You will also have many opportunities to explain American culture (as well as any other cultures you are a part of) to those same friends. They will ask many questions, and some of them will be difficult to answer. This can lead to a lot of reflection both on your own culture and yourself. Cultural exchange is one of the most important things that Peace Corps volunteers do and also one of the most interesting.

#4 You Want to Experience Something New—Every Day

Every day in your community has the potential to be an adventure. Whether it is traveling between cities with a goat in the backseat of the bus or just going to the market, you will have many unique experiences. Learning to adapt to these changes can be challenging at first, but it soon becomes second nature. I found myself looking forward to whatever would happen each day even though I had no idea what it would be. Swapping these stories with other volunteers and friends and family back home is a fun way to spend time and share your experiences with others.

#5 You May Learn Another Language

Many Peace Corps volunteers serve in a country where English is not the primary language. For individuals interested in learning another language, this is a great opportunity. Peace Corps language training is quite effective and can help almost anyone to learn another language. Training will involve many hours of language lessons, and during your service you will be immersed amongst native speakers. This intense immersion is great for developing language skills but can also be frustrating at times. It can seem like no one understands you. However, there will be other Americans there with you who are going through the same things. Upon returning home, you can be proud to be one of the bi- (or tri- or multi-) lingual Americans. And you never know when your language skills will come in handy, traveling the world or just meeting someone from your country of service.

Five Reasons *Not* to Serve in Peace Corps:

#1 You Want to Save the World

Yes, you will have the chance to make a positive impact, especially in collaboration with your host community, but it is important to be realistic about the level of impact that you will be able to make in two years' time. It may take years for your impact to be visible. For example, the impact of teachers may not be seen until the students have grown up and started their careers. The scale of your projects may also be much smaller than you imagine. While Peace Corps volunteers do have some access to funding for projects, most of what you do will be projects with no budget. This does not mean your work will be meaningless, just that individual connections are much more likely to be the lasting results of your time rather than a huge, world-changing impact.

#2 You Have No Other Plans

In order to successfully complete the full twenty-seven months of service, you will need to bring serious commitment and passion to your journey. Two years and three months is a long time. There will be very good days but also very bad days. Without a full commitment to your service, those bad days will be even worse. However, if you are dedicated to finishing what you started, those days will quickly pass—meaning the next great day is even closer! Volunteers who decided to do Peace Corps without fully considering what they are signing up for may have a much harder time than they think.

#3 You Are Attached to the Creature Comforts That Are Part of Your American Lifestyle

While everyone's country and community is different in Peace Corps, the reality is that it will also be very different from what you are used to in the US. During my service, the power went out frequently, water pressure would be extremely low for days, and everything I owned was dusty at all times. Other volunteers in my country did not even have running water, and a few of them did not have electricity (although this is rare). Some volunteers have to walk a long distance just to get cell phone service to make a call! However, all of this can make you appreciate what you do have even more. Getting a package from home with a chocolate bar in it, or having a friend bring your favorite soda when he visits will make you extremely happy. Adapting to the conditions you find yourself in while not expecting too much are both important to having a successful service.

#4 You Have Perfectionist Tendencies

Be prepared to leave them back in the States during your Peace Corps service. As a volunteer, you will experience a steep learning curve, and you will have to relearn how to do many things—from how to shop for groceries and get around town, to how to communicate with your work supervisor (most likely in another language!). Things will not always go the way you think they will. In fact, this might happen more often than not. Being flexible and willing to learn is key to overcoming these challenges. Your host-country national friends and fellow volunteers will be quick to help you when you have a problem to solve, but you must be open to taking their advice, even if you do not think it is the best solution.

#5 You Want to Pad Your Résumé

Yes, as a Returned Peace Corps Volunteer, you will have many career opportunities open to you—but it is called "the toughest job you will ever love" for a reason, and career ambitions alone are not enough to make you a successful volunteer! During your service you will change as a person, and your life and career goals may also change. Working internationally can be rewarding but also extremely frustrating. You should join Peace Corps because you want to, not because it will look good on your résumé.

TEACH FOR AMERICA

Holly Plank and Stephen Bell

Holly Plank is finishing her second year with Teach For America as an eighth-grade science and physical science teacher. Originally from Camp Hill, Pennsylvania, she teaches at Hale Junior High in Tulsa, Oklahoma. She is the science department chair, volleyball coach, and cosponsor of the Sea Perch Program (Underwater Robotics Club). After this year, she will continue to pursue her master's degree at the University of Oklahoma in educational administration curriculum and supervision and teach eighth-grade science at Hale Junior High.

Stephen Bell is finishing his second year as a seventh- and eighth-grade teacher with Teach For America. He teaches at Hale Junior High in Tulsa, Oklahoma, where he is the other cosponsor of Sea Perch and co-planner of the spring formal and where he engages with Hispanic families through the JUNTOS Program. Upon finishing this year, he hopes to return to work at his school to continue to work with his same students next year as eighth graders.

What Is Teach For America?

Teach For America is a national teacher corps consisting of recent college graduates and young professionals who commit to at least two years as a teacher leader in a low-income community in the United States. Teach For America aligns its teacher leadership development with its vision that one day, ALL children in this nation will have the opportunity to attain an excellent education. Transformational schools should be available for all students. As a data- and research-driven organization, Teach For America employs best teaching practices from around the world to develop its teachers. Incoming corps members attend a five-week intensive summer institute and continue to receive supplemental professional development and individualized coaching throughout their commitment. Teach For America seeks to make an impact in the short term and the long term with each corps member by leading their students to reach their full potential and to become lifelong leaders for educational equality.

Application Process

To be a part of Teach For America, you must be a graduate of a four-year university. While most candidates apply directly out of college, a small percent apply though alternative routes, meaning he or she had a career prior to joining the corps. The application process as well as pay and benefits can change from year to year. The application process currently involves an online application as well as a phone interview and a daylong, in-person interview.[30]

Pay and Benefits

Teach For America corps members receive the same pay and benefits as any regular educator in the district where they serve. This can vary greatly state to state, depending on how much the state values education.

#1 Transitional funding

Corps members can apply for a loan when moving to their new region as they are expected to move in June for Institute and will not begin getting paid until September. This funding is a loan that gets paid back during the corps member's service.

#2 Loan Forgiveness

Because Teach For America is an AmeriCorps affiliate, corps members are eligible for up to $5,500 in loan forgiveness for each year served.

---

[30] TFA application information: teachforamerica.org/teach-with-tfa/how-to-apply.

#3 Educational Opportunities

Opportunities vary greatly from region to region. In some areas, a master's degree is required to teach, so corps members are required to obtain it during their two-year commitment. In other places it is not necessary, just an option. Many regions offer significant scholarships to corps members wishing to obtain their master's degree, and some universities have set up partnerships with the program.[31]

Examples of Post-TFA Experiences:

1. Rachel Canter, TFA class of 2004 and a finalist for the Peter Jennings Award for TFA alumni, started Mississippi First, a policy and advocacy organization in the state of Mississippi. Mississippi First has impacted thousands of young students by creating the framework for the Early Learning Collaborative Act of 2013—the law that brought state-funded pre-kindergarten to Mississippi for the first time. Mississippi First also convinced more than thirty of the state's highest-need districts to adopt comprehensive, medically accurate sexual education programs—another first for Mississippi.

2. George Dong, TFA class of 2009 and a winner of the Social Innovation Award for TFA alumni, cofounded Education In Sight, a nonprofit that believes direct access to eye care is the right of every student in the world. Education In Sight's mission is to improve the academic performance of low-income students with poor vision by providing low-cost glasses and eye care education in the classroom

3. Hilah Barbot, TFA class of 2009 and a winner of the Excellence in Teaching Award for TFA alumni, is the highest-performing sixth-grade science teacher in the city of New Orleans with 99% proficiency and more than two years of growth. Her classroom structure puts students in a position to love science and to have content ownership and investment in the future. In addition, Hilah orchestrates a science fair each year where students write and conduct their own experiments in front of a panel of judges.

Five Reasons to Join Teach for America:

#1 It Is a Learning Process

From how to run the best professional development to how to be a better teacher, Teach For America knows that we are constantly learning how to do it best. Though you might tire from the endless surveys, I have seen in the last two years how TFA has responded based on feedback. From seeing this example, it instills in me the reminder that becoming a better teacher is also a learning/tweaking process. (It empowers leaders to approach every situation with a growth mindset.)

#2 You Want to Use Data-Driven Instruction

Teach for America removes the personal aspect of teaching and utilizes data to get results. This may sound like a cold approach, but when things are not going well in a classroom, it is easier to look at the data and try to change it than to look at yourself and put blame and negative feelings toward your teaching. Using data to drive instruction enables teachers and evaluators to hold high standards for students and to constantly find areas for improvement. Data can include test scores, but it can also look at things such as amount of time on task, amount of time teacher corrects behavior, levels of questioning used in student dialogue, percent of time teacher is speaking versus students speaking, just to name a few. This idea of data-driven instruction can have a negative connotation, but when used effectively in the classroom, it is extremely helpful.

#3 Empowering Students Is Significant to You

The partnership between teacher and students is one of the most important partnerships in a child's development (outside the family, of course). Teachers have the ability to impact a student's decision making, his or her feelings of self-worth, decisions regarding future goals, and decisions on whether or not goals are worth pursuing. This job is one of the most impactful opportunities a college graduate has.

#4 You See Development through the Lens of Social Justice and Equity

Statistics show that many of the top graduates from universities across America will be white, upper-middle class. This is not the demographic attending schools where Teach For America places corps members. This experience

---

[31] TFA discounts for educators: teachforamerica.org/teach-with-tfa/salary-and-benefits/ongoing-aid-teachers.

gives perspective and understanding that would not come through many other experiences. Working in low-income communities changes many preconceived notions of what poverty does or does not entail.

#5 You Want to Spark and Inspire a Passionate Community of Leaders

Teaching builds perspective, authentic relationships, and encourages the community to stay centered in their work toward a shared vision. Not every corps member in Teach For America will stay in the classroom for the remainder of his or her career. However, wherever each person goes, the ideals and memories of teaching in low-income schools will follow. Any other job you get past Teach For America will be strongly influenced by the lessons learned in the time spent as a corps member.

Five Reasons *Not* to Join Teach for America:

#1 Work-Life Balance Is High Priority

Oftentimes, I have felt and have heard from others that TFA treats us like robots, and life needs to be put on the back burner. Your kids are more important than you. Though I love my students and want the very best for them, I equally understand that I need to be my best self in order to be the best teacher.

#2 You Want to Have a Secure, Sustainable Position

Is this a sustainable model for participating schools? Is two years enough time to make a lasting difference in a school? What happens after a transformational teacher leaves? If a corps member decides to stay in the classroom, is this lifestyle sustainable for the long haul?

#3 You Are Seeking a Higher Status in the Education Community

There are many preconceived notions about the status of Teach For America corps members in local school districts. These ideas, which are often misconceptions, are not always discussed openly in a timely manner. This can lead to tension between traditionally educated teachers and corps members.

#4 Make a Difference Quickly

It takes more than two years to see system-wide results in a school or district. Many Teach For America corps members leave the corps not realizing the long-term impact that they have made. (TFA has responded to feedback from corps members and stakeholders that five weeks and two years is not enough, and it has recently started a program for interested college juniors.) Additionally, the first two years of teaching tend to be the most frustrating ones. It is difficult to become an expert on anything in that amount of time, so many corps members leave dissatisfied with their performance as a teacher because they do not get to see the improvement of those third, fourth, and fifth years.

#5 TFA Will Boost Your Résumé

Truth. Teach For America looks good on résumés, and it will be a great talking point when applying for jobs in the future. Is this reason alone a good enough reason to join the corps? Absolutely not. It is somewhat equitable to people going to medical school because they want the nice salary. The struggles that you face in the two years of teaching are only worth it if you have a strong belief in social justice and in your students. If you cannot get invested in your school and community, you are not going to make it through the two years. Moreover, students and communities deserve teachers who are going to be committed to the school and students that they serve.

AAAS SCIENCE & TECHNOLOGY POLICY FELLOWSHIP

Karelyn Cruz

Karelyn Cruz is an agricultural development officer and AAAS overseas fellow at USAID/ Mozambique. She works at the interface of agriculture development, research, and technology innovation contributing to Feed the Future Initiative's goal of reducing extreme poverty, hunger, and undernutrition.

What Is AAAS?

AAAS is an international nonprofit organization formed in 1848 to support the development of science, engineering, and innovation throughout the world for the benefit of all people. Albert Einstein presented his work at annual meetings and at one point received small grants from AAAS! The world's largest general scientific society, it publishes the prestigious journal *Science,* is a strong advocate for STEM in policy and society, and runs pioneering programs to achieve goals like increasing underrepresented participation in STEM and providing opportunities for scientists to use and expand their skills beyond the lab bench. One such program is the Science & Technology Fellowship, which annually places more than 130 fellows in federal government offices for one to two years.

The fellowship is for those who have a PhD in a STEM field or a master's in engineering plus three years of professional experience. If you want to be a part of AAAS but do not meet the educational requirements, consider these other opportunities they offer to expand the reach of developing undergraduate scientists.

AAAS Mass Media Science & Engineering Fellowship Program

This ten-week summer fellowship is for advanced undergraduate and graduate students to hone their skills of communicating complex scientific ideas to the general public. Fellows have worked as reporters, editors, researchers, and production assistants at such media outlets as the *Los Angeles Times* and *The Philadelphia Inquirer.*[32]

Volunteer or Intern with AAAS

Volunteer and paid internship opportunities exist for undergraduate and graduate students in *Science* magazine, science policy, and publishing and member services to allow students to develop special projects or studies for the organization. These full-time or part-time positions can earn college credit and are typically granted for a period of less than six months.[33]

Application Process

To be an AAAS Fellow, you must have a PhD in a STEM field (or a master's in engineering plus three years of professional experience) and be a US citizen, and you may not be a federal employee. You can apply to up to two of seven fellowship areas (each requiring separate applications).[34] The application process as well as pay and benefits can change from year to year. The application process currently involves an online application, letters of recommendation, and interviews.[35]

Pay and Benefits

AAAS is a prestigious organization, and you will draw upon the work-based and professional development skills gained from the science and technology fellowship throughout your life.

---

[32] Apply to become a Mass Media fellow: aaas.org/page/apply.
[33] More information on specific internship opportunities and applications: aaas.org/page/internship-opportunities.
[34] Brief descriptions of the fellowship areas: aaas.org/page/st-fellowship-program-areas.
[35] More application information: aaas.org/page/become-st-policy-fellow.

#1 Stipend

There are four different stipend levels for AAAS science and technology fellows, which are generally competitive with salaries for full-time employment but reflect the educational value the fellow will receive. Most stipends as of 2015 range from $76,000 to $100,000 and are mainly determined by the years of postdoctoral experience.

#2 Travel/Professional Training Allowance

Fellows receive a travel/professional training allowance that may be used only for preapproved fellowship-related travel and for professional training activities, such as attending scientific conferences or for courses that will enhance the fellow's skills in his/her fellowship.

#3 Relocation Reimbursement

Most first-year fellows are provided with some reimbursement for properly documented relocation expenses that are incurred to move from outside the greater Washington, DC, area.

#4 Health Insurance Reimbursement

Because fellows are not AAAS employees, they cannot be included in the AAAS group health-care coverage policy. The maximum reimbursement amounts are detailed in the fellowship offer letter.

#5 Professional Development Program

AAAS fellowships staff conduct activities to enhance the fellows' knowledge and capabilities, as well as to foster interaction and collaborative connections. Activities include orientation, educational seminars, capacity-building workshops, networking and outreach events, and the annual retreat.[36]

Examples of Science and Technology Fellow Projects:

1. Darrell Donahue, national defense and global security fellow and a professor of chemical and biological engineering at the University of Maine, was assigned to support the division director of Threat Characterization and Countermeasures within the Office of Health Affairs (OHA). One project involved exploring strategies to support local disaster preparedness initiatives.

2. Garrick Louis, National Center for Environmental Research fellow and a professor of systems and information engineering at the University of Virginia, was assigned at the US Environmental Protection Agency (EPA). As part of his work at the EPA, Garrick visited five grantee sites on behalf of the Collaborative Science and Technology Network for Sustainability Program, to identify and evaluate cases of innovation for sustainability, such as land-use sustainability, smart growth models, harbor pollution prevention programs, and tradable credit systems for storm-water management.

3. Stephanie Adams, National Science Foundation fellow and associate dean for undergraduate education in the College of Engineering and associate professor of industrial and management systems engineering at the University of Nebraska-Lincoln, was assigned at the Division of Engineering Education & Centers (EEC). Adams spent her year participating in the Engineering Education Working Group, representing NSF and the engineering directorate at nationwide outreach events; coordinating the review of seventy proposals by the Engineering Education Program Panels; planning symposia and events; and creating and implementing training materials for EEC employees.

Five Reasons to Serve with AAAS:

#1 Excellent Networking Opportunities

The original AAAS Congressional Science and Engineering Fellows Program began on Capitol Hill in 1973. Since then, more than 2,800 scientists and engineers have served as an AAAS Science & Technology Policy Fellow (STPF) in one of the dozen federal agencies or congressional placements in Washington, DC. That is a big network to be a part of! By being a fellow, you are automatically connected to this extensive network of scientists and engineers that are working all over the world in different fields. In addition to the extensive fellow network, you are exposed to peo-

---

[36] Overview of the tangible benefits of an AAAS Fellowship: aaas.org/page/become-fellow-stipend-and-support.

ple from different backgrounds and disciplines in your agency, travels, and by living in Washington, DC. As a fellow, you will also have a mentor in your agency that will help you navigate the world of government, and you can also have access to their network!

#2 Opens New Doors for PhDs Who Want to Explore Opportunities beyond the Lab Bench

For several reasons, many scientists and engineers decide to pursue a career outside academia or even traditional research and development. For many of these scientists, this can be an overwhelming transition as they might not be aware of other career opportunities out there that might be of interest to them and benefit from their skills. In many occasions, it is difficult to transition to a different sector (private, government, NGOs, think tanks, etc.) as you might not have the professional experience necessary to be competitive for that position. The fellowship opens those doors and provides the opportunity to gain experience and knowledge, to establish connections, and to develop new skills that will make you more marketable for future career opportunities.

#3 Opportunity to Impact Federal Policy Creation and Execution

Policy issues are interdisciplinary and usually very high level, which can be extremely interesting and challenging. This will provide you with the opportunity to learn about several areas, interact with new people, see the "big picture," and have a tangible impact on the issues you really care about—energy, climate change, development, or gender equity. For some scientists this can be challenging as we are used to focusing on a specific topic. However, depending on your position as a fellow, you might be able to use your academic expertise to inform the policy/decision-making process. Both circumstances can be very gratifying and intellectually challenging.

#4 Helps You Learn How the Federal Government Works (or Does Not Work)

You will have firsthand experience in the culture and *modus operandi* of the federal government. In many respects it will be different from academia and other sectors, and for many fellows this can be a steep learning curve. The good news is that the fellowship will provide you with the support and guidance you need to navigate and succeed in the federal government. The fellowship will provide workshops, mentorship, and access to an extensive network that can support you. (The weekly happy hours with the fellows also help!)

#5 Potential to Travel to and Be in Service in Remote Parts of the World

Depending on the agency they are affiliated with, fellows might have the opportunity to travel domestically and/or internationally to conferences and meetings and to visit projects (although this is mostly for diplomacy and development fellowships). This is a unique, gratifying opportunity to be exposed to new countries and cultures. For example, in addition to the fellowship in Washington, DC, AAAS provides the opportunity to fellows to serve at a USAID mission overseas as part of the AAAS Overseas Fellowship. If you are interested in living abroad, this is a unique opportunity to live as a foreign-service officer overseas.

Five Reasons *Not* to Serve with AAAS:

#1 If You Want to Stay in Academic or Bench Science

For the fellowship, you will be relocated to Washington, DC, for one or two years. This is going to be a great experience, but if you are interested in keeping in touch and continuing a career in academia, this might be difficult. Time management will be very important to stay afloat with your research and graduate student supervision back home and your new duties as a fellow. This is in addition to your personal and family responsibilities, which is something to keep in mind. This may be more than balanced out by the many benefits mentioned above, but each field and case varies.

#2 You Can Also Just Apply for Government Jobs Directly

If joining the US government is your goal and you know exactly which agency or type of work you want to do, you can apply directly to those positions. You do not have to be a fellow to get a job in government.

#3 Can Be Frustrating to Deal with Government Bureaucracy

The culture and level of bureaucracy in government is very different from academia. Usually academia is pretty "flat," and in many occasions you are your own boss. In government you will have to deal and interact with several "bosses" and a lot of processes and restrictions that can hinder the speed and reach of your work. You will have to seek approval or clearance for almost every action and documentation you do. This can be frustrating for many fellows (and non-fellows) as it hinders your capacity to do your work quickly and effectively.

#4 It Is Not a Permanent Position

You can be a fellow with AAAS for only up to four years, but you can jump from one track or program to the next within those four years. For example, you can be in the executive branch for two years in Washington, DC, and then move to the overseas fellowship for two more years (you still have to go through a competitive selection process). Even though this is not a permanent position, you will have opportunities to network and explore permanent opportunities within the government if you are interested in staying.

#5 It Might Underutilize Your Skills

Many fellows end up in positions that are not intellectually challenging or do not require the skill level from a PhD to get the job done. This is the case for many government positions that are more programmatic or managerial. This can be very frustrating and demotivating for many fellows as they feel underutilized. In reality, there are a limited number of positions that are meant for "scientists." This is something to keep in mind if your goal is to do technical or intellectually challenging work. However, if your goal is to manage programs, you will have a lot of options and opportunities for this.

part five

Professional
Competencies

BUILDING YOUR PERSONAL BRAND

Rose Cameron

Rose Cameron is the director of Innovation for Outreach and Online Education at Penn State University. Cultural anthropologist, global brand strategist, and lifelong learner, Rose's research on generations and men have been covered by The New York Times, The New Yorker, The Wall Street Journal, and Chicago Tribune to name a few. Rose is focused on identifying unmet needs in education and addressing those through partnerships and innovation that bring the brightest minds in the world together to collaborate for the betterment of learners around the globe.

Y ou are the one thing you will produce in your lifetime over which you have complete control. And you have to live with that. So, would it not make sense to spend a little time really understanding who you are and what you want to achieve? The way you project yourself to others; the way you live your life; the way you play, work, and share—they are all part of your personal branding.

#1 Start with *Why*

"My role in life would be so much easier if I had a copy of the script." You do. You are the author. And only you know your purpose—your *why*. Spend some time understanding that purpose.

I was put on this Earth to:

My purpose is to:

I believe:

The one thing I must do before I die is:

My advocates and supporters all believe I:

The evil I want to eradicate in this world is:

You should discover through your exercise one simple core truth that drives you. That is your *why*. Write it down in one line. Sit with it. Look it over. This will be your life. Are you good with that?

#2 Walk the Talk – Your *How*

If you are truly committed to your *why,* show it in your everyday behavior. It is all air until you do it. Working from your *why, how* do you prove that you are true to your *why* in all you do?

I always:

I never:

My work style is:

I try to treat people:

I approach problems by:

Victories are time to:

If another attacks my point of view, I:

If I fundamentally do not agree with what an organization or person is doing, I will:

Psychologists often talk about "personal boundaries." Your *hows* are your personal boundaries. What will I do, and what will I not do? It is important that you look at these honestly. They speak to your inner character.

Now, take your *how* to the next level. *How* are you going to make your *why* happen? Start mapping out in two-year increments *how* you will collect the right experience, connections, and equity to manifest your *why*.

How will I collect:	Year 1–3	Year 4–6	Year 7–9
Experience			
Connections			
Equity (personal and financial)			

#3 Your Credibility – Your *What*

You have just spent some considerable time at a university learning a lot of *what*s. You may do engineering, science, geography, sociology, law, or finance. These are your core credentials.

The *what*s you have collected along the way are critical to your credibility when you are entering the workforce. They signify a credible currency to which organizations can assign value. Create a list of your *what*s and then pull out the ones that are truly reflective of your *why* and *how*. You did these things because you believe (*why*), and you acquired them in the following (*how*) manner. These are the examples you will use in interviews.

What Have I Done	Long List	Short List	Support my *why* and *how* by . . .
Degrees			
Research			
Papers			
Internships			
Charitable Services			
Awards			
Sports and Competitions			
Entrepreneurial Ventures			
Inventions			
Languages			
Travel			
Extracurricular Hobbies			
Significant Achievements			

A Word on the Basics

The first twenty seconds is everything. Dress neatly, be and smell clean, make eye contact, cultivate a firm handshake, and learn to smile with your eyes. Be honest, be confident, be kind. These traits demonstrate two things: respect for your interviewer and for yourself.

Finally, there is only one you. You are unique. Do yourself proud. Be your own author. Respect your brand. We salute you.[37]

---

[37] This theory is shared and informed by Simon Sinek of startwithwhy.com and *Leaders Eat Last*.

CURIOSITY, CONNECTIONS, CREATING VALUE: AN ENTREPRENEURIAL MINDSET

Doug Melton

Doug Melton is the program director of the Kern Entrepreneurial Engineering Network (KEEN) of The Kern Family Foundation. The KEEN network includes more than twenty universities with about 1,000 engineering faculty members instructing 23,000 engineering students. The universities and colleges in KEEN have committed to fostering an entrepreneurial mindset alongside an undergraduate degree in engineering. Their mission is to graduate engineers with an entrepreneurial mindset so that they can create personal, economic, and societal value through a lifetime of meaningful work.

Put yourself in the shoes of Abdra, who has just arrived in southeast Michigan from the West African nation of Mali. You are excited about the potential of an engineering education. You speak Bambara, but no English. Michiganders do not speak Bambara. You have no family or friends. Regardless, you manage to enroll in a community college and learn English from lectures and television. Skills with a soccer ball afford some opportunities to make friends. Finally, you take the required entrance exams for the university. Success! Your skills in both math and English are sufficient for entry. You enroll in an electrical engineering program. Your path to get here has been long, tracing back to your youth when you read books by the village's single, pole-mounted light. That light was important because nighttime was the only time available to study—you had to work and go to school during the day. The electricity was provided by a gasoline-powered generator; when it was shut off for the evening, you returned home and continued to read by the light of a kerosene lantern.

Two years at the university have elapsed, and you are excelling because of your commitment and the hours you have invested. An internship helped you gain competency and confidence in circuit-board design. Now back in class, the topics seem to take on greater importance than ever. In an electronics course, the subject is high-brightness LEDs. In an energy systems course, you experiment with photovoltaic solar cells. The potential of the technical information becomes meaningful when you remember the hours spent under the single village light. In a signals and systems course, the professor invites you and other students to suggest how the technical topics from their other classes may be combined to create real-world value. The invitation seems only tenuously connected with the largely mathematical course content. Based on the grading system on the syllabus, it is not clear how the response to the professor's open-ended invitation will impact successful completion of the course.

As Abdra, what do you do?

- **Do nothing.** Ignore the invitation. Continue to study for the next exam in an effort to receive an "A" grade.
- **Demonstrate curiosity** by considering how many students in Mali (or worldwide) are limited by the scarcity of nighttime light sources. You ask: Is evening study time limited by light in many societies? What limits the electrification of underdeveloped nations? Is it the lack of resources or the lack of an economy to use the surrounding resources? Is it political?
- **Connect information** from your classes (LEDs, photovoltaics, etc.) with the insight that distributed energy systems, rather than centralized systems, may be the most viable for geographically large African nations. A quick investigation and conversation with leaders of a Canadian NGO, Light Up the World, reveals that they have been addressing the literacy need. They have learned many lessons along the way and are willing to share.
- **Create new value** by suggesting a design for a low-cost solar rechargeable light. Using your technical and business skills, estimate the feasibility and viability of the design. Prepare to investigate the desirability: your value proposition has multiple stakeholders—the villagers, NGOs, and funding organizations that target illiteracy. Does the entire idea—i.e., the complete solution that includes the design, cost, supply chain, distribution channels, cultural acceptance, etc.—have merit?

- **Capture value** by creating product prototypes, a business model, and a product pitch. Return to Mali to see if there is a "real customer" for your prototypes. Ask people to use it. With the hope of sustainability, ask people to pay for it. Incorporate a business with associates and prepare to secure funding for scaling to a full product launch.

If you have selected everything except "Do Nothing," your story matches Abdra's. And yes, this is a true story; Abdra is my former student. There are many simple, but extremely important, lessons we can we learn from Abdra's story.

#1 What Is a Mindset?

When approaching a new situation—before analyzing it, communicating about it, or making any decisions regarding it—you employ a collective set of dispositions, attitudes, and motivations that incent you to adopt particular behaviors and approaches. This composite is your mindset. It is the lens through which you see the world; it animates how you think, how you react, and what you do. Your mindset could be driven by a curiosity and desire to learn every detail; it could be driven by radical empathy, to understand and experience life from the perspective of every stakeholder involved; or your mindset could be driven by a deeper desire to connect your work—every action, every decision, every email—to broader societal impact.

#2 Mindset Matters

In her book *Mindset*, Stanford researcher Carol Dweck addresses how we view intelligence through how two distinctive groups react to challenges. Individuals with a "growth mindset" not only react positively to challenges, they seek them. Those with a "fixed mindset" manage challenges and change through self-imposed artificial limits. After following individuals in these two groups, Dweck's research reveals patterns that connect our view of intelligence, a mindset as she terms it, to long-term success and sense of personal fulfillment. In other words, mindset informs our identity, colors our attitude, and most importantly, influences how far we will go in life and what we will accomplish.

#3 Relevance to Sustainable Development Careers

Social innovation and sustainable development often involve working in low-resource contexts with multiple stakeholders with different values, resources, agendas, and thinking patterns. It can be daunting and frustrating trying to figure out how to move the project forward and concurrently meet the needs of all the stakeholders. An entrepreneurial mindset—a way of seeing, thinking, and acting that demonstrates leadership, initiative, innovation, ownership, and responsibility—can help individuals be successful in such pursuits. At times, entrepreneurially minded individuals will discover or identify unexpected opportunities. At other times, they will put in the long, hard work necessary to see their endeavors succeed.

STEM professionals with an entrepreneurial mindset are pivotal in every kind of organization, from the large corporation trying to find a way to distribute nutrient pouches to children in Africa, to the governmental agency designing a solar-power policy framework, to the nonprofit trying to cut down the cost of drilling a borewell from $5,000 to $1,000! The key point is that, irrespective of your desire to be an entrepreneur, you want to develop an entrepreneurial mindset.

#4 The Three Cs of an Entrepreneurial Mindset

An entrepreneurial mindset is the sum of three elements, each an essential component of one's dispositions, attitudes, and motivations. These are known as the three Cs of entrepreneurial mindset: curiosity, connections, and creating value. Entrepreneurially minded individuals:

- have an insatiable curiosity to understand the technical, societal, and economical aspects of problems, solutions, and opportunities within our changing world
- habitually make connections to gain insight from many sources of information, thus informing and enabling the development of creative solutions
- focus on creating value (broadly defined) for others.

The good news is that these competencies and ways of thinking and doing can be developed, and honed, over time.

#5 A Mindset Needs a Skillset

An effective mindset works in tandem with a skill set. For example, when a student is solving a calculus problem, they employ the mathematical skills they have learned in school. However, if the problem is difficult, their mindset may compel them to review old material or search the Internet. Ultimately, their ability to solve the problem is a result of their combined mindset and skill set.

Consider a police officer who has developed a variety of skills associated with law enforcement: weapons handling, defensive driving, and authoritative verbal communication. If she approaches a situation with a mindset dominated by fairness, civil safety, and rule of law, her decisions, methods, and behaviors will likely be an expression of that mindset. You can probably imagine an alternative mindset that, coupled with those skills, could produce dangerous results.

The good news is that individuals who operate with an entrepreneurial mindset and possess a powerful skill set are world changers in the making. They work in new territories and rise above established, accepted practices. An entrepreneurial mindset is the most difficult to repress. Driven by curiosity, with an uncanny ability to look for new opportunities and make connections, entrepreneurially minded individuals with strong character create value in the broadest sense, for human advancement. It is by no means a passive mental endeavor. Some people perceive entrepreneurial thinkers as mere idea generators, but ideas alone are insufficient. Once an idea has been born, an entrepreneurially minded individual will use their skills to spring it into the wild jungle of the marketplace, customers, and stakeholders. When individuals couple an entrepreneurial mindset to a technical skill set, they become extremely powerful change agents—just the kind we need to solve humanity's most complicated problems.

EIGHT WAYS TO PREPARE YOURSELF FOR A LIFE OF ENTREPRENEURSHIP

Matt Brezina

Matt Brezina is the cofounder and CEO of Sincerely Inc. and was the cofounder Xobni, two San Francisco startups acquired in 2013 by Provide Commerce and Yahoo respectively. Matt currently serves as an advisor and angel investor to multiple startups including Dropbox, Mailbox, Weebly, Gametime, MileIQ, SnapDocs, Tilt, and Wanelo. Matt has appeared in The New York Times, BusinessWeek, and The Wall Street Journal and was named one of Inc. magazine's "30 under 30." Matt also serves on the external advisory board for the Penn State Schreyer's Honors College and is a founding board member of the Penn State student-run incubator, Innoblue. Twitter: @brezina

Entrepreneurship is not for everyone. But for the right person, there is no other way to approach life. You are free to explore opportunities that excite you, you choose who you work with and when you work, and your effort and accomplishments are not averaged together with dozens or hundreds of other people that you do not control. As an entrepreneur, you have the opportunity to make a huge impact and to reap the rewards of that success.

Here are eight things that will prepare you for a life of entrepreneurship:

#1 Avoid Debt

If you owe money for a car, house, or education, you need a steady source of income to pay back that debt. That can force you to take a job instead of forgoing immediate income to work on your own idea. Or it can hold you back from quitting a job you hate because you need that steady income to pay for the car payments on your now less-than-shiny BMW M3. Stay lean. Do not spend what you do not have. Then you, not your debtors, will control your destiny.

#2 Learn to Sell

Almost all jobs require selling, and not always in the most classic sense of selling magazines door to door. Nowhere is selling more a part of your job than as an entrepreneur. Every day, you will sell your ideas to potential employees, current employees, potential investors, current investors, press, partners, and more. Entrepreneurs sell ideas more than anything else. But we also have to sell products. You will have to sell your products to consumers or your service to other businesses. Entrepreneurs are always selling, so do yourself a favor and learn the hard lessons of selling early. Get a job selling programs at football games. Or sell candy bars door to door. Or spend a summer selling credit cards over the phone. You will learn that the pain of rejection is just a step on the road to success. You will learn the victory of closing a deal. And you will learn to smile through the pain along the way.

#3 Build Expertise

Do you want to build a software company some day? Learn how to make software! Learn basic mobile or web development. Do you want to build a furniture company some day? Learn how to make furniture! As an expert in your field, you will know the opportunities in your space, you will know the best practitioners, you will know how to evaluate other practitioners, and you will know where the future of the field is heading. The business stuff? You can pick that up along the way.

#4 Explore Varied Interests

As an entrepreneur, you will have to relate to a myriad of people. You will have employees doing a wide range of roles. You will need to quickly build strong relationships with potential employees, investors, press, and partners.

Nothing builds a stronger bond than shared interests and experiences. So by all means, become the best fencer in the world. But also become experienced in a vast, diverse range of hobbies: sports, travel, art, music, science, astronomy, auto repair, sailing, flying, or chess.

#5 Read. Read Often. And Read Diverse Tomes

Entrepreneurs find opportunity in the latest and greatest. They are always on the cutting edge. Therefore, they have to be voracious learners. Find a topic you love, and go deep. Search Amazon for the top ten books on a topic and read them all (learning you do not have to read a whole book will help you pick up more books quicker). Explore esoteric niches, such as midcentury Scandinavian furniture design, backyard chicken husbandry, or art deco architecture. Often opportunity is found at the bleeding edge of a field and the intersection of two fields. And you are not going to find this information on your Facebook feed or on the *NBC Nightly News*. It is in long-form online blogs or books.

#6 Learn to Love Exercise

The best founders and CEOs are religious about their bodies—healthy mind, healthy body. As an entrepreneur, you will live a faster-paced, higher-stress life than most of your peers. You will need the body that can support this lifestyle. So embrace active transport—bike or walk to work as part of your daily life. Find active activities that you love: swimming, tennis, running. If you get injured (which you will—it is part of being an athlete), learn new activities to maintain exercise through the injury. And always bring your running shoes with you when you travel.

#7 Choose the Right Life Partner (If You Want One)

Warren Buffet said the most important decision of his, or anyone's life, is choosing a life partner. They will have more influence on your exercise habits, your eating habits, your stress levels, your intellectual pursuits, and your interpersonal relationships than anyone else on the planet. Be picky about your partner. And dear Lord, practice safe sex until you find the right person; nothing would make an ambitious life of an entrepreneur harder than bringing a child into the world with someone you are not meant to be with.

#8 Invest in Lifelong Relationships

Often people attend "networking" events when they are looking for a new job. Entrepreneurs do not attend "networking" events—life is a networking event. They maintain close relationships from childhood, from high school, from college, from grad school, and from every job they have worked and every town where they have lived. They build deep connections based on shared interests with a diverse range of people. Many of these relationships will come back to pay dividends in your business life, but they will more importantly enrich your personal life. When you are an entrepreneur, it is often pretty hard to tell these lives apart.

HOW FIELDWORK AND A COMMUNITY-CENTERED APPROACH CONTRIBUTE TO PROJECT SUCCESS

Esther Obonyo

Esther Obonyo is an associate professor of engineering design and architectural engineering at Penn State. Originally from Kenya, Esther has conducted NSF-sponsored research related to sustainable building systems for low-income communities in several African countries.

Fieldwork within the community is really a risk-management process. The lab environment, especially within any research and development system, exemplifies a utopian context. In the real world, Murphy's Law of "Anything that can go wrong, will go wrong" reigns supreme. Research ideas that are eventually translated into solutions to everyday problems must be conceived with implementations barriers and enablers in mind. A community-centered approach has several benefits.

#1 Community Outreach during Problem Identification Secures Social Acceptance

All progress in science, technology, and innovation starts as a set of assumptions, hypotheses, and some opinions that are used to maximize the opportunities available for making sustainable impact. Conducting fieldwork in communities is a mechanism for rapidly narrowing down all the possibilities into feasible solutions to things that matter to the masses. A few years ago, a group of young urban professionals in Nairobi came up with an economic empowerment idea for a rural community in Kenya's Nyanza province based on pyrethrum farming. They had a business plan for the entire operation and had even lined up angel investors. The well-meaning urban professionals overlooked an obvious fact: the community's most urgent priority was giving their children access to a quality high school education. The pyrethrum project did not take off.

#2 Dialogues at the Grassroots Promote Learning from Other People's Failures

Conventional wisdom encourages researchers to perform a thorough investigation of the existing body of knowledge. In most academic settings, this pretty much means it is necessary to read all the relevant journal papers. There is, however, a time lag of anywhere from one to three years between when the work is done and when it gets published. In addition, some of the work done within sub-Saharan Africa (SSA) is on a consultancy basis and rarely published in academic publications. That does not mean the work is not being done. In fact, many of the international agencies rely on local SSA experts to prepare their technical briefings. Because of these gaps in published knowledge, a field visit to, for example, the Kibera slums in Nairobi is a must for anyone researching low-income housing in sub-Saharan Africa (SSA). Without adopting an experience-based learning approach, it will be virtually impossible for anyone to develop a robust understanding of what has been done, the extent to which the interventions have worked, what has not worked, and the reasons behind the slow progress (where there has been progress), as well as the barriers to scale and impact.

#3 Objective Observations Can Be Used to Identify Situations "Where Less Is More"

Proponents of a low-income housing project at a location close to Nairobi in Kenya learnt the hard way that there is a financial cost associated with executing projects using a disproportionately large number of cheap, untrained laborers. In an effort to cut their construction costs and make the housing units affordable to some slum dwellers, they negotiated a deal through which part of the purchase price was to be offset using "sweat labor." Working out what would constitute a fair wage became a deal breaker at the end of the construction process. Masonry is a highly specialized skill that requires intensive training through apprenticeship. Because time was not spent in the field observing masons at work and their interactions with their apprentices, the total construction cost was grossly underestimated. To offset their loss, the asking price went up. The relocated slum dwellers who had invested "sweat labor" felt cheated when they could no longer afford the houses.

#4 Designing User-Centered Countermeasures

Andrew Hoffman's article "Isolated Scholars; Making Bricks, Not Shaping Policy" builds on Bernard K. Forscher's position that was articulated in a letter to *Science* magazine in 1963 in which professors are characterized as brick makers because of their discipline-centered focus. In a community setting, problems are facets of a social-technical system. For example, the average person in East Africa believes that a strong external wall is a solid, 200-millimeter (eight-inch) block. Any alternative walling systems that sound hollow trigger concerns about personal safety and security. Several attempts to introduce alternatives have not worked because they were marketed by stating they were in compliance with the building code in a community where the number one question is usually: "How easy will it be for a robber to break in?"

#5 Separating Facts from Fiction

After more than three decades of interactions with Western researchers, community members in some popular research destinations have become professional survey takers who give researchers from universities, nonprofits, or church missions different versions of the same story. When doing research in a different culture, first impressions are usually wrong impressions. Prior to my first field visit to Tanzania, I had assumed that the East African context was pretty much the same. After spending an entire summer in Dar es Salaam and Bagamoyo, I realized that the cultural differences between Kenya and Tanzania were not insignificant. It is against the backdrop of this realization that I have built a strong professional relationship with Tanzanians who embrace me warmly as Mzungu Mswahili (the African Foreigner)! The Africanists who hang around long enough build trust, and this guarantees them direct access to the reality on the ground.

HOW FIELDWORK PREPARES YOU FOR A CAREER IN SOCIAL IMPACT

Preeti Shroff-Mehta

Dr. Preeti Shroff-Mehta is the former dean and current senior advisor for Program Innovation and Partnership at World Learning's SIT Graduate Institute in Washington, DC. She is a global sustainable development strategy and program leader, educator, consultant, and entrepreneur with over twenty-five years expanding impact with proven design, implementation, and management accomplishments.

Graduate learning experience in the US embodies the difference between schooling and education—it is all about self-learning and transformation! It provides the global environment, people, and networks for those who are willing to engage and to transform information into knowledge and wisdom. This is achieved by stepping outside the four walls of the classrooms and mindsets to explore subject-specific or multidisciplinary learning across countries, cultures, and communities, often described as field-based experiential learning that is transformative for an individual!

A few years ago, a sustainable development program student from the US arrived in the field in a foreign country. Seeing the traffic, pollution, population, and garbage on the streets, this student's first reaction was, "This is so chaotic and difficult!" During the reflection session, we posed a question for the student: how can you address this complexity by working with the local people and communities in your capacity as a youth leader, mentor, engineer, urban planner, scientist, researcher, technology specialist, and program manager and address their daily life issues? These range from waste collection and management, pollution, traffic congestion, urban transportation, and food security, to water, health, education, housing, and access to other services.

The key to field-based experiential learning is developing the inclination and aptitude for "unlearning"— engaging in an unfamiliar, local context and going beyond the comfort of preconceived notions, the student's subject-area specific knowledge, and one's familiar and home-country specific values and understanding to "uncomfortable experiences" in diverse and different countries, cultures, and subjects that are new and challenging on multiple fronts. While struggling with the new place, culture, language, food, and people, one begins to understand, learn, and adapt.

The process of reflection and unlearning leads to new ways of knowing that form more effective, collaborative, and sustainable actions that are locally relevant and acceptable. The experiential learning cycle outlined above is adapted from David Kolb's experiential learning cycle to emphasize phases of field-based learning: engage to act, reflect, conceptualize and revise, and apply.

There are several elements that make field-based learning so critical for science and social science discipline-specific programs and participants. Here are some key lessons often learned during fieldwork.

#1 Field Reality Is Not Compartmentalized or Segmented; It Is Holistic and Interconnected

Fieldwork engages learners in interconnected realities and problems of communities enabling learners to develop cross-disciplinary, holistic skills. Developing sustainable and clean water sources and supply involves understanding historic, physical, structural, cultural, political, and social aspects of natural resources usage and management in any region or communities in a country in Asia, Africa, the Middle East, Europe, or Latin America. The analysis of macro-level water politics and policies and how they impact the struggles of local communities in slums and rural regions is critical. The most important factor is understanding various aspects of the issue of water access and then utilizing people and technology resources to build relationships across multiple stakeholders (men, women, youth, policy makers, private sector, and government leaders). This can help in leveraging global know-how for local problem solving. This global-local awareness, cross-disciplinary knowledge connections, and multi-stakeholder relationship development are the most desired skill set for any graduate entering the job market and global workplace.

#2 Field Learning Is Complex and Challenging and Necessarily Enhances Multiple Intelligences

The traditional academic learning at the graduate level has been preoccupied with IQ, intellectual quotient. Knowing a subject by reading and analyzing books or through classroom-based skills learning is not sufficient enough to prepare us for implementation on the ground or around the world. Engaging globally and with people or institutions across very distinct and different cultures requires a set of competencies. These are:

- Emotional intelligence (EQ) – to feel empathy and connect with communities in a humane way
- Cultural intelligence (CQ) – to have the patience to understand a culture's historic practices and why are they valuable and sustainable (agriculture, architecture, art, food, music, festivals)
- Global intelligence (GQ) – to understand the effects of globalization and recognize how global events and dynamics impact local policies and communities
- Relational intelligence (RQ) – to examine how we connect and relate to others who are different; this can teach us a lot even when situations are very difficult. Language, functional, intercultural, and cross-sectoral literacy are achieved only when students have the opportunity to relate to and connect with other people and experience real-life situations that impact their areas of study and work.

#3 Experience, Experience, Experience in Distinct Location, Location, Location

Field learning is all about enabling short- and long-term engagement in the "field" at home or abroad. This can range from reading a book or a case study for a class discussion to traveling to places to be on "live" situations to learn from communities. The goal is to prepare learners to take risks and explore unknown territories, whether that means home stays with a family in a specific culture and community; a field classroom in a faraway country location with local communities, institutions, and experts; a field-based project implementation and learning with a globally and culturally diverse team; or networking with government, private sector, or civil society institutions for activity and enterprise innovations to find locally affordable, cost-effective, and sustainable solutions (rather than imposing predefined agendas and programs).

At the end, one can look at field learning as an integral, essential component of academic experience or the only way of learning and staying relevant in graduate school studies and to emerge as an effective global professional. Make your choice: take the risk and plunge into any and every opportunity for field-based experience and learning!

#4 Planning Field-Based Learning: Personal Transformation and Career Path Choices!

Field-based experiential learning is by nature organic, unpredictable, and flexible. Imagine arriving for a one-month long field study, and conflict erupts or a natural disaster happens unexpectedly. What would you do in such circumstances? The challenges to be addressed in planning for any field-based learning approach are clarity in goal, well-researched local context, engagement with key stakeholders and actors, predeparture orientation, local entry and engagement preparations, logistics planning, resources management, and risk analysis for being responsible and responsive. Our presence and interventions can bring risks for the local communities and institutions.

The rest is a process of learning and unfolds on its own—that is the best part of field learning. The unknown that pushes us out of our comfort zones and challenges us to unlearn stereotypes, assumptions, and predetermined notions of what is the right answer or correct solutions. The joy of learning is to engage with a difference that will make us uncomfortable as an individual and force us to listen and learn from the collective and community contexts. Experiential learning is not just about the experience; it is how we process the experience to expand our knowledge and skills to understand our past, our current actions, and influence the future. Building learning partnerships for global collaboration and action that lead to meaningful and sustainable local impact is the way forward!

It is this personal transformation in the field that often leads to our reassessment of what our life passion is that drives us and our actions, what career will help us practice our passion, what our aptitude and skill set are, and often an early test drive to assess the reality of field-based work and careers. Ultimately, experiential learning is a personal journey of transformation that forces us to examine what worldview and value set matter and what the required skills set is to guide our actions.

HERE IS HOW YOU BECOME A BETTER STORYTELLER!

Jeff Kirschner

Jeff Kirschner is an award-winning entrepreneur who has built mobile and social media companies. Prior to entering the world of technology startups, he was a creative at TBWA\CHIAT\ DAY, developing campaigns for clients including Levi's and Sony Playstation. Before advertising, Jeff spent a year backpacking around the world, an experience he describes as "the most valuable period of his life," which opened his eyes to the challenges we face on a global scale and, in many ways, led to his most recent venture—Litterati.

Whether you are sitting around a campfire, pitching a client, or running for office, it pays to have a knack for narrative. Good storytellers grab our attention, manipulate our emotions, and foster trust. Great ones inspire us to act. Nowhere is this more evident, and arguably more important, than in social innovation. Solving our world's most pressing issues often requires an all-hands-on-deck approach, and storytelling is one of our most reliable weapons.

Consider Grameen Bank, the microfinance organization from Bangladesh. Founded in 1976 by then-little-known professor Muhammad Yunus, Grameen began as a university research project, studying how to design a credit delivery system to provide banking services to the poor. Yunus discovered that loans, as opposed to charity, were more effective in reducing poverty as they offer those less fortunate an opportunity to take initiative, which provides earnings that can then be used to pay off the debt, thereby empowering and educating these individuals.

Recognizing that those in need did not have the necessary assets required for a bank loan, Grameen turned the conventional system on its head by removing the need for collateral and, instead, fostered a bank based on accountability, participation, and trust. Today, Grameen Bank has provided over $8 billion USD in loans, and both—the bank and its founder—have been awarded the Nobel Peace Prize.

Khan Academy has similar humble beginnings. Back in 2004, Salman Kahn was remotely tutoring his cousin in mathematics by sending her lectures and practice exercises via YouTube. Warm and inviting, Sal's teaching method proved incredibly effective. Several years and thousands of micro-tutorials later, Khan Academy is widely known as one of the premier online learning resources, with a world-class organization of eighty employees and financial backing from the Bill & Melinda Gates Foundation and Google.

How does a tiny research project and family tutorial transform into two of our world's most respected institutions? One could say it is their ambitious vision, outstanding strategy, or tactical execution. While those are all true, they also share the intangible, yet undeniable, elements of a great story.

Muhammed Yunus recounts in *Creating a World without Poverty* that whenever he met a potential partner to gain support for microcredit, he would start with the story of Sufiya Begum: "It was a village woman named Sufiya Begum who taught me the true nature of poverty in Bangladesh. Like many village women, Sufiya lived with her husband and small children in a crumbling mud hut with a leaky thatched roof. . . . To provide food for her family, Sufiya worked all day in her muddy yard making bamboo stools. . . . Yet somehow her hard work was unable to lift her family out of poverty."

Yunus would then ask the person: "Why?" Although he was asking rhetorically, he was getting them to think and making them excited to hear more. He would continue, "Like many others in the village, Sufiya relied on the local moneylender for the cash she needed to buy the bamboo for her stools. But the moneylender would give her the money only if she agreed to sell him all she produced at a price he would decide. Between this unfair arrangement and the high interest rate on her loan, she was left with only two pennies a day as her income."

Now the listener had a good picture of Sufiya's struggle, and Yunus would go on to expand their view by sharing how Sufiya was not alone: "I decided to make a list of the victims of this moneylending business in the village. . . . It had the names of forty-two victims who had borrowed a total of 856 taka—at the time less than $27 [USD]. What a lesson this was for me, an economics professor! . . . I offered the equivalent of those twenty-seven US dollars from my own pocket to get these victims out of the clutches of those moneylenders. The excitement that was created among the people by this small action got me further involved in it. If I could make so many people so happy with such a tiny amount of money, why not do more of it? That is what I have been trying to do ever since."

Every time, Yunus moved his audience with his tale of the origins of microcredit. They got caught up in the emotion of the story, which came to a head in 2006 when he won the Nobel Peace Prize. To catch their support, he would end his story by asking his audience to join him in bringing affordable credit to every poor person in the world. Yunus almost always receives a standing ovation—and many pledges. That is the power of storytelling.

While there is no formula for becoming a successful storyteller, here are some helpful hints to telling a great tale.

#1 Look for Conflict

Without it, there is no story. Every film, book, and play is grounded in conflict. It does not matter if it is a romantic comedy, political thriller, family drama, or Western-horror-docu-musical—they are cemented in conflict. Why? Because conflict is interesting. Conflict forces characters to make decisions, often in moments of uncertainty or distress, in order to reach their desired outcome. Imagine this scene: An innocent boy tries to kiss a pretty older girl. He closes his eyes, puckers up, and ... nothing. That is conflict. Does he try again or give up? We are dying to know what happens next. When it comes to your story, use that tension to your advantage. Your audience will engage.

#2 Aim for the Heart, Not for the Head

Forget the facts and figures. They are hard to relate to and impossible to remember. Instead, make people care. Here is one way to craft your story: Start by posing an unexpected challenge. Next, take your audience through the struggle of overcoming that challenge. Finally, provide them with an unexpected solution and a call to action. Create an emotional connection with your audience, and you will be surprised by how many will become your ambassadors.

#3 Be Clear, Concise, and Compelling

Loquacious and garrulous anecdotes are vapid and soporific.

#4 Know Your Audience

You would not sell veal to a vegan. Nor would you sell Tempeh or Tofurkey to a carnivore. Different audiences. Different interests. In order to make your audience care, you have got to know what they care about. What are their most pressing needs? What makes them tick? What pushes their buttons? Once you know, frame your story accordingly. Make it imaginative and unforgettable. Focus not only on the content, but also the context. Where will your audience be most receptive to hearing your story? When and how should you tell them? The more you know about your audience, the better positioned you are to crafting an effective story.

#5 Let Go

As a storyteller, you must learn to give up control. Let your audience take your story and make it their own. Understandably, you may find this troubling as they reshape, alter, and edit that which you hold precious. It is okay. Let them recreate and retell. Trying to stop them would be exhausting, futile, and counterproductive. Besides the fact that you cannot control how they think and behave, the more your audience feels a sense of ownership, the more likely they are to take action.

Social innovation is not easy. You will be met with resistance, skepticism, and downright denial. After all, you are pitching transformation—ideas that require new thinking, behavioral change, and shifts in consciousness. By understanding the characteristics of a great story, you will be well positioned to affect your audience. And when you are trying to change the world, is that not the ultimate goal?

COMMUNICATING EFFECTIVELY ACROSS CULTURES

Dennis Jett

Dennis Jett is a professor in Penn State's School of International Affairs who has written widely on American foreign policy, peacekeeping, and other topics. A former career diplomat, he served as ambassador to Peru and Mozambique and on the National Security Council.

Let us start with the assumption that we are talking about a situation where you are attempting to communicate with a person from another culture in a one-on-one situation. Here are some suggestions that will help the words spoken lead to understanding.

#1 Know the Language

Communication obviously starts with the language to be used. If both of you are native speakers of the same language, communication will be easier, but not automatic. If either of you is speaking in a second language, understanding will be limited by that person's command of the language. In such a situation, or if there is no common language, an interpreter may be required. But good interpretation involves much more than translating the words in one language to the words of another. If you do not know the language of the other person, even if you do use an interpreter, learning a few phrases and the standard greetings can be a good icebreaker and show some respect for the other person's culture.

#2 Know the Person or at Least Learn

If possible, always know about the other person. Such preparation should take place before the conversation begins, but if that is impossible, much can be learned once it has begun. If you are doing the talking, however, you are neither listening nor learning, so listen carefully. Also pay attention to body language as that often speaks volumes regardless of what is said.

#3 Know What Language the Person Speaks

Listening carefully is made easier by understanding the background of the person. A peasant farmer is not going to speak the same language as a bureaucrat, a diplomat, a soldier, or a policeman. Occupation, education, social status, and more will determine how a person speaks.

#4 Know the Culture and History of the Person, the Institution, and the Country

Understanding is also aided by knowing about the things that provide the context for the person and his or her country and the institution for which that person works. Culture, history, and religion will all provide a frame of reference for the person; failing to take these into account will impede communication. Recognize that concepts of time and commitment are not the same across cultures. A 9:00 a.m. meeting may start exactly at nine or sometime around ten, or it may not start at all if a commitment is an expression of hope and not a binding promise.

#5 Know the Customs, Courtesies, and Protocol

Failing to understand the customs and norms of a society will also hinder communication. Are handshakes perfunctory or firm, long or short, expected or unacceptable? Are greetings also given short shrift, or should you inquire as to the health of everyone in the other person's family? Are business cards formally exchanged in a prescribed manner? Do people stand very close or an arm's length apart when talking? Is crossing your legs or showing the bottom of your shoe to someone acceptable or insulting?

#6 Know the Rules

Is there a strict protocol that governs how the conversation should proceed? Protocol may be looked at as the stuffy strictures of diplomats or as a set of rules that allows people from many cultures to get on with the business of communicating without unintended insults that might arise from the differences in those cultures.

#7 Final Point

This assumes that the communication takes place in the course of a face-to-face conversation. Texting and email are lousy ways to reach any degree of understanding. So ditch the ear buds and turn off the smart phone if you really want to communicate.

INTEGRATING DISPARATE WAYS OF KNOWING

Audrey Maretzki

Audrey Maretzki is a professor emerita of food science and nutrition in the College of Agricultural Sciences at Penn State University. For the past twenty years she has provided leadership for ICIK, Penn State's Interinstitutional Center for Indigenous Knowledge, a global IK resource center located in the PSU Libraries. She is also a coeditor of ICIK's new open-access, peer-reviewed, online journal IK: Other Ways of Knowing.[38]

John Todd, a biologist in the field of ecological design and the 2008 recipient of the Buckminister Fuller Challenge, has said, "Elegant solutions will be predicated on the uniqueness of place." This brief statement underlies the value of merging indigenous and Western knowledge systems. Western academic knowledge seeks universal technological solutions to "problems," while indigenous cultural knowledge seeks to explain, within a cultural cosmology, how and why conditions emerge in the unique place in which they live. The historically "young" methodologies utilized by Western scientists include hypothesis generation and experimentation that includes increasingly sophisticated techniques to control variables and quantitatively and systematically assess a stated hypothesis. In comparison, indigenous science is rooted in knowledge based on the careful observation and integration of minute characteristics of a unique place occupied by a culture that has transmitted knowledge from generation to generation over many millennia using captivating stories that are heard and repeated as children transition into adulthood.

To many Western scientists, the cultural knowledge of indigenous peoples may be interesting, but it is generally incomprehensible and impossible to validate using accepted techniques required by the process of peer review. The situation is often complicated by language, age, gender, time limitations, and the respective roles of visiting academics and local community residents. Recently, the ecological implications of global climate change and its impact on flora and fauna as well as humans in occupying discrete locations around the globe has led Western scientists to focus on the ways in which cultures adapt to change as well as how their cosmology and historical observations have combined, over time, to address ecological change. Today, as never before, Western scientists are making an effort to communicate respectfully with indigenous/native scientists, acknowledging that the many species occupying a unique ecosystem are interdependent, making Western science dependent upon the historical observations embedded in the "spirited stories" of indigenous elders.

Integrate Western and Indigenous Knowledge – The Do's and Don'ts

- DO learn everything you can about the cultures of the people in whose "places" you will be working.
- DO NOT rely solely on Wikipedia and popular movies to educate yourself about the culture.
- DO use your senses (eyes, ears, and nostrils) to help you understand a place that is new to you.
- DO NOT meet and greet your hosts as you would persons in your home community. Greetings are very important in indigenous communities, and even a few words spoken crudely in the host's language is generally interpreted as an effort to meet as equals.
- DO be respectful of the knowledge of your host. In the host's environment they know much more than you do and will share valuable information only if the authority rests within the host community.
- DO NOT ignore the respect of age in traditional communities. In a discussion group that includes younger and older individuals, the former cannot disagree with the latter.
- DO understand that in traditional communities, gender differences must be taken into account because the knowledge possessed by women and men are unique to their gender.
- DO NOT take charge of every situation if you want your host community to treat you as an equal.

---

[38] Find the IK journal at journals.psu.edu/ik.

- DO share your research findings with the community and encourage discussion of other possible ways to interpret and apply the findings.
- DO NOT forget to include, as investigators on the report or publication, those community members (women, men, and youth) that contributed in a meaningful way to the project.
- DO make clear to the community elders (men and women) what you are trying to achieve with your project. Listen carefully as they explain or demonstrate how they would undertake the project, and whenever feasible, integrate their ideas and suggestions into the methodology.
- DO NOT expect those that provide assistance to do so without reasonable compensation.

FIVE REASONS TO LEARN MULTIPLE LANGUAGES

Sher Vogel

Sher Vogel is the summit coordinator at the International Development Innovation Network (IDIN) at MIT's D-Lab. The International Development Innovation Network (IDIN) empowers a diverse, global network of innovators to design, develop, and disseminate low-cost technologies to improve the lives of people living in poverty.

If you are interested in pursuing a career in social innovation or international development, it seems self-evident why it is important to learn other languages. If you are not from the United States, you understand well that learning other languages is critical to your professional, and maybe even personal, success. The fact, however, is that English is still one of the leading world languages. And unfortunately—especially for those of us from the US—it is all too easy to sit back comfortably and rely on translators or allow our counterparts to practice their English with us without trying to learn one of their mother tongues.

As STEM innovators who dare to dream of a more creative world, I challenge you not to fall into the trap of convenience. I encourage you to make the time investment necessary to step away from your "normal" work and try learning at least one new language (if not multiple languages) even before you get to the community or office where you are planning to work. There are plenty of reasons you will thank yourself that you did.

#1 It Makes Other People Happy

Imagine being stuck in a place where you do not speak the language and do not understand all that is going on around you or the decisions being made. And then, one person comes up with a smile, speaks your language, and offers to translate for you. What relief and what joy! Someone understands you! In the same regard, when you are able to speak another language, you make that person equally as happy. In several rural communities throughout the globe, they get excited even if you know only a phrase in their language. You may not understand everything they are saying, but even the time you invested to learn the one phrase shows that you value them, and that makes them happy.

Even if you will be staying within the US, many nonprofits support local immigrant populations or international partners, both of whom may struggle with English. Even if they are fluent, making an effort to communicate in their language will give you better access to the communities, allow better understanding of their culture, and set you apart as a professional in your field.

#2 Understand What People Were Taught to Value

Oftentimes the values of a culture and community are embedded in the language. For example, some languages are similar to English and conjugate verbs based on time and when the action happened. Other languages, like some Native American languages, conjugate verbs based on truth and how true that action was. And then there are even some languages, such as Haitian Creole, that have no verb conjugations at all—actions simply just happen. Similarly, a language can have different conjugations for male, female, plural, or elder persons; a language can be written or oral, have many detailed characters or none at all, could be written horizontally or vertically, etc. Each of these are small indicators of values embedded into a people group, sometimes giving you insights into how they perceive and value different genders, ages, groups, emotions, and concepts.

#3 Think in a New Way

There is an anonymous adage that says, "If you want to see something you have never seen before, you have got to do something you have never done before." In learning another language, you typically also learn a new grammar structure. Your mind gets stretched to think about what comes first—the noun, the verb, or the subject—and why. This small exercise your brain goes through to adapt to restructuring your communication begins to awaken cognitive spaces that are typically dormant if you are living in a mono-linguistic space. Even more than going for a walk or taking a break away from your work, learning another language can "get the creative juices flowing" in a new, powerful way that can help you think in a new way about a problem and sometimes help reframe it for more innovative solution.

#4 Gain and Share More Ideas and Insights

A key step in the design process is gathering information and understanding the problem. Think of how many ideas and key insights are left out of the design process simply because they are too difficult to communicate or are not in our language. Additionally, there are so many products that fail in dissemination farther down the pipeline because people do not know how to communicate about it clearly or missed a key piece of information along the way. Ideas can be difficult enough to communicate in English, let alone another language. However, when we learn other languages, we open up more lines of communication to both hear more ideas and insights as well as share more ideas and insights.

#5 More People and Organizations Want to Partner with You

Lastly, when you speak multiple languages, more people and organizations want to partner with you. Empirically, speaking multiple languages signifies you value other people's thoughts as much as your own—a key and desirable component to successful projects and products. Practically, more people and organizations are able to partner with you because you can speak their language, including highly skilled people who have typically been marginalized, overlooked, or even uninvited because they cannot speak the dominant language.

Some new economists project that networks are the currency of the next generation. If that is true, learning multiple languages is your winning lottery ticket.

WRITING WELL: THE MASTER KEY TO UNLOCKING OPPORTUNITY IN SOCIAL IMPACT CAREERS

Elizabeth Hoffecker Moreno

Elizabeth Hoffecker Moreno has produced award-winning academic writing and over thirty successful funding proposals for community-based organizations through Social Innovation Partners, an impact-driven consultancy she founded in 2006. Currently, she conducts research at the intersection of local innovation, social impact, and sustainable regional development at MIT's D-Lab, where she leads the research program for the International Development Innovation Network, a multi-institutional consortium with over 400 grassroots innovators in fifty-two countries.

One of the most valuable skills in social impact careers across the public, private, and nonprofit sectors is the ability to communicate clearly, compellingly, and persuasively in writing. In this field, a five- or seven-page grant proposal can result in a $75,000 donation and a ten-page business plan can win a competition earning you $100,000 (or more) in seed funding. A two-page prospectus in the hands of a potential investor can lead to your first financing deals and a three-page proposal can earn you your first major contract. In the midsize city where I started my career, it was not uncommon for over 400 people to apply when a position would open at the more influential local foundations and social sector organizations. What determined if your résumé was read? A one-page cover letter, which in about three paragraphs needed to persuade a reader that you had the right combination of skills and experience to excel in the job.

While the quality of what you are offering and the degree to which it aligns with the interests of an employer, donor, investor, or client is what ultimately matters, the ability to clearly communicate that in writing is essential in order to advance your vision for impact and your career. Yet writing can be challenging and intimidating even for people who regularly produce high-quality written work. With practice, however, anyone can become a better writer, and investing time and energy in sharpening your writing skills is one of the wisest steps you can take to position yourself for a high-impact career. So what does highly effective writing look like, and how can you learn to produce it?

The Writing Skills You Will Need and How to Build Them:

#1 Offer Synthesis, Not Just Summary

Effective grants, reports, cover letters, and briefs distill data and information from many sources into the key points that are most essential to convey to the specific audiences reading the piece. This involves assessing the data and information you wish to present and asking: what about this is most necessary to convey and relevant to my readers?

#2 Be Direct, Clear, and Succinct

Whether your readers are hiring managers, grant reviewers, or government officials, they want to understand what you are proposing as quickly, clearly, and precisely as possible in what is often an extremely limited amount of space. Donors, for example, increasingly require two-page letters of inquiry (LOIs) as the first step in the proposal process. With only a few paragraphs to make your case, you must get straight to the point and address the essential information they are requesting as directly and briefly as possible.

#3 Present Arguments as Well as Analysis

Most professional writing in impact-oriented settings has dual objectives of informing as well as persuading. Whether your need your readers to change their mind about an issue, adopt a new practice, or contribute financial support to a project, you must present a rationale that is convincing enough to move them to action. This is not accomplished by presenting facts and figures alone, but rather by using evidence in support of a strong argument. One way to ensure this is present in your written work is to ask yourself the following question whenever you are presenting facts, data, or information: what point am I trying to make with this data, and have I clearly stated the point prior to and/or after offering the evidence?

#4 Tell a Coherent, Compelling Story

Social science research confirms that what motivates us to action is not simply facts and figures, but the narrative that is used to frame information. A key to creating succinct but powerful written pieces is to use a story line—a coherent narrative—to organize the data and analysis you are sharing. Frame what you are saying in terms of one main idea, thesis, or story line, and use that to organize and tie together the rest of the piece. You should always be able to answer the question "What is this document about?" with a one-sentence answer.

So how do you cultivate these essential writing skills? Research on the principles of high performance in fields ranging from sports to music to the arts confirms that the way to improve skills and build mastery is through "deliberate practice," which involves consistently engaging in the activity in a way that challenges you to stretch your limits. Just having the goal of writing better is not enough; you need to develop habits, routines, and practices that actually move you toward achieving the goal.

Four habits to develop your writing skills:

#1 Read Excellent Written Work—It Rubs Off

Regular exposure to well-crafted prose sensitizes us to what good writing looks and feels like, while exposing us to various writing styles that we can start to incorporate into our own work. A great way to start is to spend at least one hour each week reading pieces that have been screened by others for quality, such as award-winning novels, the eclectic and high-quality pieces in magazines such as *Harpers, Atlantic Monthly, Christian Science Monitor, The New Yorker*, or critically acclaimed nonfiction books. Complement this general exposure by reading one current or past article a week from publications that offer thought leadership to the fields you are interested in exploring, such as the *Stanford Social Innovation Review*. This will familiarize you both with the content and writing style of your field of interest while setting high but attainable standards to work toward in your own writing.

#2 Develop a Writing Practice that Involves Feedback

We would not attempt to run a marathon or perform a music set without regular, weekly practice beforehand and some amount of coaching. Yet we sit down to write an article, major paper, or funding application without having a regular writing practice, and we wonder why it feels so challenging. You will learn to write with more ease and better results if you establish a writing practice that involves producing short pieces under time pressure for someone else to read. One way to jump-start this routine is by taking a writing-heavy class with a teaching team that is committed to providing feedback on your work; another is to volunteer to write blog posts or funding proposals for a group you are involved with. The key is to create opportunities to write that have deadlines set by others, real consequences for missing them, and mechanisms that enable you to obtain feedback from people who are better at writing than you are. And like all forms of practice, your writing practice will yield the best results if you do it consistently at a time of day when you are most alert and focused.

#3 Organize Your Thoughts before Writing

Good writing in the social enterprise, development, and business worlds is first and foremost about clear, persuasive thinking. Whether sitting down to write a funding request, business plan, or report, the most important first step is to organize your thoughts. What is your main idea, argument, or narrative? What are the most essential points you plan to make in support of that narrative, and in what order does it make sense to address them? What examples, stories, or evidence do you need to support each of the points you plan to make? Once you know what you will say, in what order, and with what supporting material, you are in a good position to start writing. As you write, if you stay focused on the key messages you are trying to communicate, you will find that the words often take care of themselves.

#4 Use an Effective Template

Once you sit down to write, the process will be easier and produce better results if you use a template for structuring your piece that you have experienced to be effective in the past. Have you seen a cover letter that earned a friend a job? A grant that was successful in obtaining an award? A business plan that won a competition? Once you have a sense of the type of documents you will be wanting to produce, make a habit of gathering a few successful examples of these types of documents and understanding their structure in terms of what type of information is included and how it is organized. From this, you can create basic templates that you can use as starting points for various types of documents you will write. This helps you get started with a document, overcome writer's block, and ensure that you are including the type of content that will make your document most effective.

part six

Finding Your Niche

FINDING AND WORKING WITH MENTORS

Pamela Roussos

Pamela Roussos leads the Global Social Benefit Institute (GSBI®), a program of Santa Clara University.[39] She has spent most of her career as an executive starting and building software companies based in Silicon Valley. Being a mentor is a favorite part of her life, particularly working with social entrepreneurs, which she began doing with the GSBI seven years ago.

Having mentors is an important aspect of shaping your career and success. There is so much to learn, so many paths to choose and myths to dispel, it can be a lonely path. Mentors are the trusted advisors that are on the journey with you. They are there to guide, advise, share their point of view, share their wisdom, laugh and cry with you. Most importantly they are there to listen and to ask why. The reality is that most of the time the answers you are looking for are within you; they just need to be dug out. A good mentor is not someone you call up to ask a question, get a quick answer, and then go off to execute on the answer you received. They are there to walk your path with you; they are not asking or forcing you to walk their path. A good mentor will spend time with you to listen, will ask probing questions, and will let you guide yourself to an answer by tapping into their own experience and wisdom.

Finding and selecting good mentors is important—as important as getting your job done well. Sometimes you happen on to them accidently, but being thoughtful and purposeful is recommended. Here are five questions to begin your journey.

#1 Why Is a Mentor Important?

Your life and career is your path, and your path alone. However, there are people that have walked parts of your path that you can benefit from. There are people that have gifts and talents you do not have that are more than willing to help you gain from them. These people are called mentors. Good mentors are humble, respectful, encouraging, and inspiring while being engaged, an active listener, pragmatic, honest, and challenging. A good mentor will not let you settle; they will demonstrate tough love when it is needed, and they will inspire you to be your best. They will celebrate your successes with you. They will dig deep when it is necessary. Why stumble along the path by yourself when it is not necessary?

#2 When Should You Start Looking for a Mentor?

Immediately, it is never too late to start. The reality is your needs for a mentor will change over time. What you need now as a young person starting your career is not what you are going to need later in your career. Your mentors will change as you change and grow.

#3 Where to Look for a Mentor?

Work is a natural place to start identifying possible mentors. You are with your coworkers much of the day; you see what they excel at and how they interact with others. If you are working in a small environment, or perhaps you are a woman looking for a woman mentor, you might not find one at work. Asking friends is another source of possible mentors. They may have mentors or know others who could be a mentor for you. Networking events can be a great source for meeting people who could potentially be a mentor. Quite possibly friends of your parents may be the best mentors for you. The point is that mentors can be anywhere, so be open to the possibilities. Wherever you are looking, it is important to be clear about what you are looking for in a mentor.

---

[39] Mentor values articulated by the Global Social Business Incubator at Santa Clara University: scu.edu/socialbenefit/entrepreneurship/gsbi.

#4 What to Look for in a Mentor?

It is important to find someone who listens to you. Someone who will "tell" you the "right" answer is not a mentor and is not doing you a service. Trust is an important quality to have in a mentor. It is hard to gauge whether you will trust someone in a single meeting or call. It takes time, but if at any point you do not feel you can trust someone, they will not be a good mentor for you.

The more self-awareness you have, the better off you will be in identifying mentors. You will want to be looking for mentors that have skills and talents you do not have. Some of these might be hard skills, say finance or marketing. Some of these might be soft skills, for example leadership, managing others, or work-life balance. Prioritizing your "must haves" versus "nice to haves" will help you focus your search.

Finally, you might decide to have a "mentor board." Every company has a board. Their role is primarily governance, but depending on where the organization is in the life cycle, the board might be involved in other aspects—strategy, for example. A good board is comprised of different skills and talents. You could assemble a (small) group of people with different skills and talents whose role is to "govern" you.

#5 How to Ask Someone to Be Your Mentor?

Asking someone to be your mentor can be the most difficult step, especially for women. Should you ask Mr. or Ms. Very-Busy-Important-Person to be your mentor? The reality is, when you ask someone to be your mentor, they will be honored. They might still say no because they do not have the time, but they will be honored—so ask. Sometimes you will have a better chance of "yes" if you ask them to mentor you on a specific task. Say you are an engineer and have a new product you think you would like to bring to market. You are going to need a business plan, but you have not ever done one before. You can ask someone to help mentor you while you work on it. You are not asking for a long-term commitment; the task has an end point, so it can be easier to agree to it. At the end of the day, you never know where that engagement will lead. It may go beyond the business plan, or it may not; either way, you have benefitted and your mentor has too.

Mentorship can begin over coffee, beer, wine, or asking someone out to get his or her advice on a particularly difficult situation you are experiencing. Again, it maybe "transactional"; you may not go out again, or it may lead into a long-term mentoring relationship.

Bottom line: It is important to surround yourself with smart people that have talents and treasures you do not have (yet) that will listen and be your trusted advisor along your path of life and career.

Finally, you might be asking yourself:

Why do mentors mentor? What's in it for them?

I can speak from personal experience as I have mentored quite a bit. It is among my most favorite things to do. It is wonderful being surrounded by passionate people who want to create positive change in the world, and if I can help them do that, what a wonderful gift to myself. I have gained a lot of experience and wisdom—I think about it as the battle scars on my back. If I can prevent someone else from going down the same dark alleys that I know lead to these battle scars, then why would I not do that? There is a give-back aspect to mentoring: from a place of desiring to do so, not from a place of feeling required to do so.

There is a part of mentoring that never ceases to amaze me and to be a pleasant surprise: I can suggest something that seems so natural, and it is a big aha to my mentee. It is a testament to the wisdom and experience gained and to the value therein. Within a few minutes, something I say can make a big difference in someone's life. Wow! What a gift to me!

TEN TIPS FOR A BALANCED CONFERENCE

Alexander J. Moseson and Ticora V. Jones

Ticora V. Jones, PhD, is the director of the Higher Education Solutions Network within the USAID Global Development Lab. She is a social scientist and expert on creating innovation ecosystems designed to build community, enable action, and drive impact. She has spearheaded key legislative victories on energy and environment issues as a congressional fellow for Senator Russell D. Feingold (D-WI), and she helped manage the establishment of an agency-wide agenda for science and technology through policy and programming as an AAAS Science & Technology Policy (Diplomacy, Security, and Development) fellow.

Alexander J. Moseson, PhD, is an AAAS Science & Technology Policy fellow, catalyzing academia for international development at the US Agency for International Development (USAID)'s Global Development Lab. In over a decade in sustainable international development, he has codeveloped technology on four continents, been awarded a Bill & Melinda Gates Foundation grant, and starred in The Human Element.

As a STEM professional, no matter the field, conferences are inescapable. That is a good thing, and it is for good reason. Despite the electronic everything that empowers us today, relationships, cultivated through convening a bunch of like-minded people in the same place at the same time and face-to-face, are critical to how things ultimately get done. There are few better opportunities for networking, which we like to think of as making new friends, and for having those new friends and potential colleagues spill over with excitement about your niche work. So yes, it is as important as everyone says it is.

Conferences also demand time, money, and energy and can be overwhelming or downright frightening. Thus, this brief presents ten elements that you will want to consider and balance when it comes to making the most of conferences. For details, there are great less-brief resources on science communication, networking, and more.

#1 Engage Your Core Expertise ... but Stretch Yourself

- As you choose conferences, sessions, and people, balance exposure to your core expertise and "stretch" topics, especially if you are trying to be interdisciplinary or shift to a new field. Beyond traditional academic conferences, consider workshops, industry convenings, or trade shows.

- Are you not sure how interested you are? Before you dive in, look for webinars or conference proceedings from previous years to see if you would be excited (not just interested) to attend.

- A note of caution: be wary of unsolicited email invitations to conferences of open journals, even those that greet you by name. Most are scams or spams, and it is not uncommon to get half a dozen or more per day. Your peers and mentors in the field can help you discern which are legitimate, popular, or otherwise.

#2 Keep Your Old Friends . . . and Make New Ones

- Keep the rhyme in mind, as popularized by the Girl Scouts: "Make new friends, but keep the old. One is silver, the other is gold." This may be the only time each year that you see people whose company you have come to enjoy. It could also be the start of a new collaboration, friendship, or career. Enjoy your clique, but not exclusively.

- New friends may lead to a job, but unless it is a job fair, do not ask for one directly or hand out your CV/résumé unsolicited. Even new friends can smell desperation.

#3 Listen . . . and Speak

- It is true that, at a conference, you get out of it what you put into it. First, put into it listening and observation. It is a great way to equip yourself, even if the application is not immediately apparent. Also do not be afraid to speak, in conversation or on stage. The latter often justifies the funding for your attendance, but it is not required.

- Part of being a great conversationalist is listening. If you have no idea what the person you just met said because you kept yakking, try again.

#4 Bring Business Cards . . . or Master Digital Networking

- Nothing has yet bested the paper business card for universality. Bring lots, even if you print them at home. Many online print shops will print hundreds for ten dollars, given enough notice. When you receive them, write notes on the back. Conversely, if you are a digital guru, be ready with NFC, QR codes (which can also be easily added to paper cards), etc. However, there is a risk that the other person will not be ready to receive it as easily as a piece of paper. Either way, keep track of your interactions through LinkedIn, notes, a spreadsheet, etc.

- Make sure it is an exchange. If a speaker has a social media presence on Twitter, follow them. Just do not try to "friend" them on LinkedIn if you have never had an interaction outside that space.

#5 Be Confident . . . but Not Arrogant

- Do not be afraid to approach people; any excuse will do. If you prepare ahead and identify common ground in your greeting, all the better (e.g., by reading the person's journal articles or even the conference abstract). Check the attendee list in advance.

- Master the introduction: use your full name and have a "one-liner hook" to lead with. Then have a thirty-second and a two-minute elevator pitch at the ready.

- Be confident. If you like yourself, it is much more likely they will too. However, this is the only spectrum on which you do not want to be on the right side: undue humility will make you forgettable, and undue arrogance will get you spurned and remembered in an unflattering way.

#6 Attend Scheduled Sessions . . . but Not All of Them

- Side meetings, especially with those old or new friends, can be invaluable. Make time for them.

- Many people try to keep up with regular responsibilities while at a conference because of deadlines or a desire to lighten the eventual backlog. It takes away from what you accomplish at the conference itself, but if you must engage in that, consider stepping out of a session. You will be frowned upon less for that than for distracting everyone by furiously typing "notes."

- Do not feel guilty about taking a bit of rest if you need to, mental or otherwise. Conferences are exhausting before, during, and after, and you should present your best self at all times. Have dinner at a restaurant off the beaten path, see a cultural attraction, or take some time to be inspired and rest.

#7 Prepare . . . but Not Too Much

- Do make an informed decision about which conferences to attend, plan your travel wisely, have your elevator pitch (and possibly your talk) ready, study the program, and more. However, do not overwhelm yourself by investing too much time or worry. Other attendees are likely as overwhelmed as you might be.

- Know your objectives for the conference, and use them as a strategy to guide the myriad decisions you will make. However, keep your mind open to new and better opportunities; often, you could not have predicted them.

#8 Keep Your Promises . . . or Do Not Make Them

- There are many great reasons to follow up after saying good-bye: sharing a paper you wrote or a reference you used, discussing collaboration, applying to a program, and more. If you promise to do something though—do it! Follow-up is a forgotten art. We are all busy, so do not let the fear of not crafting the perfect email paralyze you. Keep it brief, make your point, wish them well, and then let go. You may not always get a response, but reliability and follow-through are great skills to flex. Do not feel obligated to promise everyone a follow-up; it manages expectations and the cloud of tasks you carry around.

#9 Save Money . . . or Increase Comfort and Opportunity

- You can often save money by staying at accommodations farther from the conference, taking less convenient flights, etc. Your time has value though, so balance that with comfort and convenience. In particular, staying at the conference hotel may enable you to attend early or evening events and—dare we say—take a power nap.

#10 Thank the Organizers . . . and Consider Becoming One

- Organizing conferences is very difficult and time-intensive. Planning each annual conference for 500 people can easily exceed 1,500 man-hours, not to mention innumerable face-palms, temper tantrums, and late nights. At least thank the organizers and volunteers when you encounter them. If the conference topic is a core area for you, consider asking if there are opportunities to join the committee. It could be a lot of (mostly thankless) work, but also an unprecedented way to join the inner circle of a community and engage with people—including VIPs—at many levels.

FINDING YOUR FIRST JOB IN THE SOCIAL SECTOR

Christina Gilyutin

Christina Gilyutin is the director of talent management at REDF, an organization whose mission is to create employment opportunities for people facing the greatest barriers to work. Operating at the intersection of private markets and social impact, REDF achieves this by investing in social enterprise employers and creating linkages between employers and employees.

Why are STEM professionals underrepresented in domestic social enterprise and the social impact space? It is not for general lack of interest: talk to any undergraduate class of engineers or scientists, and you will find a significant percentage of students looking for a meaningful career opportunity that will empower them to "make a difference." But people with this profile do not typically join the social sector. More often, they choose "caring" STEM careers: for example, medical careers working with underserved communities or engineering in the developing world.

So why then does the social sector not attract more STEM graduates? It is a mix of two interrelated factors: without a critical mass of people with STEM training, there is neither a well-worn path for people to enter the field nor a mindset that clearly values their skill sets. In the interest of growing the potential reach of the social sector (and its diversity of thought!), we need to work more actively to bring the STEM community into our work.

Of course, a transformation on this scale takes time. For people with STEM academic or professional backgrounds interested in making this type of transition, here are ten specific actions you can take in order to accelerate your move to a mission-driven career in the social sector:

#1 Find Organizations and People Who Relate to What You Know and Do

There are a number of organizations whose mission specifically ties into the technical and analytical skills that come with a STEM background. Here are a few examples with regional or national reach:[40]

- Girls who Code: A national nonprofit working to close the gender gap in the technology and engineering sectors

- Code for America: A national nonprofit that partners with local governments and citizens to foster civic innovation. By working to reinvigorate civic participation, accelerate the civic startup marketplace, facilitate collaboration among government leaders, and build new tools that enhance and strengthen communities, CfA is helping governments solve old problems in new ways.

- Techbridge: A national nonprofit that inspires girls to discover a passion for technology, science, and engineering. Through hands-on learning, they empower the next generation of innovators and leaders.

- TechSoup Global: An international network of fifty-eight NGOs serving 112 countries in Africa, the Americas, Asia Pacific, Europe, and the Middle East. For over twenty-five years, it has leveraged technology to build NGO capacity toward solving social problems in local communities and fostering global social change.

- YearUp: A national nonprofit whose mission is to close the opportunity divide by providing urban young adults with the skills, experience, and support that will empower them to reach their potential through professional careers and higher education

This is just the tip of the iceberg; there are many other organizations that fit this profile. You can search Idealist.org for a list of organizations that match your skills and geographical preferences.

---

[40] These organizations can be found at: GirlsWhoCode.com, CodeForAmerica.org, TechbridgeGirls.org, TechSoupGlobal.org, and YearUp.org.

#2 Get Experiences

This can be accomplished a number of ways, including:

- Classes: If you are still a student or entering a graduate-school program, be sure you take advantage of classes and projects that will give you real-world experience.

- Internships and fellowships: If you find the right type of internship or fellowship that will give you specific experience that you are lacking, do it. A word of caution: avoid doing too many of these, especially consecutively. If done in sequence, this can be a red flag to potential full-time employers.

- Volunteer: Donate your time to an organization whether it uses your STEM knowledge or not. Displaying your interest and passion through volunteering is a critical component of landing a job in the space. Many organizations do look for STEM mentors and tutors, so there is no shortage of volunteer opportunities that directly use your expertise. (Again, search Idealist.org for a number of options that match your skills, interests, and geographical preferences.)

#3 Network

Nonprofits typically lack the resources to recruit on campus or broadly post job opportunities. More so than in other fields, look to your connections in the social sector to make introductions for you and seek out other people who have made a similar transition, attended the same schools as you, or worked for the same companies. When reaching out to people for the first time, it is always good to make it clear that you are looking for advice given their specific experience and perspective.

#4 Translate Your Experience to Make It Relevant

This is critical. Tailor your résumé and verbal messaging to the field; specific technical details will not likely ring a bell with someone who does not share your domain knowledge. Test your wording on someone who does not have a technical background and ask them for feedback about the clarity of your descriptions and phrases. However, as part of your interview preparation, you will want to also consider how to "sell" your diversity of background, thought, and perspective and how this would add value to the organization's work. Ultimately, engineering is about designing things for people, so be ready to provide potential employers with compelling examples of how your STEM background can help solve social problems. Make sure to bring a portfolio to your interviews, and create an online portfolio that employers can review when they are considering you for an interview.

#5 Create and Maintain an Online Presence

Active blogging and LinkedIn are great venues. Make sure all relevant (and even seemingly nonrelevant) projects, internships, and volunteering are listed as part of your experience. You never know which of your interests will catch someone else's eye!

#6 Be Persistent

It is a numbers game, and you need to keep applying for jobs. A typical job search often takes six to nine months and involves applying for at least fifty different jobs. The UN often receives thousands of applications for one job opening from around the world, so it is not unreasonable to spend more time and apply for more jobs as you make your transition.

#7 Do Your Homework

Research any organization you are considering joining. This includes online research and getting in touch with people who currently work there, previously worked there, and/or have worked with the organization in question. It is important to understand the culture as much as possible to ensure you will be gaining the experience you want. There will still be inevitable surprises, but you want to minimize those by doing your due diligence ahead of time.

#8 Be Flexible on Salary

Early on, the pay may not be great, but it is a gateway to better-paying jobs. Compared to the private sector, you will often have a better work-life balance and the opportunity to pursue other interests outside work, but keep in mind that you will likely never have the same income you would have in the private sector. If that is not going to work for you, this is something to consider!

#9 Once You Are In, Help Others by Facilitating Connections and "Making the Case"

This is perhaps the most important point on our list! There is no better advocate for making the transition than someone who has done it. Be open to inquiries from people with STEM backgrounds seeking advice on their own transitions, and look for opportunities to serve as a public spokesperson. Many universities have career panels for STEM students looking to do something "beyond STEM."

#10 Keep a Mindset of Learning

Learning does not end at graduation! Even if your first opportunity in the social sector is not "perfect," just know that all jobs have ups and downs. The most important thing is to always have a mindset of learning and, no matter what, focus on continuous improvement and what you can learn from every opportunity and everybody.

HOW TO NETWORK YOUR WAY INTO A NEW JOB

Wayan Vota

Wayan Vota is a senior mobile advisor at FHI 360 and has over twenty years' experience using technology in international development. He cofounded ICT4Djobs, the premier career network for the information and communications technology for development (ICT4D) specialty, and ICTworks, ICT4Drinks, Technology Salon, Educational Technology Debate, OLPC News, Kurante, and a few other things. He also teaches ICT4D at Johns Hopkins University–School of Advanced International Studies.

Often, job seekers focus on responding to published job opportunities as the key to gaining employment. However, a formal job advertisement can be a cursory step in the hiring process; employers usually have a candidate already in mind when they publish a job ad, which means many of those that apply are really wasting their time.

See, the hiring process starts back when either an existing team member leaves or a team obtains funding to hire for a new position. At that point, a meeting is called, and everyone on the team brainstorms on whom they should bring on. In this meeting, friends and friends of friends are mentioned as potential candidates, and frequently two to three people are identified as preferred candidates. Those people are contacted and invited to submit their applications for the position.

Somewhere in here, the formal job description also goes to the human resources department to be posted online, which results in a flurry of CVs and cover letters from hopeful applications. However, the hiring team already has two to three people on their short list. These new, mostly unknown applicants are fighting for the one to two spots the hiring team might have in addition to their preferred candidates. Even then, those that applied online are at a major disadvantage—they not only have to prove their relevance, they have to prove that they are overwhelmingly better than the preferred candidates.

Now I am not saying this process is fair or ideal; I am describing what actually happens. So how can you be one of those preferred candidates—someone who is on a hiring team's shortlist from the beginning? There is one proven way: build a large professional network through informational interviewing.

Connections Matter, So Informational Interview

Back in that initial candidate brainstorm, you want someone to mention your name, to suggest you as an ideal candidate, and to push for you to be considered for the job. The best way to do that is to be known to people in the field you want to work in by networking with them before there is even a job opening. How do you do that? Here is a three-step process:

#1 Have a Solid Pitch

Many job seekers are not sure what they want to do, or they are focused on either the tasks, like business development or project management, or the sector, like health or education, that they want to work in. You actually need both.

So your first step is to think about your desires. Develop an elevator pitch about your interests—you need to be able to say that you want to have a certain role in a specific sector (e.g., a project manager working in education or in business development for health services) and explain why that is your focus in a short, targeted paragraph or less. This helps those you interview with understand your interest and relevance, and when they should think about you in that new-hire brainstorming.

Yet you do not need to fret that you have to have your end goal determined when you first start informational interviewing. A key component of the process is for you to constantly be assessing what your interviewees say and how that might change your goals.

It is quite all right to start with the expectation you want to do X with Y and then over time realize you really are interested in A with B. In fact, the worst outcome of the job-seeking process is for you to think you have just won your dream job, only to find out it is actually your hell job, and have to start this whole process all over again, while hating your workdays.

2 Start Informational Interviewing

Most recent graduates do not have a large professional network, and that is okay. You do have family and friends, so start informational interviewing with them. There are multiple online resources that tell you what an informational interview is and how to do one, though often two key points are left out: ask for names and be sure to follow up.

During an informational interview, make a point to learn about a person's professional interests and their peers. Ask what they want to work on, which may be different from what they are doing now, and for at least three people who are also in their field. You want to have three to four new contacts from every informational interview so that you can grow your network.

Add this information to a spreadsheet listing whom you have talked to, what the key points were, and whom they connected you with. This spreadsheet is core to building your professional network. You can keep it as a simple spreadsheet or get fancy and use customer relationship management software. Regardless, this database will help you continue to grow your network, understand its interconnectedness, and make connections among people.

#3 Build and Strengthen Your Network

Do not make the mistake of neglecting your contacts after you had an informational interview with them. Use your spreadsheet to track when you last contacted each person and be sure to reach back out to them and send along relevant news or connections that they would appreciate.

One of the most effective actions is to introduce them to new people in your network that you think could be relevant to them. While most peer groups are relatively small, there is constant turnover, and people are always doing new things. Making the connection between two people is both helpful to them and can be a powerful reminder that you were listening in your informational interview and still think of that person after the interview.

You want to make sure your connections remember you and think highly of you. You are not going on these interviews for fun. This is work, and you should be focused on creating long-term value for your connections so that when they are in that new-hire brainstorming session, they remember your name and put you forth as a candidate.

Work at Networking and Informational Interviewing

I run a career coaching service dedicated to my subspecialty, ICT4Djobs.com, and I tell all of those I coach to network and informational interview. Yet it is only a few who fully understand that you have to work at both. You should aim to have five to ten informational interviews a week—yes, at least one a day—to truly get the most from the interviewing experience. I practice what I preach too. I did over 400 informational interviews over two years back in 2002–2004 to break into the international development industry.

Yes, that sounds daunting, but the results speak for themselves. The conventional wisdom is that it takes one month for every $10,000 in salary to find a job. So if you want a $100,000 job, it will take you ten months to get it—if you are working at it full-time. If you put in part-time effort, expect it to take much, much longer.

Your Network Is Your Asset

Now let us fast-forward to your first day at your new job. You are so excited to start, and yet just after you walk in the door as a new employee, your boss hands you a huge project that you need to finish as soon as possible. No need to stress. You developed a wide, deep network during the informational interview process, and now it is time to put it to good use.

Open up your spreadsheet and contact those that are relevant to this new task. Thank them for helping you land this cool new job, and tell them the project you are working on and the help you need. You will find that all of those informational interviews laid the groundwork for an amazing support network that can now help you succeed at your dream job. Congratulations!

DECIDING ON A CAREER SWITCH FROM INDUSTRY TO MISSION-DRIVEN ORGANIZATIONS

John Lyon

John Lyon is president and CEO of World Hope International, a Christian relief and development organization working with vulnerable and exploited communities across the world. An attorney by trade, Lyon held senior positions at a global law firm and two privately held development companies prior to joining World Hope International. A former US Peace Corps volunteer, and as someone who has always had a penchant for missions work, Lyon made the jump from industry to mission-driven in October 2014 and has not looked back.

The idea of working for a mission-driven organization may be appealing to you, probably most of all lead by the notion of your job making an impact daily, or the feeling of your work actually helping those who need it, or the opportunity to truly make a difference for something or someone. It may undoubtedly sound much better than your forty-plus-hours-a-week job in corporate America that, let us face it, probably makes someone else more money. But before you make the switch, ensure you are ready for the commitment. The need for vast mental, physical, and emotional fortitude definitely comes along with the territory. At a mission-driven organization, days are long, resources are tight, and the work can be thankless at times. If your heart is in it though, making the jump could be one of the most rewarding and truly fulfilling decisions of your career path and your life's calling, at large.

Here are five things to consider before you make the switch:

#1 Ensure You Have Learned as Much as You Can from Your Current Role

When working for corporate America, generally your role is highly specialized, and you have a plethora of training enhancements added to your job title. Maneuvering within a traditional corporate culture, you are also likely to be exposed to structured staffing tiers and a specialized human resource department in which you can observe best practices and key learnings from other professionals in your field. Soak it all in. When you jump to a mission-driven organization, you will most likely find yourself in a more generalist role, taking on more tasks than originally outlined, learning on the job in real time, and taking on a lot of more accountability at any moment. Arrive to the mission-driven organization with as much experience as you can muster from your current role in every imaginable capacity. It will certainly be put to good use—and often.

#2 Do Not Expect to Be 100% Happy

No one job is perfect. If you are making the switch thinking the "grass is greener" and that you will be completely happy in your new role, be sure to recognize that there are problems and frustrations that come along with any job, even it if does possess a greater humanitarian purpose. While your new mission-driven role may truly help the greater good, there will still be times you leave your office for the day tired, frustrated, or up against a wall. Like life, jobs too always have ups and downs.

#3 Be Prepared for the Responsibilities

Resources—especially staffing, budget, and time—are tight in mission-driven organizations. This calls for a great deal of both creativity and responsibility as you learn how to utilize the resources you have at your fingertips. When you are working for a cause you care strongly about, yet the budget is not there to provide the help you wish you had to give, you need to know how to separate your passion from the bottom line. Do the best job you can and stretch the resources you have as far as you can. It is vital to think outside the box and push your creativity, but at the end of the day, do not beat yourself up for not being able to do enough. There will always be more work to do and aid to provide. There are times when it is okay to rest on the fact that you did the best job you could.

#4 Ensure Your Motivation Is beyond Monetary

In corporate America, your paycheck is a gratifying reward for a job well done. As you strive to advance in your corporate career through more senior titles and bigger salaries, money is often an indicator of success. This is not the same in a mission-driven organization. While upward mobility is definitely still part of succession, be prepared that paychecks will not compare to those of your private sector peers. Supplemental rewards will come through the type of work you are doing and the impact it is making on other people, on both small and larger scales. For example, your role may directly help to save people's lives from a serious disease, or provide nutrition for a child who has none, or protect a young girl from a lifetime of slavery. These accomplishments, these people you affect directly, are your reward—and from personal experience, I can say that they do make up for any difference in the paycheck.

#5 Do Not Underestimate the Workload

It will be more than you think. Actually, it will definitely be more than you think. If your heart is really dedicated to the mission though, the workload will be worth the change you are creating and the profound impact you are having. It is an old cliché, but your work will truly become a "labor of love," and the labor that goes into it is worth it, tenfold, both for yourself and others in need.

Take a step back and think about these five things, but most importantly, follow your heart and enjoy the journey.

SHOULD YOU ENGAGE ALONGSIDE YOUR JOB?

Harald Quintus-Bosz

Harald Quintus-Bosz is a visiting lecturer at MIT's D-Lab and is also the CTO at Cooper Perkins, a technology development and product engineering consulting firm. He volunteered for five years at the International Development Design Summit (IDDS) helping to organize and teach summits in the developing world. Harald partnered with a technology industry executive to pen this expert brief.

You love your industry job. The pay is great, the benefits are excellent, and your colleagues all love you. Everything is fine and dandy. But there is always this wrinkle: something is lacking. You want give back; you want to do something that makes things better for those not as privileged or fortunate as you. You have tried volunteering at the soup kitchen or mowing grass at the nonprofit around the corner. That is a good workout, but is that the best use of your time and abilities? You are an engineer, or a scientist, or an economist, or a doctor, or a public health expert. You want to contribute using the skills you worked for years to develop!

Maybe you think, "I can help the nonprofit as a webmaster, or teach kids engineering design, or volunteer at a clinic." It would be a win-win situation and help them much more than mowing grass and stuffing envelopes. Or you can teach a course on constructing small bridges in developing countries at the local university. You have spent ten years of your life doing something while the professors were studying it with their white gloves on. You have talked to the university folks, and they would love to have you teach. But before you take that plunge, here are some things to think about.

#1 Balance with Your Day Job

How, exactly, will you balance your day job with your moonlighting work? Decide how much time your work leaves you and whether you need your moonlighting commitment to be on a fixed or flexible schedule. What happens when something "comes up" at work or at the nonprofit? If you are in an important volunteer role, consider whether your job might face "scope creep" that further challenges your schedule. Are you comfortable with such a level of responsibility in a volunteer assignment? Also investigate this from the perspective of your daytime employer. Will they be supportive of schedule conflicts and potential travel, or are they more concerned about you spending too much time volunteering? Many employers encourage volunteerism, and some even offer funding and resources to support you. Find these resources if they are available, and talk to colleagues who have tried similar volunteer commitments while working for your organization.

On the other side, some volunteer opportunities can be directly useful to your career or company. Prospective employees and customers tend to respond positively to a story about your interesting, relevant volunteer opportunity and are drawn toward that type of experience. Recently, the number of candidates that are interested in social impact seems to be increasing. Even aside from new hires, building a personal network is important for both you and your company, and meeting volunteers can be very useful in that regard.

#2 Parameters of Commitment

Once you are comfortable with a potential volunteer role, discuss and assess the length of the commitment you are making. Is it multi-month or even multiyear, and does that fit with your current life and career situation? Remember that mowing a lawn is easy; you go, and three hours later you are back. Committing to revamping a website, teaching a course, or organizing a major food drive takes longer. Stepping into an organizational leadership position could require years of commitment. Find out the organization's expectations, and think hard about whether you can and want to follow through on them. Long continuous assignments, such as a four-week trip, are much more personally challenging than repeated scheduled events. Be prepared for personal vacation time and even work projects to suffer from long assignments. At the same time, one-time trips can have fewer long-term responsibilities than a steady volunteer job.

If you are taking on a major or long-term commitment, plan ahead for what will happen when you leave. Are you going to be training your replacement? Does your organization know how to handle any changes you will implement? Ensure your changes help rather than hinder a future without you there to support them, and do not underestimate how long that will take. You do not want to set up new inventory management software in a local food bank and then walk away just when people are learning how to use it. Do not run a recruiting drive at a local youth league and then leave before someone else can support the students. Consider carefully whether it is all right to be a housing construction trainer and leave before your replacement is up to speed.

Finally, consider the culture and structure of the organization itself because it will be a workplace for you. Remember that organizations primarily supported by volunteers can behave differently than for-profit businesses. You may need to be very flexible and set aside habits from your work life, such as the relatively static roles and titles and the ways in which duties are distributed, monitored, and executed.

#3 Out-of-Pocket Expenses

Consider what this volunteer opportunity will cost you. You are signing up to lend your expertise, not necessarily your money. Are you covered by the organization's insurance, whether your risk is fighting forest fires or working in a warehouse? Particularly if you are in a dangerous or emergency-response role, what happens if you miss your day job? Examine whether the organization offers reimbursement for expenses or remuneration for lost wages. What are the procedures and limitations? Read these carefully because incidental expenses can add up quickly. Gas mileage to rural clinics, printing handouts for a school team, phone calls, postage stamps, uniform cleaning—minutia can become macroscopic very quickly. On the other hand, many volunteer expenses and donations can be written off on tax returns; just ensure you have read the fine print on your volunteer job description. Try to discuss any concerns with others in the organization or your position.

#4 Conflicts of Interest

Finally, consider how the perception of your day job will reflect on your volunteering and vice versa. Understand how your work and expertise will be perceived by your fellow volunteers and organization, and how your involvement might be interpreted at work. Particularly if you are volunteering in a field close to your day job or professional expertise, investigate any potential conflicts of interest. Ensure your audience is always clear who you are advocating for. Are you an accountant trying to fundraise from nonprofit donors? Ensure that they know you are acting as an agent of the nonprofit, and encourage them to seek external financial advice. Is your company a potential vendor for this nonprofit? Whether your business sells software or designs buildings, ensure that you disclose any conflicts and avoid the appearance of favoritism. Also investigate if your company's and volunteer organization's efforts might overlap or compete in anyway. Finally, ensure any legal rights have been negotiated beforehand, particularly if you are volunteering in some official company capacity. For instance, if you are a webmaster by day and your company sends or supports you designing a new website for the local youth center, ensure everyone agrees on copyrights beforehand.

#5 Special Considerations for Travel and Fieldwork

Pay close attention if your prospective position involves travel or remote communication. If you live in Silicon Valley and the organization you want to help is in New York, you may be able to work remotely. Examine whether the organization already has a culture and history of working with remote partners and in virtual teams. This can be a very difficult and stressful thing to do, particularly with organizations who have not already streamlined the process. Even if you are working remotely, consider whether you will need to travel occasionally for an in-person meeting. Will your travel be funded or supported, and can it be written off on your taxes? Do not underestimate the need to travel, particularly if you are working with an overseas project or one in a difficult culture. In-person fieldwork is essential in order to stay grounded, to understand your stakeholders and their needs, and to keep your efforts in perspective. Do not remove yourself too far from those you aim to help, and if you cannot go in person, consider what that means. If most of your team can get to Zambia for three weeks and you will not be able to, how does that affect your contribution? While it may be tempting to contribute as much as possible without traveling, consider carefully if that is actually what is best for the team, project, and target community.

#6 Special Considerations for Academic Gigs

It is very true that a middle-aged professional likely has much more experience than a professor on particular subject matter. You may make a great visiting lecturer or adjunct professor! Universities are always looking for experts like you, and teaching can be a very rewarding opportunity. At the same time, remember that teaching is not just about knowledge: it takes special skills to connect with students, and experience counts in those skills as well. As with all new positions, be prepared to adapt and learn. Sometimes your approaches from professional life can directly enhance student learning; other times the teaching experience might help to approach new problems at work. Also remember that it can be hard to think back on what used to be difficult for you. Things that are automatic after years in industry may be entirely foreign to undergraduate and even graduate students. For example, you might need a very different way of teaching manufacturing design if your class is not fluent in a CAD package. Not only will they not be able to do hands-on drafting work, their methods and depth of thinking about interesting part geometries will be far more limited.

Where Are These Part-Time Professional Opportunities?

Professional opportunities are those that require and potentially impart transferrable skills. This does not mean that you necessarily need to be a teacher to coach a middle-school science competition or a manager to help run a breast cancer walk. The key point is that the volunteer tasks require appreciable qualifications, experience, and/or training—it is not just serving soup or driving patients to doctors' appointments. Professional volunteer opportunities can be highly rewarding for all parties, but they can also be difficult to find.

The search for professional volunteering positions depends somewhat on your expertise and interests. Starting with the local chapters of professional organizations can often provide strong leads. Educational institutions, from universities and community colleges through local public schools, are typically great places to share your experiences as a teacher or otherwise. Local nonprofits and community centers are always looking for volunteers, and engaging in the local social sector opens up a lot of networking avenues. This also applies to other socially minded organizations, such as religious institutions, social enterprises, and service clubs. Finally, there are a growing number of websites created specifically to match prospective volunteers with opportunities that meet their interests and limitations. It is just a matter of finding where you want to start!

DECIDING ON A CAREER SWITCH FROM MISSION-DRIVEN ORGANIZATIONS TO INDUSTRY

·Rebecca A. Delaney

Rebecca A. Delaney is the youngest mechanical team leader for the design firm of Skidmore, Owings and Merrill's (SOM) sustainable engineering studio in Chicago. SOM is one of the largest and most influential architecture, interior design, engineering, and urban planning firms in the world. Delaney mentors students interested in engineering careers, both locally and globally, through the ACE (Architecture, Construction, Engineering) Mentoring Program and numerous humanitarian agencies. She is a global leader for the nonprofit organization Engineers Without Borders and travels to Kenya and Uganda to teach sustainable practices to local communities.

There is a common misconception that to have the greatest impact your day job must align perfectly with your passions. If you want to change the world, then you should find an organization whose core mission matches your passions to ensure the greatest influence. However, working in industry can develop valuable skills to make you more effective in your missional pursuits.

Here are five things to consider before you make the switch:

#1 Money!

This is probably the most obvious reason, and it does not need to be a shameful incentive. You can be *in* industry without being *of* industry. Pursuing money itself will probably lead you down an unhappy path, but if you enter industry with a more selfless pursuit, the money is a nice bonus. The more money you make, the more you can financially support the organizations and passions you love. Or you could work hard and save your money in order to launch your own social enterprise, which is how Aravind Eye Care System was started in 1976 and performs 300,000 mostly free eye surgeries to prevent blindness. Either way, pursuing an industry job is not mutually exclusive from having an impact in your passion pursuit now or in the future.

#2 You Will Have a Day Job

This may not be a surprise, but working in corporate America, your first priority will most likely not be related to your mission work. Your passions will be relegated to an extracurricular activity. This can put an extra demand on your free time outside the office, leading to very long hours and slower progress. This can become very frustrating at times; however, it is important to remember "the grass is always greener on the other side." There are trade-offs whether you are in industry or missions. If you can strike the right balance, then it can be very rewarding.

A mentor once posed the following question to me: *Have you ever thought about leveraging your corporate brand to further your nonprofit passions?*

Consider the power of a corporate brand and reputation with respect to networking potential with peers, clients, and industry partners. By working with non–like-minded people, your immediate impact on those around you could be exponential. Plus, most of the people you will encounter in industry have money (see #1) and can provide further financial support to your cause(s). Additionally, corporations understand millennials are pushing forward a "capitalism-with-a-conscience" trend, reflecting their deep desire to do good. Look at the Starbucks (RED) campaign, TOMS Shoes, and Honest Tea.

#3 Learning Business . . . When You Have Resources

Industry exists to make money. Businesses invest significant resources in the form of technology and manpower to streamline processes and workflow to increase profit.

Nonprofits exist to make social change. Not-for-profit organizations invest significant resources into programs and events with the largest potential for change and are often scrutinized if too many resources are dedicated to technology or manpower. People who give money want to see the change created by their money, not the staff supported by their money.

Straddling these two worlds by working in industry and volunteering in mission work provides a unique vantage point. You can learn how to use ethos to get buy-in within the nonprofit world while learning processes created by industry to accomplish more with fewer resources. Learn from everyone you work with—including project managers, accountants, IT, marketing, HR, and the CEO/president—by asking questions and observing their best traits. And become great at your day job. Whether you master Excel, manage a team, run a research lab, or design complex structures, work to become highly proficient in your role. Successful people in industry succeed because they have developed cross-disciplinary skills while developing in their own role. Nonprofits need experts and often struggle to recruit and retain them.

You can support your mission with the resources of your industry job, including software/technology, training/conferences, and people capital. Industry projects tend to move quickly while missions projects can take quite a bit longer to complete. Industry and mission-centric organizations are certainly two different worlds with respect to priorities and operations; however, they each could benefit from a little of what the other has. Understanding these nuances positions you to have significant impact whether you choose to stay in industry long term or eventually plan to transition to a mission-driven company.

#4 You Are a PR Dream

Do-gooders create excellent public-relations opportunities for companies. Unfortunately, not everyone in corporate America feels compelled to give back to their communities and support great causes. That makes people who do give back stand out. Clients love companies that value their bottom line and their community, which attracts more clients and leads to larger revenues.

This can bring more resources your way to find stronger intersections between your industry work and the emerging social challenges you are pursuing. Those resources may be in the form of linking you within a vast people network, tapping you for company-wide thought leadership, or allowing you opportunities to interact across business units. Developing both your big-picture and detail-oriented perspectives while leveraging your resources is great for your career advancement.

#5 Launchpad for Entrepreneurship

If you have dreams of starting your own business (for profit or not) someday, then working in industry can prove to be very useful as a training ground for your future endeavors. Understanding how successful businesses are structured, attract and maintain clients, and measure their success will be critical knowledge as you start out on your own or help others start their own business.

Entrepreneurs strengthen economies by creating jobs and putting revenue back into local economies through salaries and taxes. Many mission-driven organizations believe this is the most sustainable growth strategy for developing countries/communities. Industry can provide you with a great foundation of basic business knowledge, which you can share and use to mentor organic growth at the community level.

PROMINENT CAREER ADVANCEMENT RESOURCES

Editorial Team

Most organizations have a "Careers" page on their website where they explain the kinds of opportunities they offer and how their hiring process works. Larger organizations tend to list current opportunities while the smaller ones provide contact information. In order to reach a wider talent pool, organizations typically advertise opportunities on websites that are popular with the social innovation and sustainable development community. This brief lists some of the most prominent web-based resources and forums for professional development and career advancement. Several of them host job boards that curate and disseminate internship, fellowship, and job opportunities at impact-focused organizations around the world. Increasingly, many of these web portals as well as organizations themselves use social media like Twitter and Facebook to connect with the sustainable development community and share engagement opportunities.

1. **Devex** is a phenomenal forum for career resources including international development job postings from over 1,000 organizations in 100 countries. www.devex.com

2. **Engineering for Change** is the largest community for technical professionals in social impact and provides a variety of resources. engineeringforchange.org

3. **Idealist** lists volunteer, internship, and job opportunities from 100,000 organizations across its English, French, and Spanish sites. idealist.org

4. **Echoing Green** supports rising social entrepreneurs with a monthly digest including dozens of job openings at social impact organizations. echoinggreen.org/tags/social-impact-jobs

5. **NextBillion** posts global jobs, fellowships, and internships related to sustainable development through innovation. nextbillion.net/jobsfeed.aspx

6. **Net Impact** provides job-search advice, a job and internship board, and access to their community of programs and events for 60,000 students and professionals. netimpact.org

7. **Development Net** links 600,000+ job seekers and 20,000+ international development recruiters via résumé broadcasting and job and consultancy listings. devnetjobs.org

8. **Opportunity Knocks** is a US job board and career resource center for 30,000+ nonprofits. opportunity-knocks.org

9. **Global Jobs** includes job openings in over 3,000 nonprofits, for-profits, and governments. globaljobs.org

10. **ReliefWeb Jobs** lists international humanitarian job openings in over 4,000 organizations. reliefweb.int/jobs

11. **InterAction** is the major alliance of US-based NGOs and includes job listings for its 180+ members. interaction.org

12. **USA Jobs** is the official site for all US federal job listings. usajobs.gov

13. **Social Edge** is a networking, job search, and insight sharing community by the Skoll Foundation. skollworldforum.org/jobs

14. **Escape the City** provides US and international job listings, entrepreneurial support, and transition programs. escapethecity.org

15. **Aspen Institute** runs a career center for development entrepreneurs with job listings and related resources. andeglobal.org/networking

16. **Business of Social Responsibility (BSR)** maintains a list of job openings across all their 250+ member companies. www.bsr.org/en/careers/job-openings

17. **ReWork** matches job seekers with economically sustainable social impact organizations. rework.jobs

18. **Commongood Careers** is a recruiting firm for nonprofit organizations. commongoodcareers.org

19. **Social Good Jobs** offers job, freelance work, internship, and temporary position listings in US and international social impact organizations. socialgoodjobs.org

20. **50 Ways to Get a Job That Makes Good** walks you through a guide of different ways to find your dream job. 50waystogetajob.com

part seven

7

Personal Considerations

SALARY AND COMPENSATION PRACTICES

Robert Orndorff and Blair Ciccocioppo

Robert Orndorff has advised students in higher education on career development for twenty-five years. He is currently the senior director for Career Services and an associate professor in counselor education at the Pennsylvania State University, teaching courses in career counseling for graduate students and professional development seminars for faculty and staff. While at Georgetown University, Bob's job-search program won a national award for "the best educational program related to career services in the nation."

Blair Ciccocioppo has worked in different industries and for various types of organizations ranging from the US government to nonprofits. She has worked as a mechanic for the US Army, as a mental health caseworker, and in sales and staffing. Overseas, she has deployed as a mechanic and worked as a security contractor and as duty manager with the United Services Organization (USO). She currently works for On Assignment, an international leader in placing scientific, engineering, and preclinical professionals in contract, contract-to-hire, and direct-hire opportunities.

You are in your early twenties. You cannot wait to go out and change the world. As long as you can make ends meet and pay back your student loans, you do not care much about money. You are covered by your parents' health insurance. Maybe you are single (and wild and free), or maybe you are in a committed relationship and prepared for a long-distance marathon. You are looking for exciting positions in sustainable development or have a job offer in hand. While you may not think much about your salary and benefits package right now, it is critical to start off on the right foot. The cost of living is rapidly increasing. Working in developing countries can actually end up being more expensive than living in the US! Your life is going to get even more expensive. You may want to get married or have a baby. While you may find a low-maintenance spouse, babies are always expensive! Your starting salary will stay with you, and it can be hard to break out of a salary cycle once you have set it. Your annual raises, and even your salary at the next job, will be based on your current salary. Alongside a great job where you are changing the world, you might want flexibility and the resources to pursue new opportunities and try new things. You do not want your salary to control you. People often leave jobs and careers they truly enjoy because the compensation leaves them feeling incomplete.

Do not let this be you. As you enter the real world, it is important to understand how salaries and compensation work. So far in your life, you may have worked only in wage payroll positions or internships that pay by the hour. In the professional arena, the vast majority of people work for monthly (or biweekly) salaries. You will likely have a flat paycheck every month, and you will likely have a benefits package. Your work will be driven by responsibilities and results, not the amount of time you spend working. This is typical of professional work in the US, but the kinds, amounts, and modalities of compensation vary quite a bit across jobs, organizations, and locations. This article provides an overview of the kinds of compensation that organizations offer to enable you to understand and negotiate your compensation package and perks.

Compensation in US-Based Jobs

#1 Salary

Your annual salary is the largest, and arguably the most important, aspect of your compensation package. Your skills, education, experience, and salary history are all factors in your control that affect your salary. There are other factors out of your control, like companies' locations, the supply and demand for your skill set, and the salary ranges for your organization and job position. Ultimately, the salary range is driven by supply and demand for your skill set. It is not uncommon for a twenty-five-year-old with a bachelor's degree and in-demand skills to earn substantially more than someone with a niche PhD and decades of experience. Find out how much people with your skill set make in your job location, and examine if you have any particularly marketable skills for your salary negotiation.

Location

It is more expensive to live in San Francisco, California, than State College, Pennsylvania. Thus, your salary needs to be greater in San Francisco. Be prepared for this in negotiations, and do your homework first. Read about your potential placement locations, and try to talk to people familiar with the area—particularly those with a similar life-style and family situation. You can also use online cost-of-living calculators to compare a lifestyle you are familiar with to your potential new location.

Organization Type

Part II described the various kinds of organizations engaged in social innovation and sustainable development. You can decipher from the profiles in this book that salaries vary quite substantially, even for people with similar degrees and experiences—sometimes even similar jobs. This is usually due to the nature of the employing organization. Multi-laterals, UN agencies, and governments tend to have set salary ranges based on job description, qualifications, and/or location, leaving little room for negotiation once the position and location are set. Similarly, some organizations are completely reliant on external donors for funding. These employers need to align their salaries with stipulations set by the donors and also offer few negotiation opportunities. Industry salaries tend to be higher than in corresponding nonprofit and government jobs, but this is changing in some cases. The wage gap for professionals with in-demand technical skills is shrinking among all types of organizations. At the same time, nontechnical salaries remain much lower in nonprofits than in industry.

Salaries at consulting companies are typically comparable to, or better than, their industry counterparts. However, the long hours you work and travel significantly limit your ability to have a social life. Independent consultancies are also on the rise. You may be hired for days, weeks, months, or even years. Independent consultants are often paid on an hourly basis or as a lump sum, even for longer assignments. They can command higher hourly wages, but they seldom receive the full benefits or job security that come with regular employment. For example, a consultant might be paid a lump sum of $10,000 with no benefits to conduct an assessment of a project and produce a report that aligns with donor expectations. Upon completion, they would then have to find another project with the same, or another, organization.

Entrepreneur salaries vary most of all. Startup leaders often pay themselves only after they have paid everyone else on the team, and their income depends on where the venture is in its life cycle. Although most of the money comes when an entrepreneur exits their venture, there are not many profitable exit strategies for social ventures. Selling to a for-profit can bring in a lot of money, including more capital for another project, but it is unlikely that the business would still run as a social venture. Spinning off to a larger nonprofit is also feasible, but it is unlikely to pay as well.

#2 Travel Expectations and Reimbursements

Organizations may offer vacation, sick leave, maternity leave, educational benefits, and retirement plans to stay competitive. In industry and entrepreneurial ventures, stock options and equity are also common (stock options are the ability to buy company stock at a discount; equity is part ownership). Often, companies that have limited salary ranges can make allowances on benefits. Regardless, you need to understand these common benefits, what organizations typically offer, and what questions to ask. As you read this, however, understand that you cannot ask all of these questions up front. Study the organization's policies, do your research, network with alumni and other contacts in your field, and talk to current employees.

In addition to better understanding the organization's benefits package, you should also engage in a self-assessment process for determining your professional and personal values. In short, determine what is most important to you in a job. For some, salary is by far the most important factor, and they are willing to sacrifice time off with friends and family. For others, having flexibility in office hours is the most important factor because they want to be able to get to their kids' soccer games and dance recitals. There is no right or wrong when it comes to values—only you can determine what is most important to you. The self-assessment process will help guide your decision regarding the types of benefits you should fight for the strongest.

Travel Expectations and Policies

Jobs in the social sector, especially those in international development, can involve copious amounts of travel. Before you accept a job offer, you should know what your company expects in terms of travel and consider how that fits with your personal and family preferences. While most organizations have formal travel policies, many small organizations do not. Depending on the type and culture of the organization, some of these can be negotiated.

Before you accept any offer, consider the following:

1. Where are you going? Is it within the US, in industrialized countries, in developing countries? Are you in cities or rural areas, government buildings or farm fields?

2. When are you going? How long are you gone in total? Are these long trips or short trips? Are they scheduled or short notice?

3. How will you get there? Are long flights in economy or business class? Can you fly economy instead of business and keep the financial incentive? How soon after you get out of a transatlantic economy seat do you have to give your first presentation?

4. How will you get around, and who pays for it? Transportation, whether public or rental, can set you back quite a bit. A two-hour Shinkansen train ride from Tokyo to Kyoto can set you back $300, or a car rental in Malawi can cost $300 per day.

5. How are you paid? Are you reimbursed for actual expenses or paid a flat per diem? Per diems are typically highly sought after and even negotiated as you keep the money you do not spend. They tend not to be taxed. The US government uses standard per diems that vary by location of travel.

6. Is there anything you will not be reimbursed for? Ask this question twice if you are not a US citizen—if you need a visa while an American citizen does not, will you be reimbursed for the visa?

7. Can you bring your family? If so, under what circumstances and for what trip lengths and locations? Will any of their expenses be covered, or is it completely your responsibility?

8. What resources will you have? Does the company have staff support to plan travel logistics and/or have in-country resources? How much of this is up to you to handle? Pay close attention to how visas and special travel permits are secured and by whom as these can be tricky (and costly).

9. Will you be traveling on your own passport, or are you eligible for an official one? This applies only for some governmental or UN positions and other multilateral organizations, but official passports are great for their visa-free access around the world.

#3 Vacation and Sick-Leave Policies

Companies are not legally obligated to provide vacation or sick days in the US, but most do so in order to retain employees and improve job satisfaction. According to the US Department of Labor, full-time workers earn an average of eight paid holidays per year. Paid vacation starts at an average of eight days after one year, ten after three, and eventually up to sixteen after twenty-five years. Similarly, paid sick leave also starts at eight days after one year, then nine after three years, and eleven after twenty-five years. Larger companies have begun to combine all of these days into "paid time off" (PTO) to offer more flexibility without abusing sick days. Remember, these are averages; vacation and sick-leave policies vary greatly among organizations. A new trend is for employees to take as many days off as they wish as long as all work is completed. Typically, nonprofits and government agencies have generous vacation and sick-leave policies. Most US federal employees get all ten federal holidays off in addition to other benefits. Multilaterals often take the cake, arguably due to European influences, and have very generous vacation and sick-leave policies.

As you prepare for and conduct your benefits negotiation, consider the following:

1. Does the organization have certain holidays when everyone gets PTO?

2. How much PTO do you get each year, and is it separated into vacation, sick leave, and/or other categories? How does this compare to your peers?

3. How many unused leave days (of each type) can you carry over from one year to the next? Is there a maximum number of days you can accrue?

4. Is there a maximum number of vacation days you can take at one time? How far in advance does it need to be scheduled? Does it need to be coordinated with colleagues?

#4 Work Schedules and Flexibility

Flexible hours allow you to vary when you arrive and leave work each day. This is typically a management choice rather than a standard benefit, but supervisors can offer it to help motivate staff and improve their productivity, work-life balance, and access to educational opportunities. Some organizations also offer other options such as working from home.

Consider checking the following:

1. When are you expected to be in the office? Are there common working hours when all employees are supposed to be there?

2. Can you work from home? If so, how often and under what circumstances can you work from home?

3. Are there flexible work schedules? For instance, some organizations offer a "9/80 schedule" where you work eighty hours over two weeks (nine days) and can take a long weekend.

Also understand that many specialized, high-paying jobs are not forty-hour workweeks. The stories of lawyers and financiers working around the clock are spreading to other high-skilled and high-technology jobs. Communication technology means you are available 24/7, even in austere environments. Discuss this realistically with your peers and other employees and then with anyone significant in your life.

#5 Maternity/Paternity Leave

Under the federal Family and Medical Leave Act (FMLA), many employers are required by federal law to allow their employees (both men and women) twelve weeks of unpaid leave after the birth or adoption of a child. At the end of your leave, your employer must allow you to return to your job or a similar job with the same salary, benefits, working conditions, and seniority. Depending on the state you live in, you will use a combination of short-term disability (STD), sick leave, vacation, personal days, and unpaid family leave during your time away from work.

Some US organizations also offer paid parental leave. This is a legal requirement in virtually all other countries, and a growing number of individual companies are implementing it within the US. Right now, this is seen as a major benefit and a strong leverage point for retaining and motivating quality employees. International organizations are not subject to any nation's laws and thus set their own rules for benefits, including parental leave. The UN is often used as a standard reference; its most common policy is sixteen weeks of full pay for mothers and four for fathers.

#6 Professional Development Opportunities

For each job you negotiate or accept in your career, think ahead not just about the position itself but also what it offers for your professional development (PD). Different types and sizes of organizations offer many different PD opportunities. PD is a continuous process of improving your skills and ability to perform in the workforce as well as keeping up with changes in your field. Formal opportunities can involve higher education or workshops (particularly those that offer PD credit) provided or sponsored by your organization. Informal PD can range from observing your superiors on the job, to learning by networking with peers, to volunteering.

During your job search and negotiation preparation, consider the following:

1. What do you want your career trajectory to look like? What PD do you need to get there?

2. What, if any, PD is mandatory to gain or maintain the credentials you want to hold? Many professional associations and qualifications require PD.

3. Will you be able to pursue higher education in this potential position? Will the organization help, either with work flexibility or tuition benefits?

4. Does the organization sponsor employees in your position to attend conferences, workshops, and seminars? Are there strong PD opportunities on-site as well? Are there additional resources for engaging with professional associations?

5. Does the organization allow employees in your position to spend some amount of time on projects of their choice? Some companies, most famously Google, use this "20% time" as a PD strategy for fostering creativity and innovation.

#7 Career Advancement Opportunities

Career advancement opportunities vary significantly among organizations, particularly those of different sizes. Larger employers tend to have proper processes and pathways for advancement with well-known progressions and qualifications. For instance, most universities have tenure-track systems for professors with clear guidelines on promotion and implications on compensation. Many companies will consider you for promotion on a well-defined schedule, for instance annually. However, smaller organizations may have no clear channels, and very small ones may have little to no internal advancement at all.

If you are looking to remain with an organization, consider these questions. Even if you are not comfortable with your potential career trajectory within the organization, a job with them may still be good for both of you. Your PD at the organization can lead to career advancement in a different organization or as an entrepreneur.

1. Are there clear advancement trajectories that align with your career goals? For instance, some STEM organizations may have both management and technical advancement tracks stemming from your position. Ensure that what you are researching and discussing is what you are interested in pursuing.

2. What are the pathways for advancement along this trajectory? Are they well defined, and what do they require? How often do positions open above your potential position, and how competitive are they?

3. What process does the organization use for deciding promotions? Are these processes well defined for your trajectory, and what is required of you?

4. What is the relationship among position, job responsibility, and compensation? In many organizations, one can expect that more responsibility and a higher position lead to higher compensation. This is not universally true, however. For instance, it does not apply in academia.

#8 Tuition Reimbursement

Many employers see tuition reimbursement as an investment in their employees. While the conditions depend on the company, most requirements are manageable as companies receive tax breaks for paying tuition. If you study something related to your job, then many companies will reimburse all costs up to a set limit. Some companies require you to meet a certain grade requirement and remain with that company for five years after graduation.

#9 Health Insurance

Health care is important even as a healthy young professional and will become more important as you age and your family situation changes. If you are working abroad, many countries have universal health care that may cover you as an expatriate. (See the Compensation When Abroad section for more advice about being an expatriate.) Within the US, many employers offer a variety of health-care insurance plans. For smaller organizations or independent contractor employment, you will want to look into the government health-care exchanges.

#10 Retirement Plans

Retirement plans vary depending on organization size, union affiliations, and occupation. You decide how much of your salary you want to contribute via a payroll deduction. In industry, your employer automatically puts that money into your individual retirement account and often matches your contribution. The matching contribution is usually limited to 3–6% of your salary. Companies may set a specific dollar limit, and they typically require you to work there for several years to keep the contributions. All told though, this matching is free money! It is also untaxed until you withdraw the accrued funds during retirement.

Nonprofit organizations have different types of retirement plans. As opposed to the 401(k) plans in industry, the 403(b) plans common in nonprofits typically include contributions from the employing organization. Small nonprofit groups often elect not to match employees' retirement contributions. University systems and hospitals have their own retirement plans offered by players like TIAA-CREF or the state government (in case of public universities).

US government jobs do not have either of these retirement plans but instead use pensions. The federal government will automatically set up an account and deduct 1% of your salary every year. You can also contribute more and receive matching funds. However, you can keep these savings only if you stay with the government until retirement. The details of these plans vary among organizations and even among levels of government.

Make sure you understand the following:

1. What sort of retirement account does the organization offer? Is it voluntary or automatic?

2. What are the limits on personal contributions and on matching funds? How much, if any, of your paycheck is automatically placed into the plan?

3. Can this account be transferred if you move to a new organization, and under what conditions?

#11 Stock Options

Publicly traded companies often offer stock options as a benefit to employees. These stock options give you the right to buy a certain number of shares in the company at a fixed price for a certain number of years. Although you are not required to buy these, if the value of the shares rises over that time period, you can sell for a larger profit than would be earned on the open market. Companies typically offer stock in increments over a period of four years, which serves as an incentive for you to stay with your employer. Regardless, owning stock often gives you a greater sense of responsibility to and investment in the company.

#12 Private Equity

Private equity is the term for partial ownership of a company that does not have public stock. This typically relates to smaller or younger companies. Entrepreneurs may sell their company equity for up-front capital or other contributions in the early phases of their venture's life cycle. They can use those contributions to grow the enterprise. The entrepreneur and investors can then sell their equity as the company matures and becomes more valuable. These rules rarely apply to social ventures, which are typically nonprofits, though even the for-profit versions can be difficult to scale up and sell off. Trading your equity for significant profit usually requires selling to a larger company that may or may not run it as a social venture.

#13 Employee Matching Gift Programs

Employee matching gift programs give you say in where the company allocates its corporate charity dollars. These programs are typical in large private corporations where a typical program matches the donations employees make to eligible nonprofits. Most companies match at a 1:1 ratio, but some even triple or quadruple donations. These donations improve the company's brand while allowing you to direct funds to organizations you value most. Although major corporations are more likely to offer gift matching than other organizations, other donation programs do exist. For instance, the US federal government runs the annual Combined Federal Campaign that allows employees to streamline donations to qualified charities via payroll deductions.

#14 Dual-Career Support

Dual-career couples are those where both partners have specific skill sets with difficult-to-locate employment opportunities. The US federal government (military and civilian) offers some job assistance to help your spouse when you relocate. Some universities also provide dual-career support programs, including help for job searches, résumé improvement, and family transitions. These programs are also becoming more popular in other sectors as well, and large companies may have contracts with consulting firms that specialize in relocation services. You can ask and negotiate for this support or support for long-distance commuting (e.g., schedule and telecommuting flexibility) from your company.

#15 Other Miscellaneous Benefits

Many larger organizations also offer other perks to employees. While incentives like discounts and wellness programs are usually not key selling points or negotiation subjects, programs such as spousal assistance, childcare, and other family support may be very valuable.

Compensation When Working Abroad

Professionals who live and work abroad are known as "expatriates" or "expats." This is typically a temporary living condition though it can be indefinite. Regardless, it can be tricky to handle issues such as contract negotiation, relocation, insurance, and communication with family.[41] There are some factors in particular that affect compensation of expats.

#1 Salary Issues for Expats

As with US-based employment, your salary depends on what you negotiate with your employer. You may be treated the same as local employees, with the same salary, work hours, holidays, policies, and taxes. This might happen within a local organization or within a small international organization that cannot afford to incentivize expats. Alternatively, a local employer might be willing and able to recognize you as an expat and pay you extra for your expertise and relocation. They might also offer more holidays off and could cover relocation to different extents.

In many countries, local companies shift the balance between salary and allowances versus the US standard. You may earn salary comparable to that of your US counterparts but receive allowances for local services such as travel, vacation, health, and leisure. Alternatively, large allowances for these services are common in countries where sala-

---

[41] The Expat Info Desk compiles a manual to guide you through this process: expatinfodesk.com/expat-guide.

ries are taxed and allowances are not. Large international companies can offer very nice short-term and long-term expat packages. Long-term packages might include not just a high salary but also housing and travel allowances, children's school fees, and significant holiday entitlements. Short-term packages may be similar though they will exclude long travel breaks and school fees. If you are a US citizen, also examine whether you qualify for the foreign income exclusion. In 2015, you may exclude up to $100,800 in foreign income from US income tax liability. Check the Foreign Earned Income Exclusion on the IRS's website for more information.

#2 Relocation and Living Abroad

Who pays the rent in your host country is a big deal! Depending on the organization and contract you negotiate, your employer may cover relocation costs (to and from, potentially for you and your family), a housing stipend, school fees, vehicle expenses, and even some food expenses. Living abroad is expensive, often in many ways you are not expecting. Rent is a known universal: rent for a house in Nairobi, Kenya, could run you $2,000 to $4,000 USD per month. But in Nairobi, you will also need security for your home, which tacks on another $600 each month. School fees for one child at an international or American primary/secondary school could easily exceed $30,000 per year. If you need a car, be prepared to pay import duty. This can be up to 100% in Mozambique, so buying a $40,000 SUV would cost you $80,000 USD. You will also need to examine whether you are able to drive and comfortable driving in your new country, which likely has different rules and norms for the road. Employing a driver is the norm in some places, which can run you $800 per month in Mozambique without factoring in fuel and insurance.

Questions to consider include the following:

1. What will your employer cover while you live abroad? What happens if your family situation changes while you are abroad (e.g., support for a new child or as they start attending school)?
2. What is the cost of living in your host community and why? How do housing, food, transportation, and schooling work?
3. What is the expat community like where you are moving, and what other support is available?

#3 Insurance

Insurance, particularly health insurance, depends almost entirely on your organization and country of residence. While some countries provide foreigners (especially on longer-term visas) access to their nationalized (public) health services, employers typically offer insurance coverage. Check the conditions and deductibles for your plan and whether it includes preventive checkups, routine vaccinations and tests, and additional doctor's visits. Also look into the health standards and risks for your host region. Consider logistics in addition to actual coverage—are the quality, availability, and proximity of health care to your home acceptable? Give particular emphasis to the availability (and legality) of any prescription medications or specialists you may need. Travel insurance is also important during relocation. Consider what will happen in the event of lost luggage, airline strikes, or travel company problems as well as health incidents, accidents, or family emergencies.

Consider the following questions:

1. What are the health risks and standards of your host region? What vaccines and other preventive measures are necessary and expected?
2. What are the health-care standards where you will be living? Of what quality and availability are these services?
3. Are your specific conditions treatable where you will be living? Are your medications legal and available? Are there specialists in the area?
4. What does your health insurance cover for you and your family? What are the restrictions and deductibles?
5. What does your travel insurance cover? In the event of an emergency in your country of residence, what are the protection or evacuation coverage and procedures?

#4 Additional Considerations

Some organizations offer extra opportunities to expats and their families. You may get a certain number of paid trips home if your family is not relocating with you. Most medical insurance packages will include your family as well, but always check the conditions. Some employers might find other ways to ease the transition, including having someone guide you around your new area as well as offering information on how to take pets with you and keep in touch with distant friends and family.

Process of Negotiating Compensation

The answer is always "no" if you do not ask. Negotiations can be uncomfortable, but they are too important to avoid. Help yourself by doing your research beforehand by reviewing industry-relevant salary and relocation websites[42] and talking with career counselors, alumni in the field, and other professional mentors. Consider the following points in your initial research:

1. What is the market value for the position where the job is located?
2. Who is paying your salary? Is it an entity or a donor, and what standards does the organization have?
3. How do the benefits your organization offers compare to other organizations?
4. What are you looking for? Do the offered salary range and benefits align with what you want and need? What do you want to ask about and negotiate? For example, if you need money on the front end to pay for the down payment for an apartment, you would want to negotiate for relocation/housing funding. Remember that one-time funding, such as relocation, is typically much easier to secure than annual funding requests, such as salary, where equity issues are prevalent.
5. Realize that health-care and retirement benefits can be as important as salary, especially from a long-term standpoint.

Do not feel as if you have to settle for an unsatisfactory situation just to avoid a negotiation. Negotiations are a normal part of the hiring process. It is important to prepare for and handle them with confidence because if you do not feel happy and view the process as fair, it will affect your work. Remember that once you are hired, organizations do not want you focusing on your compensation. They want you focusing on your work! A good negotiation is a win-win for you, your employer, and your family.

#1 Preparing for a Successful Negotiation

1. Research market prices. Employers base salary offers on the average of peer jobs. Investigate the average pay for professionals with your level of experience and education that are in your field and in your part of the country.
2. Calculate your fair share. Figure out how your work affects the company's financial bottom line, and ask for a share of it.

> "In a previous job, I reduced costs by X% and increased sales by Y%. These types of achievements should be transferable to your department/organization. Hence, my salary could be based in part on a share (one half or three quarters) of this contribution."

3. Determine how much risk you are willing to take and how hard you are planning to negotiate. This is a case-by-case decision, and only you can make this decision for yourself. If you have multiple offers, and the current offer is not one of your top choices, you are in a better position to negotiate more firmly and ask for a higher salary and benefits. Or, if your financial situation or current position is such that you do not need to accept the current job offer, you are in a nice position to negotiate strongly because you do not have anything to lose. On the other hand, if this current job offer is the only one in sight and you cannot afford another month without any income, you might choose to engage in a "softer" negotiation process that might look something like this: "I want you to know that I plan to accept this offer no matter what, but after extensive research, I do believe that a salary of $X best reflects the market and what I bring to this position and to your company. Anything you are willing to do to get me close to that figure will be greatly appreciated."

#2 Preparing Counteroffers

1. Use salary surveys, and share this information with your interviewer if it is favorable to you.

> "I took time to gather some information, including a survey conducted by XYZ Institute. It covers salaries paid in this area by organizations of your size in this field. It indicates that someone with my credentials and background in this job has a salary between X and Y."

---

[42] Major salary websites: glassdoor.com or salary.com.

2. Benchmark your range as being between the highest salary of your future subordinate and the salary of your future supervisor. Your research will probably show you that as a general rule, your boss will make 25% to 50% more than you and 50% to 100% more than your subordinates. You can also ask for information in the negotiation.

> "What are my subordinates' motivations, experience, backgrounds, and average salary, and specifically the highest salary paid?"

3. Ask for a job-switching bonus. This applies if someone tries to lure you from your present job.

> "I am happy where I am, and I will not consider any professional move that does not increase my salary by at least N percent (usually 10-50%)."

#3 Starting the Negotiation

1. Be enthusiastic, polite, respectful, and professional. Your tone of voice sets the impression of how this conversation will go! Be confident in speech and body language, but not too pushy. Remember that you want your employer to see this as a win-win situation.

2. Be assertive. Do not be shy about your skills, education, and experience. Know your market value, and do not be afraid to sell yourself for it!

3. Do not be the first to disclose a number. This can be tricky, but it works to your advantage to have them disclose a range first.

4. Do not feel obligated to accept the first offer. Most employers expect and leave room for a counteroffer. If you accept the first offer, you could be leaving money on the table. Instead, make a high counteroffer: start high and work toward a middle ground.

5. Be creative. Look beyond just salary but vacation time, bonuses, and an early salary review. There are many layers to compensation worth bargaining for!

#4 Working Past "This Is All We Can Afford to Pay"

1. As mentioned earlier, you must make a decision regarding how hard you negotiate and push back based on the financial and professional position in which you find yourself.

2. Mention other job offers. If you have another offer, tell your interviewer and potentially mention the highest salary you have been offered.

> "As I mentioned to you earlier, I am actively looking for a job. I am now in the final phase as I have already received two firm job offers. One of them has offered a salary of X; if your organization can match or beat this offer, I will decide on the spot. Of the two, I would immediately accept yours because I like your organization better."

3. Offer to prove your worth. If you do not have an extensive employment history or your employer will not raise an offer, consider negotiating for a time-delayed deal (usually three to six months in the future). Examples might include the following:

> "I will accept this offer under the condition that my salary will be readjusted based on my performance against X metrics in Y months. This will be retroactive to my start date."

> "What are some specific measurables that would improve your bottom line and increase my earnings?"

Just make sure you get any incentive agreements in writing!

4. Offer part-time work. For instance, if you want a monthly salary of 100 units but their offer is sixty units, try, "I will accept sixty units per month but will only work here 60% of my time."

UNDERSTANDING AND ALIGNING WITH WORK CULTURE

Choton Basu and Carol Bäckman

Choton Basu is the Irvin L. Young chair of entrepreneurship and associate professor of information technology at University of Wisconsin, Whitewater. He has been involved in entrepreneurship, innovation, and startups for over fifteen years. He is also the founder of Slipstream LLC, a mobile-based community engagement platform.

Carol Bäckman is a programme manager/specialist at the Swedish International Development Cooperation Agency (SIDA). SIDA is a government agency with a mission to find brave new ways to enhance equality, democracy, and human rights and to reduce poverty so as to foster sustainable development for all. Carol's portfolio includes capacity building and institutional development in developing countries with an emphasis on collaborating with the private sector.

As a team member, you will influence, and be influenced by, the culture of your workplace. The work culture is rarely spelled out—other than perhaps in bigger organizations where time has been devoted to the formulation of policies and guidelines. However, what is formulated need not be what is practiced. Culture is what is practiced. The skills required to tune in to the predominant culture, or to adjust to it, are rarely taught and may cause some bumps along your career path—as some lessons can only be learned the hard way.

Typically, the team leader has great influence in setting the stage for the culture of the workplace. At the same time, there is a clear trend of moving away from the traditional "command and control" culture to flat(ter) organizations where decision making and responsibilities are delegated to people on the frontlines who are empowered to make those decisions. It is important to find an organization that shares your most important values—in not only what is to be achieved but also how. Consider, for example, the value of equality in both facilitating participation and considering diverse viewpoints from other team members. The goals here are to help each other work toward a common goal as well as achieve individual development and satisfaction. This creates a culture of engagement that results in collaboration and development of shared values and leads to retention and growth of individuals within the company.

It is difficult to know which work culture you will enjoy and thrive in until you experience several firsthand. The key is to consciously assess whether the work culture of the organization in which you are working aligns with your personal values and professional ethos. There are many aspects of the workplace that are distinctly cultural, from the organization's structure and dress code to the way employees interact with peers. This chapter explains the key dimensions that shape work culture and aspects you should consider before deciding if a company is, or will be, a good fit for you.

#1 Organizational Structure

Hierarchical Structure: A hierarchical organization is structured as a pyramid in which every employee, except one, is subordinate to another within the organization. Each level of leadership is well defined, making authority and responsibility obvious. This degree of structure can be reassuring, and you will have clear opportunities for promotion. Additionally, you are likely to have a manager that is more knowledgeable and specialized in your area and who can guide you to a higher productivity level and foster your personal development. This is a win-win situation: you gain a mentor, and your manager builds a strong department of people aspiring to improve the entire organization. Some degree of hierarchy is typically necessary for large organizations with thousands of employees working on diverse products. On the other hand, there is also the danger in that "everyone rises to his or her level of incompetence," also called the Peter Principle. In essence, people get promoted for doing a good job until they reach a level in the organization where they no longer do a good job.

Flattened Structure: A flat organization has few or no levels of management between senior leaders and frontline employees. Because you are on a level playing field, you will be asked to work collaboratively in teams and will have more responsibility to make decisions. Not only will you have the ear of upper management, you will also be able to organize and conduct your own work without constantly seeking their approval. You will also experience less bureaucracy, and leaders will rely on your loyalty to the organization and mission to guide your decision making. Many organizations are flattening their structures to avoid paying middle managers, speed up decision making, and cultivate a sense of belonging among all employees. Self-motivated workers often excel when given this latitude to be creative and innovate.

Project-Based Structure: Project-based organizations are very popular in situations where companies have a limited number of specialists producing interdisciplinary products. The entire working environment is driven by ensuring that the right team and resources are in place to execute a number of projects simultaneously. The challenging aspect of this organizational structure is that you may have multiple team leaders and be pulled in multiple directions. Employees that enjoy diverse challenges and have good time-management skills may function well in project-based organizations.

Process-Oriented Structure: Process-oriented organizations have gained traction in the business world since the 1990s. This was a result of business process reengineering and process innovation popularized by Michael Hammer and James Champy. Not only did this require a focus on cross-functional business processes, but it also changed the roles of employees from being solely focused in one functional area, such as accounting, finance, marketing, etc., to participating in projects across functions. In fact, modern-day enterprise resource planning (ERP) systems that support large organizations are built on these business processes and not geared solely to functional areas. The goal is to inspire cross-functional and big-picture views, improve interconnectedness, and inspire new process innovations. An excellent example and growth of this phenomenon has led to highly developed customer order fulfillment processes that not only require cooperation across functions in an organization but has now extended to include suppliers and distributors via interorganizational systems.

#2 Leadership and Decision-Making Style

Direction-Based Leadership: A direction-based leader is one who provides the vision, guidelines, projects, plans, and future processes. This style relies on a formal chain of command and requires the leader to communicate clearly and completely. This style of leadership is particularly suited to time-critical tasks. If you work for a leader with this style, you will be asked to challenge the status quo and push through challenges. The feeling of accomplishment can be quite satisfying. However, it is important to trust that leader as some of their decisions will be based on "gut instinct" or personal feelings.

Consensus-Based Leadership: In consensus-based leadership, decision-making authority is dispersed among all group members. If you work in this environment, your thoughts will be considered, and your voice will be heard. This can enhance your sense of loyalty to the leader and organization. This style of leadership is based upon mutual respect and trust. It is particularly useful for promoting cohesiveness among teams with diverse opinions and experiences.

#3 Diversity

Surface Level: Differences that are instantly recognizable such as age, gender, ethnicity, and native language represent what is referred to as surface-level diversity. Most of today's organizations have diversified their workforce on the surface, but not all have been successful in cultivating an environment of inclusion. Without proper team building, organizations can make minorities feel like isolated subgroups, which can cause paranoia and unproductivity. It is vitally important that you investigate the level of diversity and inclusion in an organization you are thinking about joining.

Deeper Level: Deeper levels of diversity are harder to notice because differences in attitudes, beliefs, and personalities are often communicated through nonverbal behavior. Nonetheless, the ability of an organization to integrate employees with different backgrounds, perspectives, and skills can greatly enhance workplace culture and success. Many organizations strive for it, but it is difficult to attain. To investigate deeper diversity before you accept a job, ask current employees about their own perceptions of inclusion. There are also useful websites (such as Glassdoor) that include reviews by former employees. Ensure that you are comfortable with how well your organization understands the value of diverse viewpoints in both the workplace and decision-making processes.

#4 Day-to-Day Work Environment

Professionally: How people go about working with each other on a daily basis is a big indicator of the work culture. In some organizations everyone has a defined role while in others, roles change more frequently. For example, organizations may have formalized methods for handling conflicts, or they may leave the issues to the individuals involved. In addition, reward structures and systems have evolved over the years. Some organizations encourage collaboration across units, whereas others embrace competitive environments in which multiple people try to outdo each other's solutions to a problem. Consider what sort of processes and professional interactions you are looking for in your prospective organization.

Personally: Seemingly minor issues such as the dress code of your work environment can play a role in how you feel there. It is important that you feel comfortable in your workplace and with those around you. Also consider what sort of schedule you will have. How long is the commute, and does the organization support telecommuting? Does your organization or leadership allow for schedule flexibility ("flextime"), and are you able to work at the times you feel most productive? If everyone around you is working nights, going out after work, or staying in the office fifteen hours a day, you will feel an expectation to do the same. This is particularly common in startups, where work hours are a function of the team dynamics and the organization's need. Consider what day-to-day factors will most influence your happiness and productivity.

#5 Speed of Project Execution

Time-Sensitive Approach: There are multiple approaches to completing a project. Some companies focus heavily on speed and productivity. They are much more inclined to track number of projects completed or products delivered per year. Examine the organization and your particular job: What metrics are used for personnel assessment? How do deadlines work? How often is feedback given? Are you working on quick-hit tasks or long-term projects? Some workers thrive in a fast-paced environment where they work with equally efficient coworkers and get things done quickly. Being able to map out a bigger project over a longer period of time is a different feeling than that of quick-hit assignments. Taking the time to thoroughly formulate all the parts, task dependencies, and people involved results in a different atmosphere. Without as many deadlines, you need to motivate yourself to move things along, or time will pass and nothing will be accomplished.

Project-Based Approach: A different approach to execution is stricter adherence to project management principles, which is more common for longer-term projects. In this approach, considerable planning and iteration go into balancing project scope, cost, and time. This usually involves a professional project manager and can be beneficial if you are self-motivated and effective at sustaining long-term teams and tasks.

#6 Autonomy in Working

Independent: Working independently allows you to answer primarily to yourself with only loose coupling to others' projects. You get to complete your work however and wherever you want, you set your own goals, and you get full credit for your deliverables. A culture of independence aims to give you freedom as well as responsibility for your work. Though you have a greater degree of autonomy over your schedule and solution, your organization or the client holds you to those deadlines and expects efficient, successful outcomes. This means far more responsibility but also greater feelings of accomplishment and satisfaction. Forbes stated that 71% of millennials prefer a less traditional career path and would want a greater degree of autonomy at work. Independent work cultures can be found in some larger organizations, but they are chiefly used by consultants and independent contractors.

Teams: Teams allow members to share and leverage diversities of knowledge, experience, and skills. Generating ideas can be easier within a group that encourages creativity, though mismanaged groups can also succumb to groupthink. Successful team members support one another and vet each other's work during the project. Teammates can also motivate and push one another to work harder and faster as well as to take more risks. Technology has now enabled global team collaboration, but this telecommunication requires preparation, copious note taking, and the ability to work across different cultures, backgrounds, and time zones. For some people this may be an energizing experience while for others it may be a source of discomfort. In any case, it is important to build this skill set because most modern organizations have some level of digital collaboration.

#7 Room for Failure

A Lot: Failure is inevitable. Nonetheless, the attitude and reaction an organization has toward failure can define the culture. Allowing a lot of room for failure encourages risk taking, experimentation, and curiosity. Simply giving an employee a large task with the possibility of failure requires a great deal of trust by upper management. However, that trust and risk taking can also lead to great innovations. For example, academia generally accepts failure in professors' research as long as it is analyzed, documented, and improved upon.

A Little: Despite the necessity of innovation, there are some risks that a given organization cannot take. Management must keep in mind the cost of failure while simultaneously accepting mistakes and avoiding the "blame game." Rejecting all failure leads to very high-stress work environments and causes high turnover rates. On the other hand, employees that thrive under the pressure to perform may find motivation in organizations that hold high standards against failure.

Concluding Remarks

How do you discover the culture of an organization and work unit before committing? A good place to start would be an organization's or staff's Twitter feed, Facebook page, or blog. Look for TED talks by CEOs to get a sense of the leadership and how the organization thinks. Be observant in the interview by watching people interact, talk to as many people as possible, and ask questions to understand the common beliefs of the employees. Team lunches or after-hour drinks are typically a part of the interviewing process and a perfect time to understand culture as your interviewers will be in an informal space and somewhat more relaxed. If you are still not making headway, ask more directed questions. Remember, the organization wants you to be a good fit just as much as you do because it usually results in you having a longer, happier, and more productive career.

CONSIDERATIONS FOR LGBT TRAVEL AND WORK ABROAD

Bruce E. Smail

Bruce E. Smail, MA, is the executive director of The MOCHA Center, a nonprofit organization focused on improving the health and wellness of LGBT Communities of Color in Western New York. Smail has an eclectic twenty-six–year career in higher education, nonprofit, federal government, business, and secondary education with over twenty years of advocacy for people of color, LGBT, youth, and people living with HIV/AIDS.

Homophobia varies throughout the world. It is a delicate balance as one considers opportunities in locations that may have an unpredictable or hostile relationship with LGBT communities. This author is an out, bisexual, African American man living with HIV and has maneuvered in various communities in the United States, Caribbean, and South America. If you are contemplating working in a new country or even relocating to a different cultural region within the United States, I urge you to considering the following ten strategies.

#1 Research Your Destination

If you are considering a new position outside the United States, it is important that you research your destination. Review the US Department of State's briefings on that country. Utilize Google and other search engines to gather information on that country's relationship with LGBT communities. What are the laws surrounding same-sex relationships or same-gender marriages? The laws may give some indicators about the level of acceptance of LGBT communities. Find out as much as you can from reliable sources such as US Department of State's travel warnings, Amnesty International, and the International Lesbian Gay Bi Trans Intersex Association.[42]

#2 Utilize Social Media to Connect with Friends and Colleagues

Most people are connected through Facebook, LinkedIn, Twitter, and other social media sources. Send a message on your social media sites to see if anyone has lived, worked, or visited your destination. Compare your network's first-hand experience with the researched information. The comparisons may be helpful in understanding some of the nuances of that country.

#3 Visit if You Can

Before you commit to an extended work experience, try to visit the destination for yourself. With the information you obtained during the research as well as feedback from your network, you should be in a better position to assess the community. Try to reach out to the locals and avoid the touristy attractions. Find the LGBT community, and obtain their feedback about the LGBT climate at your destination. All of these sources of information will provide a better picture for you.

#4 Contact LGBT Organizations

Try to identify the local LGBT organizations, LGBT hangout spots, LGBT newspapers, and/or LGBT nightclubs. Multiple resources in a community mean visibility and a level of comfort for the LGBT community. If no resources are available, it may mean that the LGBT community is underground and experiencing a hostile climate. The lack of LGBT visibility may present challenges if you are open about your sexual and/or gender identity.

#5 Identify Potential Support Mechanism

In your research, be sure to identify the support mechanisms that are available for you. Whether it is an organization or individual, a supportive advocate will help guide you through the cultural challenges you might face during a long stay in another country.

---

[42] These resources are available at travel.state.gov (US Department of State), amnestyusa.org (Amnesty International), and ilga.org (ILGA worldwide).

#6 Safety First

Just as you are vigilant about safety in your home country, you need to be just as vigilant in another country. Constantly be aware of your surroundings, and be sure that your "difference" is not drawing unneeded attention to you. Be aware of public situations especially if they are escalating or there is a potential risk for harm.

#7 Balance Identity Development Versus Realities on the Ground

If you recently came out or you are at the "pride" level of your identity development, realize that your openness may have different consequences in another country. If you are in a very homophobic country, this is not the moment that you decide to walk around waving the LGBT flag. While it might be important to you, the environment may not be ready for the bold display of LGBT pride. This author is not suggesting that you go back into the closet; rather, be aware of the realities on the ground and sensitively handle your pride while in a different country.

#8 Remember You Are in Someone Else's Country

While you may be comfortable expressing your LGBT identity in your home country, know that your experiences may be very different in another country. Be respectful of the cultural norms, and realize that everyone may not have the same freedoms and rights as you do in the United States.

#9 Openness to Learning the Culture

You must be open to learning the culture of your destination. If you speak the native language, speak to the locals in their language. If you are not fluent, utilize alternative means like Google Translate or another online language translator. Learning a new culture may be intimidating, but making the effort builds mutual respect.

#10 Exit or Emergency Plan

Know how to get out of the country if needed. Watch the local news and monitor US Department of State travel warnings. Be sure to register with the US Embassy so that you will be notified of any travel advisories. Have a plan in case you need to exit the country.

LOGISTICAL ISSUES WHILE PURSUING CAREERS IN LESS DEVELOPED COUNTRIES

Jeffrey M. Erickson

Jeff Erickson is a clinical professor of law and director of the International Sustainable Development Projects Law Clinic at Penn State Law. The clinic supports humanitarian engineering, global health programs, and entrepreneurship ventures by providing legal due diligence and advice, drafting legal instruments, and negotiating agreements; and by developing students' "legal intelligence" in foreign, domestic, and international law in a broad range of practice areas.

As this book demonstrates, there are myriad opportunities for students and graduates to pursue work and careers on a nontraditional path focused on social value creation and international development. The variety of opportunities is astounding, a manifestation of (1) the variety of organizations involved in development projects—large companies, donor and recipient governments, nonprofits, foundations, universities, religious organizations, militaries, consulting agencies, think tanks, UN agencies; (2) the variety of work they perform—from engineering to education, global health to social entrepreneurship, from in the field to administration to policy; and (3) their worldwide distribution and individual regions of focus. While organizations and their programs may be guided by common humanitarian principles, each individual program operates differently, reflecting its individual mission, scope, scale, site, and institutional organization. While it is impossible to treat (or even anticipate) each situation, the following provides a few basic logistical (and legal) considerations for anyone preparing to embark on a development path.

Larger and more established organizations have specialists on staff to address logistical and legal concerns (theirs and yours, and the intersection). Smaller organizations may not. Where there is no organizational guide, it is incumbent on the individual to ensure that such concerns do not hinder their success. We can broadly classify a few of these concerns as (1) personal and professional risk management, (2) employment issues, (3) immigration/visa issues, and (4) local laws and conveniences.

#1 Risk Management

Personal Risk: Development organizations' risk managers' paramount concern is the safety of their personnel. Volatility is more common in the developing world, and that, coupled with less developed infrastructure and health-care capabilities, puts personnel at significant risk. An illness or injury that is easily treated in the US, for example, may be practically untreatable, particularly on the frontier in less developed countries. Despite their altruism, few development practitioners would willingly share the fate of the locals when treatment is available or vastly preferable in their home county. Reserve your judgment on this dichotomy for after your medical evacuation. Before you join a project, make sure that your employer has in place an appropriate safety and security plan for its personnel, and that either you or your employer have in place an insurance policy that covers medical emergencies and evacuations.

Your employer may be required to provide workers' compensation (WC) insurance coverage. If they maintain a WC policy in the US—great. WC coverage is mandated by the aspirational laws of many African countries, too, so you may be covered under a policy from an African insurer. Frankly, in that case, you would probably do well to consider a broad travel insurance policy or other policy that provides for medical, short- and long-term disability benefits, and to ensure that (whether the insurer would be a primary or secondary payer) there is no exclusion for work-relatedness.

Professional Risk: So you have just passed your boards, or perhaps you have been certified as an engineer-in-training. Congratulations! You undoubtedly know that those credentials are handed down by the licensing board of your state and that you cannot practice your art in a neighboring state without first jumping through some hoops. So you

367

should have no expectation that your credentials would be adequate in a foreign country. Prior to engaging in any professional practice abroad, you must obtain credentials there. In some cases, this can be relatively easy and inexpensive. Some countries offer credentials upon showing similar credentials in other countries (either more developed countries, neighboring, or regional countries). Some countries offer credentials specific to humanitarian purposes, sometimes for terms shorter than a year. For a multitude of reasons, some countries make it neither cheap nor quick to obtain credentials. Explore this issue well in advance of your departure. Also, if you will be "practicing under" someone else, make sure they have the appropriate credentials. Each country, naturally, has its own penalty schemes for professional practice without a license. You do not want to learn about them.

#2 Employment

Before you can work (or conduct business) in a foreign country, you will probably have to jump a few hurdles, namely obtaining the proper visa (more on this below) and/or work permit. Some countries are very lenient and allow for very short-term employments (i.e., up to thirty days, subject to extension) under a tourism permit.[43] Other countries have become quite strict in response to high unemployment and a perception that organizations utilizing foreign labor offer limited capacity-building opportunities for their nationals.[44]

Assuming you qualify for a work permit, you may need to provide several of the following to the host country's immigration or labor ministry:

- An invitation letter from the host company (assuming the host is in-country)
- An invitation letter from a local partner company or sponsoring individual
- A copy of your passport and valid visa
- Copies of degrees/qualifications/certifications
- Medical certificate/health examination
- Letters of reference
- Criminal record check
- Proof of funds (for living expenses, "moving on")

If you are lucky, your foray into development work will be paid. If you are getting paid, you are probably an employee. That means someone else should be ensuring compliance with all applicable employment laws—paying applicable taxes, withholding estimated taxes, and making payments into various health and pension schemes. For US citizens and residents getting paid by a US entity, in the US, it is pretty straightforward. For US citizens and residents getting paid by a foreign entity, it gets a little more complex. Yes, you will have to pay taxes in the US on your foreign earnings abroad.[45] And you will have to pay taxes in the host country, too. Dual tax and dual Social Security tax liability may become a significant expense—and demands more research—if you anticipate a longer expat career.[46]

#3 Visas

Getting into and staying in a host country is of obvious importance. For anyone not a citizen or national of a host country, that means obtaining a visa. This should be more a logistical than a legal matter. However, misrepresenting the reason for travelling is visa fraud and could subject a visa applicant to serious consequences, such as being ineligible for a visa or having a permanent record with the immigration agency—either of which might jeopardize the individual's further development work in the host country.

There are many types of visas, and each carries different regulations and a different price. Among others, types of visas include business, conference, emergency, employment, entry, journalist, medical, missionary, research, student, tourist, and transit. Those seeking a visa should research the type they need and contact the host-country's embassy or consulate if necessary. Note that all visas have a maximum stay,[47] and some visas allow reentry while

---

[43] For example, a T-3 authorization in Chile.

[44] For example, in 2012, Kenya's Ministry of Immigration announced regulations prohibiting issuance of work permits to younger (under thirty-five) and lower-paid foreigners (<$24,000/yr.), and those in medical, real estate, engineering, accountancy, and legal professions. Also in 2012, Uganda banned NGOs from employing foreigners where Ugandans possessed the requisite job skills.

[45] Check IRS Publication 54 (2014) for more information.

[46] See if your company offers a "tax equalization arrangement."

[47] Some visa terms can be quite long: India offers a ten-year business visa with reentry rights.

[48] Traveling with a spouse adds another element; consider both individuals' visas and plan accordingly.

others do not. Depending on your situation, you may have to leave the country and return to keep a visa valid (if you cannot secure an extension), or you may need to obtain a new visa. This can add significantly to your expenses and take much valuable time. Know the limitations of your visa before you go.[48] Whatever type of visa you need, you will probably have to show evidence of your "way out," for example, a return flight ticket as well as your physical location during your stay.

Students engaging in a service learning-type program (not affiliated with the host country) for a few weeks may be able to get by with a tourist visa, which is usually easily obtained, often at customs/immigration upon arrival in the host country. The ease of obtaining and the affordability of tourist visas make them attractive (student visas usually would not be required unless students are enrolled in a course at a host-country institution or a program jointly operated by host- and sponsor-country institutions). Business visas may cost two to five times as much as tourist visas, take longer to obtain, and obviously bring more scrutiny in terms of documentation.

#4 Local Laws and Conveniences

Most people who go abroad to pursue development work go with some knowledge of the cultural norms of the place. The employer should be informed of the local laws that directly affect its projects and hopefully communicates those laws to its personnel. Do not assume that being in a less developed country, perhaps on the frontier, means laws are not on the books and enforced.

Travelers should be aware of local laws that reflect cultural norms (e.g., prohibition of alcohol in Saudi Arabia, mandate of hijab in Iran, illegality of homosexuality/homosexual acts in most of Africa and the Middle East). It should go without saying that indulging in drugs and the sex trade is probably a bad idea. Likewise, insulting the government may be a serious offense. Countries' laws may prohibit taking photographs of government buildings, military installations, or infrastructure.

It is worth mentioning that both domestic law (the law of the US, for example) and the local law of the host country may regulate against corruption. If corruption is endemic to the region of your project, you should understand your employer's anticorruption policy and know your obligations, even as a victim of compulsion or extortion.

You will have to do your homework on local regulations with respect to conveniences like driving and banking privileges. A driver's license issued by a state of the US is likely to be recognized abroad; however, for longer stints in-country or for driving related to employment, you need to investigate the licensing requirements. It may also be necessary or worthwhile to obtain an international driving permit, which translates your existing license into multiple languages.[49]

Money, no doubt, is a top concern as you do not want to be stranded. Whether or not you are paid in the host country, you may want to open a bank account. Most countries allow nonresidents to maintain accounts; some may even allow domiciliary accounts, in which you can deposit certain foreign currencies, especially ever-popular US dollars. In some countries, US dollars, euros, or pounds sterling may frequently be used as cash; in other countries it may be illegal to do so. If you have to change money to the host-country currency, abide by laws that may mandate government-sanctioned exchanges, as using black-market traders is illegal in many countries.

Summary

Common sense will go a long way in preparing for your development endeavor. A comparative approach is useful; if it would be an issue here, it is probably an issue there. With that lens, do due diligence by researching requirements of the country to which you are headed. Ask questions of your prospective employer and the country's consulate until you are satisfied you know the answers. Fore-planning will help avert many potential pitfalls of doing development work abroad.

---

[49] AAA and the National Automobile Club are authorized by the US State Department to issue international driving permits.

BEATING BURNOUT

Lee Ann De Reus

Lee Ann De Reus is an associate professor of human development and family studies and women's studies. She is the cofounder of the Panzi Foundation. Panzi Foundation USA engages in strategic advocacy to end violence against women and to provide grants to Panzi Hospital in the Democratic Republic of Congo to heal women and restore their lives.

For those working abroad for long stints, especially in humanitarian, research, or other field positions, burnout is common. The high energy and passions individuals bring to the work, coupled with resource-constrained environments (e.g., no running water, electricity or Internet access, poor housing, etc.), social isolation, unrealistic expectations, safety issues, high-stakes stress, exposure to suffering, cultural differences and barriers, can take a toll if not addressed constructively. Listed below are suggestions for minimizing the potential for mental, physical, emotional, and spiritual exhaustion.

#1 Know Yourself

Developing self-awareness is the key to avoiding burnout. To that end, establishing a baseline of health can provide perspective on what being healthy looks like. The following are questions to aid in creating a personal profile:

- How many hours of sleep do I need?
- What foods make me healthiest/unhealthy?
- How much water do I need to stay hydrated?
- What is my alcohol limit?
- How much exercise do I need, and what type is best?
- How much time do I need alone? How much time do I need with friends/family?
- What best facilitates my spirituality?
- What is the best way for me to relax?
- What is the most effective way for me to handle stress or conflict?
- What brings me joy or pleasure?

#2 See the Red Flags

It can be difficult to self-diagnose burnout, and everyone has an occasional bad day. The following are examples of some common warning signs: lethargy, despair, fatigue, despondency, anger, frustration, insomnia, excessive alcohol consumption, lack of motivation, inability to concentrate, cynicism, and disillusionment. It can be helpful to enlist a trusted (and stable) friend who will compassionately point out these problems if they persist over time.

#3 Build Resilience

Fieldwork in resource-deprived, isolated, high-stakes, and/or unsafe contexts can be incredibly demanding and stressful. Developing practices that strengthen emotional and physical resilience can help prevent burnout. Yoga, meditation or prayer, exercise, hobbies, communing with nature, journaling or keeping a blog, healthy eating, even forgiveness and learning to "let go" can fortify a person's core. Drawing on past experiences of overcoming hardship or remembering when "trusting your gut" was accurate also builds confidence and reinforces resilience.

#4 Take a Break

Understanding how to work with, not against, individual needs and rhythms includes knowing when to stop work during the day or when (and how) to take a vacation. Practices such as unplugging from technology for a week or limiting screen time during meals or before bed can help. Postponing breaks to accomplish more work or using the time to rush around visiting family and friends can be exhausting. The ability to be productive at work and achieve a meaningful, balanced life, requires awareness of self and an employer who understands the value of a vacation.

#5 Stay Connected

Social isolation is common in fieldwork because of remote locations, lack of access to Internet and phone, or friends and family who do not understand this type of work. Establishing supportive networks may seem obvious but is often neglected. Peer-to-peer relationships, mentors, online communities such as AidSource on LinkedIn, coaching partnerships, trusted friends and empathetic relatives can aid in the coping process and provide a buffer to stress and burnout.

#6 Set Boundaries

People drawn to fieldwork are often the same individuals who struggle to say "no." Extreme selflessness, drive, passion, the fear of a missed opportunity or disappointing others can contribute to burnout if not kept in check. Determining healthy boundaries in personal relationships, between the personal and professional spheres, and in the workplace are paramount to a balanced life. But the ability to determine these boundaries is reliant on self-awareness about individual limits or capacities and priorities. Questions such as (1) "What is a good/not a good use of my time?" (2) "How do I know when I am in over my head?" and (3) "What does a healthy relationship look like?" can inform healthy boundaries.

#7 Manage Expectations

The desire to "make a difference" or live a meaningful life often propels people to humanitarian or aid work, typically in other countries. This outsider status can prove problematic if there is a mismatch between individual expectations and on-the-ground realities, leading to burnout. A "savior mentality" or an unconscious need to resolve or avoid personal problems are classic examples of unhealthy motivations that distort expectations. The individual who engages honestly in a critical humility about personal intentions; respects indigenous practices, knowledge, and culture; and exercises flexibility and adaptability will have realistic goals, less stress, more effectiveness, and purpose.

#8 Work for Supportive Employers

There is a prevalent culture of denial about burnout in the aid and development community, including within organizations. Toxic work environments or dismissive employers can undermine careers and damage a person's well-being. Even if individuals engage in very healthy self-care, it can be jeopardized by employers who do not provide services to address the psychological and social challenges of staff.

#9 Get Professional Help

A healthy individual has the self-awareness to know their limits and when they are in over their heads. Too often individuals struggling with burnout refuse to seek counseling or therapy until their situation is dire—or it is too late. Pride and the stigma associated with getting professional help can make us our own worst enemy. However, there is no honor in dishonoring ourselves. It is often surprising to learn how many people in our own networks have seen a therapist. Reaching out to others in search of a reputable counselor can lead to support, empathy, and relief from burnout.

#10 Value Yourself

In contexts characterized by great need or suffering, we may ignore our own well-being in deference to those we serve and in sacrifice to the larger "mission." We may be ashamed of expressing our needs or regard self-care as indulgent. Our privilege, in contrast to underprivileged people, may illicit guilt. These unconstructive reactions are a recipe for burnout. It is important to remember that a person cannot give what they do not have. Thus, we must value ourselves enough to engage in self-care so that we can provide quality and effective work in the field.

EPILOGUE: MARCHING ORDERS FOR PROFESSORS AND UNIVERSITIES

"What advice do you have for professors and universities as they educate the next generation of social innovators?" We asked each of the innovators profiled in this book and many of the expert brief contributors. Their candid responses, based on decades of living on the bleeding edge of social innovation, should come as no surprise. This epilogue synthesizes the recurrent themes and presents them in the innovators' original words.

#1 Get Students Outside the "Main Track"

"Faculty really must encourage students to take courses and get involved in activities outside their main 'track.' It may slightly slow the progress to a degree, but that extra time is negligible in terms of the career opportunities and ideas it can develop. Now that I am at NSF we find that many faculty discourage their students from doing international work because the faculty do not want to lose some of their students' productivity. Faculty really have to try to take a longer-term view—an international experience or an internship could open up a whole new world to a student and can even provide new opportunities for faculty themselves. Also, I encourage faculty to reach out to former students with nonacademic careers and get them to advise current students."

– Lara Campbell

"Let's redesign aspects of our work from the students' perspective. Traditions and growth have disconnected colleges, departments, units, and campus communities. Let's create opportunities that crosscut these man-made barriers. Let's make the maze these students are so good at getting through a little stickier so that they are required to get out of a predetermined path, have unexpected experiences, and reflect. Let's help them connect the dots between their in-class and out-of-class activities. Let's create professional development opportunities to help professors support social innovators in their teaching and research."

– Meg Small

#2 Champion Rigorous, Ethical, Evidence-Based Approaches

"I think we need to do a better job of analyzing the lessons learned of social innovation efforts in the past and linking those results to new initiatives. There is not enough quantification of results and certainly not enough cross-talk between academia and the policy makers on this side. We should create more decision spaces where needs, expectations, progress, and results are worked on jointly."

– Frances A. Colón

"Working for an incubator, one of the most consistent issues we see with early-stage entrepreneurs is that they really do not understand the problems well because they are not spending enough time in the field talking with customers. Teaching students to use human-centered design principles is a good starting point, but getting them to apply them to real-world problems and understand how vital customer insights are is the critical next step that many educational programs seem to miss. Guiding students through multiple cycles of insight gathering and product development and finally launching the product will illustrate the importance of taking this process seriously. That is an area where educators have the ability to make a big difference."

– Paul Belknap

#3 Teach Students How To Fail (And Bounce Back from Failure)

"I do not think I would be where I am today if my professors had not given me the freedom to fail and [to] learn from risk taking. Teach your students how to think, but let them fail, and fail fast. Looking back, I realize that my failures have taught me way more than my successes, and I owe it to my professors for trusting in my abilities to learn from these failures."

– Shruthi Baskaran

372

"Help your students learn to stretch themselves and to bounce back from failure. Many students have never truly failed by the time they get to college. Innovation is all about change and growth into brand new areas so you are creating the path. The only way to do this is to push beyond what has already been done. There will be losses along the way, and it is critical that new innovators do not fear the potential of loss so much that they will not take the risk. And, when they fail, it is equally critical that they are able to get up, dust themselves off, learn from the experience, and try something new."

– Andreina Parisi-Amon

#4 Toughen Up Students for a Competitive World

"Provide interdisciplinary education! Find creative ways to support student projects that cannot be supported through traditional grant/research support pipelines. Require all students in a social entrepreneurship program to enter a business plan competition—even if they do not win—so they learn in a competitive environment what goes into developing and pitching an idea. Allow them to fail and encourage them to fail so they grow a thicker skin. They should not believe they are perfect when they enter the workforce. Many new entrants to the workforce are not as hardworking as they used to be (and sometimes more entitled). You shape them during school; help to create people that are creative yet realistic, hardworking yet balanced, thoughtful yet detail oriented, great team members yet proactive! I am not saying we should be unnecessarily hard on students, but academia is not only building their knowledge in a particular area; it is preparing them for a workforce where they will need many of these practical skills. Knowledge is not enough. They will need a thick skin if they are going to be working in innovation."

– Jenn Gustetic

#5 Prepare Students to be Systems Thinkers (And Actors)

"[Universities] should help students understand systems and complexity science, and how to work under circumstances of constant and vigorous change. Technical skills are important, but more and more we need young people to be able to work effectively in a complex, interconnected, and emergent world."

– Srik Gopal

"Academic institutions should do more to present big, intangible problems to young students to encourage them to think critically and creatively about challenges that cannot be solved by simply reading a textbook or attending a lecture. Facilitating broader thinking across cultures and academic disciplines is essential in developing world-class STEM students who are prepared to enter a professional environment where there are no easy answers. More opportunities should also be made available for students to meet other young STEM people around the world and collaborate on real challenges facing humanity. This interaction provides context and importance, which is essential for taking technical development and education seriously. Without a young STEM major seeing who or where their work could ultimately impact, they are unable to think beyond what is required on their next thermodynamics assignment or chemistry lab."

– Steve DeSandis

#6 Keep It Real—Very Real

"Make sure that people are being grounded in reality. When I was in college, I was very idealistic in terms of how I wanted things to be and was a little naïve as to whether certain things were achievable or how to achieve certain things. I would have benefited from people who could have helped me understand, without diminishing my enthusiasm, but have helped me understand what is actually practical and what are the practical methods to try to achieve a goal, as opposed to pursuing impractical methods and spinning your wheels."

– Jay Goyal

"Encourage students to engage in global health work, but also help them understand that one idea, hatched in a lab somewhere, is extremely unlikely to change the world. There is lots of work, creativity, people, and, yes, money, needed beyond that initial idea, or that initial bit of lab work, before a product can be introduced, and even more so, before something can be scaled to actually have wide impact."

– Bernhard Weigl

#7 Be Willing to Question the Dominant Paradigm

"I have a soft spot for the stories of inspirational innovators from the past, of examples of people achieving greatness. I love reading about people like Louis Pasteur, John Snow, Ignaz Semmelweis, and Ada Lovelace, and how they were able to make original insights that went against conventional wisdom, because they had data that said something surprising. Most advances in knowledge do not come from a carefully planned experiment that turns out 'correctly'; they come from an unexpected finding. The willingness to question the dominant paradigm is key."

– Rick Johnston

"When senior faculty ask you to follow old trends of getting citations, push back and ask why—this will lead to an interesting conversation."

– Nigam Shah

#8 Educate Students about Nontraditional Career Pathways

"Offer as many opportunities as possible for students to get involved in social innovation. Professors can also introduce careers during their lectures that use the concepts they are teaching to engage in social value creation. Both professors and universities can work to bring social innovators to their universities to offer lectures where students can learn about their efforts."

– Tim Carter

"Provide opportunities for students to interact with social innovators. There are lots of great groups out there that support social innovation who would be happy to provide the background and get students excited about social innovation."

– Rebekah Neal

#9 Actively Help Students Find Their Niche

"Professors should be able to identify students with unique skills and talents. Examination is not the true test of knowledge. Many students who fail in class may not necessarily fail in the field. I learned more out of class than I ever learned in class. My entire undergraduate days were simply a waste for me—I just needed the degree. This is same for many students."

– Roland Fomundam

"Be careful not to sugar coat or hype the social impact arena—it is a difficult, uncertain, and competitive field. I would not encourage students to become social innovators because it sounds cool or feels good or is a dynamic and innovative new industry. Rather, I would encourage them to (1) find what they truly enjoy doing for themselves; (2) cultivate a curious, inquisitive, and questioning mind; (3) care deeply for people and the planet; and (4) go out and see for themselves what is wrong with the world expecting that they will find a way to use what they love doing to make it right."

– Tyler Valiquette

#10 Solve Problems That Matter

"Universities should offer programs focused on interdisciplinary, cooperative team experiences in which students define problems that matter and develop real solutions. This can occur through courses, cocurricular, and extracurricular activities. While students spend most of their time in classes and studying during college, it is the unconventional classroom and out-of-classroom experiences that are often critical to prepare young people to enter their careers ready to develop effective solutions to tough global challenges."

– Brian Bell

"Today's engineer must blaze a new trail in engineering ethics that prioritizes the needs of the most vulnerable members of our society and our ecosystem. Engineering education should never put the abstractions of calculus and physics ahead of the reality of the world around us, desperately in need of creative and compassionate thinkers, prepared to hear and amplify the hopes and aspirations of our brothers and sisters overcoming oppression."

– Frank Bergh

These are our marching orders.

Nothing more, nothing less.

Let's Get Going!

Made in the USA
Middletown, DE
02 April 2016